Digitalization and Industry 4.0: Economic and Societal Development

Hans-Christian Brauweiler ·
Vladimir V. Kurchenkov · Serik Abilov ·
Bernd Zirkler
Editors

Digitalization and Industry 4.0: Economic and Societal Development

An International and Interdisciplinary Exchange of Views and Ideas

Springer Gabler

Editors
Hans-Christian Brauweiler
School of Business and Economics
WHZ Zwickau
Zwickau, Germany

Vladimir V. Kurchenkov
Department of Public Administration
Volgograd State University
Volgograd, Russia

Serik Abilov
Kazakh-American Free University
Ust-Kamenogorsk, Kazakhstan

Bernd Zirkler
School of Business and Economics
WHZ Zwickau
Zwickau, Germany

The printing of this volume was supported by the DAAD with funds from the Federal Foreign Office, the Federal Ministry for Economic Cooperation and the EU within the framework of the ERASMUS+ programme.

ISBN 978-3-658-27109-1 ISBN 978-3-658-27110-7 (eBook)
https://doi.org/10.1007/978-3-658-27110-7

This Springer Gabler imprint is published by the registered company Springer Fachmedien Wiesbaden GmbH part of Springer Nature.
The registered company address is: Abraham-Lincoln-Str. 46, 65189 Wiesbaden, Germany

Preface

For several decades now it has been observed that many questions - be they political, economic, technical or scientific in a general way - can only be understood and addressed in a larger context and that proposed solutions must therefore include a very different number of aspects. This means that there is an increasing need and necessity for interdisciplinary work in overarching teams.

There are also often researchers in a specific field who have developed solutions and are looking for specific (marketable) application options. This also requires an interdisciplinary exchange and an understanding of questions and answers, i.e. in general, perspectives taken by people with a completely different experience and training profile are necessary.

In addition to interdisciplinary aspects, international and intercultural aspects must also be included to a high degree.

The possibility of recognizing new market opportunities or improvements and solutions to existing problems also means dealing occasionally or systematically with topics from other disciplines without seeing a connection at first glance. Innovative solutions and innovations are generally only possible through intensive observation, a unprejudiced approach, consideration without "operational blindness" of the associated scientific discipline, and a certain degree of "lateral thinking" and openness.

Therefore, the editors in this volume - supported by well-known scientists with an international and interdisciplinary background as a scientific committee (see list of members below) - have summarized the results of a conference and other contributions in this volume in order to achieve exactly this: A relatively colorful bouquet of scientific considerations, which are to be seen in the context of current problems.

The key questions of today are the topics of digitization, the associated changes in the environment of workplaces, and also questions of environmental pollution, which are linked to globalization - especially with the keywords transport and logistics. Unfortunately, the dramatic and dynamic effects of the Corona pandemic could not be taken into account due to the lead time of this volume, which is based on conference results from 2019. However, the editors are convinced that the fundamental questions are still valid and some issues - such as digitization - are still being given greater prominence.

Of course, the editors also have to thank many institutions, colleagues and scientists.

Firstly, there is the DAAD - German Academic Exchange Service, which has supported part of the conference participants and the printing of the volume with funds from the Federal Ministry for Cooperation, the Federal Foreign Office and the European Union.

Secondly, the WHZ under ist current rector Prof. Dr.-Ing. Stephan Kassel, in particular the Faculty of Economics under the dean Prof. Dr. Matthias Richter and the International Office under the head of Dr. Adriana Slavcheva with many helpers and participants are tob e mentioned. The majority of the burden was borne by the project and chair staff of the Chair of Business Administration, especially Corporate Accounting and Internal Auditing, Prof. Dr. Brauweiler, namely Katsiaryna Startsava, BA; Claudia Winkelmann, MA and Sören Förster, MA. In addition, there were of course many innumerable faculty employees and student assistants, often with an international background, which is particularly gratifying.

And, of course, the editors thank all participants of the international conference, who provided further important impulses for the innovative approaches through discussions, word contributions and questions.

A major contribution was put forward by the Scientific Committee, which helped to conduct the peer-review-process of the articles and thus ensured the quality of the book.

Last but not least the Editor-in-Chief thanks his co-editors for longstanding friendship, scientific support and their effort to produce this book.

The Editors, June / September 2019 and Spring 2020:

Zwickau (D), H.-Christian Brauweiler

Wolgograd (RU), Vladimir V. Kurchenkov

Ust Kamenogorsk (KAZ), Serik M. Abilov

Zwickau (D), Bernd Zirkler

Vorwort

Seit mittlerweile einigen Jahrzehnten ist zu beobachten, dass viele Fragestellungen – seien es politische, ökonomische, technische oder generell wissenschaftliche – nur in einem größeren Kontext zu durchdringen sind und Lösungsvorschläge somit eine ganz unterschiedliche Anzahl von Aspekten beinhalten müssen. Dies bedeutet, dass ein zunehmender Bedarf und eine höhere Notwendigkeit von interdisziplinären Arbeiten in übergreifenden Teams zu erkennen sind.

Auch gibt es oftmals Forscher einer bestimmten Fachrichtung, die Lösungen entwickelt haben und nach konkreten (marktfähigen) Anwendungsmöglichkeiten suchen. Hierzu ist ebenfalls ein interdisziplinärer Austausch sowie ein Verständnis für Fragen und Antworten, d.h. ganz allgemein Sichtweisen, die von Personen mit einem vollkommen anderen Erfahrungs- und Ausbildungsprofil vorgenommen werden, notwendig.

Hinzu kommt, dass neben interdisziplinären Aspekten auch in hohem Maße internationale sowie auch interkulturelle Aspekte einbezogen werden müssen.

Die Möglichkeit, neue Marktchancen oder Verbesserungen und Lösungen für bestehende Probleme zu erkennen, bedingt auch, sich gelegentlich oder systematisch mit Themenfeldern aus anderen Disziplinen zu befassen, ohne auf den ersten Blick eine Verbindung zu sehen. Erst durch intensive Betrachtung, vorurteilfreies Herangehen, Betrachtung ohne „Betriebsblindheit" der zugehörigen wissenschaftlichen Disziplin sowie ein gewisses Maß an „Querdenken" und Offenheit sind innovative Lösungen und Innovationen generell erst möglich.

Daher haben die Herausgeber in diesem Band – unterstützt durch namhafte Wissenschaftler mit internationalem und interdisziplinärem Hintergrund als wissenschaftliches Komitee (vgl. Mitgliederliste unten) – die Ergebnisse einer Tagung sowie weiterer Beiträge zusammengefasst, um genau dies zu erreichen: Ein relativ bunter Strauß an wissenschaftlichen Betrachtungen, die im Kontext aktueller Probleme zu sehen sind.

Tragende Fragen der heutigen Zeit sind die Themen Digitalisierung, damit einhergehende Veränderungen der Arbeitswelt, zusätzlich auch Fragen der Umweltbelastung, die durch die Globalisierung – hier insbesondere mit den Stichworten Transport und Logistik – verbunden sind. Die dramatischen wie auch dynamischen Auswirkungen der Corona-Pandemie konnten aufgrund des Vorlaufs der Produktionszeit des Bandes, der auf Tagungsergebnissen von 2019 beruht, leider nicht berücksichtigt werden. Die Herausgeber sind jedoch davon überzeugt, dass die grundlegenden Fragen nach wie vor Gültigkeit haben und manche Themen – wie z.B. die Digitalisierung – noch verstärkt Geltung finden.

Die Herausgeber haben natürlich auch vielen Beteiligten zu danken.

Zum einen sind das der DAAD – Deutscher Akademischer Austauschdienst, der mit Mitteln des Bundesministeriums für Zusammenarbeit sowie mit Mitteln des Auswärtigen Amtes sowie auch der Europäischen Union einen Teil der Tagungsteilnehmer sowie die Drucklegung des Bandes unterstützt hat.

Zum anderen ist die WHZ unter dem Rektor Prof. Dr.-Ing. Stephan Kassel, hier insbesondere die Fakultät Wirtschaftswissenschaften unter dem Dekan Prof. Dr. Matthias Richter sowie das International Office unter der Leiterin Dr. Adriana Slavcheva mit vielen Helfern und Beteiligten zu nennen. Den Hauptanteil der Last haben die Projekt- und Lehrstuhlmitarbeiter des Lehrstuhls für BWL, insb. Betriebliche Rechnungslegung und Interne Revision, Prof. Brauweiler, namentlich Katsiaryna Startsava, BA; Claudia Winkelmann, MA und Sören Förster, MA getragen. Daneben gab es natürlich viele unzählige Mitarbeiter der Fakultät sowie studentische Hilfskräfte, oftmals auch mit internationalem Hintergrund, was besonders erfreulich ist.

Nicht zuletzt danken die Herausgeber allen Teilnehmern der internationalen Tagung, die durch Diskussionen, Wortbeiträge und Fragen weitere wichtige Impulse für die innovativen Ansätzen erbracht haben.

Einen wichtigen Beitrag leistete das Wissenschaftliche Komitee, das den Peer-Review-Prozess der Artikel mitgestaltet und damit die Qualität des Buches gesichert hat.

Nicht zuletzt dankt der Chefredakteur seinen Mitherausgebern für die langjährige Freundschaft, die wissenschaftliche Unterstützung und ihre Bemühungen bei der Erstellung dieses Buches.

Die Herausgeber, im Juni / September 2019 sowie Frühjahr 2020:

Zwickau (D),	H.-Christian Brauweiler
Wolgograd (RU),	Vladimir V. Kurchenkov
Ust Kamenogorsk (KAZ),	Serik M. Abilov
Zwickau (D),	Bernd Zirkler

Scientific Committee

Table of Contents

Part A: Digitalization

Issues regarding cybersecurity in modern world

H. Geldiyev, M. Churiyev, R. Mahmudov

1 Introduction

Information security has always been a priority for any of the areas of human activity. Particularly acute is the issue of information security in our time - in the period of informatics and computerization. A new type of information security threat has emerged - a cyber-attack, as well as cyber war associated with it.

The authors try to define such concepts as cyberspace, cybersecurity, as well as assess the degree of danger of such phenomena as cyber-attack and cyber war. They believe that analyzing a threat with the use of information attack tools in organization of its defense is the most effective way to protect it. To do this, the work examines some properties of the registry of the operating system, used both to attack computer information and to ensure its security. In the article, special attention is paid to specially developed software that makes it possible to detect hacker and trojan attacks using the registry.

2 Cyberspace and Cyber Security

Challenges related to cyberspace and cyber security require government organizations responsible for security in the field of information technology or security in the field of communications to solve the problems of protecting the population and national interests from various kinds of influences. The ubiquity of modern computer systems and the ability to communicate or interact through various means, from mobile devices to portable computers, create a number of inherent vulnerabilities and possible attack vectors for the state and non-state parties. Using these vulnerabilities can lead to widespread consequences for national security through deliberate actions such as spying, reducing the effectiveness of command and control facilities, theft of intellectual property and sensitive personal information, disrupting the provision of essential services and functioning critical infrastructure or causing damage to the economy and industry.

News headlines contain many reports of hacking into commercial structures, data leaks, electronic fraud, disruptions in government or critical infrastructure, intellectual property theft, information leakage related to national security, and potential cyber destruction. The area that was once considered an electronic war or an information war, in which network security experts prevailed, is now being transformed into a wider area called "cybersecurity".

H.-C. Brauweiler et al. (Hrsg.), *Digitalization and Industry 4.0: Economic and Societal Development*, https://doi.org/10.1007/978-3-658-27110-7_1

Obviously, cybersecurity should aim to provide protection in cyberspace. Cybersecurity is defined as “an activity or process, ability, opportunity or condition in which information and communication systems and information contained in them are protected and / or protected from harm, unauthorized use, modification or operation”. In cyberspace, more and more dangerous and complex threats can develop. Cybersecurity aims to address these issues and ensure the normal functioning of cyberspace, protecting it from emerging threats in an effective way, including from cyber war.[1] This topic dates back to the advent of internet in the early 1990s[2], but becomes more and more prevalent.

The term “cyber war” has become firmly established not only in the lexicon of military and information security specialists, but also of politicians and representatives of the expert community. In the field of information security, the term "cyberwar" has become widely used since 2007.[3]

According to the de facto prevailing, but legally non-consolidated opinion of the overwhelming majority of military and information security specialists (regardless of their country), cyber war means deliberate actions to cause damage, seize control or destroy networks and facilities, industrial, social, military and financial infrastructure, as well as robotic and highly automated production, technological FIR lines. As a result of cyberwars, it is possible to observe the disruption of the work of business and financial centers, government organizations, the creation of disorder in the life of the country, therefore, the important life support and functional systems of populated areas suffer first. These include the water supply system, sewage, power plants, energy hubs, other communication networks.

The means of combat exposure in cyberwars is a program code that violates work, incapacitating, or providing interception of control of various kinds of material objects and networks equipped with electronic control systems.

2.1 Cyber war consists of two stages: espionage and attacks

The first stage involves the collection of data by hacking into computer systems of other states.

Attacks can be divided depending on the purpose and objectives of hostilities:

- Vandalism - posting propaganda or offensive images on web pages instead of original information,
- propaganda and information war - the use of propaganda in the content of web pages, in the distribution of messages,

---

1 See Shangin, 2013

2 See Hoffmann, Brauweiler, Wagner, 1995

3 See de Leeuw, Bergstra, 2007

- leaks of confidential data - everything that is of interest is copied from hacked private pages and servers, and secret data can also be replaced,
- DDoS attacks - attacks from several machines in order to disrupt the functioning of the site, the system of computer devices,
- disruption of computer equipment - computers that are responsible for the operation of military or civil equipment are attacked. The attack leads to the failure of equipment or to disable it,
- attack of infrastructure and critical facilities and cyberterrorism - impact on machines regulating engineering, telecommunication, transport and other systems that ensure the vital activity of the population.

3 The main features of a cyberwar

A short history of cyber-aggressions, as well as an analysis of cyber espionage and large-scale cybercrime, provide enough material to highlight the basic features of cyber war that radically distinguish them from all other types of hostilities.

First of all, the high level of anonymity of cyberwars is unquestionable. It is associated with the difficulties of determining cyber-aggressor. Partly, these difficulties are associated with the very nature of cyber war, as impacts on the computer / computer system through multi-layered and intricate electronic communication networks. In addition, there are numerous constantly improving software tools for detecting interference that hamper the detection of hacker programs.

Another distinctive feature of cyberwars is the *ambiguity of the time of their beginning*. All types of wars habitual to mankind began with well-recorded material actions and, accordingly, had a clear time reference. Multi-component programs, as the main weapon of cyberwars, can penetrate the networks and control systems of various military and civilian facilities and infrastructures in advance. In this case, the actual start of the war will be the penetration of these programs into the network, and the fixed moment of the start of the hostilities will be the activation of these programs for the purpose of destruction, or interception of control over the infected networks and objects.

A unique feature of a cyberwar is that it is potentially traceless. Any known weapon has pronounced signs of use that allow you to speak with confidence about the beginning, progress and consequences of military actions. It is well known that from the first days of the development of various kinds of hacker software, one of the main tasks was to ensure the non-detectability of the consequences of its use.

In this direction, as evidenced by the practice of imperceptibly overcoming the information security systems of both large corporations and state networks of various countries, great successes have been achieved. Accordingly, it is obvious that during the development of combat software, special attention will be paid to the masking of the consequences of its use under the imitation of the usual technical failures, malfunctions, or the consequences of errors on the part of the service personnel.

One should honestly acknowledge such an extremely unpleasant feature of cyber arms as the extreme complexity of their control by state intelligence and security systems. Many experts believe that, in its most sophisticated versions, cyber weapons are comparable in their consequences with the use of nuclear warheads.

Finally, one can't say about such a distinctive feature of cyberwars, as the absence of any framework of international regulation for them. Currently, the use of conventional weapons is regulated by the legal parties, and it is necessary to develop similar norms in relation to the conduction of cyber wars. With the help of such norms it would be possible to prohibit whole classes of cyber weapons, as is done with chemical and biological weapons.

4 Registry of the operating system as a section in the chain of computer information attack and means of its security

Registry is the heart of the operating system, its brain. One can endlessly associate it with anything emphasizing its importance, but none of those associations fully illuminate functional features of system registry, but partly they can be used to the main object of our work.

There were written many books, many forums were conducted and published on the Internet about purposes and functions of the system registry. That is why we will not talk about its work in detail, but we will note some features helping us perform these operations:
- Correct some "defects" shown in annotations of computer security methods,
- prevention of virus attacks,
- potential consequent system recovery.

4.1 Main keys of the system registry

HKEY_CLASSES_ROOT – this key consists of two data types.

1. Associations of files with programs which can open, print and edit them.
2. Registrations of classes for Component Object Model (COM –component model of objects) objects.[4]

[4] See Honeycutt, 2002

HKEY_CURRENT_USER – contains user settings of the console user.

HKEY_LOCAL_MACHINE – contatins general settings which means that settings of this branch are related to the whole computer and influence all users registrated in the system.

HKEY_USERS – contains user installations and corresponding configurating data, like window color, placement of elements on desktop, wallpapers, screensavers.

HKEY_CURRENT_CONFIG – a reference to present configurative data of present equipment profile.

Regarding data types, the most frequently used ones must be noted:

- REG_BINARY – binary data.
- REG_DWORD – two word values (32 bytes).
- REG_EXPAND_SZ – text of variables length.
- REG_MULTI_SZ – binary data containing string list.
- REG_SZ – text of constant length.

4.2 Registry as a "bridgehead" for virus and trojan attacks

Windows operating system looks like a system "closed" to program configuration at fist glance, but large numbers of WinAPI functions available for programming and functioning of the system registry creates another perspective on the issue.

Most programmers, IT-specialists and experienced users accept the system registry as an open code of the operating system.[5] They are right.

The problem is whether it is good or bad. The system registry available for direct editing by a user is an instrument if regulation and configuration of the operating system. But if it is available for program editing it may become a means of tasks directed to disfunction of operating system activity. It is a problem because the activity of an operating system can be influenced by a program whose author can be anyone.

We will take detailed look on the issue, but first we need to determine how a software can edit registry from outside. An object-oriented programming language will be used for our research (for example, Delphi).

There are standard functions for operating the system registry in the system of Delphi. In order to use **registry** module (**uses** section) must be connected in the code page of application form.[6]

---

[5] See Kokoreva, 2008

In the necessary event processing procedure registry variable needs to be introduced, for example:

Var

reg:Tregistry;

Thus, all operations related to the registry will be conducted with reg variable.

Standard program code allowing to open, close and edit one of the keys of the system registry programmatically is written below:

```
Reg := nil;
try
reg := TRegistry.Create;
reg.RootKey := HKEY_CURRENT_USER;
reg.LazyWrite := false;
.....................................................................
//Necessary operations are conducted in this section of the code.
.....................................................................
reg.CloseKey;
except
if Assigned(Reg) then Reg.Free;
end;
```

To open necessary keys and subkeys of the system registry, as well as to read them according to data types (string and integer types will be used as an example) an example of program code written below will be examined:

```
Var
reg:Tregistry;
s:string;
a:integer;
..........................................................
Reg.OpenKey(subkey path,false);
//for example, = ‚SOFTWARE\Microsoft‘
s:=Reg.ReadString(string parameter);
a:=Reg.ReadInteger(integer parameter);
Reg.WriteString(string parameter, s);
Reg.Writeinteger(integer parameter, a);
..........................................................
```

6 See Cantu, 2003

DeleteKey and DeleteValue functions are used to delete keys and their parameters, KeyExists and ValueExists functions are used to determine the existence of various keys and their parameters. Examples of their use:

If reg.ValueExists(parameter)=true then reg.DeleteValue(parameter);

If reg.KeyExists(key)=true then reg.DeleteKey(key);

For example,

if reg.ValueExists('DisallowRun')=true then reg.DeleteValue('DisallowRun');

if reg.KeyExists('System')=true then reg.DeleteKey('System');

Using examined functions a user can conduct any operations with the system registry from his/her program.

Keys responsible for autoload of programs are very some of the most important parts of the registry. There several such keys:

[HKEY_LOCAL_MACHINE\Software\Microsoft\Windows\CurrentVersion\Run]

[HKEY_LOCAL_MACHINE\Software\Microsoft\Windows\CurrentVersion\RunOnce]

[HKEY_LOCAL_MACHINE\SOFTWARE\Microsoft\Windows\

CurrentVersion\ RunOnceEx\000x]

[HKEY_CURRENT_USER\Software\Microsoft\Windows\CurrentVersion\Run]

[HKEY_CURRENT_USER\Software\Microsoft\Windows\CurrentVersion\

RunOnce]

Values containing program paths are indicated in string parameters of these keys (for example, *"C:\My_program\program.exe"*). During the load of operation system indicated keys are read and according programms are launched according to the value of their string variables.

Utilities, various service programs, antivirus programs are usually launched this way. It is easy to figure out that trojan or virus attacks can be performed this way. Carrying out according record about autoload in the necessary key of the system registry will be enough. Such a record is shown in the image below:

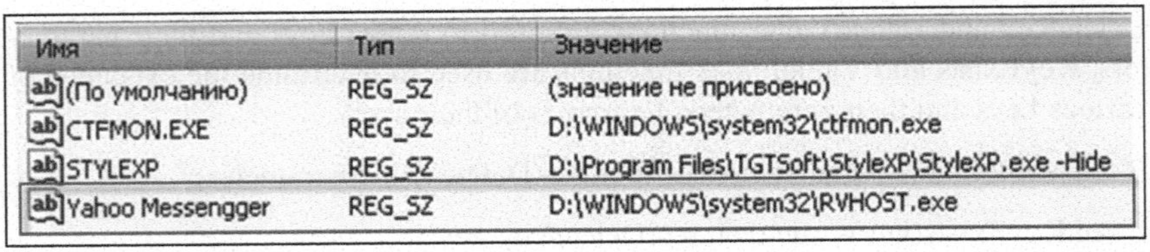

Имя	Тип	Значение
(По умолчанию)	REG_SZ	(значение не присвоено)
CTFMON.EXE	REG_SZ	D:\WINDOWS\system32\ctfmon.exe
STYLEXP	REG_SZ	D:\Program Files\TGTSoft\StyleXP\StyleXP.exe -Hide
Yahoo Messengger	REG_SZ	D:\WINDOWS\system32\RVHOST.exe

Figure 1: Record about autoload of a trojan program

Within the limits of this work some research have been carried out as a consequence of which more than a hundred virus and Trojan loaders were examined.

As a result of these research works it has been discovered that most attacks are carried out from system directories or user folders. For these purposes autoload records are skilfully masked under appropriate parameters.

In most cases loaders of viruses and trojan programs are loaded with the help of registry keys, not viruses and trojan programs themselves. Their loaders are not suspicious for antivirus programs. That is why determination of “superfluous” records in autoload keys without knowing program configuration of the operating system is quite complicated.

Besides, loaders of trojan and virus attacks can independently touch up some other keys of the registry, such as HKEY_CURRENT_USER \Software \Microsoft \Windows \CurrentVersion\Policies. Create **System** section in this key. Creating string parameters shown on the image (Figure 2) in that section will prevent the user not only from examining task panel, but also editing registry.

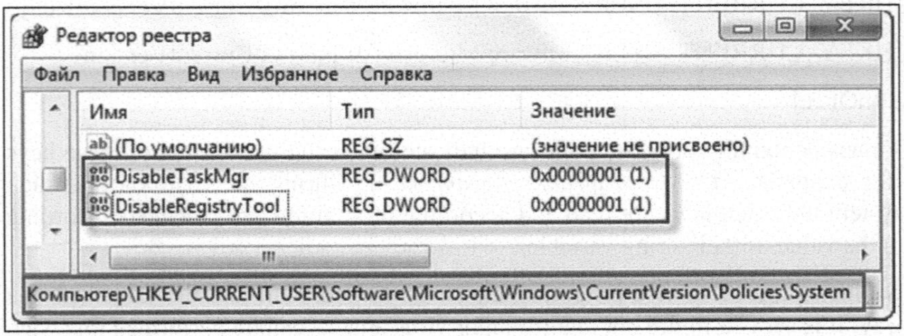

Figure 2: Blocking task panel and registry

In this case we will have to forget about visual editing of the registry, but programmatically deleting **System** key will necessary in order to amend the situation.

After that occurs another problem – ways of fighting with loaders and correct detection of autoload records. Registry monitoring should be carried out – checking autoload records with previously saved model-list, trace of new string parameters appearance, their conformity with the system tasks. It is not difficult to conduct this using program operating functions of the registry.

In recent years phantom loaders started to appear. Their detection is very difficult. Autoload of such loaders is carried out according to this principle: loader is launched by reading registry record, then it removes that record, at the moment of closure of operating system it automatically recovers the record. This process is repeated again and again.

As a result of research on these loaders it was managed to determine removal and recovery moments of registry records about their autoload as well as to create program codes preventing their load. In order to carry this out, the process of registry check must be launched after the recovery of registry record by the loader – it can be done by intercepting operating system's message about its completion. Practically, we need to act just like virus loaders themselves.

Taking into account all premises it is not difficult to understand that struggle against virus or trojan attacks conducted through the registry must be started from the system registry.

4.3 Registry as a means of development of computer information security methods

Information security has always been a priority for any of the areas of human activity. Different methods and ways of providing information security existed at different times. Some of them are still relevant.

Particularly acute is the issue of information security in our time - in the period of informatics and computerization.

Programs, files, different data carriers as diskettes, disks and etcetera are considered under the concept of information. Thus, issue of its security must also be examined from the computer technology perspective.

By examining modern methods and ways of providing computer information security, some technologies can be distinguished:

- Password security,
- limitation in launched computer programs,
- various right limitations of computer users,
- encrypting and cryptography.

Each of these methods has drawbacks and each of them allows the use of the system registry keys to a certain extent.

We aim to examine the weaknesses of the expressed information security methods. As a consequence of performed work we managed to find opportunities to fill the gaps by means of using keys and parameters of the registry.

Registry has a tree-like structure which looks Windows guide structure. It means that we can arrange some security parameters in its structure(correct password, record limiting program launch term, number of launches, unique distinctive features). Usually, these parameters are placed in a concealed file located on the disk. In some cases that file can be found by using searching resources.

In the visual design of the system registry, search on date of key or parameter creation is impossible. Often contents of files are analyzed with the help of debuggers or notebook and frequently something is found.

Contents of the registry can not be "read" by means of a debugger or another software revising byte content of files.

Search of files and their contents is frequently done by means of substitutive symbols (? – one symbol, * - several symbols) which makes the search of files and masked records inside files easier.

Substitutive symbols can not be used in the system registry

Search of multiple files can be conducted by determined criterion in file managers. Files complying that criterion are found and it assists searching results to be analyzed quickly and conveniently.

Search in the system registry is conducted consequently, keys and parameters "find" each other, which slows down "concealed" security parameter search.

In order to conceal data in a file they must be encrypted.

Data encryptment in the system registry can be conducted automatically by saving necessary data in a different data type.

Recording security parameters to a file on a physical disk, reading from it can cost some time, which slows down programm loading and that time interval becomes enough for hacking.

Reading programmatically from the registry and recording to it is carried out much faster which in turn does not influence programm loading nad allows additional records as check records for security reliability.

Well concealed security parameter is an important detail of software security. Program's consequent fate depends on that detail – whether becomes "loot" of hackers or its license period is prolonged.[7]

Premises, surely can be considered as an advantage of the system registry, allows to use its keys in software security chain, but it must be taken into account that register itself is not secured from program analyze.

5 "Antitroyan" software

In this part of the article we would like to describe a specially developed software which works with the system registry aiming against spy and trojan programs.

Antitroyan was developed as an answer to growing virus danger.

In spite of existing modern famous antivirus programs, programat virus attack makes more damage to user data. At a certain extent it is correlated with the weaknesses of the antivirus programs.

Antitroyan was developed in experimental conditions. Some of the most dangerous viruses had been launched on a computer, then methods of their manual removal were developed. These methods we programmed and compiled into machine code.

Program is developed on Delphi and contains about 100 system WinAPI functions.

Features of the program:

- Program is characterized by high speed. Program checks up to 200Mb information during 1 second. It allows to check modern computers in 40-50 minutes,
- program can detect and remove up to 200 viruses (most of which can not be detected and removed by other antiviruses),
- program works on Windows XP, Vista, Windows 7,8,10,
- works in harmony with other antivirus programs,
- program can easily be installed on contaminated computers,
- term of work is not limited,
- program conducts its own monitoring and removes itself in case of contamination,
- interface is developed in Turkmen and Russian languages,
- program provides instructions,

[7] See Churiev, Komoltsev, Muratlyev, 2012

- in case of appearance of significant operating system disfunctions various utilities working with the system registry and processes can be used.

Thus, developed software allows to effectively and quickly detect Trojans and other cyber-attacks and remove them in time.

Literature

Cantu, M. (2003). *Mastering Delphi 7, Sybex.*

Churiev, M., Komoltsev, I., Muratlyev, A. (2012). *Использование реестра в современных методах защиты. Тезисы Международной научной конференции «Наука, техника и инновационные технологии в счастливой эпохе могучего государства».* Ashkhabad.

de Leeuw, K., Bergstra, J. (2007). *The History of Information Security: A Comprehensive Handbook.* Elsevier Science.

Hoffmann, F., Brauweiler, H.-Ch., Wagner, R. (1995). *Computergestützte Informationssysteme, Einführung in die Bürokommunikation und Datentechnik für Wirtschaftswissenschaftler.* (2 ed.). Oldenbourg.

Honeycutt, J. (2002). *Microsoft Windows XP Registry Guide.* (1 ed.). Microsoft Press.

Kokoreva, O. (2008). *Реестр Windows Vista: Принципы организации и архи тектура реестра, структура и типы данных; Резервное копи рование и восстановление реестра. Устранение типовых проблем, связанных с реестром.* Petersburg: BHV.

Shangin, V. (2013). *Комплексная защита информации в корпоративных системах: Учебное пособие.*

Cyber-Crime - A strong growing Riskcategory: Prevention, Protection, Defense, Limitation of Loss

H.-Ch. Brauweiler[1]

1 Introduction

Today, in the days of the "Internet of Things", full-fledged connectivity, smart homes and so on our society – businesses, work environment, government, private homes – is dependent on electronic networks and information systems for many aspects of life.[2] The chance and sometimes easiness to enter into these information systems in order to draw on information from other people or businesses with criminal intend threatens citizens, businesses, governments and critical infrastructures: The evolution of information and communication technology has led to the development of criminal activities by using the internet resp. computers or computer networks: cybercrime.

There is much talk about cybercrime, but what exactly is it? The simplest answer is that "it's very complicated." Not unlike traditional criminality, cybercrime has various forms and can occur virtually anytime, anywhere and depends by and large on the abilities, resources and goals of the criminals. After all, cybercrime is nothing more than a criminal activity to which is added an "informatic" or "cybernetic" ingredient. However, it is important to understand the wide variety of types of cybercrimes, as it will be necessary to adopt different approaches and solutions to the respective types of cybercriminal activities in order to improve the security. Cybercrime can be industrial espionage, data loss, theft of crypto currency, credit card fraud or other forms. These notorious activities are performed by criminals in order to disrupt the harmonious society that we live in. Cybercrime is so dominant that it accounts for $ 600 bln of the world's GDP to combat the issue. Many laws and regulations have been formed in order to tackle this major issue. In a technologically advanced era like today, the laws need to be amended along with advancement of technology.[3] However, everyone must be aware, that laws will not prevent cybercrime, thus companies and responsible

---

1 Part of this work is based on various outcomes of student work in seminars related to Risk Management and Audit, conducted by the author in the past years. The author thanks numerous students of several classes and especiall Ms. Antonio Jiménez Gualda and Mr. Abhishek Raj Yadav for their work and contribution.

2 See Hoffmann, Brauweiler, Wagner, 1995

3 See Brauweiler, Risikomanagement in Banken und Kreditinstituten, 2015

H.-C. Brauweiler et al. (Hrsg.), *Digitalization and Industry 4.0: Economic and Societal Development*, https://doi.org/10.1007/978-3-658-27110-7_2

persons need to develop counteracting measures and include one focus on cybercrime into the Risk Management System.[4]

2 Definition of Cybercrime

Cybercrime can be defined as any form of criminal act that is committed online by using electronic communications networks and information systems. As it is very independent of the physical presence of the criminal or the victim and a physical location it is a borderless problem, making the prevention as well as the prosecution very difficult and only possible on an international level. Cybercrime can be classified in four broad definitions:

1. Crimes specific to the Internet, such as attacks against information systems or phishing (i.e. fake bank websites to solicit passwords enabling access to victims' bank accounts).
2. Online fraud and forgery. Large-scale fraud can be committed online through instruments such as identity theft, phishing, spam and malicious code.
3. Illegal online content, including child sexual abuse material, incitement to racial hatred, incitement to terrorist acts and glorification of violence, terrorism, racism and xenophobia.
4. Copyright-related offences (e.g. movies, music).

Another method to classify cybercrime is to look into the individuals or institutions affected. Thus cybercrime can be classified into these types:

1. Crime against individual
2. Crime against company or institution
3. Crime against society
4. Crime against the Government

The outcome of cybercrime can be extremely embarrassing for victims, and not only or singularly out of financial reasons. Victims may feel an upsetting intrusion into their privacy, and further on helplessness about the circumstances and effects.

3 History of the Development of Cybercrime

Cybercrime first started with hackers trying to break into computer networks. This, of course, can be condoned by governments in times of war or espionage, or by persons or organizations with purely criminal intend. One reason can be the curiosity or eagerness to break into high-level security networks, however, mostly the reasons are seen in gaining sensitive or classified material to exploit the data

---

4 See Brauweiler, Risikomanagement in Unternehmen, 2018

received by this. Eventually, criminals started to infect computer systems with computer viruses, which caused collapses of personal or business computers or networks. The rapid development of cybercrime is depicted in the following time-line:

1939. British cryptographer Alan Turing and his team at Bletchley Park invent the "Bombe", a code breaking machine.

1981. Ian Murphy aka Captain Zap became the first cracker to be tried and convicted as a felon (for hacking into AT&T).

1984. The US Comprehensive Crime Control Act gives the Secret Service of the USA jurisdiction over computer fraud.

1986. US Congress passes the Computer Fraud and Abuse Act which makes it a crime to break into computer systems.

1988. The Morris Worm (malware) spreads through 6,000 networked computers, debilitating government and university systems.

1989. First National Bank of Chicago is the victim of a $ 70 million computer theft.

1990. The Computer Misuse Act 1990 is passed in the United Kingdom, criminalising any unauthorised access to computer systems.

1994. Russian crackers siphon $10 million from Citibank and transfer the money to bank accounts around the world.

1996. Hackers alter Web sites of the United States Department of Justice, the CIA, and the U.S. Air Force.

1999. The Melissa worm is released and quickly becomes the most costly malware outbreak to date.

2001. The first incidences of (distributed) Denial of Service (DDoS) attacks are reported.

2004. North Korea claims to have trained 500 hackers who successfully crack South Korean, Japanese, and their allies' computer systems.

2006. Largest Defacement in Web History, at that time, is performed by the Turkish hacker iSKORPiTX who successfully hacked 21,549 websites in one sweep.

2010. Google's intellectual property is stolen by Chinese hackers in what came to be known as Operation Aurora.

2011. Sony's Playstation Network is infiltrated and brought down.

2014. The Bitcoin exchange Mt.Gox filed for bankruptcy after $460 million were apparently stolen by hackers.

Cybercrime in a narrow sense covers any prohibited or illegitimate activity directed by means of electric operation that targets the security of computer system or data contained in these.[5] A significant rise has been witnessed in the economic sector being hit by cybercrime and cyberfrauds. Around 0.7% of the world's GDP was compromised due to cybercrimes during 2014. Researchers expect a steady and significant growth. Europe is hit the hardest in terms of economic impact, which is estimated at 0.84% of the regional GDP, compared with 0.78% in North America, according to the latest report on the economic impact of cybercrime by security firm McAfee and the Center for Strategic and International Studies (CSIS).[6] The frauds related to cybersecurity have to be taken seriously. Yet most of the cyber related crimes go unreported in the business world, due to embarrassment of the victims. Researchers believe that 95% of crimes are unreported.

In the past, cybercrime was committed mainly by individuals or small groups. Today, we are seeing highly complex cybercriminal networks bringing together individuals from across the globe in real time to commit crimes on an unprecedented scale. Criminal organizations turning increasingly to the Internet to facilitate their activities and maximize their profit in the shortest time. The crimes themselves are not necessarily new (such as theft, fraud, illegal gambling, sale of fake medicines) but they are evolving in line with the opportunities presented online and therefore becoming more widespread and damaging.

According to Raj Samani, chief scientist and fellow at McAfee *"The reality is that cyber-crime is just an evolution of traditional crime and has a direct impact on economic growth, jobs, innovation and investment. Companies need to understand that in today's world, cyber risk is business risk."*[7]

4 Types of cybercrime

When any crime is committed over the Internet it is referred to as a cybercrime. There are many types of cybercrimes and the most common ones are explained below:

---

5 See Gercke, 2012
6 See Warwick, 2018
7 (Warwick, 2018)

4.1 Attacks on computer systems

Sophisticated criminals are able to exploit vulnerabilities on computers and other devices like mobile phones or tablets. Some of the techniques that they use include:

- Malware or malicious software (such as trojans, viruses and spyware) which monitor your online activity and cause damage to the computer.
- Unauthorised access or hacking. When someone gains access to your computer or device without permission.
- Denial of service attacks / Distributed Denial of service attack (Ddos). It is an attack (in the "distributed" case using a network of multiple sources) which floods a computer or website with data, causing it to overload and prevent it from functioning properly. This type of attack is more frequently targeted at businesses, rather than individuals.

Attacks can result in a criminal accessing your personal or financial details and can prevent you from being able to use your device or computer system properly.

4.2 Phishing and email spam

Phishing is a way that criminals trick people into giving out their personal or financial details. Phishing messages often pretend to come from legitimate businesses, such as banks or telecommunications providers.

Spam is electronic junk mail (unsolicited messages) sent by email, text message or instant message without the recipient's consent. Spam messages often contain offers of free goods or 'prizes', cheap products, promises of wealth or other similar offers. In many cases they try to lure the recipient to click on a malicious link, leading to a web-page, where the phishing is completed by asking for personal and financial data, or where malware will be automatically downloaded.

4.3 Illegal and prohibited offensive content

Illegal content includes, depending on the local jurisdiction, various forms of pornographic materials, especially depicting violence against other persons, often children. Further illegal contents is related to extremist political positions, advocating murder or terrorist-related acts. Extremist material online could include articles, images, speeches or videos that encourage hate or violence. Additionally, statements or posts made on social media, chat rooms or blogs that encourage hate or violence or that encourage people to commit acts of terrorism.

4.4 Identity theft

Identity theft occurs when your personal information (such as your name, address, date of birth or bank account details) is stolen – usually by phishing or by taking publicly available data from social networks etc. – and used to set up new email-addresses, bank accounts in your name. Even if you think that only few information about your live exists in public form, it might be sufficient to combine that out of several sources to set up a fraud. They can also use your personal information to create fake identity documents in your name or even apply for real identity documents in your name, but with another person's photograph.

Criminals may try to gain your personal information using a number of different techniques, including phishing. You may provide personal information over the phone or internet to what appears to be a legitimate business, but is actually a scam. Another source to illegally derive information is hacking into online accounts or business databases, where relevant information is stored. Yet the simplest form is to retrieve personal information from social media, as people often give out freely too much of their personal data.

4.5 Online trading issues

Online trading issues involve scammers targeting people who trade online. There are many types of possible fraud, all aiming at ripping off unsuspecting sellers or buyers. Online trading scammers usually advertise products at unreasonably cheap prices, tricking buyers to place orders, however never shipping the product after having the money received. Another fraudulent behavior is to pay the seller a larger amount than advertised, invent an excuse for the overpayment and then request the excess amount be repaid either back to the scammer or to a third party before the seller realizes the fraud, because the original payment is cancelled.

4.6 Cyber-bullying

Cyber-bullying or stalking occurs when someone engages in offensive, menacing or harassing behaviour through the use of technology. It can happen to people (of any age), companies and organizations anytime, and most likely anonymously. The posting of hurtful and untrue messages, images or videos online are frequent in cyber-bullying. Other forms can include the sending of unwanted messages online, often including abusive texts and emails, and again this will usually occur with high frequency. Further examples are the creation of fake social networking profiles or websites, intending to be originated by a person, which are untrue and hurtful. Last but not least, spreading of detrimental online gossip and fake news about a person or group of persons can do harm to the image and wellbeing of those affected.

4.7 Prevention of cybercrime

Cybercrime prevention can be simple and easy, attacks can easily be avoided, when you have some technical knowledge or advice and use your common sense. As online criminals try to make their money as quickly and easily as possible, the more difficult you make their job, the more likely they are to abstain from intruding or harassing you. The advices shown here will give some basic information on how to prevent online fraud.

Keep your computer current with the latest patches and updates. One of the best ways to keep attackers away from your computer is to immediately apply patches and other software fixes when they become available. Thus you block attackers from being able to take advantage of software bugs (vulnerabilities) that they could otherwise use to break into yoursystem.

Make sure your computer is configured securely. Keep in mind that a newly purchased computer may not have the appropriate level of security for you. When you are installing your computer at home, pay attention not just to make your new system function, but also focus on making it work securely. Configuring popular Internet applications such as your Web browser and email software is one of the most important areas to focus on.

Choose strong passwords and keep them safe. Strong passwords have at least eight characters that differ in type, i.e. use letters, numbers and symbols (e.g., # $ %) Keep your passwords in a safe place and try not to use the same password for every service you use. Change passwords regularly, at least every 6 months.

Protect your computer with security software. Security software includes firewall and antivirus programs.

Protect your personal information. Keep an eye out for phony email messages. Do not respond to email messages that ask for personal information. Steer clear of fraudulent Web sites used to steal personal information. Pay attention to privacy policies on Web sites and in software.

Online offers that look too good to be true usually are. The old saying "there's no such thing as a free lunch" still rings true today. While you may not directly pay for the software or service with money, the free software or service you asked for may have been bundled with advertising software ("adware") that tracks your behavior and displays unwanted advertisements or – even worse – contains a keylogger or trojan.

Review bank and credit card statements regularly. One of the easiest ways to realize that something has gone wrong is by reviewing bookings and debits on your bank account or credit card. Additionally, many banks and services use fraud prevention systems that call out unusual purchasing behaviour.

5 Challenges in fighting Cybercrime

The advancement in Internet Technology has not only helped the cyberofficers investigate crime easily but also has helped the cybercriminals to become more advanced than before. There are many ways to fight cybercrime, but combatting these has various challenges, which will be discussed in the following paragraphs.

5.1 Opportunities

The agencies involved in maintaining security and law can now easily investigate on illegal issues going on over the internet. Automation of the investigation process is difficult but there are several other ways to gear up the investigation. Keyword based search results have made it possible to takedown the illegal content off the internet. Hash value based approach is a modern and intelligent technique to track down the offenders, but distortion or modification of the original content makes it difficult to carry out the hash value based approach. Some forensic software are able to search for illegal activity in an automated way.

5.2 General Challenges

The everyday life of a common person now depends on use of ICT and various other internet communication protocols. People tend to use different applications and tools available to them without taking any security measures, especially small and medium-sized enterprises (SME) and individuals often do not have high security standards. Thus it makes the work of attackers much more easy to target only one operating system and victimize a lot of people. Strategies must be formulated to encounter those attacks and develop countermeasures including laws and software to protect the users.

The amount of users connected to the internet has had a drastic rise. There is also a rise in production and use of cheap equipment and freeware being installed in computers which makes the computer and user more vulnerable to offenders. With the rise in the amount of people it is difficult for the law enforcement agency to keep an eye on the activities and automate the law enforcement process.

The devices used for illegal hacking are found easily in the world market. Especially the developing and underdeveloped countries present a huge market for this. The password breakers or hacker system tools can be easily installed and used, they are often "plug and play", thus enabling even persons without IT knowledge, yet with criminal intend, to spy on unprotected passwords. The possibilities to use free public wifi puts the users into danger. Hackers can easily intrude these networks and get hold of private and confidential information of people accessing their email account or bank account via that network.

The investigation and prosecution of cybercrimes impose a number of challenges for law enforcement agencies (see following chapter).[8] The people involved in cybercrimes should not only be punished but also should be educated not to do so. Strict laws and regulations should be formulated and maintained in order to combat this issue.

5.3 Legal Challenges

With the development of computer related services, rise in new kinds of computer related crime has been observed. During the 1970's when computer networking was established for the first time, the first unauthorized access to computer system occurred shortly. Similarly the first ever software offence to occur was immediately after the personal computers became common to everyone.

Proper legislation is the foundation for investigation and the prosecution of cybercrime.[9] With the growing use of advanced technology it has become more difficult to update the criminal law in order to keep pace with new forms of crime. The update requires time and should be up to the point. The main challenge that the legal system faces is the delay between the recognition of potential abuse of technology and necessary amendments to criminal law. Many countries are working hard to catch up with legislative adjustments. The adjustment process can be identified into three steps as follows:

1. Recognition of abuse of new technology

Special teams such as computer incident response teams, computer security incident response teams, computer emergency response teams should be formed within law enforcement authorities to identify the potential threats before they cause any damage.

2. Identification of gaps in the penal code

Legislative amendments should be done from time to time. The laws should be checked and updated so that they can tackle the new kind of offences that emerge every day.

3. Drafting new legislation

Drafting a new legislation separately for cybercrime may result in duplication of the existing national legal framework. This could also result in waste of money and time. Nevertheless a new legislation, with the help of experts and cases studies from different organization and countries will not cause any harm. Instead it will strengthen the national legal framework of the country or the institution.

---

8 See Gercke, 2012

9 See Gercke, 2012

6 Protection of cybercrime

6.1 Prevention and defense from cybercrime

Numerous laws and regulation have been implemented to prevent cybercrimes and protect an individual or a company from cyber-attacks. Various countries have their own laws on national level. There are laws defined by a group of countries e.g. European Union at a higher level. Similarly, there are certain regulations which are defined by the strong prestigious organizations like the United Nations Organization (UNO) on an international level.

6.2 Cybercrime legislation and policies

The United Nations guidelines for the prevention of crime highlight that the government leadership plays an important part in crime prevention, combined with cooperation and partnership across the ministries and between authorities, community and organization, Non-Governmental Organization (NGO), the business sectors and private citizens.[10] While the law making bodies of government have their roles, so has the Information Communication Technology (ICT) regulators or service providers. A wider use of ICTs should be done by the telecommunication providers for a broader consumer data protection and industry development, cyber safety and mandatory implementation of cyberlaws.

Among the major global cybersecurity agenda, legal measures are considered to be the most important ones. There must be substantive criminal laws to criminalize the acts like illegal access, data interference, copyright violation and other computer fraud. A thorough analysis of the national laws should be done in order to bridge the gap between the cybercrimes done inside and outside the computer network. There is a necessity to develop a legal national framework which can strengthen the cyberpolicies. The criminal procedural law should be strong enough to punish the guilty. The tools to investigate cybercrimes should be advanced and efficient, different from those used to investigate regular crimes.

Globalization has caused cybercrimes to take a transnational dimension. There should be an international cooperation between countries to deal with these kinds of crimes and criminals. Due to internal laws and limited instruments of justice the international cooperation against cybercrime is considered to be challenging.

---

10 See Tafazzoli, n.d.

6.3 Software and cybercrime awareness

With the growth in number of people getting connected to this digital world, criminal activities have grown up in the same rate. It is not only the responsibility of the service provider to protect against cybercrimes but individuals or companies themselves should be aware of these. The company staffs should be given training on how to handle spam and unwanted mails. People should be made aware not to fall for hoax mail regarding money or any fake business plan.

Not only is awareness among people important, but also use of software can reduce falling for cybercrimes to a very large extent. The computer system or the mobile phone and tablets should always have an upgraded version of software. The software updates are rolled out in the market to enhance the security of the connected devices. The firewall system in the devices should always be enabled. It acts as a first digital barriers against bad packets being sent into the ports. Most people make a naïve mistake of using a low security common password for every account they use. This makes the user vulnerable to hackers and cybercriminals. Always use different passwords for different account. There are various sites which help you generate random strong password and store them in encrypted format. Antivirus and anti-malware software are a must for today's connected devices. Regular scans with the use of full packaged antivirus software is one of the best way to be protected against cybercrimes. Every email provider enables the users to use anti-spam feature. The users should never open unsolicited mails or any links from unknown senders. This makes the user most vulnerable to phishing attacks. The shopaholic users should always remember to shop only from well-known secured websites encrypted with HTTPS. Online shopping accounts for major amount of credit card frauds.

7 Conclusion

Cybercrime can affect our daily safety and people around us putting us in serious problems. There are numerous organizations that protect us against these cyberattacks but we must also be careful with the data that we upload to the networks. However, as long as there is a cyberspace cybercrimes will be prevailing. This is harsh but truth. Technology to act against cybercrimes will keep on advancing and so will the cybercriminals. There is always a race between the good the bad in the cyberworld. That is why we must continue to improve the protection systems in electronic devices, and especially in those containing database. There are various digital techniques to be secured from cybercrimes and cybercriminals.

An individual should act wisely while dealing with suspicious activity in the cyberworld. Never think that you are not important, your data is not important and no one has an interest to target you. The data of every single person who is connected to the internet is valuable to criminals.

While technology is increasing the criminals do not have to use weapons to commit a crime. The criminals of 21st century have their weapons on their desk and use mouse buttons, keyboards and cursors to execute their plan. Cybercrime should be taken in a serious manner and laws should be made right from the top government level to protect the cyberrights of the people.

Literature

Brauweiler, H.-Ch. (2015). *Risikomanagement in Banken und Kreditinstituten.* Springer Verlag.

Brauweiler, H.-Ch. (2018). *Risikomanagement in Unternehmen.* Springer Verlag.

Gercke, M. (2012). *Understanding Cyber crimes.* Hungary: ITU publications.

helnetsecurity. (2018). *The economic impact of cybercrime? Almost $600 billion.* Retrieved 29.4. 2020, from https://www.helpnetsecurity.com/2018/02/23/economic-impact-of-cybercrime/

Hoffmann, F., Brauweiler, H.-Ch., Wagner, R. (1995). *Computergestützte Informationssysteme, Einführung in die Bürokommunikation und Datentechnik für Wirtschaftswissenschaftler* (2 ed.). Oldenburg München.

Kaufmann, D. (2015). *German firms have learned to fear cyber-crime.* Retrieved 29.4. 2020, from https://www.dw.com/en/german-firms-have-learned-to-fear-cyber-crime/a-18308420

Tafazzoli, T. (n.d.). *Cyber Crime legislation.* Retrieved 29.4. 2020, from www.itrc.ac.ir

Warwick, A. (2018). *Economic impact of cyber crime is significant and rising.* Retrieved 29.4. 2020, from https://www.computerweekly.com/news/252435439/Economic-impact-of-cyber-crime-is-significant-and-rising

Opportunities, challenges and new competences in the digital working world

Daniel Markgraf

1 Introduction

We are currently facing new challenges in almost all areas of our lives. The extensive digitalization and the accompanying digital transformation are constantly changing our entire world. Yet change is nothing new in itself and most people will know the saying "nothing is as constant as change". So, what is currently different? What presents us with so many challenges? In a nutshell, change is accelerating and becoming increasingly disruptive. On the one hand, it provides us with many new technologies and opportunities, but also with so many options that we can no longer get out of making decisions. In addition, the changes and developments no longer affect just individuals and single regions. Digitalization in combination with globalization often leads to worldwide phenomena.

Accordingly, not only our working worlds, but all our living worlds are changing. Digitalization and digital transformation present them with new challenges and opportunities. Disruptive innovations lead on the one hand to the emergence of completely new business models that not only establish new competitors on the market, but also present established companies with the challenge of whether and how to adapt their own business models. On the other hand, these developments also mean that our individual communication and working worlds are becoming increasingly digital, making them more flexible but also more challenging.

Worldwide digital networking, new ways of communication and new working models are leading to a redefinition of social relationships, blurring boundaries between our established worlds and redefining relevant competences. In the following figure we have outlined some challenges and opportunities for the individual areas. It is now up to us as companies and individuals whether these changes are more integrative or disruptive for us.

In order to give a little more detail on the individual areas, the following article is divided into four areas. In the first step, the status quo will be presented in more detail in order to set current developments in a broader context. Followed by a description of the challenges for the companies and then for individuals. The presentation of the individual challenges ends with a brief outlook on the competencies and skills required in the future.

H.-C. Brauweiler et al. (Hrsg.), *Digitalization and Industry 4.0: Economic and Societal Development*, https://doi.org/10.1007/978-3-658-27110-7_3

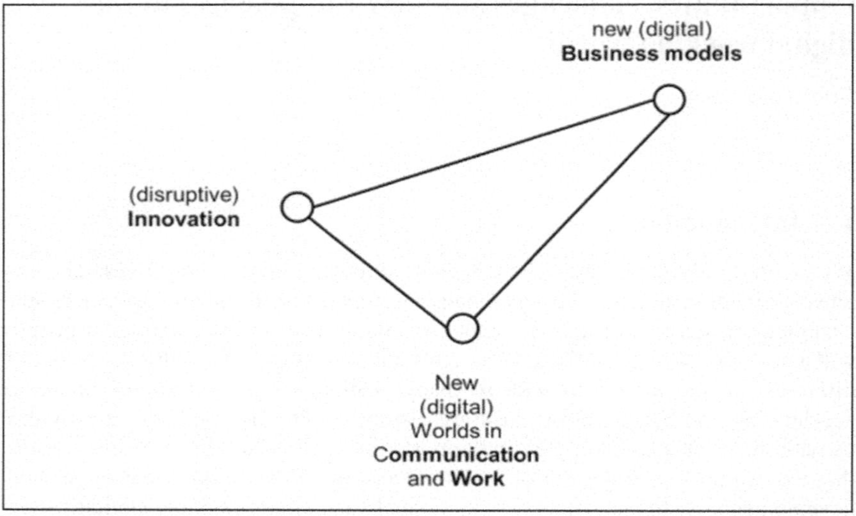

Figure 1: Fields of action in the digital Revolution

This contribution can and will only give an overview of the most important challenges and could be deepened in different directions at any point. With this in mind, we hope you enjoy reading this article and that you will be challenged to think about the points individually for yourself.

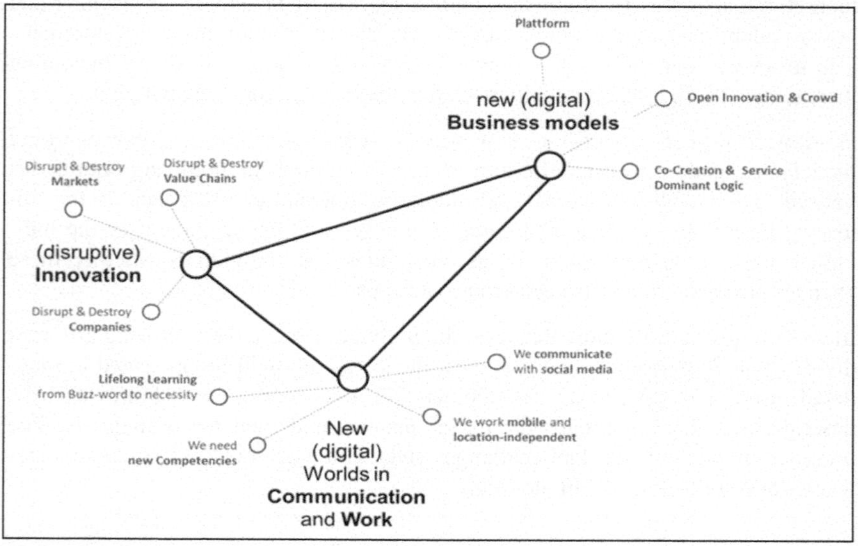

Figure 2: Exemplary challenges in the fields of action of the digital revolution

2 Digitization as driver of transformation

As in any previous industrial revolution, in transition and at this new level there will be ascenders and descenders, there will be drivers and driven ones, winners and losers. Many jobs and activities will be superfluous or taken over by robots. Others, on the other hand, will gain in importance or emerge completely new. The question that each individual must ask himself is on which side of development he wants to be and whether he can shape structural change in a positive way for himself, his company and the society. It also shows the various fields of action that arise. Digitization and the increasing interconnectedness on the basis of cyber-physical systems may be the trigger and the basis of the fourth industrial revolution, but the effects will extend to the most diverse other areas and also trigger or require revolutionary changes there.

The social change triggered by these changes can only be managed jointly over time. For ourselves, however, we can make the decision anew each day - whether we accept the challenge or not, the fourth industrial revolution will not be stopped.

Scenario 1: We can decide to hold on to the old and convince ourselves that things won't get so bad. If we are lucky, we will find a warm place in a museum or create a niche where we can survive. But let's be honest, how many companies have survived in the niche for record players, video recorders or pinball machines?

Scenario 2 (slightly shortened and adapted after Dawar 2018)[1]: Our everyday life could look something like this: Your self-driving car drops you off at home this afternoon before it drives on to the dealer for the next inspection. It will be back in time to chauffeur you to the train station on Monday morning.

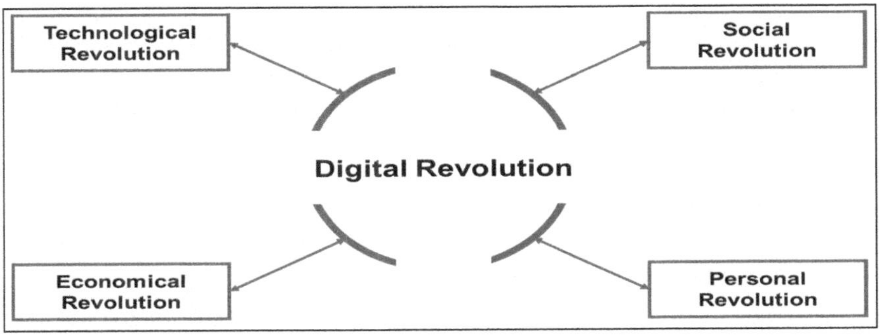

Figure 3: Fields of action of the fourth industrial revolution

1 See Dawar, 2018

On your way into the house, you'll quickly collect your drone deliveries in your front yard and the familiar voice of Eva, your intelligent personal digital assistant, will welcome you in your hallway. She friendly points out your travel plans for next Monday. Only now will you know the details of your trip to Stuttgart, where you will not be attending a web meeting as usual, but a face-to-face meeting at your company. Eva has already taken care of all the details, finding the best train connection, booking the seat and reserving the best possible hotel room.

When you unpack your deliveries, you will see that Eva has adapted your weekly purchase: This time there was considerably less perishable food, but instead hygienic articles in travel size. She also calculated that you would run out of detergent and (knowing that you would come home with your worn clothes on) ordered new ones - but now a cheaper brand that was highly praised in product reviews. And because Eva also knew that you would have little desire to cook, she ordered your favorite dish in advance, which the delivery service will bring when you return home.

Not only does your smart language assistant manage your shopping and travel, she also keeps an eye on your expenses and looks for ways to cut costs. From time to time you still have to train with your personal assistant or give her some tips on how to optimize your travel. Recently, however, these trainings and tips have become much rarer. On the contrary, Eva makes you suggestions that you might not have thought of.

Scenario 2 may still sound a bit like science fiction, but many of the aspects presented are not so far in the future. Rather, most of them are already technologically possible today and only need to be integrated into our everyday lives. The fact that the digital transformation started immediately with the advent of the internet in the early 90s, influenced our work environment immediately[2] and cannot really be stopped is something we already see in everyday life - what would we do without our little helpers such as Google, Wikipedia and smartphones? So, we are already in the middle of the digital transformation, in the fourth industrial revolution, and the question is no longer whether we want it, but rather what we make of it and how we deal with it.

3 Changing work environments

3.1 Chances and Challenges on a company level

Of particular interest in this context is the interface between professional and private life, as it connects the most important areas in our lives. In 2013 and 2018,

2 See Hoffmann, Brauweiler, Wagner, 2019

the author carried out extensive studies on the changing world of work, which also deal with the most important aspects of digitization and its effects.

The basic findings were a high number of overtime hours, which even increased over time. We spend much of our time in meetings, with e-mails and other communication tools to coordinate, share and exchange information: According to our own perception, we spend "too" much time in meetings, above all because only a little more than half of the agreed to-dos are implemented. From these points it can be seen that our working world is now very much influenced by communication and interaction. Communication is also becoming more and more digital. E-mail, for example, can no longer be assigned to modern communication channels, but rather to established ones. However, for the first time, e-mail also highlighted the challenges of increasing digitalization - we are becoming more and more flexibly reachable. Evenings and weekends are no longer automatic communication barriers.

In addition, however, we are also in a phase of upheaval in this area. The new collaboration tools like skype, slack, teams or facebook try to make e-mail obsolete with messenger-, network- and collaboration functions.[3] As in most transition phases, these developments run parallel for a while, which leads to a double burden for many of those affected. We are therefore no longer only available by e-mail, but also in messengers and social networks, both professionally and privately. This effect intensified with the social networks and instant messengers, so that you are now often reachable for colleagues and customers on weekends.

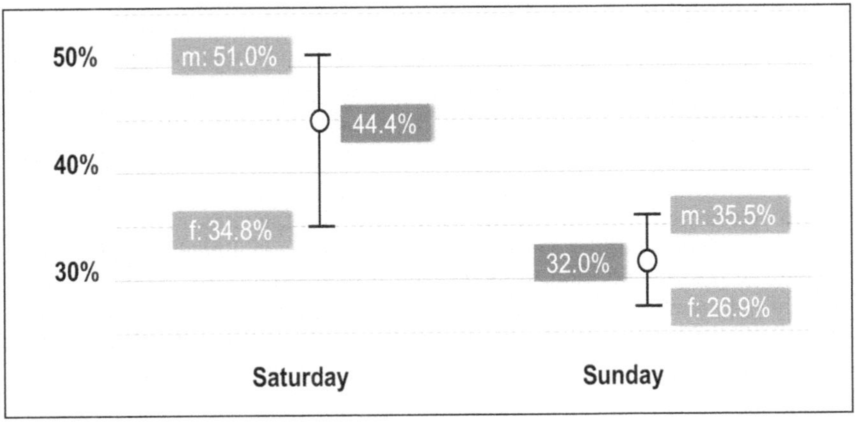

Figure 4: Share of e-mail processing at weekends (Markgraf, 2018; m=male, f=female)

[3] See Bersin, 2019

Accordingly, the main result of the 2018 study was that the 6-day week is back. We work more than contractually agreed and are often available the whole week (including the weekend) for our colleagues, business partners and customers.[4] The increasing flexibility in all areas of the working world presents both us and the company as an organization with a multitude of opportunities and challenges.

Due to the advancing digitalization in all areas, the end devices we use are not only becoming smaller and smaller, but also increasingly mobile. In the meantime, mobile devices have displaced the PC from its top position. This is reflected not only in the sales figures for the device categories, but also in the importance that mobile devices now have at the workplace. Notebooks and smartphones, in particular, have become an indispensable part of everyday working life.

Not only are the devices provided by the company becoming increasingly more portable, many employees also bring their own devices with them or use them for professional tasks. As early as in 2012, Cisco looked into this development in more detail and found that this is a practice that is often lived and will continue to gain in importance.[5]

With the increasing mobility of our devices, our data and data access will also become more mobile. Accordingly, many companies rely on cloud solutions to enable access to data and programs independent of time and location, but also to ensure necessary scaling in the business model. The market for cloud solutions is growing rapidly worldwide and increasingly offers customizable solutions for different company sizes and application areas.[6] Further growth can also be expected in this area in the future, as the distribution of cloud solutions is still expandable, and the application areas are also being continuously expanded. The following figure summarizes the current use of cloud offerings for data storage and processing.

Both the use of the cloud and the use of private devices at the workplace confront companies with completely new and different legal and technical challenges that need to be clarified. The above result also shows that the relevance has been recognized, but that actions have not yet been taken or changes are being made step-by-step and not continuously. How difficult it is for companies to cope with the changed requirements and the new situation can also be seen from the fact that only every third company has any rules at all regarding the use of private devices at the workplace.[7]

---

4 See Markgraf, 2018a
5 See Cisco IBSG 2012; See Cisco IBSG, 2013
6 See Kroker, 2018
7 See Markgraf, 2018

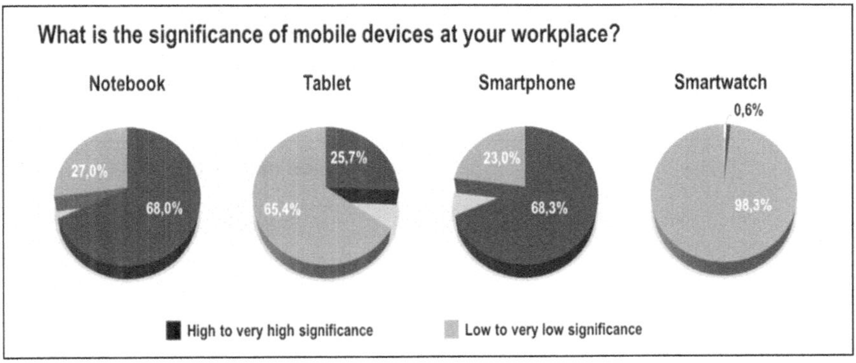

Figure 5: Use of mobile devices at the workplace (Source: Markgraf, 2018)

Analogous to the previous stages of development in the industrial revolution, the effects of digitization are not only evident in the shifts in equipment categories and the emergence of new technological possibilities, but also in the adaptation of existing processes and the establishment of new ones. These opportunities are recognized as positive effect by the companies. The new processes are quickly implemented, as the agreements on the statements on the impact of digitization on the processes show. From the companies' point of view, the processes will not only become more standardized, but also faster, more effective and more efficient. Only in the area of individualization are lower approval rates.

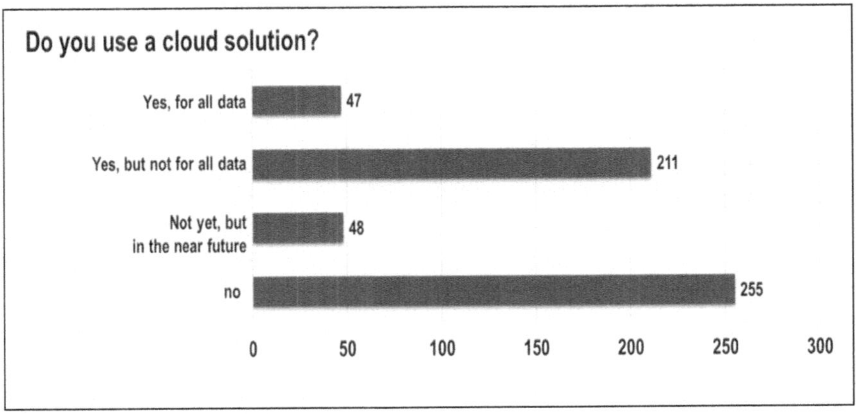

Figure 6: Usage of cloud solutions for data keeping (Source: Markgraf, 2018)

However, the approval rate for the statement that the processes are becoming more individual through digitization is still at 50 percent, which can be seen as positive given the high standardization rate in digitization. In addition, internal standardization does not necessarily have to be negative for external processes and integration of customers. Rather, established standards can be used as a common basis for standardized collaboration or further individualization. Accordingly, the effects of digitization on customer relationships are almost consistently positive.

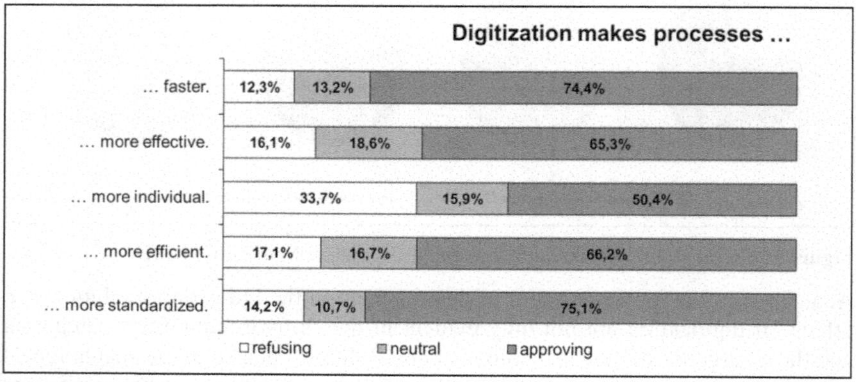

Figure 7: Impact of digitization on processes (Source: Markgraf, 2018)

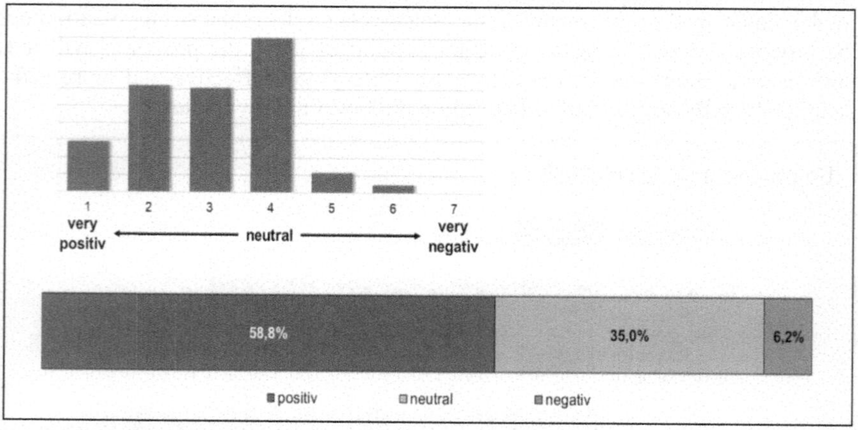

Figure 8: Effects of digitization on customer relations (Source: Markgraf, 2018)

It is particularly noteworthy that the proportion of respondents who see negative effects on customer relationships is very low. Rather, it is the case that digitization not only simplifies workflows, but also enables customers to be more closely involved in design and decision-making processes.[8]

[8] See Markgraf, 2018

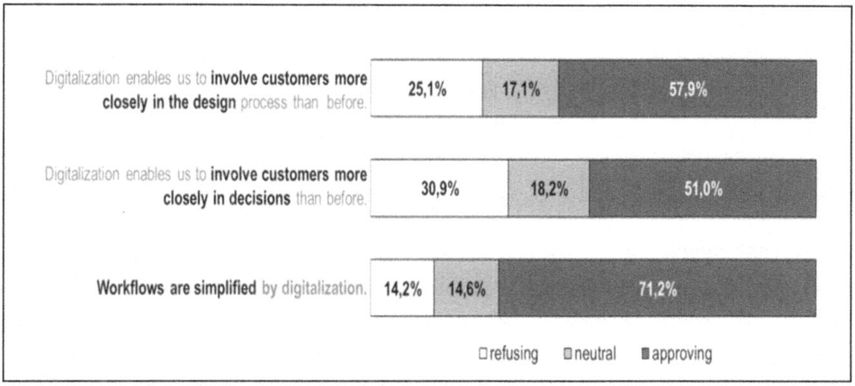

Figure 9: Effects of digitization on customer relations II (Source: Markgraf, 2018)

More than ever, from a marketing point of view, digital transformation must be based on the customer and his ability to imagine something. Or as Steve Jobs put it: "...you've got to start with the customer experience and work backwards to the technology."[9] Accordingly, we can also benefit from the digital transformation - by starting with the customer and his ability to imagine something and integrating him into our processes right from the start. There are several ways to do this at different stages of the product creation process. While digitization allows the idea of open innovation to be extended to the broad masses through crowdsourcing and co-creation within the framework of idea generation and design, digitalization often not only challenges but even disrupts the classic business models.[10,]

New digital business models are often structured as platforms and offer completely new design possibilities for suppliers, operators, owners and consumers. Even on the production and sales side, there are completely new opportunities for suppliers and consumers - the idea of a swarm production would only be one of many.

However, many of these possibilities are not really new, but rather reach their individual tipping point through the possibilities of digitization and become available, affordable and applicable for the broad mass of companies and individuals. All these individual possibilities are covered by a large number of publications which deal with individual aspects in greater depth. Accordingly, none of these areas will be discussed in more detail in the following sections. Rather, an overview is to be given and individual aspects to be considered are included. In addition, further possibilities are to be pointed out.

[9](Duarte, Sanchez, 2016, p. 256)

[10] See Christensen, Metzler, von den Eichen, 2011; See Christensen, Raynor, 2018

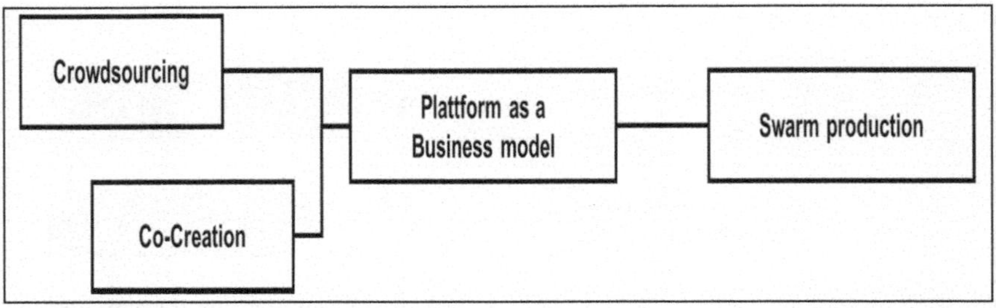

Figure 10: Opportunities through digitization in the entire value creation process of the business model

In the first step it is useful to roughly classify the areas of Open Innovation, Crowdsourcing and Co-Creation and to distinguish them from each other before we will briefly deal with the areas of Crowdsourcing and Co-Creation. A summarized presentation based on Neumann (2017) is a good way of defining the two areas.

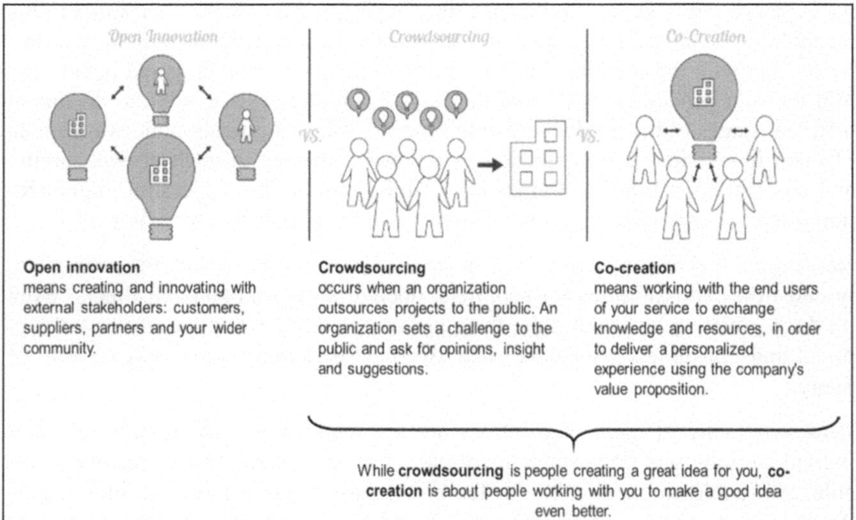

Figure 11: Open Innovation vs Crowdsourcing vs. Co-Creation (own representation based on Neumann 2017)

While Open Innovation is more of a strategy or basic attitude towards innovation behaviour, crowdsourcing and co-creation can be used as direct instruments in interaction with customers - in the sense of involving customers in design and decision-making processes.

According to the above definition, crowdsourcing is much more than "just" the wisdom of many. Rather, there are the different application scenarios, some of which are presented below as examples:

- Crowdsourcing approaches such as the Seti@Home project rely on the use and combination of many comparatively small resources for the realization of larger projects.
- Approaches such as Wikipedia primarily use the wisdom of the many to provide information or answer questions.
- Crowdfunding models like Kickstarter focus on financing larger investments through many comparatively small amounts from a larger number of investors. Often this method is also used to test the marketability of ideas. If the financing goal could be reached, the idea will be realized, if not, it will not be realized.
- Crowdtesting continues this idea and integrates early adopters and experts into a early product development and testing process. Microsoft, for example, uses different levels of test groups before upgrades and updates are delivered to the vast majority of customers.
- Mobile crowdsourcing is a result of the increasing use of mobile devices that are equipped with a location function (e.g. GPS) and thus enable the selective collection of location and movement data. One area of application, for example, is real time traffic information in navigation devices.

Especially the last two application areas - crowd testing and mobile crowdsourcing - show the smooth transition from crowdsourcing to co-creation.

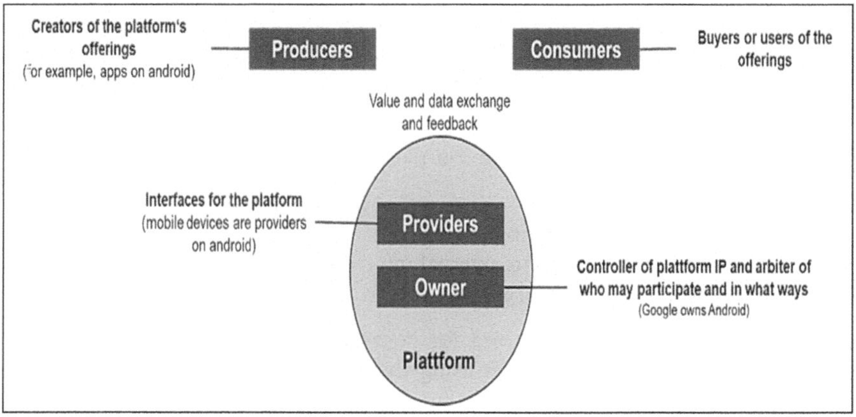

Figure 12: The players in a platform ecosystem (Source: Alstyne, Parker, Choudary, 2016)

The co-creation approach, which can be defined as "the joint creation of value by the company and the customer; allowing the customer to co-construct the service experience to suit their context"[11], is probably not a new one for all those active in the service industry. Normally, even during a regular visit to the hairdresser, there will be coordination between the service provider and the customer, quite apart from the fact that the customer is actively involved in the service provision process. Anyone who has ever set up an IKEA shelf or played with LEGO will understand that this approach can be applied not only to services but also to products. Again, the basic idea is not really new, but the possibilities that arise from the digitalization of processes and interactions are carried into areas where this was previously unthinkable. The process of co-creation can be roughly broken down into two essential steps in the early phases of idea and product development.[12]

1. the generation of new concepts and ideas
2. selection of specific concepts and ideas
3. the generation of new concepts and ideas
4. selection of specific concepts and ideas

However, the process of co-creation does not have to be limited to the idea and offer development phase. Rather, co-creation can be seen as a continuous component, as Vargo & Lusch represent in their Service Dominant Logic and postulate as FP6: "The customer is always a co-creator of value".[13]

A further opportunity for companies arising from digitization is the design of business model as a platform. This is a big opportunity for new companies but at the same time a big challenge for established companies. In this case, a platform - and thus the business model - can be seen as a marketplace that offers not only the infrastructure, but also binding rules for producers, providers, owners and consumers.

There are three major shifts due to the platform ecosystems and the associated networks.[14]

1. from controlling to organizing resources
2. from internal optimization to external interaction
3. from customer value to ecosystem value.

How important network effects are for companies and the establishment of a platform is summarized by Griffin using the example of the software business:

11 (Prahalad, Ramaswamy, 2004, p. 8)
12 See Ihl, Piller, 2010, p. 10
13 (Vargo, Lusch, 2006, p. 44)
14 See van Alstyne, Parker, Choudary, 2016

"Nothing scales as well as a software business, and nothing creates a moat for that business more effectively than network effects".[15]

Finally, even in the final stage of the process, the possibilities of digitization can be utilized, for example through swarm production. Two remarks, however, are permitted. On the one hand this area can be assigned to the crowd approach already mentioned and on the other hand it shows that this area is not fundamentally new. Rather, it is also true here that the progressive penetration of digitization makes this possibility accessible to a broader mass of companies and individuals or that it can only be used sensibly by them now. In the consulting industry, among craftsmen and construction companies, but also among programmers, this trend has been used for a long time. A large task can be transferred to different players for realization, so that more resources can be used than an individual could provide. With the increasing spread of robotics and additive manufacturing processes such as 3D printing, this can be transferred to ever new areas. For example, only the construction plans are made available instead of transporting the finished products throughout the country.

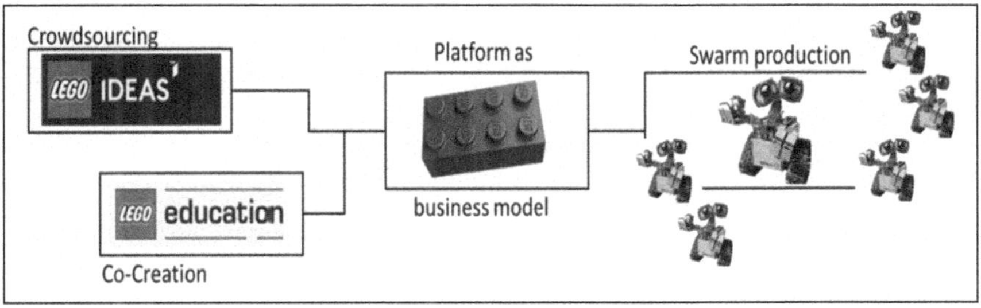

Figure 13: Possibilities of digitization and digital transformation using LEGO as an example

Let us summaries the previous points using a brief example. Most people will have been involved with LEGO before and will have found that the building blocks - if you have enough of them - are the perfect platform for realizing ideas that lie outside the building plan. In recent years, LEGO has taken advantage of these opportunities and actively used them for its own purposes.

LEGO Ideas gives LEGO the opportunity to involve customers directly in the idea generation and product development process. Fans can contribute their own ideas, and if you receive more than 10,000 votes from other fans for your ideas, LEGO will check if the idea can be realized. This is where the advantages of LEGO as a platform come into play, which no longer just consists of the bricks

15 (Griffin, 2016)

themselves but also of a large number of licenses. So, these ideas can be realized together with partners and distributed through different channels. One of the ideas was the realization of Wall-E from the Pixar film of the same name.[16]

In LEGO education, LEGO takes a slightly different approach, working with teachers and education specialists to develop assignments and teaching materials. The focus is not on exam performance, but on project results and the fun of discovery. The joint development of the sets and related teaching materials is a very good example of how co-creation can work in practice.[17]

With the spread and quality of 3D printing increasing, LEGO could ultimately move to supplement production at its main production sites with 3D printers elsewhere, especially in times of high demand. For example, certain sets could be produced on-site at the toy store or toy department. The own capacities would be relieved in such a way and different logistics services would be omitted and/or shifted into the digital area. Replacement modules would also no longer have to be ordered and shipped individually but could simply be printed out nearby.

These relatively simple examples show that digitization offers us opportunities for digital transformation in all phases of our business model. As shown in figure 13 and illustrated by the LEGO example, these benefits are already being actively exploited by many companies.

3.2 Chances and Challenges on an individual level

With the increasing use of mobile Internet access, both the devices and the work with them become increasingly location-independent. This also offers different opportunities and challenges on an individual level. How do we want to organize our work and our life in the fourth industrial revolution?

In general, the digitalization of the working environment and the use of mobile devices enables an increasingly flexible working environment in terms of time and place.[18]

These two statements briefly summaries the most important opportunities and challenges. The previous subchapter already showed that the use of mobile devices is already established in our professional environment and that the use of cloud solutions is increasingly in use. It can be assumed that both developments will continue in the future. The digital transformation uses the opportunities of increasing digitalization and applies them to existing processes, develops them

---

16 See LEGO Ideas, 2012, 2015
17 See LEGO education, 2018
18 See Markgraf, 2018

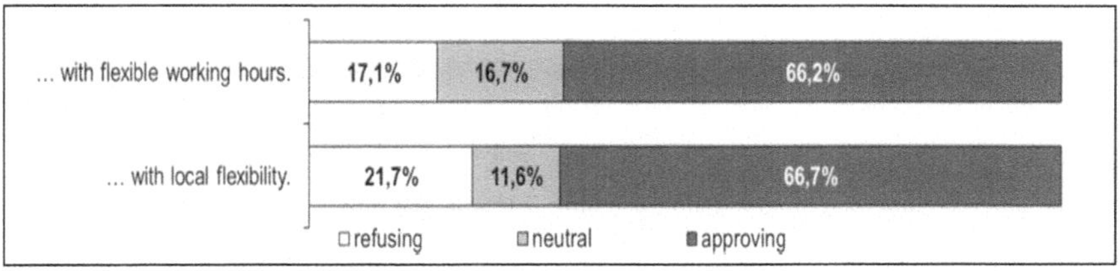

Figure 14: The digitalization of the work environment and the use of mobile end devices enable me to work ... (Source: Markgraf, 2018)

further or completely new. This shows that a high proportion of the processes can already be digitized today. Similarly, almost 60% of personal folders are already digital.[19]

If this information is combined with the possibilities of the cloud and cloud-based office programs, it becomes clear that not only our communication can now take place primarily digitally, but also that work processes can increasingly be digitized and transferred to mobile devices. It is therefore becoming easier and easier to carry out large parts of the work - even collaborative work - regardless of location. Whereby 'simple' refers to the pure possibility and not yet to the real implementation. However, it turns out that digitalization also offers the possibility of reducing a considerable stress factor in our current world of life and work - commuting to and from the place of work.[20]

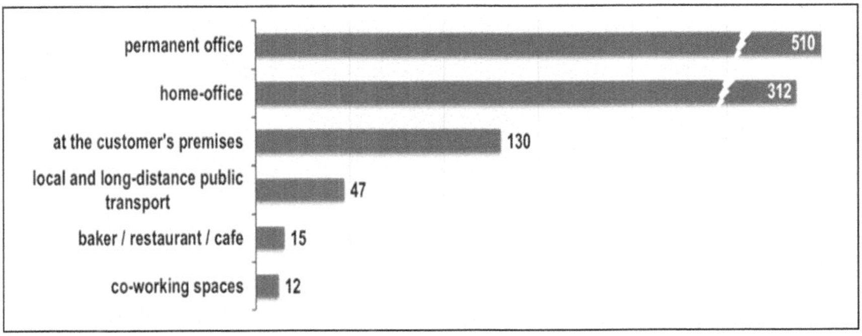

Figure 15: Where do you work regularly? (Source: Markgraf, 2018)

In addition to the increasing importance of mobile devices and the also increasing use of private devices in the professional environment, digitization, as already

19 See Markgraf, 2018
20 See Schareika, 2018

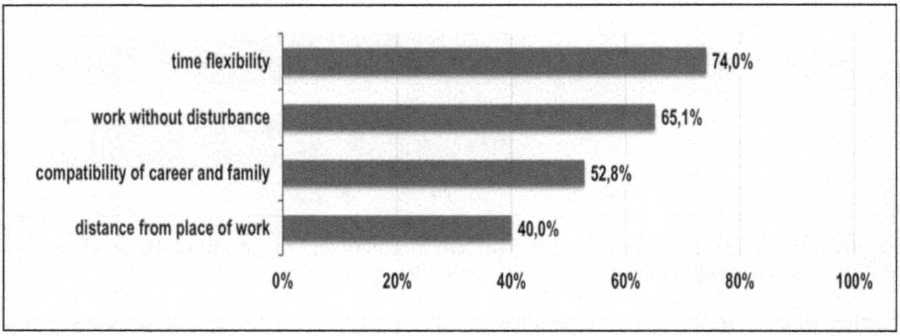

Figure 16: Reasons for working in the home office (Source: Markgraf, 2018)

noted, also makes it possible to increase the flexibility of places of work. Many tasks can already be performed from any location if the necessary technical prerequisites are created. As part of his survey, Markgraf (2018) identified the places where respondents regularly work.

As expected, it was found that most of the participants continued to indicate a permanent office as their regular workplace. However, a pronounced use of the home office is also becoming increasingly apparent. From the employees' point of view, there are various reasons for this:

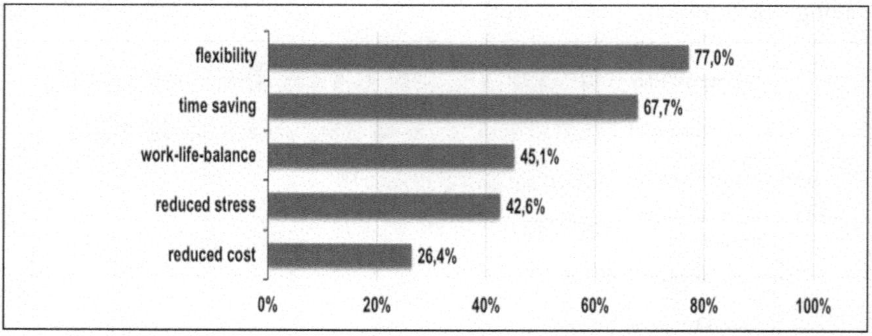

Figure 17: Advantages of working in the home office (Source: Markgraf, 2018)

Among the advantages are the high values for flexibility and work-life balance, as well as the confirmation of the two reasons already mentioned above: flexibility in time and compatibility of work and family life. With the at least partial elimination of the commuting, many participants also save time. Reduced costs are cited as the least advantage, as the following figure shows.

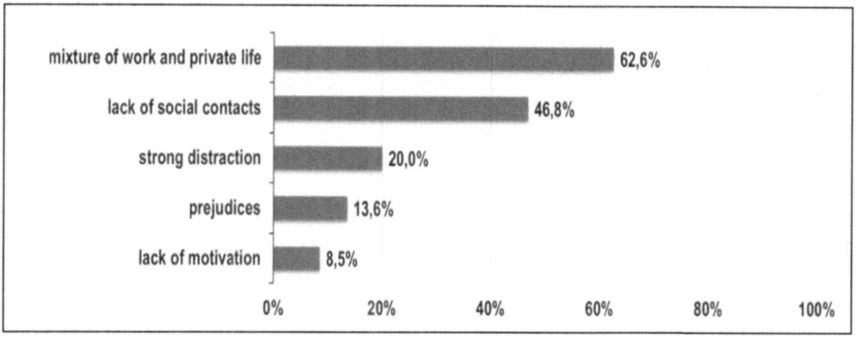

Figure 18: Disadvantages of working in the home office (Source: Markgraf, 2018)

However, the possibility of working in the home office is not perceived positively in all cases, as the disadvantages show. The results of Markgraf (2018) also coincide with those of previous studies.[21] Overall, however, it can be stated for these results that the negative aspects were mentioned less than the positive aspects. The participants in the study were particularly critical of the fact that there is a mixture of work and private life and that social contacts are lacking. These results are also quite consistent with previous results.[22]

Fundamentally, many of these disadvantages can be eliminated by fixed regulations on accessibility and support in dealing with and perceiving the home office. However, it turned out that only just under one fifth of those surveyed had such regulations in place within their company. Particularly in view of the above-mentioned possibilities of digitization and the problems that arise, among other things, from commuting, all sides should simply become more aware of the advantages and opportunities of working in a home office. With an increasing awareness of the importance of the home office and an equal recognition of the services provided there, many static regulations can be dispensed with. However, this often requires adjustments to the individual work culture as well as to the management and corporate culture.

It is currently apparent that the increasing flexibility in terms of time and location offers numerous advantages and opportunities, but also various challenges. In the last sections, the advantages were highlighted. However, it is also important to consider the impact of increasing digitization on the overall workload. This shows

21 See Schlinkert, Raffelhüschen, 2018
22 See Schareika, 2018

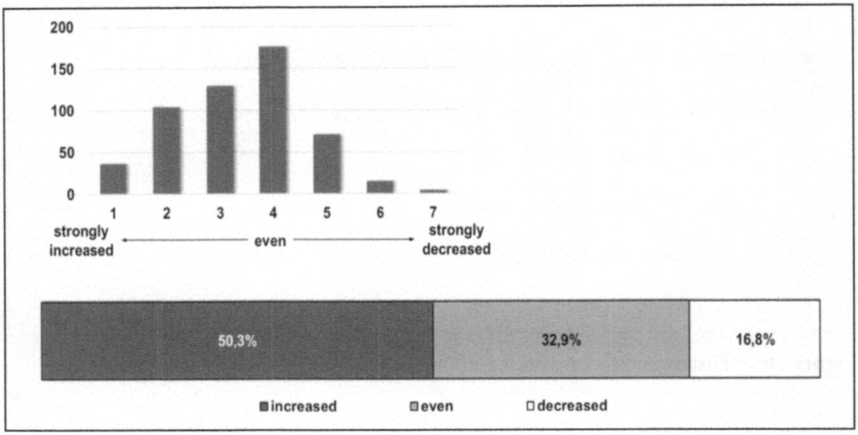

Figure 19: Effect of digitization on work life balance (Source: Markgraf, 2018)

that many of the challenges mentioned have not yet been solved. At present, the workload remains neutral at best, in many cases it even increases.

However, the increase is not only due to the flexibilization, but also to the fact that the new concepts and the social media are often not anchored in the corporate strategy. Therefore, there are no guidelines for dealing with the social media and the integration into existing or the establishment of new regulations has not yet been completed. As a result, there is often a greater burden at the present time, which is also reflected in the results on the question of the effects on the work-life balance.

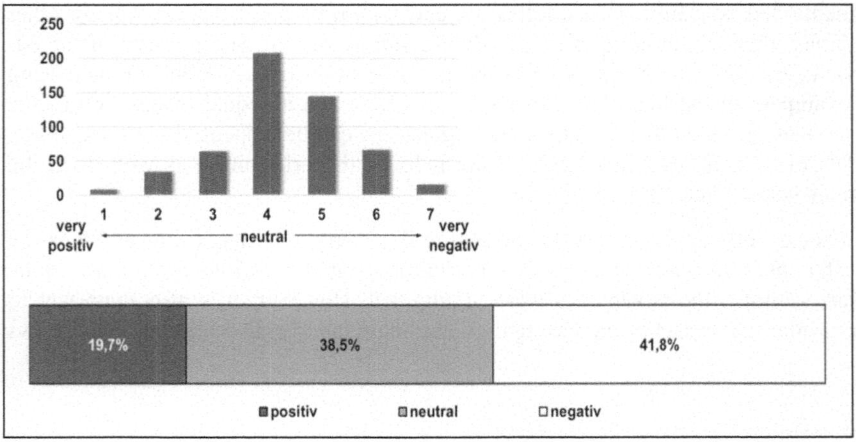

Figure 20: Change of individual workload through digital working methods and processes (Source: Markgraf, 2018)

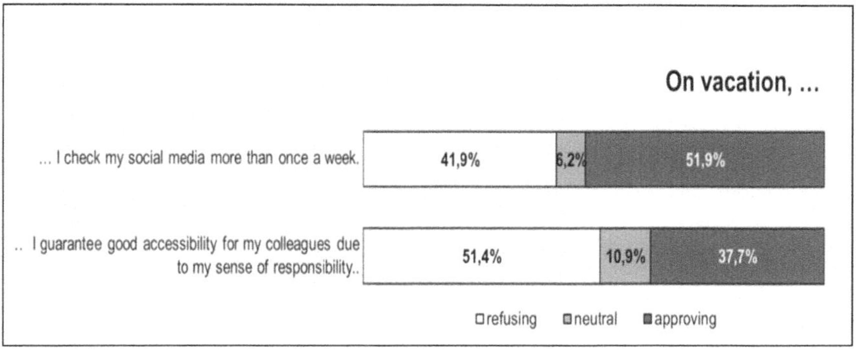

Figure 21: Processing of electronic media outside the regular working days (Source: Markgraf, 2018)

The two figures above illustrate the task facing employees as individuals but also companies as a social unit. Not only new processes have to be established, but also opportunities have to be taken and completely new competencies have to be learned and developed.

Digitalization optimizes our processes, creates a great deal of new data and information and raises expectations that we often cannot meet. The expectations are not only defined from the outside but are also placed on us by ourselves. Fundamentally, it can be said that the availability of information and accessibility are no longer the solution to our problems but are increasingly becoming a problem themselves. Whereas in the past we often had an information problem in the form of a deficit, today we have a filter problem - we are less and less able to absorb all information and filter it to the relevant ones. Markgraf's studies (2018 and 2018a) once again show this quite clearly - we can no longer switch off and are almost always reachable. The following figure is another example for the processing of e-mails and social media accounts.

The two studies on changes in workload reveal further information in both areas which will not be discussed further here. In summary, however, it can be stated that the new ways of communication in particular have not yet found their way into the regular communication and strategy processes in a coordinated manner but are usually run in addition to the established ways and processes. Accordingly, they are currently causing an even greater workload.

3.3 New competences and skills

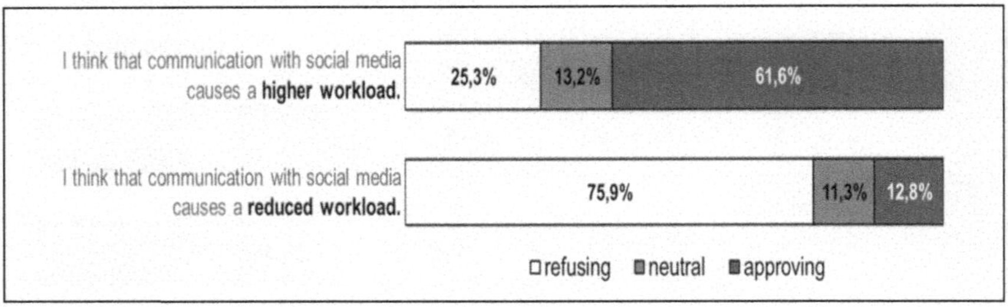

Figure 22: Impact of social media on workload (Source: Markgraf, 2018)

As the previous chapters have shown, digital transformation does not only confront companies, employees and managers with completely new challenges in the work and organizational processes themselves. Rather, new skills and competencies are needed to keep up with and respond to these rapid changes - recording and filtering information is just one example. Whereas a few years ago it was still possible to cover one's entire working life with the knowledge acquired during apprenticeships or studies, this is no longer possible today. The half-life of expert knowledge has dramatically decreased, and the challenge of lifelong learning is taking on a whole new meaning - we no longer just have to learn to get ahead, we have to learn to keep up with the permanent developments at all. Expert knowledge must be continuously developed further and must be aligned partially in the working life several times - up to the point that we will have probably every 10 years in the future completely different job profiles.[23] It is becoming increasingly important to recognize, evaluate and use relevant information. Accordingly, Markgraf's study has compiled various new competences that will gain importance in the context of the fourth industrial revolution. The respondents were asked to assess how important these will be from their point of view in the near future. The assessment was made on a scale of 1-7, with 7 corresponding to the highest significance. In total, more than 500 people participated in the evaluation of the competencies required in the future. The results are summarized in the following figure.

23 See Harari, 2018

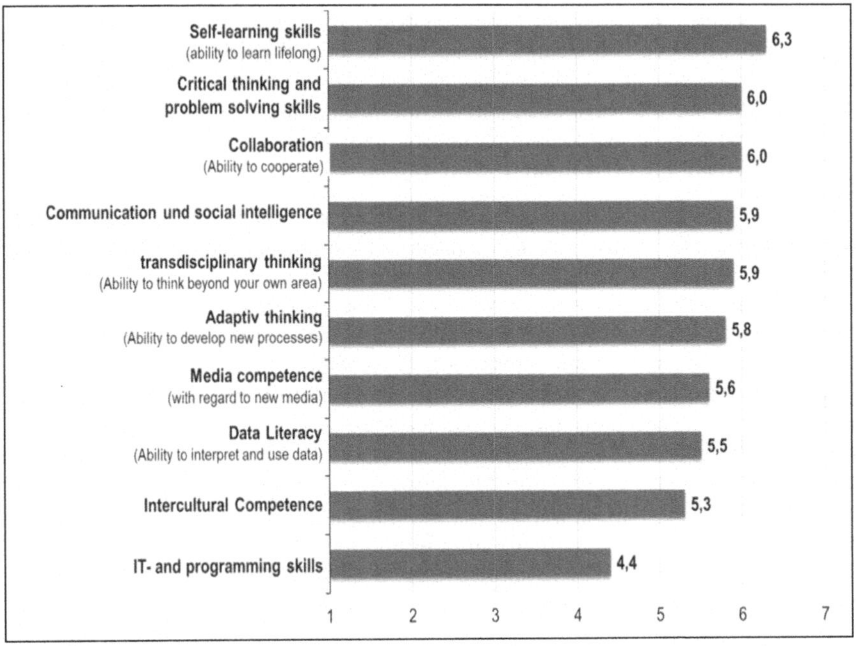

Figure 23: New competences and their importance in the near future (Source: Markgraf, 2018)

In addition to evaluating the given competencies, the participants were also able to make their own additions. This possibility was used extensively, but there was no uniform picture of what further competences would be required. In many cases, the data referred to various variations on the topics of collaboration and communication. Only the two points of self-organization and ethical action or ethical-moral responsibility can be additionally identified.

All in all, it is easy to see that it is above all those competencies that are related to new challenges, new situations and communication and interaction that are gaining in importance. Accordingly, the participants expect a continuous transformation and the associated ability to train themselves and continuously. The realization which challenges the fourth industrial revolution brings with itself is thus quite present, now it is necessary to put these also into practice.

4 Conclusion

The fourth industrial revolution influences more than just industrial processes or our professional and private lives - it goes hand in hand with various other revolutions. The social media as representatives of digital communication, the digitalization of many processes and the networking of devices and machines among each other influence and change our society at an unprecedented speed. We notice many changes only at the beginning and afterwards they spread so fast that we think they have always been part of our world. Just think back 20 years and you will find a world without smartphones, without wikipedia and with a search engine called google in its infancy.

The article also showed that we are still insufficiently prepared for many aspects of transformation. Above all, the aspects that move between professional and private life run largely without strategy, which will increasingly overtax individuals and organizations. So what do we do with the opportunities and challenges of the fourth industrial revolution? How do we deal with these developments? Here, too, we have shown different approaches. The examples and data from the studies have shown well that, at best, we are on the verge of freeing ourselves from mindless intellectual work and that, as a company as well as a customer and a private individual, we face a time full of creativity in which we can actively participate in design processes. For this, however, we must face the challenges of transformation and play an active role in shaping it. We live between old and new structures, old and new processes and old and new communication channels. In many cases you are currently running in parallel worlds that are not yet integrated, which leads to an increasing rather than a decreasing burden.

In addition, the structure of the changes in this transformation phase is different from previous industrial revolutions - the question this time is not only whether there will be more jobs being created than lost, but also whether we will be able to qualify enough employees for the resulting jobs. The newly created jobs require completely new competences and skills, which are more on a mental, psychological-emotional and creative level and often require specific knowledge up to expert knowledge. These new tasks are often not structured to learn and work through, as was the case in the previous industrial revolutions. In addition, the skills and competences required and the tasks to be performed will no longer remain constant in the long term but will change continuously. If we fail in mastering this challenge, we run into a two-sided problem - we have many vacancies for highly qualified and highly specialized people on the one hand and many people who are not sufficiently or properly qualified and therefore looking for work.

Accordingly, the major social and individual challenge is to make the best possible use of the opportunities offered by digitization and to limit the risks as far as possible by using political, corporate and social values and regulations as guard rails. One of the most important challenges will be not only to propagate lifelong learning, but also to actively support it and establish it as an individual core competence. As an individual, it is no longer just a matter of finding the individual work-life balance, but of integrating lifelong learning into this balance, so that a work-life-learn balance is created with which we feel comfortable and through which we can keep pace with the (digital) transformation, which is still accelerating.

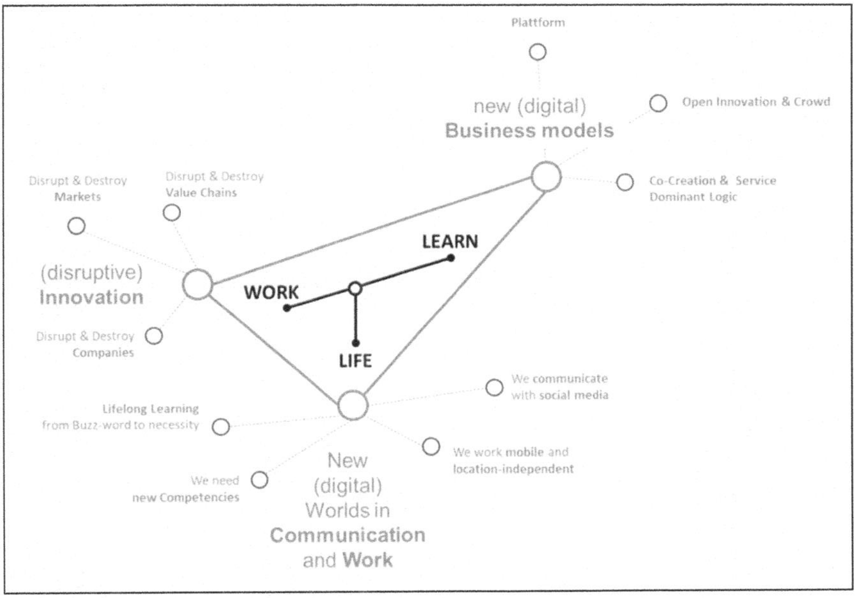

Figure 24: Work-Life-Learn Balance as a central challenge in all fields of action in digital transformation

Literature

Barthelmäs, N., Flad, D., Haußmann, T., Kupke, T., Schneider, S., Selbach, K. (2018). *Industrie 4.0 – eine industrielle Revolution? Industrie 4.0. Wie cyberphysi-sche Systeme die Arbeitswelt verändern.* (V. Andelfinger, T. Hänich, Eds.) SpringerGabler.

Bersin, J. (2019). *Technology Market 2019: Disruption ahead.* Retrieved 3.3.2019, from https://joshbersin.com/wp-content/uploads/2014/07/Tech_Disruptions_Final.pdf

BMWi. (n.d.). *Industrie 4.0: Digitale Transformation in der Industrie.* Retrieved 23.12.2018, from https://www.bmwi.de/Redaktion/DE/Dossier/industrie-40.html

Brauweiler, H.-Ch. (2017) Internal Audit in a Multinational Perspective; Wroclaw University of Economics, Conference Proceedings, 2nd International Research Symposium: "Global Challenges of Management

Control and Reporting", in: Research Papers of WUE, Wroclaw, S. 25 - 32Christensen, C., Raynor, M. (2018). *The Innovator's Solution: Warum manche Unternehmen erfolgreicher wachsen als andere.* Vahlen.

Christensen, C., Metzler, K., von den Eichen, S. (2011). *The Innovators Dilemma: Warum etablierte Unternehmen den Wettbewerb um bahn brechende Innovationen verlieren.* Vahlen.

Cisco IBSG. (2012). *BYOD: A Global Perspective.* Retrieved 23.12.2018, https://www.cisco.com/c/dam/en_us/about/ac79/docs/re/BYOD_Horizons-Global.pdf

Cisco IBSG. (2013). *Finanzielle Auswirkungen von BYOD: Ein Modell der Vorteile von BYOD für globale Unternehmen.* Retrieved 23.12.2018, from https://www.cisco.com/c/dam/global/de_de/assets/pdfs/byod_economics_top_10_insights.pdf

Dawar, N. (2018). Marketing im Zeitalter von Alexa. *Harvard Business Manager 08/2018.*

Duarte, N., Sanchez, P. (2016). *Illuminate: Ignite Change Through Speeches, Stories, Ceremonies and Symbols.* Portfolio/Penguin.

Fürst, R., Bügner, T., Frohberg (Eds.). (2019). *Deglobalisierung: Risiko oder Rettung?* Springer.

Griffin, T. (2016). *Two Powerful Mental Models: Network Effects and Critical Mass.* Retrieved 25.12.2018, from https://a16z.com/2016/03/07/network-effects_critical-mass

Harari, Y. (2018). *21 Lektionen für das 21. Jahrhundert.* C.H.Beck.

Hoffmann, F., Brauweiler, H.-Ch., Wagner, R. (1995). *Computergestützte Informationssysteme, Einführung in die Bürokommunikation und Datentechnik für Wirtschaftswissenschaftler* (2 ed.). Oldenbourg/ München.

Ihl, C., Piller, F. (2010). Von Kundenorientierung zu Customer Co-Creation im Innovationsprozess. *Marketing Review St. Gallen 4/2010.*

Kroker, M. (2018). *Big Bang im Cloud Computing: Wachstumsrate von AWS, Microsoft & Google legt wieder zu.* Retrieved 31.10.2018, from http://blog.wiwo.de/look-at-it/2018/06/05/big-bang-im-cloud-computing-wachstumsrate-von-aws-microsoft-google-legt-wieder-zu/

LEGO education. (2018). *Mehr ausprobieren, mehr entdecken.* Retrieved 12.26.2018, from https://education.LEGO.com/de-de

LEGO Ideas. (2012). *How does it work.* Retrieved 12.26.2018, from https://www.LEGO.com/dede/ideasproducts/explore/about

LEGO Ideas. (2015). *WALL·E: Interview with LEGO Ideas Fan Designer Angus MacLane.* Retrieved 26.12.2018, from https://www.LEGO.com/de-de/ideasproducts/videos/walle-5095979e4469458a87d8cea0ad8aa69b

Losse, B. (2018). *Wer von der Digitalisierung profitiert – und wer verliert.* Retrieved 23.12.2018, from https://www.wiwo.de/politik/konjunktur/ist-der-roboter-ihr-feind-wer-von-der-digitalisierung-profitiert-und-wer-verliert/23666044.html

Markgraf, D. (2018). *Arbeitswelten im Wandel. Auswirkungen der digitalen Transformation auf Effizienz und Arbeitsbelastung.* Retrieved 30.12.2018, from https://www.akad.de/ueber-akad/wissenschaft-und-forschung/

Markgraf, D. (2018a). *Arbeitswelten im Wandel. Auswirkungen etablierter Kommunikationsmittel auf die Effizienz modernen Arbeitens.* Retrieved 30.12.2018, from https://www.akad.de/ueber-akad/wissenschaft-und-forschung/

Markgraf, D. (2019). *Es war einmal ... Storytelling als Schlüssel zur deglobalen Zielgruppe.*

n.n. (2017). *Historie der industriellen Revolution.* Retrieved 23.12.2018, from https://viernull.blog/detail/Blog/Post/zeige/historie-der-industriellen-revolutionen

Neumann. (2017). *Open Innovation vs Crowdsourcing vs Co-creation.* Retrieved 29.11.2018, from https://nextstart.fr/en/2017/05/22/open-innovation-vs-crowdsourcing-vs-co-creation-by-m-neumann/

Prahalad, C., Ramaswamy, V. (2004). *The Future of Competition.* Harvard Business School Press.

Schareika, N. (2018). *Pendler könnten es besser haben.* Retrieved 26.12.2018, from https://www.wiwo.de/erfolg/trends/gluecksatlas-zeigt-wider sprue che-pendlerm-koennten-es-besser-haben/23174868.html

Schlinkert, R., Raffelhüschen, B. (2018). *Deutsche Post Glücksatlas 2018.* Penguin Verlag.

Van Alstyne, M., Parker, G., Choudary, S. (2016). Pipelines, Platforms, and the new rules of strategy. *Harvard Business Review April 2016.*

Vargo, S., Lusch, R. (2006). Service-dominant logic: What it is, What it is not, What it might be. The service dominant logic of marketing: Dialog debate and directions. *Journal of the Academy of Marketing Science 6(3).*

Yokogawa. (n.d.). *Bausteine der Industrie 4.0.* Retrieved 23.12.2018, from https://www.yokogawa.com/de/loesungen/industrie-4-0.htm#anchor-top

Digitization of the Health and Education Sectors in the Palestinian Society, in View of the United Nations Sustainable Development Goals

Hilmi S. Salem

1 Introduction

Policy- and strategy-makers, governments, and societies, in general, are facing nowadays, worldwide, a stage of transformation towards the digitization era through information and communications' technology (ICT). People today, around the world, have access to mobile phones more than to life's necessary basics, such as electricity and water. In addition, the amount of information generated globally is expanding exponentially at exceptional rates, as a result of the benefits offered by the ICT. Leaders of countries, prime-ministers of governments, ministers of ministries, chief executive officers (CEOs) of businesses, and directors of universities and research institutions are deciding — through policies and strategies for ICT, Internet access, communications' media, and digital applications — how to promote and to structure the digitization of their countries, societies, institutions, companies, and economies at large. These decisions and choices have produced enormous impacts and consequences on the way how people are living in those countries and societies, and on how economies are functioning.

Industrialized countries, which have achieved advanced levels of digitization and have greatly adopted a great deal of connected digital technologies and ICT applications by consumers, enterprises, governments, and industrial and academic institutions, have achieved significant economic, social, political, educational, and health-related benefits. Those countries have shown that digitization is a pathway to prosperity, while, on the other hand, other countries are falling disproportionately behind, as they do not utilize and apply digitization's techniques.

By looking more closely at the ways of how people use digital technologies and applications, it can be concluded that the greatest social and economic benefits depend on factors related to adoption and usage of ICT, such as pricing, reliability, commercialization, speed, and ease of use and access to. In any geography around the world, these factors determine the level of digitization and its rate of success in societies, which, in turn, have proven impacts on reduction of rates of unemployment, improvement of life quality, and boosting access of citizens to services, such as health, education, banking, travel and tourism, research and development, industry, trade, etc.

H.-C. Brauweiler et al. (Hrsg.), *Digitalization and Industry 4.0: Economic and Societal Development*, https://doi.org/10.1007/978-3-658-27110-7_4

Therefore, people around the world have now what is known as e-government, e-finance, e-commerce, e-banking, e-trade, e-health, e-learning, etc. For instance, e-government (short for electronic government) is the use of electronic communications' devices, computers, and the Internet to provide public services to citizens and other persons in a country or a region. The other e's provide a wide spectrum of services through the Internet or online. E-commerce, for example, is the process of buying and selling produce by electronic means, including mobile applications and the Internet, which (e-commerce) has become a very successful way of making great profits, globally. E-commerce refers to both online retail as well as electronic transactions. Remarkably, e-commerce (or mobile commerce) has been on a continued rise with the availability of a range of online shopping preferences for consumers that include online purchases of grocery, toys, books, music, movies, video games, clothing, footwear, household appliances, consumer electronics, and so on.

The average value of global online shopping orders placed using a smartphone, for instance, stood at approximately USD 105 per person during the third quarter of 2017. In a 2016-survey, it was found that about half of mobile shoppers turn to smartphone or tablets for purchasing products for convenience – 46% of them opted for the mobile platform to save time.[1] One of the remarkable advantages of digitization is that digitization, in essence, allows governments to operate with greater transparency and efficiency, and it also has a great effect on economic growth. Countries which are at the most advanced stage of digitization, including e's (e-government, e-finance, e-commerce, e-banking, e-trade, e-health, e-learning, etc.), derive 20% more in economic benefits than other countries that are just at the beginning stage of digitization.[2]

In 1990, there were 100 million personal computers (PCs) worldwide, 10 million mobile phone users, and less than 3 million people (about the population of the city of Berlin, Germany) on the Internet. By 2010, there were 1.4 billion PCs, 5 billion mobile phone users, and an Internet population of 2 billion.[3] According to the Internat. Telecommunication Union (ICU), in 2015 it was estimated that about 3.2 bn. people (or almost half of the world's population then) would be online by the end of that year (2015). Of them, about 2 b. would be from developing countries, including 89 million from least developed countries. As of June 2018, 55.1% (about 4.21 billion) of the world's population has Internet access.[4]

---

1 See Statista, 2019

2 See El-Darwiche, Singh, Ganediwalla, 2012

3 See El-Darwiche, Singh, Ganediwalla, 2012

4 See BBC, 2015; See ITU (International Telecommunication Union), 2017; See IWS (Internet World Stats), 2018; See Wikipedia, 2019a; See Wikipedia, 2019b; See Zappedia, 2019; See Figure 1

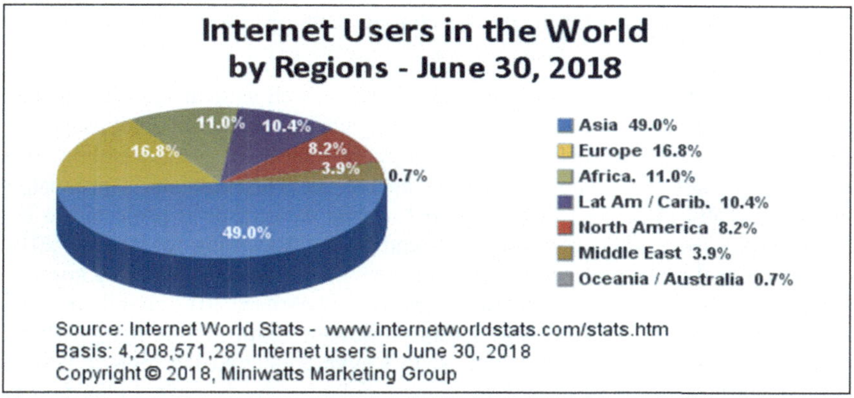

Figure 1: Internet users in the world by the region – June 2018 (Source: IWS (Internet World Stats), 2018)

The usage of the Internet has been considerably increased during the period of 2005–2017.[5] It has increased over that 12-year period (2005–2017) by three times worldwide; by more than 5 times in the developing countries; and by approximately 1.6 times in the developed countries.[6] Remarkably, 70% of the world's youth are online.[7]

Table 1: Internet users: worldwide; in the developing countries; and in the developed countries for the period of 2005–2017 (Source: ITU (International Telecommunication Union), 2017)

USERS	2005	2010	2017
World's Population (billion)	6.5	6.9	7.4
Users' Worldwide (%)	16	30	48
Users in the Developing Countries (%)	8	21	41.4
Users in the Developed Countries (%)	**51**	**67**	**81**

The number of the Internet users has increased, over the last 20-year period (1997–2017), considerably. It has increased from 11% to 81% in the developed

5 See Table 1 & Figure 2
6 See Table 1
7 See ITU (International Telecommunication Union), 2017

countries; from 0% to 41% in the developing countries, and from 2% to 48% globally.[8]

The use of the mobile smart-phones and tablets, as well as their applications has considerably increased the use of the Internet, globally. Mobile Internet usage has worked its way into the daily life of smart-phone and tablet users, enabling consumers to access and share information on the go. This portends a promising future for mobile Internet usage, as global mobile data traffic is projected to increase nearly seven-fold between 2016 and 2021. According to January 2018 data, the global mobile population amounted to 3.7 billion users, forming approximately 48% of the world's population then. As of February 2017, mobile devices accounted for 49.7% of web-page views worldwide, with mobile-first markets, such as Asia and Africa leading the pack. Kenya registered the highest rate of Internet traffic coming from mobile devices; followed by Nigeria, India, Singapore, Ghana, and Indonesia, which are classified as developing countries. The Americas and Europe have the highest mobile broadband subscription penetration rate, which is around 78.2% and 76.6%, respectively. In 2016, the global average stood at nearly 50%.[9]

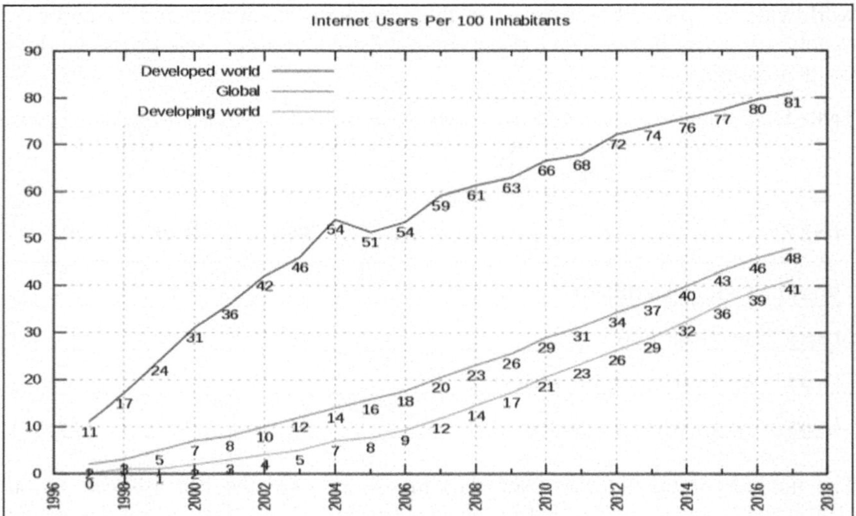

Figure 2: Worldwide Internets users per 100 inhabitants (Source: Wikipedia, 2019a)

8 See Figure 2
9 See Statista, 2019

Social media mobile networking, consisting of social networking and mobile messaging applications (Apps), is one of the most popular activities of mobile Internet users. 'Facebook Messenger' is the second most popular mobile messaging Apps behind 'Whatsapp,' which is the world's leading messaging App with more than 1.3 billion monthly active users as of July 2017.[10] Other popular mobile messaging Apps include QQ Mobile (which is the official App of China's most popular social network), WeChat (which is a Chinese multi-purpose messaging, social media, and mobile payment's App developed by Tencent), and Skype (which is a telecommunications App, established, in August 2003, in Denmark, specializing in providing video chat and voice calls between computers, tablets, the Xbox one console, and other mobile devices via the Internet).

As regarded to healthcare sector and digitization, the quality of the healthcare sector is measured by various factors, including, among others, life expectancy's rate (LER). Accordingly, every nation is vying to improve its LER, as being an indicator of any nation's wholesome development. To achieve a greater LER, the quality of the healthcare services needs to be constantly checked and, consequently and frequently, improved. Most likely, the quality of healthcare services is directly proportional to the healthcare expenditures, which are a problematic issue and a major challenge for most (if not all) countries around the world. Accordingly, reducing the expenditures of the healthcare sector without jeopardizing the quality of services provided represents a great challenge. However, many countries have been already introduced digitization's technologies and applications to reduce the healthcare's expenditures. Therefore, digital transformation and digitization processes have been used by many countries around the world as a stepping stone to reduce the excessive healthcare's expenditures. Now, the big players (governments, industries, companies, etc.) in the healthcare system are all pushing and pressing for the need of digital transformation. However, the success of this effort relies on the vast reach of the digitization's technology and applications.

As regarded to the education sector and digitization, typically education is one of the last sectors to make extensive changes, which means holding on and keeping antiquated methods and practices. But through the digital transformation and the rise of educational technologies, teachers have begun making drastic changes to their instructions and assessments' tools and techniques of teaching. Accordingly, it is believed that teachers and other professionals who work in the education sector have come to the conclusion that a better education system means digitization's technologies and applications have to be introduced more and more to the education sector.

10 See Statista, 2019

In this paper, the digitization process of the healthcare and education sectors in the Occupied Palestinian Territories (OPT) is investigated and analyzed, in view of the strategic plans 2017–2022 of both sectors. Also, the digitization process of both sectors is evaluated and assessed with respect to the services provided by the telecommunications and information technology institutions, the Palestinian government, and the local companies. The digitization process of both sectors is also analyzed and evaluated in view of the United Nations' (UN) Sustainable Development Goals (SDGs) to be globally achieved by 2030.

2 Study Area

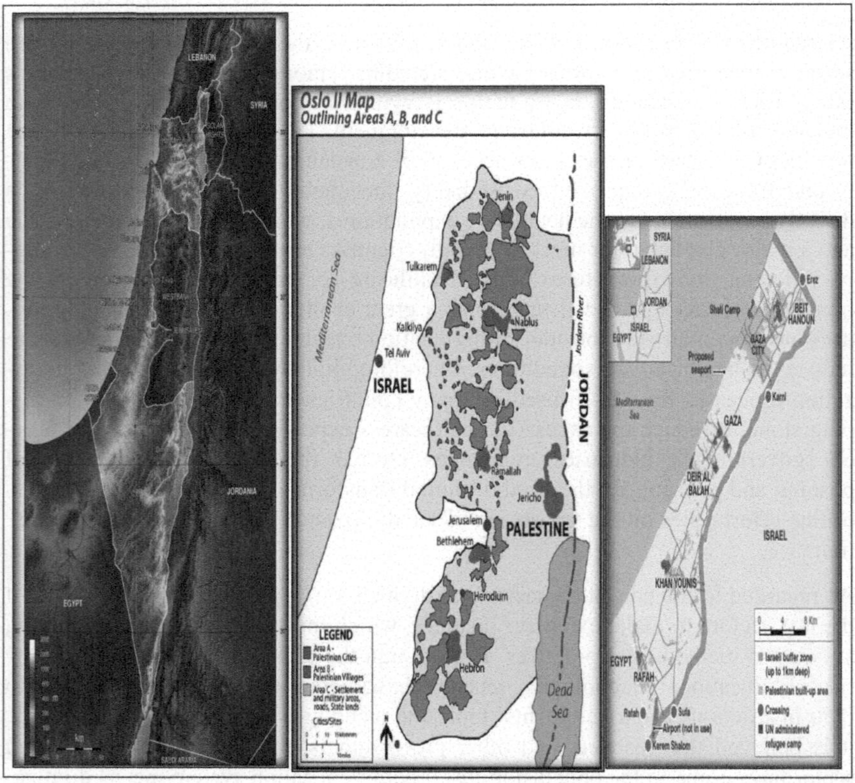

Figure 3: Historic Palestine (left), including West Bank (middle), and the Gaza Strip (right)

This study was carried out to explore the status of digitization and the obstacles and challenges facing it, with respect to the healthcare and education sectors in the Occupied Palestinian Territories (OPT), including the West Bank (including East Jerusalem) and the Gaza Strip, as part of Historic Palestine.[11]

As it is the first of its kind, this study opens eyes on the possibilities, including obstacles, problems, challenges, and opportunities, of digitizing the healthcare and education sectors in the OPT, in view of the national (Palestinian) healthcare and education strategies for the period of 2017–2022, as well as in view of the United Nation's Sustainable Development Goals (SDGs).

The Occupied Palestinian Territories (OPT), occupied by Israel in June 1967, has an area of around 6,000 km^2, forming approximately 22% of the total area of Historic Palestine, which is about 27,000 km^2.[12] The OPT[13] has a Palestinian population of approximately 5.1 million, living under the Israeli military occupation for more than half a century (i.e. since June 1967), in addition to approximately one million Israeli settlers living illegally in the OPT. The occupied West Bank[14] was divided, according to the Oslo Agreements, signed in 1993/1995 by the Palestinian and Israeli leaderships, into three areas.

These are *Area A* (≈18% of the total area of the West Bank), which is under the Palestinian control, security-wise and administration-wise; *Area B* (≈22% of the total area of the West Bank), which is under the Palestinian control, administration-wise, and under the Israeli control, security-wise; and *Area C* (≈60% of the total area of the West Bank), which is totally under the Israeli control, security-wise and administration-wise.[15] The Gaza Strip[16] has an area of approximately 365 km^2 and a population of more than 2 million, and is totally besieged by the Israeli occupation authorities since June 2007.

In addition to the direct impacts of the Israeli military occupation on the Palestinian people living in the OPT, the division of the occupied West Bank into the three areas (mentioned above) has made their life more complicated and even miserable, regarding all aspects of life, including healthcare and education, as well as telecommunications and information technology, in relation to digitization of the healthcare and education sectors, as being the focus of this study.

---

11 See Figure 3
12 See Figure 3 left
13 See Figure 3 middle and right
14 See Figure 3 middle
15 See Salem, 2019
16 See Figure 3 right

3 Telecommunications' Sector in the Occupied Palestinian Territories (OPT)

Before discussing the status of the healthcare and education sectors in view of their digitization's status in the OPT, it is important to understand the situation of the OPT's telecommunications sector. The development of the Palestinian Information and Communications Technology (ICT) sector, like everything else in the OPT, has been a subject to the asymmetrical power relationship between the Israeli occupation authorities and the Palestinian people under occupation, represented by the Palestinian National Authority (PNA). The PNA was founded in the OPT, based on the Oslo Agreements signed in 1993/1995 between the Israeli and Palestinian leaderships, in order to administrate the affairs of the Palestinians living in the OPT, and finally to establish a Palestinian state in the OPT, by ending the long-standing Israeli military occupation of the 1967-Occupied Palestinian Territories (OPT).

The Telecommunication's Agreement (TA), as being part of the Oslo Agreements signed in 1993/1995, while acknowledging the Palestinian rights to build and operate their own telecommunication's sector, gives the Israeli authorities a total control over the international telecommunication's gateways, the electromagnetic field (frequency spectrum), the telephone numbering's plan, and the access to all of the geopolitical zones of the occupied West Bank, especially *Area C*[17], as well as the importation of equipment.[18]

Until 1995, the telephone lines and other communications' facilities were all under the control of the Israeli-state owned company, known as 'Bezeq.' In 1996, Israel awarded the Palestine Telecommunications (Paltel) a license to build, operate, and own all land-lines, cellular networks, data communications, paging services, and public telephones. The Paltel Group (PG), as a public shareholding company, is now comprised of Palestine Telecommunications (Paltel), Palestine Cellular Communications Ltd. (Jawwal), Hadara company (Internet provider), and Reach (call center). However, the TA and the establishment of Paltel did not put an end to the Palestinian reliance on Israel for domestic and international connections, although Article 36B(4) of Annex III of the 1995-Interim Agreement of the Oslo Agreements outlines the TA, and states that the Palestinians have the right to build and operate a separate and independent telecommunications' system.[19] However, the TA simultaneously introduced conditions that have made the building of an independent telecommunications' system profoundly

---

17 See Figure 3 middle

18 See Abudaka, 2017

19 See IMFA (Israel Ministry of Foreign Affairs), 1995

impossible.[20] This simply means that the Palestinian telecommunications' network has been, since 1995, totally dependent on the Israeli decisions and networks.

In 1999, Israel granted the PNA (and, thus, PG) frequencies to launch 'Jawwal' – the first Palestinian mobile-phone service operator in the West Bank and the Gaza Strip. The second Palestinian mobile-phone operator – 'Watania' – was granted its license in 2006, but actual operation started in 2008 after Israel agreed to free frequencies for its operation only in the West Bank.[21] Both mobile-phone operators (Jawwal and Watania) provide the Second Generation's (2G) services, while they could not, until recently, provide the Third Generation's (3G) services in the West Bank and the Gaza Strip, which was due to the Israeli restrictions on the allocation of frequencies. In January 2018, the Israeli occupation authorities agreed to allow the PNA (and, consequently, PG) to launch the 3G services in the West Bank only (without the Gaza Strip) after years of wrangling with the Israeli occupation authorities to persuade them to lift their ban on Palestinian mobile-phone companies, and grant them the necessary frequencies related to the 3G services.[22]

The ICT sector consists of a 100% digital telecommunication's infrastructure that has been entirely developed by the Palestinian private sector and hosts more than 250 companies specialized in the field of information and communications' technology. The Palestinian market in the OPT (West Bank and Gaza Strip) has over 4.3 million mobile phone's subscribers and over 470,000 fixed-line's subscribers, in addition to 100 radio stations and local television stations, as well as 17 companies that operate in the field of telecommunications and the Internet.[23] This is despite the fact that the Israeli occupation authorities have besieged the Palestinian telecommunications' sector; have enforced an unfair competition from the Israeli operators; and have also enforced strict restrictions on infrastructure development in the OPT, in general, and in *Area C* of the occupied West Bank[24], in particular.

In 2010, the Palestinian Ministry of Telecommunication and Information Technology (MTIT) started to initiate fixed-line liberalization by separating the Internet services from line access – a process called Bit-Stream Access (BSA). For the first time, the Internet Services' Providers (ISPs) were able to compete in the Internet market, while Paltel services in the area of data remained confined to providing line of access. Today, 17 companies compete to provide Internet ser-

---

20 See Abudaka, 2017
21 See Abudaka, 2017
22 See CBG (Courtesy of Paltel Group), 2019
23 See CBG (Courtesy of Paltel Group), 2019
24 See Figure 3 middle

vices in the Occupied Palestinian Territories (OPT),[25] which have increased from 10 companies in 2016.[26]

In Europe, for instance, unlike unbundled access, the provision of BSA's services is not mandated under European Union's (EU) law, but where an incumbent operator provides BSA's Digital Subscriber's Line (DSL) services to its own services, subsidiary or third party, then, in accordance with community's law, it must also provide such forms of access under transparent and non-discriminatory terms or conditions to others (Directive 98/10/EC Article 16).[27] In view of the situation in Europe, and according to the World Bank (2016)[28], the ISPs in the Occupied Palestinian Territories (OPT) do not have open, transparent, and non-discriminatory access to Paltel's infrastructure; and in addition, there is no Reference Interconnection Offer (RIO), or a Catalogue's Price List (CPL).[29]

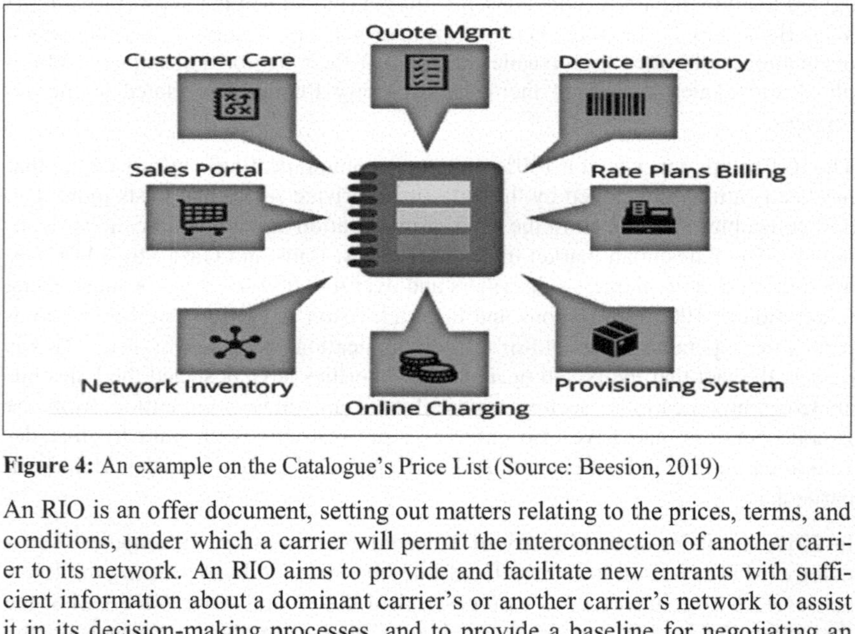

Figure 4: An example on the Catalogue's Price List (Source: Beesion, 2019)

An RIO is an offer document, setting out matters relating to the prices, terms, and conditions, under which a carrier will permit the interconnection of another carrier to its network. An RIO aims to provide and facilitate new entrants with sufficient information about a dominant carrier's or another carrier's network to assist it in its decision-making processes, and to provide a baseline for negotiating an interconnection agreement.[30] A CPL is a list that includes faster innovation and

25 See CBG (Courtesy of Paltel Group), 2019; See Nassereldin, 2019
26 See Abudaka, 2017
27 See Nikolinakos, 2006
28 See World Bank, 2016
29 See Figure 4
30 See TRBR (Telecommunications Radiocommunications and Broadcasting Regulator), 2018

elimination of problems caused by inconsistent product information. With a CPL, ICT and marketing teams can create and manage technical definitions for every product and service, even if they reside in third-party sites or billing systems. As indicated by the World Bank (2016)[31], the RIO and CPL are not available in the OPT, and, thus, there is no control or adjustment of the access of the Internet services among ISPs. Accordingly, there is no adequate and proper delivery of the Internet service to the end-users (Palestinian consumers) in the OPT.

When the competing ISPs do have access to Paltel's fixed infrastructure, the contractual conditions do not allow for strong and commercial freedom. As a consequence, the ISPs claim that they are better off by deploying their own fiber infrastructure, which implies inefficient infrastructure duplication. Even though the MTIT introduced the BSA's service in 2010 that has improved the broadband penetration, the end-users are required to subscribe to a broadband line to Paltel before selecting an ISP to provide them with the Internet access. So, the Palestinian end-users in the OPT are paying three times in order to have access to the Internet, which is absolutely unfair and illogic.

These three payments are: 1) A considerable amount of money paid to Paltel for the line access; 2) Another considerable amount of money paid to the ISPs for the Internet service; and 3) A third payment paid to Paltel and ISPs on the speed of the Internet. Despite the fact that the Internet service is very expensive in the OPT, because of lack of competition, the Internet penetration within Palestinian society reached, in 2017, 51.7%. This means that more than half of the Palestinian households have Internet access at their homes: 60.6% in the West Bank and 38.0% in the Gaza Strip.[32] This means that, according to latest statistics (in 2017), approximately 52% of the Palestinian households have Internet access and, thus, the Palestinian society can be described as a 'digitized' society.

Because the Palestinian consumers in the OPT pay very high prices on telecommunications' services (including fixed phone, mobile phone, the Internet, and the Internet's speed they choose), the Author of this study sent, on 31 July 2015, a comprehensive letter, in the form of a complaint, to the Minister of MTIT, addressing in it many problems facing the Palestinian consumers, with respect to the high prices on the services provided by the local (Palestinian) telecommunications' companies, bad services, wrong and unaccepted behaviors towards the Palestinian consumers, and so forth.[33] In addition, a group of Palestinian activists launched, on 1 March 2017, a public campaign, protesting the high prices of the telecommunications' services and the unethical practices of the local companies,

---

31 See World Bank, 2016

32 See PCBS (Palestinian Central Bureau of Statistics), 2018a

33 See Salem, H. S., 2015

considering the facts that: 1) the Palestinian consumers are paying the highest prices in the MENA (Middle East and North Africa) region, as indicated by the World Bank (2016)[34]; and 2) The Palestinians, who are living under very harsh conditions, politically, geopolitically, financially, and economically, should be treated fairly regarding the telecommunications' services – at least similar to their neighbors in the MENA region. Nowadays and after three years of the launching of the campaign, approximately a quarter a million Palestinians are following and strongly supporting the campaign, named:

Enough Is Enough: You Telecommunications' Companies.[35]

It is worthy to mention that the prices of telecommunications' services made by the Palestinian companies (Paltel, Jawwal, Watania, Hadara and other ISPs) in the OPT are the highest in the MENA region. According to a study on telecommunications in the OPT, issued by the World Bank in 2016, the price of fixed and mobile services is still high, and mobile data is particularly expensive, especially compared with the offers of unauthorized Israeli operators.[36]

Despite the fact that Paltel Group started in 2011 a project to lay out to a fiber-optic cable between Jordan and the West Bank, in order to both support its international traffic and reduce the prices of the Internet service for Palestinian consumers, the Internet prices are sky-high, though the international link is now activated, but through an Israeli registered company. Retail prices of mobile and fixed services are higher in the Occupied Palestinian Territories (OPT) than in similar markets when taking into account either the Purchasing Power Parity (PPP) or the GDP per capita. According to the World Bank (2016), based on extensive interviews with Palestinian operators, the creation of the Palestinian Telecommunications Regulatory Authority (PTRA) would mitigate the risk of anti-competitive practices by Paltel Group (PG), who could leverage its dominance on the Palestinian wholesale and retail telecommunications' markets, whereas monitoring dominance is usually part of the mandate of a regulatory authority.

The competitors identify three potential anti-competitive practices, which are: 1) Limited access to Paltel's infrastructure; 2) Differentiated prices for 'on-net/off-net'; and 3) Cross-subsidized fixed broadband and mobile services. These Paltel's practices identify the lack of an efficient and effective regulatory agency with the proper framework, mandates, capabilities, and tools to deal with them. According to the World Bank (2016), an evidence of these Paltel's practices and its sky-high

---

34 See World Bank, 2016
35 See TCC (Telecommunications' Community Campaign), 2019
36 See World Bank, 2016

prices for fixed and mobile phones' and Internet services can be found in the Alpha International survey, showing that 71.7% of Palestinian respondents:

Agree that they limit their phone calls to mobile or fixed phones of another network operator, because they are concerned with the higher communication charges than when making a phone call to others on the same network operator.

For fixed-telephony prices, Palestinian consumers in the OPT face higher prices than the MENA average with monthly costs of USD 44 for 60 calls / month, compared to an average of USD 29 per month for the MENA average (taxes included). As for mobile telephony, Palestinian consumers also face significantly higher prices for calls compared to the average in the MENA region. In addition, the Palestinian consumers face the highest fixed-to-mobile prices.[37] For fixed-broadband, a connection with a download speed of at least 2 Mb/s (mega-bite per second) is 30% more expensive than the MENA average. More details on the prices in the OPT compared with the average MENA prices are given in Table 2. For this comparison, 20 markets in the MENA region were taken into consideration.

Table 2: The Occupied Palestinian Territories' (OPT) retail price's ranking among 20 MENA markets and comparison with MENA average (June 2015, USD/month (taxes included)) (Source: BTRA-ARGENET, 2015, World Bank, 2016)

Service	Basket (monthly consumption)	2015 Palestinian ranking	2010-2015 Palestinian ranking evolution	Palestinian price	MENA price average	Palestinian price / MENA average
Mobile telephony	40 calls + 60 SMS	17		$ 18	$ 11	1.6
	30 calls + 100 SMS + 100Mb data	19		$ 176	$ 31	5.8
Fixed telephony (PSTN)	60 calls	14		$ 44	$ 29	1.5
	140 calls	14		$ 89	$ 55	1.6
Fixed BB	2Mbps - 10Mbps connection	14		$ 84	$ 62	1.3
Leased lines	2Mbps circuit	10		$ 2 697	$ 2 699	1.0

The high prices of telecommunications' services (Internet, fixed phone, and mobile phone) made by the Palestinian companies, mainly Paltel Group (PG), have enforced many Palestinian consumers to obtain their services from Israeli companies. According to PG, the number of Palestinian subscribers with Israeli providers reached 600,000 in 2018, and this number is predicted to jump to one million

37 See World Bank, 2016

subscribers by 2020.[38] Israeli operators have an illegal market share of 17% in the OPT, and 73% of the Palestinian subscribers with Israeli providers use prepaid plans.[39]

According to the World Bank (2011), another anti-competitive behavior is a process of 'cherry picking' major institutions, conducted by PG. Those major institutions, such as Hadara, which is one of the Paltel-subsidiary companies, were receiving leased-line services from Paltel, and providing the services to consumers at expensive costs, as being possible due to their ownership of the Internet's infrastructure. This process is carried out by Paltel Group (including Hadara) in a manner that they marginalize the existing ISPs. Such anti-competitive behavior by PG would require an extensive regulatory and competition's assessment.[40] In the interim, fiber infrastructure is visibly deployed in the West Bank by Paltel's competing ISPs, as mentioned earlier. This raises a double question of economic efficiency and economic rationality as the competing ISPs consider it more cost-effective to duplicate the fixed infrastructure rather than access Paltel's infrastructure.[41] This is something that the MTIT needs to considerably think about, and, thus, to work immediately on reducing the telecommunications' prices in the OPT. Accordingly, if happened, the Palestinian consumers will stop obtaining telecommunications' services from Israeli companies that provide their services at lower prices and even of better quality than the services provided by Palestinian companies, considering the fact that the Israeli telecommunications' operators cover most of the OPT, while the Palestinian operators have no control on *Area C*, which forms more than 60% of the occupied West Bank.[42]

The coverage of the Israeli operators of the OPT is in contrary to the signed TA between Israel and the PNA. The Israeli operators cover most of the OPT, without licenses from the PNA, and without paying fees or taxes, and without contributing additional technologies to be particularly used by the Palestinian consumers in the OPT. In addition, some of the Israeli operators use confiscated privately-owned Palestinian land to erect their towers. In the meantime, the Palestinian operators are not allowed to build telecommunications' or otherwise infrastructure in *Area C*, leaving the Palestinian residents with no alternative but to use the available telecommunications' services provided by Israeli operators.

Similar to any growing economy, the development of the Palestinian telecommunications' industry leads to the need to use advanced IT services. Despite the severe Israeli restrictions on technology import and export, the IT industry in the

38 See CBG (Courtesy of Paltel Group), 2019
39 See CBG (Courtesy of Paltel Group), 2019
40 See World Bank, 2011
41 See World Bank, 2016
42 See Figure 3 middle

OPT has witnessed rapid growth since 1994. The sector employs around 8,500 individuals, working in 600 companies. It is estimated that the telecommunications' sector has a total volume of production of around USD 600–900 million annually, forming 5.5%–6.1% of the Palestinian Gross Domestic Product (GDP), and is still growing rapidly, with an annual increase of around 10%.[43]

All of the 13 universities in the OPT have currently ICT's departments, with a total enrollment of over 8,000 students, graduating 2,500 students annually to meet the demand for a qualified workforce able to drive the new ICT's industry.[44] With human capital regarded as the most important input for ICT's development, modernizing the education system is vital to the creation of a suitable and sustainable work's environment. However, recent studies revealed that the private sector is unable to absorb a sufficient number of ICT's graduates. This phenomenon has resulted in a very high unemployment's rate among graduates in computer science and engineering, as well as in related disciplines, which is estimated at 17.6% in the West Bank and at 45.8% in the Gaza Strip.[45]

As a last note on the telecommunications' status in the OPT, the Cyber space in the OPT is described as being 'militarized'[46], because the online activity and access on the Cyber space in the OPT are censored and monitored. AbuShanab (2018)[47] documented violations of the Palestinian digital rights by various authorities: Israel (the occupying power of the West Bank and Gaza Strip), the Palestinian National Authority (the ruling power in the occupied West Bank), and Hamas (the ruling power in the besieged Gaza Strip by the Israelis), stating:

All three authorities, including Israel, the Palestinian Authority and Hamas authorities, targeted Palestinians for their activism on various social media networks, specifically Facebook. In 2017, Israel arrested about 300 Palestinians in the West Bank, including East Jerusalem for charges related to posts on Facebook. On the other hand, 530 violations against media freedoms were reported in the OPT, including 376 violations committed by Israel and 154 attacks carried out by the Palestinian factions.

Most notable violations, related to the Palestinian Authority's censoring and monitoring the Cyber space, include the blocking of 29 websites in the occupied West Bank in June 2017, and the adoption of the 'Cybercrime Law' in July 2017 to justify the arrest of journalists, activists, and political dissidents.[48]

---

43 See Abudaka, 2017; See CBG (Courtesy of Paltel Group), 2019
44 See Abudaka, 2017
45 See Abudaka, 2017
46 See AbuShanab, 2018
47 See AbuShanab, 2018
48 See AbuShanab, 2018

4 Healthcare Sector and Digitization in the Occupied Palestinian Territories (OPT)

In this section, four topics are analyzed and discussed, which are: status of the healthcare sector, the National Health Strategy 2017–2022, healthcare as the 3rd Goal of the UN's Sustainable Development Goals (SDGs), and digitization of the healthcare sector.

4.1 Status of Healthcare Sector

The National Palestinian Authority (PNA) took responsibility for the supervision, regulation, licensing, and control of the entire healthcare sector beginning in 1994 (i.e. since it took administration's control over the OPT directly after the signing of the Oslo Agreements in 1993). The health services are mainly provided by the Palestinian Ministry of Health (MoH), and through the private sector, non-governmental organizations (NGOs), and the United Nations Relief and Works Agency for Palestine Refugees in the Near East (UNRWA).

The OPT ranks 113th in the Human Development Report 2015 published by the United Nations, putting the OPT in the Medium Development Category (MDC).[49] However, the OPT's (Occupied State of Palestine's) rank was not much changed in 2016 and 2017, as it was 114 in the MDC,[50] and in 2018 it moved back to become 119.[51] The UNDP's indicators suggest that, during these years (2015–2018), the situation in the OPT deteriorated, though, relatively speaking, it is still better than in other countries, regionally and internationally.

The Palestinian population in the OPT get their health services from primary healthcare clinics and centers (PHCCs), and from hospitals. In the OPT, until 2005, there were 667 PHCCs, with an average ratio of persons per clinic (or center) equal to 5,752/1. In addition, there were 76 hospitals in the OPT.[52]

The percentage of the Palestinian population that had health insurance in 2004 was 76.1%, distributed as 65.8% in the West Bank and 93.8% in the Gaza Strip.[53] According to a recent report issued by the PCBS in 2018[54], the OPT has 80 hospitals, with a total of 6,006 beds, whereby 26 of these are governmental hospitals, offering 2,979 beds or 54.3% of the total number of beds. Also, 54 hospitals are private, with 2,508 beds or 45.7% of the total number of beds. In addition, there are 750 PHCCs, including 603 in the West Bank and 147 in the Gaza Strip. The

---

49 See UNDP (United Nations Development Programme), 2015
50 See UNDP (United Nations Development Programme), 2016, same 2017
51 See UNDP (United Nations Development Programme), 2018
52 See MoH (Ministry of Health), 2006
53 See PCBS (Palestinian Central Bureau of Statistics), 2005a
54 See PCBS (Palestinian Central Bureau of Statistics), 2018b

governmental PHCCs account for approximately 61.3% of the total number of the PHCCs in the OPT.[55]

In 2012, the number of physicians registered with the Palestinian Doctors' Association (PDA) was 8,810. The average number of physicians per 1,000 people was 2.2 (2.3 in the West Bank and 2.2 in the Gaza Strip). In the same year (2012), there were 11,633 registered nurses. The average number of nurses per 1,000 people was 2.7 (2.2 in the West Bank and 3.4 in the Gaza Strip). A more recent statistics for 2015 showed that the average number of the health sector's workers rose significantly, with the number of general practitioners and specialists reaching 10,562. However, the ratio of hospitals and hospital beds to the population has largely stayed the same.[56]

Regarding the Gaza Strip, in particular, the health conditions are really catastrophic, as they have been severely deteriorating for a long period of time, especially since the blockade (military siege) was enforced on the Gaza Strip by the Israeli occupation authorities in June 2007. According to Dr. Gerald Rockenschaub, WHO's Head of Office for the West Bank and Gaza[57]:

The deteriorating humanitarian situation is extremely worrying. Hospitals in Gaza are overwhelmed with the influx of injured patients. With further escalations expected during the coming weeks, the increasing numbers of injured patients requiring urgent medical care is likely to devastate Gaza's already weakened health system, placing even more lives at risk.

Another alarming health issue in the OPT is the widespread use of drugs among youth in Palestinian society. According to surveys conducted recently,[58] substance use exists especially among youth, even in socially conservative communities. The reasons behind drug use and drug addiction and abuse, as well as alcohol drinking in the OPT include the following: 1) To cope with stress, for fun, and out of curiosity; 2) To challenge society, due to the influence of media, peer pressure, poverty, unemployment, and chronic and acute exposure to political violence, as being under the Israeli military occupation for more than half a century; 3) To increase productivity in an environment of hard-work and long working hours; 4) The availability and easy access to drugs; 5) Myths about the effect of some drugs on improving sexual performance; and 6) Being a wife or a child of someone addicted to drugs.[59]

---

55 See PCBS (Palestinian Central Bureau of Statistics), 2018b

56 See Fanack, 2016

57 See WHO (World Health Organization), 2018

58 See Massad, et al., 2016; See PNIPH (Palestinian National Institute of Public Health), 2017

59 See Massad, et al., 2016; See PNIPH (Palestinian National Institute of Public Health), 2017

The level of drug use [in the occupied West Bank] today is really scary. It increases day by day. The seriousness of these drugs is like a nuclear bomb; like dropping a nuclear bomb on a small country.[60]

4.2 National Health Strategy (NHS) 2017–2022

According to the National Health Strategy (NHS) 2017–2022[61], the vision of the Palestinian healthcare sector is based on integrated comprehensive health system that contributes to improved quality health services and sustainable promotion of health status and that addresses the key determinants of health in Palestine.

The 2017–2022 NHS' values are:

1. Justice and Equality: Fair opportunity for all citizens to attain health services without any hindrance or discrimination.
2. Sustainability: Ensure sustainability of the Palestinian health system in its various components (health services, human resources, health information, medicines' and health technology, health finance, leadership and governance).
3. Right to Healthcare: The right to enjoy the highest attainable standards of healthcare and healthy environment for all citizens.
4. Integration & Partnership: Partnerships between different healthcare providers and other sectors to achieve integrated health services.
5. Financial Protection: National commitment to work towards universal healthcare coverage.
6. Quality: Safe and high quality of healthcare services matching the approved national standards that ensure continuous development.
7. Privacy: This is with respect to the Palestinian situation regarding the Israeli occupation's obstacles, the growing community needs, and caring for the marginalized vulnerable groups.

The 2017–2022 NHS' objectives are:

1. Ensure the provision of comprehensive healthcare services to all Palestinians, heading towards localization of healthcare services in Palestine.
2. Promote the management of non-communicable diseases, preventive healthcare, community health awareness, and gender-related programs.
3. Institutionalize quality systems in all aspects of health services.
4. Promote and develop health workforce management system.
5. Strengthen health governance, including effective health sector management, laws and legislations' development and enforcement, cross-sectoral coordi-

---

60 See McQueeney, 2017
61 See Aker, 2016

nation, intra-sectoral coordination, and integration towards achieving the localization of services and universal healthcare coverage.
6. Enhance healthcare financing system and protection of citizens against financial hardship of paying healthcare costs.

4.3 Healthcare as the Third Goal of the UN's Sustainable Development Goals (UN's SDGs)

The 3rd Goal of the UN's Sustainable Development Goals is 'Good Health and Well-Being'.[62] This means that by 2030, nine sub-goals or targets related to this goal have to be globally achieved.[63] It is believed, however, that this goal will be unachievable in the OPT (State of Palestine under Israeli occupation) by 2030, as promoted by the UN. The high growth rate will increase the Palestinian population in the OPT to 6.9 million by 2030 and to 9.5 million by 2050. This growth will increase the pressure on delivering basic services, especially health, education, and labor market, which challenges the Palestinian government's ability to sustain and develop the standards of living in the OPT.

In 2013, 11% of the Palestinian children under the age of five years suffer from chronic malnutrition (stunting – low height for age). This includes 11.5% in the West Bank and 10.4% in Gaza Strip. It should be noted that the percentage was 7.5% in 2000.[64] These children are malnourished with vitamin and other mineral deficiencies. Simultaneously, in 2013, 22.1% of adult males and 23.1% of adult females were suffering from overweight.[65] So the situation in the OPT signals double burden of nutrition (decrease in weight among children, and increase in weight among adults), which results in health problems.

In addition, according to the national definition, 29.2% of Palestinians live under the national poverty line as of 2017: 13.9% in the West Bank and 53% in the Gaza Strip, while 16.8% of Palestinians live in deep poverty: 5.8% in the West Bank and 33.8% in the Gaza Strip.[66] The facts on the ground in the OPT, especially in the presence of the continuing Israeli occupation, suggest that the 3rd Goal (Good Health and Well-Being) of the United Nations' SDGs will be really difficult to achieve by 2030.

62 See Figure 5
63 See WHO (World Health Organization), 2019
64 See PCBS (Palestinian Central Bureau of Statistics), 2013
65 See PNVR (Palestinian Nat. Voluntary Review on the Implementation of the 2030 Agenda), 2018
66 See PNVR (Palestinian Nat. Voluntary Review on the Implementation of the 2030 Agenda), 2018

Figure 5: The 17 United Nations' Sustainable Development Goals (UN's SDGs), including the two goals that are the focus of this study: The 3rd Goad: 'Good Health and Well-Being,' and the 4th Goal: 'Quality Education' (Source: UN News, 2015)

However, in the Palestinian National Voluntary Review on the 'Implementation of the 2030 Agenda,' with respect to the SDGs, issued in June 2018, there is no mention at all of digitization, as related to the health sector in the OPT.[67]

4.4 Digitization of Healthcare Sector

One of the main challenges that face decision- and policy-makers in countries around the world is how to reduce expenditures of the healthcare sector while keeping good quality of the services provided. This has been translated into reality in many of the developed countries by the digital transformation in the healthcare sector. Digital transformation is not just about buying new technologies and advanced tools that can ease the process of healthcare procedures, but also about changing the operational process in the healthcare sector and making it more automatic and efficient, which should lead to reducing costs and, thus, to money saving.

As a matter of fact, despite the goodness of the vision and values, as well as the strategic objectives of the Palestinian National Health Strategy (NHS) 2017–2022, there is no single mention of digitization or digital transformation towards a digitization process or plan towards having a digitized healthcare sector in Palestine (the Occupied Palestinian Territories – OPT). Therefore, it is required from the decision- and policy-makers in the healthcare sector to energize, activate, and implement the digitization's process within the healthcare sector, which can be done through creation of a digital public health system or observatory, in order to integrate concepts, tools, and methodologies towards implementation of the digitization process of the healthcare sector.

---

67 See PNVR (Palestinian Nat. Voluntary Review on the Implementation of the 2030 Agenda), 2018

A digital public health process or observatory should focus on integrating different sources of information. These sources may include surveys, questionnaires, technical reports, and publications to analyze the relationship between demographic, socioeconomic, and the health status of the Palestinian population in the OPT. The surveys and questionnaires should include data and information to be provided by people who are directly involved in the healthcare sector, including physicians (medical doctors), nurses, instruments' technicians, pharmacists, physiotherapists, nutrition's specialists, and administration's staff, as well as patients. In this way, data and information are provided to monitor the healthcare status from different perspectives, such as medical; service-wise; environmental, social, and demographical factors; health and mental status; habits and way of living (including sport activities); rehabilitation; common and other kinds of diseases; and so forth. This will allow to successfully meeting the goals that will be established with respect to the plans of the healthcare system, and the objectives of sustainable development of the healthcare sector provided in the NHS 2017–2022.

The availability of a public health observatory that uses digitization's techniques and tools will allow the integration, visualization, and manipulation of the data and information collected and stored in the healthcare sector. A healthcare observatory must be very static, so it can present, categorize, and save the data and information in special forms that cannot be manipulated or intruded. The lack of such a healthcare observatory in the OPT, and the difficulty to have a clear strategy to build such an observatory that motivates the initiative to have a Public Health Digital Observatory (PHDO) are obstacles towards having a digitized healthcare system in the OPT.

The PHDO integrates business intelligence (BI) and visual analytics (VA). Both BI and VA provide mechanisms to support organizational decision-making processes. The BI focuses on collecting, organizing, and managing information from several sources; providing updated, consistent, and complete data and information for the generation of knowledge; allowing the discovery of patterns, trends, and monitoring indicators; and providing different levels of analysis. The VA provides interactive, easy-to-use visual interfaces that aid in the intuitive exploration of information. The VA also offers options for manipulating information (filtering, grouping, sorting, eliminating, refining, etc.), and options for interacting easily and quickly with it. The integration of BI and VA has been successfully applied to the healthcare sector in different countries. Successful examples on the BI and VA integration and application to the healthcare sector are given, for instance, by Simpao et al. (2015)[68] and Lozano and Villamil (2018).[69]

---

68 See Simpao, Ahumada, Rehman, 2015

Another way of digitization of the healthcare sector might be the application of TRACnet, which has been used in several countries around the world to improve the quality of service in primary healthcare institutions, by providing public safety software solutions.[70] This system has been widely used since 2004 in some African countries, like Rwanda, and has approved to be effective and successful.[71] This Electronic Disease Surveillance System (EDSS) has improved timeliness and completeness of reporting, and it extremely supports early detection and notification of outbreaks for timely response. The EDSS has also demonstrated advantages in the cross-border disease surveillance.

The Palestinian Ministry of Health (MoH), the Ministry of Telecommunication and Information Technology (MTIT), ICT companies, healthcare service providers, research and development institutions, and donor organizations should work together to develop innovative ICT-based approaches to healthcare service delivery to the Palestinian people in the OPT, which will, in turn, lead to gradual transformation towards digitization of the healthcare sector in the OPT.

5 Education Sector and Digitization in the Occupied Palestinian Territories (OPT)

In this section, four topics are analyzed and discussed, which are: status of the education sector, the National Education Strategy 2017–2022, education as the 4th Goal of the UN's Sustainable Development Goals (UN's SDGs), and digitization of the education sector.

5.1 Status of Education Sector

In 1994, and according to the Oslo Agreements signed in 1993 between the Palestinian and Israeli leaderships, the Palestinian Ministry of Education and Higher Education (MoEHE) took control over the educational system in the OPT after 27 years of the Israeli military control. Since then, the MoEHE has been trying to modify the system to match the current needs of the Palestinian population, and to develop the Palestinian curricula to acceptable standards. As a result, the literacy rate in the OPT has increased from 84.3% to 92.9% for the period 1995–2005.[72] This 8.6 percentage increase in the literacy rate in about a 10-year period is considerably high, especially it was achieved under difficult geopolitical conditions affecting the Palestinian population in the OPT. Remarkably, this literacy rate was higher among females than among males, as it noticeably increased, for the

[69] See Lozano, Villamil, 2018
[70] See AVASANT, 2013
[71] See Kizito, et al., 2012
[72] See PCBS (Palestinian Central Bureau of Statistics), 2005

same period (1995–2005), by 15.5% among females and by 5.9% among males.[73] It is, however, believed that these increases represent a shift in attitude concerning females' education, along with better financial resources before the economic downturn that followed the outbreak of the 'Second Intifada' (public uprising).

The 2016 data revealed that the percentage of individuals who completed university education (a Bachelor degree and above), was 14% while the percentage of individuals who did not complete any stage of education reached 9%. In 2016, the female illiteracy rate was three and half times higher than that of males. The illiteracy rate among individuals aged 15 years and over in the OPT was 3.1% in 2016.[74]

However, generally speaking and despite the encouraging education figures given above, education in the OPT has been getting worse. In her study conducted in 2015, Ramahi states:

Public schools are failing our youth. The quality of education has been worsening rapidly... Students are promoted to higher grades despite inabilities to read and write... It's intolerable. Several university faculty members reported that their students are not capable of performing basic analytical and communication skills necessary for a post-secondary education. Alarmingly, one [university lecturer] indicated that up to 90% of her students did not meet basic university level academic standards. The vast majority of my students can't do a research paper. They're so used to memorization that they can't think for themselves. There is no self-confidence or ability to think critically. How can they advance in life or contribute to society? How did we let things get so bad?[75]

The main supervising authority for schools in the OPT is the governmental sector that belongs to the Palestinian National Authority (PNA), although some schools are supervised by UNRWA, and some others are private. All the Palestinian localities have governmental schools, meanwhile, the UNRWA schools are distributed in the refugee camps and in some small villages, and the private schools are primarily distributed in the cities. The statistics of the scholastic year 2005/2006 indicates that there were about 2,276 schools in the OPT, providing educational services to about 1,078,500 students. According to recent reports, the number of schools in the OPT is 2,963 schools, including basic and secondary schools, distributed as 2,249 schools in the West Bank and 714 schools in the Gaza Strip. For the school year 2016/2017, the number of students in the OPT was 1,376,589,

---

73 See PCBS (Palestinian Central Bureau of Statistics), 2005b

74 See MoEHE (Ministry of Education and Higher Education), 2017a

75 See Ramahi, 2015

distributed as 783,871 students in the West Bank, and 592,718 students in the Gaza Strip.[76]

The number of students enrolled in the Technical and Vocational Education and Training (TVET) system, belonging to the MoEHE of the PNA, for the year 2014 was 2,644 students, including 2,428 students in the industrial stream and 216 students in the agriculture stream.[77] In 2014, the total number of TVET schools in the OPT was 76 institutions, funded by various ministries of the Palestinian Authority (such as the MoEHE, Ministry of Labor, and Ministry of Agriculture); UNRWA; the private sector; and NGOs; as well as international organizations, such as the GIZ (Deutsche Gesellschaft für Internationale Zusammenarbeit, GmbH – German Society for International Cooperation, Ltd.). The programs offered to trainees/students by these schools range in time length from less than 2 days to 2 years.[78]

Table 3: The approximate ratios of students/teacher, students/computer, and students/classroom for all stages in private schools, public schools, and UNRWA schools (Source: MoEHE (Ministry of Education and Higher Education), 2017a, PCBS (Palestinian Central Bureau of Statistics), 2017b)

	≈ Students/ Teacher Ratio	**≈ Students/Computer Ratio**	**≈ Students/ Classroom Ratio**
Private Schools	16/1	16/1	24/1
Public Schools	21/1	22/1	34/1
UNRWA Schools	29/1	47/1	42/1
Total's Average	22/1	28/1	33/1

Regarding the higher education in the OPT, until 2005/2006 there are 43 institutions, including 11 universities, 13 university collages, and 19 community colleges, hosting more than 135,000 students.[79] In 2015/2016, the number of higher education institutions in the OPT jumped to approximately 50, including universities, university colleges, and community colleges distributed in the West Bank and Gaza Strip, with up to 221,000 students (approximately 40% males and 60% females).[80]

---

76 See PCBS (Palestinian Central Bureau of Statistics), 2017b
77 See MoEHE (Ministry of Education and Higher Education), 2014
78 See MAS (Palestine Economic Policy Research Institute), 2015
79 See MoEHE (Ministry of Education and Higher Education), 2006
80 See RecoNow, 2016; See Wikipedia, 2018

In the OPT, for the year 2015/2016 the average students/teacher, students/computer, and students/classroom ratios in the private schools were lower than those in the public (governmental) schools, which, in turn, are lower than those in the UNRWA schools.[81] Table 3 demonstrates that the classes are relatively crowded with not enough teachers and not enough computers, as well as insufficient classrooms' space to meet acceptable standards of education.

5.2 National Education Sector Strategic Plan (NESSP) 2017–2022

The National Education Sector Strategic Plan (NESSP) 2017–2022 has the Vision of "A Palestinian society that possesses values, knowledge, culture, science and technology, and is able to produce knowledge and employ it for liberation and development".[82] This plan is based on the United Nations' Sustainable Development Goals (UN's SDGs) and the Palestinian National Policy Agenda of 2017–2022. Transforming the education system to realize this vision requires that the educational system and schools be viewed as:

1. Community-based schools owned by the society and designed and established to be educational organizations, where employees are knowledge-producers and students are treated as key-individuals of the educational process.
2. Schools free from the bureaucratic structures that hinder utilizing multiple paths necessary for achieving targets.
3. Schools encouraging all students on free reading, research, and self-learning.
4. Open-minded and developed leadership that respects the other.
5. All operational processes of the system are subject to development and continuing improvement.
6. The leaders of the system and schools concentrate on prevalent social norms which govern the behavior, including those related to beliefs, development, and knowledge; and those that orient the employees and students towards the values and the vision of the educational system.

The NESSP 2017–2022 objectives are:

1. A society where governmental, non-governmental, and private organizations can work together to provide quality education at all levels.
2. Safe child-friendly schools with diversified education and technology methods able to build effective relations with the society to meet students' needs.
3. Qualified and committed schools' staff that enjoy respect and appreciation, knowing that their first priority is to provide service for students.

---

81 See Table 3

82 (MoEHE (Ministry of Education and Higher Education), 2017a)

4. Schools working in partnership with the directorates and the MoEHE which, in turn, supply them with financial and human resources, as well as with technical needs. They also set forth learning standards and objectives, and empower assessment and accountability systems, which inform the society of the education quality at schools and the levels of successes achieved by students.

5.3 Education as the Fourth Goal of the UN's Sustainable Development Goals (UN's SDGs)

The 4th Goal of the United Nations' Sustainable Development Goals (SDGs) is 'Quality Education'[83], stating: "Ensure inclusive and equitable quality education and promote life-long learning opportunities for all".[84] Achieving inclusive and quality education for all reaffirms the belief that education is one of the most powerful and proven vehicles for sustainable development. This goal ensures that all girls and boys complete free primary and secondary schooling by 2030. It also aims to provide equal access to affordable vocational training, and to eliminate gender and wealth disparities with the aim of achieving universal access to a quality higher education.

Regarding the OPT, the high growth rate, as indicated above, will increase the population to 6.9 million by 2030 and to 9.5 million by 2050. This population's increase, in view of the dramatic geopolitical situation in the OPT, will put more pressure on delivering basic services, especially education, health, and labor market, which will challenge the Palestinian government's ability to sustain and develop the standards of living of the Palestinians living in the OPT. Nevertheless, despite all of these difficulties, education is considered one of the main pillars of the Palestinian society and its values, and, thus, the Palestinian government shares this view with its citizens, based on the fact that education is a tool for empowerment and resilience. Hence, the government provides free primary and secondary education for all, and has ratified 'Education Law 2017' – a mandatory minimum of 10 years of schooling for all its citizens. This is reflected in the fact that the provision of net school enrolment rates in 2016 was 98.2% for primary education (1–4 grades), 98% for upper basic education (5–10 grades), and 63% for secondary education (11–12 grades).[85]

The illiteracy rate among individuals (15 years and above) in the Occupied Palestinian Territories was 3.3% in 2017. Illiteracy gap is significantly noticed among males and females at 1.7% and 5.0% respectively.[86] Meanwhile, the gender gap in

---

83 See Figure 5
84 (SDGF (Sustainable Development Goals Fund), 2019)
85 See PCBS (Palestinian Central Bureau of Statistics), 2017b
86 See PCBS (Palestinian Central Bureau of Statistics), 2018a

education has been bridged, where the number of females who are enrolled in education has surpassed males, where 96.6% of males and 99% of females are enrolled in compulsory education.[87] Unfortunately, persons with disabilities remain left behind in the Palestinian educational system, where illiteracy rates amongst them is 31.7% (34% in the West Bank and 29% in the Gaza Strip), as for 2017.[88] Approximately 25.8% of youth, aged 18–24, are enrolled in higher education institutions, meanwhile enrolment in the technical and vocational educational training (TVET) remains low at 2.6%.[89]

It seems that the MoEHE moves steadily towards establishing the foundations for a better and stronger and, thus, sustainable education system in the OPT. However, there is still a lot to do towards achieving the 4th Goal (Quality Education) of the United Nations' SDGs. This is with the consideration of the ongoing Israeli military occupation of the Palestinian Territories since June 1967, as well as the many problems and obstacles created by the Israeli occupation authorities, which hinder achieving sustainable development in the OPT.[90] However, it is hoped that digitization of the education sector in the OPT will enable the sector to move forward towards sustainability.

5.4 Digitization of Education Sector

The MoEHE has implemented several steps during the past few years towards reforming the educational system.[91] One of the MoEHE's main achievements was producing an action plan for curricula's development, as the MoEHE began to develop the curricula for grades 1–4. It also began to implement a policy of digitization in the Palestinian educational system in line with latest technological developments, regarding the teaching and learning processes. At the same time, the MoEHE approved a new modern system for the secondary education called in Arabic 'Injaz' (meaning 'Completion,' Fulfilment,' or 'Accomplishment') that replaced the old name 'Tawjihi' (meaning 'Directive'). The MoEHE also incorporated the technical and vocational educational training (TVET) in public education for grades 7–9. This integration constitutes exposing students of the 7–9 grades to vocational subjects that illustrate the relationship between theoretical knowledge and practicum. Additionally, the MoEHE encourages students to join the vocational stream during their secondary educational stage.

The MoEHE has adopted the system of digitization in order to overcome the costly infrastructure investments, and also to allow improving educational ser-

87 See MoEHE (Ministry of Education and Higher Education), 2017b
88 See PCBS (Palestinian Central Bureau of Statistics), 2018a
89 See RecoNow, 2016
90 See Salem, H. S., 2019
91 See MoEHE (Ministry of Education and Higher Education), 2017a

vices at effective cost. The MoEHE moves towards digitization of the education sector to make essential changes in the educational process. It intends to employ technology for the service of education based on four components. Three of these components depend on the infrastructure of information and communications technology (ICT), as well as technology equipment (Internet, portals, and computers). The fourth component is training and rehabilitation of teachers.

Also, the MoEHE has moved forward in cooperation with local governments and municipalities. The MoEHE views municipalities and local governments as pivotal partners for digitizing education and improving its quality in the OPT.

The percentage of classes in which educational technologies are used rose from 21% in 2014 to 22.2% in 2015, and it is planned to rise to 40% in 2019.[92] These technologies and their usage percentages are: 1. Digital tools (30.1%); 2. Non-digital tools (41.5%); and 3. Specialized tools (28.4%). The rate of students who use computer labs is 56.2%; while the rate of students who use educational portals is 17%; and the rate of students who use school library is 13%.[93] One of the goals of digitizing the education sector in the OPT is nurturing an investment-friendly environment, which means bolstering and encouraging digital and technical industries and enhancing digital content.

The MoEHE supports and enhances industrialization especially in the technical and digital fields and reinforcement of the digital content. It also boosts digitization of education at various levels. This includes providing all schools with free access to the Internet (under an agreement with the MTIT); reinforcement of digitization of the educational content through an educational portal which all schools, teachers, and students should have access to; and providing schools with sufficient computers and tablets containing the Palestinian curriculum. However, as noticed in Table 3 (above), the students/computer ratio, for the scholastic year 2016/2017, was 16/1 for private schools, 22/1 for public schools, and 47/1 for UNRWA schools, with an average ratio of 24/1.[94] These ratios are still very high in comparison with schools in other countries, where the students/computer ratio is 10/1, which is also embraced by UNESCO.[95]

Learning through tablets is currently being experimented at two basic schools in each of the directorates of education (grades 5–6) in the OPT, where implementation will be expanded gradually at a later date. The MoEHE also supports activation of the usage of traditional teaching methods and modern technology; the usage of smart tablets for digital display of the educational material during class;

---

92 See MoEHE (Ministry of Education and Higher Education), 2017b
93 See MoEHE (Ministry of Education and Higher Education), 2017b
94 See PCBS (Palestinian Central Bureau of Statistics), 2017a, 2017b
95 See UNESCO (United Nations Educational, Scientific and Cultural Organization), 2016

and the production of computerized educational methods that enhance the teaching and learning processes.

Another example on digitizing the education sector in the OPT is the e-learning, which is already applied in some Palestinian universities for some time now, particularly in the Al-Quds Open University (QOU). Established in 1991, the QOU is the first open and distance learning (including e-learning) institution in the Occupied Palestinian Territories.[96] According to the NESSP 2017–2022, developing e-learning programs in the OPT means elevating the education system to the era of digitization, which includes the following targets[97]:

1. Increasing the rate of usage of education and learning technologies in the education process, beginning with the classrooms. It also includes the library, science lab, computer lab, other teaching methods and means, etc.
2. Promoting the usage of modern tools and equipment, such as interactive projectors at schools.
3. Expanding and encouraging the digitization of education.
4. Improving the process of e-learning and distance learning.

However, the digitization process in the education sector has several problems, obstacles, and challenges. Most prominent obstacles to achieving the targets of digitization include the following ones[98] that represent geopolitical and financial issues:

1. The Israeli occupation's withholding of electronic equipment and tools (sometimes for long periods of time). It is worth-mentioning that the Israeli occupation authorities have full control over imports and exports in the OPT, considering the fact that the equipment and tools are donated or imported from abroad.
2. Budgets earmarked for development of the e-learning programs are insufficient to popularize the initiative of digitization of education. Therefore, the MoEHE will endeavor to mobilize funding for this initiative through other sources, such as municipalities and donor countries, as well as international organizations.

6 Conclusions and Recommendations

The speedy development of wireless communications and digital and technological equipment has enabled developed and developing countries alike to overcome the hurdles associated with the costly financial investment in infrastructure that is

---

96 See QOU (Quds Open University), 2019
97 See MoEHE (Ministry of Education and Higher Education), 2017a
98 See MoEHE (Ministry of Education and Higher Education), 2017a

needed for the two major sectors in societies, which are the health sector and the education sector. Such development has been mobilized by developed countries in the 20th Century and is continuing in the 21st Century, which has led to digitization of the health and education sectors, including the administrative aspects of both sectors. Advances in computer science, engineering and technology, as well as in patient monitoring systems, access to the Internet, and electronic health record systems have all enabled rapid accumulation of patient data, especially big data, in electronic form. Some of these things have also facilitated digitization of the education sector, which have enabled the improvement of both teaching and learning processes at schools and universities, worldwide.

Despite the obstacles, problems, and challenges facing the Palestinian people in the Occupied Palestinian Territories (OPT), these territories have been no exception in the field of digitization, though at lower rates than the digitization's rates of other countries in the MENA region, in particular, and worldwide at large. Access to the Palestinian market and free movement of people and goods (such as computer hardware), as well as the Israeli restrictions on the usage of the Internet, and the strict and total Israeli control of borders, especially in the case of the Gaza Strip, have greatly hindered the progress of the health and education sectors towards having digitization's transformation of the health and education sectors, as well as other sectors that have heavy influence and impact on the daily life of Palestinian people in the OPT.

As discussed in this paper, the Palestinian health sector in the OPT is still far behind the digitization era, while the Palestinian education sector has already made some appreciated progress towards digitization's transformation. However, it is noteworthy to mention that the education system in the OPT gives students minimal interaction with communications and information technology, including the usage of the Internet, and does not stimulate students' problem-solving skills or their innovative thinking.

Various in-depth analyses of the Palestinian education system have revealed serious flaws in the system represented in four main components of the education process. These educational components are: 1. Methods of assessment and evaluation of the students; 2. Teaching and learning methodologies, means, and processes; 3. Design of the curriculum at the different schooling and university levels; and 4. Advanced digitization process of the education system. At the higher education levels, for instance, these serious flaws have resulted in the phenomenon where the skills of graduates are currently falling below the skills required by local and international companies, though some (but not many) Palestinian graduates have succeeded in obtaining jobs abroad.

Moreover, the high cost and long hours required to train new graduates in the information and communications technology areas (ICT), with respect to the health and education sectors, in particular, as concerned in this study, have discouraged companies from investing in capacity building and technology transfer, as those companies cannot expect a quick return on their investments, especially when considering the volatile environment, politically, geopolitically, and economically. However, the good news is that the international community (represented in some governments, NGOs, and big companies, dealing with ICT, such as Cisco Systems Inc., Google, Microsoft, and others) has invested in training Palestinian graduates. By investing in the Palestinian infrastructure and in training graduates in the ICT sector, Cisco helped startup companies in the OPT compete for outsourcing work with other international markets.

For the ICT industry to seriously advance, move forward, and make considerable progress by providing services to the health and education sectors and other sectors in the OPT, and, thus, supplying the Palestinian market with jobs that are desperately needed by thousands of unemployed young graduates, the Israeli restrictions must be ended. On the other hand, the Palestinian National Authority (PNA) needs to provide a capable environment for ICT, in order to take the lead in building the e-government's infrastructure, and to move this matter beyond the political division between the West Bank and the Gaza Strip. Such forward's movements towards a better situation of the ICT sector to be effectively functioning in the Occupied Palestinian Territories (OPT) need immediate intervention from the international community, including organizations from the United Nations (UN), the USA, and the European Union (EU).

Literature

Abudaka, M. (2017). *The telecommunication and IT sector in Palestine. This Week in Palentine, Issue 251*. Retrieved 9.3.2019, from http://thisweekinpalestine.com/telecommunication-sector-palestine/

AbuShanab, A. (2018). *A Hashtag Palestine 2017: Palestinian Digital Activism Report. 7amleh – The Arab Center for Social Media Advancement.* Retrieved 10.3.2019, from https://7amleh.org/2018/04/03/press-release-palestine-2017-report-palestinian-online-content-targeted-through-mass-surveillance-digital-occupation-and-biased-content-moderation/

Aker, O. (2016). *National Health Strategy 2017–2022. Draft English Summary. Ministry of Health, General Directorate of Health Policies and Planning, October 2016, Ramallah, Palestine.* Retrieved 10.3.2019, from http://www.lacs.ps/documentsShow.aspx?ATT_ID=29996

AVASANT. (2013). *Palestinian ICT market penetration study. Final Report. Palestinian Information Technology Association of Companies and the French Development Agency (AFC).* Retrieved 10.3.2019, from file:///G:/international_market_penetration_study%20(1).pdf

BBC. (2015). *Internet used by 3.2 billion people in 2015.* Retrieved 9.3.2019, from https://www.bbc.com/news/technology-32884867

Beesion. (2019). *Simplify product management with Beesion's telecom product catalog: Easy to update and expand – Multiple deployment modes.* Retrieved 10.3.2019, from https://beesion.com/product-catalog/

BTRA-ARGENET. (2015). *Kingdom of Bahrain Telecommunications Regulatory Authority (TRA), Strategy Analytics, 2013 Telecommunications Retail Price Benchmarking Report for Arab Countries, Report from the AREG-NET Price Benchmarking Study.* Retrieved 10.3.2019, from http://www.tra.org.bh/en/press-releases/tra-releases-its-final-report-on-strategic-market-review.html

CBG (Courtesy of Paltel Group). (2019). *The evolution of the telecommunications sector in Palestine: A sustainable Palestinian success story. This Week in Palestine.* Retrieved 9.3.2019, from http://thisweekinpalestine.com/evolution-telecommunications-sector-palestine/

El-Darwiche, B., Singh, M., Ganediwalla, S. (2012). *Digitization and Prosperity. The economic growth of nations is linked to one factor: adoption of information and communications technology.* Retrieved 10.3.2019, from https://www.strategy-business.com/article/00127?gko=efe69

Fanack. (2016). *The health sector in Palestine.* Retrieved 9.3.2019, from https://fanack.com/palestine/governance-and-politics-of-palestine/the-health-sector-in-palestine/

IMFA (Israel Ministry of Foreign Affairs). (1995). *THE ISRAELI-PALESTINIAN INTERIM AGREEMENT-Annex III.THE ISRAELI-PALESTINIAN INTERIM AGREEMENT ON THE WEST BANK AND THE GAZA STRIP Annex III. Protocol Concerning Civil Affairs.* Retrieved 9.3.2019, from https://mfa.gov.il/mfa/foreignpolicy/peace/guide/pages/the%20 israeli-palestinian%20interim%20agreement%20-%20annex%20iii.aspx

ITU (International Telecommunication Union). (2017). *ICT Facts and Figures 2017. The World in 2015. ICT Data and Statistics Division, Telecommunication Development Bureau. International Tele-communication Union, Geneva, Switzerland.* Retrieved 9.3.2019, from https://www.itu.int/en/ITU-D/Statistics/Documents/facts/ICTFacts Figures2017.pdf

IWS (Internet World Stats). (2018). *Internet usage statistics. The internet big picture world Internet users and 2018 population stats.* Retrieved 9.3.2019, from https://www.internetworldstats.com/stats.htm

Kizito, K., Adeline, K., Baptiste, K., Anita, A., Agnes, B., Johnson, P., Thierry, N. (2012). *TRACnet: A national phone-based and web-based tool for the timely integrated disease surveillance and response in Rwanda. ISDS Conference 2012 Abstracts. Online Journal of Public Health Informatics, ISSN 1947-2579, 5(1):e202, 2013.* Retrieved 10.3.2019, from https://journals.uic.edu/ojs/index.php/ojphi/article/view/4598/5047

Lozano, L. A., Villamil, M. d. (2018). *Strategy to develop a digital public health observatory integrating business intelligence and visual analytics. In: Rocha, Á., and Guarda, T. (Eds.) Proceedings of the International Conference on Information Technology & Systems (ICITS 2018).* Retrieved 9.3.2019, from https://link.springer.com/chapter/10.1007 %2F978-3-319-73450-7_42

MAS (Palestine Economic Policy Research Institute). (2015). *Training provision and employment in Palestine: Gaza, East Jerusalem, Refugee Camps, Area C; Jerusalem and Ramallah, Palestine. A study funded by GIZ.* Retrieved 9.3.2019, from http://www.mas.ps/files/server/201517 11140259-1.pdf

Massad, S., Shaheen, M., Karam, R., Brown, R., Glick, P., Linnemay, S., Khammash, U. (2016). Substance use among Palestinian youth in the West Bank, Palestine: A qualitative investigation. Public Health, 16: 800, Open Access. (https://www.ncbi.nlm.nih.gov/pmc/articles/ PMC498 8009/, Ed.) p. 9.

McQueeney, K. (2017). *Hydro: The drug epidemic sweeping through the West Bank.* Retrieved 9.3.2019, from https://www.thenational.ae/world/ mena/hydro-the-drug-epidemic-sweeping-through-the-west-bank-1.610097

MoEHE (Ministry of Education and Higher Education). (2006). *Education Statistical Yearbook 2005/2006. Ramallah, Palesttine.*

MoEHE (Ministry of Education and Higher Education). (2017a). *Education Sector Strategic Plan 2017–2022. An Elaboration of the Education Development Strategic Plan III (2014–2019). April 2017, Ramallah, Palestine.* Retrieved 10.3.2019, from http://www.lacs.ps/ documents Show.aspx?ATT_ID=34117^

MoEHE (Ministry of Education and Higher Education). (2017b). *Educational databases for schools and kindergartens for the academic year 2015/2016. Ramallah, Palestine.*

MoH (Ministry of Health). (2006). *Health Status in Palestine – Annual Report 2005. Gaza, Palestine, August 2006.*

Nassereldin, S. (2019). *Lost opportunities and future prospects telecommunications' physical infrastructure in Palestine. This Week in Palestine, Issue*

251. Retrieved 9.3.2019, from http://thisweek inpalestine.com/lost-opportunities-future-prospects/

Nikolinakos, N. (2006). *EU Competition Law and Regulation in the Converging Telecommunications, Media and IT Sectors. International Competition Law Series, Kluwer Law International, Alphen aan den Rijn, The Netherlands*. Retrieved 9.3.2019, from http://www.kluwer competitionlaw.com/book-toc?title=EU%20Competition%20Law%20and%20Regulation%20in%20the%20Converging%20Telecommunications%2C%20Media%20and%20IT%20Sectors

PCBS (Palestinian Central Bureau of Statistics). (2005a). *Demography and health survey 2004. Ramallah, Palestine*. Retrieved 10.3.2019, from http://www.pcbs.gov.ps/

PCBS (Palestinian Central Bureau of Statistics). (2005b). *Education–Time Series Statistics. Ramallah, Palestine*. Retrieved 10.3.2019, from http://www.pcbs.gov.ps/

PCBS (Palestinian Central Bureau of Statistics). (2013). *Child Statistics Series (No. 16) Palestinian Children –Issues and Statistics Annual Report, 2013. Ramallah, Palestine*. Retrieved 9.3.2019, from http://www.pcbs.gov.ps/Downloads/book1971.pdf

PCBS (Palestinian Central Bureau of Statistics). (2017a). *Number of schools by region, stage and school gender, 2016/2017. Ramallah, Palestine*. Retrieved 9.3.2019, from http://www.pcbs.gov.ps/Portals/_Rainbow/Documents/Education2016-01E.htm

PCBS (Palestinian Central Bureau of Statistics). (2017b). *Number of students in schools and kindergartens by region and supervising authority, 1994/1995–2016/2017. Ramallah, Palestine*. Retrieved 9.3.2019, from http://www.pcbs.gov.ps/Portals/_Rainbow/Documents/Education-1994-2016-02E.htm

PCBS (Palestinian Central Bureau of Statistics). (2018a). *On the occasion of the International Population Day 11/7/2018. Ramallah, Palestine*. Retrieved 9.3.2019, from http://www.pcbs.gov.ps/post.aspx?lang=en&ItemID=3183

PCBS (Palestinian Central Bureau of Statistics). (2018b). *Palestine in Figures–2017. Ramallah, Palestine*. Retrieved 10.3.2019, from http://www.pcbs.gov.ps/Downloads/book2362.pdf

PNIPH (Palestinian National Institute of Public Health). (2017). *Illicit drug use in Palestine: A qualitative investigation. A formative phase study report. Palestinian Ministry of Health, United Nations Office on Drugs and*

Crime (UNODC), Korea International Cooperation Agency (KOICA). Retrieved 9.3.2019, from https://www.unodc.org/documents/publications/Illicit_Drug_Use_in_Palestine.pdf

PNVR (Palestinian National Voluntary Review on the Implementation of the 2030 Agenda). (2018). *Sustainable development goals. Ramallah, Palestine.* Retrieved 9.3.2019, from https://sustainabledevelopment. un.org/content/documents/20024VNR2018PalestineNEWYORK.pdf

QOU (Quds Open University). (2019). *Research on e-learning.* Retrieved 4.3.2019, from https://www.qou.edu/home/en/sciResearch/research On Elearning.jsp

Ramahi, H. (2015). *Education in Palestine: Current challenges and emancipatory alternatives. The American School of Palestine and University of Cambridge. A study funded by the Rosa Luxemburg Stiftung's Regional Office Palestine.* Retrieved 10.3.2019, from http://www.rosaluxemburg.ps/wp-content/uploads/2015/11/RLS-Study-29.11.15-final.pdf

RecoNow. (2016). *The higher education system in Palestine. National Report.* Retrieved 10.3.2019, from http://www.reconow.eu/files/fileusers/ 5140_National-Report-Palestine-RecoNOW.pdf

Salem, H. S. (2015). *Correspondence between Hilmi S. Salem and the Palestinian Ministry of Telecom and Information Technology (MTIT) – 31/7/2015 and 9/9/2015 –, Regarding Public Concerns against Local Communication Companies (Document in English and Arabic.* Retrieved 9.3.2019, from https://www.researchgate.net/publication/342110072_No_Sustainable_Development_in_the_Lack_of_Environmental_Justice_Full_Paper; https://home.liebertpub.com/publications/environmental-justice/259/overview

Salem, H. S. (2019). *No sustainable development in the lack of environmental justice. Environmental Justice. DOI: 10.1089/env.2018.0040.* Retrieved 4.3.2019, from https://www.liebertpub.com/doi/10.1089/env.2018.0040; https://www.researchgate.net/publication/330847246_No_Sustainable_Development_in_the_Lack_of_Environmental_Justice; https://home.liebertpub.com/publications/environmental-justice/259/overview

SDGF (Sustainable Development Goals Fund). (2019). *Goal 4: Quality Education.* Retrieved 9.3.2019, from https://www.sdgfund.org/goal-4-quality-education

Simpao, A., Ahumada, L., Rehman, M. (2015). Big data and visual analytics in anaesthesia and health care. British Journal of Anaesthesia. (https://www.sciencedirect.com/science/article/pii/S0007091217311479, Ed.) *ScienceDirect*, pp. 350–356.

Statista. (2019). *Mobile internet usage worldwide - Statistics & Facts*. Retrieved 3.3.2019, from https://www.statista.com/topics/779/mobile-internet/

TCC (Telecommunications' Community Campaign). (2019). *Enough is Enough with You: Telecommunications' Companies.* Retrieved 7.3.2019, from https://www.facebook.com/groups/428446937499489/

TRBR (Telecommunications Radiocommunications and Broadcasting Regulator). (2018). *Reference Interconnection Offer. What is a Reference Interconnection Offer (RIO).* Retrieved 10.3.2019, from https://www.trr.vu/en/telecom-industry/market-and-competition/reference-interconnection-offer

UN News. (2015). *Sustainable Development Goals to kick in with start of new year.* Retrieved 9.3.2019, from https://news.un.org/en/story/2015/12/519172-sustainable-development-goals-kick-start-new-year

UNDP (United Nations Development Programme). (2015). *Human Development Report–2015. Work for Human Development. UN, New York, N.Y., USA.* Retrieved 10.3.2019, from http://hdr.undp.org/sites/default/files/2015_human_development_report.pdf

UNDP (United Nations Development Programme). (2016). *Human Development Report 2016. Human Development for Everyone. UN, New York, N.Y., USA.* Retrieved 10.3.2019, from http://hdr.undp.org/sites/default/files/2016_human_development_report.pdf

UNDP (United Nations Development Programme). (2017). *Human Development Report–2017. Human Development Index and its Components. UN, New York, N.Y., USA.* Retrieved 10.3.2019, from https://www.pharmacoepi.org/pub/?id=dab17eb7-0dc4-489f-66b6-a59dbc4010df

UNDP (United Nations Development Programme). (2018). *Human Development Report–2018. Human Development Indices and Indicators. 2018 Statistical Update. UN, New York, N.Y., USA.* Retrieved 10.3.2019, from http://hdr.undp.org/sites/default/files/2018_human_development_statistical_update.pdf

UNESCO (United Nations Educational, Scientific and Cultural Organization). (2016). *Internationally comparable statistics on information and communication technology (ICT) in education: The role of the UNESCO Institute for Statistics (UIS) – Capacity Building Workshop on Information and Communication Technology in Education Statistics.* Retrieved 9.3.2019, from file:///G:/brazil-2016-role-uis-2-1-en.pdf

WHO (World Health Organization). (2018). *WHO concerned over increasingly overwhelmed health services in the Gaza Strip.* Retrieved 9.3.2019, from http://www.emro.who.int/palestine-press-releases/2018/who-concerned-over-increasingly-overwhelmed-health-services-in-the-gaza-strip-april-2018.html

WHO (World Health Organization). (2019). *Sustainable Development Goals – Third Goal: Good Health and Well-Being. SDG 3: Ensure healthy lives and promote wellbeing for all at all ages. The goals within a goal: Health targets for SDG 3.* Retrieved 10.3.2019, from https://www.who.int/sdg/targets/en/

Wikipedia. (2018). *List of Universities and Colleges in the State of Palestine.* Retrieved 10.3.2019, from https://en.wikipedia.org/wiki/List_of_universities_and_colleges_in_the_State_of_Palestine

Wikipedia. (2019a). *Global Internet usage.* Retrieved 23.2.2019, from https://en.wikipedia.org/wiki/Global_Internet_usage

Wikipedia. (2019b). *International Telecommunication Union.* Retrieved 22.2.2019, from https://en.wikipedia.org/wiki/International_Telecommunication_Union

World Bank. (2011). *West Bank and Gaza – Improving governance and reducing corruption. Report No. 61701 GZ, The World Bank, Washington D.C., USA.* Retrieved 9.3.2019, from https://openknowledge.worldbank.org/handle/10986/2814

World Bank. (2016). *Telecommunication sector note in the Palestinian Territories: Missed opportunity for economic development note for the Palestinian Ministry of Telecommunications and Information Technology. Carlo Maria Rossotto, Anat Lewin, Xavier Decos.* Retrieved 9.3.2019, from file:///G:/World%20Bank%20Telecom%20sector%20note%2004042016.pdf

Zappedia. (2019). *Internet usage stats: How many people use the Internet?* Retrieved 3.3.2019, from https://zappedia.com/global-internet-access/

New Approach to the Economic Measurement in Terms of Digital Economy

Andrey Shevandrin

1 Introduction

The traditional cycle of research in the regional economy involves the formation of a hypothesis of research or a theoretical model, the choice of methods for analyzing its verification, the collection and analysis of the data obtained, the final conclusion with regard to verification of the assumptions made.[1] In economic research of Russian regions, until recently, reliable analysis, diagnostics, and hypothesis verification could be based only on the final annual (for selected indicators of quarterly) data included in the published information resources of Rosstat. The data of official statistical bulletins in the context of accelerating the dynamics of economic processes are characterized by the following significant shortcomings: low level of relevance (data are published with a delay of 3 months to 2 years), distortion due to the quality of the primary statistical material (enterprises tend to underestimate their official reporting, statistics); conservative composition of statistical indicators (new economic phenomena and processes are not observed by official statistics); different degree of depth of detail and analytical slices of indicators (does not allow for comparative studies); fragmentary time series; refinement of previously published values (makes conclusions of researchers initially not reliable).

Ensuring reliable selective research is associated with high costs, which research teams, even taking into account grant support, objectively cannot bear.

The development of information technologies, the introduction of methods of artificial intelligence and machine learning, the need to search for heuristic solutions in the modern creative economy led to the spread of new approaches to obtaining a factual basis in economic research. Conventionally, we can distinguish two alternative official statistics and selective studies of the data extraction approach - obtaining "live" data from the Internet (Web Mining) and Big Data.

Modern resources of the Internet contain huge arrays of poorly structured information. Since the advent of Web 2.0 technology, according to which users themselves create content on Internet sites, the worldwide network increasingly re-

---

1 See Borisova, Kalinina, Buyanova, 2016; See Petrova, Tarakanov, Kalinina, 2017; See Brauweiler, 2002

H.-C. Brauweiler et al. (Hrsg.), *Digitalization and Industry 4.0: Economic and Societal Development*, https://doi.org/10.1007/978-3-658-27110-7_5

flects interests, preferences, sensitivity to the properties of various goods and the characteristics of their users. Therefore, the modern economy is increasingly called the "Digital Economy".

Effective methods of Web Mining are:

- obtaining data from Internet sites through a specially created software interface (API). Such interfaces have the majority of social networks and data banks (citation systems, ad placements, registries, etc.);
- "parsing" sites, i.e. the analysis of texts of pages of Internet sites, special programs-robots with the purpose of extracting information according to pre-established rules. "Parsing sites", as a rule, apply in the absence of API-interfaces; the most interesting for parsing are sites of online stores, job banks, exchanges and organizations.

Obviously, the disadvantage of Web Mining is the need for the researcher to have the relevant competences in the field of software engineering or to involve the relevant specialist in the research.

Big Data technology involves processing a significant amount of data recorded by information systems and analog-to-digital converters, or obtained from processing unstructured data (images, video, audio data). Unlike the "parsing" of sites, the Big Data array is not formed for a specific query and is designed to search for new (not obvious) patterns in socio-economic phenomena and processes. In this regard, large owners of such data sets (corporations, national governments) are interested in providing researchers with access to their data banks or publish them in aggregate form. The most popular open data projects include Data.gov (US Government, http://data.gov), US Census Bureau (US Census Bureau portal, http://www.census.gov/data.html), European Union Open Data Porta (Open Data Portal of the European Union, http://open-data.europa.eu/en/data), Government of the United Kingdom Open Data Portal (http://data.gov.uk/), Amazon Web Services public datasets (Amazon Internet store datasets, http://aws.amazon.com/datasets), UnData (UN Open Data Portal, http://data.un.org/Default.aspx), DBPedia (Database Publishing Service , http://wiki.dbpedia.org/).

The most popular Russian public Internet resources include the Open Data Portal of the Russian Federation (http://data.gov.ru/), the open data portals of the subjects of the Russian Federation (for example, the official portal of the open data of the Volgograd Region http://opendata.volganet.ru), open data of the Savings Bank of the Russian Federation (http://www.sbebank.com/en/analytics/opendata).

The latter is of particular value for research in the regional economy, since it offers a set of aggregated monthly data for all regions of Russia.

The cognitive potential of using big data of the Internet in social research has already been recognized by many researchers.[2] Published a large number of studies of social, political and financial issues based on the stream data of social services and platforms[3] the results of which were confirmed later.

2 Materials and Methods

Based on the analysis of the practice of using the technology of collecting and processing data on the Internet for sociological research, the methodology of such studies can be built in the sequence of phases presented in table 1.

Table 1: Methodology of economic measurements in a digital economy

Phase	Aim	Tasks
1. Acquisition	Collecting data from various Internet sources	Building dictionary of words (hashtags, search phrases, text mining) Collect streaming data from different internet sources Retrieving data from the API different sources
2. Preprocessing	Obtaining a data set of the required quality	Data quality assessment
3. Analytics	Data processing in order to obtain new knowledge about the properties, trends, and patterns of the studied area	Classification (Categorization) – lexicon based approach or machine learning Relevancy evaluation Counting analysis Building complex metrics
4. Interpretation	Explain new knowledge in the context of already known information	Search for relationships that could create a model of economic behavior
5. Prediction	Predicting the state of the object of study on the basis of identified patterns or a trained neural network	Development of a program for forecasting economic processes

In the majority of well-known studies carried out according to a similar scheme, Twitter was used as a source for text mining. This is due to the fact that the Twit-

2 See Kitchin, 2014; See Elragal, Klischewski, 2017; See Müller, Junglas, Brocke, Debortoli, 2016

3 See El Alaoui, et al., 2018; See Pääkkönen, Jokitulppo, 2017; See Cerchiello, Giudici, 2016; See Budiharto, Meiliana, 2018; See Fang, Zhan, 2015

ter API provides the ability to obtain the necessary data, including for contextual analysis (positive, negative or neutral responses).

The API of other resources does not provide enough data attributes for such an analysis, although we should expect the development of Internet resources in this direction.

The problem of using Twitter for such research in Russia lies in its low popularity, and hence the representativeness of such research. Table 2 shows that the share of Twitter in the overall traffic of social networks and platforms is 2.14% (in February 2019).

Table 2: Popularity of social networks and platforms in Russia
*share of traffic generated by this social network on the Russian Internet
(Source: Seo Auditor, 2019)

Rank	Social media or platform	Percentage*
1	Vk.com	65.67%
2	Facebook	14.25%
3	Odnoklassniki	10.97%
4	Youtube	4.99%
5	Twitter	2.14%

Therefore, with respect to the Russian advisable to consult the data search systems, e.g., yandex.ru, which fraction was 57.04% in February 2019 (for comparison google.com - 39,7%).[4]

In order to include keyword metrics that users use to satisfy their information needs, it is necessary to find patterns of their use from users' economic behavior.

In the present study, an array of aggregated big data of PJSC "Sberbank" was used for this purpose.

An array of data published by PJSC "Sberbank" and intended for free use as of February 2019 contains more than 45.5 thousand records for 83 regions of the Russian Federation for the period from January 2015 to December 2019, inclusive. The set includes the following indicators:

---

4 See Yandex, n.d.

- The number of applications for consumer loans (NACL);
- The average loan amount requested (ALR);
- The number of applications for mortgage loans (NAM);
- The average mortgage amount requested (AMR);
- The number of new deposits (NND);
- The average amount of a new deposit (AND);
- The average salary (AS);
- The average pension (AP);
- The average rub. on the current account per person (AA);
- The average deposits in rubles. per person (AD);
- The average spending on cards (ASC);
- The average spending in a restaurant (ASR);
- The average spending in a fast food restaurant (ASFF);
- The average bill in the restaurant (ABR);
- The average bill in fast food (ABFF).

PJSC "Sberbank" is the largest financial institution of the country, according to the Frank Research Group as of 01.07.2017, the share of private lending is 38.8%, in the credit card market - 40.5%, in the current account and term deposits market – 44.2%, mortgage lending - more than 50%[5], having offices in all constituent entities of the Russian Federation, a bank of these indicators of its activities can be qualified as representative for the study of the economy of Russian regions.

Based on the available data set, it seems appropriate to carry out the analysis in the following areas:

1. Having a monthly data array, it is relevant to analyze the seasonality of a number of income indicators of the population, since official statistics do not publish such data.
2. The data in the context of the regions of the Russian Federation will make it possible to draw a number of conclusions on the differentiation of subjects in terms of income indicators of the population.
3. It is of interest to analyze certain aspects of the social and economic well-being of the population, which, according to official statistics, is difficult to ascertain.
4. Expediency classification of regions according to a set of indicators that will allow to establish not only differences, but also to identify common groups of regions.

[5] See Frank RG, 2019

The purpose of this study is to search for trends and features that are significant for the economy of the Russian regions based on a comparison of the aggregated data of the country's largest financial institution, Sberbank, and the search queries of Internet users reflecting the state of the economy in a particular region of Russia.

3 Results and Discussion

The Google Adwords and Yandex Wordstat services were used to search for the corpus of key queries reflecting the state of the “bad economy”. Semantic analysis allowed us to select the following triggered words "bad economy": 'Crisis', 'Vacancy', 'Cause of the crisis', 'Allowance', 'Loan', 'Bankruptcy', 'Close Ltd.', 'Employee reduction' (in Russian).

Selected keywords have different frequencies. To compare the data, their values were normalized to the average. The dynamics of the frequencies of the first four words are presented in figure 1. According to these words, it is impossible to note positive or negative dynamics in the observed period. We can single out the seasonality of Internet users' interest in the topic of the crisis, its causes and vacancies: these topics cause the greatest interest in the fall, the traditional decline in interest occurs in the summer season.

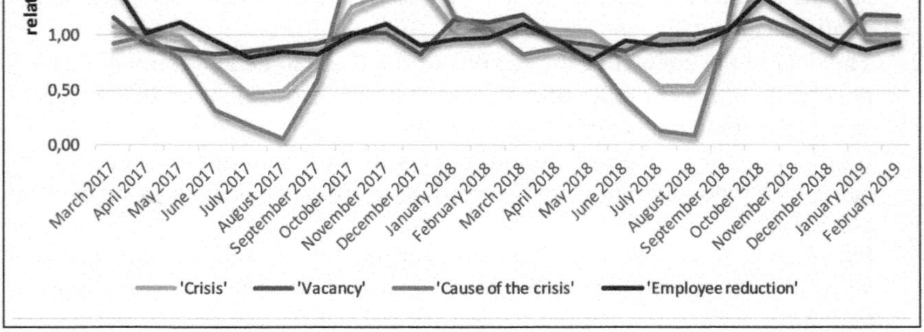

Figure 1: Dynamics of the normalized values of search queries for yandex.ru users in the Volgograd region for the period from March 2017 to February 2019

Next, we consider how the economy of the regions of Russia looks in terms of the array of large aggregated data of Sberbank.

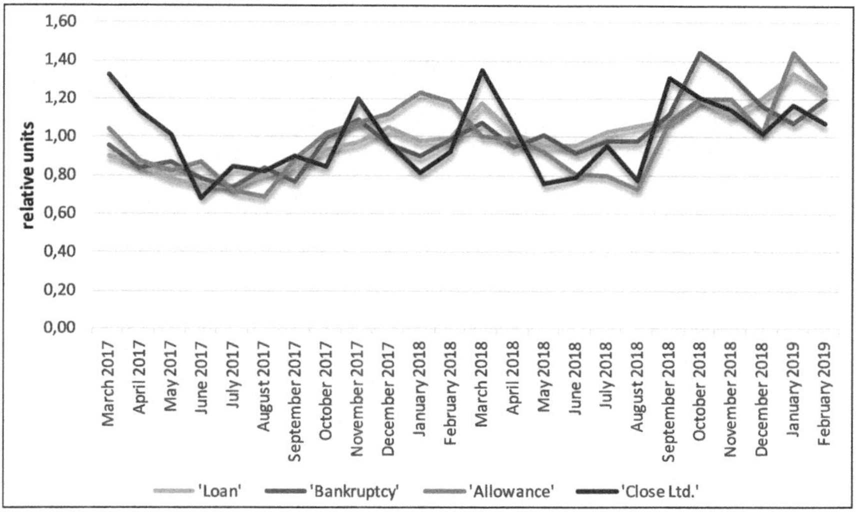

Figure 2: Dynamics of the normalized values of user searches in the Volgograd region on yandex.ru for the period from March 2017 to February 2019

The dynamics of the average wage in the RF as a whole, separately for the Volgograd region and the ratio of salary and transferred to the accounts of PJSC "Sberbank" pensions are shown in figure 3.

According to the diagram above, the observed seasonality and rhythmicity of time series by average wage should be noted: traditionally the largest payments fall in December (seasonality ratio is 1.6), less significant growth is observed in July (seasonality ratio 1.1), and the minimum payments are made in the first months of the year (seasonality ratio ≈ 0.7).

In the ratio of salary and pensions, using the linear approximation, the regression coefficient will have a negative sign, i.e. on the observed period; there is an increase in the gap between the average pension received and salary.

The study of the differentiation of the regions of the Russian Federation in terms of these indicators was carried out by means of generally accepted statistical indicators for estimating the regional inequality: mean value, variation range, coefficient of variation, asymmetry and kurtosis coefficients. The values obtained are presented in table 3.

The greatest differentiation of the regions of the Russian Federation is observed in terms of the average volume of deposits per person, since 2015 the relative range of variation here has increased by 46.2%. It should be assumed that the population of the regions has different propensities to savings, which will be considered separately.

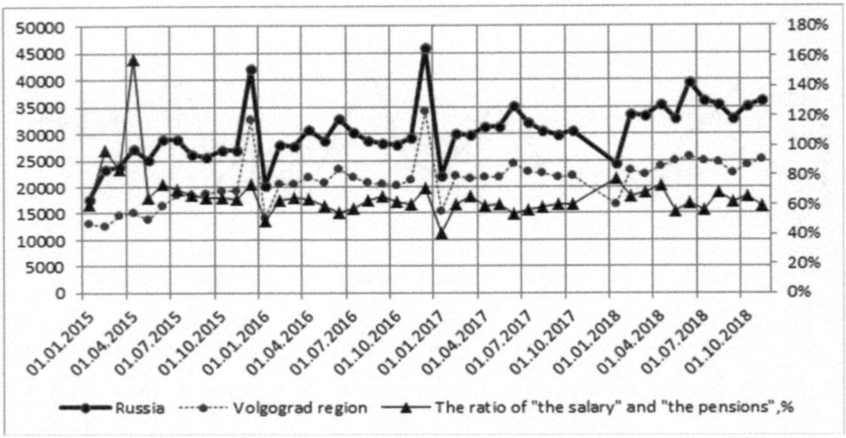

Figure 3: Dynamics of the average salary transferred to the accounts of PJSC "Sberbank"

By the level of salary, pensions received and the average application for consumer credit, regions show a reduction in heterogeneity. In 2017, the smallest transferred average pension in the Tula region is 8587 rubles; the largest in the Kamchatka Territory is 22588 rubles. The lowest average wage is observed in the Republics of Karachaevo-Cherkessia and Kalmykia, Ivanovo and Kostroma regions. The highest salary are typical for the Chukotka Autonomous District (72022 rubles), the Magadan Region (67697 rubles), the Kamchatka Territory (60552 rubles) and Moscow (55661 rubles). For these indicators, if the kurtosis index is not high, asymmetry has a positive value, and therefore the distribution of clients' income of PJSC "Sberbank" is still shifted to the right. Thus, on this set of data, the hypothesis of increasing differentiation of regions according to the incomes of the population in the observed period is not observed.

Analysis of hidden relationships between the indicators considered is carried out through factor analysis (main components method).

As a result, 2 factors have been identified, which can explain 85% of the variation in the initial values. The first factor includes the variable salary and the size of pensions, i.e. this is the income factor of the population, it gives only 16% of the explained variance. The second factor consists of variable-value applications for consumer and mortgage loans, a new deposit and card expenses - 69% of the explained variance. Thus, salary (together with the value of the average pension) are not determinative in the financial activity of the population.

Table 3: Statistical data for the evaluation of differentiation for indicators on services received in pjsc "Sberbank" on january 01, 2015 and october 15, 2017

The coefficients	Average salary		Amount of the pension		Average volume of deposits in rub. per person		Average amount of applications for consumer loans in rub.	
Period	01. 2015	10. 2017	01. 2015	10. 2017	01 .2015	10. 2017	01. 2015	10. 2017
Relative range of variation, %	311,3	124,2	253,6	196,1	409,2	455,4	166,0	144,7
Excess	7,8	3,8	4,4	4,5	21,1	23,5	4,3	3,3
Asymmetry	2,4	1,6	1,9	2,1	4,1	4,3	2,0	1,9

To analyze the data array and solve the problem of classification of regions by the set of indicators of PJSC "Sberbank", a multidimensional statistical grouping based on the application of the Kohonen neural network was applied. This method allows you to identify latent rules and patterns in the data set.

Table 4: The cluster analysis of the level of registration of regions of Russia

Cluster number	Level of crediting
2	Low (55 regions)
1	Below the average (16 regions)
3	Abow the average (9 regions)
0	High (3 regions)

As a result of processing the data array, Kohonen self-organizing maps were built, whereby the regions of Russia were combined into clusters, each of which characterizes the extent to which the savings, investment or credit strategy of the population is implemented.[6]

The credit strategy is typical for the population of the cities of St. Petersburg, Moscow and the Moscow Region, which are classified in the zero cluster. The

[6]See Table 4

Volgograd Region is included in the second cluster with a low level of applications for consumer and mortgage loans, which indicates the prevalence of a savings strategy with low salary relative to other regions.

Considering the profiles of clusters in terms of average salary, the amount of the application for mortgage and consumer loans[7], it can be noted that the most "secured" regions form the main portfolio of mortgage loans, in regions with lower incomes, the share of consumer loans in the aggregate portfolio of applications.

Figure 4: The diagram of clusters in the context of average values of the population's wage and the loan amount.

Analyzing the profiles of clusters in the context of the average values of the turnover of funds on bank cards and the average size of the new deposit, it can be seen that the population of regions classified as a cluster with a propensity for credit behavior is actively using bank cards.

The analysis of the relationship between the frequency of search queries and indicators of the economic behavior of the population of the region was carried out by means of the correlation coefficient. The resulting matrix of coefficients is presented in table 5.

According to the data presented, the largest correlation is shown between the average household expenditure per restaurant (ASR) and the average bill in a

---

[7]See Figure 4

Table 5: Matrix of correlations of the frequency of keywords reflecting a "bad economy" and indicators of the state of the economy in the Volgograd region, 2018

Indicators / Key word	'Crisis'	'Vacancy'	'Cause of the crisis'	'Allowance'	'Loan'	'Bankruptcy'	'Close Ltd.'	'Employee reduction'
AD	0,31	0,11	0,41	0,46	0,24	0,24	-0,27	-0,22
AA	0,19	-0,05	0,23	0,19	0,64	0,43	-0,05	-0,18
NAM	0,15	0,25	0,11	0,14	0,31	0,12	-0,02	-0,09
NACL	-0,46	-0,13	-0,56	-0,41	0,11	-0,27	-0,18	-0,32
NND	0,28	-0,45	0,23	0,02	-0,08	0,07	-0,14	-0,22
ASC	0,14	-0,04	0,3	0,14	0,47	0,43	-0,22	-0,21
ASR	-0,66	-0,43	-0,73	-0,62	-0,54	-0,8	-0,51	-0,53
ASFF	0,06	0,15	0,2	0,16	0,72	0,6	-0,01	-0,14
ABR	-0,42	-0,29	-0,55	-0,29	-0,51	-0,79	-0,51	-0,5
ABFF	-0,46	-0,21	-0,51	-0,32	-0,63	-0,7	-0,32	-0,2
AS	0,18	-0,45	0,15	-0,04	0,23	0,16	-0,1	-0,17
AP	0,31	-0,3	0,23	0,11	0,23	0,07	0,04	-0,02
ALR	0,22	0,31	0,19	0,38	0,77	0,48	0,02	-0,13

restaurant (ABR) and all words of a dedicated search query corpus, with the exception of "vacancy". The sign in front of the correlation coefficient shows that the more Internet users access the search engine with "bad economy" queries, the less they are willing to spend on food in a restaurant. At the same time, the cost of visiting fast food restaurants is growing (ASFF).

Thus, the search for the most sensitive search phrases reflecting certain aspects of household behavior in a digital economy can be performed.

4 Conclusion

To summarize, the following points should be noted regarding economic measurements in the digital economy:

1. Studies of regularities and features of the economy of the regions can now be performed not only on the basis of an array of official statistical information and sample studies, but also on the basis of data collected or published on the

Internet. The need to search for heuristic solutions in management, as well as using the capabilities of artificial intelligence and machine learning leads to the formation of an open access to a new class of information resources obtained by information owners on the basis of aggregation of large data.

2. In this study, based on the open data set of PJSC "Sberbank", certain features of the socio-economic status of the regions have been identified, which it is difficult to identify on official open statistics, including: the seasonality and rhythm of time series of salary and pensions have been established; the reduction of differentiation of regions according to the incomes of the population was revealed, with their insignificant growth; it is shown that salary (together with the value of the average pension) are not decisive in the financial activity of the population; for the relatively "poor" regions, the savings strategy of the population is characteristic, the "rich" - the credit strategy; the higher the incomes of the population in the region, the more demanded mortgage lending.
3. Expansion of the indicators, which is announced on the website "Open data of Sberbank", will allow solving other analytical problems of the regional economy, and the addition of time series will make them suitable for forecasting, which will make such information resource for researchers as valuable as official ones statistical bulletins.
4. A new approach in economic measurements in conditions when official statistics do not meet the requirements of accuracy and relevance of information in the digital economy is the collection and analysis of big data of the Internet (Web mining).
5. A promising approach is to isolate keywords — triggers of a "bad economy" based on a comparison of data on economic processes and frequencies of search queries at equal short time intervals.

Literature

Borisova, A., Kalinina, A., Buyanova, M. (2016). "The mechanism for detecting and controlling regional socio-economic risks".

Brauweiler, H.-Ch. (2002). Innovationen im peripheren Raum. Wiesbaden: Gabler.

Budiharto, W., Meiliana, M. (2018). Prediction and analysis of Indonesia Presidential election from Twitter using sentiment analysis. Journal of Big Data.

Cerchiello, P., Giudici, P. (2016). Big data analysis for financial risk management. Journal of Big Data.

El Alaoui, I., Gahi, Y., Messoussi, R., Chaabi, Y., Todoskoff, A., Kobi, A. (2018). A novel adaptable approach for sentiment analysis on big social data. Journal of Big Data.

Elragal, A., Klischewski, R. (2017). Theory-driven or process-driven prediction? Epistemological challenges of big data analytics. Journal of Big Data.

Fang, X., Zhan, J. (2015). Sentiment analysis using product review data. Journal of Big Data.

Frank RG. (2019). *The biggest players in the retail banking market [Krupneishie igrokirynka roznichnykh bankovskikh uslug] [Electronic resource]*. Retrieved 1.3.2019, from https://frankrg.com/index.php?new_div_id=145

Kitchin, R. (2014). Big Data, new epistemologies and paradigm shifts. Big Data & Society.

Müller, O., Junglas, I., Brocke, J., Debortoli, S. (2016). Utilizing big data analytics for information systems research: challenges, promises and guidelines. European Journal of Information Systems.

Pääkkönen, P., Jokitulppo, J. (2017). Quality management architecture for social media data.Journal of Big Data.

Petrova, E., Tarakanov, V., Kalinina, A. (2017). Methodological Toolset of Regional Authority Bodies' Cluster Policy. Russia and the European Union. Development and Perspectives. Contributions to Economics.

Seo Auditor. (2019). *Social Network Ratinghttp [Rejting social'nyh setej] [Electronic resource]*. Retrieved 1.3.2019, from gs.seo-auditor.com.ru/socials/

Yandex. (n.d.). *Search engines in Russia [Poiskovye sistemy v Rossii] [Electronic resource]*. Retrieved 1.3.2019, from https://radar.yandex.ru/search

Comparision of field measurement data with propagation models, and modification of COST 231-Hata and Cost 231-Walfisch-Ikegami propagation models for UMTS2100 mobile network in Ashgabat, Koshi

Nokerov Suleyman

1 Introduction

The Universal Mobile Telecommunications System (UMTS) is a third generation wireless telecommunication system based on W-CDMA technology, and is normally the solution generally preferred by most countries. Nowadays UMTS has become an everyday technology from the user perspective in most countries. Over the years, the UMTS radio network system has been significantly enhanced and now offers broadband speeds far beyond the original design. Over time, many more frequency bands have been opened to UMTS radio network system around the world. In our case, UMTS radio network system operates at the uplink direction, that is, from the user to the network, in the frequency range between 1920 MHz – 1980 MHz and at the downlink direction, that is, from the network to the user, in the frequency range between 2110 MHz – 2170 MHz. In UMTS radio networks, it is necessary to properly define and manage the relationships between the neighboring cells. Incorrectly defined neighboring cells are not immediately noticeable but later on create difficulties for handovers and cell reselections of moving subscribers.[1]

If the parameters of existing cellular network are changed according to need, that is, optimized, or a new cell is installed to increase the bandwidth in an area that is already covered by other cells, the most important task in a UMTS network is to decrease the transmission power of the neighboring cells. Then, it is necessary to obtain radio propagation information to characterize path loss and interference geometries to guide link budgeting and site engineering.[2] Having an accurate realistic picture of the RF interference geometry resulting from candidate sites that are selected in sets is highly critical before actual deployment, to make sure that adequate cell isolation is obtained. In the mobile communication environment, signal propagation takes place through reflections, diffraction, and scatter-

---

1 See Holma, Toskala, 2010; See Sauter, 2014

2 See Sauter, 2014

H.-C. Brauweiler et al. (Hrsg.), *Digitalization and Industry 4.0: Economic and Societal Development*, https://doi.org/10.1007/978-3-658-27110-7_6

ing of signals from multiple obstacles, such as vehicles, hills, buildings, etc. This results in propagation characteristics that require modeling and parameterization.[3]

Radio signal propagation models are used to predict the expected (mean) value of the signal path loss at a certain distance from the transmitter. The path loss depends on the distance from the BS, the antenna heights of the BS and MS, the radio signal frequency, and the specifics of the terrain and the morphostructure (buildings type and density, clutter such as vegetation, forestry, open areas, water, etc.). There are three different categories of propagation models, referred to as statistical (or empirical), deterministic, and semi-deterministic. The empirical models are formulas that describe the path loss versus distance on an average scale. They are based on statistical analysis of a large number of measurements obtained in typically distinct environments such as urban, suburban and rural. Deterministic models use building and terrain databases to estimate the signal strength at the receiving point resulting from multiple reflections. The semi-deterministic (or semi-statistical) models are based on a mixture of a deterministic method of following individual signal propagation effects and calibration of model parameters based on collected path loss measurements.[4]

In urban environment the radio signal propagation is much more complex because the transmission path between the MS and the BS can vary from simple direct line-of-sight to one that is severely obstructed by buildings, foliage, and the terrain and the propagation paths of the radio wave are therefore more difficult to determine. In such cases, an empirical or semi-empirical model is more usable.[5]

Studies on the characteristics of the propagation of radio signals were studied in Seyitnepesov, Hydyrov, 2015 and Seyitnepesov, Nokerov, 2017. In this work, empirical models of the propagation of radio signals COST 231-Hata and COST 231-Walfisch-Ikegami were studied for applicability under corresponding conditions. On the basis of statistical data processing, it is proposed to use a correction coefficient for these models.

2 Radio Wave Propagation Models

2.1 COST 231-Hata Model

COST 231-Hata radio wave propagation model is extension of the Okamura–Hata model.[6] COST 231 Project extended the Okamura–Hata model to the frequency

3 See Rahnema, 2008
4 See Rahnema, 2008; See Laiho, Wacker, Novosad, 2006
5 See Laiho, Wacker, Novosad, 2006
6 See Okumura, Ohmori, Kawano, Fukuda, 1968; See Hata, 1980

bands of 1500…2000 MHz. COST 231-Hata propagation model takes note of four terrains/areas as shown below[7]:

1. small and medium-size cities
2. metropolitan areas.

Four parameters are used in COST 231-Hata model for estimation of the radio wave propagation loss. Range of validity for the COST 231-Hata model: carrier frequency $f = 1500...2000$ MHz, base station (BS) antenna height $h_{BS} = 30...200$ m, mobile station (MS) antenna height $h_{MS} = 1...10$ m, distance $d = 1...20$ km. The COST 231-Hata model formula for calculating the radio wave path loss has the following form[8]:

$$PL = A + B\log(d) + C \tag{1}$$

$$A = 46.3 + 33.9\log(f) - 13.82\log(h_{BS}) - a(h_{MS}) \tag{2}$$

$$B = 44.9 - 6.55\log(h_{BS}) \tag{3}$$

$$a(h_{MS}) = (1.1\log(f) - 0.7)h_{MS} - (1.56\log(f) - 0.8) \tag{4}$$

$$\begin{cases} C = 0 & \text{for medium sized city and suburban} \\ & \text{centres with medium tree density} \\ C = 3 & \text{for metropolitan areas} \end{cases} \tag{5}$$

If the BS antenna height is below the rooftop level of the surrounding buildings, the COST 231-Hata model is not suitable for predicting cellular transmission path loss.

2.2 COST 231-Walfisch-Ikegami Model

The COST 231-Walfisch-Ikegami propagation model is the most widely used model for calculating path losses in cellular transmission. COST 231-Walfisch-

---

7 See Damosso, Correia, 1999; See Molisch, 2011
8 See Damosso, Correia, 1999; See Molisch, 2011

Ikegami Model is a combination of the F.Ikegami and J.Walfisch models[9] and it developed by COST 231 project. The model assumes that the signal propagates over roof-tops and is diffracted by the roof-top edges in reaching the receiver.[10] The illustration of COST 231-Walfisch-Ikegami model parameters is shown in figure 1.

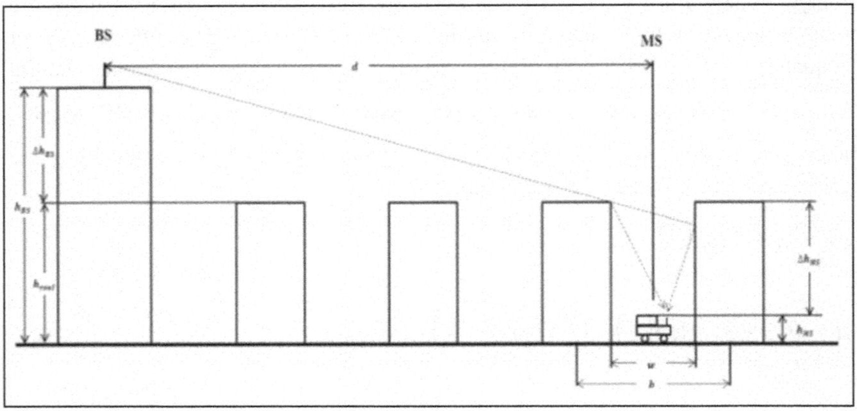

Figure 1: Illustration of COST 231-Walfisch-Ikegami Model parameters

The model presents two different formulas for cases: LOS (line-of-site) and Non-LOS (NLOS). The formula for LOS is simple and only depends on the carrier frequency f in MHz and the distance d in km between the BS and the MS. In this case path loss is calculated as follows[11]:

$$PL_{LOS} = 42.6 + 26\log(d) + 20\log(f) \quad \text{for} \quad d \geq 20 \tag{6}$$

The radio wave path loss formula for NLOS case is composed of a free-space path loss L_0, roof-top-to-street diffraction and scatter loss L_{rts}, and multiple screen diffraction loss L_{msd}. The parameters of the model for the NLOS case are: carrier frequency f in MHz, BS antenna height h_{BS} in m, MS antenna height h_{MS} in m, distance d between BS and MS in km, building height h_{roof}

9 See Ikegami, Yoshidas, Takeuchi, Umehira, 1984; See Walfisch, Bertoni, 1988
10 See Damosso, Correia, 1999
11 See Damosso, Correia, 1999; See Molisch, 2011

in m, width of the street w in m, distance between buildings b in m, orientation angle φ between the direction of propagation and street axis in degrees.

In this NLOS case path loss is calculated as follows[12]:

$$PL_{NLOS} = \begin{cases} L_0 + L_{rts} + L_{msd} & \text{for } L_{rts} + L_{msd} > 0 \\ L_0 & \text{for } L_{rts} + L_{msd} \leq 0 \end{cases} \tag{7}$$

where the free-space path loss L_0 is given by:

$$L_0 = 32.4 + 20\log(d) + 20\log(f) \tag{8}$$

The roof-top-to-street diffraction and scatter loss L_{rts} is given by:

$$L_{rts} = -16.9 - 10\log(w) + 10\log(f) + 20\log(\Delta h_{MS}) + L_{ori} \tag{9}$$

where Δh_{MS} is the difference between the building height h_{roof} and the MS antenna height h_{MS}.

$$\Delta h_{MS} = h_{roof} - h_{MS} \tag{10}$$

Correction factor L_{ori} depend on the orientation of the street and given by:

$$L_{ori} = \begin{cases} -10 + 0.354\varphi & \text{for } 0^\circ \leq \varphi < 35^\circ \\ 2.5 + 0.075(\varphi - 35) & \text{for } 35^\circ \leq \varphi < 55^\circ \\ 4.0 - 0.114(\varphi - 55) & \text{for } 55^\circ \leq \varphi \leq 90^\circ \end{cases} \tag{11}$$

where φ is the angle between street orientation and the direction of incident wave in degrees.[13]

---

12 See Damosso, Correia, 1999; See Molisch, 2011

13 See Figure 2

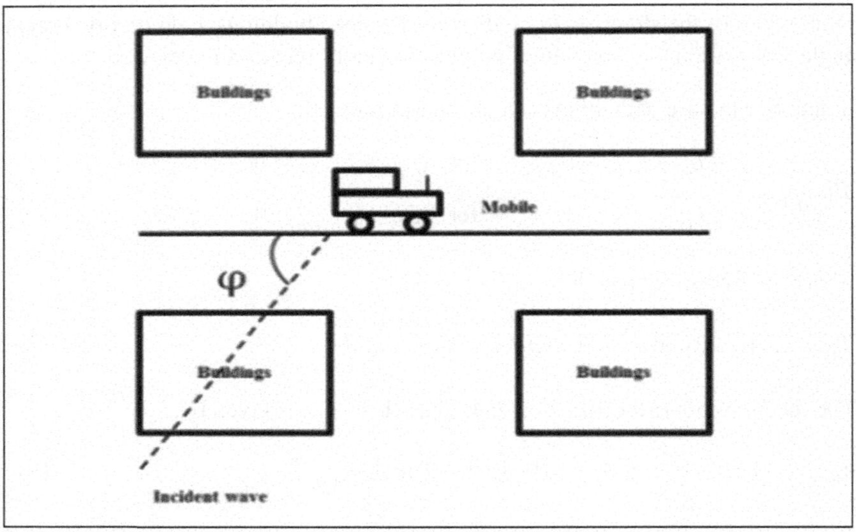

Figure 2: Definition of the angle φ between street orientation and the direction of incident wave

The multiple screen diffraction loss L_{msd} is given by:

$$L_{msd} = L_{bsh} + k_a + k_d \log(d) + k_f \log(f) - 9\log(b) \tag{12}$$

where L_{bsh} is the shadowing gain that appears when the $h_{BS} > h_{roof}$ and given by:

$$L_{bsh} = \begin{cases} -18\log(1+\Delta h_{BS}) & \text{for} \quad h_{BS} > h_{roof} \\ 0 & \text{for} \quad h_{BS} \le h_{roof} \end{cases} \tag{13}$$

where Δh_{BS} is the difference between the BS height h_{BS} and the building height h_{roof}.

$$\Delta h_{BS} = h_{BS} - h_{roof} \tag{14}$$

The factor k_a increases when the $h_{BS} \le h_{roof}$ and given by:

$$k_a = \begin{cases} 54 & \text{for } h_{BS} > h_{roof} \\ 54 - 0.8\Delta h_{BS} & \text{for d} \geq 0.5\,\text{km and } h_{BS} \leq h_{roof} \\ 54 - 0.8\Delta h_{BS}\dfrac{d}{0.5} & \text{for d} < 0.5\,\text{km and } h_{BS} \leq h_{roof} \end{cases} \quad (15)$$

The distance factor k_d is given by:

$$k_d = \begin{cases} 18 & \text{for } h_{BS} > h_{roof} \\ 18 - 15\dfrac{\Delta h_{BS}}{h_{roof}} & \text{for } h_{BS} \leq h_{roof} \end{cases} \quad (16)$$

The frequency factor k_f is given by:

$$k_f = -4 + \begin{cases} 0.7\left(\dfrac{f}{925} - 1\right) & \text{for medium - sized cities and} \\ & \text{suburban centres with medium tree density} \\ 1.5\left(\dfrac{f}{925} - 1\right) & \text{for metropolitan areas} \end{cases} \quad (17)$$

Range of validity for the COST 231-Walfisch-Ikegami model: carrier frequency $f = 800...2000$ MHz, BS antenna height $h_{BS} = 4...50$ m, MS antenna height $h_{MS} = 1...3$ m, distance $d = 0.02...5$ km.

3 Measurement of radio signal power

To determine the applicability of models, relevant studies have been conducted on UMTS 2100 MHz cells. The measurements were carried out on the territory of the Oguz Han Engineering and Technology University of Turkmenistan. 1,2,3 and 4-storey buildings are located on the measurement area. The buildings are quite tight. Despite the fact that the measurements were carried out in a small area, its relief is heterogeneous and and sharply variable. Between the station and the terminal is located a many trees. The station is designed as a 3 sector Node B class antenna. The antenna is located at a height of 17 meters, the measuring device (terminal) is located at a height of 1.5 meters. A map of the location of measurements and measurement results (color scheme) are shown in figure 3.

Figure 3: A Google Earth map of the location of measurements and measurement results

The Lenovo A7000-a mobile phone with NetMonitor Android software installed was used for measure the received signal power. The software allows to archive measurement results in .csv and .kml formats. Discrete time of intensity of measurements 1 second. The measurements were carried out at a distance from the base station within 260 m to 526 m. The .csv file contains the received signal strength (RSSI), operating frequency, and GPS coordinates. Screen shots of some received signal power measurements shown in figure 4.

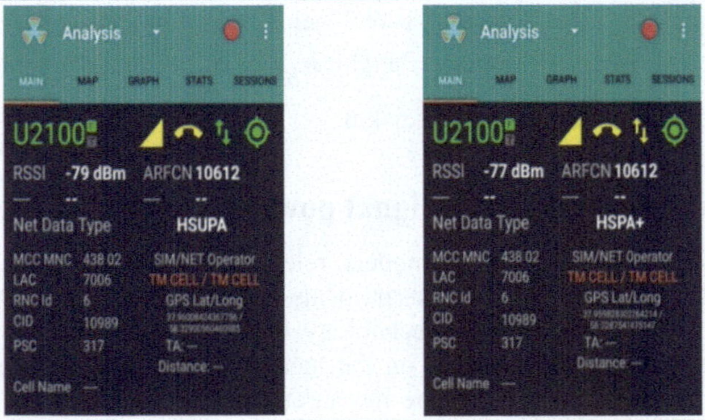

Figure 4: Screen shots of some received signal power measurements

The results of field measurements versus distance between Node B and MS is shown in fig. 5. The vertical axis represents the Signal Power in dBm, the horizontal axis the distance between Node B and MS in km.

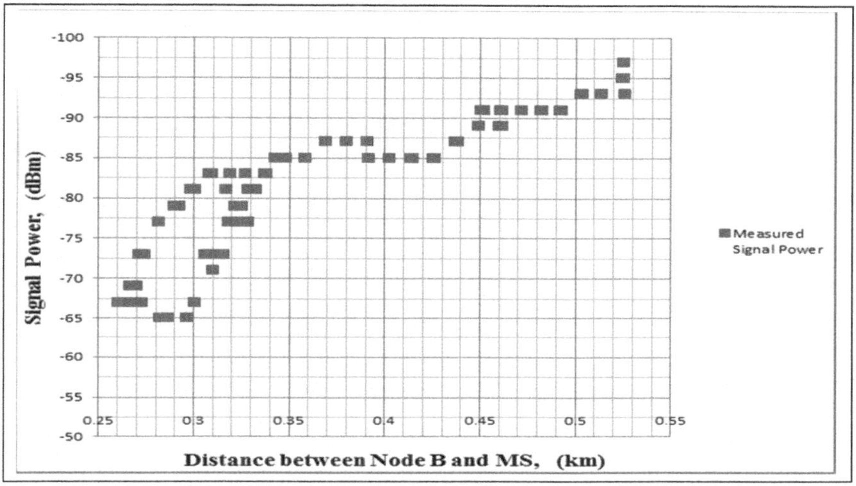

Figure 5: The results of field measurements versus distance between Node B and MS

4 Comparison of field measurement results with signal power prediction

To predict the average signal power at the receiving point we used formulas for "small and medium-size cities" environment from all propagation models shown above. For the parameters and their values for propagation models see table 1.

Table 1: The propagation models parameters and their values

Parameters	Values
carrier frequency, (f)	2122.4 MHz
Node B antenna height, (h_{BS})	17 m
MS antenna height, (h_{MS})	1.5 m
distance, (d)	0.26 – 0.526 km
widths of the street, (w)	20 m
distance between buildings, (b)	30 m
orientation angle, (φ)	54°

The results of the path loss prediction used to calculate the average signal power based on transmitted power, transmitter and receiving antenna gains, and cable losses. Predicted average signal power results and measurement results are compared with each other and graphically illustrated in figure 6. A comparison was done using Microsoft Excel software. The vertical axis represents the Signal

Power in dBm, the horizontal axis represent the distance between Node B and MS in km.

From the below illustrated graphical construction, we can investigate that predicted signal power results are higher than measured signal power results.

This is due to:

1. despite the available line of sight, in these zones signals are weakened by reflection from obstacles
2. the presence of trees in the measured area
3. at the area where we made field measurement buildings are very closer to each other
4. despite the fact that the measurements were carried out in a small area, its relief is heterogeneous and sharply variable.

Obtained signal power results by COST 231-Walfisch-Ikegami propagation model is nearest to the measured data than COST 231-Hata model.

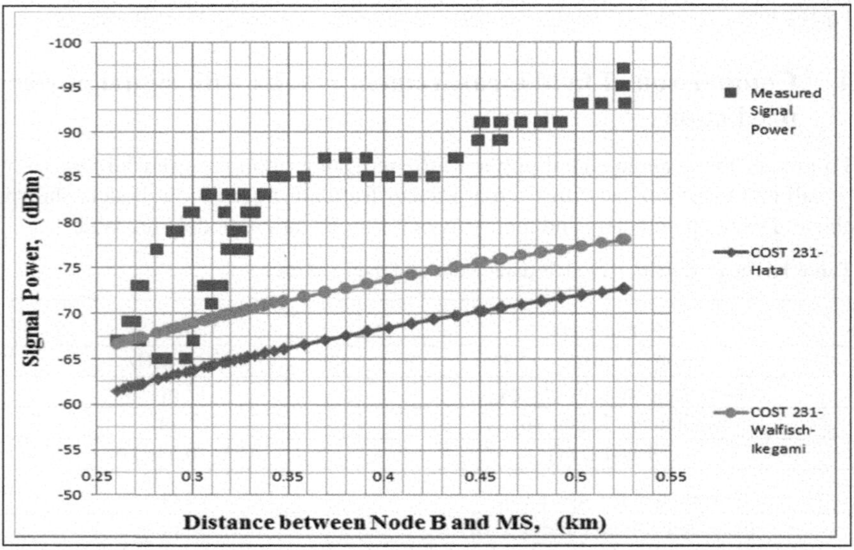

Figure 6: Comparison of measured and predicted signal powers

For evaluating spread of results between propagation models and measured data commonly used statistical tool is the Root Mean Square Error (RMSE). The acceptable RMSE value is up to $6-7$ dB for urban area. The formula for RMSE is given by[14]:

$$RMSE = \sqrt{\frac{\sum_{i=1}^{n}\left(X_{\text{obs},i} - X_{\text{model},i}\right)^2}{n}} \tag{18}$$

where X_{obs} – observed values and X_{model} – modelled values at time/place i, and n is number of measured and obtained data at the same points.

Evaluated data of spread of results between propagation models and measured data by RMSE shown below in the table 2.

Table 2: Evaluated data of spread of results between propagation models and measured data

Propagation Models	RMSE values
COST 231-Hata	16.4 dB
COST 231-Walfisch-Ikegami	11.6 dB

The COST 231-Walfisch-Ikegami model is the best model than COST 231-Hata, for path loss prediction in the investigated area which can be tuned with respect to RMSE value with 11.6 dB.

We can modify propagation models by adding obtained RMSE values to the Hata equation for "medium sized city" environment. Modified propagation models are shown below.

Modified COST 231-Hata propagation model:

$$PL = 62.7+33.9\,log(f) - 13.82\,log(h_{BS}) - a(h_{MS})+(44.9 - 6.55\,log(h_{BS}) * log(d) \tag{19}$$

where the function $a(h_{MS})$ is the same as (4).

Modified COST 231-Walfisch-Ikegami propagation model:

$$PL_{NLOS} = L_0 + L_{rts} + L_{msd} + 11.6 \tag{20}$$

where L_0, L_{rts}, and L_{rts} losses are the same as (8) – (17).

---

14 See Oluwafemi, Femijemilohun, Oluwasola, Owolabi, 2018; See Ogbeide, Edeko, 2013

Modified propagation models are validated by applying it to the measurement data in order to obtain accurate predictions closer to the field measurements for these environments. The comparison of prediction results of modified propagation models and field measurement data are shown in figure 7. The vertical axis represents the Signal Power in dBm, the horizontal axis represent the distance between Node B and MS in km.

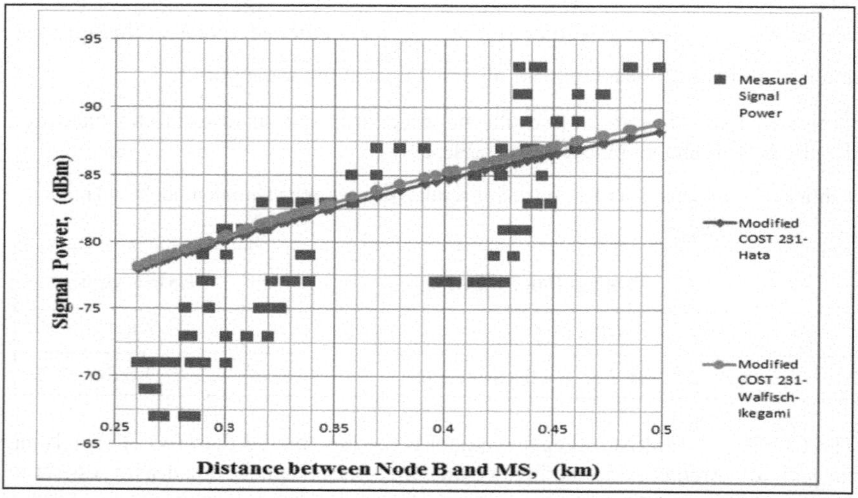

Figure 7: Predicted Signal Power by modified propagation models and measured Signal Power

Evaluated data of spread of results between modified propagation models and measured data shown below in the table 3.

These results are within the acceptable range of up to 6–7 dB for good signal prediction.

Table 3: Evaluated data of spread of results between modified propagation models and measured data

Propagation Models	RMSE values
COST 231-Hata	5.4 dB
COST 231-Walfisch-Ikegami	5.6 dB

5 Conclusion

As a result of the conducted research, a correction factor was proposed for the models describing the propagation characteristics of radio signals COST 231-

Walfisch-Ikegami and COST 231-Hata. The error of the models using the correction factor does not exceed 5.4-5.6 dB, which confirms the possibility of using this correction factor to predict the signal characteristics with sufficient accuracy.

Literature

Damosso, E., Correia, L. (1999). *COST Action 231: Digital Mobile Radio Towards Future Generation Systems: Final Report.*

Hata, M. (1980). Empirical formula for propagation loss in land mobile radio services. *IEEE Transactions on Vehicular Technology, VT-29(3)*, pp. 317-325.

Holma, H., Toskala, A. (2010). *WCDMA for UMTS: HSPA Evolution and LTE.* (5 ed.). Chichester: John Wiley & Sons.

Ikegami, F., Yoshidas, S., Takeuchi, T., Umehira, M. (1984). Propagation factors controlling mean field strength on urban streets. *IEEE Transactions on Antennas and Propagation AP-32(8)*, pp. 822-829.

Laiho, J., Wacker, A., Novosad, T. (2006). *Radio network planning and optimization for UMTS.* (2 ed.). Chichester: John Wiley & Sons.

Molisch, A. (2011). *Wireless communications.* (2 ed.). Chichester: John Wiley & Sons.

Ogbeide, O., Edeko, F. (2013). Modification of the Hata empirical propagation model for application in Vhf band in Edo State, Nigeria. *International Journal of Engineering Science Invention.*, pp. 35-39.

Okumura, Y., Ohmori, E., Kawano, T., Fukuda, K. (1968). Field strength and its variability in the VHF and UHF land mobile service. *Electronic Communication Laboratories 16(9/10)*, pp. 825-873.

Oluwafemi, I., Femijemilohun, O., Oluwasola, S., Owolabi, I. (2018). Inýestigation of error bounds of empirical path loss models at UHF band in Ondo State, Nigeria. *ARPN Journal of Engineering and Applied Sciences.*, pp. 3172-3181.

Rahnema, M. (2008). *UMTS network planning, optimization, and inter-operation with GSM.* Singapore: John Wiley & Sons.

Sauter, M. (2014). *GSM to LTE-advanced: an introduction to mobile networks and mobile broadband.* (2 ed.). Chichester: John Wiley & Sons.

Seyitnepesov, C., Hydyrov, A. (2015). Research of the expansion characteristics of cellular communication systems in the Mary city. *Science and technology in Turkmenistan*, pp. 72-78.

Seyitnepesov, C., Nokerov, S. (2017). Calculations propagation loss of radio signals of mobile communication systems based on statistical models. *Science and technology in Turkmenistan.*, pp. 86-91.

Walfisch, J., Bertoni, H. (1988). A theoretical model of UHF propagation in urban environment. *IEEE Transactions on Antennas and Propagation, AP-36(12)*, pp. 1788-1796.

Clean sweeping the modelling languages jungle — Overview of commonly used modelling languages in software development, transformability, and pros and cons of model-to-model transformation

Felix Suda, Frank Grimm, Sofia Meacham

1 Introduction

Software models are used to capture knowledge about some domain (aka problem space). In order to be useful, models should focus on a particular domain and should not be mixed up with information from other domains. For instance, a model defining how bank transfers work should be focused on the business (banking) domain and should not contain technological concepts (required for implementing bank transfers in software). In other words, models should capture what is becoming to be known as "Fachlichkeit". This Term was borrowed from the German language because there is no suitable alternative in the English language.[1] *Fachlichkeit* refers to the part of a software implementation, which is not concerned with software-technical details, but with the business domain this software belongs to Stahl, Völter.[2] So *Fachlichkeit* describes all the aspects of a certain software system that are of interest to the end user, i.e., concepts that are part of the end user's mental model, but are not related to the technical details of implementing/developing the software itself.

Fachlichkeit should be clearly visible in the software implementation. It should not be buried under or mixed with technical software implementation details. It is, therefore, beneficial to extract the *Fachlichkeit* of a domain into its own model. Because such models focus on concepts from a particular (business) domain, they are called domain-specific models.

Software that provides a solution for a business will usually consist of more than one domain-specific model because this software contains *Fachlichkeit* from several domains. These models should be understandable to the end user or domain expert. If done right, the domain expert will be able to define Fachlichkeit herself domain-specific models using appropriate modelling tools.

---

1 "Fachlichkeit" is similar to "Kindergarten" for which no suitable term exists in the English language either.
2 See Stahl, Völter, et al., 2005

H.-C. Brauweiler et al. (Hrsg.), *Digitalization and Industry 4.0: Economic and Societal Development*, https://doi.org/10.1007/978-3-658-27110-7_7

Domain-specific models can take various forms of appearance. In order to be useful for domain experts, they have to present the domain concepts in a way that is familiar to the domain expert.

Different domain-specific models will build upon each other. One model will reference elements from other domain models belonging to the same software system. Since different domain-specific models will be built on different meta-models (discussed below), there have to be mechanisms to transform *Fachlichkeit* from one model adhering to a certain meta-model into *Fachlichkeit* in another model adhering to a completely different meta-model. This is why model transformations, especially model-to-model transformations are important for this paper.

2 Overview of commonly used Modelling Languages

Model-driven software engineering (MDSE) is a widely used approach for developing software and software-intensive systems (SIS). Modelling such software provides many advantages and benefits. In this paper, we want to give a short overview of certain aspects of model-driven software development with regard to class- and fact-based modelling languages and model transformations.

2.1 Class-based modelling (Ecore, UML class modelling)

Object-oriented programming (OOP) acts as base concept for class-based modelling languages. The *Unified Modeling Language* (UML) with its class concept is a very popular framework for engineers to design software. With the *Ecore* modeling language, the *Eclipse Modeling Framework* (EMF) provides a similar framework. Both UML class model specification and Ecore are similar structured and described in the following section.

UML in its latest version 2.5.1 is a standard developed by the *Object Management Group* (OMG).[3] The Ecore meta-model is developed by the Eclipse Foundation and is currently available in version 2.9.0.[4] Both modeling languages are described by the *Essential Meta-object Facility* (EMOF)[5], which is another standard defined by the OMG to describe class-based modeling languages.[6] The focus of EMF is mainly the modeling of data structures. It is purposely similar designed as UML class modeling to provide an easy and pragmatic entry point for the design of systems.[7] Because of similarities of the UML class modeling language

3 See Object Management Group Inc., 2019
4 See eclipse, n.d.
5 See Steinberg, Budinsky, Paternostro, Merks, 2009
6 See Object Management Group Inc., 2019
7 See Steinberg, Budinsky, Paternostro, Merks, 2009

and the Ecore modeling language, we will describe both in the same course. Most concepts are named the same, Ecore prefixes a capital E. So, a UML concept called *Class* has the Ecore equivalent called *EClass*.

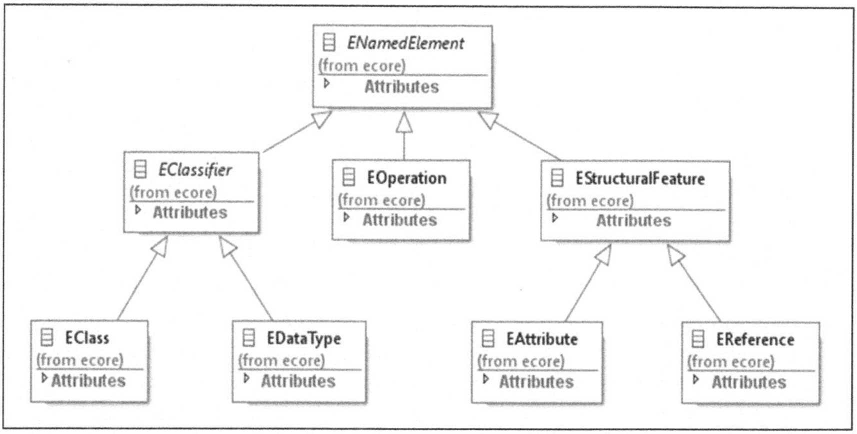

Figure 1: Ecore meta-model starting from ENamedElement modelling concept (incomplete)

Both, Ecore and UML define a common concept named *NamedElement* (*ENamedElement* in Ecore), which acts as a base concept for most other concepts.[8] This is, to easily identify model elements. Also, most references between concepts are bidirectional, so the model descriptions can be navigated easily. The use of compositions helps to structure the description further and introduces a hierarchy of elements.

For a semantic structure of models, *packages* are used. One package can contain multiple subpackages, but each package (except the root package) has exactly one super package. Packages contain *Classifiers*, which distinguish in *Classes* (to represent object types) and *Datatypes* (to represent value types). Datatypes map either to primitive types (such as Integer or Boolean) or to a more complex type, that should be used as a value (such as a unified unique identifier, UUID). Instances of Ecore's *EDataType* can be mapped to any Java class.

To describe properties and associations, classes contain *Structural Features*. Those are split into *Attributes* and *References*. Attributes represent properties and have usually primitive values (or quasi-primitive values, e.g. a UUID). References in contrast define a reference target to a class and are used to represent associations. Multiplicity can be expressed for both attributes and references.

8 See Figure 1

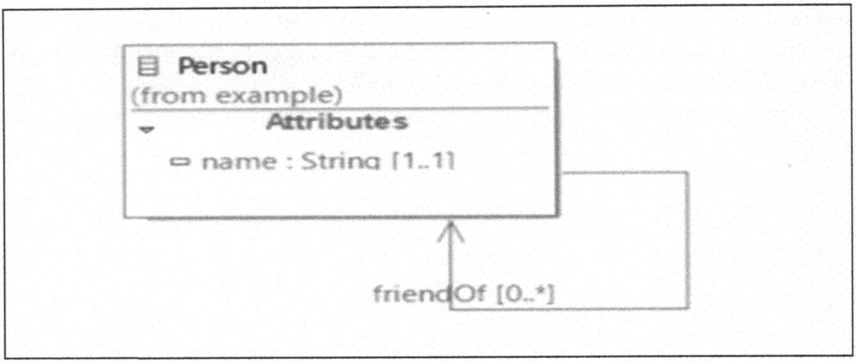

Figure 2: Simple example to illustrate class-based modeling

A very basic class model is shown in figure 2. It demonstrates the concepts *class*, *package*, and *features* of UML and Ecore. The class *Person* is represented as box, containing its containing package (in this case *example*) and lists all attributes (here only *name* with its attribute type and multiplicity). Person defines a reference *friendOf* to itself. Valid instances of this model can be described as follows: Person with name Alice is friend of Person with name Bob. Person Bob is friend of Person with name Charlie. Person Dave exists. Person Alice is friend of Person Alice. The intuitional semantics of *friendOf* imply that the last statement is invalid, but this cannot be expressed in pure UML/Ecore.[9]

Inheritance is an important tool to improve cohesion and reusability. Inheritance can be defined between classes and leads to an acyclic inheritance hierarchy. Multiple inheritance is supported by UML and Ecore. A set of subclasses of the same superclass (i.e. generalization set) is in Ecore always disjoint, in UML such a set may overlap.[10]

One speciality of EMF is a built-in feature to generate an Ecore model based on annotated Java classes, UML models or an XML schema definition (XSD). EMF also provides a built-in persistence layer by using XML metadata interchange (XMI). The XMI contains all necessary meta-data to to form the corresponding data model (instance model) based on the referred Ecore model. Was the Ecore model generated from an XSD, then EMF ensures, that the persistence of that model conforms the origin XSD.[11]

---

9 It can, however, be expressed using the Object Constraint Language (OCL).
10 See Object Management Group Inc., 2019
11 See Steinberg, Budinsky, Paternostro, Merks, 2009

2.2 Fact-based modeling (FBM)

Fact-based modelling languages are mostly used for conceptual modelling by describing a Universe of Discourse (UoD) in simple terms and phrases. The UoD contains all terms and relations relevant for a model. It is often used for the data view, when designing and analysing information systems.[12]

Object Role Modeling (ORM)—the base for Fact-based Modeling—was first developed by Eckhard D. Falkenberg in 1976. Its idea is the relationship of objects represented by roles, which are acted by the corresponding object. This forms a binary association of entities (e.g. a person drives a car and a car is driven by a person). ORM was developed further by Falkenberg, Terry Halpin and others and formalized in 1989.[13]

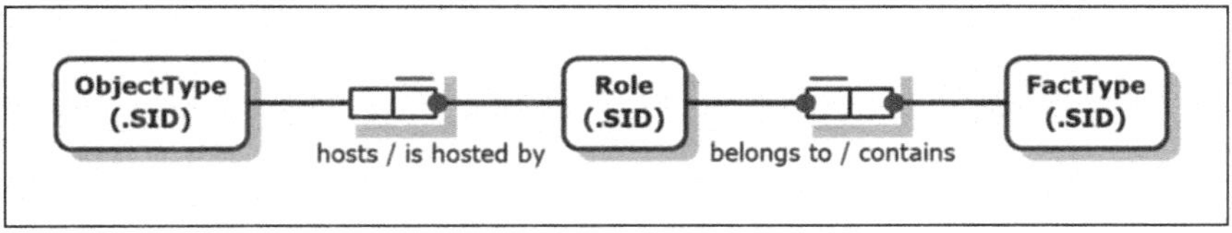

Figure 3: Basic concepts of the FBM meta-model

Fact-based modelling (FBM) is the progression of ORM.[14] The structure of ORM and FBM is quite similar. Both consist of *Entity Types* (which are divided into *Object Types* and *Value Types*), *Roles*, *Fact Types*, and *Constraints*. The base concept of fact-based modelling is the population of Roles by Entity Types. Roles are connected with each other by Fact Types.[15] Fact Types can be of an arbitrary arity, the most common used are *unary* and *binary Fact Types*. While binary Fact Types establish associations of two Entity Types, unary Fact Types are used to model Boolean properties (although Boolean properties can be modelled via binary Fact Types as well). Less common, but powerful, are n-ary Fact Types (e.g. a Temary Fact Type), which associates n Entity Types to express complex associations (e.g., a developer uses some programming language in some project, connecting the Entity Types *Developer*, *Programming Language*, and *Project* and expressing further constraints for this complex association).

FBM provides a huge set of constraints, which can be applied to several model elements. Constraints involve expression of multiplicity (Mandatory Constraint and Internal Uniqueness Constraint, Frequency Constraint) or value ranges (Value Constraint). But advanced relational constraints are supported as well, summa-

12 See Halpin, 1998
13 See Halpin, 1998
14 See Halpin, On the Move of Meaningful Internet Systems 2205. OTM 2005 Workshops, 2005
15 See Figure 3

rized by the Ring Constraints. Those Ring Constraints can be used to define acyclic, antisymmetric, etc. relationships of Entity Types.

Another main characteristic of FBM is the substitution of properties by Value Types. This increases the maintainability of models, improves reusability, and strengthens the semantic of such advanced properties. Assume a model with the Entity Types *Student* and *University*. A student lives in a country, a university is located in a country. Assume further, that country is used as a primitive concept. In class-based modelling languages one can model country as a string. In fact-based modelling, country is represented as a Value Type. So, the Value Type country has a stronger semantic as two attributes called country. Yet, the country Value Type can be instantiated as a textual value.

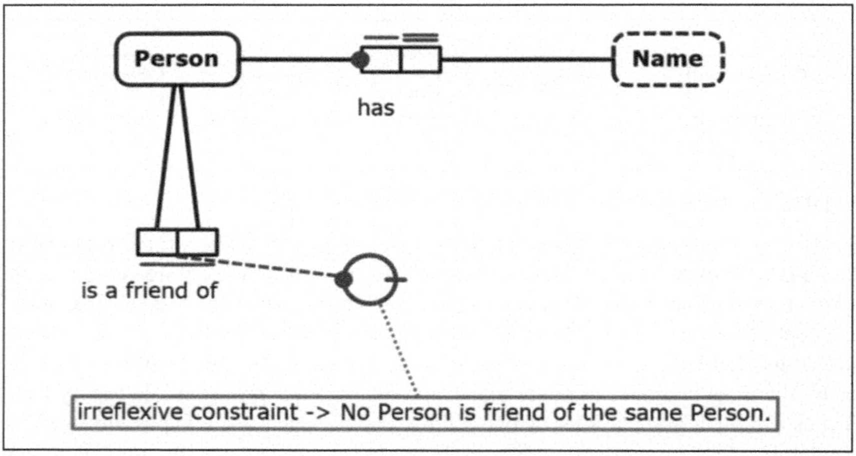

Figure 4: Simple example to illustrate fact-based modelling

There are two approaches to build a model. The classical way of modelling a domain by examining the structure of the inspected domain and identifying entity types, properties and associations. But fact-based modelling also provides the ability to abstract a model from a fact base, i.e. an existing collection of entities and facts as observed in the Universe of Discourse.[16] Applying the statement from the abstract model level, that a Fact Type states something about Entity Types, a fact describes a statement involving entities. For example, the statement *Alice is a friend of Bob*. *Alice* and *Bob* are entities and can be abstracted to the Entity Type *Person* with a property *Name*. The entities are connected by the fact *is a friend of*, which is then generalized to a binary Fact Type, connected to the

16 See Halpin, Object Role Modeling (ORM/NIAM), 1998

Entity Type Person. From domain knowledge it can be stated further, that a person is never friend of herself.

The previous can be modelled as shown in figure 4. The Entity Type *Person* is connected to the Value Type *Name* by a Fact Type *has*. The Fact Type defines a Mandatory Constraint (the dot denoted left at the Fact Type has) and an Internal Uniqueness Constraint, stating that one Person has at most one Name and a Name is related to at most one Person (the two dashes above the Fact Type). Additionally, the Fact Type *is friend of* represents the friendship relation. It defines an Internal Uniqueness Constraint, which states Person A can be friend of more than one Person and some Person is friend of more than one Person (note the implicit zero lower bound). The circle connected to the Fact Type is an Irreflexive Ring Constraint, which permits the friendship of one person with herself.

3 Characteristics of modelling languages and benefits of using them

3.1 Common concepts

"All models are wrong, some are useful" as the British statistician George Box famously wrote with reference to statistical models.[17] However, this statement can be made for software models as well. The usefulness of a software model is based on the model's ability to clearly capture aspects of the problem and/or solution space the model was created for. In order to do so, models usually describe abstract aspects (e.g., a certain aspect of the real world, such as a concept or process). These aspects usually share a common set of characteristics. Usually modelling languages provide, on their most basic level of abstraction, three basic concepts for defining higher-level abstractions: entities, properties and relationships. Entities describe things or concepts that are meaningful for modellers of a certain domain, e.g., a Person entity. Properties allow for entities to be described in more detail, e.g., the First Name property for specifying that each Person has a name. Relations define relationships between entities, e.g., a Person entity is related to an Address entity.

The modelling languages discussed above (Ecore and FBM) offer concepts for enabling domain-specific modelling. Modelling languages offering these concepts become more expressive and allow modellers to express certain aspects of their models more direct and concisely, i.e., to express concepts of the problem domain more directly and with less "translation loss" in models. For Ecore and FMB, these language features are:

---

17 See Box, 1976

- Modelling concepts provided by Ecore, but not FBM:
- Package (model hierarchy)
- Containment (Parent-child hierarchy)
- Can be applied on model (M1) and meta-model (M2) level
- Modelling concepts provided by FBM, but not Ecore
- n-ary Fact Types
- Objectification (i.e., Fact Types can be used as Entity Types)
- Cardinality Constraints
- External Uniqueness Constraints
- Ring Constraints
- Set Comparison Constraints
- Subtype Constraints
- Verbalization (i.e., human-understandable textual descriptions of an FMB model can be automatically created from this model)
- Modelling concepts provided by FBM and Ecore
- Entity Types
- Binary Fact Types (References)
- Data Types (Attributes)
- Internal Uniqueness (Cardinalities)
- Constraints
- Subtype (Inheritance)

3.2 Meta-models

To describe the syntactics and semantics of a model (and all models of the same focus, used model elements, and domain---or in general of the same *Fachlichkeit*) a meta-model is used. A meta-model characterizes the structure of a compliant model in a formal way, i.e. a meta-model combines allowed model elements and their usage (syntactic) as well as meaning (semantic). So, every model is a valid instance of a related meta-model. Model and meta-model are in an *instance-of* relationship. This relationship enables the formal verification of models and offer several other advantages like model transformation or text generation.

A meta-model describes the structure of a model by means of *concepts*, *properties*, *relationships* of defined concepts and *constraints* (e.g. value ranges or multiplicities). An *abstract syntax* defines allowed model elements and their relation among each other and assigns a fixed semantic to those elements. Textual and visual representations of a model are described by a *concrete syntax*. One meta-model can be represented by one or more concrete syntaxes. For instance, a UML class element can be graphically depicted as a box with an attached class name. The very same element can be described in a fictional UML DSL with the keyword *class* following its name. So, a meta-model can be represented by multiple conforming modelling languages, as shown in figure 5.[18]

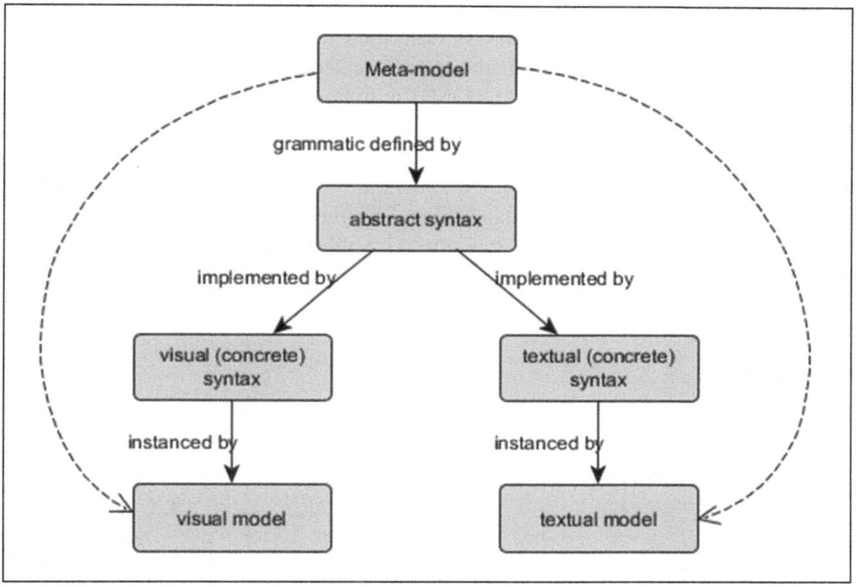

Figure 5: Abstract and concrete syntax in context of models

The OMG (Object Management Group) consortium develops and maintains standards relevant for modern software engineering. Among others, MOF (Meta Object Facility) was designed by the OMG. MOF covers a generic description of meta-models and defines with EMOF (Essential MOF) similar concepts as the UML class specification, i.e. *classes*, object-, and value-types as well as a description of internal characteristics and behaviours by *properties* and *operations*.[19]

Theoretically, the loop of *model-is-instance-of-meta-model* is infinite, but at some point, it is useless to further generalize the concepts (since the generalized concepts will conclude in similar, abstract concepts). Instead, the top most model level describes itself. This self-reference avoids the need for infinite meta-models. So, the MOF recommends a total of four abstraction levels: *M0* (level of instances) to *M3* (level of the meta-model's meta-model, short meta-meta-model or meta²-model).[20] The instance level (M0) is familiar to every developer, since it

18 See Object Management Group Inc., 2019; See Stahl, Völter, et al., 2005
19 See Object Management Group Inc., 2016a
20 See Object Management Group Inc., 2016b

corresponds to an application's runtime, e.g. a person object with name *Alice*. The M0 level is described by M1, which is the model level and may correspond with a data structure implemented in a code file. This corresponds to the class definition of all person objects. Further, M1 is described by M2, the meta-model level. Here, UML and language specifications are located. To be able to describe language specifications themselves, the OMG defined a fourth level, the meta-meta-model, M3. MOF and EMOF are examples of M3 modelling languages. Ecore is often used as M2 modelling language, but since Ecore reflexively describes itself, Ecore is its own meta-model. Figure 6 shows the MOF stack (on the left) and the correspondence to the actual instances used by developers (on the right). Ecore and EMOF are similar structured and aim to complement and simplify MOF.[21]

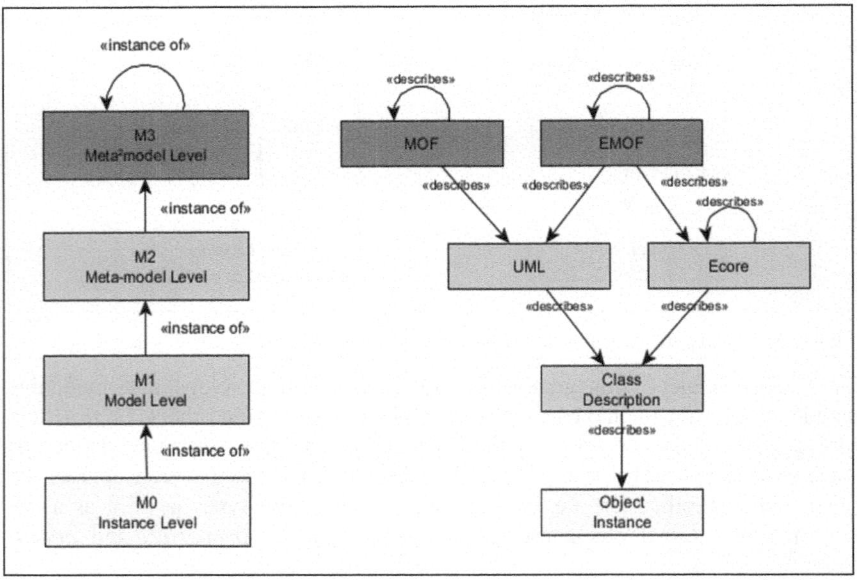

Figure 6: MOF model levels

Meta-models describing the same or a similar domain can have some overlapping concepts or characteristics. For example, a management system for cafeteria visitors and employees of the cafeteria's enterprise. Both meta-models will describe the concept of a person with attributes like *name* or *registration number*, but they are used in different domains. Besides overlapping concepts of meta-models, it is also possible, that one model is an instance of two distinct meta-models. For example, the textual representation of a UML class model written in

[21] See Steinberg, Budinsky, Paternostro, Merks, 2009

a fictional UML DSL is at the same time an instance of the UML meta-model and an instance of the UML DSL.

The application of meta-models is the general description of recurring concepts. This includes the definition of user interfaces, *Fachlichkeit*, and programming languages, such as DSLs. The formal conformance of models to their meta-models allows the use of code generators, the definition, validation and verification of data models and improves the maintenance and documentation of code.[22]

Examples for meta-models are the UML and Ecore specification. Programming languages can be considered as meta-model of their program code, too. The java language specification defines the syntax and semantics of java code elements and is considered as the meta-model of the java code.[23]

3.3 (Inter-)Transformability

Many software development tools process models in various formats. Generally, every data format itself can be seen as a meta-model of each data file. Such models are often exchanged between team members or processed by tools, e.g. to extend or refine a model. Depending on used tools or preferences of team members, it might be useful to translate a model into another format (i.e. meta-model). To realize such translations, model transformation is used.[24]

MDA (Model Driven Architecture) divides model transformations into three layers. An abstract model without any implementation specific information is declared as *PIM (Platform Independent Model)*. Adding details to such a PIM results in a *PSM (Platform Specific Model)*. Finally, artefacts such as code or documentation are generated from the PSMs. Transformations can happen within one layer or change the abstraction layer. For instance, a model refactoring happens always on the same abstraction layer. In contrast, a specialization will change the level of abstraction.[25]

A transformation tool (*transformator*) should create from a correct source model a semantically and syntactically valid target model, i.e. the transformation description creates valid elements of the target model. Further, a transformator should treat inconsistencies of a source model in a transparent way, e.g. by logging or reporting any issues. With regard to fault tolerance and avoiding loss of information, this is a very important feature.

---

22 See Demelt, 2007
23 See Stahl, Völter, et al., 2005; See Brambilla, Cabot, Wimmer, 2017
24 See Tratt, 2005
25 See Stahl, Völter, et al., 2005

As stated in section 3a, models of different meta-models can share common concepts, so overlapping might exist. However, is it possible to transform models from each and every source to target modelling language? As long as the involved meta-models share common concepts (as described above in Sec. 3.1, Common Concepts) this task is straight forward. Transforming UML (class models) to Ecore and vice versa is quite an easy task. But if there is only a partial overlapping of concepts, the transformation description becomes harder to implement. Finding suitable mappings, which might be not bijective (due to indirect consequences in the target model) and dealing with information loss caused by unmapped concepts are challenges to conquer. One example is the transformation of a UML package structure into FBM. FBM provides no suitable concepts to represent a namespace hierarchy, so this information has to be either dropped (which blocks the back transformation from FBM to UML) or the namespace information has to be translated in another way (e.g. by annotations, if supported by the target meta-model).

There might thus be loss of information when transforming a model M conforming to some meta-model A to a model M' conforming to a different meta-model B. If meta-model B does not provide mechanisms for modelling concepts defined by meta-model A and used by the to-be-transformed model M, then this part of M cannot be transformed into M' without losing information.

3.4 Tool Support

Since models are described by their meta-model in a formal way, tools can easily take advantage of this formal specification. The applications range from code generation (Xtext, EMF GenModel, Acceleo) to validation and verification frameworks, persistence according to the meta-model (CDO, EMFStore), as well as complete runtime environments (ECP). Model-based development also enables the reuse of components or introducing model transformation, if needed.

4 Model-to-Model Transformation

Model transformation in general is the conversion of a source model into a target model, while a set of transformation rules is applied either in a *declarative* (by pattern matching) or *imperative* style to the model elements. Those transformation rules define, how to translate a source model element to a target model element.[26]

In Tratt, 2005, a model transformation is defined as a program which transforms a *source model* into another *target model*. This definition is extended in Mens,

---

26 See Kleppe, Warmer, Bast, 2003

Czarnecki, Gorp by a *transformation description* which adds transformation rules. A *transformation rule* qualifies how to translate a model element of the source model into one or more elements of the target model. A transformation can process one or more source models and also produces one or more target models. The transformation program can be written in a general-purpose language (such as Java or C++) or in a Domain-specific language (e.g. ATL, QVTo).[27]

In general, model transformations are distinguished by the resulting artefacts. A *Model-to-Model* (M2M) transformation produces one or more target models. Text artefacts (e.g. source code or documentation) are produced by a *Model-to-Text* (M2T) transformation. The amount of source and target artefacts can vary. Also, it is not necessary that all artefacts conforming one meta-model.[28]

A comfortable execution of transformations requires certain functionality from a transformation tool, also called *transformator*. Basic CRUD functions and an (at least basic) management of elements (storing, querying, referencing) are minimal requirements. Such features are essential for multi-step transformations or more advanced procedures.[29]

Depending on the context of a model, some model transformation requires a flexible transformation flow. So-called *higher-order transformations* (HOT) are a useful paradigm. They allow to transform the transformation itself and so enable a dynamic approach. The base idea of a HOT is the assumption, that the transformation itself can be considered as a model. The transformation of a transformation allows the analysis, composition or modification of a transformation. It is even possible to synthesize a transformation from input artefacts. HOTs apply the advantages of model transformations to transformations.[30]

4.1 Approaches

Model transformations (MT) aim at various objectives and are used in several use cases. So, the amount of source and target models can differ, syntactic or semantic transformation executed, or models being synced via bidirectional MT. The description of MT can be in an imperative or declarative style and realized with a General-Purpose Language (GPL, such as Java or C++) or Domain Specific Language (DSL, like ATL or QVTo).

Independent of the realization and use case of a model transformation, it is to be considered, that information of the source model is integrated into the target model. This integration happens during the transformation execution by applying

27 See Mens, Czarnecki, Gorp, 2005
28 See Trunkunas, Vasilecas, 2009
29 See Mens, Czarnecki, Gorp, 2005
30 See Tisi, Jouault, et al., 2009; See Mens, Czarnecki, Gorp, 2005

the defined transformation rules to a source model element. The information can be integrated on a syntactical level (e.g. convert all existing tokens into camel case style), on a semantical level (e.g., supplement an element with context information). Also, information can be replaced or removed from the target model. Those characteristics imply significant model changes with the risk of information loss.

A constant level of abstraction in the course of transformations is called *horizontal transformation*. Here, the syntactic level is changed. It is distinguished between *endogenous* and *exogenous* transformation. The source and target meta-models of an endogenous transformation stay the same. Reasons for such a transformation are manifold. Optimization, refactoring, and simplification[31], each without changing the semantics of model details are use cases. A refinement of a model element is both a syntactic and a semantic transformation (e.g. transforming syntactic sugar into more primitive model elements). However, an exogenous transformation affects the source and target meta-models. Exogenous transformations mostly change besides the meta-models also the abstraction layer. Model-to-Text (M2T) transformations are count also into exogenous transformations.

The MDA method starts with a platform independent model (PIM), which describes formally a domain. This initial model is independent of any platform details and forms the source for the following transformations. During the development process, more and more implementation details are added to the initial model and a platform specific model (PSM) is formed. Every transformation adds details to the source model, so it is refined with every step. Those refinements extend the semantics of the actual source model. This is called *vertical transformation*.

Transformation rules can be applied only *unidirectional*. This is, the transformation definition T_{AB} creates from a source model M_A the target model M_B. This transformation definition cannot be used to create the model M_A by applying the transformation to model M_B.

$$T_{AB}(M_A) \rightarrow M_B$$

$$T_{AB}(M_B) \nrightarrow M_A$$

A bidirectional transformation description creates a correspondence between two meta-models and processes models conforming one of the involved meta-models. The result of such a transformation is a model, conforming the corresponding

31 See Stahl, Völter, et al., 2005

meta-model of the source model's meta-model. This approach can be used to propagate model changes in both directions, so synchronizing the models.[32]

Depending on the used technology, a transformation description can be either declarative or imperative. Many transformation frameworks use a declarative style, since here model element mappings are expressed explicitly. The transformation engine determines the transformation process and applies matching rules to recognized model elements. This way, transformation descriptions are understandable, the transformation process can be only partly affected (e.g. by using a higher-order transformation).

In contrast, with an imperative definition it is easy to customize the process of transformation. Model elements to be transformed are explicitly mentioned in the transformation flow. The imperative style describes every transformation step explicitly (i.e. the sequence of steps as well as which model elements to transform) and is executable by the used framework or tool.

4.2 Pros and cons of model transformations

The previous section described several features and techniques to spice up the use of models. The MDSD approach benefits from horizontal transformations, when a general model is more and more refined. Generating code and other artefacts like documentation is done by means of vertical transformations. Further, model migration is implemented by using horizontal, exogenous transformations.

So, there is a wide area of application, but especially model migration, used to communicate between different groups of project participants (e.g. software engineers and domain experts), facilitates the exchange of models by means of bidirectional transformations.

But cutting both ways, model transformations can be a huge challenge. As already mentioned in Sec. 3d, finding adequate mappings of different meta-models is sometimes hard and has to deal with the potential loss of information. In the context of transformations to exchange a model in different modelling languages, one has to define point-to-point transformations for every used meta-model.

To conquer some of those drawbacks, a unified metamodeling language could be established. As worked out in Sec. 3a, most modelling languages share a common set of concepts but provide also language specific constructs. Formalizing these common concepts could result in an overall meta-model, which is able to map all kinds of information and provide mechanisms to represent the remaining meta-model specific constructs (e.g. n-ary Fact Types from FBM).

---

32 See n.n., 2008

5 Summary

This paper described how software models are used to capture knowledge about some problem domain. These models should be understandable to the end user or domain expert. The first part of the paper described approaches to modelling knowledge with so-called class-based modelling and fact-based modelling. The second part of the paper discussed common characteristics of modelling languages and how modellers can benefit from them. It also introduced the concept of meta-models as a way of formal defining the concepts available in models conforming to a certain meta-model. The last part of this paper described the need for transforming models conforming to a certain meta-model into models conforming to a different meta-model. These model-to-model transformations are important because different domain-specific models are based on different meta-models and, thus, there have to be mechanisms to transform *Fachlichkeit* from one model adhering to a certain meta-model into *Fachlichkeit* in another model adhering to a different meta-model.

Literature

Box, G. (1976). Science and statistics. Journal of the American Statistical Association.

Brambilla, M., Cabot, J., Wimmer, M. (2017). *Model-Driven Software Engineering in Practice.* (2 ed.). Morgan & Claypool.

Demelt, A. (2007). *Ubiquitous MDSD - Bringing together Modeling and Coding.* Retrieved 1.3.2019, from https://www.eclipsecon.org/summiteurope2007/presentations/ESE2007_Model-Demelt-UbiquitousMDSD.pdf

eclipse. (n.d.). *Eclipse Modeling Framework (EMF).* Retrieved 1.3.2019, from https://www.eclipse.org/modeling/emf/

Halpin, T. (1998). *Object Role Modeling (ORM/NIAM).* Retrieved 1.3.2019, from http://orm.net/pdf/springer.pdf

Halpin, T. (2005). On the Move of Meaningful Internet Systems 2205. OTM 2005 Workshops. Springer Berlin Heidelberg.

Kleppe, A., Warmer, J., Bast, W. (2003). *MDA Explained. The Model Driven Architecture: Practise and Promise.* Addison-Wesley Professional.

Mens, T., Czarnecki, K., Gorp, P. V. (2005). Discussion – A Taxonomy of Model Transformations. In J. Bezivin, R. Heckel (Eds.), *Language Engineering for Model-Driven Software Development.* Dagstuhl, Germany.

n.n. (2008). *Journal of Object Technology.* Retrieved 1.3.2019, from A change propagating model transformation language: http://www.jot.fm/issues/issues20083/article4

Object Management Group Inc. (2016a). *OMG Meta Object Facility (MOF). Core Specification.* Retrieved 1.3.2019, from Version 2.5.1.: http://www.omg.org/cgi-bin/doc?formal/2016-11-01.pdf

Object Management Group Inc. (2016b). *OMG Meta Object Facility (MOF). Core Specification Version 1.4.* Retrieved 1.3.2019, from http://www.omg.org/cgi-bin/doc.cgi?formal/2002-04-03.pdf.

Object Management Group Inc. (2019). *UML specification 2.5.1.* Retrieved 1.3.2019, from https://www.omg.org/spec/UML/2.5.1/

Stahl, T., Völter, M., et.al. (2005). *Modellgetriebene Softwareentwicklung.* (R. Schönfeldt, Ed.) dpunkt Verlag.

Steinberg, D., Budinsky, F., Paternostro, M., Merks, E. (2009). *Eclipse Modeling Framework EMF.* (E. Gamma, L. Nackman, J. Wiegand, Eds.) Addison Wesley.

Tisi, M., Jouault, F., et.al. (2009). *On the Use of Higher-Order Model Transformations.* Retrieved 1.3.2019, from https://modeling-languages. com/wp-content/uploads/hot1.pdf

Tratt, L. (2005). Model transformations and tool integration. In *Journal of Software and System Modelling 4.* (pp. 112-122).

Trunkunas, J.Vasilecas, O. (2009). *Ontology Transformation.* Retrieved 1.3.2019, from From Requirements to Conceptual Model: http://www.lu.lv/materiali/apgads/raksti/751_pp_52-64.pdf

Erfassung von Gründächern auf der Grundlage fernerkundlicher Luftbilddaten und digitalen Gebäudemodellen am Beispiel der Hansestadt Rostock

Görres Grenzdörffer

1 Hintergrund und Problemstellung

Zu den großen kommunalen Herausforderungen des 21. Jahrhunderts gehört es, die negativen Auswirkungen der zunehmenden Urbanisierung und des sich verstärkenden Klimawandels auf den städtischen Lebensraum abzupuffern. Im Unterschied zu verschiedenen technischen Maßnahmen (z.B. Reduzierung des urban heat island-Effektes durch Dächer mit reflektierender weißer Färbung, Pufferung von Starkregenereignissen durch Regenrückhaltebecken etc.) wirken Dachbegrünungen dabei nicht nur in Einzelbereichen. Egal, ob es sich um Regenwasserrückhalt, sommerliche Hitzeabwehr oder Aspekte der Artenvielfalt handelt – alle diese Aspekte werden durch begrünte Dächer gleichzeitig angesprochen. Eine aktuelle Übersicht zu den zahlreichen Ökosystemleistungen begrünter Dächer findet sich bei Berardi et al., 2014. Für die Hansestadt Rostock ergibt sich zusätzlicher Handlungsbedarf, da mehrere kommunale Weichenstellungen anstehen, in denen diese Informationen einfließen können.

In dem Beitrag wird in einem ersten Schritt dargestellt, wie auf Grundlage aktueller multispektraler Luftbilddaten des Landesvermessungsamts Mecklenburg-Vorpommern aus dem Sommer 2016 und Gebäudeumringe des Stadtmessungsamts alle vorhandenen Gründächer erfasst und kategorisiert werden können. An die Erfassung der Gründächer schließt sich als zweiter Schritt die Potentialanalyse an. Dabei gehören Flachdächer und leicht geneigte Dächer bis 10° Dachneigung zu den präferierten Dachtypen für eine nachträgliche Begrünung, da hier in der Regel keine besonderen Vorkehrungen zur Aufnahme der Schubkräfte berücksichtigt werden müssen. Als besonders geeignet gelten außerdem Kiesdächer, da dieser Dachtyp eine höhere statische Belastbarkeit aufweist.

Dadurch lässt sich die Anzahl der Dächer, die in einem nachfolgenden Schritt – der nicht Gegenstand dieses Beitrags ist – einer konkreten bau-und kostentechnischen Analyse unterzogen werden müssen, einschränken. Dachneigung und Gebäudestatik liefern erste Anhaltspunkte für eine potenzielle Begrünbarkeit. Allerdings dürfen diese beiden Kriterien auch nicht überschätzt werden. Weitere bautechnische Erfordernisse, die sich nicht mit der vorliegenden fernerkundlichen Methode ermitteln lassen, betreffen zum Beispiel den Zustand der Dachabdichtung, Wärmedämmung, Dachrandhöhen und Zugänglichkeit der Dachfläche. Die

H.-C. Brauweiler et al. (Hrsg.), *Digitalization and Industry 4.0: Economic and Societal Development*, https://doi.org/10.1007/978-3-658-27110-7_8

tatsächliche Begrünbarkeit eines Gebäudes und deren voraussichtliche Kosten müssen deshalb zusätzlich auch im Rahmen von Vor-Ort-Besichtigungen überprüft werden, wobei die dargestellte Potenzialanalyse im Vorfeld die Anzahl der zu überprüfenden Gebäude deutlich reduzieren kann. Die nachfolgend detailliert beschriebene Methodik ist nicht grundsätzlich neu und wird prinzipiell in anderen deutschen Städten seit wenigen Jahren angewandt.[1]

1.1 Vorgehensweise zur fernerkundlichen Erfassung von Gründächern

Für die fernerkundliche Erfassung von Vegetation im Allgemeinen und von begrünten Dächern im Speziellen werden so genannte Falschfarbeninfrarot-Luftbildaufnahmen verwendet, welche neben der Reflektion im sichtbaren Spektralbereich (rot, grün, blau) auch den Bereich des nahen Infrarots (NIR) abdecken. Der zusätzliche NIR-Bildkanal bietet nicht nur die Möglichkeit, Vegetationsflächen im Luftbild zu identifizieren, sondern auch deren Qualität über die Berechnung eines speziellen Vegetationsindexes (NDVI) zu bewerten. Der mögliche Wertebereich des NDVI liegt zwischen -1 und 1, wobei der Wert 1 eine sehr dichte und vitale Vegetation mit hoher photosynthetischer Aktivität widerspiegelt, während negative Werte nahezu vegetationsfreie Flächen oder Flächen mit toter Vegetation und negative Werte vegetationslose Oberflächen wie etwa Wasser repräsentieren. Mithilfe des NDVI können demnach vegetationslose Flächen von vegetationsbedeckten Flächen unterschieden werden. Ein exakter Rückschluss auf die Vitalität der identifizierten Vegetation ist aber nur bedingt möglich, da ein niedriger NDVI-Wert sowohl durch eine geringe photosynthetische Aktivität der vorhandenen Vegetation als auch durch eine spärliche Vegetationsbedeckung (Mischbild Vegetation und Substrat) verursacht werden kann.

Das Kataster-, Vermessungs- und Liegenschaftsamt der Hansestadt Rostock hat vierkanaligen Luftbilder aus der Sommerbefliegung des Jahres 2016 vom Landesvermessungsamt bezogen und in Form eines Mosaiks der gesamten Hansestadt aufbereitet. Von diesem 6.1 GB große Datensatz im *.ecw Format wurde der NDVI pixelweise, d.h. mit einer Bodenauflösung von 40 cm berechnet.

Als zweiter Datensatz für die Inventarisierung und Potenzialanalyse von Dachbegrünung sind die Hausumringe als Gebäude-Polygone verwendet worden, die aus dem amtlichen Liegenschaftskatasterinformationssystem (ALKIS) stammen. Dieses umfasst aber aufgrund seiner Methodik nicht den gesamten Gebäudebestand der Hansestadt Rostock. Das betrifft insbesondere kürzlich errichtete Gebäude, die noch nicht in das amtliche Kataster eingepflegt sind. Luftbildsichtbare Gebäude, die nicht in den amtlichen Datensätzen enthalten sind, sind im Rahmen des Projekts nicht manuell erfasst worden.

1 Vgl. Ansel, Zeidler, Esch, 2015

Zunächst erfolgte auf Grundlage der Falschfarbeninfrarot-Luftbildaufnahmen aus 2016 die Berechnung des NDVI. Als Schwellenwert für die Abgrenzung der Klassen *Vegetation* und *keine Vegetation* wurde 0.25 gewählt. Alle Pixel mit Werten oberhalb des Schwellenwertes werden als Vegetationszellen eingestuft, während alle übrigen Zellen für die weitere Untersuchung nicht mehr beachtet werden. Die Dachflächen entstammen den Polygonen der Hausumringe, wobei alle Dachflächen <25 m² aufgrund ihrer geringen Fläche aus dem Datensatz entfernt wurden.

Innerhalb jedes Polygons wurden anschließend alle Vegetationszellen addiert und die Grünfläche sowie die Flächenanteile der Grünfläche an der gesamten Dachfläche berechnet. Um schließlich als Gründach eingestuft zu werden, müssen folgende Kriterien erfüllt werden:

- Allgemeine Mindestgrünfläche: 10 m²
- Mindestanteil Grünfläche für Dachflächen ≥ 100 m²: 10%
- Mindestanteil Grünfläche für Dachflächen < 100 m²: 20%

Im nächsten Schritt werden Dachflächen welche die vorstehenden Kriterien erfüllen mit „ja" attributiert. Das betrifft ca. 4.200 Gebäude. Anschließend folgt eine manuelle Überprüfung der Gründächer um Fehlklassifikationen zu berichtigen. Potentielle Fehlerquellen, die manuell kontrolliert und verifiziert werden müssen, sind:

- Vollständige oder teilweise Überschirmungen durch Bäume und Sträucher, die zu fehlerhaft klassifizierten Gründächern führen können.[2]
- Verkippungseffekte bei Luftbildaufnahmen, was insbesondere bei hohen Gebäuden problematisch sein kann.[3]
- Fehler in den ALKIS-Gebäudedaten, da die amtlichen Gebäudedaten aufgrund der Methodik teilweise der Wirklichkeit etwas hinterherhinken und alte, mittlerweile abgerissene Gebäude nicht automatisch aus dem Datensatz entfernt wurden.[4] Zudem befinden sich einige Gebäude derzeit in Planung / im Bau. Deren Dachbegrünung kann folglich nicht im Luftbild festgestellt werden (ZUS_TXT = „im Bau").[5]
- Unterirdische Objekte mit begrünten Dächern, wie Tiefgaragen werden gesondert ausgewiesen (OFL_TXT = „Tiefgarage").[6]

Nach diesen Korrekturmaßnahmen bleiben nur 193 Gebäude mit vollständiger oder anteiliger Dachbegrünung übrig. Hinzu kommen 53 begrünte Tiefgaragen

---

2 Vgl. Abbildung 1 und 2
3 Vgl. Abbildung 5
4 Vgl. Abbildung 4
5 Vgl. Abbildung 3
6 Vgl. Abbildung 6

und ein Speicher. 285 Dachflächen der ursprünglich 4.200 Gebäude befinden sich unterhalb des Kronendachs von Bäumen, sodass eine manuelle Prüfung mittels der vorliegenden Orthofotos nicht möglich war.

Abbildung 1: Vollständige Überschirmungen der Dächer durch Bäume

Abbildung 2: Teilweise Überschirmungen der Dächer durch Bäume

Abbildung 3: Nach 2016 gebaute Gebäude, die zum Zeitpunkt der Befliegung (2016) noch nicht vorhanden waren

Abbildung 4: Geometriefehler im ALKIS-Datensatz am Beispiel einer begrünten Tiefgarage

Abbildung 5: Verkippungseffekte bei hohen Gebäuden durch Orthoprojektion

Abbildung 6: Oberflächlich begrünte Tiefgarage

1.2 Ergebnisse der Gründachinventur

Die Ergebnisse sind in einer Shape-Datei zusammengefasst, bzw. als zusätzliche Attribute der Gebäudedatei angehängt worden.[7]

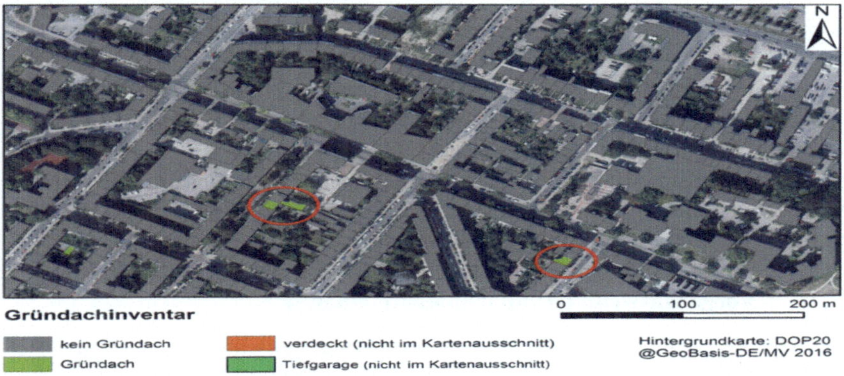

Abbildung 7: Auszug aus der Shapedatei der Gründachinventur der Hansestadt Rostock.

2 Potenzialanalyse Gründächer

Die Potenzialanalyse befasst sich mit der nachträglichen Begrünbarkeit bereits existierender Gebäude. Die Eignung der Dachflächen wird dabei von der Dachform, der Dachneigung und der vorhandenen Oberflächenbeschaffenheit beeinflusst. Der Gebäude-bestand wird deshalb nach drei Kriterien hin untersucht:

- Dachneigung: Analog zur Gründach-Inventarisierung werden auch für die Potenzialanalyse nur Gebäude mit flachen oder leicht geneigten Dächern (bis ca. 10 °) berücksichtigt. Die dafür notwendigen Daten der Flachdächer sind vom Kataster- und Vermessungsamt in Form von CityGML Dateien zur Verfügung gestellt worden.
- Kiesdächer/Gebäudestatik: Neben der Dachneigung gehören die statischen Lastreserven zu den konstruktiven Anforderungen, die einen besonders starken Einfluss auf die potenzielle Begrünbarkeit von Dachflächen besitzen. Da diese Information nicht in den üblichen amtlichen Katastern hinterlegt ist, ist versucht werden, aus den vorhandenen Flachdächer mithilfe einer multispektralen Klassifikation Kiesdächern gegenüber anderen Dachbedeckungen abzugrenzen.
- Solardächer: Dächer mit PV-Anlagen sind als potentielle Gründächer von besonderem Interesse, da Gründächer im allgemeinen kühler sind und durch

[7] Vgl. Abbildung 7

eine Kombination die Leistungsfähigkeit der PV-Anlagen noch gesteigert werden kann. Solaranlagen auf Flachdächern sollen im Zuge der Dachtypenklassifikation der Flachdächer mit erfasst werden. Das wird automatisch allerdings nur bis zu einem gewissen Grad funktionieren. An der Erfassung der Dächer mit PV-Anlagen wird aktuell im Rahmen des Projekts e_Regie MV gearbeitet.

Im Ergebnis der Potentialanalyse sind alle potentiell geeigneten Dachflächen identifiziert worden. Die identifizierten Gebäude sind in Abhängigkeit der aus den Katasterdaten verfügbaren Informationen zur tatsächlichen Nutzung der Gebäude gemäß dem ALKIS-Objektartenkatalog (AX_Gebaeudefunktion)[8] klassifiziert worden, um z.B. eine Aussage zu bekommen, wie viele Dächer von Industrie- und Gewerbeflächen potentiell als Gründächer in Frage kommen.

2.1 Vorgehensweise Gründachpotentialanalyse

Die von der Hansestadt Rostock zur Verfügung gestellten LoD2-Daten (CityGML) enthalten im tag <bldg:roofType> Informationen zur Dachform. Mittels der Software FME wurden die CityGML-Daten in ESRI-Shapefiles umgewandelt um die Attribute aus den CityGML-Datensätzen mit den Gebäude-Daten verknüpfen zu können. Die Codeliste für Dachformen stammt von Code-Listen der Special Interest Group 3d, welche explizit für 3D-Stadtmodelle entwickelt wurde (<https://www.sig3d.org/codelists/Handbuch-SIG3D/building/2.0/CL-V1.0/_AbstractBuilding_roofType.xml>).

Grundsätzlich gelten alle Flachdächer als geeignet für Gründächer, weshalb diese im ersten Schritt extrahiert wurden. Ausnahmen sind nur Parkhäuser, da diese ihre Dächer üblicherweise als weiteres Parkdeck nutzen. Wenn Gebäude-Shapefile und CityGML gegensätzliche Informationen enthielten, wurde im Luftbild geprüft oder im Zweifelfall die CityGML-Information akzeptiert. Die **8.981 identifizierten Flachdächer** im Stadtgebiet werden demnach aufgrund ihrer vollständigen (bzw. in einem Gebäudeteil) geringen Dachneigung als potenzielle Gründächer betrachtet. Für viele kleinere Gebäude innerhalb von Kleingartenanlagen (i. d. R. Schuppen und Gartenhäuser) ist weder im CityGML-Datensatz noch im Gebäude-Datensatz eine Information zur Dachform enthalten. Aus diesem Grunde wurden diese Gebäude nicht weiter betrachtet.

Anhand des Luftbildes wurden dann Trainingsgebiete für weitere Dachausprägungen erstellt, um dann mittels Klassifikation Dächer mit Kiesdächern (höheres Gründachpotenzial) oder mit Kollektoren für solare Energie (geringeres Grün-

8 Vgl. o.V., 2016

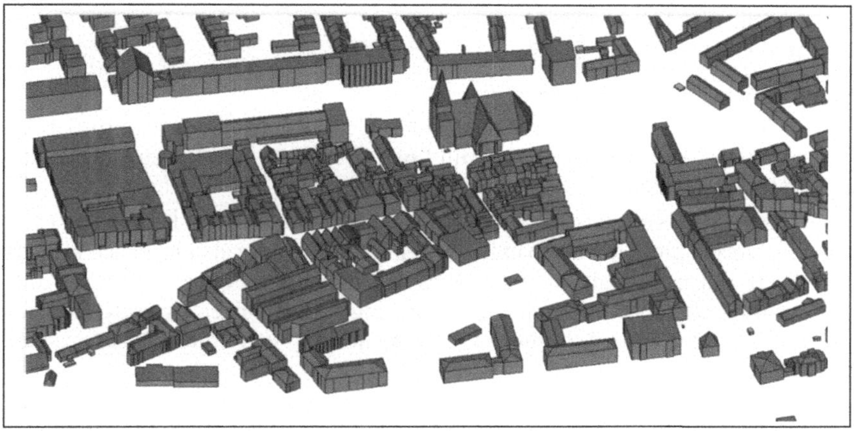

Abbildung 8: Rostock 3D- LOD 2 – Aus Luftbildern / Laserscanning abgeleitete 3D-Dachformen am Beispiel der Innenstadt von Rostock

dachpotenzial) zu ermitteln. Zu den gewählten Klassen zählen Vegetation, Solar-/Photo-voltaikanlage, Kies und verschiedene weitere Dachoberflächen. Die Klassifikationsergebnisse wurden in die Attributtabelle der Hausumringe als Potenzialbewertung integriert. Wie bereits zuvor bei der NDVI-Berechnung existieren einige Unsicherheiten, wenn Gebäudegeometrien nicht deckungsgleich mit den Dachflächen im Luftbild sind. Deshalb wurde auch bei der Potentialanalyse eine visuelle Prüfung der Resultate durchgeführt, wobei die Unterscheidung von Kiesoberflächen und anderen hellen Dachoberflächen nicht gewährleistet werden kann. Von den 8.981 Flachdächern besitzen **90 eine Kiesaufbringung** und **186 Solar- oder Photovoltaikanlagen**.

2.2 Ergebnisse AP2

Abbildung 9: Automatisch klassifizierte Solarpanels auf einem Flachdach

Beschreibung relevanter Spalten in der Attributtabelle der Shapefile Gründachpotenzial:

Potenzialb [= Potenzialbewertung]:

- „kein Flachdach / keine LoD2-Dachform“: Entweder die Dachform ist gemäß LoD2 kein Flachdach oder im LoD2-Datensatz sind hierzu keine Informationen verfügbar
- „Flachdach“: Gebäude ist im LoD2-Datensatz als Flachdach kategorisiert
- „Flachdach mit Kies“: Gebäude ist im LoD2-Datensatz als Flachdach kategorisiert und nach multispektraler Klassifikation besitzt die Dachfläche (vollständig oder teilweise) eine Kiesausbringung (unsicher, weil Kiesdächer spektral und visuell (mittels DOP) nicht klar von Betondächern unterschieden werden können)
- „Flachdach mit Solar- / Photovoltaik-Anlage“: Gebäude ist im LoD2-Datensatz als Flachdach kategorisiert und nach multispektraler Klassifikation und manueller Prüfung besitzt die Dachfläche (vollständig oder teilweise) eine Solar- oder Photovoltaikanlage.

Gründach = Gründachbewertung aus AP1 nach manueller Prüfung anhand des Luftbilds. Entweder „ja“, wenn eindeutig ein Gründach erkannt wurde oder „verdeckt“ wenn die manuelle Prüfung anhand der Luftbilds aufgrund Vegetationsüberdeckung nicht möglich war.

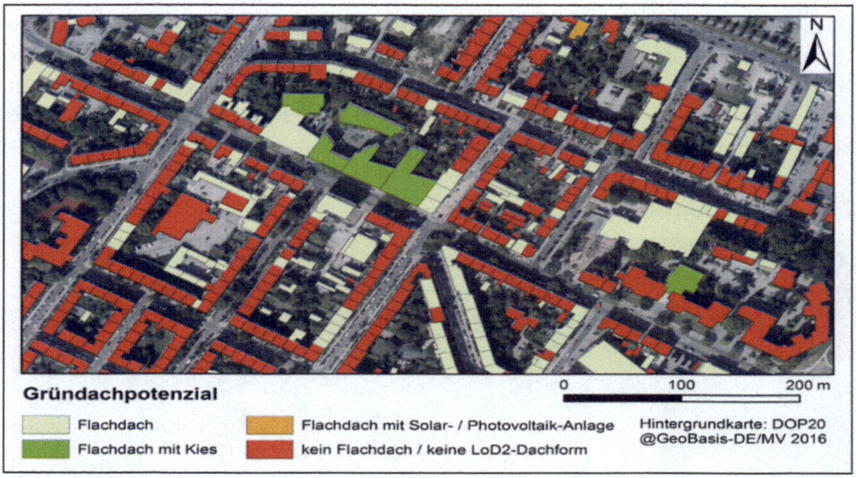

Abbildung 10: Auszug aus der Shapedatei des Gründachpotentials der Hansestadt Rostock

3 Kennwerte der Gründachpotentiale bezogen auf das Stadtgebiet

Vor einem detaillierten Blick auf die Ergebnisse eine kurze Zusammenfassung der wichtigsten Ergebnisse auf der gesamtstädtischen Ebene:

- Anzahl aller Dächer mit Dachbegrünung im Stadtgebiet (193) zzgl. 54 Tiefgaragen/Speicher
- Prozentualer Anteil der Gründächer an der Gesamtzahl aller Dachflächen (aller Dachflächen größer als 25 m²) (ca. 0,45%)
- Vegetationsfläche aller begrünten Dachflächen (ca. 3,4 ha)
- Anzahl aller potenziell begrünbaren Gebäude im Stadtgebiet (alle Flachdächer, Flachdächer mit Kies sowie Flachdächer mit Kollektoren für solare Energie, ohne Parkhäuser) (8.955)
- Prozentualer Anteil der potenziell begrünbaren Dachflächen an der Gesamtzahl aller Dachflächen (aller Dachflächen größer als 25 m²) (ca. 21%)
- Gesamtfläche der potenziell begrünbaren Dächer (ca. 372 ha)

Zur näheren Betrachtung der potentiell geeigneten Dachflächen sind diese in Abhängigkeit der ALKIS-Gebäudefunktion differenziert und in Abbildung 11 zu verschiedenen übergeordneten Kategorien zusammengefasst worden. Dabei zeigt sich, dass die flächenmäßig größten Potentiale für Gründächer auf Gebäuden mit gewerblicher Nutzung liegen (ca. 157 ha). Dabei ist an dieser Stelle noch zu erwähnen, dass dies auch große Industriegebäude und Lagerhallen mit beinhaltet, die in einer Leichtbaukonstruktion erbaut sind und als Gründächer nur bedingt

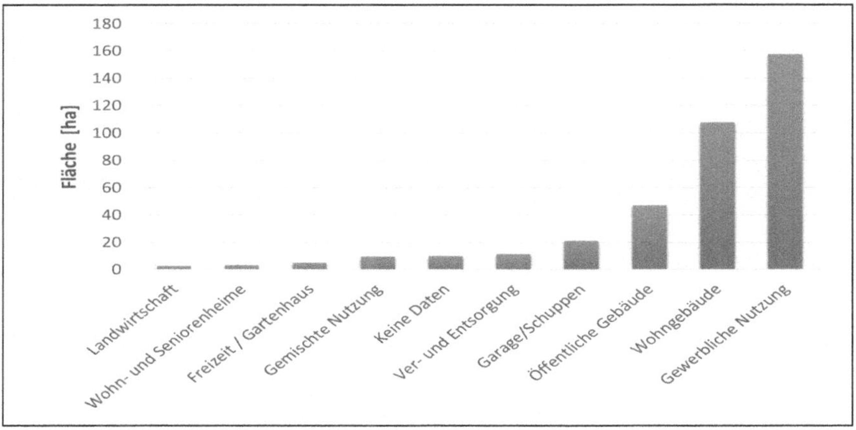

Abbildung 11: Gesamtfläche der potenziell begrünbaren Dächer, aufgeschlüsselt nach der Nutzung der Gebäude

geeignet sind. Die zweitgrößte Kategorie sind Wohngebäude mit einer Fläche von ca. 107 ha. Die Kategorie der öffentlichen Gebäude mit einem Potential von max. 46 ha ist nicht mit den kommunalen Gebäuden gleichzusetzen, vielmehr sind in dieser Rubrik alle öffentlichen Gebäude, angefangen von Behörden bis hin zu militärisch genutzten Immobilien, enthalten.

Wenn man nicht nur die Fläche in Betracht zieht, sondern auch die Größe der Gebäude, ändern sich die Verhältnisse ein wenig, wie die Abbildungen 12 und 13 zeigen. So sind es nur wenige öffentliche Gebäude, die aber im Mittel über eine große Dach-fläche verfügen. Wohngebäude hingegen sind im Durchschnitt wesentlich kleiner, da dies neben den Plattenbauten auch Ein-familienhäuser mit Flachdächern umfassen kann.

Die Anzahl und Fläche potentieller Gründächer verteilt sich sehr ungleichmäßig über das Stadtgebiet Rostocks. In einigen Stadtteilen sind sehr viele Gebäude mit Flachdächern zu finden und in andere kaum welche. Die Abbildung 14 zeigt die gesamten potentiell in Frage kommenden Gebäude. Die Abbildungen 15 und 16 schlüsseln die Gebäude in Wohngebäude und gewerblich genutzte Immobilien auf. Dabei zeigt sich, dass es große Unterschiede gibt. Während bei den gewerblich genutzten Gebäuden ein lokaler Schwerpunkt im Überseehafen, entlang der Warnow und in den innerstädtischen Stadtteilen zu beobachten ist, konzentrieren sich die Wohngebäude mit Gründachpotential in denjenigen Stadtteilen, in denen viele Großblockgebäude, sprich Plattenbauten zu finden sind.

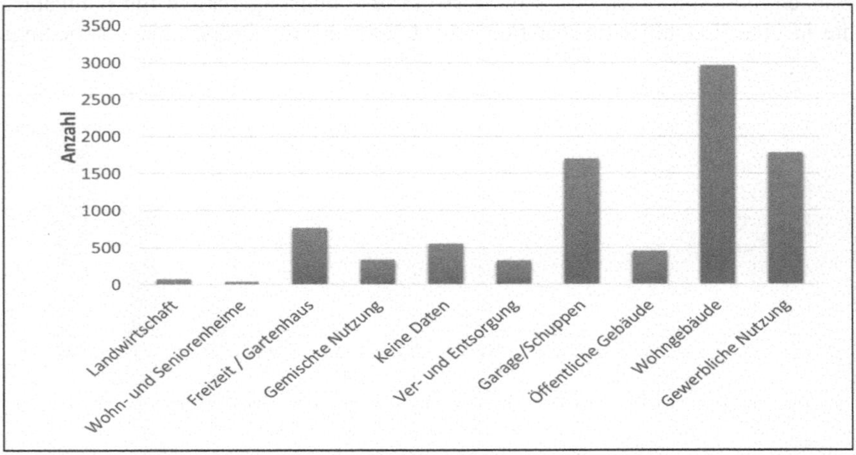

Abbildung 12: Anzahl der potenziell begrünbaren Dächer, aufgeschlüsselt nach der Nutzung der Gebäude

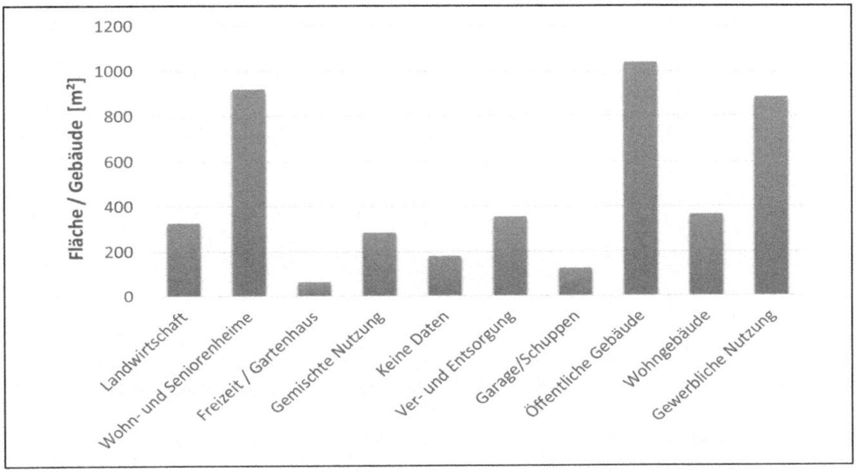

Abbildung 13: Mittlere Dachfläche der potenziell begrünbaren Dächer, aufgeschlüsselt nach der Nutzung der Gebäude

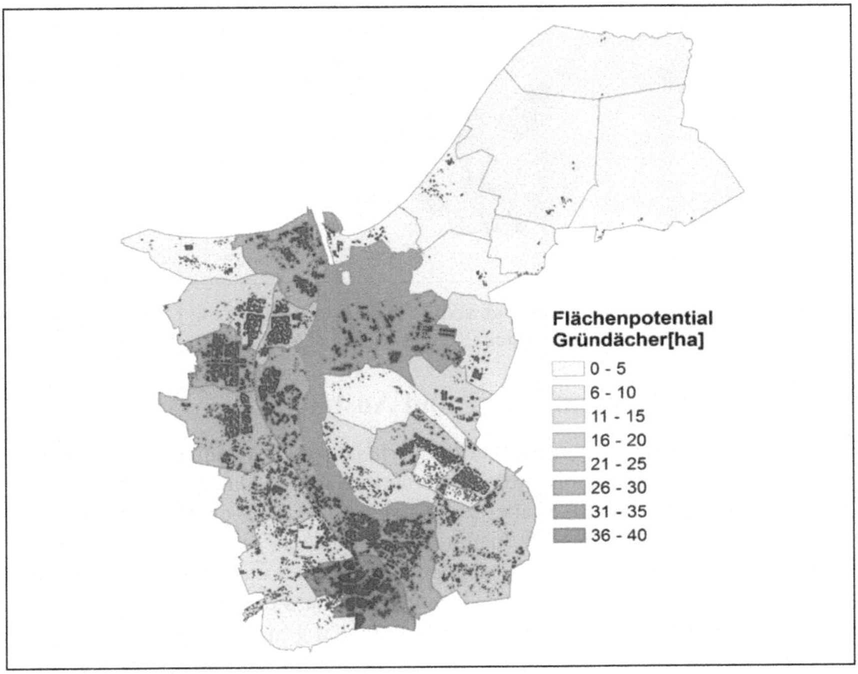

Abbildung 14: Potentiell geeignete Gebäude mit Flachdächern in der Hansestadt Rostock, untergliedert nach Stadtteilen

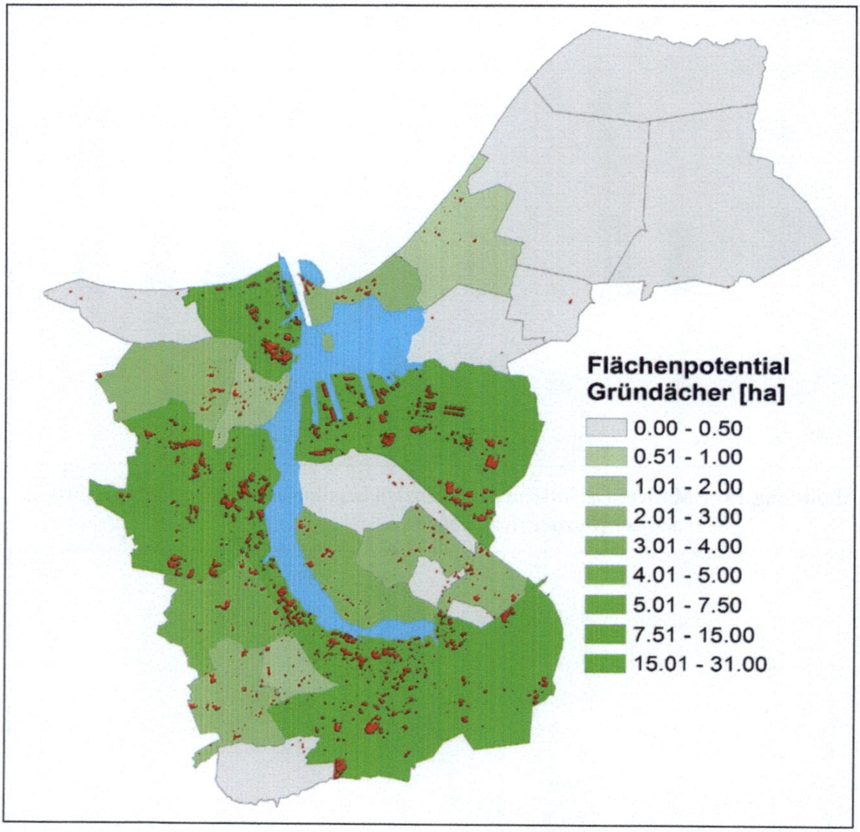

Abbildung 15: Potentiell geeignete gewerblich genutzte Gebäude mit Flachdächern in der Hansestadt Rostock, untergliedert nach Stadtteilen

4 Fazit / Zusammenfassung und Ausblick

Im Rahmen der Untersuchungen wurden vorhandene Gründächer der Hansestadt Rostock mittels einer Kombination aus fernerkundlichen Daten und vorhandenen Gebäudegeometrien erfasst. Dabei zeigte sich, dass es sich nur im eine verschwindend kleine Zahl handelt, nämlich 247 Gebäude einschließlich begrünter Tiefgaragen, was etwa 5 ‰ der gesamten Dachflächen ausmacht. Die Potentialanalyse auf der Grundlage amtlicher Daten ergab, dass es im Punkto Gründächer in Rostock ein sehr großes flächenmäßiges Potential gibt, was maximal 21% aller Dächer der Hansestadt ausmachen könnte. Die Gründachpotentiale betreffen

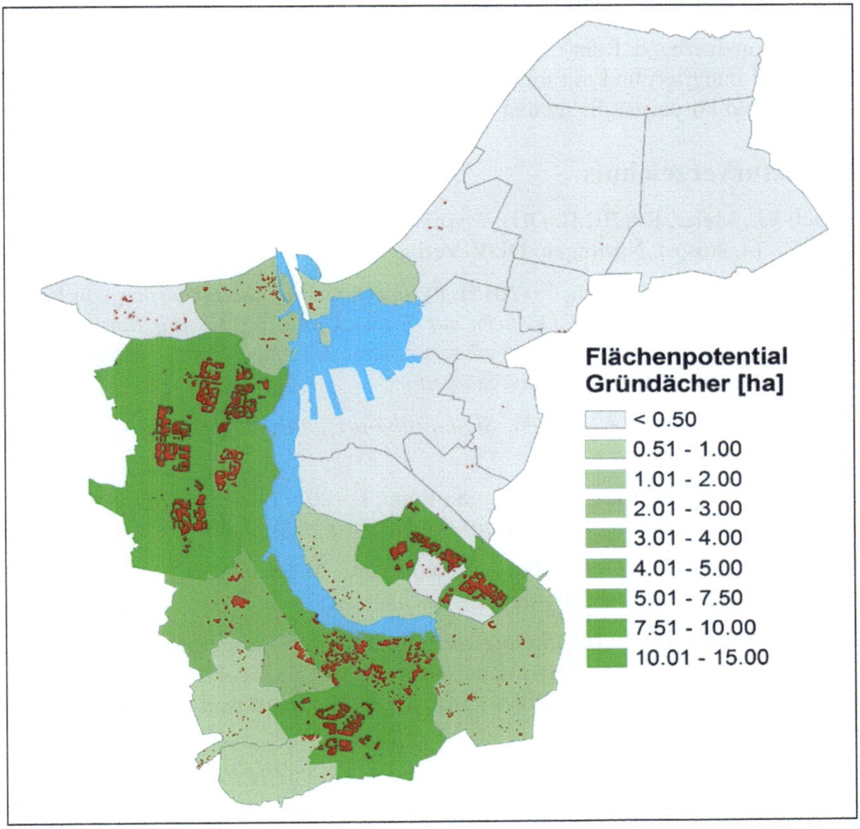

Abbildung 16: Potentiell geeignete Wohngebäude mit Flachdächern in der Hansestadt Rostock, untergliedert nach Stadtteilen

natürlich nicht alle Gebäude und Stadtteile, vielmehr sind es vornehmlich Plattenbauten, gewerbliche Immobilien und öffentliche Gebäude. Diese sind im Schnitt auch am größten.

Die Erschließung dieses Potentials, das haben Erfahrungen anderer deutscher Städte gezeigt, gelingt am besten durch einen Mix aus gezielten und passgenauen Informationen und einer an die Bedürfnisse der Stadt angepassten Förderrichtlinie für den Umbau eines herkömmlichen Dachs in ein Gründach.[9]

[9] Vgl. Klärle, Langendörfer, Lanig, Popp, 2017

Dazu haben andere Städte in der Bundesrepublik, z.B. Marburg[10], Aachen[11] oder der Regionalverband Ruhr[12] die hier vorgestellten Fachdaten in ihr jeweiligen Geoportal integriert und mit unterschiedlichen Daten und Informationen über die Vorteile und Fördermöglichkeiten ergänzt.

Literaturverzeichnis

Ansel, W., Meier, R. (2014). *DDV-Praxisratgeber: Das 1x1 der Dachbegrünung.* (4. Ausg.). Nürtingen: DDV-Verlag.

Ansel, W., Zeidler, J., Esch, T. (2015). *Fernerkundliche Identifizierung von Vegetationsflächen auf Dächern zur Entwicklung des für die Bereiche des Stadtklimas, der Stadtentwässerung und des Artenschutzes aktivierbaren Flächenpotenzials in den Städten.*

Berardi, U., Hoseini, A. (2014). *State-of-the-art analysis of the environmental benefits of green roofs.*

Klärle, M., Langendörfer, U., Lanig, S., Popp, F. (2017). *GREEN-AREA – Intelligentes Gründachkataster auf der Basis von GIS-Daten.*

Marburg Universität. (o.J). *Gründachkataster.* Abgerufen am 2.3.2019 von https://www.marburg.de/gruendachkataster

o.V. (2016). *Anlage 5: ALKIS-Objektartenkatalog M-V.* Abgerufen am 2. 3.2019 von https://www.laiv-mv.de/static/LAIV/Abt3.Geoinformation/Medienobjekte/ALKISVV%20M-V-Anlage_5_Entwurfsstand_%202016-10-11.pdf

Regionalverband Ruhr. (2019). *AUF DER SUCHE NACH INHALTEN ZUM REGIONALVERBAND RUHR?* Abgerufen am 2.3.2019 von http://www.metropoleruhr.de/regionalverband-ruhr/umwelt-freiraum/klima/klimaanpassung/startseite-gruen dachkataster.html

StädteRegion Aachen. (o.J.). *Eignet sich mein Dach für eine Begrünung?* Abgerufen am 2.3.2019 von https://www.staedteregion-aachen.de/de/navigation/aemter/umweltamt-a-70/klimaschutz/m-itmachen-und-informieren/gruendachpotenzialkataster/

---

10 Vgl. Marburg Universität., o.J.
11 Vgl. StädteRegion Aachen, o.J.
12 Vgl. Regionalverband Ruhr, 2019

Modulare Datenbrille

Rigo Herold

1 Datenbrillen-Architekturen

Um die hier vorzustellende Datenbrille besser einordnen zu können soll folgend ein kurzer Überblick von generellen Datenbrillen-Architekturen gegeben werden. Bei dieser Aufstellung werden gleichzeitig die Vor- und Nachteile dieser Architekturen erläutert. Diese Gerätetypen findet man unter den Bezeichnungen „Smart Glasses", „High-Immersive-Datenbrillen" sowie „modulare Datenbrillen".

1.1 Smart Glasses

Da klassische Datenbrillen in der Vergangenheit meist sehr schwer und voluminös waren, ist die Kategorie Smart Glasses entstanden. Smart Glasses sind praktisch leichte Datenbrillen. Das Ziel war, ein optisches Aussehen ähnlich einer Lesebrille zu erzielen, damit auch eine Nutzerakzeptanz im Konsumerbereich erzielt werden kann. Charakteristisch für Smart Glasses ist, dass als Basis ein Lese- bzw. Schutzbrillengestell genutzt wird. An diesem Basisgestell werden dann die erforderlichen Komponenten einer Datenbrille wie Optik, Display, Akku, Schnittstelle, Kopfhörer, Mikrofon, Sensoren sowie ein Prozessor integriert. Der integrierte Prozessor mit zugehöriger Peripherie gestattet somit prinzipiell ähnliche Funktionalitäten wie bei Smartphones.

Wie bei Smartphones können auch die Smart Glasses überall als Stand Alone Geräte betrieben werden. Die meist integrierten WiFi- und Bluetooth Schnittstellen erlauben eine Verbindung zu W-LAN Hotspots oder einen einfachen kabellosen Datentransfer. Der Vorteil, dass bei Smart Glasses quasi das Smartphone in die Lesebrille integriert ist, bringt jedoch auch verschiedene Probleme mit sich. Am Gestell einer einfachen Lesebrille werden zusätzliche Komponenten angebracht, welche jeweils ein Mehrgewicht, Volumen und eine Verkabelung erfordern. Die Stabilität von Smart Glasses ist deshalb bei einem Einsatz in industriellen bzw. rauen Umgebungen nicht zu hoch zu bewerten. Ein technischer Nachteil ist, dass Smart Glasses nicht über Lese- bzw. Schutzbrillen getragen werden können.[1] Die Hersteller schlagen vor in Smart Glasses individuelle Korrekturgläser anfertigen zu lassen bzw. Kontaktlinsen zu nutzen. Diese Möglichkeiten sind jedoch in der Praxis schlecht umsetzbar und schließen meistens den Einsatz von Smart Glasses bei Brillenträgern aus. Ebenfalls sind Einsatzbereiche, in denen

---

[1] Vgl. Abbildung 1

H.-C. Brauweiler et al. (Hrsg.), *Digitalization and Industry 4.0: Economic and Societal Development*, https://doi.org/10.1007/978-3-658-27110-7_9

eine Schutzbrille gefordert ist problematisch. Da einerseits am Gestell der Datenbrille energiefordernde Komponenten wie der Prozessor, Sensoren und Funkschnittstellen integriert sind, ab auf der anderen Seite durch den begrenzten Integrationsraum der Smart Glasses nur kleine Akkus eingebaut werden können ist die Betriebszeit oft sehr kurz und die Datenbrillen-Software muss zum Akkuwechsel herunter und wieder hochgefahren werden.

Abbildung 1: Problematik beim Tragen von Smart Glasses über Lesebrillen

Der Vorteil der kompakten Integration eines Prozessors, welche Smart Glasses zu einen kompakten autarken mobilen Informationsgerät macht, muss von zwei Seiten betrachtet werden. Der eingebettete Prozessor ist fest mit der Datenbrille verkoppelt. In Analogie zu Smartphones besteht hier auch die Problematik, dass der Prozessor mit Peripherie und das Betriebssystem nach relativ kurzer Zeit veraltet sind. Ein Hardware- bzw. Software-Update ist in den meisten Fällen nicht möglich. Bei industriellen Anwendungen könnten die Komponenten wie Optik, Display, Brillengestell und Akku für längere Zeiträume eingesetzt werden. Prozessor und Betriebssystem sind deshalb die Komponenten, welche die Lebensdauer begrenzen. Bezüglich des Datenschutzes sind auch Einschränkungen zu berücksichtigen, da Smart Glasses digitale Spuren wie Browser-Verläufe, persönliche Videoaufnahmen oder Pausenzeiten speichert. Eine Weitergabe des Gerätes z.B. zum Schichtwechsel ist aus Datenschutzgründen sehr kritisch zu betrachten.

1.2 High-Immersive-Datenbrillen

High-Immersive-Datenbrillen kann man als ein mobiles VR-, AR- oder Mixed-Reality-System mit erweiterter Nutzerinteraktion betrachten. Im Gegensatz zu Smart Glasses basieren High-Immersive- Datenbrillen nicht auf einem einfachen Gestell einer Lese- bzw. Schutzbrille, sondern haben den Aufbau eines Helms oder zumindest das Innenleben eines Bauhelms. Somit gibt es auch mehr Integrationsmöglichkeiten für komplexere Komponenten. Es kann somit ein sehr großes

Field of View FOV (>30° diagonal) erzielt werden. Je nach optischer Technologie ist die Ausgabe in 3D also Hologramm möglich. Der Einbau von Tiefensensoren erfasst ein Tracking der Umgebung in 3D und somit ist auch eine Nutzerinteraktion in 3D möglich. Das bedeutet, dass Objekte im Raum erkannt und die virtuelle Überlagerung der AR-Inhalte z.B. mit der Hand manipuliert werden. Diese Kategorie von Datenbrillen können somit auch einen leistungsfähigen Prozessor und die zugehörige Stromversorgung aufnehmen.

High-Immersive- Datenbrillen sind sehr gut geeignet, wenn z.B. Firmen auf Messen ein neues Produkt vorstellen und dieses in 3D zu einer Umgebung überlagert dargestellt werden soll. Ebenfalls sind diese Datenbrillen gut geeignet, wenn ein Konstrukteur sich einen Entwurf im Büro in 3D von allen Seiten ansehen möchte. Es ist dafür keine teure Cave als 3D Ausgabemedium erforderlich. Betrachtet man die High-Immersive- Datenbrillen im Kontext eines industriellen Einsatzes z.B. für Logistiker oder Mitarbeiter in der Fertigung, dann müssen verschiedene Begrenzungen beachtet werden. Ein Sicherheitsproblem ist insbesondere das meist eingeschränkte Sichtfeld auf die reale Umgebung, bedingt durch die Helmform.[2] Durch das eingeschränkte Sichtfeld können mögliche Gefahren wie z.B. Treppenstufen oder fahrende Stapler nicht erkannt werden und es erhöht sich die Unfallgefahr.

Abbildung 2: Problematik beim Tragen von High-Immersive-Datenbrillen über Lesebrillen

Neben diesen Restriktionen gibt es bis jetzt noch keine Studien, ob z.B. Fertigungsarbeiter in einer normalen Arbeitsumgebung mit einem solch immersiven System den Arbeitsalltag ohne psychische Auswirkungen bestreiten können. Man kann ähnlich wie beim 3D-Kino aktuell nur davon ausgehen, dass es vom jewei-

[2] Vgl. Abbildung 2

ligen Individuum abhängt, wie gut die 3D Inhalte aufgenommen werden können. Ergonomisch muss ebenfalls noch geprüft werden, welche Tragedauer bei High-Immersive- Datenbrillen zumutbar ist, da diese im Gegensatz zu Smart Glasses ein deutlich höheres Gewicht aufweisen.

2 Modulare Datenbrille

Modulare Datenbrillen sind eine weitere Kategorie. Smart Glasses und High-Immersive-Datenbrillen müssen für die jeweilige Anwendung nach dem Top-down Ansatz skaliert werden. Das bedeutet, dass von vielen Funktionsmöglichkeiten nur einzelne Funktionen wie z.B. die reine Displayausgabe oder nur die Kamerafunktion per Software aktiviert werden. Modulare Datenbrillen sind als ein modulares System zu betrachten und verfolgen den Bottom-up Ansatz. Es handelt sich dabei um separate Ein- und Ausgabegeräte, welche in einer gewünschten Konfiguration an verschiedene Träger wie Schutzbrillen, Schutzhelme, Stoßkappen, Kopfhörer oder Headsets montiert werden können.[3] Die modularen Komponenten kann man mit Bluetooth-Headsets oder WiFi Überwachungs-Kameras vergleichen, welche wie ein Client fest mit einem Computer gekoppelt sind.

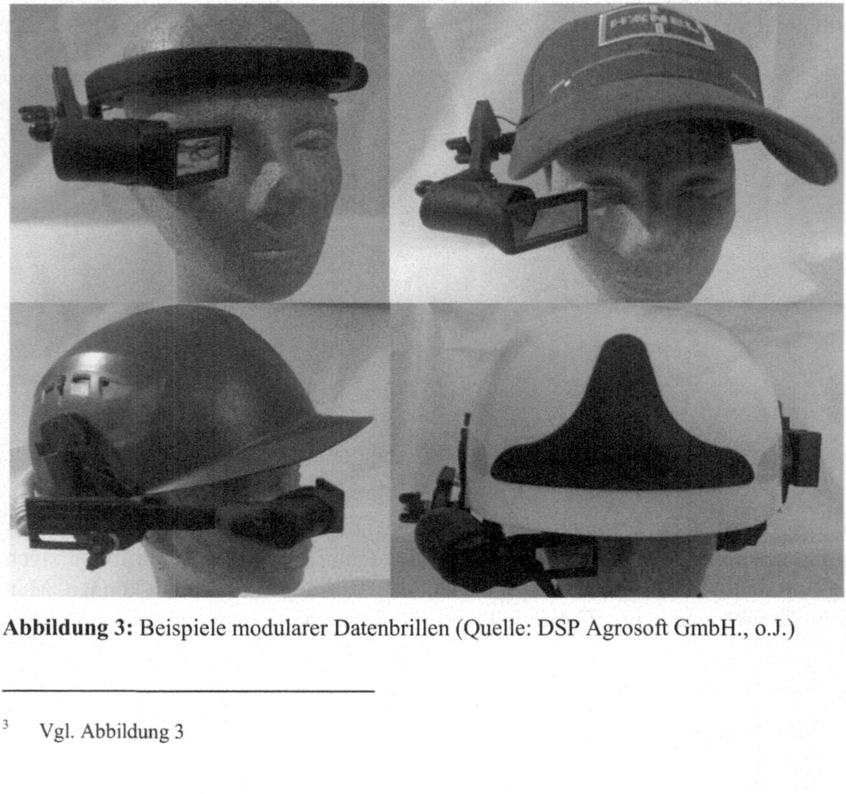

Abbildung 3: Beispiele modularer Datenbrillen (Quelle: DSP Agrosoft GmbH., o.J.)

[3] Vgl. Abbildung 3

Der Nachteil ist, dass Modulare Datenbrillen nicht ohne eine separate Compute-reinheit nicht autark arbeitsfähig sind. Die einzelnen Module müssen mit einem sogenannten Applikationsrechner gekoppelt werden. Die Entkopplung von einem fest verbauten Rechner ermöglicht jedoch den Freiheitsgrad, dass über Standard-Schnittstellen ein aktueller Rechner eingesetzt werden kann. Im praktischen Einsatz kann das ein Smartphone, Tablet, Smart Watch oder ein bereits in der Fertigung vorhandener PC sein. Der Anwender kann sich somit seine Datenbrille für die Anwendung und die bestehende IT-Struktur selbst konfigurieren. Die Modulare Datenbrille kann deshalb auch langfristig eingesetzt werden, da die einzelnen Module an einen aktuellen bzw. bereits in der Fertigung vorhandenen Rechner unabhängig vom Betriebssystem gekoppelt werden können. Durch die Entkopplung von Datenbrille und Computermodul fallen somit auch keine Folgekosten für Neuanschaffungen veralteter Datenbrillen mit integrierten Computersystemen an. Die Systemkonzeption der modularen Datenbrille ist in Abbildung 4 dargestellt.

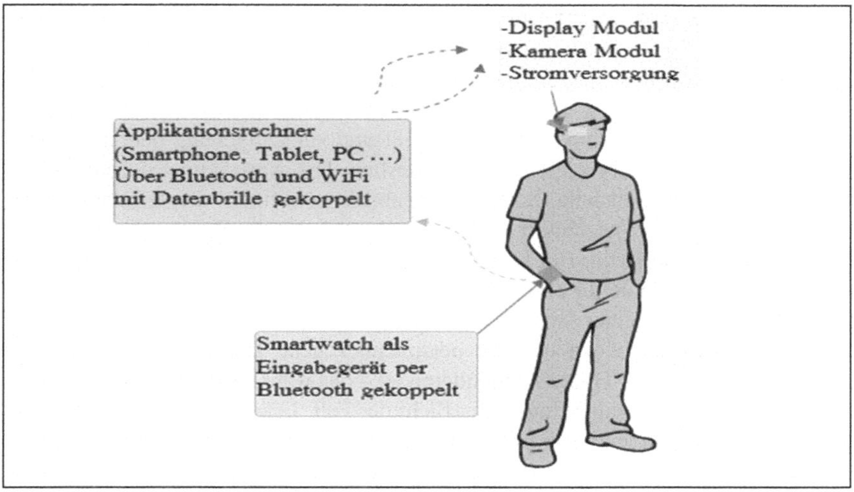

Abbildung 4: Systemkonzeption des Modularen Datenbrillen (Quelle: dgZ (data glasses Zwickau UG), o.J.)

3 Vorgehensweise zur Auswahl von Datenbrillen für den Praxiseinsatz

Aufgrund der Vielfältigkeit von möglichen Anwendungen für Datenbrillen müssen verschiedene Restriktionen berücksichtigt werden, um geeignete Datenbrillen für die jeweilige Ziel-Anwendung einsetzen zu können. In einer Studie wurden 38 Teilnehmer in insgesamt 14 verschiedenen Einsatzszenarien bei 84 Variationen untersucht. Das Resultat der Studie zeigt, dass für jede spezifische Anwendung auch eine geeignete Hardware eingesetzt werden muss. Abbildung 5 veranschaulicht die wichtigsten Entscheidungskriterien, die ein Nutzer für die Auswahl der Datenbrille für die spezielle Anwendung berücksichtigen muss.

Im ersten Schritt muss die konkrete Anwendung analysiert werden. Hierbei ist zu berücksichtigen, ob es eine Indoor- oder Outdoor-Anwendung ist. Bei Outdoor Anwendungen muss sichergestellt sein, dass die Datenbrille vor Wasser geschützt ist und insbesondere, dass der Kontrast der virtuellen Projektion ausreichend groß ist. Die Art der Anwendung bestimmt auch die erforderliche Betriebsdauer. Soll die Datenbrille z.B. im Logistik- oder Fertigungsbereich eingesetzt werden, ist eine Betriebsdauer von 8h gewünscht. Soll die Datenbrille z.B. für einen Remote Service genutzt werden, sollte eine Einsatzdauer von 2h auch ausreichend sein. Ebenfalls ist die Arbeitsumgebung für die Robustheit der Datenbrille entscheidend. In einer sauberen Arbeitsumgebung wie z.B. im Reinraum einer Chipfertigung muss die Datenbrille nur eine geringe Robustheit sowie einen Staubschutz aufweisen. Wird hingegen die Datenbrille in rauen Arbeitsumgebungen wie z.B. einem Stahlwerk eingesetzt, muss die Hardware vor Hitze, Staub und mechanischen Stößen geschützt sein. Ein weiterer Aspekt ist die Menge der darzustellenden Informationen. Bei einem Logistik-Szenario wo nur einfache Pick Inhalte als Textinformation angezeigt werden, ist ein kleines Field of View ausreichend. Soll hingegen eine Maschinenkonstruktion in 3D dargestellt und zur Umgebung überlagert werden, ist ein Wide Field of View oft erforderlich. Die Anwendung definiert dann auch die Nutzer-Schnittstelle. Soll die Datenbrille von einem Staplerfahrer eingesetzt werden, muss eine handfreie Bedienung z.B. durch Sprachsteuerung oder Eyetracking möglich sein. Bei Fertigungs- oder Logistikarbeitern, bei denen zwischenzeitlich die Hände für eine Nutzereingabe eingesetzt werden können, ist z.B. die Tasteneingabe an einer Smart Watch oder eine Gestensteuerung möglich. Ebenfalls ist zu berücksichtigen ob eine personenbezogene Datenbrille während der Arbeit an verschiedene Träger zu montieren ist – das wäre beispielsweise der Übergang in einen Bereich mit Schutzhelmpflicht der Fall. Letztendlich ist bei der Auswahl der Datenbrille auch das Individuum zu betrachten. Piloten oder Spezialeinsatzkräfte dürfen berufsbedingt keine Sehschwäche aufweisen, sodass eine Datenbrille ohne Sehhilfe direkt getragen werden kann. Im industriellen Bereich benötigt ein Teil der Belegschaft eine Sehhilfe, die Datenbrille sollte so ausgewählt werden, dass diese in Kombination mit einer Lese- bzw. Schutzbrille getragen werden kann. Ein nichttechnisches Problem ist der Datenschutz. Mit Datenbrillen können einerseits andere Mitarbeiter über die Kamera erfasst werden. Auf der anderen Seite kann auch die Leistungsfähigkeit des Mitarbeiters erfasst werden. Es wird daher empfohlen rechtzeitig Betriebsrat und Datenschutzbeauftrage zu involvieren und genau die technischen Features einer Datenbrille festlegen zu können.[4]

[4] Vgl. Herold, 2018

Tabelle 1: Auswahlhilfe zur Bewertung der Anwendungsanforderungen und der Eignung der zugehörigen Datenbrillen-Architektur (Quelle: dgZ (data glasses Zwickau UG), o.J.)

Datenbrillen Architektur	**Smart Glasses**	**High-Immersive Datenbrillen**	**Modulare Datenbrille**
Anforderung der Anwendung			
Darstellung			
Virtual Reality	+	+++	+
Head-up-Inhalte	+++	+	+++
Augmented Reality	+	+++	++
Mixed Reality	+	+++	+
Technische Parameter			
Betriebsdauer	+	+++	+++
Funktionsdichte	++	+++	+
Skalierbarkeit für die Anwendung	+	+	+++
Computersystem			
Rechenleistung	+	+++	++
Administrationsaufwand	++	+++	+
Betriebssystemupdate	+	+	+++
Hardwareupdates	+	+	+++
Flexible Ankoppelung an Computersystemen	+		+++
Anpassbarkeit für den Datenschutz z.B. Deaktivierung der Kamera	+	+	+++
Mechanik			
Aufnahme an verschiedenen Trägern (Modularität)	+		+++
Mechanische Stabilität	+	++	+++
Tragekomfort / Gewicht	++	+	+++
Eignung für Lese- und Schutzbrillenträger	+		+++
Kosten	Mittel	Hoch	Niedrig

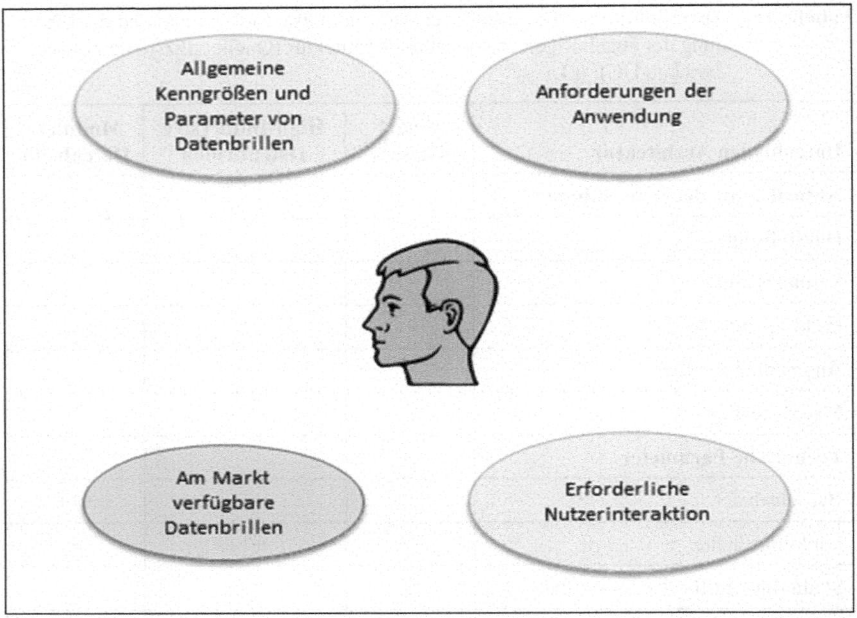

Abbildung 5: Restriktionen zur Auswahl von Datenbrillen für eine Anwendung

Literaturverzeichnis

dgZ data glasses Zwickau UG. (o.J.). *data glasses.* Abgerufen am 3.3.2019 von www.datenbrillen.org

DSP Agrosoft GmbH. (o.J.). *Datenbrille für die Klauenpflegesoftware KLAUE.* Abgerufen am 3.3.2019 von https://www.herde-net.de/service/neuheiten/

Herold , R. (2018). *Modularer Systemaufbau erforderlich, Elektronik 2018.*

Herold, R. (2011). *Ein Beitrag zur Realisierung von Systemarchitekturen für Head-Mounted Displays auf Basis bidirektionaler OLED-Mikrodisplays. Dissertation, Universität Duisburg-Essen.*

Experience of introducing digitalization into the economy of foreign countries

I. Kh. Tuseeva, A. A. Azhibaeva, D. T. Askarov

1 What is the role of the state in the process of digitization in the US economy?

The United States is one of the world leaders in the digital economy, which refers to "the economy, which mainly operates with the use of digital technologies, especially electronic transactions carried out using the Internet".[1]

The US Department of Commerce is the lead agency responsible for the implementation of the program. 12 offices of this department participated in the creation of the program, and 4 of its structural divisions participated in its implementation: The National Agency for Telecommunications and Information (NATI), the National Institute of Standards and Technology (NIST), the US Patent Office and the International Trade Administration. To ensure inter-agency management, the Digital Economy Leadership Team was created in 2015, with the participation of the Internet Policy Task Force.

In order to develop recommendations for expanding opportunities in the digital era, in March 2016, the Digital Economy Board of Advisors was created, including representatives from a number of major US companies (General Electric, Electrical and electronics engineering, Microsoft, Silicon Valley Bank, YouTube, McKinsey Global Institute, Home Shopping Network, and others), civil society and academia.[2]

Since March 2016, a pilot program has been implemented to create "digital attaché" positions in US trade offices abroad responsible for trading in digital products and services.

The main areas of the US digital economy are:

- Promoting a free and open Internet worldwide;
- Promoting trust and security online;
- Ensuring access for workers, families, and companies;

---

1 (U.S. Departament of Commerce, n.d.)
2 See Revenko, 2017

H.-C. Brauweiler et al. (Hrsg.), *Digitalization and Industry 4.0: Economic and Societal Development*, https://doi.org/10.1007/978-3-658-27110-7_10

- Promoting innovation, through smart intellectual property rules and by advancing the next generation of exciting new technologies.[3]

2 Which way does China choose development of the digital economy?

As noted in the report of the Global Institute of the international consulting company McKinsey "How does China's digital economy define a new global trend?" China has the world's largest e-commerce market. China has become the main force shaping the structure of global digitalization, digital globalization is rapidly developing in the country, and China is creating new global trends in many areas: industrial investment, business models and global governance.[4]

In particular, an active system of digital investments and innovative enterprises has been created in China. The Chinese e-commerce market is the largest in the world. According to analysts of the research company Forrester, in its latest report, Electronic Commerce in China: Trends and prospects for the largest e-Commerce market "The online trading market will grow to $ 1.8 trillion by 2022. For example, in the US, the online retail market will reach only $ 713 billion by 2022, and in Japan only $ 159 billion. By the end of 2018, Chinese e-Commerce will reach $ 1.1 trillion. It is expected that by 2022, online retail sales in the country will grow steadily at 8.5% per year. The main influence on the industry have two giants: Alibaba and JD.com which constitute more than 85% of local online commerce. New companies are emerging, such as Pinduoduo and Xiaohongshu, using new social trading platforms.

In addition, China ranks third in the world in terms of venture capital in various areas. In 2016, in terms of the volume of venture investments in the financial science and technology sector, China ranked first in the world (this is the total investment of the United States and the United Kingdom, which ranked second and third.[5]

According to a McKinsey report, three main factors determine the development of the digital economy in China.

1. The large size of the Chinese market and a significant number of young Internet users contribute to the rapid commercial use of digital business models. Digital start-ups are entering the market and are developing rapidly due to the growth in production.

---

3 See Revenko, 2017
4 See n.n., n.d.
5 See n.n., n.d. a

2. Three Chinese Internet giants (Baidu, Alibaba, Tencent) have created an "ecosphere" favorable to digitalization, which continues to expand continuously. Venture investments of three Internet giants in 2016 accounted for 42% of the total venture capital in China (for comparison: The volume of venture capital investments of the four largest US Internet companies Facebook, Amazon, Google and Netflix in 2016 amounted to only 5% of the US venture capital market.
3. Realizing the importance of information transformations, the government became the main driving force behind the development of digitalization in PRC. In order to create a favorable atmosphere in the field of informatization, the Government regulates the situation by strengthening and weakening control over digital enterprises.[6]

In terms of the level and scale of the development of the digital economy, China has ranked second in the world. According to Ren Xulin, director of the State Internet Information Office, the scale of China's digital economy in 2015 was estimated at 18.6 trillion yuan (about $ 2.7 trillion, or almost 14% of China's GDP).[7]

It was stated in the report of the Tencent Research Institute that the digital economy today makes up approximately 22.77 trillion yuan ($ 3.3 trillion), or 30.6% of China's GDP. According to forecasts of the Boston Consulting Group, by 2035 China's digital economy will create more than 400 million jobs.[8]

In general, as Chinese expert Zhang Xinhong (Jinji Jibao) states, "today, China has peculiar advantages and favorable conditions in the development of the digital economy, which started quickly and showed a favorable trend. In many areas, our country has begun to compete with developed countries and lead simultaneously, in the future in large areas there is still a large potential for huge development."[9]

3 The role of the state in the formation of the digital economy in Russia

In Russia, pursuant to the list of instructions of the President of the Russian Federation on the implementation of the Message to the Federal Assembly (Npr-2346 of December 6, 2016), the Digital Economy of the Russian Federation Program was approved.

---

6 See n.n., n.d. a
7 See Katasonov, n.d.
8 See n.n., n.d. b
9 (Theory China Resource of Understanding China, 2019)

The main digital technologies included in the Russian Program are: "Big data; neurotechnology and artificial intelligence; distributed registry systems; quantum technologies; new production technologies; industrial internet; components of robotics and sensorics; wireless technology; technologies of virtual and augmented reality".[10]

At the same time, the Program recognizes that the Russian Federation ranks 41st place in readiness for the digital economy with a significant margin from dozens of leading countries, such as Singapore, Finland, Sweden, Norway, USA, Netherlands, Switzerland, Britain, Luxembourg and Japan. Russia ranks 38th in terms of the economic and innovative results of using digital technologies, with a large lag behind leading countries such as Finland, Switzerland, Sweden, Israel, Singapore, the Netherlands, the United States, Norway, Luxembourg and Germany.[11]

For the development of the digital economy, this Program includes 5 basic directions for the development of the digital economy in the Russian Federation for the period up to 2024, which include: regulation; personnel and education; the formation of research competencies and technical reserves; information infrastructure and information security.

The tasks are accomplished by the Digital Economy Autonomous Non-Profit Organization, with the participation of the founders, which were 16 leading Russian companies - Rostelecom, MegaFon, Rosatom, Rostec, Sberbank, ASI, Yandex, Open Mobile platform, 1C, Mail.ru Group, MTS, Skolkovo Foundation, VEB Innovation, Rambler, Russian Post and VimpelCom.[12]

Under the State Duma Committee on Economic Development, Industry, Innovative Development and Entrepreneurship, a Digital Economy Expert Council was established.[13] All interested foreign companies, universities and R & D centers were invited to take part in the implementation of the Digital Economy of the Russian Federation Program.[14]

Having studied the experience of developing and implementing digitalization programs in foreign countries, we can draw one very important conclusion. It consists in determining the role of the state in this process and the degree of its participation in this process.

---

10 (n.n., Concerning the Approval of the Digital Economy of the Russian Federation Program, 2017)
11 See n.n. Concerning the Approval of the Digital Economy of the Russian Federation Program, 2017
12 See Krasnushkina, 2019
13 See PlusMagazine, 2019
14 See TACC, n.d.

Currently, issues of digitalization of the economy are being addressed in many developed countries. Similar questions are posed by developing countries. A large number of countries have developed and approved similar programs, and there is a sufficient amount of information for a detailed study of various approaches. For example, Russia approved its program "The Digital Economy of the Russian Federation" five months before Kazakhstan.

In our opinion, the Russian program is fully consistent with international experience. It also, like the programs of other states, defines the role of the state in the digitalization process. On the basis of a thorough study of the Russian experience, it can be concluded that the main role of the Russian state in the field of digitalization is to create an ecosystem, ensuring the effective interaction of the scientific and educational community, business, government and citizens to digitize the economy. In addition, the government must ensure the necessary and sufficient institutional and infrastructural conditions.

The Digital Kazakhstan program implies two vectors for the development of digitalization. The first vector in the program is:

"Digitalization of the existing economy providing a pragmatic start consisting of specific projects in the real sector; launching projects on digitalization and technological re-equipment of existing sectors of the economy, government structures and the development of digital infrastructure."

This means that the Kazakh government plans not indirect, but direct participation in the processes related to the digitization of the economy. First of all, we are talking about the technological re-equipment of existing sectors of the economy and the introduction of digitalization projects.

However, analysis of international experience shows that one of the key recommendations is that government interventions in the digitalization of the economy should be indirect. The government should act as a moderator of the process, but not a manager and a full-fledged investor and performer. The leading role in digitalization should be assigned to private business and human capital. Private initiative should prevail over the public one.

An analysis of the Digital Kazakhstan program shows that the state, while actively participating in the digitalization process, does not take into account this key recommendation. At present, projects for the digitalization of a certain business have been selected, funding is being provided for this, and the state will carry out this digitalization (automation). Let's give some examples from the program.

According to the first vector of development of the program, the government has planned the implementation of the state company RD Kazmunaygaz at its own expense of the project Intellectual Field, and the state company Kazatomprom, the project Digital Mine. In our opinion, these projects will be very expensive and require a detailed and in-depth analysis of their payback.

For the above reason, the state plans to buy out the share of private minority shareholders in RD Kazmunaygas. If the project "Intellectual field" does not give the required rate of return, this may lead to the fact that minority shareholders will stop financing this project, and it has already been approved in the state program.

Therefore, we believe that this project can be effective in the case of not the sole participation of the state, but by attracting private business, which has a wealth of experience in evaluating the effectiveness of projects under tough competition.

An analysis of the current situation shows the presence of the main structural problems of Kazakhstan.

One of the main problems is too large a share and the role of the state in a market economy.

The second important problem, in our opinion, is undeveloped entrepreneurship, free competition and market relations. Therefore, we believe that in order to successfully meet the challenges posed by the digitalization program, first of all, one must carry out political liberalization in accordance with the "Kazakhstan 2050" strategy, which allows to create healthy, real political competition. In addition, the prerequisite for success is a final and irrevocable victory over corruption and existence of the rule of law.

The third major problem is the lack of full broadband Internet coverage in many areas. To solve the problem, huge financial investments are needed, and they can be provided only by the state.

Another important problem that arises as a result of the development and implementation of the latest information technologies is security.

First, the introduction of digitalization is a global trend and it affects all countries of the world and Kazakhstan is no exception. Modern digitalization can be compared with the industrial revolution that occurred 100 or more years ago.

Secondly, we believe that digitalization will have a positive impact on increasing the transparency of the processes taking place in the economy. For example, the blockchain as a mechanism is convenient and it allows everyone to control their request from the moment of its assembly and delivery to the final customer as well as the movement of any service or product. Digitalization has many advantages, but at the same time it initiates a large number of vulnerable zones. This applies to the security of personal information, secret information, etc. In turn, the increasing complexity and improvement of the data protection system will inevitably lead to the growth of hacker professionalism. Unfortunately, in this regard,

Kazakhstan is on the periphery, because we do not have our own developments in the cyber security system. For example, even in countries with powerful cyber defense systems, a much larger staff of professional, competent and experienced IT specialists, hackers hack and gain access to secret data. Kazakhstan's cyber defense system lags far behind in terms of security and vulnerability from the aforementioned countries. There are real problems with the level of professionalism of those professionals who provide such security. It can be stated that Kazakhstan specialists still need to learn a lot in order to gain the professional skills that many foreign hacker groups have. It should be noted that so-called international hacker groups are being created. Over the past decade, legal practice has resulted in many cases of accusing top-notch specialists from different countries who deal a powerful blow to secret databases in various fields.

In Kazakhstan, there are problems related to corruption. Under such conditions, it is very difficult to guarantee complete security in the protection of any personal data. Countries where there is a longer tradition of ensuring the security of information data suffer from the human factor, which plays a key role. An example is the situation with Snowden, who worked for a long time in the special services, the national security agency, then for one reason or another, he decided to go against the system and began to merge secret information that the United States considers secret.

Literature

Katasonov, V. (n.d.). *China digitized.* Retrieved 4.3.2019, from https://www.fondsk.ru/news/20/02/22/kitay-ocifrovannyj-43590.html

Krasnushkina, N. (2019). *The White House started digitalization. The government is ready to start the program.* Retrieved 4.3.2019, from https://www.kommersant.ru/doc/3423672

n.n. (2017). *Concerning the Approval of the Digital Economy of the Russian Federation Program.* Retrieved 4.3.2019, from http://static.government.ru/media/files/9gFM4FHj4PsB79I5v7yLVuPgu4bvR7M0.pdf

n.n. (n.d. a). *China's Digital Economy A Leading Global Force.* Retrieved 4.3.2019, from file:///C:/Users/Leonid/Downloads/MGI-Chinas-digital-economy-A-leading-global-force.pdf

n.n. (n.d. b). *Digital economy big job creator.* Retrieved 4.3.2019, from http://www.shanghaidaily.com/business/finance/Digital-economy-big-

PlusMagazine. (2019). *The Council on Digital Economy and Blockchain Technologies was created in the State Duma.* Retrieved 4.3.2019, from http://www.plusworld.ru/daily/tehnologii/sovet-po-tsifrovoj-ekonomike-i-blokchejn-tehnologiyam-sozdali-v-gosdume-2//

Revenko, N. (2017). *US Digital Economy in the Age of Information Globalization. Current Trends. USA - Canada: Conomy - Politics - Culture.* (8 ed.).

TACC. (n.d.). *Dvorkovich invited foreign companies to participate in the digital economy program.* Retrieved 4.3.2019, from http://tass.ru/ekonomika/4606722

Theory China Resource of Understanding China. (2019). *Digital Economy: China's new transformation growth variable.* Retrieved 4.3.2019, from http://ru.theorychina.org/xsqy_2477/201701/t20170111_349538.shtml

U.S. Departament of Commerce. (n.d.). *Digital Economy. Information of the U.S. Departament of Commerce.* Retrieved 4.3.2019, from https://www.commerce.gov/news/blog/2015/11/commerce-departments-digital-economy-agenda

Exit from degenerate mode in linear programming

H. Geldiyev, Y. Seyisov, M. Churiyev, J. Geldiyev

1 Introduction

We will note the system of limitations within the problem of linear programming (LP)

$$\begin{cases} x_1 + a_{1,m+1} x_{m+1} + \ldots + a_{1n} x_n = b_1, \\ \ldots\ldots\ldots\ldots\ldots\ldots\ldots\ldots \\ x_\nu + a_{\nu,m+1} x_{m+1} + \ldots + a_{\nu n} x_n = b_\nu, \\ \ldots\ldots\ldots\ldots\ldots\ldots\ldots\ldots \end{cases} \quad (1)$$

$$x_m + a_{m,m+1} x_{m+1} + \ldots + a_{mn} x_n = b_m,$$

$$x_i \geq 0, \ i = \overline{1,n}. \quad (2)$$

A linear form is a criteria of optimality

$$L(\boldsymbol{X}) = (\boldsymbol{C}, \boldsymbol{X}) \quad (3)$$

We will designate

$$\Delta_\mu = c_\mu - \sum_{i=1}^{m} a_{i\mu}$$

When $\theta_\mu > 0$ the presence of non-basis vector provides $\Delta L = \theta_\mu \, \Delta_\mu$ increase. That is why when the task is solved, a linear programming problem occurs when for all A_μ c $\Delta_\mu > 0$ non-basis vectors are corresponding $\theta_\mu = 0$. We will call this situation *problematic*. For a problematic situation to occur presence of a zero element b_iy of the *b* vector is enough. Let, $b_1 = 0$, other b_i are positive only. Then the first equality of the system (1) looks like this

$$x_1 + a_{1,m+1} x_{m+1} + \cdots + a_{1n} x_n = 0. \quad (4)$$

If all $a_{1j} > 0, \ j = \overline{m+1,n}$ then it turns out that,

$$\theta_\mu = \min\left\{\frac{b_i}{a_{i\mu}}: \ a_{i\mu} > 0, \ i = \overline{1,\mathrm{m}}\right\} = 0, \ \ \mu = \overline{\mathrm{m}+1,\mathrm{n}} \quad (5)$$

Presence of at least one b_i zero element of the $\boldsymbol{b}$ vector corresponds to degeneracy of the supporting plan in the theory of linear programming. Thus, it turns out that

H.-C. Brauweiler et al. (Hrsg.), *Digitalization and Industry 4.0: Economic and Societal Development*, https://doi.org/10.1007/978-3-658-27110-7_11

the demand of the absence of degenerate modes in works on linear programming obviously presumes absence of problematic situations. But there is no guarantee that the whole process of consequent approaches to the solvation of linear programming (e.g. by simplex method) will pass only through non-generate supporting plans.

2 Equations for variations

Equations (1) can be interpreted as decomposition of $b \in R^m$ to $A_j, j = \overline{1,n}$,c vectors with negative coefficients x_j.

This vector has a decomposition on vectors $A_i = e_i,\ i = \overline{1,m}$

$$b = \sum_{j=1}^{m} x_j A_j,\ \ x_j \geq 0.$$

We are interested in possible participation of a non-basis in decomposition of determined vector $b \geq 0$. The main question: what if for all A_j c $\Delta_j > 0$ it is $\theta_j = 0$? Let $0 \leq k < m$, k be number of zeroes of $\boldsymbol{b}$ vector. Without belittling commonality of the considered problem, let's assume, that the first k coordinates of $\boldsymbol{b}$ vector are equal to zero, while other *m-k* coordinates are *positive only*. The system of limitations-equations in the task looks like this

$$\begin{cases} x_1 + a_{1,m+1} x_{m+1} + \ldots + a_{1n} x_n = 0, \\ \ldots\ldots\ldots\ldots\ldots\ldots\ldots\ldots\ldots \\ x_k + a_{k,m+1} x_{m+1} + \ldots + a_{kn} x_n = 0, \\ x_{k+1} + a_{k+1,m+1} x_{m+1} + \ldots + a_{k+1,n} x_n = b_{k+1} \\ \ldots\ldots\ldots\ldots\ldots\ldots\ldots\ldots\ldots \\ x_m + a_{m,m+1} x_{m+1} + \ldots + a_{mn} x_n = b_m. \end{cases} \quad (6)$$

$\boldsymbol{I_0}$ - plan is obviously the vector below

For smaller variations

$$\begin{aligned} x_i &= \vartheta_i, & i &= \overline{1,k}, \\ x_i &= b_i + \vartheta_i, & i &= \overline{k+1,\ m}, \\ x_i &= \vartheta_i, & i &= \overline{m+1,\ n}, \end{aligned} \quad (7)$$

we will get correlations

$$\begin{cases} \vartheta_1 + a_{1,m+1}\vartheta_{m+1} + \ldots + a_{1n}\vartheta_n = 0, \\ \ldots\ldots\ldots\ldots\ldots\ldots\ldots\ldots\ldots\ldots \\ \vartheta_k + a_{k,m+1}\vartheta_{m+1} + \ldots + a_{kn}\vartheta_n = 0, \\ \vartheta_{k+1} + a_{k+1,m+1}\vartheta_{m+1} + \ldots + a_{k+1,n}\vartheta_n = 0, \\ \ldots\ldots\ldots\ldots\ldots\ldots \\ \vartheta_m + a_{m,m+1}\vartheta_{m+1} + \ldots + a_{mn}\vartheta_n = 0, \end{cases} \tag{8}$$

which are in conference with the conditions

$$\begin{aligned} x_i &= \vartheta_i \geq 0, & i &= \overline{1,k}, \\ x_i &= b_i + \vartheta_i \geq 0, & i &= \overline{k+1,\ m}, \\ x_i &= \vartheta_i \geq 0, & i &= \overline{m+1,\ n}, \end{aligned} \tag{9}$$

determine possible variations of ϑ_i , $i = \overline{1,n}$ in point $\boldsymbol{X_0}$. Because $b_i > 0$ when $i = \overline{k+1,\ m}$ then in smaller variations ϑ_i , $i = \overline{k+1,\ m}$, inequalities will be considered, so only these limitations will be active

$$\begin{aligned} \vartheta_i &\geq 0, & i &= \overline{1,k}, \\ \vartheta_i &\geq 0, & i &= \overline{m+1,\ n}, \end{aligned} \tag{10}$$

and ϑ_i , $i = \overline{k+1,\ m}$ variations are free and can positive and negative values. Thus, smaller variations are characterized only with the first k equations of the system (1).

Now we will get an expression for ΔL variation of quality function L($\boldsymbol{X}$). taking into accounts the equations (8).

$$\begin{aligned} L(X) &= \sum_{i=1}^{n} c_i x_i = \sum_{i=1}^{k} c_i \vartheta_i + \sum_{i=k+1}^{m} c_i(b_i + \vartheta_i) + \sum_{i=m+1}^{n} c_i \vartheta_i = \\ &= -\sum_{i=1}^{k} c_i \sum_{j=m+1}^{n} a_{ij}\vartheta_i + \sum_{i=k+1}^{m} c_i b_i = \sum_{i=k+1}^{m} c_i \sum_{j=m+1}^{n} a_{ij}\vartheta_j + \sum_{i=m+1}^{n} c_i \vartheta_i = \\ &= L(X_0) + \sum_{i=m+1}^{n} c_i \vartheta_i - \sum_{j=m+1}^{n} \sum_{i=1}^{m} a_{ij} c_i \vartheta_j = L(X_0) + \sum_{i=m+1}^{n} c_i \vartheta_i - \sum_{i=m+1}^{n} \sum_{j=1}^{m} a_{ji} c_j \vartheta_i = \\ &= L(X_0) + \sum_{i=m+1}^{n} \left(c_i - \sum_{j=1}^{m} a_{ji} c_j \right) \vartheta_i = L(X_0) + \sum_{i=m+1}^{n} \Delta_i \vartheta_i \end{aligned}$$

Thus,

$$\Delta L = L(X) - L(X_0) = \sum_{i=m+1}^{n} \Delta_I \vartheta_i$$

We will designate

$$\vartheta_0 = \Delta L, \quad a_{0i} = -\Delta_i, \quad \left(i = \overline{m+1, n}\right)$$

Then expression (11) can be rewritten like this

$$\vartheta_0 + a_{0,m+1}\vartheta_{m+1} + \dots\dots\dots + a_{0n}\vartheta_n = 0$$

Now occurs the issue of possible direction on point X_0, during the movement along which linear form L(X) will get positive ΔL increment, comes to finding out the solution of the system:

$$\begin{cases} \vartheta_0 + a_{0,m+1} \ \vartheta_{m+1} + \dots + a_{0n}\vartheta_n = 0, \\ \vartheta_1 + a_{1,m+1} \ \vartheta_{m+1} + \dots + a_{1n}\vartheta_n = 0, \\ \dots\dots\dots\dots\dots\dots\dots\dots\dots\dots \\ \vartheta_k + a_{k,m+1} \ \vartheta_{m+1} + \dots + a_{kn}\vartheta_n = 0, \\ \vartheta_0 > 0, \end{cases} \tag{11}$$

$$\vartheta_i \geq 0, \quad i = \overline{1, k}, \quad i = \overline{m+1, n}. \tag{12}$$

It is assumed that $V^\circ = \left(\vartheta_0, \vartheta_1, \dots \vartheta_k, \vartheta_{m+1}, \dots \vartheta_n\right)$ is the solution of the system, which satisfies the limitations (12). Due to the homogeneity of the equation (11), vector $\mu V^\circ, \mu \geq 0$ is also the solution, that is why when

$$x_i = \mu\vartheta_i, \quad i = \overline{1, k}, \quad i = \overline{m+1, n}$$

first *k* equations of the system are done (6), other equations (m-k) will be written in this form

$$\begin{cases} x_{k+1} = b_{k+1} - \mu\left(a_{k+1,\,m+1}\vartheta_{m+1} + \dots + a_{k+1,n}\vartheta_n\right) \\ \dots\dots\dots\dots\dots\dots\dots\dots\dots\dots\dots\dots \\ x_m = b_m - \mu\left(a_{m,\,m+1} \ \vartheta_{m+1} + \dots + a_{m,n}\vartheta_n\right) \end{cases} \tag{13}$$

Because $b_i > 0,\ i = \overline{k+1, m}$ positivity of those coordinates when μ=0 is provided. And, if если $V^\circ \neq 0$ then the computation process of continuous improvement of I_0-plan can be done, meanwhile selecting the value $\mu = \overline{\mu}$ from the condition

$$\overline{\mu} = \min_{k+1 \le j \le m} \frac{b_j}{\sum_{i=m+1}^{n} a_{ji} \vartheta_i} = \frac{b_v}{\sum_{i=m+1}^{n} a_{vi} \vartheta_i} \tag{14}$$

While quality function ***L(x)*** will get positive increment

$$\Delta L = \overline{\mu} \vartheta_0,$$

An important distinctive feature from the standard simplex must be noted: not one, but some kind of a linear combination of non-basis vectors are entered into basis.

3 Criteria of optimality of generate mode

We will write out a task which is connected to the analysis of possible variations in case of appearance of generate modes during the solution process of the LP task.

Derivative task: Find the solution of the equation system (11) in the presence of limitations (12).

We will enter *(k+1)*-dimensional Euclidean space $\boldsymbol{R}^{k+1}$ with $\boldsymbol{U} = (u_0, u_1, \ldots, u_k)$ elements. Singular orts R^{k+1} will be designated $e_0, e_1, \ldots, e_k$. With help of vectors

$$\Gamma_j = (\Delta_j, a_{1j}, \ldots, a_{kj})^T,\ j = \overline{m+1,\ n},$$

$$\Gamma_j = (0, e_j), \qquad j = \overline{1, k},$$

we will build a cone

$$K^\# = \{\, U: U = \textstyle\sum_{j=1}^{k} \vartheta_j \Gamma_j + \sum_{j=m+1}^{n} \vartheta_j \Gamma_j,\ \vartheta_j \ge 0, \},$$

Lemma 1. If $e_0 \notin K^\#$, then $\boldsymbol{\psi} = (\Psi_1, \ldots, \Psi_k)$: $\Psi_j \ge 0$, $j = \overline{1, k}$ exists, which in turn means

$$-\Delta_j + \textstyle\sum_{i=1}^{k} \Psi_i a_{ij} \ge 0,\ j = \overline{m+1,\ n}; \tag{15}$$

Proof. If $e_0 \notin K^\#$, then on any $\varepsilon > 0$ point $U(\varepsilon)=\varepsilon e_0 \notin K^\#$. According to separability theorem[1] are a reference plane exits

$$(\boldsymbol{\psi}^\#, U) = 0; \tag{16}$$

which is

$$(\boldsymbol{\psi}^\#, U) \geq 0 \quad \text{для} \quad U \in K^\#,$$

$$(\boldsymbol{\psi}^\#, U(\varepsilon)) < 0\,. \tag{17}$$

From the last inequality we have

$$(\boldsymbol{\psi}^\#, U(\varepsilon)) \;=\; (\boldsymbol{\psi}^\#, \varepsilon e_0) \;= \varepsilon\, (\boldsymbol{\psi}^\#, e_0) = \varepsilon\, \Psi_0 \; < 0$$

at any $\varepsilon > 0$. This implies that $\Psi_0 < 0$. That is why we can place $\Psi_0 = -1$ and show equation (16) like written below

$$-\vartheta_0 + \sum_{j=1}^{k} \Psi_j\, \vartheta_j = 0.$$

When $\varepsilon \to 0$ condition (17) takes this look

$$(\boldsymbol{\psi}^\#, U) = -\vartheta_0 + \sum_{j=1}^{k} \Psi_j\, \vartheta_j \geq 0 \quad \text{для всех } U \in K^\#.$$

Because $\Gamma_j = (0, e_j) \in K^\#$,, $j=\overline{1,k}$, we will have

$$\Psi_j \geq 0 \quad \text{для} \quad j=\overline{1,k}, \tag{18}$$

and from the attribute $\Gamma_j = (\Delta_j, a_{1j}, \ldots, a_{kj})^T \in K^\#$, $j=\overline{m+1,\, n}$, derives $-\Delta_j + \sum_{i=1}^{k} \Psi_i\, a_{ij} \geq 0$, $j=\overline{m+1,\, n}$,

What is required to prove.

Lemma 2. If vector $\boldsymbol{\psi} = (\Psi_1, \ldots, \Psi_k)$: $\Psi_j \geq 0$, $j=\overline{1,k}$, which is

$$-\Delta_j + \sum_{i=1}^{k} \Psi_i\, a_{ij} \geq 0,\; j=\overline{m+1,\, n}, \tag{19}$$

then $e_0 \notin K^\#$.

Proof. Condition (19) means, that $K^\#$ cone is fully located in "positive" half-space

$$(\boldsymbol{\psi}^\#, U) \geq 0$$

---

1 See Beale (1955)

If $(\psi^{\#}, e_0) = -1$, then $e_0 \notin K^{\#}$. Lemma is proven.

The only solution of the task (11-12) is

$$\vartheta_i = 0, \quad i = \overline{0, k}, \quad i = \overline{m+1,\ n},$$

Theorem 1.3. For optimality of the generate *I*-plan it is necessary and enough for vector $\psi = (\Psi_1, \ldots, \Psi_k)$ exist:

$$\Psi_j \geq 0 \text{ для } j = \overline{1, k},$$

which is

$$-\Delta_j + \sum_{i=1}^{k} \Psi_i a_{ij} \geq 0, \quad j = \overline{m+1,\ n}.$$

Proof. Optimality of the generate *I*-plan implies the absence of possible directions in the first LP task, which in turn is equal to $e_0 \notin K^{\#}$ condition. When *lemma 1* is used the necessity of the conditions of the theorem will be proven.

Adequacy. We will assume that $X_0 = (0,0,\ldots,0, b_{k+1}, \ldots, b_m, 0,\ldots,0)$ - some I-plan in the initial LP task and for $j = \overline{1, k}$ exists $\psi = (\Psi_1, \ldots, \Psi_k): \Psi_j \geq 0$ vector, which is

$$-\Delta_j + \sum_{i=1}^{k} \Psi_i a_{ij} \geq 0, \quad j = \overline{m+1,\ n}.$$

According to lemma 2, vector e_0 does not belong to $K^{\#}$ cone and possible variation do not exist in the initial task. It means that X_0 – an optimal plan.

Theorem is proven.

4 Normalization

Task of the linear programming in its canonic form is written in this form:

$$\max \{ L(X) : AX = b,\ X \geq 0 \},$$

where A-matrix ($m \times n$) with a_{Ij} elements,

$$L(X) = (C, X), \quad C = (c_1, c_2, \ldots, c_n)^T,$$

$X = (x_1, x_2, \ldots, x_n)^T$ - vector with non-negative components.

It will be assumed that k is the number of zeroes of b vector. Without detracting commonality of the considered problem, presuming that the first k coordinates of the ***b*** vector are equal to zeror, while the other are *m-k* coordinates are *positive only*.

The issue of possible directions on the point $\boldsymbol{X_0}$ during the movement along which linear form L(***X***) will get positive increments, comes to finding out the existence of the solution of the derivative task (11,12).

Let's assume that,

$$A_j = (a_{0j}, a_{1j}, \ldots, a_{kj}), \qquad j = \overline{m+1, n},$$

$\|A_j\|$ - Euclidean length of A_j vector.

Presumably

$$A_j^* = \frac{A_j}{\|A_j\|}, \quad j = \overline{m+1, n}$$

$$\vartheta_j^* = \|A_j\| \vartheta_j, \quad j = \overline{m+1, n}.$$

Then the system (11)-(12) will be written in this form

$$\begin{cases} \vartheta_0 \qquad\qquad + a_{0,m+1}^* \vartheta_{m+1}^* + \cdots + a_{0n}^* \vartheta_n^* = 0 \\ \qquad \vartheta_1 \qquad + a_{1,m+1}^* \vartheta_{m+1}^* + \cdots + a_{1n}^* \vartheta_n^* = 0 \\ \quad \ldots \quad \ldots \quad \ldots \quad \ldots \quad \ldots \quad \ldots \quad \ldots \quad \ldots \\ \qquad\qquad \vartheta_k + a_{k,m+1}^* \vartheta_{m+1}^* + \cdots + a_{kn}^* \vartheta_n^* = 0 \end{cases} \tag{20}$$

$$\begin{cases} \vartheta_0 > 0 \\ \vartheta_i \geq 0, \quad i = \overline{1, k} \\ \vartheta_i \geq 0, \quad i = \overline{m+1, n} \end{cases}$$

and there will be this equality

$$\|A_j^*\| = 1, \qquad j = \overline{m+1, n}.$$

Noticing that the system (20) differs from the system (11)-(12) only with the existence of the index , henceforth we will assume that the derivative task is given by the system (1)-(2) and normalization conditions are done, i.e

$$\sum_{i=0}^{k} a_{ij}^2 = 1; \quad j = \overline{m+1,n}\,.$$

By designating $\boldsymbol{e_0}$, $\boldsymbol{e_1}$, ...,$\boldsymbol{e_k}$ are singular orts in the $\boldsymbol{R^{k+1}}$ space, then (11) system can be written in this form

$$\sum_{i=0}^{k} \vartheta_i e_i + \sum_{i=m+1}^{n} \vartheta_i A_i = 0\,. \tag{21}$$

5 Characteristics of the generate mode

With the letter $\boldsymbol{S}$ we will designate the sphere of the singular radius in the space $\boldsymbol{R^{k+1}}$. The ends of the $\boldsymbol{e_i}$, $i = \overline{0,k}$ orts and $\boldsymbol{A_i}$, $i = \overline{m+1,n}$ vectors are located in the sphere $\boldsymbol{S}$. Convex hull of these vectors will be a polyhedron with tops on points $\boldsymbol{e_i}$, $(i=0,k)$ and $\boldsymbol{A_i}$, $(i=m+1,n)$ written in the $\boldsymbol{S}$ sphere. It is known that any point of the convex limited polyhedron in $\boldsymbol{R^n}$ is shown in the form of a linear combination with coefficients α_i , but not more than $(n+1)$ tops of this polyhedron.

$$\sum_{i=1}^{n+1} \alpha_i = 1.$$

In this case the derivative task (1-2) comes to finding out the next issue: Is the center $\boldsymbol{O}$ of the $\boldsymbol{S}$ sphere an element of $\boldsymbol{M}$ polyhedron. Positive answer to this question means that there is a representation (21) with non-negative coefficients ϑ_i, $i=\overline{0,k}$, $i=\overline{m+1,n}$. If $\vartheta_0 > 0$ then the discovered variation provides positive increment to the criteria of the quality ΔL.

It turns out that the main feature of the generate mode is this value

$$S = \min\left(S_j = \sum_{i=0}^{k} a_{ij}, j = \overline{m+1,n} \right). \tag{22}$$

We will differentiate three situations according to that value:

1. $S \geq 0$;
2. $-1 \leq S < 0$;

3. S < -- 1.

Lemma 1. If S≥0, then possible variations providing positive ΔL increment are absent.

Proof. Taking into account these designations

$$\Delta_j = -a_{0j}, \qquad j = \overline{m+1,n}$$

we will rewrite the condition of the lemma like this

$$-\Delta_j + a_{1j} + \ldots + a_{kj} > 0, \qquad j = \overline{m+1,n}$$

i.e conditions of the optimality of the generate mode are fulfilled with

$$\Psi_i = 1, \; i = \overline{1,k}$$

Lemma is proven.

Consequence. If this condition is fulfilled

$$S = \min\left(-\Delta_j + \sum_{i=1}^{k} a_{ij},\; j = \overline{m+1,n}\right) \tag{23}$$

I – the plan of the initial task is optimal.

Lemma 2. If there exists A_j fulfilling these conditions

$$S_j = \sum_{i=0}^{k} a_{ij} < -1,$$

$$a_{ij} \le 0, \; i = \overline{1,k},$$

$$a_{0j} < 0,$$

then possible variations.

Proof. We will show that the *0* center of the *S* sphere is located in the convex hull of the vectors $e_0, e_1, \ldots e_k$ and A_j. The formula written below

$$A_j = \sum_{i=0}^{k} a_{ij} e_i, \quad \| A_j \| = 1,$$

means that

$$\sum_{i=0}^{k} a_{ij} e_i - A_j = 0.$$

Dividing both sides of this equation to $(S_j - 1)$ we will have

$$\sum_{i=0}^{k} \mu_i e_i + \mu_i A_j = 0. \tag{24}$$

According to the conditions of the lemma

$$\mu_0 = a_{0j}/(S_j - 1) > 0,$$
$$\mu_i = a_{ij}/(S_j - 1) \geq 0, \ i=\overline{1,k} \tag{25}$$
$$\mu_j = -1/(S_j - 1) \geq 0, \ i=\overline{1,k}$$

While

$$\sum_{i=0}^{k} \mu_i + \mu_j = (\sum_{i=0}^{k} a_{ij} - 1)/(s_j - 1) = 1.$$

Thus, we have shown that the beginning of $\boldsymbol{0}$ coordinates of the R^{k+1} space belongs to convex hull of the $e_0, e_1, \ldots e_k$ and $\boldsymbol{A}_j$ vectors, which means that $\boldsymbol{0} \in \boldsymbol{M}$, where $\boldsymbol{M}$ is the convex hull of $e_0, e_1, \ldots e_k, \boldsymbol{A}_{m+1}, \ldots, \boldsymbol{A}_n$ vectors.

By comparing (24) equality with (11) equations we will notice that

$$\vartheta_0 = t\mu_0 > 0,$$
$$\vartheta_i = t\mu_i \geq 0, \ i=\overline{0,k} \tag{26}$$
$$\vartheta_j = t\mu_j \geq 0,$$
$$\vartheta_i = 0, i = \overline{k+1, n}, i \neq j$$

can be possible variations at any $t > 0$. μ_i values are set with formulas (26). As noted before, inequality $\vartheta_0 > 0$ provides positive increment to ΔL quality criteria.

Lemma is proven.

Thus, when the S value of the generate mode set by formula (22) appears, in case 1 it indicates to the ending of the initial LP task, in case 3 – to existence of the possibility of further search of the optimal plan by classical simplex method. Case 2 remains a problem.

6 Search of the possible variations

We will assume that $a_{0\mu} > 0$. We will make transformation (1:356) of the system (1) by recording it in the new basis, formed from the basis $\boldsymbol{e_0}, \boldsymbol{e_1}, \ldots, \boldsymbol{e_k}$ by switching e_0 to $\boldsymbol{e_\mu}$. $\boldsymbol{A_\mu}$ vector has a coordinate $a_{0\mu} = 0$, a $a_{\nu\mu} > 0$, then it will be necessary to replace the equation of the system (1) to the first place.

$$\begin{cases} \alpha_{00}\, \vartheta_0 + \alpha_{0,m+1}\, \vartheta_{m+1} + \ldots + \vartheta_\mu + \ldots + \alpha_{0n}\, \vartheta_n = 0, \\ \ldots\ldots\ldots\ldots\ldots\ldots\ldots\ldots\ldots \\ \alpha_{\nu 0}\, \vartheta_0 + \vartheta_\nu + \alpha_{\nu,m+1}\, \vartheta_{m+1} + \ldots + 0 + \ldots + \alpha_{\nu n}\, \vartheta_n = 0, \\ \ldots\ldots\ldots\ldots\ldots\ldots\ldots\ldots\ldots \\ \alpha_{k0}\, \vartheta_0 + \vartheta_k + \ldots + \alpha_{k,m+1}\, \vartheta_{m+1} + \ldots + 0 + \ldots + \alpha_{kn}\, \vartheta_n = 0, \end{cases}$$

$$\alpha_{00} = 1/a_{0\mu},$$

$$\alpha_{0j} = a_{0j}/a_{0\mu}, \qquad j = m+1, \ldots, n, \tag{27}$$

$$\alpha_{i0} = -a_{i\mu}/a_{0\mu}, \qquad i = 1, \ldots k,$$

$$\alpha_{ij} = a_{ij} - a_{i\mu}\, a_{0j}/a_{0\mu}, \qquad i = 1, \ldots, \kappa.$$

In (k+1)-dimensioned Euclidean space $\boldsymbol{R}_1^{k+1}$ with orthonormal basis $\boldsymbol{e_\mu}, \boldsymbol{e_1}, \ldots, \boldsymbol{e_k}$ form an orthonormal basis. Equation of the hyperplane $\Pi_0^{\#}$ which moves through the ends of these vectors will be written in this form

$$\vartheta_\mu + \vartheta_1 + \vartheta_2 + \ldots + \vartheta_k - 1 = 0.. \tag{28}$$

Indeed, by using formulas (26) we will have

$$1/a_{0\mu} - a_{1\mu}/a_{0\mu} - \ldots - a_{k\mu}/a_{0\mu} - 1 = (1 - a_\mu)/a_{0\mu} - 1 =$$

$$= (1 - S_\mu + a_{0\mu})/a_{0\mu} - 1 = (1 - S_\mu)/a_{0\mu} > 0.$$

Elementary transformation used before defines some display $\boldsymbol{A}_j \to \boldsymbol{A}_j^{\#}$. We will have normalization of $\boldsymbol{A}_j^{\#}$ vectors and review a display

$$\boldsymbol{A}_j \to \boldsymbol{A}_j^{\#} / \| \boldsymbol{A}_j^{\#} \| . \tag{29}$$

We will designate the sum of the coordinates of $\boldsymbol{A} \in \boldsymbol{R}_1^{k+1}$ vector through $S^{\#}(\boldsymbol{A})$. Coordinates of $\boldsymbol{e}_0^{\#}$ vector fulfills the inequality (12), i.e

$$\alpha_{00} + \alpha_{10} + \ldots + \alpha_{k0} \geq 1.$$

Consequently, for singular vector $\boldsymbol{e}_0^{\#} / \| \boldsymbol{e}_0^{\#} \| \in \boldsymbol{R}_1^{k+1}$.

$$S^{\#}(\boldsymbol{e}_0^{\#} / \| \boldsymbol{e}_0^{\#} \|) =$$

$$= \alpha_{00} / \| \boldsymbol{e}_0^{\#} \| + \alpha_{10} / \| \boldsymbol{e}_0^{\#} \| + \ldots + \alpha_{k0} / \| \boldsymbol{e}_0^{\#} \| \geq 1 / \| \boldsymbol{e}_0^{\#} \| > 0 \qquad (30)$$

Summary. As a result of an elementary transformation with further normalization while fulfilling the conditions of the theorem 1 when $v = 0$, the next switch will take place:

$$\boldsymbol{A}_\mu \rightarrow \boldsymbol{e}_\mu,$$

$$\boldsymbol{e}_0 \rightarrow \boldsymbol{e}_0^{\#} / \| \boldsymbol{e}_0^{\#} \|,$$

and $\boldsymbol{e}_i$ ($i = \overline{1, k}$) vectors remain unchanged. We managed to build a hyperplane in $\boldsymbol{R}_1^{k+1}$ space,

$$S^{\#} = \vartheta_\mu + \vartheta_1 + \vartheta_2 + \ldots + \vartheta_k = 0, \qquad (31)$$

so that the figures of $\boldsymbol{A}_\mu$, $\boldsymbol{e}_0, \boldsymbol{e}_1, \ldots, \boldsymbol{e}_k$ points are in positive half space

$$S^{\#} = \vartheta_\mu + \vartheta_1 + \vartheta_2 + \ldots + \vartheta_k \geq 0,$$

while, $S_\mu < 0$, and the ends of $\boldsymbol{e}_1, \ldots, \boldsymbol{e}_k$ vectors are located at $S > 0$.

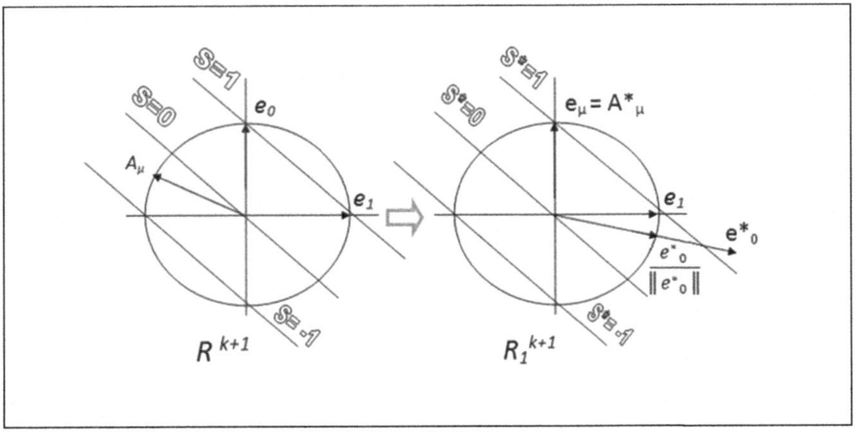

Figure 1: Elementary transformation with normalization

Henceforth we will analyze the situation in the space $\boldsymbol{R}_1^{k+1}$.

1. If S# $\geq$ 0, then possible variations providing positive ΔL increment are absent (lemma 1).
2. If Aμ fulfilling conditions written below exists:

   $S^{\#} < -1, \quad a_{0\mu} > 0,$

   $a_{i\mu} \leq 0, \quad i = \overline{1,k}\,,$

then various variations that allow to give ΔL positive increment in linear form are found.

3. Finally, if condition 1 or condition 2 is not fulfilled, then the problem will remain. It will be necessary to repeat the operations expressed in p.3 – it will the second step on finding possible variations if they exist.

In conclusion, we note that $\boldsymbol{A}_\mu$ vector giving minimum

$$S = \min\,(S_j = \textstyle\sum_{i=0}^{k} a_{ij}\,,\, j = \overline{m+1,n}),$$

is selected for entering into basis, then the number of steps necessary to find out the problematic situation is reduced to minimum. This statement comes from the next theorem.

Theorem 2.6.

1. Aμ - vector fulfills the condition a0μ > 0,--1 $\leq$ S < 0,
2. --1 $\leq$ S < 0,
3. Aj vector is located in the positive half space Π0 μ+, i.e

$$\psi_0\, a_{0j} + a_j - 1 \geq 0, \tag{32}$$

where

$$\Psi_0 = (1 - a_\mu)/\, a_{0\mu}\,, \qquad a_j = a_{1j} + \ldots + a_{kj} = S_j - a_{0j},$$

then figure $\boldsymbol{A}_j^{\#}$ of the $\boldsymbol{A}_j$ vector is located in the half space (31).

Proof. We will rewrite the inequality (32).

$$a_{0j}\,(1 - S_\mu + a_{0\mu})/\, a_{0\mu} + S_j - a_{0j} - 1 = a_{0j}\,(1 - S_\mu)/\, a_{0\mu} + S_j - 1 \geq 0. \tag{33}$$

By using formulas (28) and (33) we will have

$$\alpha_{0j} + \alpha_{1j} + \alpha_{2j} + \ldots + \alpha_{kj} - 1 = a_{0j}/\, a_{0\mu} + S_j - a_{0j} - (S_\mu - a_{0\mu})\, a_{0j}/\, a_{0\mu} - 1 =$$

$$= (1 - S_\mu)\, a_{0j}/\, a_{0\mu} + S_j - 1 = (1 - S_\mu)\, a_{0j} + (S_j - 1)\, a_{0\mu} \geq 0.$$

Theorem is proven. This theorem has a common character and is usable if $\boldsymbol{A}_{\mu}$ vector has at least on $a_{v\mu}$ element. If the v. equation of the system (1) is moved to the first place condition of the 1 theorem will be fulfilled.

We will review an example Beale (2:270):

$$Max\ (10x_1 - 57x_2 - 9x_3 - 24x_4),$$

$$\begin{cases} 0{,}5\,x_1 - 5{,}5\,x_2 - 2{,}5\,x_3 + 9\,x_4 + x_5 = 0, \\ 0{,}5\,x_1 - 1{,}5\,x_2 - 0{,}5\,x_3 + x_4 + x_6 = 0, \\ x_1 + x_7 = 1, \end{cases} \tag{34}$$

$$x_i \geq 0, \quad i = \overline{1{,}7}.$$

Let's form a derivative task

Basis	A1	A2	A3	A4	A0	A5	A6
0	-10	57	9	24	1	0	0
5	0,5	-5,5	-2,5	9	0	1	0
6	0,5	-1,5	-0,5	1	0	0	1
‖*‖1	10,025	57,2864	9,3541	25,6515			

We will execute an operation of normalization.

BASIS	A1	A2	A3	A4	A0	A5	A6
0	-0,99751	0,995036	0,96214	0,935617	1	0	0
5	0,049875	-0,09601	-0,26726	0,350857	0	1	0
6	0,049875	-0,02619	-0,05345	0,038984	0	0	1
S	-0,89776	0,872838	0,641427	1,325458			

It turned out that the least S belongs to column A_1. Because there are two equal positive elements in that column, we choose the first of them. After the elementary transformation we will have.

BASIS	A1	A2	A3	A4	A0	A5	A6
0	0	-0,92521	-4,38308	7,952748	1	20	0
A1	1	-1,92504	-5,35857	7,034652	0	20,04994	0
6	0	0,069827	0,213809	-0,31187	0	-1	1
‖*‖2	1	2,137	6,9261	10,6221	1	28,3372	1
‖*‖×‖*‖	10,025	122,421	64,7878	272,473	1	28,3372	1

The first step is finished. We execute the normalization process again:

BASIS	A1	A2	A3	A4	A0	A5	A6
0	0	-0,43295	-0,63283	0,748696	1	0,705785	0
A1	1	-0,90082	-0,77367	0,662263	0	0,707547	0
6	0	0,032676	**0,03087**	-0,02936	0	-0,03529	1
S		-1,3011	***-1,37564***	1,381598		1,378042	

Min S is reached at A_3, which has only positive component that is located on the third string. After the elementary transformation we will have

BASIS	A1	A2	A3	A4	A0	A5	A6
0	0	0,236899	0	0,146803	1	***-0,01764***	20,5
A1	1	-0,08189	0	-0,07358	0	***-0,17689***	25,06242
A3	0	1,058497	1	-0,95111	0	***-1,14316***	32,39406

Min S is reached at A_5 , all of its components are negative.

So,

$$x_0^{\#} = 0{,}01764\ \mu,$$

$$x_1^{\#} = 0{,}17689\ \mu, \qquad x_2^{\#} = x_4^{\#} = x_6^{\#} = 0,$$

$$x_3^{\#} = 1{,}14316\ \mu,$$

$$x_5^{\#} = 1{,}00000\ \mu,$$

is the solution of twice transformed derivative task at any $\mu \geq 0$. The solution of the derivative task is:

$$x_0 = x_0^{\#} / \|A_0\|_1 \times \|A_0\|_2 = 0{,}01764\ \mu,$$

$$x_1 = x_1^{\#} / \|\mathbf{A_1}\|_1 \times \|A_1\|_2 = 0{,}01764\ \mu,$$

$$x_3 = x_3^{\#} / \|A_3\|_1 \times \|A_3\|_2 = 0{,}01764\ \mu,$$

$$x_5 = x_5^{\#} / \|A_5\|_1 \times \|A_5\|_2 = 0{,}03529\ \mu$$

$$x_2 = x_4 = x_6 = 0.$$

For performing the last equality of the system (34)

$$x_1 + x_7 = 1$$

and $x_7 \geq 0$ condition

$$0{,}01764\ \mu \leq 1,$$

is necessary.

So,

$$max\ \mu = 56{,}6893$$

and the solution of the initial task is written out:

$$x_0 = x_1 = x_3 = 1,$$

$$x_2 = x_4 = x_6 = 0,$$

$$x_5 = 2,$$

$$Max\ (\ 10x_1 - 57x_2 - 9x_3 - 24x_4\ ) = x_0 = 1.$$

It took us to make two steps for solving the derivative task.

Using Bland's rule (3:103) Beale task is performed in seven steps (4:67).

Literature

Beale, E. (1955). *Cycling in the dual simplex algorithm. Naval Research Logistics Quarterly 2.*

Bland, R. (1977). *New finite pivoting rules for the simplex method. Mathematics of Operations Research 2.*

Ferris, M., Mangasarian, O., Wrigt, S. (2007). *Linear Programming with MATLAB. MPS – SIAM Series on Optimization.*

Yudin, D., Holstein, E. (1969). *Линейное программирование (теория, методы и приложения). (in Russian).* Наука.

Part B: Economy

Wirtschaftlich optimale Heizöltechnologie auf Basis von Heatpipes

Hajymuhammet Geldiyev, Patshakuli Atayev, Nuraly Hudaykuliyev, Durjahan Atayeva

Heute ist Öl einer der wichtigsten Bestandteile des Weltmarktes für Brennstoffe und Energieressourcen und wird in vielen Bereichen der Weltwirtschaft verwendet. Infolge dieser Tatsache ist es eine der wichtigsten Aufgaben für das Erdöl exportierenden Länder, einen qualitativ hochwertigen Öltransport auf der Grundlage energiesparender und feuersicherer Technologien durchzuführen.

Die Zusammensetzung des abgepumpten Öleinsatzmaterials umfaßt nicht nur Öl, sondern auch andere mechanische und hydraulische Verunreinigungen wie Sand, Wasseremulsion, Schwefel und andere. Daher überschätzt die Ölviskosität die erforderliche technologische Rate zu sehr, was sich negativ auf den Pipeline-Transportprozess auswirkt. In diesem Zusammenhang werden in der Nähe der Felder Ölheizöfen installiert, die auf der Grundlage der Verbrennung großer Mengen an Begleitgas oder anderer Brennstoffe betrieben werden. In speziellen Ölheizöfen wird das Öl auf eine Temperatur von +60°C und höher auf die geforderte Leistung erhitzt, wodurch der Ölfluss durch die Rohrleitungen normalisiert wird.[1]

In Turkmenistan sowie in anderen Ölstaaten, werden hauptsächlich Ölheizöfen des Typs PTB-10 verwendet. Diese Öfen können pro Stunde 416 Tonnen Öl auf +60°C erwärmen und pro Stunde 1940 m^3 Gas verbrennen. In diesen Öfen wird natürliches oder zugehöriges Erdöl-Gas als Brennstoff verwendet.[2] Experten zufolge ist dies ein großer Energieverlust entlang der Pipelines der Pipeline und schädigt gleichzeitig das ökologische System der Umwelt. Aus wissenschaftlicher Sicht ist es daher sehr wichtig, dass das Öl mit minimalem Energieverlust schnell und effizient erhitzt wird. Um dieses industrielle Problem zu lösen, haben wir uns ein Ziel gesetzt – eine absolut neue Technologie für Heizöl, das durch Rohrleitungen transportiert wird, mit minimiertem Energieverlust, mit hoher Heizleistung und minimalen Finanz- und Materialkosten sowie ohne Umweltbelastung.

Geleitet von den grundlegenden technischen Informationsmaterialien zu Wärmerohren, haben wir diese Rohre mehrere Jahre lang wiederholt auf Wärmeleit-

---

1 Vgl. Geldiyev, Atayev, Hudaykuliyev, 2017
2 Vgl. Geldiyev, Atayev, Hudaykuliyev, 2017

H.-C. Brauweiler et al. (Hrsg.), *Digitalization and Industry 4.0: Economic and Societal Development*, https://doi.org/10.1007/978-3-658-27110-7_12

fähigkeit, Verschleißfestigkeit und die Fähigkeit getestet, in verschiedenen Umgebungen zu arbeiten. Wir haben die optimale Variante des Heat Pipe gewählt.

Ein "Heatpipe" ist ein Element eines Heiz- oder Kühlsystems, dessen Prinzip auf der Tatsache beruht, dass eine niedrigsiedende Flüssigkeit (zum Beispiel Wasser) in einem wärmeleitenden geschlossenen Rohr (zum Beispiel in einem zylindrischen Kupferrohr) verdampft. Die Wärmeübertragung in diesem Gerät erfolgt aufgrund der Tatsache, dass die Flüssigkeit auf ihrer heißen Seite verdampft, der Dampf sich entlang der Länge des Arbeitshohlraums ausbreitet, auf der kalten Seite des Rohrs kondensiert und in die erste Heizzone zurückfließt.[3]

Für Tests unter Laborbedingungen wurde ursprünglich ein Wärmerohr aus einem zylindrischen Kupfermetall mit einer Länge von 35 cm und einem Außendurchmesser von 2 cm hergestellt und ein Gitter aus Messing als Docht in das Wärmerohr eingeführt. Das entstehende Wärmerohr wurde mehrmals von innen mit Alkohol und doppelt destilliertem Wasser gereinigt. Dann werden beide Rohrenden mit Kupfer verschweißt. Nach dem Schweißen wurde mit der Vakuumpumpe VUP-5 (also "VUP-5 – Vakuum Universal Post-5") ein Vakuumraum im Wärmerohr von 10^{-3} Torr geschaffen.

Als Arbeitsfluid wurde doppelt destilliertes Wasser mit einer Kapazität von 15 ml in das Innere des Wärmerohrs eingeführt, und ein Kanal aus einem Kapillar-Kupferrohr, das zum Injizieren einer Flüssigkeit vorgesehen war, wurde komprimiert und verschweißt. Ansonsten ein elektrisches Heizelement hergestellt wurde, um die thermophysikalischen Parameter eines experimentellen Wärmerohrs zu untersuchen. Dieses Heizelement wurde hergestellt, indem ein Kupferrohr mit einer Länge von 10 cm und einem Außendurchmesser von 2,2 cm verwendet wird, auf das eine Asbestseilschicht als Isolierung aufgewickelt wurde, dann eine elektrisch leitfähige Spule aus Nichromdraht und zwei weitere Schichten Asbestseil. Nach der Herstellung des Heizelements wurden die von der Innen- und Außenwand innerhalb von 10 Minuten erreichten Temperaturen in verschiedenen Indizes des angewandten elektrischen Reglers gemessen.

Als Ergebnis der Messungen wurde bestimmt, dass in Bezug auf "6" (23,2°C; 23,5°C), "7" (122,2°C; 98,7°C) und "8" (180,5°C; 124,4°C) optimale Temperaturen für die Versuche erreicht werden. Die maximale Temperatur, die dieses Heizelement erreicht, beträgt 180°C. Um die Wärmeleitfähigkeit des hergestellten Wärmerohrs zu testen, wurde das Heizelement an seinem unteren Teil befestigt, woraufhin die in verschiedenen Indikatoren des elektrischen Reglers erreichten Temperaturen bei Vorhandensein und Abwesenheit von Arbeitsfluid im inneren Hohlraum des Wärmerohrs gemessen wurden.

[3] Vgl. Geldiyev, Atayev, Hudaykuliyev, 2016a

Als Ergebnis der Messungen hat sich gezeigt, dass die maximale Temperatur, die erreicht wird, wenn im inneren Hohlraum des hergestellten Wärmerohrs kein Arbeitsfluid vorhanden ist, 72,4°C beträgt. Der Temperaturunterschied zwischen seiner anfänglichen Heizzone (72,4°C) und der Endkondensationszone (44,2°C) beträgt 32°C. Diese Ergebnisse zeigen, dass die Wärmeleitfähigkeit eines herkömmlichen Kupferrohrs ohne ein Arbeitsfluid im Inneren gering und ineffizient ist.

Als Ergebnis der Durchführung der gleichen Tests unter Verwendung eines Wärmerohrs mit einem Arbeitsfluid im Inneren wurde festgestellt, dass die erreichte Maximaltemperatur 115,4°C betrug. Die Temperaturdifferenz in diesem Fall zwischen der anfänglichen Heizzone des Wärmerohrs (115,4°C) und seiner Endkondensationszone (115,7°C) beträgt 0,3°C, das heißt, aufgrund seiner thermophysikalischen Grundlagen ist dies ein Hinweis darauf, dass das Wärmerohr hergestellt wurde technisch korrekt.[4]

Abbildung 1: 1. Herstellung eines experimentellen Wärmerohres. Hier bezeichnen die Zahlen: 1 – Heizelement, versehen mit einer Spirale aus Nichrome und einer Isolierung aus Asbestfasern; 2 – inneres Kupfergehäuse des Heizelements; 3 – Einbringen eines Messingnetzes in das Kupferrohr, das als wärmeleitende Kapillarstruktur verwendet wird; 4 – die endgültige Form der fertigen Heatpipe

Während der Experimente zeigte sich, dass die innere Kapillar-Docht-Struktur auf der Basis eines Messingnetzes mit einem äußeren Kupferkörper in Form eines Zylinders im Vergleich zu herkömmlichen Thermosyphonen oder Kupferrohren die beste Energieeffizienz aufweist. Nachdem das Wärmerohr hergestellt und seine thermischen Parameter gemessen worden waren, wurde das Design des Wärmetauscher Tanks erstellt. In der Mitte der Flansche wurden Löcher mit einem Durchmesser von 2 cm vorgebohrt, in die Kunststoffrohre für den Wasserfluss mit unterschiedlichen Geschwindigkeiten entlang der inneren Arbeitskammer des Wärmetauscher Tanks angebracht wurden.

4 Vgl. Geldiyev, Atayev, Hudaykuliyev, 2016b

Der Innendurchmesser der Heizeinrichtung beträgt 20 cm, der Außendurchmesser beträgt 21 cm, die Länge beträgt 40 cm Der Durchmesser des Lochs in seinem unteren Teil in der Mitte, das zum Einsetzen eines Wärmerohrs vorgesehen ist, beträgt 2,2 cm, und die Länge des ausgehenden Außendeingangs beträgt 4 cm Der Außendurchmesser des Einlasses beträgt 4,8 cm, der Innendurchmesser der Tankflansche beträgt 22 cm, der Außendurchmesser beträgt 30 cm, die Wandstärke der Flansche beträgt 0,8 cm, und für jeden Flansch werden im Voraus 8 Schraubenlöcher vorbereitet. Zusätzlich wurde die hergestellte Struktur mit zwei 12 cm langen und 28 cm breiten Eisenfüßen versehen, deren Gesamtmasse für Experimente 85 kg betrug. Fotos der hergestellten Testausrüstung sind in Abbildung 2 dargestellt.

Abbildung 2: Experimentelles Modell einer Ölheizungsanlage auf der Grundlage eines Wärmerohrs

Aufgrund der thermischen Parameter des Wärmerohrs, das für die experimentelle Ausrüstung hergestellt wird, die den Ölheizprozess simuliert, ist es technisch vorgesehen, Indikatoren 6, 7 und 8 des elektrischen Reglers des Heizelements zu verwenden, wenn der Fluidstrom durch den inneren Hohlraum des Wärmetauscher Tanks aktiviert wird.

Im Labor "Kompressor pump Einheiten und –Stationen" haben wir mit Hilfe einer speziellen Pumpe kaltes Wasser mit drei verschiedenen Geschwindigkeitsstufen in unsere Geräte eingeleitet und Temperaturparameter des Durchflusses in einem genau definierten Zeitraum erfasst: niedrige Geschwindigkeit (8 Liter/min oder 480 Liter/Stunde), durchschnittliche Geschwindigkeit (12 Liter/Minute oder 720 Liter/Stunde) und hohe Geschwindigkeit (20 Liter/Minute oder 1200 Liter/Stunde).

Wasserleitungsrohre aus Kunststoff wurden an Heizungsanlagen auf der Basis eines Wärmerohrs befestigt, und vor dem Einschalten des elektrischen Heizelements wurde am Eingang des Wärmetauscher Tanks eine Wassertemperatur von 18°C aufgezeichnet. Nach dem Beginn einer gestaffelten Wasserversorgung mit bestimmten Indikatoren der Strömungsgeschwindigkeit durch den inneren Hohlraum des Wärmetauscher Tanks wurde die Wassertemperatur am Auslass des Tanks alle 15 Minuten für jeden Indikator der Strömungsgeschwindigkeit getrennt gemessen. Die Ergebnisse der Versuche sind in der folgenden Tabelle dargestellt.

Tabelle 1: Ergebnisse der Versuche

Die Anzeige des Reglers des Heizelements	**Die erreichte Wärme in Bezug auf die aktuellen flüssigen Medium, °C, (t = 15 Minuten).**		
	Niedriger Niveau (8 Liter/min oder 480 Liter/Stunde)	**Durchschnittliches Niveau (12 Liter/min oder 720 Liter/Stunde)**	**Hohes Niveau (20 Liter/min oder 1200 Liter/Stunde)**
6	39,7	37,2	36,8
7	36,2	38,5	35,3
8	32,3	38,8	32,5

Als Ergebnis der Messungen der erforderlichen Parameter zeigte sich, dass mit zunehmender Anzahl von Wärmerohren in Anlagen (dh bis zu 4 Wärmerohre) ihre Anwendung in der Ölindustrie energieeffizient und technisch optimal sein wird.

Diese Erfindung, von uns entwickelte und patentierte, kann verwendet werden, um die erforderliche Viskosität von Öl und Ölprodukten beim Durchführen von Kraftstoff auszulassen, in Abschnitten der Rohrleitung und in Gefahrenbereichen, in denen eine Erwärmung von Transport Öl erforderlich ist, im Bereich der Energietechnik sowie zur Warmwasserversorgung in Wohngebäuden Haushalts-, Verwaltungs- und Industriegebäude, Strukturen, in denen elektrische Energiequellen zur Verfügung stehen. Sofern eine entsprechende Schutzisolierung vorhanden ist, können diese Heizgeräte in Onshore-, Untergrund- und Unterwasserleitungen installiert werden, um eine stabile Temperatur des beförderten Rohöls und der dicken Erdölprodukte zu schaffen.

Die Erfindung wird durch Abbildung 3 veranschaulicht, die den gesamten Umfang der Ansprüche dieser technischen Lösung nicht abdecken und auch nicht einschränken, sondern lediglich veranschaulichende Materialien für einen bestimmten Ausführungsfall sind. Hier werden bezeichnten mit Zahlen: 1 – Heatpipe; 2 – Tank mit Flanschanschluss; 3 – Wärmerohrheizkörper; 4 – leitfähiges Kabel; 5 – Wärmeisolierung der Heizzone des Wärmerohrs; 6 – Verbinder (Teil des Designs, bei dem das leitfähige Kabel an den Wärmerohren befestigt ist, besteht aus einem Metallgehäuse mit interner elektrischer Isolierung); 7 – Isolierschicht aus Polyurethanschaum mit einer Außenhülle; 8 – Ölpipeline und/oder Pipeline.

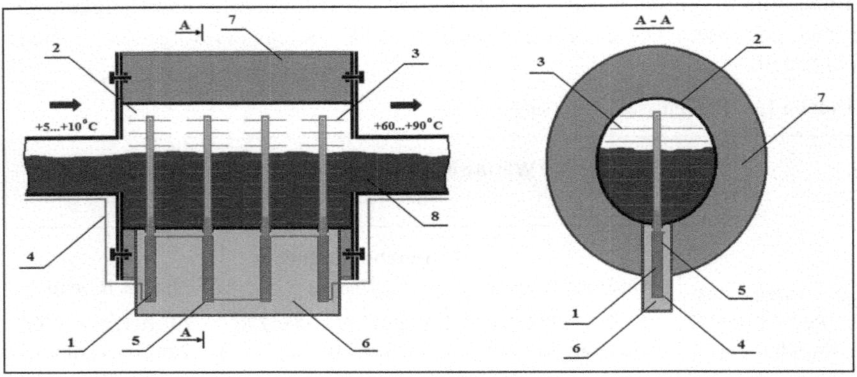

Abbildung 3: Funktionsprinzip der Ölheizungsanlage auf Basis einer Wärmerohrleitung

Die Ölheizungsanlage, von uns entwickelte, arbeitet wie folgt: Das durch die Rohrleitung 8 strömende Produkt durchströmt den Vorratsbehälter 2 der Heizvorrichtung und erwärmt sich aufgrund der Wärmeeinwirkung der Heizkörper 3 auf die Wärmeströme 1 auf die Strömung des transportierten Produkts, während aufgrund der thermodynamischen Eigenschaften der Heizungsrohre 1 der Energieverlust zu Heizung wird minimal sein.

Wenn der Durchmesser des Tanks, beispielsweise, 2000 mm beträgt, beträgt die Länge des Wärmerohrs 2600 mm, und der größte Teil der Länge des Rohrs, das 1800 mm entspricht, befindet sich in vertikaler Position im zylindrischen Tank. Die Anzahl der Heatpipe-Kühler hängt von der Größe des Tankdurchmessers ab.

Die Konstruktion der Heizvorrichtung, bei der im Wärmetauscher Tank elektrische Heizwärmerohre zum Transport von Rohöl und Dickölprodukten durch die Rohrleitung eingebaut werden, kann die Betriebskosten, die mit der Reinigung verbunden sind, erheblich reduzieren. Gegebenenfalls wird der Tank wie folgt gereinigt: Abnehmbare Polyurethanschaum-Isolierung mit äußerer Schutzhülle 7 wird mit Flanschanschluss 2 aus dem Tank entfernt. Anschlussteil 6 wird geöffnet und das leitfähige Kabel 4 wird von den Heizteilen der Wärmerohre 1 getrennt aufgeräumt.

Nach Experimenten mit Wärmerohren, die zunächst mit elektrischer Energie arbeiteten, beschlossen wir, die Möglichkeit einer nächsten Minimierung des Energieverbrauchs aufgrund des experimentellen Ausschlusses der Stromquelle und der Einführung der Technologie zur Nutzung thermischer Energie der Sonnenstrahlung zu untersuchen. Es wurde beschlossen, einen Parabol-Solar energie konzentrator durch mechanisches Polieren der erforderlichen Arbeitsfläche der

Metallantenne herzustellen. Zusätzlich zu den Polierarbeiten wurden chemische, flüssige und Temperaturreinigungsarbeiten durchgeführt, um eine spiegelartige Arbeitsfläche des herzustellenden Konzentrators zu erhalten.

Im Fokus eines parabolischen Konzentrators für Sonnenstrahlung mit einem Durchmesser von 1,3 Metern bei trübes Novemberwetter konnten wir bereits 314°C erreichen.

Die Technologie zur Herstellung von Wärmerohren, die zur Verwendung in Wärmetauschern von Ölheizungsanlagen geeignet sind, wurde entwickelt. Es wurde eine energieeffiziente Technologie für Heizöl geschaffen, das mit minimalen Energie-, Finanz- und Materialkosten durch Pipelines fließt und für den Einsatz in der Ölindustrie geeignet ist.

Abbildung 4: Der hergestellte Konzentrator der Sonnenenergie, der für die Anwendung in Experimenten bestimmt ist.

Entwickelte und patentierte Geräte zum Erwärmen des aktuellen Öls in oberirdischen, unterirdischen und Unterwasserleitungen. Unter Berücksichtigung der Besonderheiten unseres Landes (Sonnenjahr pro Jahr für 290 Tage) wird die beheizte Zone der Wärmerohre zusätzlich mit Hilfe von Sonnenenergie erhitzt, die auf Sonnenstrahlung konzentratoren konzentriert ist. Dadurch können Sie viel mehr Kraftstoff sparen, was wiederum eine umweltfreundliche und energieeffiziente Energieeinsparung bedeuten würde.

Die Ergebnisse der Forschungsarbeiten gelten für die Temperaturregelung flüssiger und dichter Strömungsmittel in der Wärme- und Energietechnik, der Petrochemie sowie in anderen Branchen, in denen ein energiesparendes Heizverfahren erforderlich ist. Wirtschaftlichkeit wird eindeutig durch Energieeinsparung und Minimierung von technischen Verbrauchsmaterialien für die von uns entwickelte Vorrichtung erreicht. Die von uns vorgeschlagene Methode und Vorrichtung ist eine kostengünstige Lösung für dieses Problem.

7 Zusammenfassung

1. Für Experimente wurde ein Wärmerohr mit bestimmten Abmessungen hergestellt. Die erzielbaren Temperaturen wurden während des Betriebs mit und ohne Wärmeübertragung im inneren Arbeitsraum gemessen. Es wurde experimentell gezeigt, dass die Verwendung einer Heatpipe mit Kühlmittel die optimale Lösung für dieses Problem ist.
2. Unter Laborbedingungen wurden Heizungsanlagen mit Wärmerohren zum Erhitzen von Erdöl und dicken Erdölprodukten hergestellt, die durch die Rohrleitung fließen. Mit Hilfe bestimmter Mess- und Testarbeiten wurden die thermischen Parameter untersucht. Basierend auf den Experimenten wurde in Turkmenistan eine energieeffiziente und energiesparende Technologie für Heizöl entwickelt.
3. Die Möglichkeiten der Nutzung von Sonnenenergie in den von uns entwickelten Versuchsanlagen mit Wärmerohren wurden untersucht, wobei ein Solar strahlungs konzentrator mit optimalen geometrischen Eigenschaften hergestellt wurde.
4. Aufgrund der Versuche, die mit Hilfe von Heizgeräten mit Wärmerohren durchgeführt wurden, wurde ein Patent von Turkmenistan Nr. 696 für die Erfindung "Vorrichtung zum Erwärmen eines durch eine Rohrleitung transportierten flüssigen Mediums" (Autoren: Hajymuhammet Geldiyev, Patshakuly Atayev) erhalten.

Literaturverzeichnis

Atayev, P., Hudaykuliyev, N. (2014). Ölheizung für den Transport mithilfe von Heatpipes verbessern. Die wissenschaftliche und technische Kreativität junger Menschen ist der Weg zu einer auf Wissen basierenden Gesellschaft. *Sammlung von Berichten der IV. Internationalen Konferenz für Wissenschaft und Praxis*, S. 748-752.

Geldiyev, H., Atayev, P., Hudaykuliyev, N. (2016a). *Energieeffiziente Technologie der Ölheizung. Herausgegeben Volumen der inter-nationalen wissenschaftlich-praktische Konferenz von Studenten, Diplomanden und Doktoranden. Markt- und Produktivitätseffizienz-13.*

Geldiyev, H., Atayev, P., Hudaykuliyev, N. (2016b). Vorrichtung zum Erwärmen der transportierten Flüssigkeit durch die Rohrleitung. *Patent für die Erfindung von Turkmenistan № 696.*

Geldiyev, H., Atayev, P., Hudaykuliyev, N. (2017). Ausarbeitung einer energiesparenden Technologie zum Heizen von Erdöl durch Ölpipeline. Wissenschaft und Technologie in Turkmenistan. *Wissenschaftlich-theoretisches Journal der Akademie der Wissenschaften von Turkmenistan. Nr. 1*, S. 83-87.

The Future of the European Union – an Overview on Implementation of SDGs for Sustainable Social and Economic Development in EU

Goran Bandov, Nikolina Herceg Kolman

1 Socio-economic development in the 2030 Agenda

The 2030 Agenda for Sustainable Development, adopted in 2015 by all UN Member States, is unprecedented in its ambition and universality. Throughout three dimensions of the Document – social, economic and environmental – five themes crosscut all of 17 sustainable development goals: people, planet, prosperity, peace, partnership.

The 17 Sustainable Development Goals and 169 targets aim to end poverty and hunger and to ensure dignity and equality for all people on Earth; to protect the planet from degradation; ensure that social and technological progress occurs in harmony with nature; peaceful and inclusive societies; and global partnership and solidarity on achieving SDGs.

17 Sustainable Development Goals:

Goal 1. End poverty in all its forms everywhere

Goal 2. End hunger, achieve food security and improved nutrition and promote sustainable agriculture

Goal 3. Ensure healthy lives and promote well-being for all at all ages

Goal 4. Ensure inclusive and equitable quality education and promote lifelong learning opportunities for all

Goal 5. Achieve gender equality and empower all women and girls

Goal 6. Ensure availability and sustainable management of water and sanitation for all

Goal 7. Ensure access to affordable, reliable, sustainable and modern energy for all

Goal 8. Promote sustained, inclusive and sustainable economic growth, full and productive employment and decent work for all

Goal 9. Build resilient infrastructure, promote inclusive and sustainable industrialization and foster innovation

H.-C. Brauweiler et al. (Hrsg.), *Digitalization and Industry 4.0: Economic and Societal Development*, https://doi.org/10.1007/978-3-658-27110-7_13

Goal 10. Reduce inequality within and among countries

Goal 11. Make cities and human settlements inclusive, safe, resilient and sustainable

Goal 12. Ensure sustainable consumption and production patterns

Goal 13. Take urgent action to combat climate change and its impacts

Goal 14. Conserve and sustainably use the oceans, seas and marine resources for sustainable development

Goal 15. Protect, restore and promote sustainable use of terrestrial ecosystems, sustainably manage forests, combat desertification, and halt and reverse land degradation and halt biodiversity loss

Goal 16. Promote peaceful and inclusive societies for sustainable development, provide access to justice for all and build effective, accountable and inclusive institutions at all levels

Goal 17. Strengthen the means of implementation and revitalize the global partnership for sustainable development

Socio-economic dimension of the Agenda is reflected in goals 1-12 and goal 16. Each goal sets targets and indicators for their achievement, dealing with issues from poverty, hunger, education, sustainable growth and innovation, to reducing inequality and building peaceful, inclusive societies.

2 Implementation of socio-economic dimension of the 2030 Agenda in EU

In line with the EU commitment to implementing the 2030 Agenda, in 2016 new sustainable development strategy "New steps on Europe's sustainable future" was adopted, with several key actions[1]:

Including the SDGs into all EU policies and initiatives, with sustainable development as an essential guiding principle for all European Commission policies;

Providing regular reporting of the EU's progress as of 2017;

Developing partnerships and including EU governments, the European Parliament, other European institutions, international organizations, civil society organizations, citizens and other stakeholders into implementation of the 2030 Agenda;

---

1 See European Commission, 2016

Launching a high-level multi-stakeholder platform, with the goal of exchanging best practices on implementation of the Agenda;

Introducing a longer term vision with a post 2020 perspective.

When it comes to implementing the socio-economic dimension of the Agenda, the EU has two overarching instruments: European Pillar of Social Rights and the EU 2020 Strategy.

2.1 The European Pillar of Social Rights

The European Pillar of Social Rights was signed by the European Parliament, the Council and the Commission on 17 November 2017, at the Social Summit for Fair Jobs and Growth in Gothenburg, Sweden. The signing of the Pillar, which was a symbol of recommitment to social Europe after economic crisis and austerity policy, was preceded by broad public discussion in 2016, which included citizens, members of civil society, representatives of Member States and EU institutions. The Pillar comprises of 20 principles in three chapters, dealing with equal opportunities, work conditions and social protection.

Chapter I: Equal opportunities and access to the labor market[2]: 1.Education, training and life-long learning - quality and inclusive education, training and life-long learning; 2.Gender equality – equal treatment and opportunities for women in the labor market, conditions of employment and career progression, including equal pay; 3.Equal opportunities – equal treatment and opportunities regarding employment, social protection, education and access to services available to the public, regardless of gender, racial or ethnic origin, religion or belief, disability, age or sexual orientation; 4.Active support to employment - timely and tailor-made assistance to improve employment or self-employment prospects. Special emphasis is on young people and their right to continued education, apprenticeship, traineeship or a job offer of good standing within 4 months of becoming unemployed or leaving education.

Chapter II: Fair working conditions[3]: 1.Secure and adaptable employment - fair and equal treatment regarding working conditions, access to social protection and training, the necessary flexibility for employers to adapt swiftly to changes in the economic context, entrepreneurship and self-employment and occupational mobility; 2.Wages - fair wages that provide for a decent standard of living, adequate minimum wages and prevention of in-work poverty; 3.Information about employment conditions and protection in case of dismissals – rights and obligations stemming from employment contract, informed dismissal with reasonable

[2] See European Commission, 2017b, pp. 11-12
[3] See European Commission, 2017b, pp. 14-17

period of notice and adequate compensation; 4.Social dialogue and involvement of workers - consulting social partners on economic, employment and social policies; 5.Work-life balance - suitable leave, flexible working arrangements and access to care services for parents and people with caring responsibilities, encouraging men and women to use parental leaves of absence in a balanced way; 6.Healthy, safe and well-adapted work environment and data protection - high level of protection of health and safety at work, working environment adapted to professional needs and which enables workers to prolong their participation in the labor market, protection of personal data in the employment context.

Chapter III: Social protection and inclusion[4]: 1.Childcare and support to children - affordable early childhood education and good quality care, protection of children from poverty, specific measures to enhances equal opportunity for underprivileged children; 2.Social protection - adequate social protection for workers and self-employed; 3.Unemployment benefits - adequate activation support from public employment services to (re)integrate in the labour market and adequate unemployment benefits of reasonable duration; 4.Minimum income - adequate minimum income benefits ensuring a life in dignity at all stages of life, and effective access to enabling goods and services; 5.Old age income and pensions - a pension commensurate to contributions of workers and self-employed, ensuring an adequate income for living in dignity; 6.Health care - timely access to affordable, preventive and curative health care of good quality; 7.Inclusion of people with disabilities - income support that ensures living in dignity, services that enable them to participate in the labor market and in society, and a work environment adapted to their needs; 8.Long-term care - long-term care services of good quality, in particular home-care and community-based services; 9.Housing and assistance for the homeless - Access to social housing or housing assistance of good quality shall be provided for those in need; appropriate assistance to vulnerable people and protection against forced eviction; adequate shelter and services to the homeless; 10.Access to essential services - access to essential services of good quality, including water, sanitation, energy, transport, financial services and digital communications.

Implementation of the European Pillar of Social Rights is a joint responsibility of the EU and the Member States, but also of civil society organizations and social partners. The progress on implementing the Pillar is monitored through European Semester, with three new elements added for this purpose, as outlined in Commission's Communication on monitoring the implementation of the European Pillar of Social Rights: mainstreaming the priorities of the Pillar in the European Semester while selecting themes for detailed reporting on an annual basis; providing technical assistance, promoting benchmarking and exchanging good practic-

4 See European Commission, 2017b, pp. 19-22

es; assessing and monitoring performances with the help of the new Social Scoreboard, designed to help monitor performance of Member States in the field of social policy, covered by the Pillar.[5]

2.2 Europe 2020

The Strategy for sustainable growth, adopted in 2010 by the European Council, is another major EU instrument for enhancing socio-economic development. The Strategy defined three priorities - smart growth, through the development of an economy based on knowledge, research and innovation; sustainable growth, through the promotion of resource-efficient, green and competitive markets; inclusive growth, through policies aimed at fostering job creation and poverty reduction.[6] Within these three priorities it has set goals to be achieved by 2020 in six major areas: employment, research and development, climate change and energy, education and poverty and exclusion.[7]

In the area of employment, Europe 2020 Strategy set the goal of 75% of EU citizens to be employed by 2020. For research and development, the Strategy set a very ambitious goal of 3% of the EU's GDP to be invested in R&D. Climate and energy section called for greenhouse gas emissions 20% lower than 1990 levels, 20% of energy coming from renewables and 20% in-crease in energy efficiency. In the field of education, the Strategy aimed for the rates of early school leavers to be below 10% and at least 40% of people aged 30–34 having completed higher education. And finally, by 2020 the Strategy planned to take action to have at least 20 million people fewer in, or at risk of, poverty and social exclusion.[8]

Areas and goals on which Europe 2020 focuses are reinforced in seven flagship initiatives of European Commission: "Innovation Union"; "Youth on the move"; "A Digital Agenda for Europe"; "Resource efficient Europe"; "An industrial policy for the globalisation era"; "An Agenda for new skills and jobs"; "European Platform against Poverty".[9] The Strategy is implemented in cooperation between EU and Member States, which set national targets and annual reform plans on the Strategy goals, reported on in the process known as European Semester.

Eurostat publishes regular comprehensive progress reports on the targets. The 2018 edition "Smarter, greener, more inclusive" concluded that since the adoption of the Europe 2020 Strategy substantial progress has been achieved in the area of climate change and energy by reduction of greenhouse gas emissions and increase

---

5 See European Commission, 2018, pp. 11-12
6 See Kramer, Brauweiler, 2002
7 See European Commission, 2010
8 See European Commission, 2010
9 (European Commission, 2010)

in renewable energy use. In the area of socio-economic dimension of the Strategy, the employment target (75% employed) is still reachable, however, poverty alleviation and research and development investment goals look far less promising.[10]

3 The future of socio-economic development in EU

At the Rome Summit on 1 March 2017 the Commission presented a White Paper on the EU's future, with five potential scenarios: 1. Carrying On — the EU-27 focuses on delivering its positive reform agenda.; 2. Nothing but the Single Market — the EU-27 is gradually re-centered on the single market; 3. Those Who Want More, Do More — the EU-27 allows willing Member States to do more together in specific areas; 4. Doing Less, More Efficiently — the EU-27 focuses on delivering more and faster in selected policy areas, while doing less elsewhere; 5. Doing Much More Together — Member States decide to do much more together across all policy areas.[11]

The White Paper has been accompanied by several reflection papers on issues vital for the future of the EU: the social dimension, harnessing globalization, the deepening of the economic and monetary union, the future of European defense policy and the future of EU finances. In January 2019 the paper on sustainable Europe by 2030 was published, focusing on how to use Agenda 2030 and Sustainable Development Goals to promote sustainable development in the EU.

The reflection paper on the social dimension of Europe tackles the issue of how to preserve the principles of social Europe at the backdrop of the current challenges, namely those brought about by demographic changes, technological progress and globalization. Following the logic of the White Paper on the Future of EU, the paper sets out three possible scenarios: limiting the social dimension to free movement; those who want to do more do more in the social field; the EU-27 deepens the social dimension together.[12]

- Limiting the social dimension to free movement

Under this option, the Union would keep the rules within the single market, such as rules on social security rights, on posting of workers, on cross-border health care and the recognition of diplomas. On the other hand, there would no longer be EU minimum standards on many social rights.[13]

---

10 See Eurostat, 2018b, p. 8
11 See European Commission, 2017a
12 See European Commission, 2017b, p. 25
13 See European Commission, 2017b, p. 26

- Those who want to do more in the social field do more

This scenario entails closer cooperation by a group of Member States, namely the Eurozone member states, which could adopt legal acts that bind only the countries that take part. These common standards could apply to labour markets, competitiveness, the business environment and public administration, or tax policy. The euro area would be better supported and its citizens better protected and national employment and social policies would be more aligned. This enhanced cooperation could be also done by some other groups of countries.[14]

- The EU27 deepen the social dimension of Europe together

In this scenario Member States would give much more authority to the EU in the field of social policy. Legislation would not only set minimum standards but, in selected areas, could fully harmonize citizens' rights across the EU, with the aim of focusing on convergence in social outcomes.[15]

The Reflection paper on the deepening of the Economic and Monetary Union focuses on steps forward towards completing the economic and monetary union by 2025. The first phase, till the end of 2019, would entail completing Banking Union and Capital Markets Union. A number of new instruments, such as better economic and social convergence standards, could be introduced. The second phase, from 2020-2025, would complete the EMU architecture.[16]

Reflection Paper 'Towards Sustainable Europe by 2030' set out three possible scenarios for the implementation of the 2030 Agenda: an overarching EU strategy on SDGs guiding actions of EU and Member States; continued mainstreaming of SDGs in all relevant EU policies by the commission, but not enforcing member states' actions; enhanced focus on external action, while consolidating current sustainability ambitions at the EU level.[17]

All of the above mentioned papers consider different scenarios for sustainable development in certain policy fields, following the logic outlined by the White Paper on the Future of Europe. Therefore, for the future of any EU policy to be evaluated, especially policies at the core of the EU project – social model and economic cooperation – one should have in mind that their success predominantly depends on the future institutional framework of the EU.

---

14 See European Commission, 2017b, p. 28
15 See European Commission, 2017b, p. 30
16 See European Commission, 2017c, p. 29
17 See European Commission, 2019, pp. 34-39

4 Conclusion

At its meeting on 20 June 2019 European Council adopted a new strategic agenda for the next five years, as an overarching guiding paper for the policies and programes that will be put forward by other EU institutions during the 2019 – 2024 term. The new agenda set four general priorities – protection of citizens and freedoms, strong economy, green and fair and social Europe and promoting European interests and values globally.[18] Within priorities addressing economy and social dimension, the European Council agenda gives a very prominent role to the implementation of the Pillar of Social Rights, as well as to the project of completing the EMU, with key principles being sustainability and inclusivity.

It is, therefore, to be expected that the new Commission, upon final evaluation of the Europe 2020 Strategy, will put forward a new strategy of sustainable growth with emphasis on the Pillar of Social Rights and EMU. And, while the EMU project is pretty straightforward in its scope and implementation (which is not to say easy), the implementation of the Pillar is more questionable and more complicated matter. To begin with, the Pillar is a set of principles, proclamation on desired course of action, signed jointly by Commission, Council and the European Parliament. In order for it to have an actual effect for the lives of EU citizens, relevant policies on the EU level and the level of Member States have to be adopted and implemented. There are some steps in that direction at the EU level, such as the recent Directive on work-life balance for parents and carers, which gives Member States three years to align their legislation to its provisions.

However, it is futile to expect a substantial progress without political will and policy initiative by Member States. Furthermore, in order for the EU to be able to build sustainable, shock resilient and inclusive economy, with strong social safety net for its citizens, there needs to be more policy convergence between Member States. And that again brings us to the issue of the future EU architecture. Which scenario outlined in Juncker's White Paper will prevail? The answer to those questions is inevitably the answer to the question on the future of Europe's social model and economic development. Taking all of the elements into the account, including the results of the last European Election, it is sound to expect that maintaining the institutional *status quo* will be the choice of preference. In such circumstances, the implementation of the 17 goals of the 2030 Agenda could prove as a valuable tool for socio-economic development in EU within the following decade.

All EU Member States have pledged to implement the Goals and voluntarily report on it every year at the High Level Political Forum on Sustainable Devel-

---

[18] See European Commission, 2019, p. 2

opment. There is a clear and unequivocal commitment to the implementation of the SDGs on the side of the EU institutions. That convergence of will could serve as a strong motivator to forward sustainable development in EU, without having to risk political stability of the Union by transferring more power to the EU level, or failing to achieve progress due to the lack of motivation by Member States.

This opportunity is, finally, recognized by the Commission's Reflection Paper "Towards a Sustainable Europe by 2030". It remains to be seen how much will the EU institutions rely on that idea in the next five and ten years.

Literature

European Commission. (2010). *Europe 2020. A strategy for smart, sustainable and inclusive growth.* Retrieved 5.3.2019, from https://ec.europa.eu/eu2020/pdf/COMPLET%20EN%20BARROSO%20%20%20007%20-%20Europe%202020%20-%20EN%20version.pdf

European Commission. (2016). *Commission Communication on Next steps for a sustainable European future.* Retrieved 5.3.2019, from https://ec.europa.eu/europeaid/commission-communication-next-steps-sustainable-european-future_en

European Commission. (2017). *European Pillar of Social Rights.* Retrieved 5.3.2019, from https://ec.europa.eu/social/main.jsp?catId=1226&langId =en

European Commission. (2017a). *White paper on the Future of Europe: Reflections and Scenarios for the EU 27 by 2025.* Retrieved 5.3.2019, from https://ec.europa.eu/commission/sites/beta-political/files/white_paper_on_the_future_of_europe_en.pdf

European Commission. (2017b). *Reflection Paper on Social Dimension of Europe.* Retrieved 5.3.2019, from https://ec.europa.eu/commission/sites/beta-political/files/reflection-paper-social-dimension-europe_en.pdf

European Commission. (2017c). *Reflection Paper on the Deepening of the Economic and Monetary Union.* Retrieved 5.3.2019, from https://ec.europa.eu/commission/sites/beta-political/files/reflection-paper-emu_en.pdf

European Commission. (2019). *Reflection Paper Towards Sustainable Europe by 2030.* Retrieved 5.3.2019, from https://ec.europa.eu/commission/sites/beta-political/files/rp_sustainable_europe_30-01_en_web.pdf

Federal Ministry for Economic Cooperation and Development. (2015). *The 2030 Agenda for Sustainable Development.* Retrieved 5.3.2019, from http://www.bmz.de/de/ministerium/ziele/2030_agenda/index.html

Kramer, M., Brauweiler, H.-Ch (2002). *Naturschutz und Nutzungskonflikte - Ein Vergleich zwischen Deutschland, Polen, Tschechien.* Gabler.

Application of neural network technologies for analyzing and forecasting the natural movement of the territory's population

E. A. Petrova, M. S. Lapina

1 Introduction

The problem of analyzing and forecasting the dynamics of demographic indicators is widely considered and studied both in the domestic and in foreign literature. A number of fundamental studies which consider various methods of modeling demographic processes and build prognostic hypotheses are devoted to these questions. However, experts search for the most accurate and effective ways to solve the problem in connection with the emergence of new concepts and methods of analysis.

The demographic forecasts currently being developed by government agencies confirm the relevance and significance of demographic forecasting. One of the modern approaches to solving the problem of forecasting and the most perspective tool for managing complex systems is the application of artificial neural networks.[1]

Artificial neural networks are a prospect of information and computing technology using new approaches to the study of dynamic systems. The possibility of their use for solving a wide class of managerial and economic tasks is conditioned by the ability to model non-linear processes in working with adaptability and "noisy" information.[2]

In accordance with these advantages, application of artificial neural networks that allow to model the processes of various systems, the object of this research is the forecasting of demographic processes, in particular the birth rate in the regions of the Russian Federation.

2 Modeling the birth rates in the economic systems of meso-level based on neural networks

At present time, both in Russia and abroad, the technique of forecasting the number and structure of the population has been sufficiently developed. One of the

---

1 See Krug, 2002, p. 10
2 See Petrova, 2018, p. 158

H.-C. Brauweiler et al. (Hrsg.), *Digitalization and Industry 4.0: Economic and Societal Development*, https://doi.org/10.1007/978-3-658-27110-7_14

tasks facing demography is to build demographic forecasts allowing to build an effective socio-economic policy.[3]

The practical significance of demographic forecasts is that, based on scientific research, management bodies are given recommendations on the need to take measures to stabilize or improve the current demographic situation, to take into account population reproduction trends when solving important national economic tasks, to make adjustments when conducting demographic policy.[4]

The demographic forecast allows to obtain estimated data on the population and its individual parts of the future numbers of births and deaths, marriages and divorces, migration, its impact on the size and structure of the population, the number of families and family composition of the population, the possible impact of demographic policy on reproduction of the population.[5]

The exact definition of possible perspective scenarios for changing the parameters of demographic processes, and how close they are to the dynamics that will occur, determines the accuracy of the demographic forecast, both in terms of the total population and its age and sex structure.[6]

Thus, to predict demographic processes, it is advisable to choose a non-standard method of research defining its relevance and the advantages of its application. Such methods represent the artificial neural networks that have recently been more actively used in time series forecasting.

2.1 Application of neural networks to research the dynamics of demographic processes

Demographic processes are complex systems characterized by a high degree of uncertainty. Neural networks are used to model complex systems and are considered the most perspective tool for control such systems.[7]

Neural networks are one of the directions in the development of artificial intelligence systems, the idea of which is to model the work of the human nervous system (its ability to learn and correct errors) as closely as possible. The main feature is the ability to learn and act independently on the basis of previous experience, each time making fewer mistakes.

Intelligent systems based on artificial neural networks (ANN) allow solving the problems of pattern recognition, forecasting, optimization, associative memory

---

3 See Koroleva, n.d.
4 See Vorontsov, Glotov, 2016
5 See Gerasenko, 2015
6 See Basovskiy, 2014
7 See Krug, 2002, p. 10

and control. There are traditional approaches to solving these problems, but they do not have the necessary flexibility beyond the limited conditions.[8]

Unlike traditional methods, in which only predetermined characteristics proven by developers should be used, neural networks contain an important property of elasticity, allowing to generate features that are not developed explicitly, as they are resistant to noisy data. As long as the interference does not affect the main line of the modeling process, the network will develop in the right direction.[9]

Currently, various types of neural networks have been developed and tested, many of which may be necessary in approximation and modeling of demographic monitoring information. The principles of construction and training of the neural network may differ from each other and give different results when they are applicable to demographic data. Thus, neural networks have sufficient advantages over traditional methods of forecasting, and represent a stable method of approximation of the objective functions by means of training pairs and such networks are used to describe the complex processes.

The choice of this method is mainly due to such advantages as: the ability to model non-linear processes in working with adaptability and "noisy" information; solving problems with unknown patterns; noise resistance in the input data; adaptation to environmental changes; potential ultrahigh speed; fault tolerance in hardware implementation of the neural network.

In the case of analyzing and forecasting demographic processes, the application of neurotechnologies is perspective, despite their high demands on input data sets and their quality.[10] Using neural networks it is possible to obtain reliable models of processes and on their basis to create a variety of alternatives to management solutions for the demographic sphere of the region.

2.2 Designing a neural network to forecast birth rates in the regions of the Russian Federation

Among various types of population movement, natural and mechanical (migration) occupy a central place, since these types of movement represent a quantitative aspect of population reproduction, and are complex social processes that affect many socio-economic aspects of population life.

---

8 See Babich, Kozieva, Vertakova, 2016

9 See Krug, 2002, p. 20

10 See Zhukov, Reshetnikova, 2007

One of the main components of natural population movement is the birth rate.[11] The process of birth is influenced by groups of factors - natural, social, which can be adjusted to reduce adverse effects in the future or improve the position of an object in its present state. For this purpose, forecasting is used, which allows to undertake an effective analysis of the situation and make the management decisions.[12]

As part of this research, 12 birth indicators have been identified, which individually have the same structure and nature of origin in the regions of the Russian Federation. The data source is Rosstat (Federal State Statistics Service), which every year publishes data not only countrywide, but also in each region. These indicators characterize the certain sphere of human activity.

On the basis of the initial observations, a model was built that is able to forecast the birth rate of the population with known values of the input parameters, and also to describe the dependencies of the input and output parameters in the form of graphs. The basis of the software product is the Deductor Academic analytical platform, as the technologies implemented in it based on a single architecture allow to go through all the stages of building an analytical system, from creating a data warehouse to automatic selection of models and visualization of the results. Deductor Studio makes it possible for the analytics to automate routine data processing operations and focus on intellectual work: formalizing decision-making logic, building models, and forecasting.

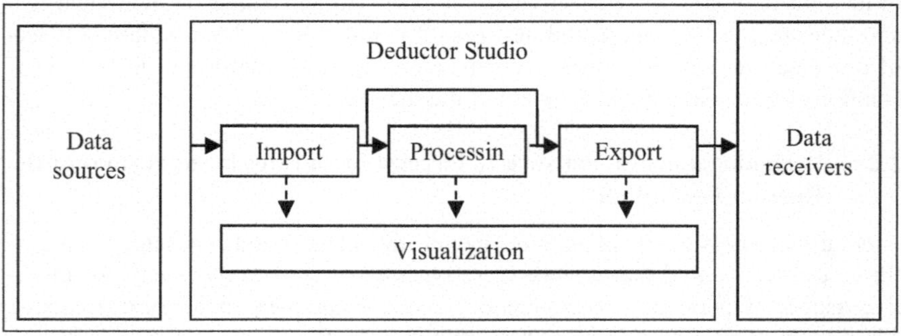

Figure 1: Scheme of work in Deductor Studio (compiled by the author)

---

11 Birth rate is a massive statistical process of childbearing in the aggregate of people constituting a generation, or as a whole of generations — the population. See Medkov, 2002

12 See Petrova, Shevandrin, Kalinina, 2017, p. 391

Working with Studio is reduced to the visual construction of scenarios that is a sequence of actions allowing one to obtain knowledge from data.[13] The execution algorithm consists of the operations depicted in figure 1[14]:

Thus, to build a model at the first stage, it is necessary to collect data for training. A training data set is a set of observations for which the values of input and output variables are indicated. Based on the research of the birth rate of the population 12 indicators presented in table 1 were selected for the design of the neural network.

Table 1: Indicators for forecasting birth rate (Source: compiled by the authors)

Name of indicators	Description
Total birth rate	Y
Total marriage rate per 1,000 people	X1
Total divorce rates per 1000 people	X2
Unemployment rate	X3
Per capita income of the population	X4
The total area of dwellings per person on average	X5
Number of organizations involved in educational activities in educational programs for pre-school education, child care and supervision, and the number of pupils in them	X6
Number of hospital beds	X7
The load on the health workers	X8
Termination of pregnancy (abortions)	X9
The ratio of men and women	X10
Emissions of pollutants into the air from stationary sources, by type of economic activity	X11
Discharge of polluted wastewater to surface water bodies. The volume of wastewater discharges into surface water bodies by types of economic activity	X12

For the network's training, 425 observations were collected over 5 years from 85 subjects of the Russian Federation, and data were later excluded for some regions (Republic of Crimea, Sevastopol, Nenets Autonomous Okrug, Khanty-Mansi Autonomous Okrug, Yamalo-Nenets Autonomous Okrug). This was done in view

13 See Gorozhanina, 2017, p. 39

14 See Figure 1

of the fact that the statistics for these regions is not stable and could distort the results of the model. As a result, 400 observations for 12 indicators were used for analysis.

One of the main points when setting up a neural network is the choice of input and output variables. For this research, the “Region” parameter is an information field, the X1-X12 indicators are input, and Y is the output variable.

To build a neural network, data must be standardized, i.e. lead to a general view, as they have a different range and units of measurement. Next, the percentage of training and test sets is determined. 95% were defined for the training set, 5% for the test set, which is 380 and 20 lines, respectively.[15]

The next step is to configure the network structure, select the number of layers, the type of function and the slope. For the data set under study, a model with one hidden layer, a type of sigmoid function and a slope unit is suitable.

The next step is to configure the neural network learning process. For training, an offline training option was chosen, in which the weights are corrected after all examples of the training variety are presented.

The final stage before the launch of network training is setting parameters at which network training will be stopped. An error of 0.05 or an achievement of 10,000 epochs was selected for this research. An important point in setting these parameters is that the network can be retrained and reduce the dependence to zero.

After conducting network training, the Visualization Wizard offers available ways to display data.

To analyze the results of building this model, it is necessary to display the following graphs and tables[16]:

- graph of the neural network displays the neural network in the form of a graph;
- scatter plot is a chart that displays the deviation of the predicted
- values from the actual ones;
- what-if - is a tool that allows to calculate the output parameter by entering the available data;
- training set is a table displaying the lines selected as a training and test variety;
- table displays the data, including predicted values and an error;
- statistics displays general statistical data about parameters.

---

15 See Figure 12

16 See Figure 15

Thus, a neural network was constructed, which describes the degree and type of dependence of the selected variables on the birth rate.

2.3 Interpretation of the results of neural network modeling

Having built a neural network for the birth rate of the population, we will consider the results of its construction through the various reflection methods selected at the network setup stage.

As a result of building a neural network, Deductor Studio generates a mapping of a neural network in the form of a graph.[17]

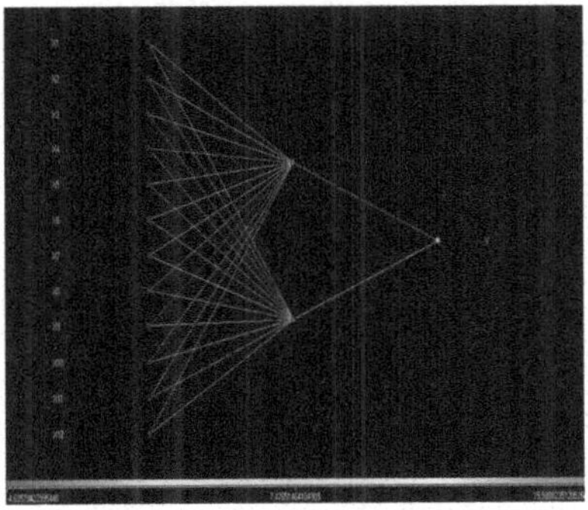

Figure 2: Generated neural network graph

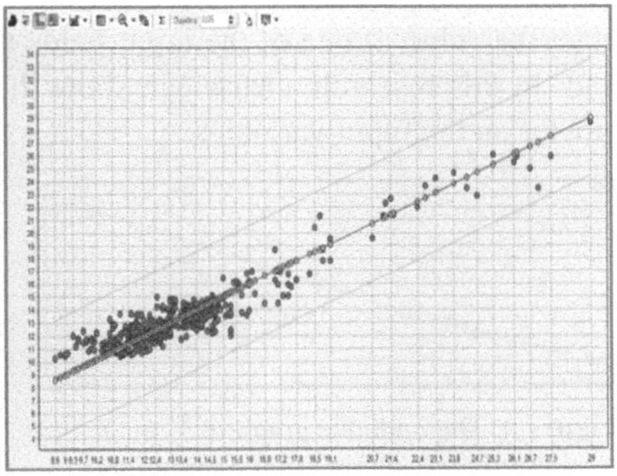

Figure 3: The scatter plot with a given error value of 0.05

The graph has vertices that correspond to the modules of the network, as well as edges describing the connections between the modules. Under the graph a measuring scale corresponding to the strength of the connection between the modules is situated.

When constructing a neural network, a scatter plot is indicative, which displays observations on the graph, the error of the predicted values of which is more than a given value (0.05 in this model). The scatter diagram[18] shows that the predicted values from 400 observations do not exceed the error of 0.05, that is, all observations fall within the specified limits.

The next tool displaying the results of building a network is the "Training Set" table, which displays the observations of the training and test variety, as well as the obtained predicted values and the error. The "Table" tool also displays pre-

17 See Figure 2

18 See Figure 3

dicted values and error, but, unlike the Training variety it does not divide observation into test and training sets. The "Statistics" table describes general statistical indicators for parameters, such as, minimum, maximum, average, standard deviation, amount, etc.

Particular attention should be paid to the "What-if" tool, since it can be used to apply the generated model for 2016 data.

The "What if" tool allows to enter data for a region and get the value of the output parameter. It is also possible to apply the generated model to the data of the next year. In addition, the "what-if" tool has dependency diagrams of indicators for the output parameter under other equal conditions. Charts are mainly used to select the value of one of the input fields to obtain the desired value of the output field. In this research, charts can show the type of dependence of the output parameter on the input variables.

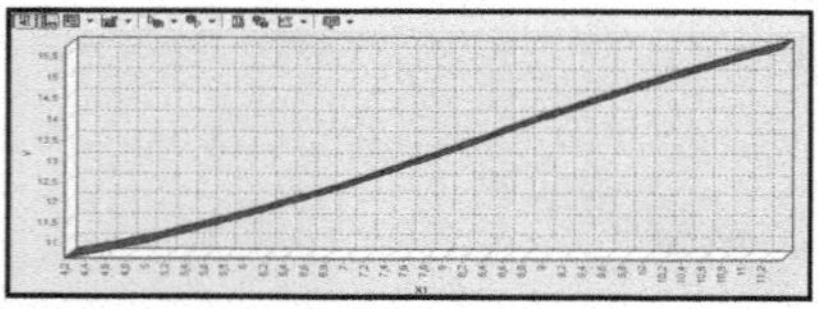

Figure 4: Dependence graph of Y on X – total marriage rate per 1000 population (compiled by the authors)

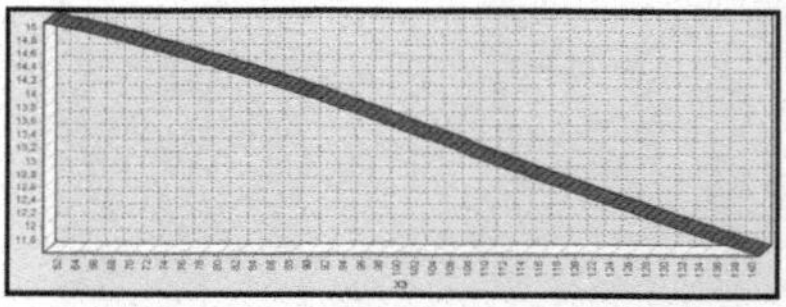

Figure 5: Dependence graph of Y on X3 – load on health care workers (compiled by the authors)

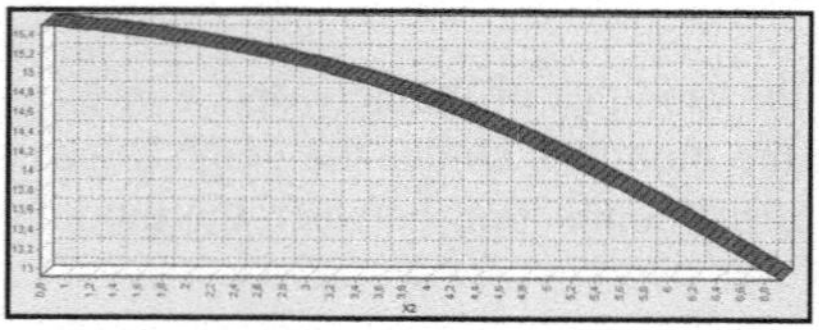

Figure 6: Dependence graph of Y on X2 – total divorce rate per 1000 population (compiled by the authors)

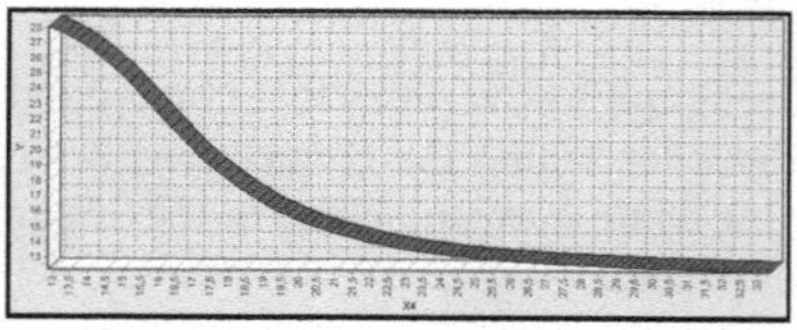

Figure 7: Dependence graph of Y on X4 – the total area of dwellings per person on average (compiled by the authors)

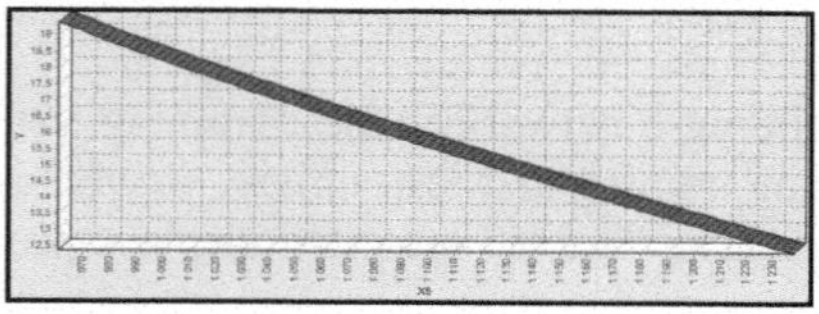

Figure 8: Dependence graph of Y on X5 – ratio of men and women (compiled by the authors)

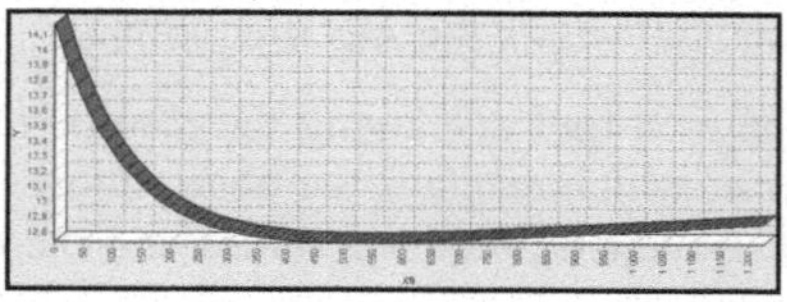

Figure 9: Dependence graph of Y on X9 – discharge of polluted wastewater to surface water bodies (compiled by the authors)

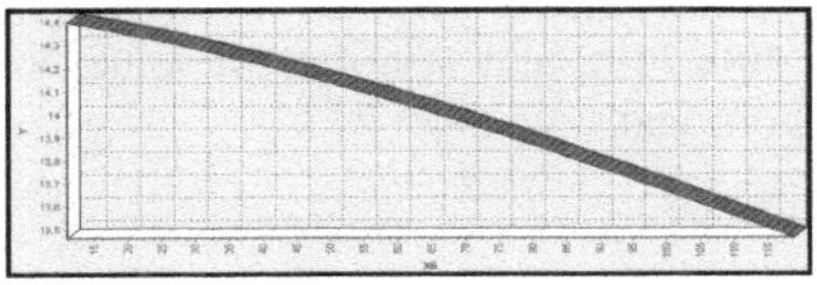

Figure 10: Dependence graph of Y on X6 – termination of pregnancy (compiled by the authors)

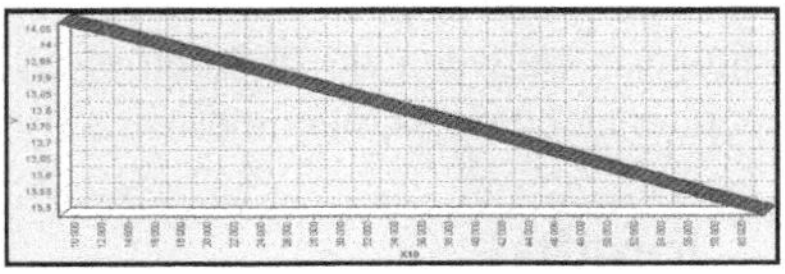

Figure 11: Dependence graph of Y on X10 – per capita income of the population (compiled by the authors)

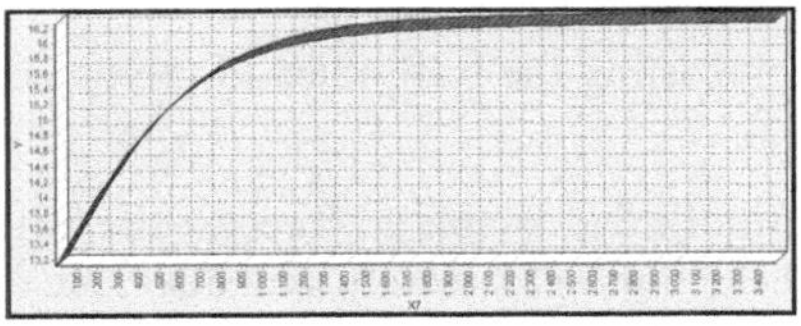

Figure 12: Dependence graph of Y on X7 – emissions of pollutants into the atmospheric air coming from stationary sources (compiled by the authors)

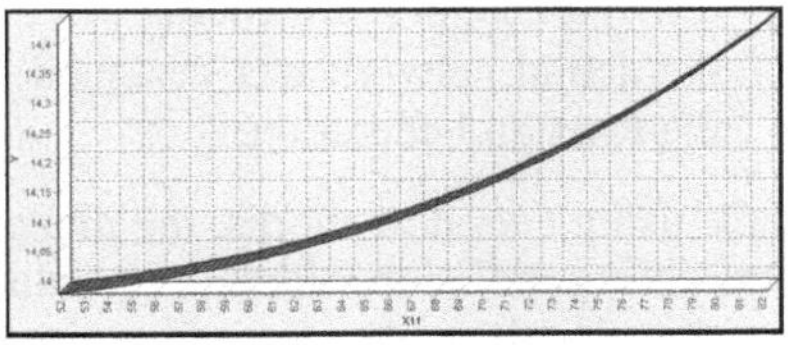

Figure 13: Dependence graph of Y on X11– level of economic activity (compiled by the authors)

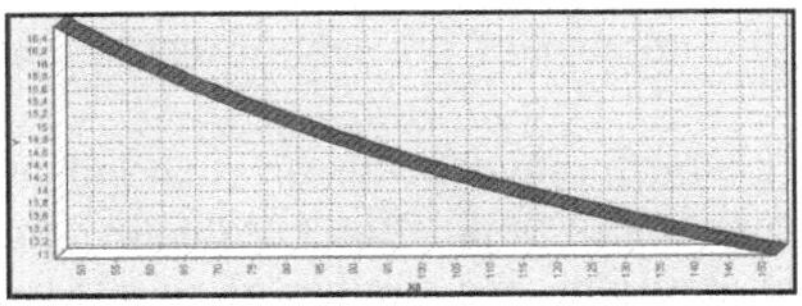

Figure 14: Dependence graph of Y on X8 – number of population per hospital bed (compiled by the authors)

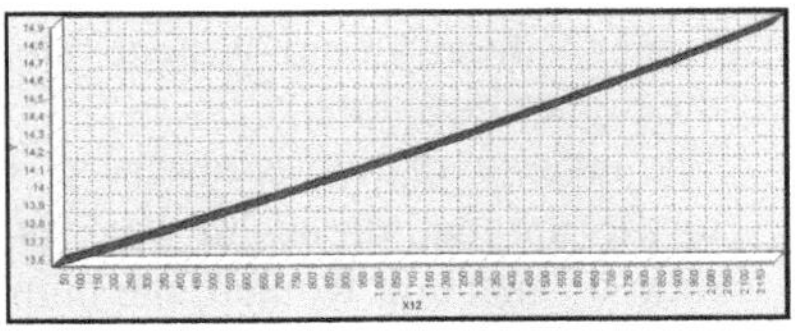

Figure 15: Dependence graph of Y on X12 – number of pre-school educational institutions (compiled by the authors)

In figure 4, the graph shows that in regions where the overall marriage rate is 1,000 more than in other regions, the birth rate is higher, and vice versa, the dynamics can be traced; if the total divorce rate is 1,000 less, then the birth rate is lower.[19] The graph in figure 12 shows the dependence of the birth rate on a variable up to a certain point in a straight line, and then remains in one position. Thus, it can be concluded that in regions with a birth rate above 16.2, emissions of pollutants into the air coming from stationary sources are not an influencing factor. Analyzing the graph in figure 10 we can note the ambiguous dependence between the indicators. To a certain value (X9 = 400), the dependence is inversely proportional - the higher the discharge of polluted wastewater into surface water bodies,

19 See Figure 5

the lower the birth rate, then this dependence decreases to zero, that is, there is no connection between the indicators (X9 = 400..700), and at a certain value, the dependence changes, becomes directly proportional.

3 Results

- The study of theoretical questions on this research led to the following results, containing elements of scientific novelty:
- a balanced scorecard has been developed for the birth rate of the population, based on factors influencing this process;
- the neural network was designed for forecasting the birth rates in regions of the Russian Federation.

Thus, using neural networks, the model was built that is able to forecast the birth rate of the population with known values of the input parameters, and also able to describe the dependencies of the input and output parameters in the form of graphs. After studying the dependency graphs for each indicator, the following results can be noted:

1. Direct dependence is observed in such indicators as "the level of economic activity of women", "the number of pre-school educational institutions". The higher women's employment rate and the number of pre-school institutions the higher birth rate.
2. The inverse relation is observed when the birth rate depends on such indicators as the load on health workers (the number of population per doctor), the ratio of men and women, the number of abortions, the number of people per hospital bed (per 10,000 population), monetary incomes per capita. The higher the values of these indicators, the lower the birth rate.
3. Analyzing the dependence data between indicators, the following regularities can be identified. The smallest number of births is observed in those families where housing supply is critically low, the highest rates are in middle groups. Among the urban population, the birth rate is significantly lower than among rural residents, due to the peculiarities of lifestyle and attitudes to the reproductive behavior of the population. The birth rate is directly dependent on the organization of medical care for the child population, the possibilities of medicine to ensure the survival of children. In families with a higher budgetary level, the birth rate in all age groups is lower than in families with lower incomes, which is a consequence of the higher economic needs of women with high incomes and their greater employment. Involving women in social production has a negative effect on the birth rate. The wide possibilities of the population to solve problems with kindergartens, with the additional education of children, have a positive effect on the motivation for increasing the birth rate.

4 Conclusion

As part of the research, the methodological foundations of modeling the population birth rate in the economic systems of the meso-level based on neural networks were considered, since this method has several advantages over traditional ones.

1. The essence of forecasting demographic processes was studied, the research of the economic content of the natural movement of the population was conducted, as well as an analysis of its quantitative measurement systems of international and Russian organizations.
2. The main methodological approaches for forecasting are considered, the rationale for the choice of the method of artificial neural networks for solving the problems of the present research is given, a software product for building a neural network is selected.
3. The processes of setting up and training of the neural network are described, the values of the forecast of demographic indicators and the interpretation of the obtained simulation results are presented.

The studied technology of analysis and forecast for making management decisions allows building adequate neural network models of processes and using them to carry out forecast of demographic indicators with higher accuracy. Thus, in the case of analyzing and forecasting demographic processes, the use of neurotechnologies is perspective. Using neural networks, it is possible to obtain reliable models of processes and on their basis to create a variety of alternatives to management solutions for the demographic sphere of the region.

Literature

Babich, T. N., Kozieva, I. A., Vertakova, Y. (2016). *Forecasting and planning in the conditions of the market: study guide.* Kuzbozhev: SSRC INFRA-M.

Basovskiy, L. (2014). *Forecasting and planning in market conditions: Textbook.* INFRA-M.

Gerasenko, V. (2015). *Forecasting and planning of the economy: practical manual: study guide.* Minsk: New Knowledge Publishing House.

Gorozhanina, E. (2017). *Neural networks. Study guide.* Samara: Povolzhskiy State University of Telecommunications and Informatics.

Kharchenko, L. (2012). *Demography: study guide for university students studying in the specialty "Statistics" and other economic specialties.* Omega-L Publishing House.

Koroleva, T. (n.d.). *Problems and methods of forecasting in demography. Electronic text data.* Retrieved 6.3.2019, from http://politika. snauka.ru/ 2015/08/3335

Krug, P. (2002). *Neural networks and neurocomputers: A manual for the course "Microprocessors".*

Medkov, V. (2002). *Demography: Study guide. Series "Textbooks and study guides".* Phoenix Publishing House.

Petrova, E. (2018). *Regional Life Quality Management: Methodological Approaches to its Forecasting using Neural Networks. Advances in Economics, Business and Management Research (AEBMR).* (Vol. 39).

Petrova, E., Shevandrin, A., Kalinina, V. (2017). *Effectiveness of State Territorial Administration in Provision of Sustainable Economic Growth of the Region. Integration and Clustering for Sustainable Economic Growth.*

Tikhonov, E. (2006). *Methods of forecasting in market conditions.* Nevinnomyssk.

Vorontsov, A., Glotov, M. (2016). *Demography: a textbook and a practical manual for applied bachelor.* Yurayt Publishing House.

Zhukov, L., Reshetnikova, N. (2007). *Neural network applications: A manual for students, students of the Lyceum and Winter Polytechnic School on neuroinformatics.* Krasnoyarsk: KSTU.

Business competences in the provincial region

Olga Grozova, Galina Tsevtkova

1 Introduction

Global competition for all types of resources, digitalization of socio-economic and technological processes, but the remaining disparities in the development of Russian regions, determine the relevance of the search for new theoretical designs that can set the innovative development of regional systems. From our point of view, the concept of key competencies has a large research potential. This theoretical platform allows the territory to design development strategies primarily with the use of its own resources – including the resource potential of the main subjects of the region. The resource-based, processing economy is replaced by the knowledge economy, in which the source of competitiveness of the region is not natural resources, but human capital, and therefore, the key competencies of the subjects conducting their business in this territory. Under institutional units, subjects of the region, we understand the population, business, authorities, science and education, public organizations. The carriers of the region's business competencies are the population of the region engaged in small and medium-sized businesses and ready to start their own business. Studies have shown that only 28.4% of Russian respondents positively assess their level of knowledge and experience to start their own business. Unfortunately, our country ranks 63rd in this indicator, which positions it as a country with a low level of development of business competencies.[1]

Understanding of the role and place of Russian entrepreneurship in the economy of the country and regions is reflected in the documents adopted by the Federal authorities, in particular:

1. National project "Small and medium-sized enterprises and support of individual entrepreneurial initiative". The project aims to increase the number of entrepreneurs and those employed in small and medium-sized businesses to 25 million people, to ensure the growth of the share of small and medium-sized businesses in GDP to 32.5% by 2024. We pay attention to such sections of the project as acceleration of small and medium-sized businesses, promotion of entrepreneurship, which are directly related to the design and development of business competencies of business entities.[2]

---

1 See n.n., 2017
2 See n.n., 2019

H.-C. Brauweiler et al. (Hrsg.), *Digitalization and Industry 4.0: Economic and Societal Development*, https://doi.org/10.1007/978-3-658-27110-7_15

2. Federal law No. 422 provides a special tax regime "Tax on professional income". This tax is introduced from January 1, 2019 for self-employed persons who do not have an employer and do not attract employees. The experiment included Moscow, Moscow and Kaluga regions, and Tatarstan Republic. The period of validity of the law is until 31 December 2028.[3]

The important role of entrepreneurship in economic development is confirmed by numerous empirical studies. In most developed countries, business entities make a significant contribution to the gross domestic product of the state, create jobs and promote competition. The creation of new jobs leads to an increase in income in the economy, increases effective demand, which creates conditions for sustainable economic development. Competition created by business entities stimulates the improvement of the quality of goods and services, productivity growth, and innovation.

The business sector contributes significantly to the innovative development of the economy by generating innovations to ensure competitive advantages. Higher innovative activity of small and medium-sized businesses is confirmed by researches.[4] Thus, a study conducted in the United States showed that 16 times more patents per employee are created in small and medium-sized businesses than in large businesses.[5]

However, the potential of small and medium-sized businesses in the innovative development of Russian regions remains underutilized. All this confirms the relevance of the research topic.

The purpose of the study is to determine the list of business competencies that ensure the innovative development of the region.

The object of the study is the provincial region, Mari El Republic, which is part of Volga Federal district of the Russian Federation. The population of the Republic is only 682.33 thousand people. The economy of the region has an industrial and agricultural orientation, the share of industry in the gross regional product (GRP) is 34%, the share of agriculture is 16%. Mari El Republic has no reserves of hydrocarbon raw materials or natural resources suitable for the production of export-oriented products. The Republic traditionally belongs to the number of subsidized regions. In terms of quality of life in the ranking of Russian regions in 2017, Mari El Republic takes only 63rd place. Yoshkar-Ola, the capital of the region, is at a distance of 862 km to Moscow, 334 km to Nizhny Novgorod, 151 km to Kazan. In the conditions of mobility of labor resources, logistics, lack of

---

3 See Federal law, 2018
4 See Brauweiler, 2002
5 See Titov, 2018

investors, this leads to the fact that more successful regions as points of growth "pull" the resources that could be invested in the peripheral region.[6]

Open data placed in professional and statistical bases of the Organization for economic cooperation and development, the World intellectual property organization, the Federal state statistics service, the Association of innovative regions of Russia, the Federal portal of small and medium enterprises, the Rating Agency Expert were used as the information base of the study.

2 Theoretical basis of the study

In the study of business competencies as a factor of innovative development of a provincial region, we relied primarily on the theory of systems, the theory of the firm, the resource theory of the firm, evolutionary theory, spatial theory, and institutional approach. Systems theory and systems approach formed the understanding of the provincial region as a self-forming, dynamic system with the potential for self-development, with the links of coordination between the main actors.[7] A region as a non-standard socio-economic system is characterized by the third type of self-organization processes, which means that the system of a provincial region is able to develop, accumulate and use past experience.[8] In accordance with the firm's theory, we considered the region as a "quasi-firm" or "quasi-Corporation" capable of forming competitive advantages independently, turning them into key competencies.[9] The resource theory of the firm made it possible to understand that the competitive advantages of the firm (region) are the key competencies, that is, the unique resources and organizational abilities of its subjects.[10]

Among the Russian scientists whose ideas and works have had a significant impact on the understanding of the dynamics of regional development we distinguish Zubarevich N. V.[11] and Tatarkin A. I.[12] In accordance with the provisions of the spatial economy, the national economy is not a mono-object, it is a multiregional organism, functioning on the basis of vertical (from the center to the regions) and horizontal (interregional) economic, social and political interactions and included in the system of global economic relations.[13]

---

6 See Brauweiler, 2002; See Tsvetkova, 2018
7 See Kleiner, Mayevsky, Kirdina, 2016
8 See Livschits, 2013
9 See Granberg, 2004
10 See Prahalad, Hamel, 2003
11 See Zubarevich, 2017
12 See Tatarkin, 2016
13 See Granberg, 2004

2.1 The concept of business competences

In modern management theory and practice, the concept of key competencies is widely used, which is associated with its huge research potential. This concept is a kind of response to the organizational changes that have taken place in large international companies since the early 70's of the XX century. The analysis of scientific literature has shown that competence studies distinguish the American approach (which focuses on the behavior of subjects), the functional approach (which is typical for the English school), the third integrated approach (shown by researchers in Germany, Austria and France). In Russia, the understanding of competencies as a result of educational and practical activities of the subject, its personal characteristics is formalized in the Federal state educational standards.[14] A more detailed presentation of our understanding of competences was presented in other articles.[15] As part of this research phase, we focus only on business competencies.

The choice of a group of business competencies as a subject of research arises from the fact that they are an element of the creative potential of the region, a factor in the development of the economy and characterize the ability of the region to create added value. The basic category for understanding the business competencies of the region for us was the definition of entrepreneurial competence, presented in the recommendations of the European Council: «entrepreneurship competence refers to the capacity to act upon opportunities and ideas, and to transform them into values for others. It is founded upon creativity, critical thinking and problem solving, taking initiative and perseverance and the ability to work collaboratively in order to plan and manage projects that are of cultural, social or financial value».[16]

In our study, we consider the business competencies of the region, by which we understand the ability of the population of the region to organize effective business activities, including the ability to ensure self-employment and stable income generation, organization of the process of production and marketing of a competitive product, organization of new jobs and management of labor collectives.

2.2 Review of international practice

To determine the composition of the region's business competencies, we relied on the world practice of competence research.[17] Among the works that caused our interest, we note a study of the requirements of the German employers to the

14 See Federal state, 2018c
15 See Murtazina, Tsvetkova, 2018
16 (Council recommendation, 2018)
17 See World economic forum, 2015

graduates of educational institutions[18], a collective work of American scientists, "Four-dimensional education".[19] Next, we present the studied approaches to the formation and content of competencies.[20]

Table 1: The projection of competences of the main groups (compiled by the authors on the basis of sources: Adam, S., 2009, OECD, 2005, EUR - Lex, 2006)

	Competence groups			
Approaches	**Personal Communication**	**Cooperation**	**Self-development**	**Entrepreneurship**
Union of Industrial and Employers' Confedera-tions of Europe – UNICE	competences in native and foreign (preferably English) languages; intercultural understanding and competencies	ability to work in a team; skills in analysis and synthesis; creativity and flexibility in the application of knowledge and skills	life-long learning skills; management techniques and feedback, etc.	entrepreneurial thinking and behaviour
Development and Selection of Key Competencies - DeSeCo	ability to interact effectively with the environment: use language, symbols and texts interactively; use knowledge and information interactively; use technologies interactively	ability to interact with heterogeneous groups, including the ability to build good relationships with others, to cooperate and work in a team, to resolve conflicts	ability to manage one's own life, being aware of social dynamics, environments and one's own role in society	ability to implement life plans and personal projects, and to act autonomously
Finland	interaction and multi-literacy; ICT literacy	engagement and building a sustainable future	thinking and learning; cultural competence, self-expression; self-care and management of daily life	career development and entre-pre-neurship
China	working with information and meaning	acceptance of responsibility: public responsibility, national identity, understanding of international context	ability to learn: learning in joy, effective learning, attention to self-esteem	innovation and practicality: value of work, problem solving, knowledge of applied technologies

[18] See Arthur, Brennan, de Weert, 2007

[19] See Fadel, Bialik, Trilling, 2015

[20] See Table 1

Approaches	Personal Communication	Cooperation	Self-development	Entrepreneurship
Republic of Korea	communication: respectful listening to the opinions of others and effective expression of own thoughts and feelings in a variety of situations	civic literacy: active involvement in changing societies for the better, with the values and attitudes necessary to be part of the local, national and global community	self-management: management of one's own life, personal identity and self-confidence, based on the abilities and qualifications necessary for life and career	creative thinking: exploration of new things, integration of knowledge, skills and experience from different professional fields on the basis of deep fundamental knowledge
Federal state educational standards, Russia	ability to carry out business communication in oral and written forms in the state language of the Russian Federation, and foreign language(s); ability to perceive the intercultural diversity of society	ability to carry out social interaction and realize a team role	ability to manage time, build and implement a trajectory of self-development based on the principles of education throughout one's life	ability to determine scope of tasks within the framework of the goal and to choose the best ways to solve them, based on the existing legal norms, available resources and limitations

The study has shown that all experts identified competencies related to entrepreneurial skills and emphasized the importance of innovative thinking, creativity, and willingness to act independently. At the same time, experts pay considerable attention to technological education and digital tools.[21]

These characteristics are related to business competencies. The authors were convinced that the Russian practice of implementing the competence approach, in general, corresponds to the main trends of the modern educational process. Since 2017, a new generation of Federal state standards of higher education (GEF 3++) has been formed in Russia, which include requirements for creation of universal competence. Generalization of the above approaches allowed us to identify and formulate ten competencies that characterize people's ability to carry out an effective business activity, that is, business competencies (cf. table 2).From our point of view, the presence of these competencies should be not only representatives of the business community (entrepreneurs and heads of organizations), but also the population of the provincial region, which can potentially become an entrepreneur, to start a business. The international study "global entrepreneurship monitoring" assesses entrepreneurial intentions as the willingness of the population to create their own business in the near future.[22] This indicator seems to reflect, to some extent, the assessment of the development of business competencies.

21 See Boston Consulting Group, 2018
22 See n.n., 2017

Table 2: Business competences of subjects of entrepreneurship

(*compiled by the authors on the basis of Federal state, 2018c)

Competences	Content of competences
Universal competencies	
1) interaction with people, teamwork	ability to carry out social interaction and realize their role in the team, taking into account the understanding of the intercultural diversity of society in the socio-historical, ethical and philosophical contexts
2) multilingualism and multiculturalism	ability to carry out business communication in oral and written forms in the state language of the Russian Federation and foreign languages
3) digital literacy	ability to collect, process and analyze data necessary for solving management tasks, including the use of modern tools of information technology and software, intelligent information and analytical systems
4) self-management, self-development	ability to manage their time, build and implement a trajectory of self-development, including vocational education throughout their life
5) creative thinking	ability to generate new ideas and knowledge, find non-standard solutions to problems, quickly solve problem situations
Specific business competencies	
1) economic literacy	ability to choose the best ways to solve professional problems, based on available resources and constraints, the ability to evaluate the effectiveness of solutions
2) legal literacy	knowledge and ability to use the regulatory framework of their activities
3) technological entrepreneurship	basic technological knowledge in the field of specialization: understanding of technologies, processes and the market situation in the industry, related and non-related industries
4) project skills	ability to define and logically articulate the goals and objectives of their activities, identify methods and develop plans to achieve them
5) marketing competences	ability to identify and evaluate new market opportunities, identify and predict market trends, develop projects for the creation and development of new products and activities of the company that are most relevant to the market situation

2.3 The economy of the provincial region and business competences

The study of theoretical concepts allowed the authors to present a logical model for the study of business competencies and their impact on the economy of the region, which reflects the main relationship between the resources and the results of the institutional units of the region.[23]

As a practical demonstration, we consider the real values of indicators of socio-economic development of the region, which, from our point of view, clearly demonstrate the level of development of region business competencies. The main object of the study was the provincial region, Republic of Mari El, which is part of Volga Federal district of the Russian Federation.

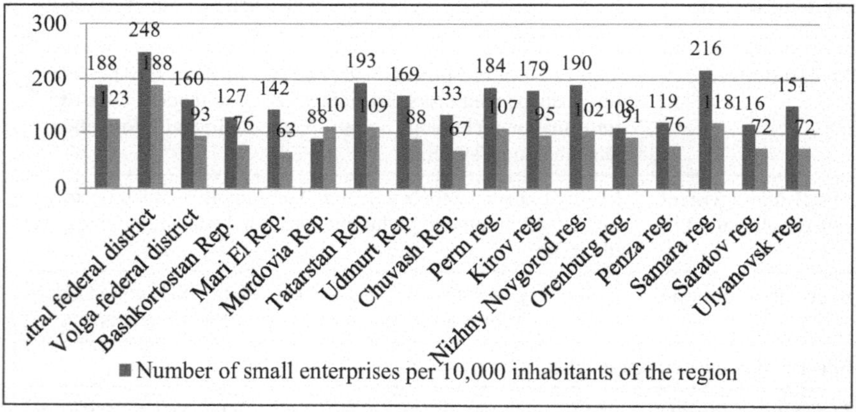

Figure 1: Structural profile of regions in the context of small - medium - large business. (compiled on the basis of data from the Federal state, 2018b)

*Abbreviations hereafter: Rep. – Republic, reg. - region

First of all, let us consider the statistics of the number of enterprises per 10,000 people.[24] This indicator gives an idea of the production potential of the region, the quality of institutional design of the production function of the region. Comparison of the number of small enterprises with the number of large and medium-sized enterprises allows us to see the structural profile of the region.

The number of small enterprises in Volga Federal district per 10,000 people is below the Russian average. The highest values of the indicator are in Samara, Kirov, Nizhny Novgorod regions, Republic of Tatarstan, Udmurt Republic, Perm region. These regions lead in the national ranking in terms of economic and inno-

---

23 See Figure 2

24 See Figure 1

vative development, have a significant share of the resource industry in the structure of the economy. The largest ratio of the number of medium and large businesses with the population is observed in the regions with a large share of the resource industry in the structure of the economy – Republic of Tatarstan, Perm, Nizhny Novgorod and Samara regions.

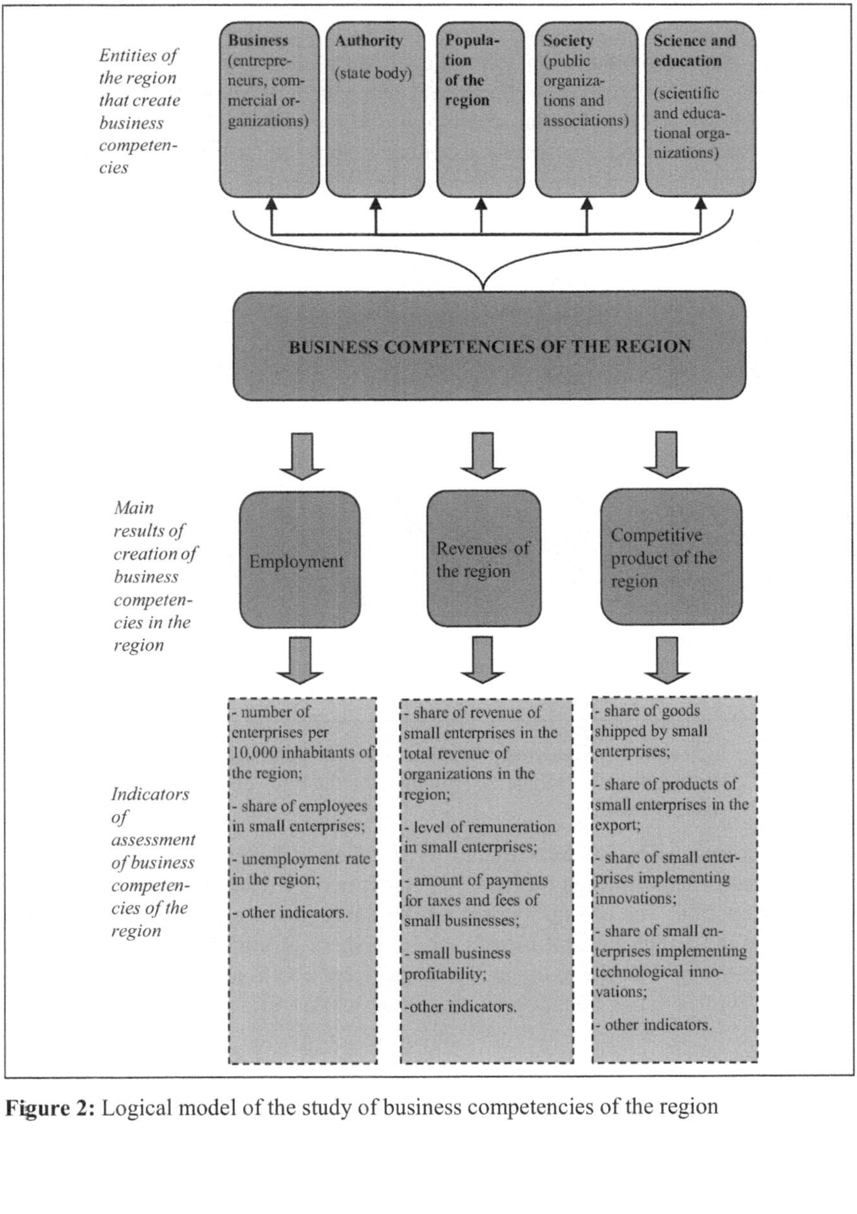

Figure 2: Logical model of the study of business competencies of the region

The number of small businesses per 10,000 people in Mari El Republic is close to the median. It should be noted that the Republic has the lowest number of medium and large organizations per 10,000 people. This indicates the limited opportunities for development of small businesses in Republic of Mari El and their "growth" into medium and large. In the context of the study of business competencies, this situation characterizes a lack of readiness of the population of the region to engage in business activities and to take the risks of doing business. A large part of the population of Republic of Mari El is more comfortable to be employees, avoiding risky entrepreneurial behavior strategies. This partly stems from the legacy of the industrial structure of the region, which was dominated by large machine-building enterprises associated with the military-industrial complex during the planned economy. We can say that the population prefers jobs in medium and large businesses, which is a feature of this provincial region.

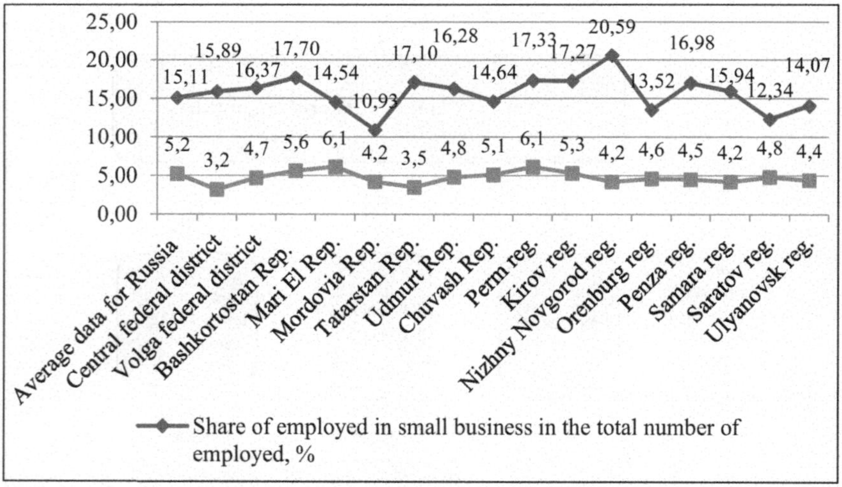

Figure 3: Indicators of employment in small enterprises and unemployment in Volga Federal district regions, %. (compiled on the basis of data from the Federal state, 2018b)

Formal acceptance by subjects of the territory of such structural profile of the region "small-medium-large business" is confirmed by data on unemployment in Mari El Republic. The unemployment rate in the region is higher than the national average and Volga Federal district, and the share of employment in small enterprises is lower than the average.[25] Mari El Republic is included in the List of territories with a tense situation in the labor market at the end of 2016-2017,

25 See Figure 3

which indicates not only the presence of problems in the labor market in the region, but also the insufficient level of development of business competencies of the region's population.

In Mari El Republic the contribution of small businesses to the turnover of the manufacturing industry amounts to 40.8%, the highest in Volga Federal district. This results in a high value of revenues of small enterprises per capita of Mari El Republic.[26] This figure is above the average of Volga Federal district. At the same time, both in Republic of Mari El and in all Volga Federal district, the revenue of small enterprises per capita is lower than the average value in Russia and more than 2 times lower than in Central Federal district. The reasons for this phenomenon can be both lower effective demand in provincial markets, and lower capacity of businesses to produce a competitive product which would be demanded in foreign markets.

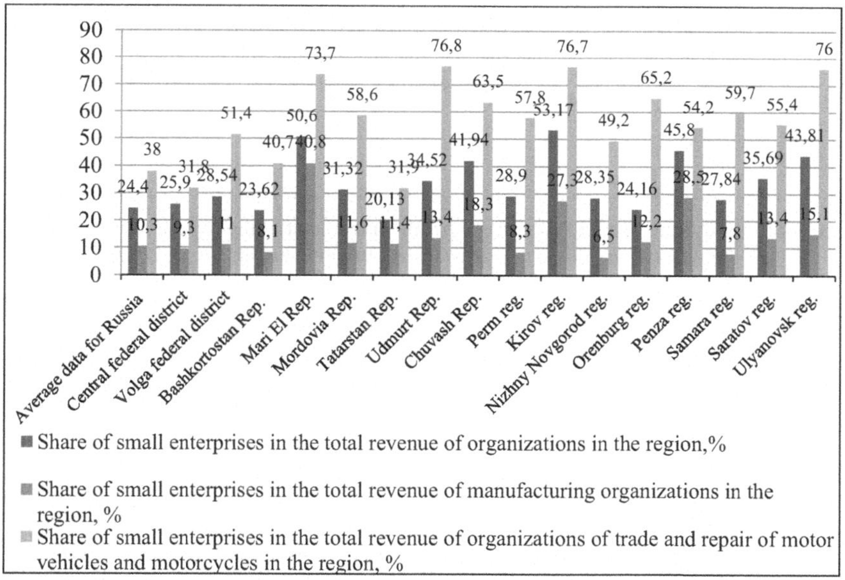

Figure 4: Contribution of small enterprises to the total revenue of organizations in the region, %. (compiled on the basis of data from the Federal state, 2018b)

The ability of small enterprises to produce a competitive product is an indicator of business competence. Data on introduction of innovations in the manufacturing of products by enterprises of the region, including small businesses, were used as

26 See Figure 5

indicators of assessing the capacity of businesses to produce a competitive product.[27]

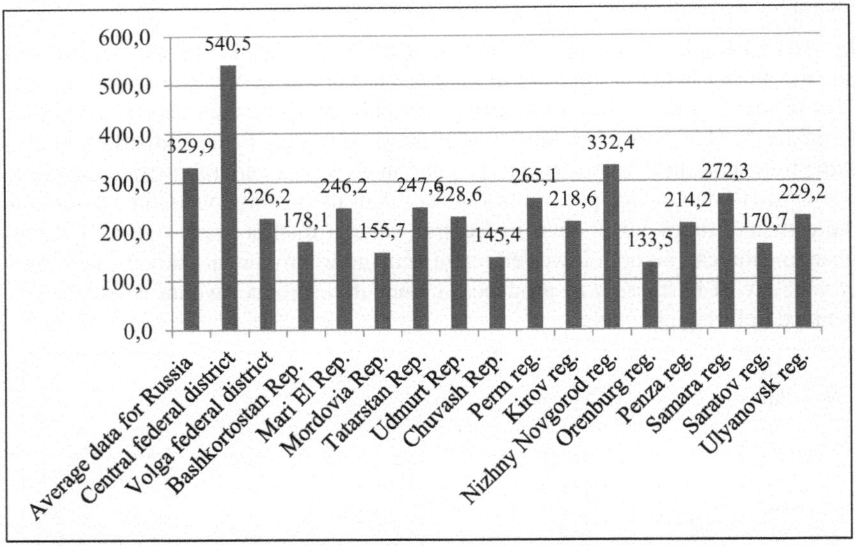

Figure 5: Revenue of small enterprises per one inhabitant of the region, thousand rubles. (compiled on the basis of data from the Federal state, 2018b)

The ability of small enterprises to produce a competitive product is an indicator of business competence. Data on introduction of innovations in the manufacturing of products by enterprises of the region, including small businesses, were used as indicators of assessing the capacity of businesses to produce a competitive product.[28]

On average, in Volga Federal district, the indicators of innovative activity of organizations are close to the median, but within the region there is a significant differentiation of indicators. The greatest innovative activity is witnessed in Mordovia, Tatarstan and Chuvashia, Nizhny Novgorod and Penza regions. Traditionally, low rates are observed in the provincial regions of Mari El Republic, Orenburg and Ulyanovsk regions.

27 See Figure 6
28 See Figure 6

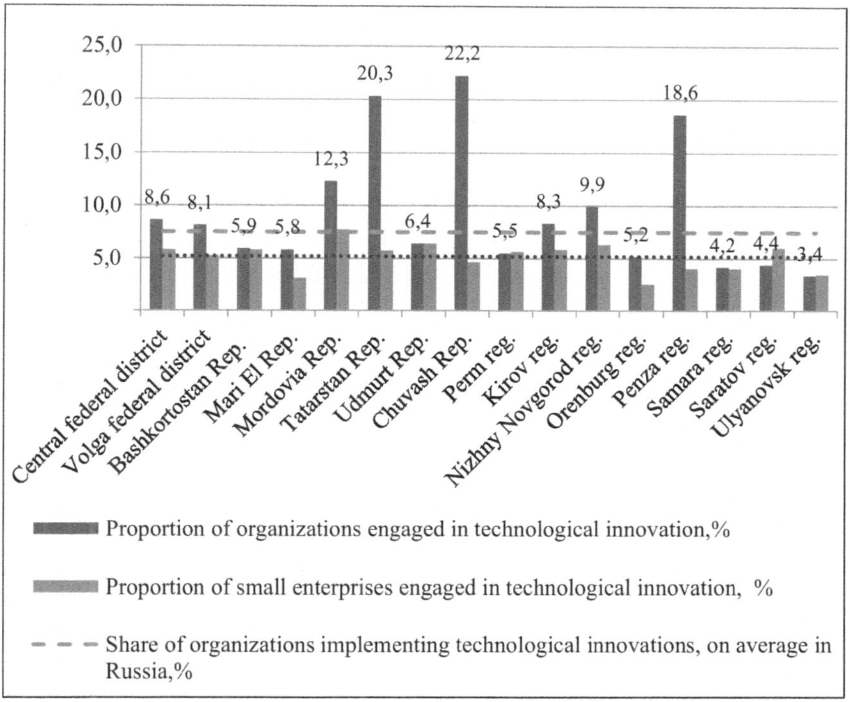

Figure 6: Indicators of innovation activity of enterprises of Volga Federal district regions. (compiled on the basis of data from the Federal state, 2018b)

3 Conclusion

Modern trends in socio-economic and technological development require a rethinking of classical approaches to regional development. The analysis of theoretical concepts, practical studies of foreign and domestic scientists revealed the prospects of studying regional systems on the basis of the concept of key competencies. The authors propose a logical scheme for the study of business competencies of the provincial region, which focuses on the institutional units of the region (business, government, science and education, population, and public organizations) and indicators that reflect the implementation of business competencies (employment, revenues of the region, competitive product), and their impact on the development of the region's economy.

Analysis of statistical data of the provincial region, Mari El Republic, has shown that the small business sector employs about 14.5% of the population of the region. This is below the average data for Russia, and together with the increased unemployment rate, it does not characterize the competence of small businesses in the field of job creation as satisfactory. The inclusion of the region in the list of territories with a tense situation in the labor market and low rates of innovative activity of small enterprises confirm the insufficient level of development of business competencies and entrepreneurial skills of the population. The results indicate the need to continue research on the problem of development of business competencies of the provincial region and their impact on its economic development.

Literature

Adam, S. (2009). *Learning Outcomes: state of the art in Europe. New in the application of learning outcomes in the context of the Bologna process. Bologna process: learning Outcomes and competence approach (book-Annex 1).*

Arthur, L., Brennan, J., de Weert, E. (2007). *Employer and Higher Education Perspectives on Graduates in the Knowledge Society – A Report for the European Commission VI Project: 'The flexible professional in the knowledge society.*

Boston Consulting Group. (2018). *The Value of Digital Learning in Higher Education.* Retrieved 12 10, 2018, from https://www.worldgovernment summit.org/api/publications/document?id=a76994c4-e97c-6578-b2f8-ff0000a7ddb6

Brauweiler, H.-Ch. (2002). *Innovationen im peripheren Raum.* Wiesbaden: Gabler.

Council recommendation. (2018). *Council recommendation on key competences for lifelong learning of 22 May 2018.* Retrieved 21.11.2018, from https://eur-lex.europa.eu/legal-content/EN/TXT/?uri=CELEX%3A32018 H0604%2801%29

EUR - Lex. (2006). *The Key Competences for Lifelong Learning.* Retrieved 25.11.2018, from A European Framework is an annex of a Recommendation of the European Parliament and of the Council of 18 December 2006 on key competences for lifelong learning that was published in the Official Journal of the European Union.: https://eur-lex.europa.eu/legal-content/EN/TXT/?qid=1551880593927&uri=CELEX:32006H0962

Fadel, C., Bialik, M., Trilling, B. (2015). *Four-dimensional education: The competencies learners need to succeed. Boston: Center for Curriculum Redesign.* Retrieved 28.10.2018, from http://curriculumredesign.org/our-work/four-dimensional-21st-century-education-learning-competencies-future-2030

Federal law. (2018). *Federal law of 27.11.2018 N 422-FZ.* Retrieved 10.2.2019, from "On conducting an experiment to establish a special tax regime "Professional income tax" in a federal city of Moscow, in Moscow and Kaluga regions, as well as in the Tatarstan Republic (Tatarstan)".: http://www.consultant.ru/law/hotdocs/55771.html

Federal state. (2018a). *Federal state educational standards.* Retrieved 22.9.2018, from https://fgos.ru

Federal state. (2018b). *Federal state statistics service.* Retrieved 24.9.2018, from http://www.gks.ru.

Federal state. (2018c). *Portal of Federal state educational standards of higher education.* Retrieved 24.9.2018, from http: fgosvo.ru

Granberg, A. (2004). *Socio-economic space of Russia: transformational trends and prospects: a series of public lectures.*

Kleiner, G., Mayevsky, S., Kirdina, M. (2016). *System coordination in Economics: towards the formation of the General theory of coordination. New research in heterodox Economics: Russian contribution.* Institute of Economics.

Livschits, V. (2013). *Fundamentals of system thinking and system analysis.* Institute of Economics.

Murtazina, A., Tsvetkova, G. (2018). *Basic subjects that form the core competencies of the region. Bulletin of the faculty of management.* St. Petersburg state economic University.

n.n. (2017). *National Report. Global entrepreneurship monitor Russia.* Retrieved 17.11.2018, from http://smb.gov.ru/files/images/gem_russia_2016-2017.pdf

n.n. (2019). *National project "Small and medium-sized enterprises and support of individual entrepreneurial initiative".* Retrieved 10.2.2019, from http://government.ru/projects/selection/654

OECD. (2005). *The definition and selection of key competencies: Executive summary.* Retrieved 20.11.2018, from http://www.oecd.org

Prahalad, C., Hamel, G. (2003). *Core competence of the Corporation.* Vestnik St. Petersburg University.

Tatarkin, A. (2016). *The Regional focus of the economic policy of the Russian Federation as Institute for spatial development. Economy of region.* (12 ed.).

Titov, B. (2018). *Sector of small and medium enterprises: Russia and the World.* Retrieved 15.10.2018, from http://stolypin.institute/wp-content/uploads/2018/07/issledovanie-ier-msp-27.07.18.pdf

Tsvetkova, G. (2018). *External and internal threats to economic security peripheral region Innovative development of the economy.*

World economic forum. (2015). *New Vision for Education. Unlocking the Potential of Technology. World Economic Forum report.* Retrieved 12.10.2018, from http://www3.weforum.org/docs/WEFUSA_NewVisionforEducation_Report2015.pdf

Zubarevich, N. (2017). *Development of the Russian space: barriers and opportunities of regional policy. World of new economy.*

Mergers and Acquisitions: Share Deal vs. Asset Deal – Risks and Impediments

Vedran Alickovic, H.-Ch. Brauweiler

1 Acquisitions

1.1 Share Deal

A share deal contains the purchase of all company shares or the purchase of a certain rate of shares which empowers the buyer to exercise control over the company. Thereby all rights and obligations and with that, all assets and liabilities were transmitted to the buyer.[1] Based on that fact, the corporate investment represents the legal object of purchase and meets the criteria of a legal purchase in accordance with § 433 (1) sentence 2 BGB (Bürgerliches Gesetz-Buch, German Civil Law Code)[2] read in conjunction with article § 453 (1) BGB.[3] The advantage of such an acquisition is that the assets don't have to be transferred one by one, but rather in one transaction.

In case of buying just a rate of shares without the ability of exercising control, the transaction fulfils the definition of an acquisition of assets. The term share embodies all kind of shares of legal entities, despite their legal structure and contains especially shares of limited partnerships, joint-stock companies, limited companies or corporations.[4]

The following figure shows the general idea of an acquisition on a share deal basis.

---

1 See Engelhardt, 2017, p. 5
2 See Jansen, 2016, p. 291
3 See Picot, 2012, p. 301
4 See Picot, 2012, p. 301

H.-C. Brauweiler et al. (Hrsg.), *Digitalization and Industry 4.0: Economic and Societal Development*, https://doi.org/10.1007/978-3-658-27110-7_16

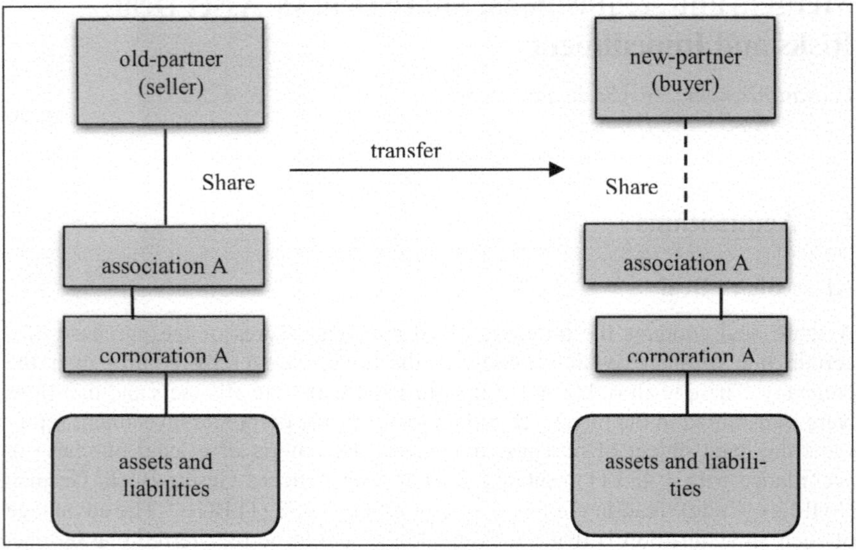

Figure 1: Share Deal, own representation based on Engelhardt, 2017, p. 6

1.2 Asset Deal

As in chapter 1 explained a share deal contains the purchase of all company shares or the purchase of a certain rate of shares which empowers the buyer to exercise control over the company. An asset deal recognises the purchase of all[5], or individual assets, held by an individual or company and not the purchase of company shares in any case. In some cases, it is possible to obtain also liabilities or portions of liabilities, when discussed with the creditors in advance.[6] Each asset and liability is transferred accordingly to the singular succession from the seller to the buyer. Hence it meets the criteria for being a purchase in accordance with § 433 (1) sentence 1 BGB.[7]

The following figure shows the general idea of an acquisition on a asset deal basis.

---

5 See Picot, 2012, p. 301
6 See Engelhardt, 2017, p. 6
7 See Jansen, 2016, p. 291

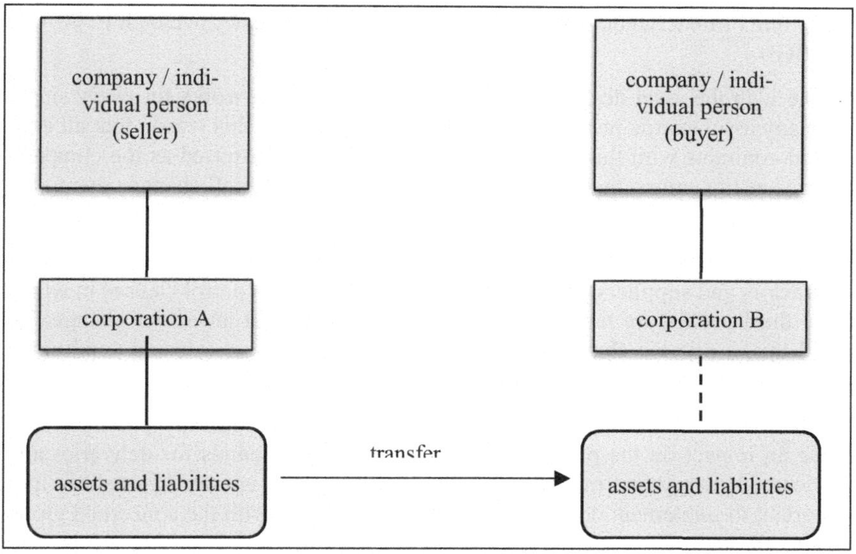

Figure 2: Asset Deal, own representation based on Engelhardt, 2017, p. 7

2 Contractual Item

2.1 Share Deal

As in the previous sequence described a share deal generally contains the purchase of shares and not individual assets. For that reason, it is mandatory that the purchase object complies to the transactional structure and the contractual item must be defined precisely.[8] As in figure 2 already mentioned, the buyer obtains a direct participation in the assets of the company or rather the legal entity. Hence the identity of a company stays untouched, legal entities are legal persons, partnerships or even individual companies. However, the important part is that the company assets are strictly separated from the private assets of the company member if the companies legal form is a corporation or partnership. Based on that fact, the share deal meets the criteria of a legal purchase in accordance with § 453 BGB. So, the seller of the ownership rights is not only liable for the legal validity of the sold rights, but also for their economic value, considering specific risk,[9] as the purchase of rights got extended by the provisions for the purchase of goods which shall apply accordingly. Therefore, the seller is obliged to transfer the

---

[8]See Engelhardt, 2017, p. 30
[9] See Brauweiler, 2018

rights free of material defects and defects of title to the buyer, pursuant to §§ 434, 435 BGB.[10]

Unlike with the asset deal, there is no need of transaction works for every single company asset as it is just a change in the owner. It is for this reason that all concluded contracts with third parties do not need to be transferred as the company remains as the contractual partner. This is also the case for all changes due to the changes of undertaking as pursuant in § 613a BGB.

As it is not unusual for companies to have contracts with licensors, banks, subcontractors and suppliers, they may have some change of control clauses in which these third parties are terminating the contract in case of an owner change. To avoid this, a proviso clause regarding the transfer of shares (closing-conditions) should be implemented within the sale purchase agreement.[11]

It is also necessary to take account of the fact that the company purchase may cause an impact on the purchased group company's demands for deliveries and services of energy and raw materials from other group entities. Therefore, it is important to implement delivery contracts (term-sheets) with the concerned group entities through the transition period to ensure proper supply within the present framework.[12]

2.2 Asset Deal

The acquisition of a company within an asset deal can be even more than just buying all assets a company offers in its books. Furthermore, it can contain a total of goods, knowledge, customer relations and legal or tangible rights. It is generally a legal purchase in accordance with §§ 433 et seq. BGB. In addition, the buyer has a claim for performance as pursuant in § 433 (1) BGB in which the seller on the one hand transfers the ownership to the buyer and on the other hand does it free of material defects and defects of title. Regarding § 23 HGB, a company cannot be sold without its trade transaction for which it has been constituted.

Notwithstanding from selling goods, if the purchasable objects are intellectual property rights, patent rights or copyright treaties the company purchase meets the criteria of being a purchase of rights in accordance to § 453 BGB, the buyer must ensure that the enterprise / shareholder value equals the total of wanted tangible and intangible assets. Furthermore, the seller is obliged to

- transfer all related company know-how to the seller within a competition agreement,

---

10 See Picot, 2012, p. 303 f.
11 See Picot, 2012, p. 304
12 See Picot, 2012, p. 303 f.

- give the acquirer any instruction and information about the company's fields of activity.

Same as with the share deal, the asset deal requires an individual transfer of all third-party contracts (suppliers, customers, lessors or leasing companies). If the acquirer wishes to release himself from the obligation, a tripartite agreement with all contractual partners is inevitable. This can be even more critical in cases of continuing obligations as a third-party member denies the transfer of the contract to the transferee. In such a case, it is only possible to solve that issue via internal relationship between the contractual partners.[13] In some cases it can be hard to identify all transferrable assets, due to missing machines or parts, or incomplete lists of transferrable assets. Due to this fact catch-all-clauses were implemented within the sale purchase agreement.[14]

However, defining the object of purchase has a direct effect on the transfer of employment relationships. Since the purchaser buys the company and gains the total ownership, he also acquires the rights and obligations within the employment relationships in accordance to § 613a BGB.

Aggravating this situation, the company cannot be part of the transfer process regarding the company purchase, but rather the company's items and rights in the sense of the singular succession according to general civil law. So, within the principle of legal certainty it is precisely defined which individual parts of the company are being transferred within the property transaction process. There is a considerable difference between acquiring a manufacturing or a service company, as various levels of know-how, staff, machinery, customer lists are involved and are forming the basis for the supply of goods or services.[15]

3 Due Diligence

In everyday life, it happens that customers are buying goods from manufacturers "as seen" and under a systematic asymmetry of information. Germany tried to solve the problem by using special warranty clauses implemented in their selling contracts until the 1990s, in which the Anglo-Saxon concept of the due diligence has prevailed.[16]

As every acquisition comes with risk, whether a reliable evaluation is possible or not, it is always reasonable to execute a due diligence, due to getting a true and fair view of the financial position, financial performance and cash flow in ad-

---

13 See Picot, 2012, p. 302
14 See Engelhardt, 2017, p. 30
15 See Picot, 2012, p. 303
16 See Jansen, 2016, p. 314

vance. It is advisable to execute this activity in an early stage of the negotiation process and right before making an official offer. Although there is a distinction between the Buyer Initiated Due Diligence and the Vendor Initiated Due Diligence, in most of the cases the due diligence is requested by prospective buyers.[17] Hence the BIDD is only executable after signing a confidentiality agreement, due to the fact of classified business information, the VIDD is reasonable when trying to meet a larger number of buyer needs. To be as trustworthy as possible and to evade unjustified security demands from perspective buyers, the VIDD is mostly done by third party companies, as their core competency is company valuation. In terms where a due diligence is not done or not done correctly, the manager of the acquiring company is guilty of delinquency[18] in accordance with §§ 76, 93 (1) AktG (Aktiengesellschaften-Gesetz, German Stock Corporation Act) and must pay an indemnity as in conjunction with article § 93 (2) AktG.[19]

Before acquiring a company or even starting to bid, the buying party must determine if there are any synergy effects when purchasing a company. Furthermore, every company purchase means that risks are also part of the transaction which must be taken. Therefore, a correct evaluation of the purchase price recognizing these points is vital for the buyer. To do so, the buyer needs certain information, which the seller can contribute. The due diligence can an approach of willingness of the seller to deliver the information needed, and to adjust the asymmetrical distribution of information between the two parties.[20] However a bigger amount of information given to the buyer, leads to more detailed demands regarding the contractual warranty obligation from the seller, and vice versa.

So, in the first place the due diligence gets all relevant information needed for determining a correct purchase price for a company as for the company valuation. The procedure adjusts the asymmetrical distribution of information between both contractual parties and gives the buyer a better a chance of allocating risks and weaknesses of the transaction target. It assesses all needed warranties arising from recognised risk positions and lack of information.[21] In the end, it consolidates all discussed points and records them for evidentiary purposes and implementation into the purchase agreement.[22]

The following figure shows the initiator of a due diligence, the main target, the individual forms of a due diligence and the general effect.

---

17 See Picot, 2012, p. 256
18 See Engelhardt, 2017, p. 12
19 See Picot, 2012, p. 256
20 See Picot, 2012, p. 257
21 See Pomp, 2015, p. 9
22 See Engelhardt, 2017, p. 12

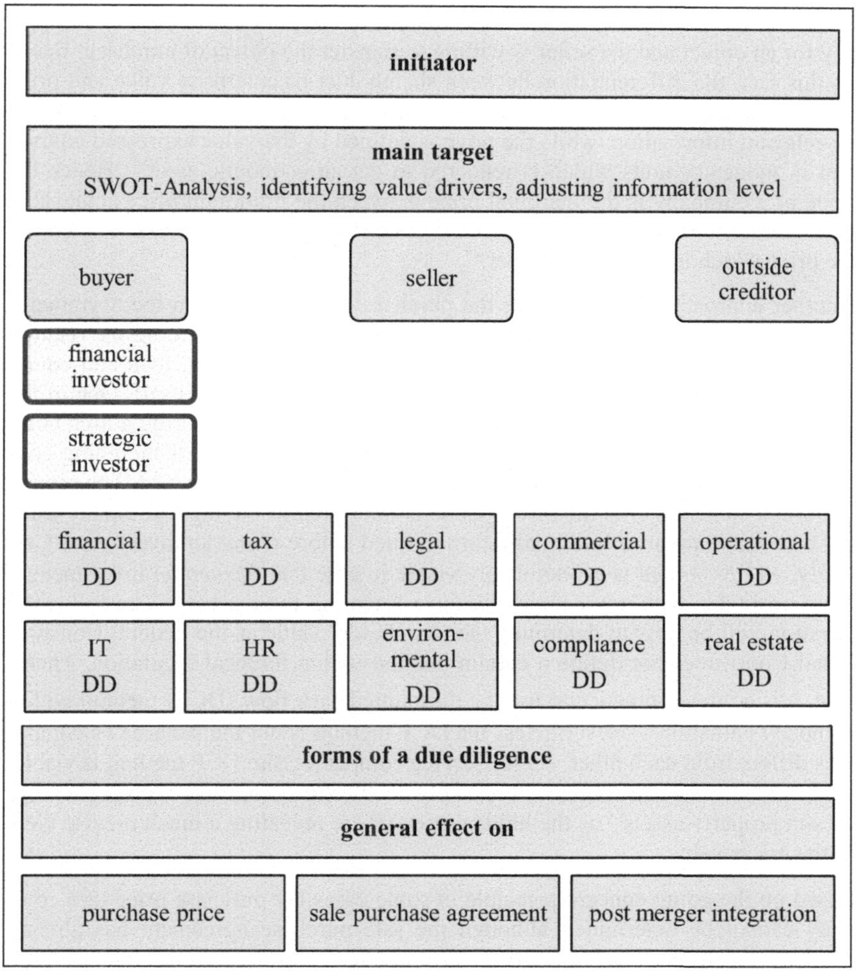

Figure 3: Due Diligence: target, initiator, forms and effect, own representation based on Pomp, 2015, p. 10

4 Purchase Price

As already in the previous section discussed the due diligence has a general effect on the purchase price determination. So, in this segment the major topic is the proper differentiation between value and price and the determination of a purchase price.

However, the purchase price is defined as the actual price the buyer is willing to pay for an object and the seller is willing to transfer the object of purchase. Based on this fact, the differentiation between shareholder or enterprise value and price of the company is vital, as the value is defined by the monetary evaluated company-relevant information, while the price is defined by the value expressed equivalent in monetary units which is rendered to get an economic asset.[23] Hence the price of a company is the marginal price between the minimum price achievable by the seller without gaining economical disadvantages and the maximum available price which is paid by the buyer.[24]

Another approach of determining the purchase price, aside from the asymmetry between supply and demand within a heterogenous market regarding the relation between value and price, lies by the stakeholders (seller, buyer, loan and equity providers, advisors) involved in the transaction of an enterprise itself. One of the most important stakeholder is the seller, as he is interested in getting a high compensation for the company (shareholder value) due to the fact of the going concern principle and the future associated discounted cash flows earned. The second important stakeholder is the buyer, as he is interested in buying a company earning a certain amount of minimal return defined before doing an investment. Certainly, an investment is economically viable in case that the capital investment is more profitable than any comparable investment on the market.[25] The following question will be how to determine the shareholder value as the Federal Constitutional Court does not define a certain method within its legal regulation. Therefore, it is common practice to use the discounted cash flow (DCF) method within company valuation.[26] Nevertheless the DCF method is not the panacea as companies differs from each other. As for service companies, the DCF method is viable, the net asset value method is more likely usable for companies with higher figures in property assets[27] as the hidden reserves are revealing a much precise view of the assets value.

Based on the going concern principle in some cases the purchase price of a company cannot be determined although the sale purchase agreement has already been signed as the company is still running operations. Due to that fact the sale purchase agreement is enlarged by price adjustment clauses. These clauses are recognising future adjustments regarding the company's value within the contract

23 See Jansen, 2016, p. 320
24 See Sinewe, 2015, p. 50
25 See Jansen, 2016, p. 321
26 See Picot, 2012, p. 306
27 See Engelhardt, 2017, p. 31

and allowing the seller a participation in future company earnings. Common price adjustment clauses are[28]:

- trust accounts, which are distributing the contractual price after a contractual period
- earn-out clauses are giving a reimbursement to the buyer in case of missing contracted income goals
- purchase price clauses which are adjusting a decrease in the customer base due to the transaction
- locked-box concepts which are determining the purchase price based on a contracted effective date balance sheet or a future transition date

5 Post Merger Integration (PMI)

One of the last procedures which is crucial for the success of an acquisition is the integration procedure. This process is vital for the company, and if done correctly the determined synergy effects will occur during the integration phase.[29] Therefore a proper preparation and discussing essential integration topics before the signing or transaction process is necessary and contributes in strengthening the organizational structure as well as ensuring business operations, preventing initial difficulties which are narrowing revenue.

Possible integration models can be bolt-on, in which the current company remains its structure and is an affiliate company. Another possibility is the takeover, where the acquiree is totally incorporated into the company. Best-of-both describes that the qualities of both companies are merged and implemented, whether the transformation process combines the two companies into one new company.

Any of these methods are divided into two phases. In the design phase, which is critical for the success of any model, the management is defining the company's strategy and determines a structural plan for the integrational process.

This phase includes the following tasks, all contributing to an easier integration process:

- determining the aspirational level of the company and defining business goals
- identifying all short, middle, and long-term value-creation potentials
- planning any further integrational procedure
- ensuring the company's future effectivity[30]

---

[28] See Engelhardt, 2017, p. 31; See Picot, 2012, p. 308 f.
[29] See Jansen, 2016, p. 362
[30] See Picot, 2012, p. 535

In the implementation stage the structural plan is being executed and deviations are controlled. An appropriate IT infrastructure and staff training is essential in this stage for the integrational success.[31]

6 Conclusion

In summary, it can be said that it is not possible to say if a share or asset deal is the ultimate decision for a company. More likely it is the company's strategy which can determine which kind of acquisition method it uses. In this seminar paper the general idea of the share and asset deal was given pointing in the second section out, that there are risks about the change of control clauses in which creditors like e.g. banks can terminate a contract in case of an owner change. This can lead to a termination of loan contracts and may have an impact on the company's financial structure or even the current cash situation. Another point is that the acquisition may have an impact on the purchased group company's demands for deliveries and services of energy and raw materials from other group entities for ensuring its operations. So, it is important to implement term-sheets with the concerned group entities through the transition period to ensure proper supply within the present framework

It was shown that a due diligence is vital for the acquisition process as it helps determining the purchase price, and leads to a much smoother integrational procedure. Neglecting a due diligence or executing it incorrectly, the manager of the buying company is guilty of delinquency and may face legal action in terms of the business judgment rule. Furthermore, the planned synergy effects won't occur, as a proper strategy was not developed by the management in prior stages before the transaction process.

Risks and impediments regarding the purchase price can arise in the correct valuation of the shareholder value. As there are plenty of methods, like the DCF method or the net asset value method, every stakeholder can determine which approach he prefers and what is maximum or minimum price he is willing to pay. Another big point is the fact that price adjustment clauses can damage the contract or even cause a reverse transaction of the contract, as the price is adjusted due to the higher risks of the seller, who is revealing vast amounts of information to the prospective buyer.

Literature

Brauweiler, H.-Ch. (2018). *Risikomanagement in Unternehmen.*

---

31 See Picot, 2012, p. 534 f.

Coenenberg, A. G., Haller, A., Schultze, W. (2016). *Jahresabschluss und Jahresabschlussanalyse.* Stuttgart: Schäffer Poeschel.

Engelhardt, C. (2017). *Mergers & Acquisitions.* Wiesbaden: Springer Gabler.

Jansen, S. A. (2016). *Mergers & Acquisitions.* Wiesbaden: Springer Gabler.

Küting, K., Weber, C. (2012). *Der Konzernabschluss.* Stuttgart: Schäffer Poeschel.

Meckbach, A. (2013). *CMS International.* Retrieved 2.3.2019, from https://www.cmshs-bloggt.de/gesellschaftsrecht/m-a/legalese-folge-10-share-deal-oder-asset-deal/

Pellens, B., Fülbier, R. U., Gassen, J., Sellhorn, T. (2014). *Internationale Rechnungslegung.* Stuttgart: Schäffer Poeschel.

Petrik, O., Filipe, M., de Abreu e Silva, J. (2014). The Influence of the Volume – Delay Function on Uncertainty Assessment for a Four-Step Model. *Advances in Intelligent Systems and Computing.*

Picot, G. (2012). *Handbuch Mergers & Acquisitions.* Stuttgart: Schäffer Poeschel.

Pomp, T. (2015). *Praxishandbuch Financial Due Diligence.* Wiesbaden: Springer Gabler.

PTV-Ag. (2017). PTV VISSIM 9 User Manual. Karlsruhe: PTV-Ag.

Sinewe, P. (2015). *Unternehmenskauf in der Steuerpraxis.* Wiesbaden: Springer Gabler.

Spiess, H. (1990). Technical note—conical volume-delay functions. *Transportation Science.*

Statista. (2019). *Institute for Mergers, Acquisitions and Alliances (IMAA).* Retrieved 27.9.2019, from Volumen der weltweiten M&A Deals von 1985 bis 2018 (in Milliarden US-Dollar) [Graph].: https://de.statista.com/statistik/daten/st

Wiehl, M. (2016). *Rödl & Partner.* Retrieved 2.3.2019, from http://www.roedl.de/themen/unternehmenskauf-im-ausland/unternehmenskauf-share-deal-versus-asset-deal

Modelling of traffic flow characteristics of traffic calmed roads

Matthias Richter, Jan Paszkowski

1 Traffic calming

According to a definition by Institute of Transportation Engineers[1] traffic calming is a set of measures, the purposes of which is to reduce the negative effects of motor vehicle use, alter driver behaviour and improve conditions for non-motorised street users. That includes reduction of traffic volume, thus noise and air pollution, improvement of road safety level, and the quality of life. The beginning of traffic calming reaches 1960s and 1970s in Great Britain, Germany, Netherlands and Denmark and is connect ed with pedestrianisation – an idea to prioritise walking by closing the streets or to slow car speed down to walking pace.[2]

Traffic calming can be divided by the scales of influences into three levels[3]:

Level I – actions restricted to local, residential level with low traffic volumes and capacities to restrain traffic speeds and to reduce traffic impacts

Level II – actions extended to a corridor, which has an influence on a traffic on that corridor, but not on the network

Level III – actions at macro-level, introduced on a greater area and having an influence for the traffic network.

2 Measurement methods

To reproduce driver behaviour to a high level of precision, it was necessary to have precise vehicle motion recorded including data relating to speed, acceleration and braking. Moreover, for further investigation of the problem, it was important to note interactions between vehicles; these interactions between vehicles include the distances between successive vehicles, braking forces when noticing the approach to the car in front, and the speed and distance fluctuations when following. These parameters can be adopted in the Wiedemann model, used in PTV Vissim software.

---

1 See ITE/FHWA, 1999
2 See Barbosa, 1995
3 See Brindle, 1992

H.-C. Brauweiler et al. (Hrsg.), *Digitalization and Industry 4.0: Economic and Societal Development*, https://doi.org/10.1007/978-3-658-27110-7_17

In general, the measurement types can be divided into two categories: inside and outside the vehicle. **Measurements inside the vehicle**, known also as floating car, stands, that there is a measurement car, equipped with movement tracking device, such as car computer, recording distance travelled and speed of the car, or additional values, such as acceleration and braking pedal press. Another solution for floating car motion recording is the use of GPS devices, which record not only the speeds of the vehicle, but also its trajectory; this means that in every time stamp (for example one second), the position of the vehicle is recorded. When using this method, it should be noted that GPS has an accuracy of 2-5 meters[4], which can have a negative influence on the results. **Measurements outside the vehicle**, unlike the methods above, are able to record the behaviour of more than one vehicle. These methods include strategies such as pneumatic tubes for speed measurement or radar control[5] and can be connected to speed control, photographing or video recording facilities. Unfortunately, most of these methods are only working in one specific point of the measured road or area; therefore, it is needed to provide measurements in more points. However, gaps between measurement points still exist.

In order to ensure continuity in the recording of every vehicle in the traffic flow, video recording can be used. Previously, analysis of the video and identification of the vehicles trajectories were performed manually and this was a very time-consuming task. Nowadays, with the use of deep machine learning through creating classifiers, it is possible do detect vehicles automatically, trace them, and produce trajectories.

The area which can be recorded depends on the angle of the camera and the obstacles which cover the traffic, as well as the shape of the road, which can limit the size of that area. The optimal solution is to position the camera in such a manner that it is recording from above in order to minimize the amount of obstacles, as well as to simplify the trajectory calculations. This would mean installing the camera at a point high above the street or to record from the air. To provide coverage of a great area, when only low buildings are present, an unmanned quadcopter was used, hovering 80 meters above ground level, and recording the traffic along an approximate length of 110 meters of road. The quadcopter used is able to fly for around 25 minutes, which, taking into account a safe reserve of battery time, take off, positioning above the street and landing, leaves around 15-20 minutes of traffic recording at any one time. Recordings were made at a high definition of 1920*1080 pixels resolution, and 40 frames per second.

---

4 See GPS, 2017
5 See Barbosa, 1995

The trajectories from the video were processed by the company DatafromSky.[6] The result of processing is delivered in two files – one of these is the file for the DatafromSky viewer software which is used to visualise the results, and the other is the .csv-file with all the data, containing timestamp, coordinates, object ID, and object type (car, heavy vehicle, bus, bicycle, pedestrian). A screenshot of the DatafromSky viewer software is presented in figure 1.

Figure 1: DatafromSky viewer software screenshot with car detection and trajectory data displayed (source: own)

3 Measurement results

The data acquired from recordings was processed. The street visible in figure 1 was divided into 10 cm sections and for each section instantaneous velocities were identified for every vehicle, divided to vehicle classes, such as cars (standard and van), busses and heavy vehicles. From these speeds, charts showing the speed profiles have been created for different points along the analysed road, including the installed speed cushions. The following measurement results are based on approx. 20 minutes recording and contain trajectories of a total of 192 vehicles: 165 cars, 18 vans, 3 heavy vehicles, and 6 buses. There were also 90 pedestrians detected, but for the purposes of the model, only vehicles have been taken into the consideration. Charts of speed profiles are presented below in figures 2 and 3.

6 See DatafromSky, 2018

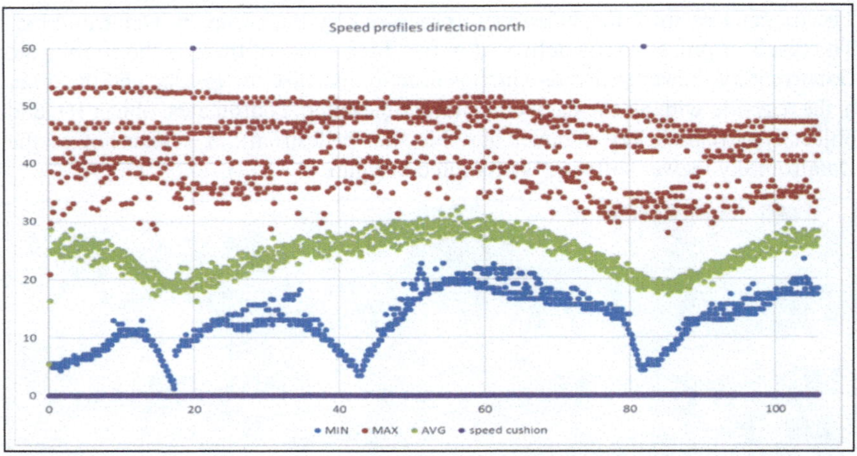

Figure 2: Speed profile for Stachiewicza street, direction northbound (source: own)

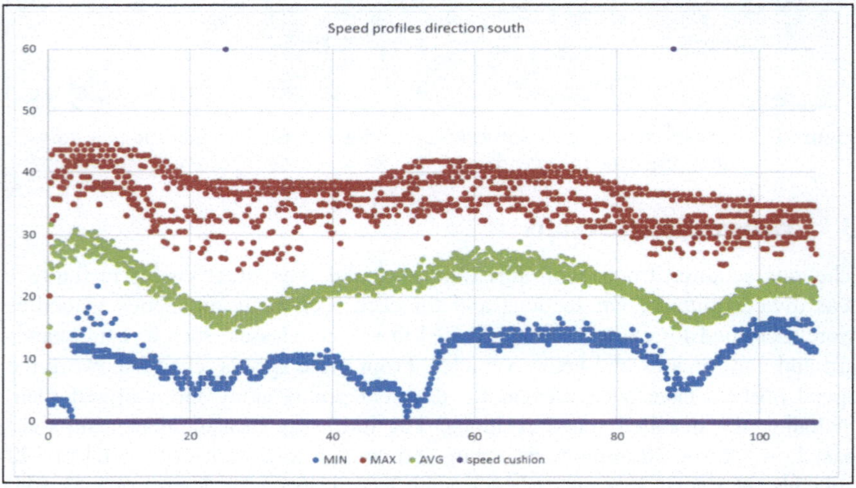

Figure 3: Speed profile for Stachiewicza street, direction southbound (source: own)

On the charts, the studied 107-metre length of Stachiewicza Street can be seen. Speed cushions, as indicated by the violet line, are located at 20 and 82 metres along this section northbound, whereas southbound – on 26th and 88th meter. The blue points indicate the minimum speed. The decrease of the minimal speed between the speed cushions (between 40 and 60 metres) depicts the car stopping on the pedestrian crossing. The green points show average speeds – slowing down in the area of speed cushions are clearly visible. Maximal speeds, marked with red points, show that not every vehicle is decelerating on speed cushions, especially, on the first device in the northbound.

4 Microsimulation modelling

In microsimulation model, every vehicle is analysed separately, considering its features, such as speed, acceleration, etc. and represents the driver behaviour in current traffic situation in every frame (time stamp) of the simulation.[7] For correct functioning of microsimulation model it is essential, that it is calibrated to reproduce the real situation (unimpeded speed, interactions, reactions). Based on this parameters demand (traffic) is moving along the path during the simulation. Path choice or traffic assignment usually takes place outside of the microsimulation model – the most important calculations of the microsimulation model are costs (travel times). Microscopic models are dynamic models – the result (state of the traffic on network) is a function of time. The result of the simulation depends on many parameters, so it is difficult to describe the influence of separate parameter to model. Every vehicle can be described by following, basic parameters: position, velocity, acceleration in time. Usual time of simulation is long (ex. 30 min) and discretised of simulation time is dense (ex. 1s). Because of the above, microsimulation models require a lot of computing power, and precise network reproduction, requiring a great amount of information, which is very hard or impossible to achieve for the bigger area, such as the city. Each simulation run represents one stochastic situation taken from the whole set of every possible situations. The result of the simulation could be presented as, for example: animation, trajectories, (spatial and movement data) average travel times or speeds, unimpeded traffic speed or delay as an effect of growing density.

4.1 Preparation

A microsimulation model was created on the basis of the measurements. The model was prepared using the PTV Vissim software. Vissim's traffic flow model is a stochastic, time-step based, microscopic model that treats driver-vehicle units as the basic entities. The car following model is based on the Wiedemann model. Driving behaviour in this model is divided to four states: free driving, approaching, following, braking. Driving behaviour in detail is described with Wiedemann model parameters: Wiedemann 74, such as safety distances, lack of attention duration or lack of attention probability and Wiedemann 99: time distribution of the speed-dependent part of the desired safety distance, time of deceleration before reaching safe distance, influence of distance on speed oscillation, desired acceleration when starting from standstill. Initially in this paper, the standard

7 See Kucharski, 2013

(default) parameters of the model, such as speeds and accelerations, were taken into consideration without modifying the Wiedemann parameters describing interactions between vehicles.[8]

For each vehicle type, speed distributions have been created according to measured, cumulated frequencies, for two kinds: near or away the speed cushions. On the slowing down and speeding up areas around the speed cushions, the accelerations and decelerations were identified. The model consists of two links, representing two directions of the road and four reduced speed areas, one for each speed cushions. Speed distributions parameters for both links and all four reduced speed zones were inputted. Two examples of speed distributions are presented in figure 4.

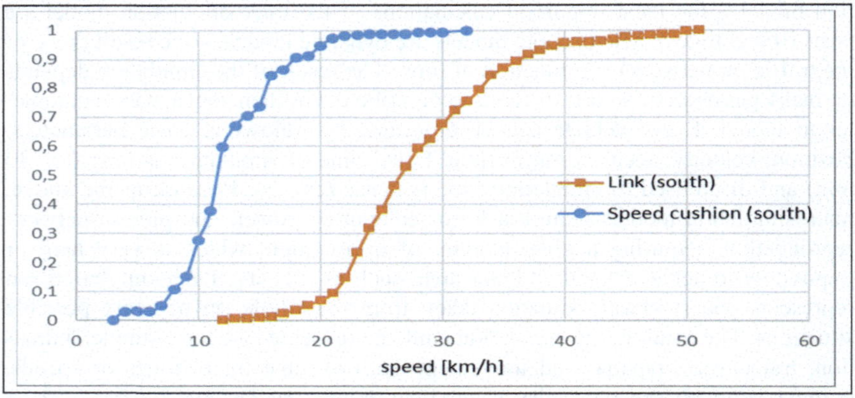

Figure 4: Car speed distributions for the link, direction southbound (orange) and its second speed cushion (blue)

4.2 Comparison and calibration

After inputting all of the speed distributions to the Vissim model, the simulation was started for the same traffic flow as was observed during the measurement. The results of the simulation were exported and extracted as average speed profiles of all vehicles in order to compare them with the measurements. Calibration of the model required using only the speed distributions of unimpeded vehicles – otherwise, the simulated speeds were higher than measured, because of that fact speeds in the simulation have been adjusted to meet measurements. The shape of the speed profile was calibrated by estimating the acceleration and the braking characteristics of the vehicles. For the first direction (northbound), the correlation

8 See Kucharski, Drabicki, 2017

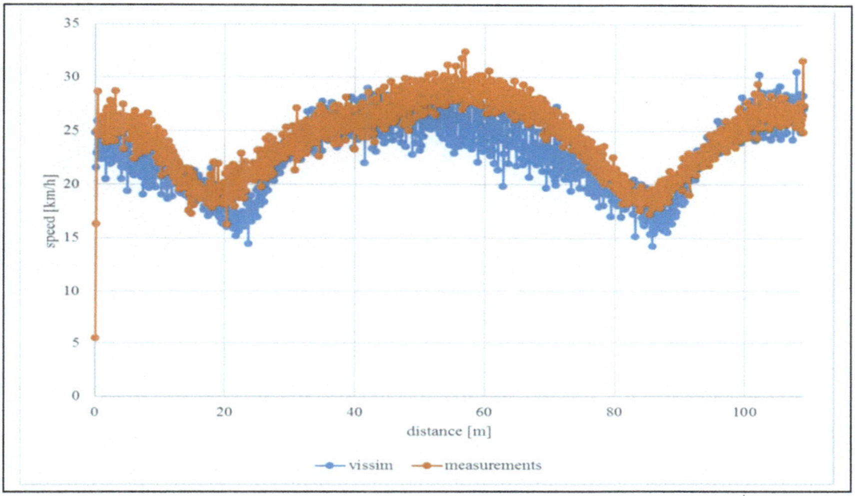

Figure 5: Comparison of speed profiles on the measured street section, heading northbound

between the model and the measurement is 0.79. The compared speed profiles are presented in figure 5.

For the second direction southbound along Stachiewicza street, the correlation between the measured and modelled speed profiles is 0.71. Figure 6 shows this comparison.

Comparing the measured and simulated speed profiles, a strong correlation between the speeds both in and out of the area of the traffic calming device can be observed. However, there is a difference in the shape of the speed profiles between the speed cushions. To minimise this difference, further activities should be undertaken, such as adaptation of the Wiedemann model parameters, acceleration and braking, or dividing the link into more speed zones.

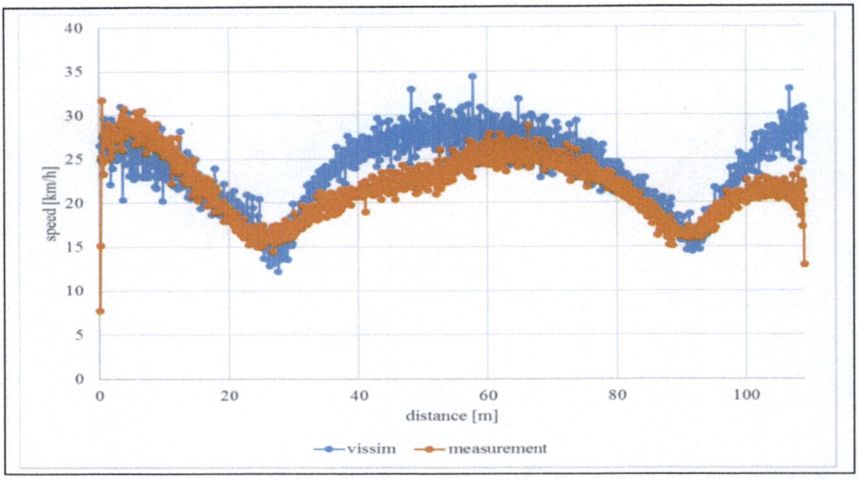

Figure 6: Comparison of speed profiles on the measured street section, heading southbound

5 Volume-delay functions

The volume delay function (VDF) is a macrosimulation approximation of fundamental traffic phenomena occurring in dynamic traffic models, such as gridlocks, spillbacks etc.[9] Primarily, fundamental diagrams of traffic flow were used in modelling of a highway traffic, helping to understand capacity effects, different traffic states, etc. More complicated diagrams, useful for urban areas were based on traffic density or a relationship with kinematic wave theory.[10] However, VDF, contrary to fundamental diagram, has a form of function, and contains hypocritical part (where the traffic volume is less than capacity) and hypercritical.

One of the oldest and commonly used formulations of VDFs are BPR functions, published in 1964 by Bureau of Public Roads in USA.[11] Example of others can be Conical[12] or Akcelik[13] functions.

---

9 See Kucharski, Drabicki, 2017

10 See Daganzo, Geroliminis, 2008; See Helbing, 2008

11 See Bureau of Public Roads, 1964

12 See Spiess, 1990

13 See Akcelik, 1991

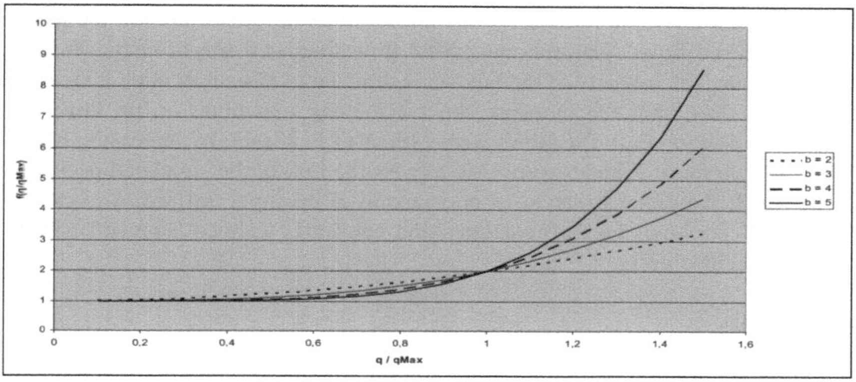

Figure 7: Example of Volume-delay functions (Source: Kucharski, 2013)

In macrosimulation model, the network is described as a graph, in which links (sometimes also nodes) makes a resistance. The resistance of the links is described as a relation between saturation grade and travel time, known as volume-delay function. Volume-delay function is a non-descending, continuous, differentiable function, usually calibrated based on assumptions or observations of the travel time and the corresponding volume data.[14] For minimal traffic flow, the result of the volume-delay function is equal to 1, meaning, that travel time is equal to free flow travel time. With the growth of traffic flow expressed in vehicles per hour, the function is growing. When saturation grade is equal 1, meaning, that traffic flow has reached capacity, the function usually starts to grow dramatically thanks to exponential parameter of that function. On the figure 7. Examples of VDFs are shown differing with exponential parameter. For all BPR functions travel time is doubled (compared to minimal travel time) when q is equal to q_{max}.

6 Modelling a volume-delay relation

6.1 Capacity

Table 1: Comparison of maximal traffic flow for both directions with and without traffic calming

Direction	1 (north)	2 (south)
Traffic calmed [veh/hour]	1068	1044
Standard [veh/hour]	1308	1158

[14] See Petrik, Filipe, de Abreu e Silva, 2014

As mentioned above, the Vissim microsimulation model was tested for the whole range of traffic flows. The minimal traffic flow simulated was around 100 vehicles per hour. The capacity of the link was estimated in Vissim through increasing the traffic flow until the message about achieving maximum traffic flow was displayed. Maximum traffic flows were estimated in Vissim by increasing traffic flow until no more vehicles were able to pass the link in the simulated period of time, which stands for capacity. A comparison of maximal traffic flow, counted as vehicles per hour, for traffic-calmed and non-traffic-calmed (standard) streets is presented in table 1.

6.2 Delay

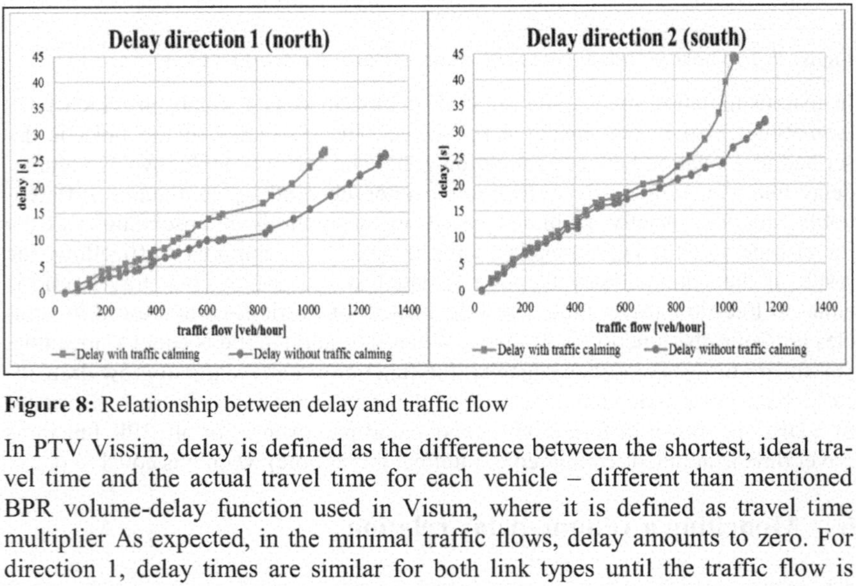

Figure 8: Relationship between delay and traffic flow

In PTV Vissim, delay is defined as the difference between the shortest, ideal travel time and the actual travel time for each vehicle – different than mentioned BPR volume-delay function used in Visum, where it is defined as travel time multiplier As expected, in the minimal traffic flows, delay amounts to zero. For direction 1, delay times are similar for both link types until the traffic flow is around 500 veh/hour, then the delay for the traffic-calmed roads starts to increase more sharply. At the maximal traffic flow, the delay is 26 seconds for both link types. For the opposite direction, delay amounts are the same until the traffic flow is around 800 vehicles per hour, then the delay on the traffic calmed road increases sharply to reach a maximum delay of 45 seconds, whereas the non-traffic-calmed street reaches 32 seconds of delay.

On this charts it can be seen, that together with increase of traffic volume, the delay of a traffic-calmed road is growing more sharply. This difference in relation between traffic volume and travel time requires a change not only a parameter of capacity and average speed, but also parameters responsible for volume-delay function shape.

6.3 Visum volume-delay function

Travel times were calculated in such a manner, to correspond with the form of volume-delay function available in PTV Vissim, thus showing the relationship between saturation grade (traffic flow divided by maximum traffic flow) and the travel time gain compared to $x \cdot t_0$ (t_0 - free flow travel time). In the Kraków transport model, volume-delay function were estimated based on BPR2 volume-delay function shape, with five sets of parameters. The formula of the volume-delay function is:

$$t_{cur} = \begin{cases} t_0 \cdot \left(1 + a \cdot \text{sat}^{b}\right), & \text{sat} \leq \text{sat}_{crit} \\ t_0 \cdot \left(1 + a \cdot \text{sat}^{b'}\right), & \text{sat} > \text{sat}_{crit} \end{cases}$$

Where:

t_0 - free flow travel time

a, b, b' – shape parameters

sat – saturation grade

sat_{crit} – capacity, q_{max}

As seen above, BPR function consists of two parts: when the traffic volume is lower than capacity, and when it is higher. BPR function is a macroscopic simplification of traffic phenomena, which enables to calculate traffic volumes bigger than capacity in order to meet traffic assignment results. In reality It is not possible to measure traffic scenario of the traffic volume higher than a capacity, because, according to fundamental diagram, the traffic enters the congestion state, speed and capacity decreases dramatically, as seen on figure 9, which represents measurements result of increasing traffic and exceeding capacity, thus decreasing a speed and traffic volume.

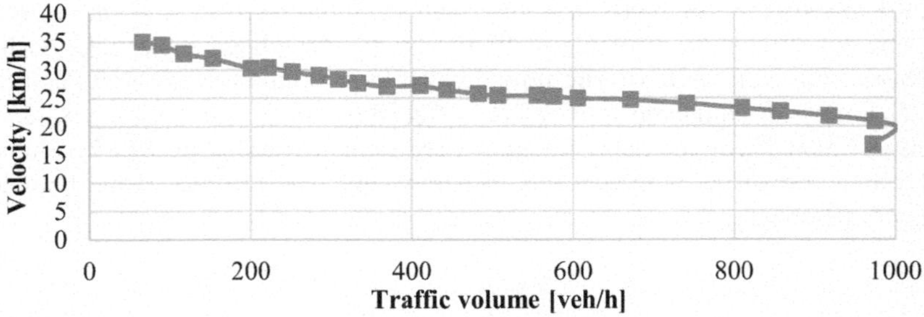

Figure 9: Relation between traffic volume and velocity showing decrease of velocity in congested road

In order to solve that problem, let's see basic relations between density, traffic volume and speed:

$$D = \frac{Q}{V}$$

where: V is a velocity (km/h), D is density (veh/km) and Q is traffic volume (veh/h). In order to avoid traffic volume in this relation, we use density instead.

After that transformation, relations looks as follows:

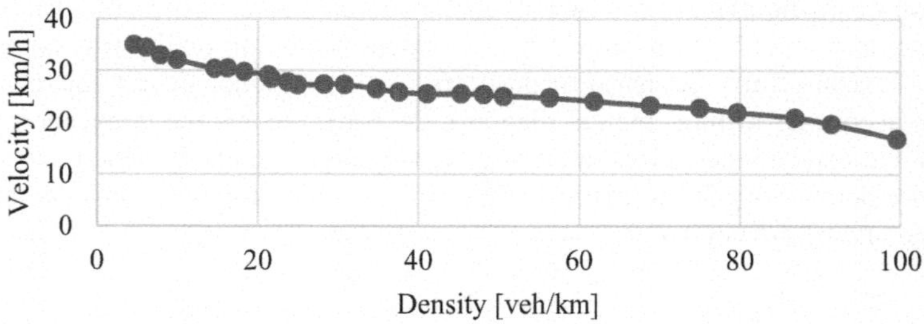

Figure 10: Relation between traffic volume and density

In that case, even in a state of congestion, density is constantly growing, which means, it maintains a form of function. After that transformation, it is possible define new traffic volume (Q_d) and saturation grade (sat_d) representing traffic volume divided by capacity with density divided by density at capacity:

$$sat = \frac{Q}{Q_{max}} \quad Q_d = D \cdot V \quad sat_d = \frac{D}{D(Q_{\max})}$$

6.4 Selecting parameters to fit the Volume-delay function

As written above, BPR2 function shape was used. In order to fit the parameters, squared difference minimisation method was applied, and calculated in Solver. Below, there is a table with parameters calculated:

Table 2: Calculated parameters of volume-delay function

	With traffic calming		**Without traffic calming**	
	direction 1	**direction 2**	**direction 1**	**direction 2**
a	0.544712	0.626661	0.527618	0.611864
b	0.946787	0.848014	0.905478	0.646525
b'	7.133219	5.533088	7.080322	2.591875

Average correlation of the parameters is 0.98.

For direction 1, BPR2 function parameters are similar for both traffic-calmed and non traffic-calmed road. This may be caused by a traffic composition of the heavy vehicles, which doesn't change their speed. That type of relations will be further researched in the future.

However it is noticeable, in direction 2, that parameters responsible for steepness of the function, have bigger values for links with traffic calming. This means, that when we compare travel times of traffic-calmed and non traffic-calmed road, for low traffic volume they will be similar, but for bigger ones, travel time for traffic-calmed road is significantly higher.

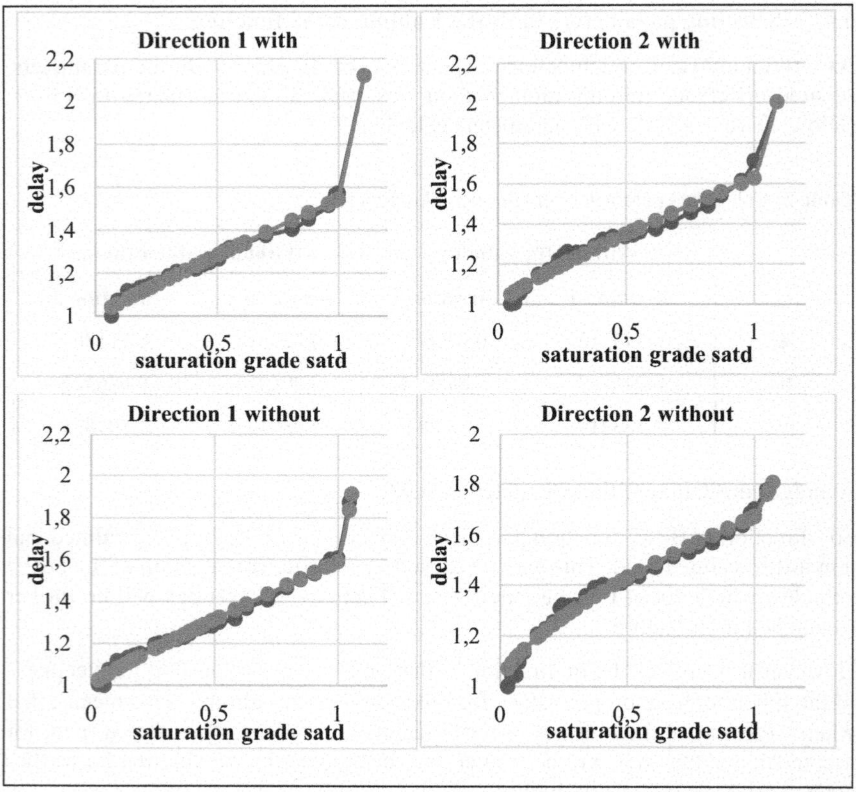

Figure 11: Shape of modeled (orange) and measured (blue) volume-delay functions

7 Summary

This paper shows a method to use video recordings and trajectory extraction softwar to create a microsimulation model of the traffic-calmed street. From the data, only dynamic behaviour of drivers was extracted, this included speed distributions, together with braking and acceleration when entering and leaving the reduced speed area. Modelling of volume-delay functions, including situations with traffic flow bigger than capacity, shows, that traffic-calmed roads are more sensitive to traffic volume increase. This makes the reason to use different parameters of volume-delay functions for traffic-calmed roads in order to improve the correlation of macrosimulation model.

Literature

Akcelik, R. (1991). Travel time functions for transport planning purposes: Davidson's function, its time dependent form and alternative travel time function. *Australian Road Research.*

Barbosa, H. M. (1995). *Impacts of traffic calming measures on speeds on urban roads.* Leeds: University of Leeds.

Brindle, R. (1992). *Australia's Contribution to Traffic Calming.* Pearson: PTRC.

Bureau of Public Roads. (1964). *Traffic Assignment Manual.* Washington, DC: Department of Commerce, Urban Planning Division.

Daganzo, Geroliminis. (2008). An analytical approximation for the macroscopic fundamental diagram of urban traffic. *Transportation reseatch part B: Methodological.*

DatafromSky. (2018). *Advanced traffic analysis of video data.* Retrieved 18.3.2018, from http://datafromsky.com/

GPS. (2017). *GPS Accuracy. What is the government's commitment to GPS accuracy?* Retrieved 18.3.2018, from https://www.gps.gov/systems/gps/performance/accuracy/

Helbing, D. (2008). Derivation of a fundamental diagram for urban traffic flow. *THE EUROPEAN PHYSICAL JOURNAL B.*

ITE/FHWA. (1999). *Traffic Calming: State of the Practice ITE/FHWA, August 1999.* Retrieved 18.3.2019, from http://www.industrializedcyclist.com/trafficcalming.pdf

Kucharski, R. (2013). MAKROSKOPOWY MODEL PRZEPŁYWU RUCHU W SIECI DRUGIEGO RZĘDU – ALTERNATYWNY OPIS STANU SIECI.

Kucharski, R., Drabicki, A. (2017). Estimating Macroscopic Volume Delay Functions with the Traffic Density Derived from Measured Speeds and Flows. *Journal of Advanced Transportation.*

Petrik, O., Filipe, M., de Abreu e Silva, J. (2014). The Influence of the Volume – Delay Function on Uncertainty Assessment for a Four-Step Model. *Advances in Intelligent Systems and Computing.*

PTV-Ag. (2017). PTV VISSIM 9 User Manual. Karlsruhe: PTV-Ag.

Spiess, H. (1990). Technical note—conical volume-delay functions. *Transportation Science.*

Mathematic modeling for dynamics of transport flows

H. Geldiyev, R. Nepesov, A. Amanov, J. Geldiyev, M. Churiyev

1 Introduction

With the increase in the intensity of traffic, the existing street and road networks (UDS) fail to cope with traffic flows. On the roads, there are so-called traffic jams, resulting in the loss of both drivers' working hours and the disruption of timely deliveries of goods to consumers, which leads to a loss of enterprise productivity. To solve the emerging problems, it is necessary to develop the entire transport and road infrastructure, in particular, the construction of high-speed, city-wide highways. This requires significant investment, although it leads to global improvement.

The problem is closely related to the well-being and lives of people. Road traffic accidents cost the economy an average of 3% of GDP.[1] In 1999, the economic losses from road accidents in the world amounted to 500 billion dollars. The amount of annual damage in Russia, according to the Internet, exceeds 1 billion $. The generally accepted criteria for road quality are the reduction of environmental pollution and excessive noise levels, minimizing fuel consumption, preventing the formation and spread of traffic congestion.

In the early 1990s, the study of transportation systems in the USA was raised to the rank of a national security problem. The best "physical minds" and computer equipment of the National Los Alamos Research Laboratory (LANL)[2] were involved in this task. By now, automated traffic control systems have been developed, the technical means of which is being continuously improved. The special relevance of the development of methods for solving network traffic organization problems (HLM) should be noted.

Actions aimed at solving such problems are optimizing the work of traffic lights at autonomous intersections to ensure their maximum throughput in all directions conflicting with each other, organizing the movement of vehicles along certain routes, monitoring the current traffic situation and making decisions to prevent traffic accidents, congestion, etc. The combination of these actions is called traffic management.

---

1 See Petrov, 2007
2 See Robertson, 1997

H.-C. Brauweiler et al. (Hrsg.), *Digitalization and Industry 4.0: Economic and Societal Development*, https://doi.org/10.1007/978-3-658-27110-7_18

Reducing the level of delay of vehicles at intersections, due to the optimization of control signaling traffic lights - is the main factor determining the effectiveness of the HLM program. In the task of traffic control, the object of study is considered as a directed graph, the vertices of which correspond to intersections, and the arcs - to the crossings of the traffic controller.

Management of individual intersections with adaptation to changes in traffic volumes on the approaches to them was implemented in the 30s of the twentieth century and found particularly widespread use in Europe. A significant effect was obtained already by controlling the signals of traffic lights at the following intersections of one main street, and obtaining the effect of the so-called "green wave".[3]

We present some of the provisions that we establish as the base of the construction of a mathematical model of the movement of vehicles at intersections.

1. When approaching an intersection, each stream $\mathbf{\Pi}_j$ (j=1,4) spontaneously splits into three types depending on the driver's intention to go straight on $\mathbf{\Pi}_{2j}$, turn left $\mathbf{\Pi}_{1j}$ or to the right $\mathbf{\Pi}_{3j}$.
2. The presence of sensors that provide real-time information about the current state of the object - the value of $\mathbf{\Pi}_{ij}$ $\left(i=\overline{1,3}\right)\left(j=\overline{1,4}\right)$.

Let $\boldsymbol{T}$ - the period of the traffic light. Usually $\boldsymbol{T}$=60 s. To ensure complete controllability of traffic at the intersection, we divide $\boldsymbol{T}$ into 8 parts, as shown in figure 1.

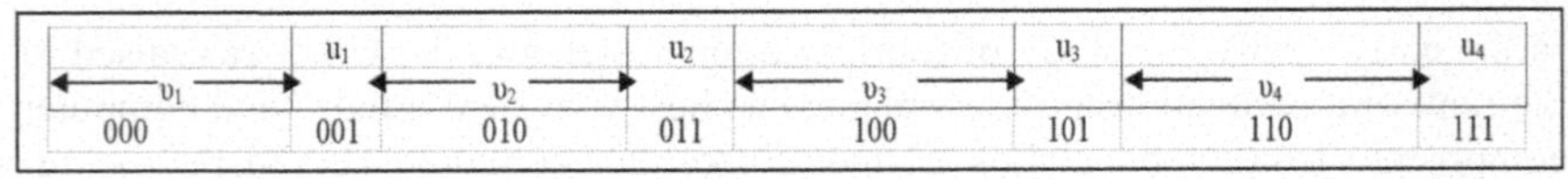

Figure 1: υ1, υ2, υ3, υ4, u1, u2, u3, u4 – the duration of the sections designated as 000, 001, 010, 011, 100, 101, 110, 111. The traffic on each site is shown in figure 2 (a-h).

2 Calculation of the capacity of the intersection

Let $\mathbf{\Pi}^*$ - the number of cars standing in line in front of the intersection by the time *t=0*, at which the green light of a traffic light lights up, allowing passage. Considering the movement of vehicles from the start is equally accelerated with acceleration α, for the distance traveled we have the ratio.

$$S = \frac{at^2}{2}$$

3 See Petrov, 2007

In figure 2, the bold curve shows the graph of the movement of the first car. Neglecting some delay in starting subsequent machines and assuming that each machine takes 7 meters of the way, it is easy to obtain addiction.

$$7\Pi = \frac{a\Delta^2}{2},$$

where Π – is the number of cars entering the intersection during the time Δ of the green signal light.

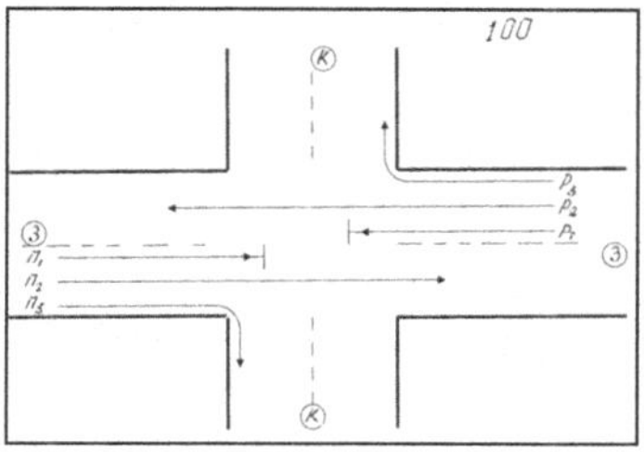

Figure 2a

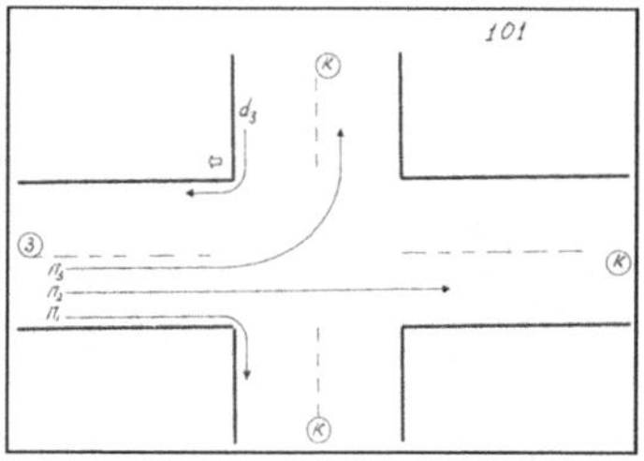

Figure 2b

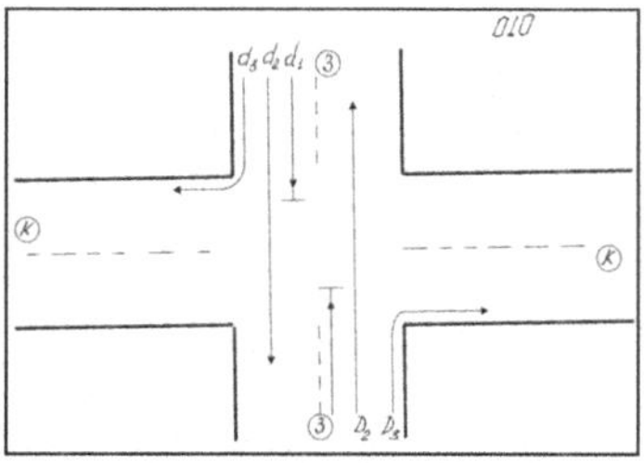

Figure 2c

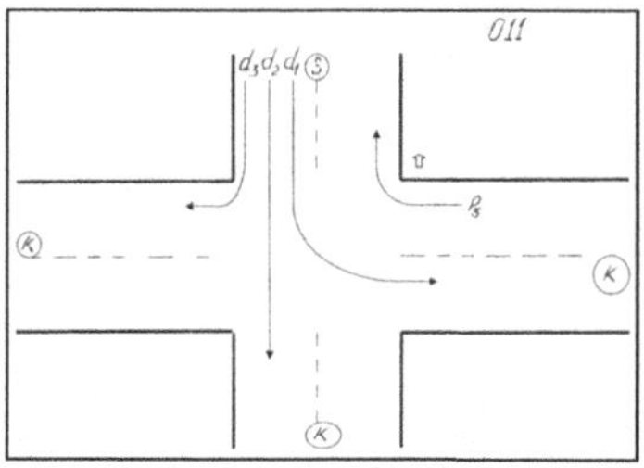

Figure 2d

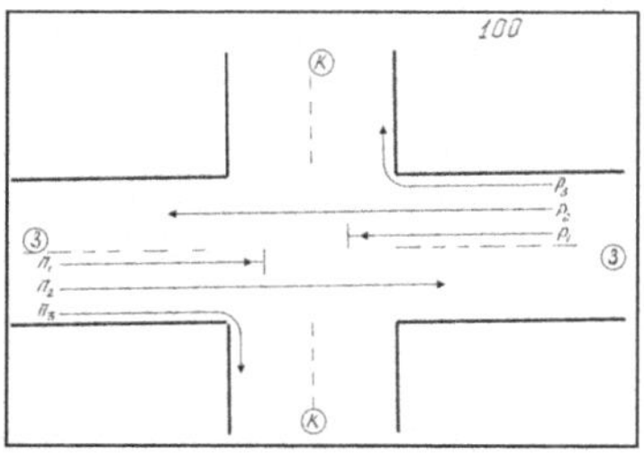

Figure 2e

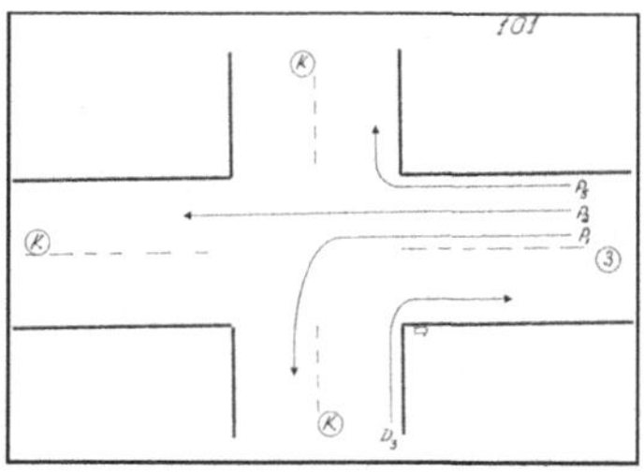

Figure 2f

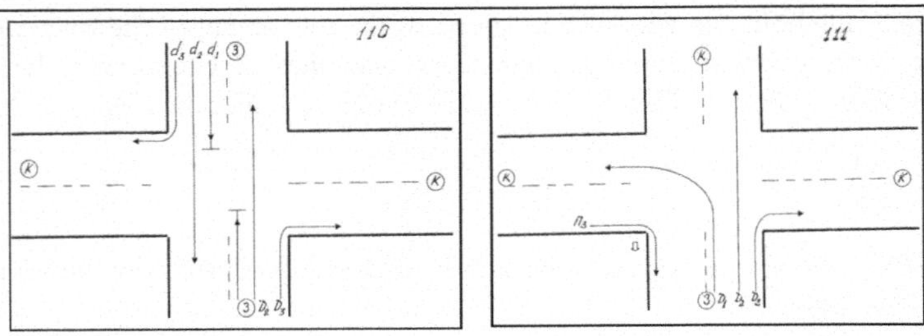

Figure 2g *Figure 2h*

Figure 2: (a-h). Designation: Пi - the number of cars from the stream, crossing the intersection along the corresponding streams. The variables Pi, Di, di have a similar meaning.

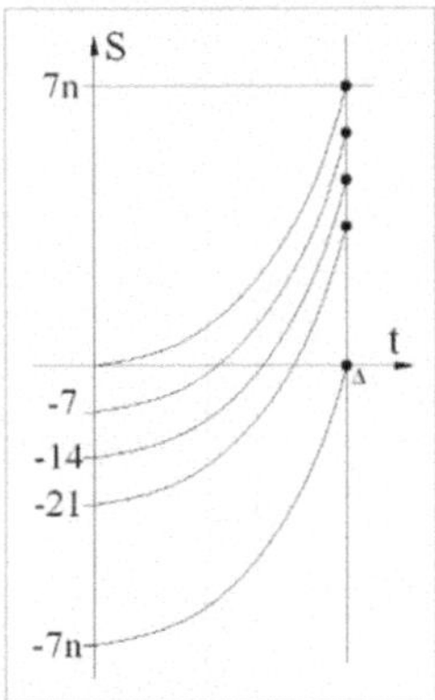

Figure 3: The schedule of movement of cars from the start

Thus, the dependence of the number of cars crossing the intersection during the Δ time under the assumption that the movement occurs at zero initial speed is given by the formula, $n \approx \tau \cdot \Delta^2$, $\tau = \dfrac{a}{14}$

Henceforth, we will assume that τ is constant.

Table 1 is filled in accordance with this formula. It can be said that table 1 represents a mathematical model of an object - an adjustable intersection. In this case, the quantities υ_i, u_i should be considered control parameters, and the variables $\mathbf{\Pi}_i$ - coordinates of the object. The last column shows the sum of values in the corresponding rows, which is the number of cars crossing the intersection in one ***T*** period depending on the mode of operation of the traffic light. Note that dividing the ***T*** period into 8 parts is a necessary measure. Otherwise, there is no possibility to control the value of the queue of cars that intend to make a left turn (flows $П_1$,p_1,D_1,d_1).

Let $\left(\Pi_1^*,\Pi_2^*,\Pi_3^*,P_1^*,P_2^*,P_3^*,D_1^*,D_2^*,D_3^*,d_1^*,d_2^*,d_3^*\right)$ be the indexes of the current state sensors of the intersection, that is, the number of cars in each stream at the moment the green signal turns on. It is required to determine the mode of operation of the traffic light, which ensures the passage of these cars through the intersection in the shortest possible time.

Table 1: Mathematical model of an object

		000	001	010	011	100	101	110	111	
		V_1	U_1	V_2	U_2	V_3	U_3	V_4	U_4	and
1	$П_1$	2	τU_1^2	0	0	2	0	0	0	$4+\tau U_1^2$
2	$П_2$	$\tau\,(V_1+U_1)^2$		0	0	τV_3^2	0	0	0	$\tau\,(V_1+U_1)^2+\tau V_3^2$
3	$П_3$	$\tau\,(U1+V1+U4)^2-\tau U_4^2$		0	0	τV_3^2	0	0	τU_4^2	$\tau\,(V_1+U_1+\tau U_4)^2+\tau V_3^2$
4	P_1	2	0	0	0	2	τU_3^2	0	0	$4+\tau U_3^2$
5	P_2	τV_1^2	0	0	0	$\tau\,(V_3+U_3)^2$		0	0	$\tau\,(V_3+U_3)^2+\tau V_1^2$
6	P_3	τV_1^2	0	0	$\tau\,(U_2+V_3+U_3)^2$			0	0	$\tau\,(U_2+V_3+U_3)^2+\tau V_1^2$
7	D_1	0	0	2	0	0	0	2	τU_4^2	$4+\tau U_4^2$
8	D_2	0	0	τV_2^2	0	0	0	$\tau\,(V_4+U_4)^2$		$\tau\,(V_4+U_4)^2+\tau V_2^2$
9	D_3	0	0	τV_2^2	0	0	$\tau\,(U_3+V_4+U_4)^2$			$\tau\,(U_3+V_4+U_4)^2+\tau V_2^2$
10	d_1	0	0	2	τU_2^2	0	0	2	0	$4+\tau U_2^2$
11	d_2	0	0	$\tau\,(V_2+U_2)^2$		0	0	τV_4^2	0	$\tau\,(V_2+U_2)^2+\tau V_4^2$
12	d_3	0	$\tau\,(U_1+V_2+U_2)^2$			0	0	τV_4^2	0	$\tau\,(U_1+V_2+U_2)^2+\tau V_4^2$

Now we formulate the main task:

Using table 1, we write the main task in the form

$$T = \sum_{i=1}^{4} (v_i + u_i) \to \min,$$

$$\begin{aligned}
&\Pi_1(\upsilon,u) = 4 + \tau u_1^2 \geq \Pi_1^* \\
&\Pi_2(\upsilon,u) = \tau(\upsilon_1 + u_1)^2 + \tau\upsilon_3^2 \geq \Pi_2^* \\
&\Pi_3(\upsilon,u) = \tau(\upsilon_1 + u_1 + u_4)^2 + \tau\upsilon_3^2 \geq \Pi_3^* \\
&p_1(\upsilon,u) = 4 + \tau u_3^2 \geq p_1^* \\
&p_2(\upsilon,u) = \tau(\upsilon_3 + u_3)^2 + \tau\upsilon_1^2 \geq p_2^* \\
&p_3(\upsilon,u) = \tau(\upsilon_3 + u_3 + u_2)^2 + \tau\upsilon_1^2 \geq p_3^* \\
&D_1(\upsilon,u) = 4 + \tau u_4^2 \geq D_1^* \\
&D_2(\upsilon,u) = \tau(\upsilon_4 + u_4)^2 + \tau\upsilon_2^2 \geq D_2^* \\
&D_3(\upsilon,u) = \tau(\upsilon_4 + u_4 + u_3)^2 + \tau\upsilon_2^2 \geq D_3^* \\
&d_1(\upsilon,u) = 4 + \tau u_2^2 \geq d_1^* \\
&d_2(\upsilon,u) = \tau(\upsilon_2 + u_2)^2 + \tau\upsilon_4^2 \geq d_2^* \\
&d_3(\upsilon,u) = \tau(\upsilon_2 + u_1 + u_2)^2 + \tau\upsilon_4^2 \geq d_3^*
\end{aligned}, \qquad (1)$$

under the assumption

$$\upsilon_i \geq 0, u_i \geq 0, i = \overline{1,4} \qquad (2)$$

Let T_0 be the solution of the main problem. This means that if over the next T_0 sec. the same number of cars (1) arrives, there will not be a queue at the intersection, and the average waiting time of any car is $T_0/2$, since for period T (as can be seen from the table), the cars start twice with a green signal. Now it is possible to point out the connection of the quantities (1) with the speed of cars in each stream, namely Π_i/T - there is the average number of cars passing per unit of time in the stream Π_i. The main problem formulated above is the object of the theory of extreme challenges. Unfortunately, it does not fit into the framework of well-developed challenges of linear or convex programming. Nevertheless, taking into account the specifics of the constraints (2), it is possible to construct an efficient algorithm for its solution.

3 Geometric interpretation of the task

First of all, we note that from inequalities 1.1, 1.4, 1.7, 1.10 we have:

$$u_1 \geq \sqrt{\frac{\Pi_1^* - 4}{\tau}}; \qquad u_3 \geq \sqrt{\frac{P_1^* - 4}{\tau}};$$
$$u_2 \geq \sqrt{\frac{d_1^* - 4}{\tau}}; \qquad u_4 \geq \sqrt{\frac{D_1^* - 4}{\tau}} \tag{3}$$

Since the variables u_i enter the quality function T additively, we take

$$u_1^* = \sqrt{\frac{\Pi_1^* - 4}{\tau}}; \qquad u_3^* = \sqrt{\frac{P_1^* - 4}{\tau}};$$
$$u_2^* = \sqrt{\frac{d_1^* - 4}{\tau}}; \qquad u_4^* = \sqrt{\frac{D_1^* - 4}{\tau}} \tag{4}$$

After that, the remaining inequalities are divided into two independent groups:

$$\left.\begin{aligned}
&(v_1 + u_1^*)^2 + v_3^2 \geq \frac{\Pi_2^*}{\tau} && (5.1)\\
&(v_1 + u_1^* + u_4^*)^2 + v_3^2 \geq \frac{\Pi_3^*}{\tau} && (5.2)\\
&(v_3 + u_3^*)^2 + v_1^2 \geq \frac{P_2^*}{\tau} && (5.3)\\
&(v_3 + u_3^* + u_2^*)^2 + v_1^2 \geq \frac{P_3^*}{\tau} && (5.4)
\end{aligned}\right\} \tag{5}$$

$$\left.\begin{aligned}
&(v_4 + u_4^*)^2 + v_2^2 \geq \frac{D_2^*}{\tau}\\
&(v_4 + u_4^* + u_3^*)^2 + v_2^2 \geq \frac{D_3^*}{\tau}\\
&(v_2 + u_2^*)^2 + v_4^2 \geq \frac{d_2^*}{\tau}\\
&(v_2 + u_2^* + u_1^*)^2 + v_4^2 \geq \frac{d_3^*}{\tau}
\end{aligned}\right\} \tag{6}$$

The first group includes only the variables v_1 and v_3, and each inequality in R^2 defines the exterior of a circle of a given radius with center located at points on the $0v_1$ or $0v_2$ axes. The intersection of these sets is obviously a non-convex set. Therefore, the standard methods of convex programming with minimization of the sum $T_1=v_1+v_3$ on the set defined by system (5) and restrictions $v_1 \geq 0, v_2 \geq 0$ are not applicable. However, this problem can be solved. We write the equation of a circle defining the boundary of the set defined by the j-m inequality (5j) of system (5). Depending on j, 4 cases are presented:

I. j = 4. The boundary of the set defined by inequality (5.4)

$$(v_3 + u_3^* + u_4^*) + v_1^2 = \frac{P_3^*}{\tau} \tag{7}$$

is a circle of radius $R_4 = \sqrt{\frac{P_3^*}{\tau}}$ centered at a point $v_1 = 0, \quad v_3 = -u_3^* - u_4^*$.

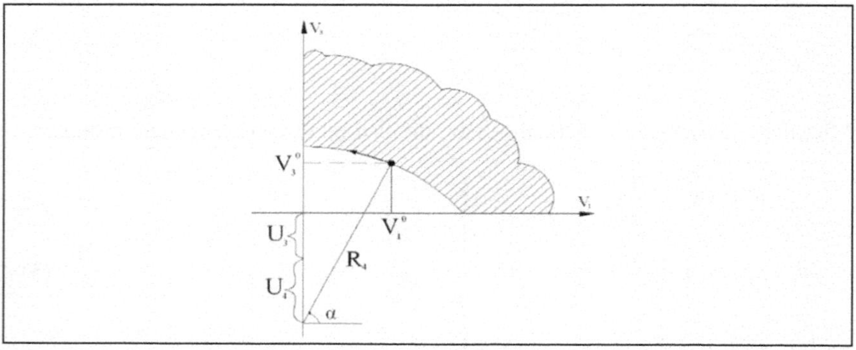

Figure 4

Movement along the border (v_1^0, v_3^0), starting from the point, is carried out by increasing the angle α, starting from

$$\alpha_0 = arctg\frac{v_3^0 + u_3^0 + u_2^0}{v_1^0} \tag{8}$$

according to equalities

$$v_1 = R_4 \cos\alpha$$

$$v_3 = R_4 \sin\alpha - u_3^* - u_2^*$$

II. j = 3.

$$(v_3 + u_3^*)^2 + v_1^2 = \frac{P_2^*}{\tau} \qquad R_3 = \sqrt{\frac{P_2^*}{\tau}} \tag{9}$$

$$\alpha_0 = arctg\frac{v_3^0 + u_3^*}{v_1^0} \qquad v_1 = R_3\cos\alpha \qquad v_2 = R_3\sin\alpha - u_3^* \tag{10}$$

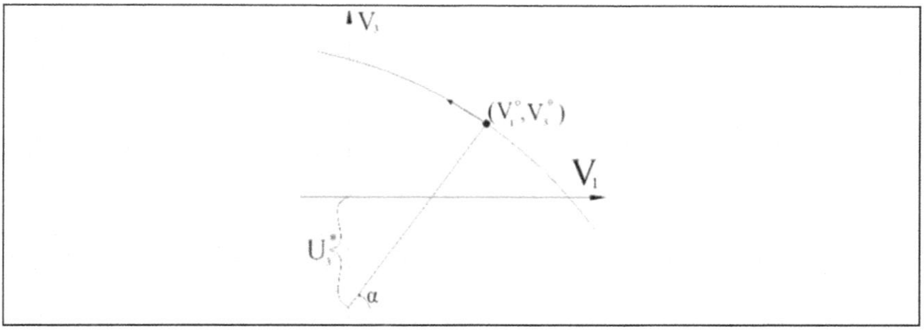

Figure 5

III. j=1.

$$\left(v_1 + u_1^*\right)^2 + v_3^2 = \frac{\Pi_2^*}{\tau} \qquad R_1 = \sqrt{\frac{\Pi_2^*}{\tau}} \tag{11}$$

$$\alpha_0 = arctg\frac{v_3^0}{v_1^0 + u_1^*} \qquad v_1 = R_1\cos\alpha - u_1^* \qquad v_2 = R_1\sin\alpha \tag{12}$$

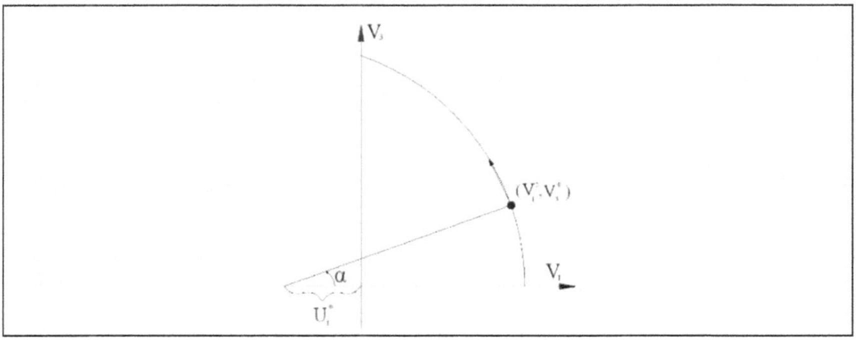

Figure 6

IV. j=2.

$$\left(v_1 + u_1^* + u_4^*\right)^2 + v_3^2 = \frac{\Pi_3^*}{\tau} \qquad R_2 = \sqrt{\frac{\Pi_3^*}{\tau}} \tag{13}$$

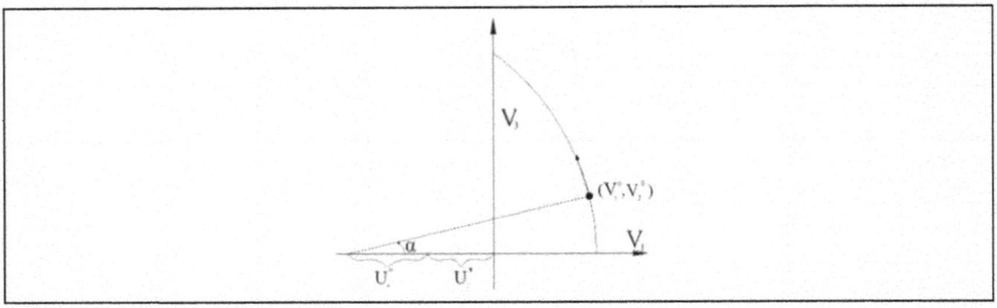

Figure 7

$$\alpha_0 = arctg\frac{v_3^0}{v_1^0 + u_1^* + u_4^*} \qquad v_1 = R_2\cos\alpha - u_1^* - u_4^* \qquad v_2 = R_2\sin\alpha \tag{14}$$

The set D_1 defined by inequalities (5), in the general case, can have the form shown in figure 8.

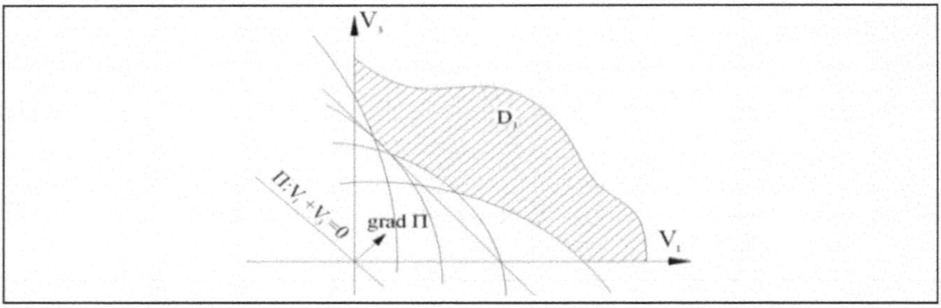

Figure 8: D1 set

The geometric problem was reduced to a parallel movement of the plane ***П***: $v_1 + v_3 = 0$ before the first contact of the boundary of the set D_1.

4 Standard traffic light

To assess the performance of a "smart" traffic light, consider the possibilities of a typical traffic light with a two-phase mode.[4] The time of activity the yellow signal is not taken into account. The presence of such a signal is provided to complete the movement of vehicles that have passed the footpath with a green signal at the intersection. Typically, the duration of the yellow signal is relatively small and is approximately 3 seconds. Let's consider the problem. At the time of the green signal turning on in the east-west direction[5], the sensors record the state:

4 See Figure 2a und 2b

5 See Figure 2

$$\left(\Pi_1^*, \Pi_2^*, \Pi_3^*, P_1^*, P_2^*, P_3^*, D_1^*, D_2^*, D_3^*, d_1^*, d_2^*, d_3^*\right).$$

Let us estimate the time T required for the passage of the intersection of all the cars in line. We will not take into account the flows Π_3, P_3, D_3, d_3, since usually their passage is within the time allotted to the flows Π_2, P_2, D_2, d_2, especially if we take into account intersections equipped with a separate passage for those who want to make a right turn.

Travel time for the Π_1 and P_1 machines will be

$$\overline{v_1^*} = \max\left\{\sqrt{\frac{\Pi_2^*}{\tau}}, \sqrt{\frac{P_2^*}{\tau}}\right\}$$

After that, take time

$$\overline{u_1^*} = \max\left\{\sqrt{\frac{\Pi_1^*}{\tau}}, \sqrt{\frac{P_1^*}{\tau}}\right\}$$

for cars making a left turn. In total, it will take time for an east-west journey $\overline{v_1^*} + \overline{u_1^*}$, after which time is allocated for vehicles moving in north-south directions.

We have

$$\overline{v_2^*} = \max\left\{\sqrt{\frac{D_2^*}{\tau}}, \sqrt{\frac{d_2^*}{\tau}}\right\}$$

$$\overline{u_2^*} = \max\left\{\sqrt{\frac{D_1^*}{\tau}}, \sqrt{\frac{d_1^*}{\tau}}\right\}.$$

So, the total travel time of the flow (*) will be

$$T_0 = \overline{v_1^*} + \overline{u_1^*} + \overline{v_2^*} + \overline{u_2^*}.$$

5 Algorithm

1. Putting in inequalities (5) $v_3 = 0$, we determine the values

$$v_{11} = -u_1^* + \sqrt{\frac{\Pi_2^*}{\tau}}, \quad (15.1)$$

$$v_{12} = -u_1^* - u_4^* + \sqrt{\frac{\Pi_3^*}{\tau}}, \quad (15.2)$$

$$v_{13} = \sqrt{\frac{P_2^*}{\tau} - \left(u_3^*\right)^2}, \quad (15.3)$$

$$v_{14} = -\sqrt{\frac{P_3^*}{\tau} - \left(u_3^* + u_2^*\right)^2} \quad (15.4)$$

Find $V_1^0 = \max_{i=1}^{4} v_{1i} = v_{1j}$

2. We assume $v_1^0 = v_{1j}$, $v_3 = 0$ and carry out movement along the boundary of the set D_1 in one of their 4 variants, determined by the index j. The pitch is given by changing the angle α by the Δ value. At each step, relations (5) are checked. The first stage is completed either when a violation of any of these inequalities is detected, and its number μ, the point reached $\left(\overline{v_1}, \overline{v_3}\right)$, and the sum are fixed $\overline{v_1} + \overline{v_3}$. Otherwise, the process ends with a condition $\overline{v_1} = 0$.
3. Further bypassing the boundary of the set D_1 is determined by the number μ, according to which, one of the 4 methods described above is selected. Note that the number of possible "switchings" is no more than 3. Moreover, the sequence of switchings can only be in ascending order of the methods $I \to II \to III \to IV$ described above.
4. On the basis of certain v_1 and v_3 at the switching points of both the initial $\left(v_1^0, 0\right)$ and final points $\left(0, v_3^k\right)$, $T = v_1 + v_3$ is calculated and as the optimal ones v_1^* we v_3^* choose those values of v_1 and v_3 that minimize ***T***.
5. System (6) differs from (5) only in the indexes of incoming variables and right-hand sides. Therefore, using the approach described above, we determine the optimal values of the variables v_2^* and v_4^*.
6. The block diagram of the algorithm is shown in figure 9. The program is implemented in **Visual Basic**. The effectiveness of the method is on average 9%.

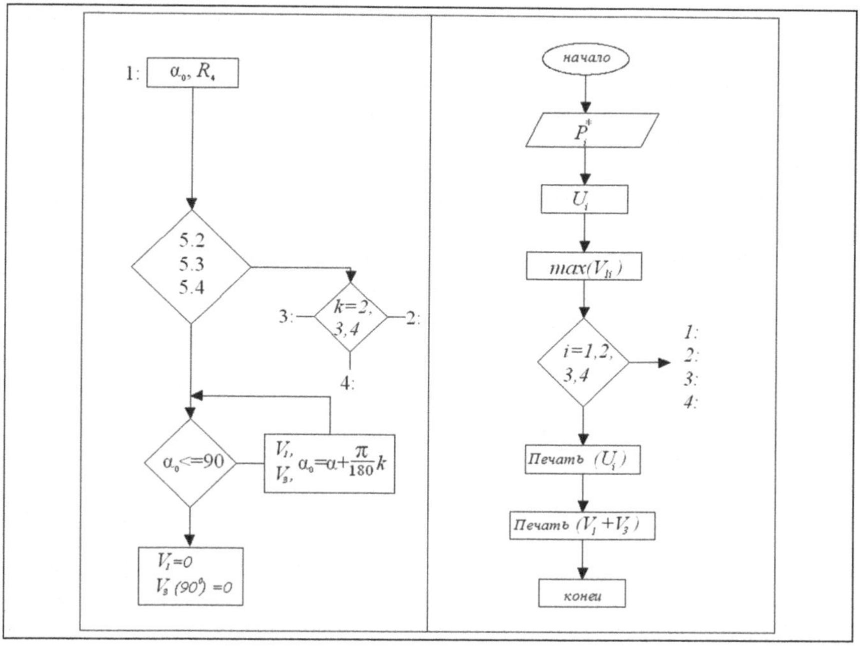

Figure 9: Block diagram

6 Simulation of traffic flows in cities

With medium and high intensity of movement and small distances between intersections (up to 500-700 meters) a group form of movement is formed. It is caused by the alternation of the phases of traffic light signaling. Crossroads become interdependent in control, thus there is a need to coordinate signals by maximizing the periodic, grouping nature of the traffic flow. Coordination of forms randomly emerging transportation means (TM) into dynamically homogenous car groups. The most efficient and affordable method of traffic organization in terms of its algorithmic and technical implementation is the coordination management of transport flow movement. The emergence of a new generation of technical means of organizing traffic on a microprocessor element base makes it possible to solve traffic control problems not only according to pre-calculated coordination programs, but also in real time, which is more efficient. Using simulation modeling allows you to conduct a model experiment and adjust the control parameters of the coordination program (PC). The software using the simulation model of the group movement of the vehicle is intended to determination of optimal parameters of coordinated control. Motion simulation is performed in an arbitrarily specified transport network of the city. The transport network is represented as a directional graph, whose arcs are spans (directions), and at the nodes there are intersections with traffic lights. The road network graph contains the following elements: **Crossroads**. It has a number of properties, the main of which is the number of phases, phase duration, first phase offset, etc. **External intersection**. It does not participate in modeling, it is necessary to indicate the directions included in the network. In all incoming directions, the intensity is a value which is constant in time. **The extra point**. Necessary to simulate such elements of the UDS as a narrowing of the carriageway, an adjustable merging of the TP, the division of flow between two adjacent intersections into components. **Direction**. Interconnects intersections, the main properties are intensity, maximum throughput or saturation flow, average travel time, length, etc.

Each network element is represented in the program by a separate class with its own unique attributes and methods. The setting of properties for each of the network elements is performed in the dialogue mode. For an intersection, the user sets parameters such as number, name, number of phases, initial phase shift, duration, and minimum the duration of the phases. There can be several intersection groups in the network, for which the phase shift relative to each other will be constant. For the direction, the following is specified: number, saturation flow, intensity, length span, the time of displacement of the beginning and end of the green light for complex promotions, the number of permissive phases for a given direction, the type of direction (normal or percolating).

This program has the ability to create an arbitrary number of routes. Route of movement is understood as a set of connected directions of movement. As a rule, in the UDS of the city there are such sets of directions, the movement along which is most intensive at a certain time, for example, in the city center in the morning rush hours and from the center to the areas in the evening. Each route is assigned a weighting factor indicating the importance of this route. The program has developed a procedure that optimizes the travel time for a given route, taking into account its importance. Thus, the program allows you to determine the optimal control parameters for the automatic system of coordinated traffic management.

Literature

Petrov, V. V. (2007). *Управление движением транспортных потоков в городах: Монография. (in Russian)*. Омск: Изд-во СибАДИ.

Robertson, D. (1997). The TRANSYT method of coordinating traffic signals. *Traffic Eng. + Contr.*, pp. 76-77.

Kostengünstige Produktionstechnologie für Verbund-Schwefel-Betonrohre auf der Grundlage lokaler Materialien

Hajymuhammet Geldiyev, Patshakuli Atayev, Nuraly Hudaykuliyev, Durjahan Atayeva

Derzeit sind große Brennstoff- und Energieländer wie Turkmenistan, Russland und andere Länder dabei - die Menge des produzierten technischen Schwefels übersteigt den Bedarf um ein Vielfaches. Auf dem internationalen Markt sind Nachfrage und Preis für technischen Schwefel extrem niedrig, und Länder, die Schwefel in ihren chemisch-technologischen Produktionsprozessen verwenden, importieren dieses Produkt nicht, da sie bereits über ausreichend große natürliche und industrielle Schwefelreserven verfügen.

Dieses industrielle Produktionsproblem ist nicht das Ergebnis der Gewinnung dieses Rohstoffs in einzelnen Schwefelsteinbrüchen oder Bergwerken, sondern ist das Ergebnis des Produktionsprozesses der chemischen Reinigung von wiedergewinnbaren Kohlenwasserstoffbrennstoffen in Öl- und Gasförderländern. Es ist bekannt, dass Öl und Gas zur weiteren Verwendung einer Vielzahl von Produktionsprozessen einschließlich mehrstufiger Reinigungsstufen unterzogen werden.[1]

In vielen Ländern wird in den meisten Fällen mangels großflächiger Nutzung – technischer Schwefel in bestimmten Gebieten gelagert - Freilagerhäusern auf unbestimmte Zeit gelagert. In der Natur gibt es solche Prozesse wie die aerodynamische Aktivität von Windströmungen, die hydromechanischen Auswirkungen von Niederschlag, eine hohe Intensität der Strahlung der Sonnenstrahlen, gefolgt von thermodynamischen Effekten. Aufgrund dieser Faktoren – die Lagerung von Schwefel im offenen Raum und die mangelnde Nutzung – ist dies ein großes Problem für das ökologische System der Umwelt.[2]

Dieser wissenschaftliche Artikel stellt die Experimente und Ergebnisse der Forschung zur Entwicklung von Technologien vor – die Herstellung von Verbundbaustoffen aus Schwefel mit hoher mechanischer Festigkeit sowie die Entwicklung neuer energie- und materialsparender Technologien für die Herstellung von langen und nahtlosen Verbundrohren aus Schwefel.

---

1 Vgl. o.V., 2014
2 Vgl. Strebel, et al., 2003

H.-C. Brauweiler et al. (Hrsg.), *Digitalization and Industry 4.0: Economic and Societal Development*, https://doi.org/10.1007/978-3-658-27110-7_19

"Schwefelbeton" ist ein künstlicher steinartiger Baustoff, der durch thermische Einwirkung auf Schwefel und Hinzufügen verschiedener inerter Füllstoffe erhalten wird. Die Zusammensetzung von Schwefelbeton ist ein Verbundwerkstoff, der verbindenden Schwefel, inerte Füllstoffe und Modifizierungsmittel enthält.[3]

Im Gegensatz zu anderen Betonbautechniken erfordert Schwefelbeton in keiner Weise die Verwendung von Wasser und Zement für die eigene Produktion, dass die Kosten der hergestellten Produkte erheblich senkt oder Installations- und Wartungsarbeiten erleichtert. Anstelle von ihnen wird Schwefel (20-40%) verwendet - modifiziert mit verschiedenen Modifizierungsmitteln, wie beispielsweise Styrol, Pentadien, Dicyclopentadien.

Die Hauptvorteile von Schwefelbeton im Vergleich zu den üblichen sind: schnelle Festigkeit, Haltbarkeit und höhere Festigkeitseigenschaften (Druck und Biegung), die Fähigkeit dieses Materials, unter Spannung effektiv zu arbeiten, hohe chemische (korrosive) Beständigkeit, Haltbarkeit in sauren und salzhaltigen Umgebungen und Frostbeständigkeit, ein Vielfaches des traditionellen Betons. Die Palette der verwendeten inerten Füllstoffe sowie anderer Massenadditive ist sehr breit. In ihrer Qualität man kann gewöhnlichen Bruchstein, Kies, Sand, feinkörnige Steine verschiedener Mineralien, metallurgische Schlacken sowie andere trockene und lose Materialien verwenden.

Andere Eigenschaften können niedrige Wärmeleitfähigkeit, Wasserbeständigkeit, Aushärtung in der Kälte, die Möglichkeit des Recyclings, leichte Schrumpfung und hohe Adhäsion (Effekt der Adhäsion von Oberflächen verschiedener Körper) sein.[4]

Abbildung 1: Die erhaltenen Kopien von Verbundwerkstoffen basieren auf Schwefelbeton unter Verwendung verschiedener Füllstoffe im Verlauf der Forschungsarbeit.

3 Vgl. Geldiyev, Atayev, 2016b
4 Vgl. Geldiyev, Atayev, 2017

Die Eigenschaften von Schwefelbeton sind eine Folge seiner inneren Struktur, die von Wissenschaftlern in Industrieländern eingehend untersucht wurde. Schwefel ohne Zusatz eines Füllstoffs ist eine Substanz mit einer homogenen Struktur, was eine dichte Anordnung von Molekülen relativ zueinander bedeutet. Die Anwesenheit des Füllstoffs führt dazu, dass Schwefelmoleküle die Füllstoffmoleküle „befestigen" und die Innenräume der erhaltenen Substanz so ausfüllen, dass die Porosität (sogar unter einem Mikroskop) fast unsichtbar wird. Für die Gasindustrie kann auch Schwefelbeton von Interesse sein, da er ein ideales Material für Gaspipelines, Straßenplatten und -pfähle ist, die in der Feldentwicklung verwendet werden usw.[5] Die resultierenden Schwefelbetonbaustoffe, die aus langjähriger, von uns durchgeführter Forschungs- und Entwicklungsarbeit resultieren, weisen hohe physikalisch-mechanische Eigenschaften auf. Sie sind in der folgenden Abbildung dargestellt.

Zur Gewinnung von Schwefelbeton im Labor wurde zunächst technischer Schwefel in einem geschlossenen Elektroheizofen auf eine Temperatur von 140°C geschmolzen. Nachdem der Schwefel im flüssigen Zustand erhalten worden war, wurde der Dicyclopentadien-Modifikator in bestimmten Mengen als modifizierende chemische Verbindung zugegeben. Nachdem der flüssige Schwefel mit dem Modifikator versetzt worden war, wurden sie 5 Minuten lang in einem geschlossenen Behälter mit einem "Utest" -Mixer gemischt. Um die erforderliche Schwefelmodifikation zu erhalten, wurden gleichzeitig die Erwärmungsvorgänge von Karakum-Sand, der zuvor gereinigt und im Verhältnis von 70% des gesamten Sandes auf nanoskalige Werte zerkleinert worden war, unter Verwendung eines elektrischen Heizofens auf eine Temperatur von 140°C durchgeführt. Nach der Aufbereitung des modifizierten Schwefels wurde er mit Sand in das Innere der beheizten Tanks gegossen. Danach wurden Mischvorgänge durchgeführt, um das Mischen unter Verwendung der elektrischen Heiz- und Mischausrüstung "Utest" für 10 Minuten zu maximieren. Bei den Heiz- und Mischarbeiten wurden auch kubische Formen mit Standardabmessungen mit einem Elektroofen auf 120°C erhitzt. Die fertige Mischung aus Schwefelbeton wurde in die Metallform gegossen. Für die Untersuchung und Bestimmung der technischen Eigenschaften wurde aus Proben von Schwefelbetonmaterial ein Komplex von Mess- und Prüfgeräten "Utest" hergestellt. Die Druckfestigkeit der erhaltenen Proben von Schwefelbeton erreicht 80 MPa. Ein derartiger Parameter für die hohe Festigkeit kann erhalten werden, indem das folgende Verhältnis der Komponenten der Zusammensetzung der hergestellten Produkte umgesetzt wird: Füllstoff/Schwefel/Modifizierungsmittel = 50,0%/41,7%/8,3%. Die Ergebnisse der Mess- und Forschungsarbeiten mit experimentellen Proben von hergestelltem Schwefelbeton sind in der folgenden Tabelle dargestellt.

---

[5] Vgl. Geldiyev, Atayev, 2016b

Um experimentelle Proben von Rohren aus Schwefelbeton mit Standardmaßen zu erhalten, wurden diese aus zylindrischen verzinkten Blechen mit der glattesten Oberfläche von innen geöffnet. Der Prozess der Herstellung von Schwefelbetonrohren besteht aus dem Eingießen von Schwefelbetongemisch in den inneren Hohlraum einer zylindrischen Form und anschließender Abkühlung mit kaltem Wasser. Nach dem Abkühlen können die Rohrproben ohne mechanische Defekte leicht aus der Form entnommen werden.

№ Bestellnummern	Technische Eigenschaften	Numerische Indikatoren
1.	Probengewicht I, Gramm Probengewicht II, Gramm	2245 2120
2.	Probengrößen, mm	100*100*100
3.	Probendichte I, kg/m³ Dichte der Probe II, kg/m³ Die durchschnittliche Dichte von Beton, kg/m³	2245 2120 2183
4.	Stärke der Probe I, kgf/m² Die Stärke von Probe II, kgf/m² Die durchschnittliche Festigkeit von Beton, kgf/m²	390,5 391,4 390,9

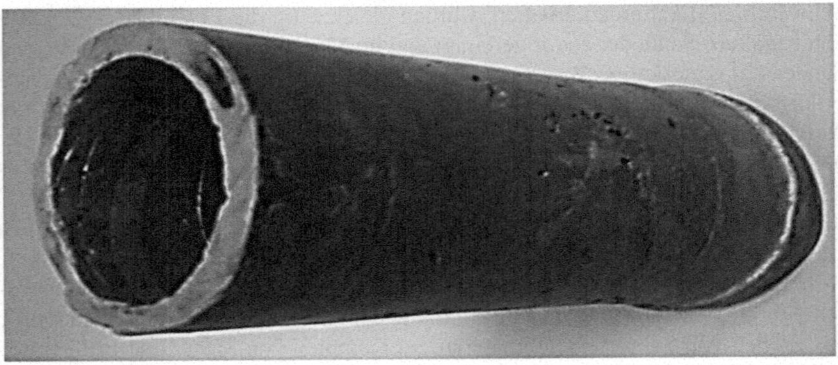

Abbildung 2: Herstellung von Verbundrohren auf der Basis von Schwefelbeton für Testversuche: eine allgemeine Übersicht über experimentelle Proben von Schwefelbetonrohren mit Standardgrößen.

Als Ergebnis unserer wissenschaftlichen Arbeit haben wir ein Verfahren und eine Vorrichtung zur Herstellung nahtloser Verbundrohre auf der Basis von Schwefelbeton entwickelt. Diese von uns patentierte Erfindung bezieht sich auf die Bauindustrie, insbesondere auf die Herstellung von Bauprodukten aus Gemischen auf der Basis von Schwefelbeton, und ist zur Verwendung bei der Herstellung von Rohren bestimmt, insbesondere zur Abwasser, Wasserversorgung und Müllentsorgung. Das Verfahren zur Rohr-herstellung besteht in der Vorbereitung der Schwefelbetonmischung, die Schwefel als Bindemittel, Sand, Schotter oder andere trockene Füllstoffe enthält, als Füllstoff. Gießen von Schwefelbeton in einen trichterförmigen Arbeitsraum, Formen aus Schwefelbeton mischungs produkten, wie Kolben mit O-Ring-Dichtung, der das aus dem Hohlraum austretende fertige Schwefelbetonrohr zwischen einem elektrisch beheizten Zylinder und einem zylindrischen Kanal abkühlt Schrott, ein Kühlrohr mit einer Quelle für kaltes Wasser verwendet wird.

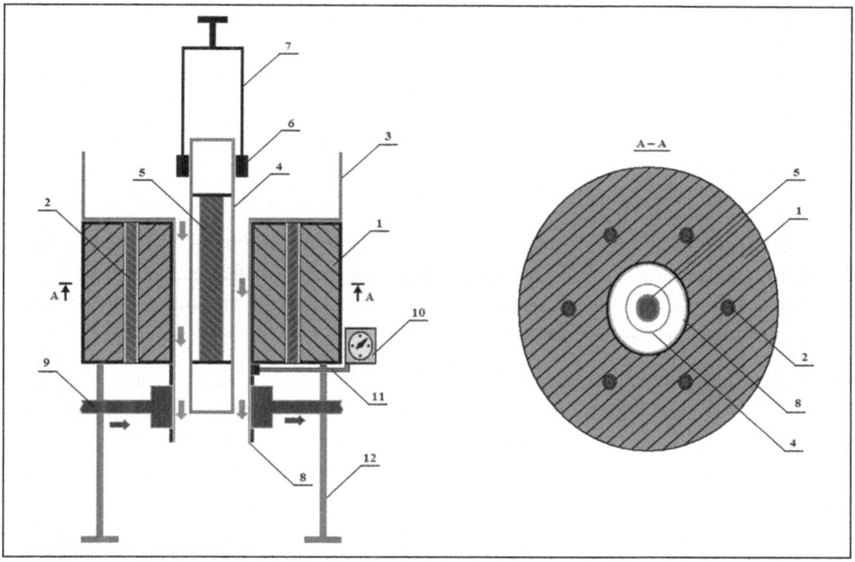

Abbildung 3: Vorrichtung zur Herstellung nahtloser Bauprodukte wie Rohre aus schwefelhaltigen Gemischen.

Die von uns entwickelte Vorrichtung wird durch Abbildungen in Abbildung 3 veranschaulicht, die den gesamten Schutzumfang der Ansprüche dieser technischen Lösung nicht abdecken und auch nicht einschränken, sondern lediglich beispielhafte Materialien für einen bestimmten Ausführungsfall sind. Hier bezeichnen die Zahlen: 1 - einen zylindrischen Körper aus Asbestzement; 2 - Spule für die elektrische Beheizung von Chromel; 3 - Arbeitsbereich zum Gießen von vorbereiteter Schwefelbetonmischung; 4 - Edelstahlzylinder zum Verleihen eines Hohlraums; 5 - Spule zum elektrischen Aufheizen von Chromel; 6 - Ringdichtung aus Edelstahl; 7 - mechanischer Kolben für die Kraft; 8 - zylindrischer Kanal aus Edelstahl; 9 - Rohr mit Kaltwasserquelle zur Kühlung der Endprodukte; 10 - Thermostat; 11 - Thermostatleiter mit einem thermischen Sensor; 12 - Eisengestelle.

Bei der Herstellung von langen Rohren mit kleinem Durchmesser (beispielsweise bis zu 300 Millimeter) erfolgt die Kraft auf den mechanischen Kolben manuell, und bei der Herstellung von langen Rohren mit großem Durchmesser (beispielsweise über 300 Millimeter) kann die Kraft auf den mechanischen Kolben unter Verwendung eines automatisierten elektrischen Antriebs erreicht werden. Bevor das Bauprodukt die Vorrichtung verlässt, wird es auch mittels einer Leitung mit einer Kaltwasserquelle gekühlt, die an den Wänden des zylindrischen Kanals befestigt ist und seine ringförmige Form von außen umgibt.

Das technische Ergebnis der von uns entwickelten Erfindung besteht darin, eine optimale Technologie für die Herstellung nahtloser Langrohre aus Mischungen auf der Basis von Schwefelbeton zu schaffen, um die Anzahl der Arbeitsschritte im Produktionsprozess zu minimieren, die Produktivität dieses Produkttyps zu erhöhen, um Rohre mit verbesserten physikalisch-mechanischen Eigenschaften wie Biegefestigkeit herzustellen, geringe Flüssigkeitsaufnahme, Frostbeständigkeit, geringe Porosität sowie Erhöhung der Lebensdauer der hergestellten Produkte.

Als weitere technische Ergebnisse können Sie die Erweiterung des Produktumfangs hinzufügen, die Größe (Abmessungen) des Geräts reduzieren und die Komplexität des Arbeitsvorgangs, die geringen Baukosten und die kurze Zeit reduzieren, dies erleichtert die Installation erheblich.

Einer der Hauptparameter, der höchste Genauigkeit bei der Herstellung von Bauprodukten auf der Basis von Schwefelbeton erfordert, ist die Heiztemperatur. Wenn sich die Erwärmungstemperatur während des Produktionsprozesses um zwei oder drei Grad Celsius ändert, haben die aus Schwefelbeton resultierenden Produkte nicht die erforderlichen Eigenschaften und können nicht für Bauarbeiten verwendet werden. Deshalb wurde ein empfindlicher thermoelektrischer Regler an das Gerät angeschlossen.

Das von uns entwickelte Gerät arbeitet nach seinen technologischen Grundsätzen folgendermaßen: Das zuvor aufbereitete Schwefel-Beton-Gemisch tritt in den trichterförmigen Arbeitsraum (3) ein. Dann wird unter Verwendung eines mechanischen Kolbens (7) mit einem ringförmigen Verdichter (6) eine Kraft aufgebracht, mit deren Hilfe das Bauprodukt freigesetzt wird. Der Austritt des Rohres erfolgt in vertikaler Richtung in der unteren Seite des Hohlraums zwischen dem Zylinder (4) mit elektrischer Heizung (5) und dem zylindrischen Kanal (8). Sie befinden sich im Inneren des Asbestzements (1), der mit mehreren Chromel-Spiralen (2) zum elektrischen Erhitzen des Stromgemisches ausgestattet ist. Die erforderliche Heiztemperatur wird von einem Thermostat (10) gesteuert, der mit einem Temperatursensor (11) ausgestattet ist. Mit Hilfe einer Leitung mit kaltem Wasser (9) wird der Produktausstoß gekühlt.

Das konfektionierte Schwefelbetonrohr ist glatt, wobei die Wände entlang der gesamten Länge des Bauprodukts gleich dick sind. Die Verwendung der Erfindung erlaubt es, die Technologie der kontinuierlichen Herstellung von Gebäudestrukturen wie Rohren zu vereinfachen sowie die Produktionsgeschwindigkeit und Haltbarkeit der resultierenden Produkte zu erhöhen.

Basierend auf der von uns entwickelten Produktionstechnologie für Schwefel-Beton-Bauprodukte können die Finanz- und Materialkosten in der Öl- und Gasindustrie und im Bauwesen minimiert, die Einsatzfähigkeit von Schwefel erhöht und die Energie- und Umweltleistung verbessert werden. Neben der Erhöhung des physischen Produktionsvolumens von Baustoffen wird die Verwendung von Schwefelbeton in der Bauindustrie unter den Bedingungen einer ständig wachsenden Nachfrage die Zuverlässigkeit der daraus hergestellten Objekte erheblich erhöhen.

Als Ergebnis der Experimente sowie der Durchführung mathematischer Berechnungen wurden die folgenden Eigenschaften der Verbundrohre auf der Basis von Schwefelbeton identifiziert, die sich von anderen Produktionsanaloga unterscheiden: Korrosionsbeständigkeit; Die maximale Lebensdauer beträgt ca. 50-55 Jahre. gesundheitliche und hygienische Sicherheit; natürliche und ökologische Sicherheit; extrem geringe Rauheit sowie eine hohe Glätte der inneren und äußeren Oberfläche; das praktische Fehlen von Algen und anderer biologischer Vegetation im inneren Arbeitshohlraum von Rohren während des Betriebs unter Bedingungen thermisch passiver hydraulischer Strömungen mit niedrigem Druck; hohe Beständigkeit gegen hydroabrasive Defekte; hohe Beständigkeit gegen chemisch aggressive Umgebungen; hoher mechanischer Widerstand; hohe Widerstandsfähigkeit gegen extremen Druckabfall der Hydraulikströmungen; hoher Widerstand gegen elektrische Ströme; optimales Gewicht der Rohre bei Transport, Montage und Demontage; hohe Festigkeit der ringförmigen Verbindungen zwischen Rohren; geringe technologische Komplexität beim Wiederaufbau und Recycling.

Neben Umweltsicherheit und Materialeinsparungen wird finanzielle Effizienz durch die Minimierung der Kosten der erforderlichen Ausgangsmaterialien für die Herstellung von Verbundrohren auf der Basis von Schwefelbeton erreicht. Die Möglichkeit des Recyclings im Bedarfsfall mit minimalem Energie-, Zeit- und Arbeitsaufwand macht diese Technologie sehr attraktiv für den Einsatz als wettbewerbsfähiges Produkt, das auf internationalen Märkten sehr gefragt ist.

Zusammenfassung

Unter Laborbedingungen wurde eine Reihe von Versuchen durchgeführt, um Versuchsproben aus Schwefelbeton durch Zugabe einer Vielzahl trockener, pulverförmiger mechanischer Füllstoffe zu erhalten. Es zeigte sich, dass die Festigkeit der erhaltenen Schwefelbetonproben von den Korngrößen der verwendeten Füllstoffe abhängt. Als Ergebnis der Tests wurde festgestellt, dass die größte Festigkeit unter der Bedingung erreicht wird, dass das Verhältnis der Verbundfüllstoffe wie folgt ist: Füllstoffe im Nanomaßstab – 70%, feinkörniger Sand und 30% Splittstein.

Eine hitzebeständige Form wurde mit einer chemisch beständigen und glatten Oberfläche von innen hergestellt, um Versuchsproben von Rohren aus Schwefelbeton herzustellen. Die physikalisch-chemischen Eigenschaften der erhaltenen Rohre aus Schwefelbeton nach internationalen technischen Standards wurden untersucht und das Fehlen ihrer Umweltbelastung wurde aufgezeigt. Durchführung von Studien zu den Möglichkeiten des Recyclings von Baustoffen auf der Basis von Schwefelbeton.

Eine thermoelektrische Vorrichtung mit vertikalem Auslass zur Herstellung nahtloser und langer Verbundrohre auf der Basis von Schwefelbeton wurde entwickelt. Es wurde daran gearbeitet, es weiter zu optimieren, zu automatisieren und zu automatisieren, und es wurden auch Möglichkeiten zur Kontrolle der Dicke und des Durchmessers der hergestellten Produkte untersucht. Basierend auf den durchgeführten experimentellen Arbeiten wurde ein Patent für die Erfindung von Turkmenistan Nr. 707 mit dem Namen "Eine Methode zur Herstellung nahtloser Schwefelbetonrohre und eine Vorrichtung zu deren Implementierung" (Autoren: H. Geldiyev, P. Atayev und andere; 27. Dezember 2016) erhalten, und es wurden Dokumente für die Erteilung eines Patents für die Erfindungen Turkmenistans mit dem Namen "Verfahren zur herstellung von gebäuden wie rohren aus schwefelbeton und einer maschine mit elektrischer heizung zu deren umsetzung" (Autoren: H. Geldiyev, P. Atayev; 24.07.2017).

Literaturverzeichnis

Geldiyev, H., Atayev, P. (2016a). Eine Methode zur Herstellung nahtloser Schwefelbetonrohre und eine Vorrichtung zu deren Implementierung. *Patent für die Erfindung von Turkmenistan № 707.*

Geldiyev, H., Atayev, P. (2016b). Herstellungstechnologie für Bauprodukte auf der Basis von Schwefelbeton. Herausgegeben Volumen der internationalen wissenschaftlich-praktische Konferenz von Studenten, Diplomanden und Doktoranden. *Markt- und Produktivitätseffizienz-13.*

Geldiyev, H., Atayev, P. (2017). Entwicklung der Anwendungstechnologie der Schwefelbauproduktion zur ökologischen Neutralisierung. *Wissenschaftlich-theoretisches Journal der Akademie der Wissenschaften von Turkmenistan. Nr. 4*, S. 83-86.

o.V. (2014). Tonnen Schwefelbeton. *Gazprom Corporate Journal. Nr. 1-2.*

Strebel, H., Eifler, P., Brauweiler, H.-Ch., et al. (2003). *Umweltorientierung in Betrieblichen Querschnittsbereichen. Internationales Umweltmanagement. Operatives Umweltmanagement im internationalen und interdisziplinären Kontext, Band III*, Gabler-Springer, S. 313-358.

Analysis of computer modeling tools for assessing the risk of flooding in the East Kazakhstan region

R. K. Chettykbayev, N. F. Denisova

1 Introduction

Throughout the history of mankind, the problem of forecasting natural disasters has occupied one of the most important places in planning, construction, agriculture and other aspects of life activity.[1] One of these phenomena is undoubtedly river floods. For thousands of years, huge rivers carrying thousands of cubic meters of water were at the same time a source of well-being, and a sufficiently large danger for many large settlements. At this stage of development, mankind adapted and learned to some extent to cope with river plagues, by adjusting the flow of the most important rivers, observing changes in the water level in the river, etc.

More than 40% of all water resources of the Republic of Kazakhstan and 5 large hydropower stations are concentrated in East Kazakhstan region. Every year in the region there are emergency situations with floods; in the flood zone there are a large number of villages, houses and flood water threatening hydroelectric power stations, which are located in the region. In this connection, the task was to create an information and analytical system for forecasting the flooding of territories in emergency situations, which could predict possible damage during the flood period.

This article is a part of a study that is devoted to the creation of an information and analytical system for forecasting the flooding of territories in emergency situations in East Kazakhstan region. The aim of the study is the conceptual development of theoretical foundations, the development of methodological principles and the solution of practical problems of monitoring and forecasting the flooding of territories during a seasonal increase in water levels in the rivers of East Kazakhstan region. One of the objectives of the study is to choose a tool for constructing a computerized digital model.

In the modern world there are many software systems whose main task is to simulate river hydraulics and simulate flooded areas. For the purposes of hydraulic calculations, software packages have been developed that are widely spread both

---

[1] See Kramer, Brauweiler, 2000

H.-C. Brauweiler et al. (Hrsg.), *Digitalization and Industry 4.0: Economic and Societal Development*, https://doi.org/10.1007/978-3-658-27110-7_20

abroad and in the CIS countries. The most common programs are: the MIKE 11 program and the HEC-RAS (US Army Corps of Engineers).

2 Basic physiographic and hydrological characteristics of East Kazakhstan region

East-Kazakhstan region occupies the southwestern part of Altai, the Zaisan basin, the Kalbinsky highlands, the Saur-Tarbagatay ranges, the Irtysh plain and the Eastern part of the Kazakh Uplands. Currently, the area of East Kazakhstan region is 283.3 thousand km^2. Three European countries, such as Bulgaria, Greece and Albania, could be freely accommodated in this territory.

Figure 1: The Republic of Kazakhstan

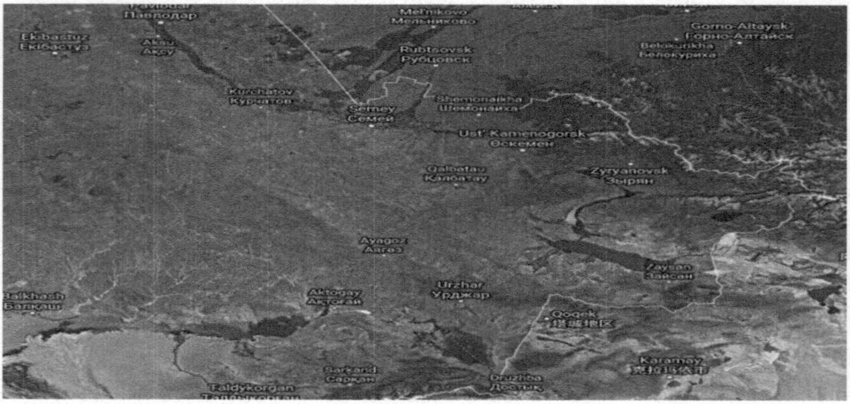

Figure 2: East-Kazakhstan Region

The position of East Kazakhstan region in the central part of Eurasia, as well as the Altai Mountains located on its territory determined its main climatic features. In general, it is a distinctly continental climate with large seasonal and daily temperature differences. Summer is hot and moderately dry, while winter is cold and snowy, moderately cold in the foothills. According to the meteorological station of Ust-Kamenogorsk city, the average temperatures of the winter months vary from −12 ° C to −15 ° C, in the foothills of the Altai from −9 ° C to −11 ° C. However, during the irruption of the Arctic air masses, the temperature can drop to −42 ° C. Snowfalls are a regular occurrence in winter in semi-deserts and steppes of the region, and inversion fogs are frequent in intermountain basins. The average maximum July temperatures range from + 25 ° C to + 30 ° C. Maximum summer temperatures can reach + 45 ° C. The average annual rainfall is from 300 to 600 mm, in the mountains – about 900 mm, in some places up to 1500 mm.

A small territory of East Kazakhstan is occupied by the Altai and Saur-Tarbagatai mountains with eternal glaciers on the tops, the Kalbinsky mountain range, small-hilly plains, the Kazakh Uplands, wide basins and extensive plains along the rivers.

About 885 rivers more than 10 km long flow on the territory of East Kazakhstan. Among the largest ones are the Black Irtysh, Bukhtarma, Kurchum, Kalzhyr, Narym, Uba, Ulba. The main waterway of the region is the Irtysh, on which 3 hydroelectric power stations are located – Bukhtarma, Shulbinsk and Ust-Kamenogorsk.

In East Kazakhstan there are about a thousand lakes larger than 1 hectare. They are unevenly distributed across the territory – the largest number of lakes are concentrated in the northern and northeast parts of the region. The largest lakes of East Kazakhstan are Zaisan, Markakol, Bukhtarma, Ulmes, Caracol, Turangakol, Dubygaly, Kemirkol, and also lakes located on the border of East Kazakhstan and Almaty regions: Alakol and Sasykkol.

3 General methods of hydraulic calculations

For hydraulic calculations using various software systems, initially, it is required to have all the initial information for building a river model directly in a computer program. Background information is varied and diverse. According to its structure and value, it can be divided into two types: basic information and hydrological information for rapid calculations. According to its method of constructing a digital model of a river, this is a complex process that includes several stages: isolating design sections on a river and determining the locations of settlement sections, measuring and checking the distances between the sections, digitizing cross sections of the riverbed, determining the roughness values for the sections (often this may be background information). Finally, entering data into the model manually or from a downloadable file of a specific format and content, that is, filling the data into the tables of specialized forms presented in the calculation program on a computer screen, completes the preliminary preparation of a digital basic river model for hydraulic calculations.[2]

Hydrological information for rapid calculations of the steady-state movement of water is set in the form of water flow rate, which is a characteristic of the inflowing stream from each considered river station to the next river station along the river course. Boundary conditions are introduced without taking into account temporary changes. When calculating using a block of steady-state motion, the boundary conditions can be specified in the form of unitary levels and water flow rates, lateral inflowing stream, or as a curve of water flow rate versus levels (Q = f (H)).

Rapid hydrological information is of the greatest value and is of particular value in the calculation, as it is the most recent and accurate (taking into account the modern development of methods of observation at the remaining hydrometeorological stations and hydroelectric facilities, where observations are made). This information forms the basis for calculating the hydraulic and hydrodynamic model. Specific types of information can be distinguished from operational hydrological information, such as maps of the velocity field of a stream, observations of sediment yield.

4 The main characteristics of the software systems HEC-RAS and MIKE

The HECRAS program (Hydrologic Engineering Center - River Analysis System)[3] was developed at the Hydrological Engineering Center of the U.S. Army Corps of Engineers (1995). The software package implements a one-dimensional approach to the hydraulic modeling of river flows, works in the Windows environment and includes a graphical interface, hydraulic analysis components, data storage and management, graphic and reporting tools.

The version of the HEC-RAS program includes four calculation modules:

1. calculation of water surface profiles for steady-state water movement;
2. calculation of the unsteady movement of water;
3. modeling of sediment transport in deformed channels;
4. water quality analysis.

The HEC-RAS software package models the flow hydraulics of natural river beds and channels for uniform flow. Used to simulate the calculation of water surface profiles. The software complex is one-dimensional. The main calculation path is

2 See Levit-Gurevich, 2009; See Nikiforov, 2012; See Nikiforov, 2015; See Nikiforov, 2014

3 See HEC-RAS, n.d.

based on solving the energy flow equation. Loss of energy due to friction, contraction, expansion of the channel of a water body is estimated. The equations of impulses are used for cases of abrupt changes in the surface profile of a water body, such as calculations during a hydraulic jump, flow hydraulics at bridge crossings, confluence of rivers or inflowing streams. For the calculation of unsteady water movement in the channel of a water body (such objects are calculated continuously and are the main objects of research, due to the work with open river beds), the Saint-Venant equation (see Formula 1) is used in the form of a final calculation using the finite difference method.

$$\begin{cases} \dfrac{\partial Q}{\partial s} + \dfrac{\partial W}{\partial t} = q \\ i - \dfrac{\partial H}{\partial s} = \dfrac{\alpha}{g}\left(V\dfrac{\partial V}{\partial s} + \dfrac{\partial V}{\partial t}\right) + \dfrac{V^2}{C^2 R} + \dfrac{qV}{gW} \end{cases} \tag{1}$$

In the calculations, the software complex uses the equations of continuity (see formula 2), energy (see formula 3) and resistance to flow (see formula 4).[4]

$$Q = v_1 A_1 = v_2 A_2 \tag{2}$$

$$H = z + y + \frac{\alpha v^2}{2g} \tag{3}$$

$$Q = K S_f^{1/2} \tag{4}$$

The capabilities of the HEC-RAS program can be used to calculate the hydraulic characteristics in the entire complex channel network in the river system section. This calculates the averaged (weighted) for each living section of the hydraulic characteristics: mark the curve of the free surface, hydraulic slope, speed, area of the living section, depth, etc.

MIKE is a professional software package for modeling flows (including dam breaks), water quality and sediment transport, the main feature of which is a modular structure having the following basic (basic) modules: - hydrodynamic (HD), which implements an implicit differential scheme for calculating unsteady water movement in watercourses, based on the equations of Saint-Venant; - advection-dispersion and coherent sediment transport (AD), based on the one-

4 See Ross, 2010; See Hunt, Brunner, 1995; See Sharkey, 2014

dimensional equation of mass conservation of dissolved and suspended matter (salt, coherent sediment, etc.). As the initial data are used the result of the calculation in the hydrodynamic module (HD); - water quality (WQ), describing the main aspects of water quality in a river as a result of human impact. Used in conjunction with the module advection-dispersion and transport of coherent sediment (AD); - morphology and transport of incoherent sediment (NST), allowing to calculate the transport of incoherent sediment, morphological changes and changes in the resistance of the channel.

The design model is applicable to the conditions of a uniform vertical flow, varying from the conditions of river flows with large slopes to tidal currents in estuaries. Means of the numerical scheme of the HD-module can be described as subcritical and supercritical flow regimes with appropriate adaptation to local conditions.[5]

The complete non-linear Saint-Venant equations for flow in open channels can be numerically solved for all points of the chosen grid and for given time intervals and boundary conditions. In addition to the complete hydrodynamic description of the flow, it is possible to use a simplified description of the flow, which makes it possible to estimate diffusion waves, kinematic waves, and quasistationary flow. In the structure of the standard HD-module, computational methods are formulated and developed, making it possible to perform calculations of flow passage through culverts of various types:

- broad crested weir;
- bottom water outlet;
- other types of structures selected by the user of the system.

The HD module implements an implicit differential scheme for calculating unsteady water movement in watercourses, based on the equations of Saint-Venant. The original mathematical model includes the one-dimensional equation of water motion and the continuity equation.

The MIKE model provides the possibility of describing the resistance of a channel of a complex shape with non-uniform roughness, as well as dependence calibration, describing hydraulic resistance, according to field data.

In the MIKE hydrodynamic module, it is possible to take into account the flooding of lands adjacent to a watercourse as connected tanks (they are not taken into account when calculating the flow dynamics, but are taken into account in the continuity equation). The area of the attached tanks at different water levels is set when describing the transverse profiles.

[5]See DHI Group MIKE 11, 2019

If necessary, the following parameters can be taken into account in the model calculations:

- wind effect (additive to hydraulic resistance);
- distributed lateral inflow;
- filtration losses in the floodplain and return of seepage water.

5 Conclusion

Work on the study has just begun and at the moment there is a collection and accumulation of necessary information. Also, at the moment, the main software systems that allow you to create digital models of river systems and enable the simulation of the flooding process in the region have been studied. This article outlined the main physiographic and hydrological characteristics of East Kazakhstan region, as well as the main features of the HEC-RAS and MIKE software packages. After examining all the advantages and disadvantages of software systems, it was decided to use both programs to create a digital model of the river system of East Kazakhstan region, which should lead to more accurate results.

Literature

Agroskin, I., Dmitriev, G., Pikalov, F. (1964). *Hydraulics.* (4 ed.).

DHI Group MIKE 11. (2019). *A modeling system for rivers and channels.* Retrieved 7.3.2019, from https://www.dhigroup.com/)

HEC-RAS. (n.d.). *Hydrologic Engineering Center-documentation and data.* Retrieved 7.3.2019, from http://www.hec.usace.army.mil/software/hec-ras/

Hunt, J., Brunner, G. (1995). *Flow Transitions in Bridge Backwater Analysis (RD-42).*

Kramer, M., Brauweiler, H.-Ch. (2000). *Gewässerschutz- und Hochwasserschutzrecht: Regelungen zum Hochwasserschutz an der Oder.* Wiesbaden: Gabler.

Kuchment, L. (2008). *River flow (genesis, modeling, prediction).*

Levit-Gurevich, L. (2009). *Simulation of cross sections along river stations and flowing water reservoir based on observed flow dependencies on water level. Proceedings of the conference "Modeling Sustainable Regional Development".* Nalchik: KBSU.

Nikiforov, D. (2012). *Calibration of digital computer models for hydraulic calculations of rivers and water storage reservoirs. Collection of scientific papers of the Russian scientific conference "Water and water resources: system-forming functions in nature and economics.* Tsimlyansk/ Novocherkassk: South-Russian State Polytechnic University.

Nikiforov, D. (2014). *Problems of creating hydrochemical models of rivers and water storage reservoirs on the example of the Moscow River using the HEC-RAS software package.* (Vol. 16). Samara: Publishing House of the Samara Scientific Center of the Russian Academy of Science.

Nikiforov, D. (2015). *Method of calibration of hydraulic models of rivers and water storage reservoirs. Proceedings of the Samara Scientific Center of the Russian Academy of Sciences.* (Vol. 17). Samara: Publishing House of the Samara Scientific Center of the Russian Academy of Sciences.

Ross, D. (2010). *Calibration of HEC-RAS models for rating curve development in semi-arid regions of Western Australia.* AHA Conference.

Sharkey, J. (2014). *Investigating Instabilities with HEC-RAS Unsteady Flow Modeling for Regulated Rivers at Low Flow Stages.* Retrieved 7.3.2019, from Master's Thesis, University of Tennessee: http://trace.tennessee.edu/utk_gradthes/3183

Online-recruiting as an element of the development of Kazakhstan within the framework of the program "Kazakhstan 2050"

Ernest Sirotin, Adina Musrepova, , D. T. Askarov

1 Introduction

With the rapid development of Internet technologies and a comprehensive process of globalization, the Republic of Kazakhstan does not stand aside and follows global development trends. Thus, the Tax Code of the Republic of Kazakhstan, approved in 2018, implies the most convenient taxation conditions for entrepreneurs, whose main activities can be attributed to electronic entrepreneurship. This step should have been expected from the government, since, firstly, an increasing number of Kazakhstanis have access to the Internet, about 74.6% of the country's population, according to the World Economic Forum[1], and secondly, Kazakhstanis are showing increasing confidence in online shopping, which is manifested in the amounts spent and, as a result, the constant growth of the e-commerce market. The current e-commerce market share in the country's economy is $ 1 billion.[2] The development of the e-commerce market and the exemption of this market from taxes shows that Kazakhstan intends to further develop in the direction of Internet technologies. In the message of the President of the Republic of Kazakhstan N.Nazarbayev to the people of Kazakhstan, dated January 10, 2018, one of the points states that "the integrated program" Digital Kazakhstan[3] was adopted. This fact once again proves the importance of the development of the ICT sector for the Republic of Kazakhstan. The program "Digital Kazakhstan" itself involves 4 key areas of development, namely:

1. "The implementation of the digital Silk Road. This is the development of a reliable, affordable, high-speed and secure digital infrastructure;
2. Development of a creative society. These include the development of competencies and skills for the digital economy, the work to improve the digital literacy of the population, the training of ICT specialists for industries;
3. Digital transformations in industries. This is the widespread introduction of digital technologies to improve the competitiveness of various sectors of the economy;

---

1 See World Economic Forum, 2018
2 See Khabar 24, 2018
3 See Akorda, 2018

H.-C. Brauweiler et al. (Hrsg.), *Digitalization and Industry 4.0: Economic and Societal Development*, https://doi.org/10.1007/978-3-658-27110-7_21

4. Transition to a proactive state. This is an improvement of the electronic and mobile government system, optimization of the provision of public services."[4]

As you can see, especially from the first three points, this program involves some digitalization of not only individual sectors of the economy, but also of the whole society. Consequently, in the foreseeable future, the Republic of Kazakhstan expects a transition to partial digitalization and automation of the simplest processes. This trend can already be traced in the economic and everyday areas of activity, such as in the banking sector and in the field of taxi-ordering. There are also quite positive developments in the field of HR. The so-called Internet recruiting functions quite well in the territory of the Republic of Kazakhstan through such services as HeadHunter, HiPO, various firms engaged in direct recruitment: Fircroft, Antal Group. However, in the future, the development of Internet recruiting in the Republic of Kazakhstan may deviate from the current level, at which the recruiting specialist is engaged in searching for candidates through the resume database provided by HeadHunter, and also manually selecting candidates for the first time to the level when recruiting is mainly responsible for controlling the execution of a search and the initial selection of a candidate, providing the search and primary selection work itself to the bot, or artificial intelligence. Thus, the process of selection and initial selection of the candidate is automated and the HR specialist can, to a greater extent, pay attention to things that only a person can perform.

Now let's take a closer look at this concept and highlight the main advantages and disadvantages of it.

2 Basic principles of online recruiting today

First of all, in order to consider the concept of Internet recruiting, it is necessary to clarify and, in principle, find out what recruiting is. First of all, if this term is explained briefly, then this is a completely ordinary staff recruitment, which almost all firms with an HR department have in their structure. The main task of recruiting is to attract and hire those professionals whose personal and professional characteristics meet the requirements of the company at the moment. And, as a result of the subjectivity of the requirements of companies, the methods for achieving the main task of recruiting in different companies coincide, in general, with their content, but differ in details.

There are a number of methods that allow searching for new employees in the company:

---

4 (Zerde, 2018)

1. "to search among friends. The selection criterion in this case may be the recommendations of these trusted people;
2. poaching staff from other companies;
3. tosearch by print and on the Internet;
4. attracting promising graduates;
5. to search using social networks".[5]

As you can see from this list of methods, at least 4 of them are usually implemented using the Internet today.

It's easier for a friend to write an e-mail with a request to recommend someone to a specific position. Luring employees can also be done using the Internet. For the most part, recruiting staff for middle-level positions is luring away employees who work for a competitor by providing better conditions than competitors. As a rule, such employees are usually not satisfied with their current position and enter the labor market in order to change jobs, but remain approximately in the same professional area in which they worked. There are very rare cases when a person radically changes the direction of his work activity, however there are such cases.

The third method, which includes searching through print publications and the Internet, makes sense to reduce to a simple "Internet search", as in the modern realities of the development of Internet technologies, more and more print publications either close down or switch to an electronic version with a paid subscription and mailing numbers to customers. If earlier, at the beginning of 00x, the search for suitable candidates took up a large amount of time (especially taking into account the factor of technology development, in 2000 only "70 thousand inhabitants"[6] of the Republic had full access to the Internet), then now a relatively small number of HR department managers will resort to searching for the applicant, using any printed editions. This process takes too many time resources, which will certainly affect the productivity of a particular manager. Therefore, for sampling among applicants, the HR manager will most likely resort to the most popular Internet resource containing a database of candidates' resumes, rather then using printed publications. In addition, online resources contain a very extensive database of summaries. The site HeadHunter.kz has "1911168 resumes and 21901 vacancies from 52453 companies as of October 16, 2018".[7] The number of resumes posted on this service is 10.5% of the current number of residents of the Republic of Kazakhstan, which, of course, means that:

1. HR departments are more expedient to conduct a search and initial selection of candidates through the Internet;

---

5 See Podborkadrov, 2018; See Eberbach, Brauweiler, 1993
6 (Centrel, 2016)
7 (HeadHunter's, 2019)

2. This fact, again, proves that print publications are not the most suitable way of searching compared to newer methods.

As for the fourth method of searching for new employees, one cannot definitely say that this can be fully implemented via the Internet. Naturally, there are special internship programs for third and fourth year students, where you must send a resume using the Internet. Of course, there is an option of just bringing a resume to the company's office, but the extra waste of temporary resources in the current realities is not in demand even from young professionals. However, for the most part, companies attract students not by posting a vacancy on an Internet resource, or posting an internship program on their website, but working closely with universities and non-profit organizations (for example, AIESEC) and presenting their internship programs at university job fairs or the “Leadership Development Day” organized by AIESEC. This tool is fairly problematic to introduce into the framework of Internet technologies, since the main feature of this tool is the direct communication between the employer and graduate students, who are already potential applicants in the future.

The fifth method of searching for new employees is completely tied to the use of Internet technologies and the search for additional information about the applicant in social networks, which will show its more informal side of the applicant's personality. The main problems with this search method are the complete absence, the content of hidden, or completely changed information about the applicant. And as it often happens, information about the applicant is missing due to completely changed data by the applicant. However, as it was said earlier, this method is completely tied to the use of Internet technologies. Specifically, the search for information is conducted through social networks popular in the Republic of Kazakhstan likeVKontakte, Instagram, and Facebook.

Now that the basic recruitment methods have been considered, we can go to the algorithm for the selection of personnel.

First, it is necessary to realize what kind of person is needed and what Soft and Hard skills should be combined in that person in order to solve current business - the company's tasks.

Next, it is needed to make a portrait of a suitable candidate. This stage is best done with the one who initiated the application for a vacancy, since only the “customer” represents what the candidate should be, what functional responsibilities should be performed, what personal competencies and professional skills should have, in order not to affect the work of this or that department is negative, and as a maximum - to increase the efficiency of the department and the company as a whole.

The next step, after realizing what kind of candidate the company needs, is to describe the vacancy itself, which is being searched for a candidate. And at this stage it is important to understand that the job description, ideally, is better regarded as writing a commercial offer. After all, the vacancy text itself should attract those candidates that are needed by the company. This means that in addition to the functional job description, the vacancy text should include the principles and values that the company follows in the course of its activities; key company features from competitive companies; possible prospects of the candidate in the near future.

Ideally, this description should be as truthful as possible. This is done in order to immediately show the candidate the realities. Otherwise, faced with these realities of the company, the candidate simply does not accept your offer. Or he will, but he either will start looking for a new job, or he will influence the team, or the department itself will have a negative effect.

Other errors, apart from not writing a relatively honest job description, are:

1. Reluctance to prescribe functional requirements;
2. Lack of understanding and ignorance of personal competencies inherent in the position for which the candidate is looking for.

The unwillingness to qualitatively prescribe functional requirements for vacancies is often manifested in the fact that the recruiter / HR specialist allegedly has a clear idea of the functional requirements, and, based on his knowledge, prescribes functional requirements independently. Or, a recruiter / HR specialist, due to his ignorance of the functional requirements for the position, begin to engage in copying the information of functional requirements from other similar vacancies. It is important to understand that the functional requirements should be prescribed either by an expert in the subject area of the vacancy, or by a recruiter / HR specialist, but jointly with an expert in the subject area of the vacancy. The algorithm works here - the more the vacancy is described, the chance that the right company specialist will respond to it increases.

The next mistake, which consists in misunderstanding or ignorance by a recruiter / HR specialist of personal competencies inherent in the position being searched, has a deeper effect on the company than the lack of functional requirements in a vacancy. This, above all, will affect the adaptation of the employee who was hired. As a consequence of this, if the adaptation process takes place in a negative way and the new employee hurries to change jobs, the recruiter / HR specialist will have to start the process of recruiting a new employee again, which may lead to a loss of department performance.

If we look into this error even more deeply, it is necessary to give an example. The company lays down in the corporate culture that an employee of the company must be innovative, always be in search of new methods of solving problems and always try to introduce any innovations in the company's activity. This implies that the company will give preference to those who are willing to take responsibility for the risks incurred, highly motivated and focused on achieving the best results. At the same time, a recruiter / HR specialist prescribes in vacancies that non-conflicting people who avoid failures and punishments are best suited for this vacancy. The return on such candidates will be minimal for the company, since the newly arrived employee will not direct his energy to introduce any innovations, but to avoid conflict situations with his superiors. In this case, in the description of the vacancy it is necessary to clearly state the requirements for candidates, that the company is looking for a person who is ready to solve atypical tasks; take responsibility and be innovative.

After the vacancy is done and satisfies all the requirementslisted above, it is necessary to proceed to the choice of methods for finding new employees. The description of search methods is already covered in this article. It should only be added that the majority of companies choose a more acceptable search path - this is placement of a vacancy on various Internet resources for finding a job. Naturally, when choosing such an Internet resource, it is important to take into account the popularity of this very Internet resource in society. The chance that the company's HR department will select the right person for the company increases several times if the vacancy is posted on the popular job site. Of course, for a more efficient search, you can and should use all available search channels, but the results of such a search may coincide in some places. This is primarily due to the fact that a certain number of people can also use several "job" sites for job search. It is also worth noting that HR departments seek to conduct searches not only as efficiently as possible, but also as quickly as possible, especially when recruiting goes to mass positions. Therefore, in these conditions, using only the services of the most popular "job" site is quite logical and reasonable.

Another tool that can be used to select the necessary personnel, however, only to a high level of positions is to hold any conferences and events that are supposed to attract the right specialists in the field covered by the conference.

The next step, after the channel / method of searching for candidates has been chosen, is to establish contacts with the most suitable candidates. This stage is very important, as it allows personal communication with the candidate and evaluating him from the point of view of verbal communication (if you use the classic method of communication with the candidate, used in many companies - telephone interview). Of course, for the company it is a great advantage if the HR department tries to pick a candidate, not only using the classic "telephone interview", but other, alternative communication channels. Candidates are also valued if the company tries not only to call, but also to contact the candidates through any instant messengers and other modern communication channels, since communication through the instant messenger, for the most part, saves time, not only the HR department, but also candidates. However, it is important to understand that the preservation of personal boundaries and adherence to the principle of respect for the candidate are the most important working points during the transition to this stage. Since respect for the candidate by the HR department of the company at this stage will show how, in principle, the company treats the candidates. This will directly affect the company's reputation, since if a candidate does not like communication with the HR department, then naturally the candidate will convey information to his friends looking for work that a particular company is not very competent about communication with candidates, and it's better to have a resume for consideration not to send.

And the final step in this chain of personnel selection algorithm is - an interview. This stage is necessary to verify the candidate at the time of meeting the company's expectations. The purpose of the interview is to create conditions for the full disclosure of the candidate, so that the HR specialist can assess the level of the personal and professional qualities of the candidate. Various techniques are used to achieve the goal of the interview, but the frequently used technique is a technique of open questions that cannot be answered unambiguously with "yes" or "no." Usually, such questions are offered elements of a "case study", when a candidate is given a situation directly related to his, possibly, future activity in the company, and is given the task to solve this situation. And in the process of forming the answer to the task, the HR specialist makes certain conclusions about the professional and personal qualities of the candidate, forms the opinion and the final answer to the candidate for employment. However, another important point in the interview is to give the candidate the opportunity to ask questions. This action is useful because the HR specialist will find out through the questions of the candidate, what the candidate cares about and what are his values and motives. At the same time, by answering candidate questions, the HR specialist can and should create better conditions for the "sale" of the company to a candidate. It is also necessary to correctly complete the interview itself. Even if the candidate does not fit the company, it is important to understand that the candidate must leave positively charged. This is an important part of the interview, as the candidate will carry the information about the company that came to him to the masses, which will further form the image and reputation of the company, as well as rumors circulating around the company. And if the information entering the interview will have a negative connotation, then, as a result, the candidate will be a carrier of negative feedback and attitude towards the company. And if the candidate is asked by friends / colleagues / relatives about that company, then the candidate will accordingly share a negative impression, which of course will affect the perception of the company by the people with whom the candidate shared his opinion about the company.

As an example, let's take a look at the situation at Ernst & Young. Ernst & Young is the largest auditing and consulting firm in the world with an almost impeccable reputation in the service market. As for the labor market, Ernst and Young has rather controversial feedback from employees, who, on one hand, motivate people to try to get a job at Ernst and Young, and, on the other, make them think about the correctness of their choice of employer. According to the international research company Universum[8], in 2018 business disciplines students recognized Ernst and Young as the most attractive employer among the Big Four companies and the 7th in the overall rating of 100 companies. It would seem that statistics show that Ernst and Young is one of the most attractive employers in the labor market of the Republic of Kazakhstan. And this is logical, because Ernst and Young has a very strong "employer brand", which potential candidates associate with trust, stability, prestige and responsibility. However, judging by the reviews and rumors circulating around this company, it can be concluded that not everything is so good with the working conditions inside the company and with the terms of the interview. Of course, these rumors and reviews are do not describe Ernst & Young as a good employer, and Ernst & Young, in theory, loses potential candidates who in the future could improve the work of the company itself, only because of rumors around working conditions. However, this percentage of loss is extremely small, but still should not be ignored, and you should take any action to minimize damage to the "employer brand."

In addition to the above said, it is necessary to add that not only the company's reputation in the external market is an important factor for attracting potential employees to the company. Another important factor is the internal reputation of the company. If external reputation influences the likelihood of a candidate's response to a company vacancy / accepting a company's invitation to an interview / accepting a company's job offer increases in direct proportion to the company's reputation in the labor market, then internal reputation influences the flow of good candidates on the recommendation of employees. After all, if employees have a positive attitude towards the company itself and are involved in the company's activities, then naturally employees will recommend working in the company to their acquaintances who are currently looking for a job, or thinking about changing jobs, because the employees themselves like to work in the company and why I would not create even more comfortable conditions for myself, recommending the HR department to a friend who basically corresponds to the values of the company. And here it is important to understand that the employees themselves in this case will perform such HR specialist functions as: selection and assessment of competencies. After all, if a certain employee has several acquaintances,who are looking for a job, then it is logical that the employee will not

8 See Universum, 2018

recommend that acquaintance to whom the company's activities will not work because of professional skills or values promoted in the company. An HR specialist for the most part acts as an overseer at the initial stage, because an HR specialist will need to double-check the candidate himself, send references to the recommended candidate, and, in principle, conduct a full selection cycle in order to proceed from objective considerations with possible hiring the recommended candidate for a company.

So, to summarize, it should be noted that today, online recruiting is a classic recurring, only using Internet resources to speed up the recruitment process. And at the moment, in most companies, people are engaged in the search and initial selection, which is certainly time consuming. However, using the latest technology, these two stages - search and primary selection - can be fully automated and free up time resources for HR specialists to solve other problems of the department, or monitor the system, which will be discussed below.

3 The Internet Recruiting Of The Future

As it was already written above, by introducing new technologies into the HR department's work, it will almost completely automate some aspects of the HR department's work - specifically, the search for candidates and the initial selection of candidates; reduce the time of closing, in the future, almost all open vacancies; to transfer the activity of an HR specialist from the mainstream of active search for candidates to a kind of evaluation of the answers of candidates for further interviews with selected candidates. The essence of this automation is simple - it is the use of artificial intelligence in the process of searching, initial selection and inviting a potential candidate for an interview by making contact with a candidate using popular instant messengers.

The use of instant messengers in this concept is more than justified, since communication through the instant messenger is increasingly replacing communication through telephone conversations. This is primarily due to the fact that with the advent of instant messengers, people's communication has become more convenient and more efficient than communication through a telephone conversation. Currently, a phone call is the most inconvenient form of commu-nication, as the phone call is convenient for the caller, who frees up time for the call, or it is part of the caller's professional activity. At the same time –the convenient time for the answerer almost never coincides. Since now there is a tendency that time is the most important resource for a person, it is logical that if the respondent is can not answer the call, and as it often happens, the telephone numbers of the HR departments are defined as a normal number not recorded in the phone book, the respondent will answer the call. Even further, will not even call back on an unknown number. This fact can be confirmed, as well as in theoretical and practical orientation. In a practical direction, it is possible to analyze how many calls were made in the HR department, how many of the calls made were answered, and how many people called back when they were not answering the phone call. So, out of 107 calls made, the answer was 50% of the cases, and only 3 of the non-respondents called back to the missed call. That means - this is only 5.6%. The findings from this study are disappointing for phone calls. Also, these disappointing conclusions can be traced to the theoretical component of this issue. There are 8 theoretical reasons, which, in principle, are supported by the everyday experience of other people:

1. People are constantly busy.
2. People are not comfortable talking at the moment.
3. Loss of faith in an even word
4. My diary - my smartphone
5. Talk is long
6. Memory is short
7. Communication?
8. I do not understand you

So, following the order, the first reason called "People are constantly busy" describes that a call usually distracts a person from any activity performed by a person at the moment of receiving a call. And usually the topic of this call is not more relevant than the activity performed by the person at the time of the incoming call. In fact, the person does not want to be distracted from the current actions and, as a rule, misses the incoming call.

The second reason - "People are not comfortable talking at the moment" – intersects with the first one. However, here the problem is considered from the point of view of the caller. The caller, as already mentioned, makes a call at a time when it is convenient for the caller to call, or calls are included in the professional activity of the caller. Consequently, in most cases, answering a call is not always convenient to receive a call at the very time when it is convenient for the caller to make a phone call. But the caller does not want to call back to an unknown phone number. This is primarily due to the fact that with the existing variety of ways of communicating with a person, the conditional caller uses only one communication channel with the respondent. The respondent, having missed a call from an unknown number, does not strive to call back, as he thinks that if the caller would need to contact the answering party, after the missed call, the caller would use another communication channel, such as sending an e-mail, or a message in the messenger to communicate with the respondent. Consequently, the respondent does not have the desire to waste his time to receive information that is not important for the responding. And it also shows the degree of interest of the caller. You can consider this statement on the example of the HR department. If an HR specialist has found a candidate whose work experience fits in perfectly in order to close a position, then accordingly in Kazakhstan's realities, the first thing the HR specialist will call is the number indicated in the resume. Suppose the candidate did not take the phone. Consequently, the actions of the average HR specialist may look as follows - the HR specialist will call the candidate even after some time, and if there is no answer, he will probably call the next day, or end attempts to establish communication after the second missed call. Such a time delay may contribute to the loss of this "ideal" candidate. Perhaps the candidate for the time lost by the HR specialist will receive a job offer by e-mail from a competitor's company and will accept the offer of a competitive company. Although, after the first missed call, the HR specialist can immediately write a candidate to some instant messenger, or use an SMS message to inform the candidate that a certain company is contacting the candidate for a job offer.

The third reason is characterized, for the most part, by the fact that decisions made during a telephone conversation may not be implemented, or will be implemented with some amendments. Words, for the most part, in the modern world mean little if these words are not documented and notarized. Consequently, even under the condition that the call will contain information about the invitation for an interview, the candidate will still have some doubts about the reality of this invitation. Messengers in this regard are more reliable, since it is possible to trace the chain of messages and, in the event of a conflict situation, have, let's say, written, or better, electronic confirmation of the conversation. For example, if an HR specialist got through to a candidate and scheduled an interview at one time, and upon arrival at the company the candidate discovers that there is no waiting for the candidate at all, then the candidate cannot prove that he was specifically told to arrive at the appointed time. However, if the communication was carried out via an instant messenger, the candidate in principle can show that yesterday such an employee invited him to the appointed time for an interview. In any case, for the company this situation is unpleasant, since this situation directly affects the brand of the employer.

The fourth reason for the most part is the problem of functionality. If during a telephone conversation any appointments are made, or some list is dictated, it is rather difficult, or even impossible, to simultaneously talk on the smartphone and make any changes to the smartphone in your schedule. Smartphones, for the most part, are now replacing paper diaries and in fact it is easier to enter the incoming information into your smartphone, rather than looking for a paper carrier and writing subject. It is also convenient to open a message in the messenger, where the HR specialist indicated all the details, from the place to the time of the interview, and to come to the scheduled interview.

The fifth reason why a telephone conversation in the modern world is no longer as effective as it was before is the waste of too much time resources compared to communication via instant messengers. In order to read a short message in the messenger takes half a second. In order to say "Good afternoon, you are disturbed by the HR department of any company" by phone, it takes 5 seconds. If, of course, another phrase is added to this phrase that clarifies whether the respondent is comfortable talking, then the time will increase to 9 seconds. Therefore, the instant messenger is best used for quick communication, as the instant messenger allows you to send a message to the convenient timeframe for the sender, and to reply to the sender's message at a convenient timeframe for the respondent. And the time of the communication process itself is significantly reduced, which is good both for the HR department itself and for the candidate himself.

The sixth reason is mostly connected with both the first and the second reason, and it is explained by the fact that the average person cannot remember the details dictated by telephone if they are not recorded. A person who is involved in his own business, being distracted by a phone call, in his subconscious wants to return to his business and quickly end a telephone conversation. Accordingly, the likelihood that a person will forget about the details of the conversation, as well as about the telephone conversation itself increases. And in the messenger you can select and save the desired message, set a reminder and, in principle, at the set time, the smartphone will remind the person that an interview should take place at a certain time today. Accordingly, the chance that a person will forget about any event, the same interview, is reduced, since there will be a notification about this event on the smartphone screen.

The seventh reason is the quality of communication. In fact, the quality of communication in Kazakhstan leaves much to be desired. Interference and interruption of communication are observed everywhere, even in major cities of the Republic. And it is logical that when it comes to important phone talks, it's better to be safe and just arrange a personal meeting. Otherwise, there is a risk not to hear important information, or to make a mistake in an important aspect of the question. Especially in matters when an HR specialist suggests a candidate to go on a television interview, thereby increasing both his risks not understanding what the candidate said, and the risks of the candidate not understanding what the HR specialist said. However, this is not the only risk of a candidate in this case, since if the candidate does not correctly understand the question of an HR specialist, or the HR specialist does not understand it, this will affect the general impression of the HR specialist about the candidate, and therefor affect the assessment of the candidate himself. Of course, in the present conditions, messengers do not allow for, say, a message-interviews, but in the future this development is possible.

The eighth and last reason for the inefficiency of telephone calls at the present time is the incomprehensibility of the interlocutor himself. If the caller cannot convey briefly and concisely the information to the respondent, the conversation may drag on for a long time and eventually the information will still be communicated, but the respondent will never understand what the caller wanted from him . Therefore, it is easier and less time-consuming to write a message in the messenger with brief but important information.

As you can see, the effectiveness of telephone calls decreases from year to year. But, nevertheless, most of the HR departments in the Republic of Kazakhstan use this channel of communication with potential candidates, which, of course, shows that HR departments are not too exposed to global trends.

In order to develop a "smart recruitmentsystem", hereinafter referred to as "SRS", it is necessary to determine several things: First, determine the messenger that will be used to contact potential candidates. Secondly, to determine how the SRS will work, either as a separate program or already integrated into any "job site" of type like HeadHunter.

For the first goal, it will ideally fit into this concept of using the Whatsapp messenger. According to a study by SimilarWeb[9] on February 5, 2018, the most popular instant messenger in the world, which is also relevant for Kazakhstan, is Whatsapp. As the # 1 messaging app in 104 countries, WhatsApp Messenger ranks first in more countries than any other application. Involvement is a key indicator of the effectiveness of messaging applications. WhatsApp Messenger is very popular in countries where WhatsApp is ranked first - WhatsApp is installed on more than 90% of devices in 45 countries. In particular, the application is installed on 95% of Android devices in India, where 75% of users use the application daily. South African users are as active as Indian users, although the installation speed is slightly lower by 92%. In the United Kingdom, WhatsApp Messenger is installed on 84% of Android devices, and 56% of them use it daily. As for statistics for Kazakhstan, there are no specific figures for using WhatsApp Messenger. Nevertheless, world statistics show the general picture. After all, the choice of the most popular messenger is due to the fact that at the initial stage it is necessary not to disperse technical capabilities, but to concentrate on the effective use of one channel of communication with candidates. Moreover, WhatsApp has a separate business application called WhatsAppBusiness, which basically allows you to create a company profile in WhatsApp and use it for communication with potential customers. Therefore, in principle, to strengthen the brand of the employer, for the SRS, it is necessary to use the profile in WhatsApp Business, so that potential candidates do not have the impression that a specific job offer in the messenger does not bear serious intentions, and represents manipulative actions.

Just as it was said earlier, it is necessary to determine whether the SRS will work as a separate program, or whether it should be integrated into the job-site of type likeHeadHunter. In fact, integration into the job-site operation looks more con-

[9]See SimilarWeb, 2018

venient than developing a separate program for many reasons. The main reason is the lack of a current database. The absence of a database of an up-to-date and updated database for an employer is characterized by the fact that the employer has only the data of those people who are employees of the company, or were once employees of the company. Information about candidates, in the modern world, for the most part, the employer takes, paying a certain amount of money for providing such information from a job-site, to which people themselves voluntarily upload or create their resumes in order to find a job. And as it was said earlier, the main reason for entering the SRS is to automate the search and initial selection of candidates. That is, the SRS, at the initial stage, is a bot, which is given keyword search algorithms, and this bot independently selects a resume of candidates based on keywords. This bot needs access to a specific summary database in order for this search to take place. And of course, it would be best of all to ensure that this bot, without circumventing any security protocols, absolutely legally gets access to this database. And in this situation, full integration with the job-site is necessary. Consequently, the moment of integration of this bot must be resolved in some way - it already depends on the company. If you do not integrate the SRS into the job-site for some reason, then the company, of course, has a way to solve this problem - this is developing the SRS into a separate program. However, a logical question arises - how this program will function if the SRS does not have access to the database of candidates. It is necessary to take into account the fact that companies pay job-sites just for providing a database of candidates' resumes. And the companies are free to decide what to do with the resume data. Accordingly, in this situation, some unnecessary actions will be added, however, in theory, the result would be identical if the SRS would be integrated into the job-site.It is necessary to load a certain number of resumes from the job-site into the SRS, set the search algorithm, and the SRS will do its job.

Accordingly, the principle of operation of the SRS looks as follows: first, the operator sets an algorithm for searching candidates for the SRS. It is necessary to make a reservation that at the initial stage of the SRS's operation the role of the operator himself will be important, which will perform the function of controlling. After all, "job-sites" also provide an advanced search and keyword search function, but not always such a search gives the desired results. Therefore, if we consider the further activity of the SRS with minimal operator intervention, then at the early stages it is also necessary to introduce a neural network into the SRS in order for the SRS to develop itself over time.

The next step, after the search algorithms have been set, is the search itself and the selection of candidates. At this stage, the result will depend on the specified search algorithms and on how the SRS can select the right candidates from the entire data set. As it has already been written, here, especially at the initial stages, control by the operator is necessary, who will either reject the proposed resumes or accept the proposed resumes, while not forgetting to train the neural network implemented in the SRS.

The third stage is the process of the message interview, which will be carried out via the WhatsApp messenger. In fact, everything is practically very simple here. The candidate's resume usually contains the contact details of the candidate, in particular the telephone number. Having determined this phone number, SRS will write to the candidate, at the operator's command, in WhatsApp, presumably the majority of Almaty residents have WhatsApp registered to the phone number and, as the candidate answers, will begin a conversation with the candidate. The introductory offer may vary from company to company, but its text may be something like this: "Good morning / afternoon / evening Name, a certain company is looking for a specialist for a certain position (link to position description) and your resume seemed very interesting and suitable for this positions. Would you like to consider our offer? Please answer yes or no. If the candidate answers "no", the SRS wishes him a pleasant day and this is where the dialogue ends. If the candidate answers "yes", the dialogue continues, and the SRS either conducts a message of the interview directly in this dialog box, or asks the candidate to follow the link, and in the new dialog box begins the message of the interview. The message interview is a standard set of questions that an HR specialist usually asks when conducting a telephone interview. In the perspective of the development of the SRS, it is assumed that over time, the candidate will answer the questions of the SRS not in writing, but verbally, recording voice messages. At the initial stage, for SRS, it is best to use textual information analysis in order to speed up the process of learning the perception of the text and the selection of candidates according to the resume and message interview. After the SRS conducted the message of the interview with the candidate, after informing the latter that the subsequent answer will follow after the processing of the incoming information from the candidate, the candidate will also answer the questions on the SRS and the operator. This, again, is very important at the initial stage of development of this system, so that it is controlled. Moreover, the subsequent comparison of inspections of the operator and the SRS will allow the neural network of the SRS to study the selection criteria in more depth and then make more "informed" decisions.

After the results of the message interview are formed, the SRS informs the candidate that either the candidate has passed the message of the interview and can now come to the interview to the head of the department at a specific address, at a specific time in a particular office, or that the candidate has not passed the message interview, but the candidate should not despair and try to improve their skills, or gain experience.

It is also necessary to take into account the written wording of the questions and answers that the chat bot will send to candidates, because this will affect the brand of the company's employer. The wording of questions and answers chat bot must be adequately spelled out and not carry any restrictive information for the candidate.

In the future, it is possible and necessary to add the function of drawing up the personal file of the newcomer employee and the preparation of documentation for the newly arrived employee to the SRS. It also automates one of the important processes of personnel office work. But the best thing to start is to select new employees and conduct a message interview with them, and only then develop the bot in the logical order of the functions of the HR department.

4 Conclusion

Today, very few companies in Kazakhstan use this concept of recruitment. And in principle, now there is an idea that it would be good to introduce such a system. In particular, RamilMukhoryapovon his Instagram account posted a video from the meeting, where a similar concept was already discussed. Therefore, it can be concluded that in the near future, many HR departments of companies will be developing in this promising direction. Of course, if each company develops its own SRS, it will not be bad in the sense that each company that develops SRS independently will contribute to the development of SRS. However, in this case, this system will have a completely different basis and structure, which of course is a negative fact for those companies that want to introduce the SRS into the activities of their company, but have no idea how to develop this system. Therefore, the SRS needs to be standardized when developing, in order to make the SRS more accessible. In the ideal case, the following scenario is acceptable - companies in the initial stages are independently involved in building a SRS, and after the SRS more or less stably functions, the companies that created the SRS on their bases can hold a series of meetings in order to share their experience in building the SRS and approve some technical standards for the construction of the SRS. At this stage of the research, it is already possible to single out certain standards that were covered in this article:

1. The system should not adversely affect the brand of the employer. This means that the language that the candidate sees should be adequate. Also, this is the creation of an official chat bot of the company, so that the candidate can understand that this is not a lie.
2. The system should always be under the supervision of the operator (person), even after the neural network embedded in the SRS, learned how to do the job properly. This is necessary so that in case of critical situations, the person is aware of what is happening, and in which case he takes over the management of the system.
3. SRS must comply with the principles of the HR department.

4. SRS should be constantly improved. It is impossible to limit only the SRS by the primary selection of personnel. As already mentioned, in the long term, the SRS can learn how to conduct personnel records management and, in principle, but this is already for the long term, SRS can fully automate the activities of the HR department, and in generaal, play an important role in conducting interviews live.

From the point of view of the automation of human labor activity, the development of the SRS looks very promising. It is only necessary to start taking the right steps in the development of the SRS and the introduction of the SRS in the labor activity of the HR department of companies. As for the Republic of Kazakhstan, the introduction of the SRS into the work activities of companies fully complies with the tasks set in the development program of Kazakhstan "Kazakhstan 2050". In addition to this, it should also be noted that when introducing the HR SRS, a specialist of any company should not only have the professional skills of a psychologist, but also have knowledge of basic programming and training of neural networks, which greatly expands the scope of activities of future HR specialists.

Literature

Akorda. (2018). *State of the Nation Address by the President of the Republic of Kazakhstan NursultanNazarbayev.* Retrieved 10.10.2018, from http://www.akorda.kz/ru/addresses/addresses_of_president/poslanie-prezidenta-respubliki-kazahstann-nazarbaeva-narodu-kazahstana-10-yanvarya-2018-g

Centre1. (2016). *Интернет в ЦентральнойАзии: досихпорплетемся в хвосте. (in Russian).* Retrieved 29.10.2018, from https://centre1.com/ kazakhstan/internet-v-tsa-do-sih-por-pletemsya-v-hvoste/

chatbotslife. (2018). *Top 5 Benefits of deploying Chatbots in Human Resources.* Retrieved 29.10.2018, from https://chatbotslife.com/top-5-benefits-of-deploying-chatbots-in-human-resources-cf1f436dbbcd

chatbotsmagazine. (2018). *7 Ways Chatbots and AI are Disrupting HR.* Retrieved 29.10.2018, from https://chatbotsmagazine.com/7-ways-chatbots-and-ai-are-disrupting-hr-3989ad1c1fed

Eberbach, W., Brauweiler, H.-Ch. (1993). *Arbeitsrecht, Systematische Darstellung.* (3 ed.). Oldenbourg/München.

EY. (2018). *Студентыбизнес-дисциплинпризнали EY вКазахстанесамымпривлекательнымработодателемсредикомпаний «большойчетверки». (in Russian).* Retrieved 29.10.2018, from https://www.ey.com/kz/ru/newsroom/news-releases/news-ey-universum-ranking-2018

HeadHunter's. (2019). *HeadHunter's official site.* Retrieved 29.10.2018, from https://hh.kz/?nocookies

Khabar 24. (2018). *Рынокэлектроннойкоммерции в Казахстаневыросна 30%. (in Russian).* Retrieved 29.10.2018, from https://24.kz/ru/news/economyc/item/246840-rynok-elektronnoj-kommertsii-v-kazakhstane-vyros-na-30

MacDigger. (2017). *Звонитьневежливо: почемумессенджерызаменилителефонныеразговоры. (in Russian).* Retrieved 29.10.2018, from https://www.macdigger.ru/news/post/zvonit-nevezhlivo-pochemu-messendzhery-zamenili-telefonnye-razgovory

messengerpeople. (2018a). *Chatbots: What Is A WhatsApp Bot, Actually?* Retrieved 29.10.2018, from https://www.messengerpeople.com/ chatbots-what-is-a-whatsapp-bot-actually

messengerpeople. (2018b). *WhatsApp, WeChatAnd Facebook Messenger Apps – Global Messenger Usage, Penetration And Statistics.* Retrieved 29.10.2018, from https://www.messengerpeople.com/global-messenger-usage-statistics/

Mir24. (2018). *Почемумессенджерывытесняюттелефонныеразговоры? (in Russian).* Retrieved 29.10.2018, from https://mir24.tv/articles/16288303/menshe-slov-bolshe-bukv-messendzhery-vytesnyayut-telefonnye-razgovory

neuronus. (n.d.). *Обучениенейроннойсети. (in Russian).* Retrieved 29.10.2018, from https://neuronus.com/theory/nn/238-obucheniya-nejronnoi-seti.html

Novostivoronezha. (2017). *7 важныхпричиннаписатьсообщение в мессенджервместотого, чтобыпозвонитьпотелефону.(in Russian).* Retrieved 29.10.2018, from https://novostivoronezha.ru/2017/04/ 16/80269

Podborkadrov. (2018). *Рекрутинг: основныезадачи. (in Russian).* Retrieved 10.10.2018, from http://podborkadrov.com/poisk-personala/rekruting/rekruting.html

Prohr. (2018). *Проще, чемвыдумаете: 5 шаговпривлечениянужныхсотрудников. (in Russian).* Retrieved 29.10.2018, from https://prohr.rabota.ua/rekruting-proshhe-chem-vyi-dumaete-5-shagov-privlecheniya-nuzhnyih-sotrudnikov/

SimilarWeb. (2018). *Mobile Messaging App Map – February 2018. 5 февраля 2018 года.* Retrieved 29.10.2018, from https://www.similarweb.com/blog/mobile-messaging-app-map-2018

Twilio. (2016). *How Consumers Use Messaging Today.* Retrieved 29.10.2018, from https://www.twilio.com/learn/commerce-communications/how-consumers-use-messaging

Universum. (2018). *Kazakhstan's most attractive employers – Trends and Rankings 2018.* Retrieved 29.10.2018, from https://universumglobal. com/ rankings/kazakhstan/

World Economic Forum. (2018). *The Global Competitiveness Report 2018.* Retrieved 29.10.2018, from http://reports.weforum.org/global-competitiveness-report-2018/competitiveness-rankings/#series=NETUSERPCT

Zerde. (2018). *State Program "Digital Kazakhstan".* Retrieved 10.10.2018, from https://zerde.gov.kz/activity/management-programs/digital-kazakhstan/

Development of energy efficiency accounting tools at subregional level in the Russian Federation (The case of the Volgograd region)

Lyudmila Yu. Bogachkova, Yulia B. Zaytseva, Elena E. Zaytseva, Irina V. Usacheva

1 Introduction and literature review

Digitalization and improvement of energy efficiency are among the global long-term trends of economic and social development. The global nature of these trends has got reflection in the special term *megatrends* introduced into scientific use by John Naisbitt.[1] These two megatrends are closely interconnected. Indeed, such well-known energy efficiency technologies as smart electrical networks (Smart Grid), Building Information Modeling (BIM), smart city and smart housing and utilities sector – all of them are manifestations of digitalization.

In 2017 the Government of the Russian Federation developed and approved the program of transition to the digital economy.[2] In particular, the program outlines the need to develop the procedures of data collection, processing and analysis as well as data exchange which should be used in the course of socio-economic management. As for the system of monitoring the State policy of energy efficiency, we should mention the relevance and urgency of developing energy consumption accounting tools, especially at the regional and subregional levels, which is substantiated in the Complex plan of measures on increasing energy efficiency of the Russian economy, approved by the Government of the Russian Federation in 2013.[3] The Complex plan provides for implementation of a number of measures in the short-term, including modernization of the order and scope of works on official statistical accounting of energy efficiency indicators; development of State information system for energy efficiency monitoring (ensuring its constant updating, data verification and integration of data from allied information systems). However, today the analysis of energy efficiency at the regional level has

---

1 See Naisbitt, 1988

2 Digital economy is the economic activity, the key production factor of which is represented with the digital data. The processing of large volumes of digital data and analyzing their results allow to substantially increase the performance of productions, technologies, equipment, as well as goods and services' storage, sale and delivery as compared to the traditional forms of economic management. See Government of the Russian Federation, 2018

3 See Government of the Russian Federation, 2018

H.-C. Brauweiler et al. (Hrsg.), *Digitalization and Industry 4.0: Economic and Societal Development*, https://doi.org/10.1007/978-3-658-27110-7_22

been carried out on the basis of limited data due to the lack of analytical tools, and we aim to fill this gap in the present research.

Numerous theoretical and empirical research serve a substantial proof that increasing Energy Efficiency (EE) in all spheres of human activity is a driver for economic development and population welfare.[4] In this connection, the measures aimed at EE increase are indispensable and vital components of State economic policies of various countries and their associations.[5] Various energy efficiency accounting systems (EEAS) which imply the use of economical-mathematical and econometric methods are applied in world practice for monitoring the performance of EE policies.[6] Research and practical problems of developing and monitoring the State policies of energy efficiency are covered in.[7]

In modern Russia as well as in other countries, EE increase measures refer to the priority area of State economic policy.[8] The State programs for energy saving and EE increase have already been worked out and implemented at the federal, regional and municipal levels. Since 2015, the annual monitoring of EE State policy has been carried out in sectoral and regional contexts, and the obtained results have been covered by State reports.[9] The monitoring is based on the data of the Federal State Statistics Service (Rosstat), State information system 'Energy Efficiency', and other information provided by the entities of the Russian Federation. However, the Russian energy consumption accounting system and its regional subsystems are still at the stage of development.[10]

The monitoring of energy consumption at the regional and subregional levels in the Russian Federation is associated with such problems as the lack of a unified methodology for collecting, processing and analyzing data; non-transparency of EE estimation techniques; and the use of unreliable information. Due to these factors, the information about implementation of regional and municipal programs for EE increase is not taken into account while preparing State reports at the federal level. Thus, the improvement of EE monitoring system in the Russian

---

4 See Baatz, 2015; See Brauweiler, 2002; See Cambridge Econometrics, 2015; See EC Directorate-General for Energy, 2016; See IEA (International Energy Agency), 2017; See Ivanov, Matveev, 2017; See Kramer, Brauweiler, Urbaniec, 1999; See Makarov, Grigoryev, Mitrova, 2016; See Naess-Schmidt, Hansen, von Below, 2015; See Saldanha, Gouvea da Costa, de Lima, 2016; See Strebel, Eifler, Brauweiler, et al., 2003

5 See Inshakov, Bogachkova, Popkova, 2019

6 See Bashmakov, Myshak, 2012, p. 10

7 See Braungardt, et al., 2014; See EPA (Environmental Protection Agency), 2017a; See EPA (Environmental Protection Agency), 2017b; See Bashmakov, 2013

8 See Government of the Russian Federation, 2009

9 See Ministry of Energy of the Russian Federation, 2015, 2016, 2017; See Ministry of Economic Development of the Russian Federation, 2018

10 See Bogachkova, 2018

Federation represents both an important national and economic task and an urgent research and practical problem.

Energy intensity, which is calculated by dividing the total volume of consumption of all energy resources by the volume of the gross regional product (GRP), is the most widely used aggregated indicator of territories' EE. In the regional context (entities of the Russian Federation), the annual values of GRP energy intensity over the period 2012-2016 are now available at the website of the Rosstat. However, in the context of municipalities (at the subregional level), the indicators of energy intensity of the Gross Municipal Product (GMP) are not calculated by official statistics bodies since there is no data necessary for this procedure. Firstly, the Rosstat and its territorial bodies do not estimate the GMP; secondly, there is no official data about total volumes of municipalities' energy consumption.

Despite the difficulty of data collection for EE indicators estimation, the scientific area associated with quantity analysis of energy consumption in Russian regions, including the level of municipalities, is being actively developed.[11] The review of literature on this subject is presented in Bogachkova, Khurshudyan, 2017.[12]

Thus, researchers pay special attention to analyzing energy efficiency of the Russian regions, but still there is a number of issues that need to be faced. For instance, we can observe the demand for methods allowing to group municipalities according to the sectoral structure of the GMP (production specialization) and to the levels of economic development for ensuring the correctness of interregional comparison of EE indicators; to form integrated ranking estimates of municipalities' EE on the basis of available official data about specific energy consumption indices; to conduct comparative analysis of the dynamics of municipalities' EE integrated ranking estimates taking into account production specialization and the levels of economic development for decision-making support as far as the relative performance of EE policies implemented at subregional level is concerned.

The present research is aimed at developing and implementing the tools for decision-making support in the sphere of subregional EE policies performance through increasing the accuracy of municipalities' EE estimates and carrying out correct comparative analyses of territories' EE by means of comparing municipalities characterized by homogeneous GMP structure and similar levels of economic development. Stage-by-stage investigation let us achieve the given aim.

At the first stage, municipalities of the Volgograd region have been grouped into territories homogeneous in the GMP sectoral structure. For this purpose we have

---

11 See Bashmakov, Myshak, 2016; See Gasho, Puzakova, Stepanova, 2013; See Popov, Dobrodey, Veselova, Konyaeva, 2012; See Khurshudyan, 2018; See Popov, Gainalov, 2015

12 See Bogachkova, Khurshudyan, 2017

obtained the estimations of GMPs and their sectoral structure for 38 municipalities of the Volgograd region. The grouping of territories has been carried out by means of cluster analysis in the software package Statistica-10. Then we have calculated and analyzed the GMP values per capita – the indicator reflecting the levels of economic development in a given territory. All the municipalities in each group are characterized by practically the same level of economic development. Intergroup differentiation of GMP value per capita turns out to be significantly higher than the intragroup one. The further comparative analysis of territories' energy efficiency has been conducted taking into account the obtained groupings.

At the second stage, we have compared the data on specific indicators of energy efficiency in the context of municipalities. On the one hand, these data are generated by the Territorial Body of State Statistics in the Volgograd region (Volgogradstat) and disclosed in the so-called passports (profile certificates) of municipalities. On the other hand, the data include the list of energy consumption indicators used by executive authorities of the Volgograd region for making up regional State reports on energy saving and EE improvement.[13] At the end of 2018, the executive authorities of the Volgograd region prepared such report for the first time, and this can be considered as a step forward to updating of the region's EE monitoring. Over the longer term it is planned to annually make up regional reports which would contain the results of EE State policy monitoring conducted at the regional and subregional levels. We pro to expand the list of energy consumption indicators used at preparing the State reports and supplement it with a number of parameters from municipalities' passports. We also put forth the practice of annual integrated ranking among municipalities by the index of their energy efficiency as part of regional EE monitoring. The ranking is supposed to be formed on the basis of an expanded list of specific energy consumption indicators.

At the third stage, we have obtained integrated ranking estimates of Volgograd municipalities' EE for several years and compared them taking into account municipalities' production specialization and economic development. The results can be used for evaluating the performance of regional EE policy conducted at the subregional level.

---

13 The regional report on energy saving and energy efficiency improvement in the Volgograd region in 2017 (Signed by O.D. Nikolaev, chairman of the Committee for Housing and Communal Services and the Fuel and Energy Complex of the Volgograd region. Volgograd 2018). Provided by the State Budget Institution "Volgograd Center for Energy Efficiency".

2 Methods and statistical data

2.1 The method of grouping municipalities according to their production specialization and to the level of economic development

The production specialization of municipalities is characterized by the sectoral structure of the GMP. To estimate the GMP and its sectoral structure, we have applied the methodology of the Global Urban Observatory (GUO), carrying out its activities under the United Nations Human Settlements Programme.[14] The GUO methodology is based on the hypothesis that the regional gross product is distributed among municipalities approximately in the same proportion as the payroll fund of the region. Therefore, if we dispose of the data about the GRP, the payroll fund of the region and the payroll funds of municipalities, we may estimate the GMP of a territory. The similar principle has also been realized in relation to the GMP distribution by sectors (types of economic activity).

Our previous research present the GMPs of municipalities of the Volgograd region obtained through the abovementioned method but without the account of small and medium-sized enterprises' (SMEs) contribution into the GMPs of the region. [15] The present research fills this gap. We have obtained a more accurate estimate of the GMP taking into account the SMEs contribution which was evaluated by means of the Volgograd SMEs total survey conducted by the Volgogradstat in 2015. The SMEs total surveys were conducted in the Russian Federation only twice – in 2010 and 2015. The grouping of the Volgograd municipalities according to production specialization is based on the data for the latter period – 2015 year.

Despite the fact that the GUO methodology provides rough estimates of the GMP and its sectoral structure, its application is very productive against the background of limited data available for analysis. Figure 1 illustrates 5 integrated economic sectors which represent the gradations of the GMP sectoral structure.

Then, by means of cluster analysis of municipalities by five characteristics – gradations of the integrated sectors in the GMP structure (agrarian-bioresource, raw-material, industrial, trade-financial, budget-dependent sectors), we have grouped territories according to their production specialization. The sector which share prevailed in the GMP structures of other territories is considered to be the profiling sector in the GMP structure of a given territory. The cluster analysis has been carried out in the software package Statitica-10.

---

14 See UN, 2004

15 See Bogachkova, Zaytseva, Usacheva, 2018a; See Bogachkova, Zaytseva, Usacheva, 2018b; See Bogachkova, Zaytseva, Usacheva, 2019

Integrated sectors of GMP structure	*Sectors of the GMP according to the official data on payroll funds by the types of economic activity*
Agrarian-bioresource:	ariculture, hunting and forestry; fishing, fish-farming
Raw-material:	extraction of mineral resources
Industrial:	manufacturing industries; production and distribution of electricity, gas and water; construction activities
Trade-financial:	wholesale and retail trade; maintenance of motor vehicles, household goods and personal appliances; financial activities; real estate operations, leasing, provision of municipal, social and personal services; hotels and restaurants; transportation and communication
Budget-dependent:	public administration and military security; social insurance; education; health and social services health and social services

Figure 1: Formation of integrated sectors of the GMP. Authors' classification used in the previous works (Source: Bogachkova, Zaytseva, Usacheva 2018a; Bogachkova, Zaytseva, Usacheva 2018b; Bogachkova, Zaytseva, Usacheva 2019).

The index of the GMP per capita has been investigated to characterize the levels of municipalities' economic development. Using the methods of descriptive statistics allowed to find out that the grouping according to the GMP structure also ensures an adequate division of territories according to the level of economic development.

2.2 The method of integrated ranking estimation of municipalities' energy efficiency by a number of specific energy consumption indicators

The available official data on municipalities' energy consumption is limited by the economic sectors which are the most prospective from the viewpoint of energy saving (the budget sphere and the housing and utilities sector). The regional report on energy saving and energy efficiency improvement of the Volgograd region prepared for the first time at the end of 2018 contains these data only for 2016-2017. Moreover, they cover mostly regional level, not municipal one.

It seems to be reasonable to supplement the list of used data on energy consumption with a number of indicators mentioned in municipalities' passports or calculated on the basis of these passports over the period 2012-2016. The proposed expanded list of specific indicators of municipalities' energy consumption in the housing and utilities sector and the budget sphere is presented in table 1. The first 5 indicators are used at making up the regional report, and indicators 1-13 are supposed to supplement them.

EE indicators in apartment blocks

1. Electricity consumption (kWh per capita)
2. Heat energy consumption (Gcal/m^2)
3. Hot water consumption (m^3 per capita)
4. Cold water consumption (m^3 per capita)
5. Natural gas consumption (m^3 per capita)

EE indicators in Municipal Budget Institutions

6. Electricity consumption (kWh per capita)
7. Heat energy consumption (Gcal/m^2)
8. Hot water consumption (m^3 per capita)
9. Cold water consumption (m^3 per capita)
10. Natural gas consumption (m^3 per capita)

EE indicators in the housing and utilities sector and in the communal infrastructure (may be calculated using the indicators estimated by Volgogradstat)

11. The length of heat and steam networks that need to be replaced, in the total length of heat and steam networks in the territory of the municipality (in double-pipe terms, meter)
12. The area of residential premises in dilapidated and failing buildings in the total area of residential premises in the territory of the municipality
13. The share of expenses on housing and communal services in the total actual expenses of the local budget

Figure 2: Expanded list of specific indicators of energy consumption by municipalities in the housing and utilities sector and the budget sphere. (compiled by the authors)

The fundamental authors' methodology of integrated ranking estimation of EE based on specific indicators of municipalities' energy consumption is described in detail in our previously published work.[16] However, earlier this methodology was used only in relation to the first 10 specific indicators listed in table 1. In the present study, the ranking estimates of municipalities' EE have been specified taking into account three new specific indicators in the housing and utilities sector and in the communal infrastructure (shown at the bottom in figure 2).

[16] See Bogachkova, Zaytseva, Usacheva, 2018a

2.3 The methods of estimating the relative levels of municipalities' energy efficiency

The relative levels of municipalities' EE have been estimated by means of comparing the integrated ranking estimates of EE taking into account production specialization and the levels of territories' economic development. This required the application of descriptive statistics methods and data graphic visualization.

3 Results and discussion

3.1 Diversification of municipalities of the Volgograd region according to the GMP sectoral structure and the level of economic development

1. Industrial and trade - financial municipalities

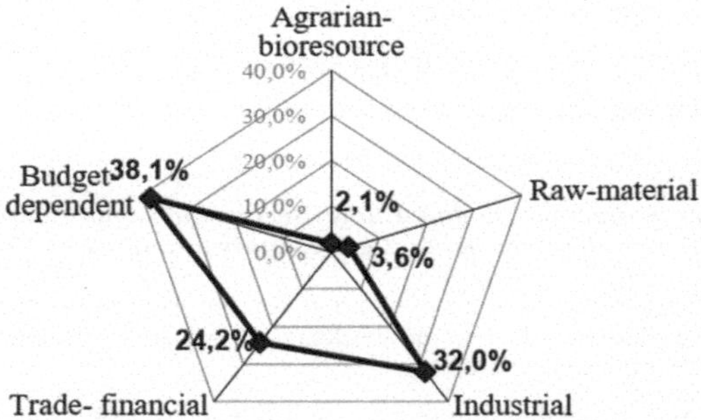

Cities and towns: 1) Volgograd, 2) Volzhsky, 3) Kamyshin, 4) Mikhaylovka, 5) Uryupinsk, 6) Frolovo. **Municipal districts:** 7) Gorodishchensky, 8) Zhirnovsky, 9) Kamyshinsky, 10) Kotelnikovsky, 11) Kotovsky.

Figure 3: Average structure of the GMP and the nominal list of the Ind&TF-group with indication of consecutive numbers of the municipalities.

The Volgograd region consists of 38 municipalities, including 6 city districts, or cities, and 32 municipal districts. All municipalities are characterized by different GRP structure and the level of economic development connected with production specialization of the territories. We have classified them into 3 groups by means of cluster analysis.

The first group unites the municipalities with significantly larger shares of industrial and trade-financial sectors as compared to other territories. These municipalities will be referred to as industrial and trade-financial (*Ind&TF-group*).[17]

The second group includes the municipalities with larger shares of agrarian-bioresource sector (*AB-group*).[18]

2. Agrarian-bioresource municipalities

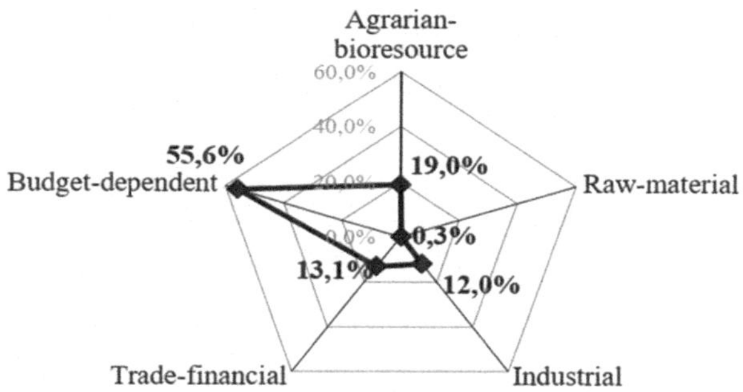

Municipal districts: 1) Alekseevsky, 2) Danilovsky, 3) Elansky, 4) Ilovlinsky, 5) Kalachevsky, 6) Kletsky, 7) Nikolaevsky, 8) Novoanninsky, 9) Novonikolaevsky, 10) Oktyabrsky, 11) Pallasovsky, 12) Svetloyarsky, 13) Sredneakhtubinsky, 14) Uryupinsky, 15) Frolovsky.

Figure 4: Average structure of the GMP and the nominal list of the AB-group with indication of consecutive numbers of the municipalities.

The third group consists of the municipalities outrunning other territories by the contribution of the budget-dependent sector to the GMP structure (*BD-group*).[19]

The differences in the levels of economic development depending on production specialization of the territories are reflected in table 1 which presents descriptive statistics of the GMP indicator per capita for 2015 with regard to the distinguished groups of municipalities.

[17] See Figure 3
[18] See Figure 4
[19] See Figure 5

3. Budget-dependent municipalities

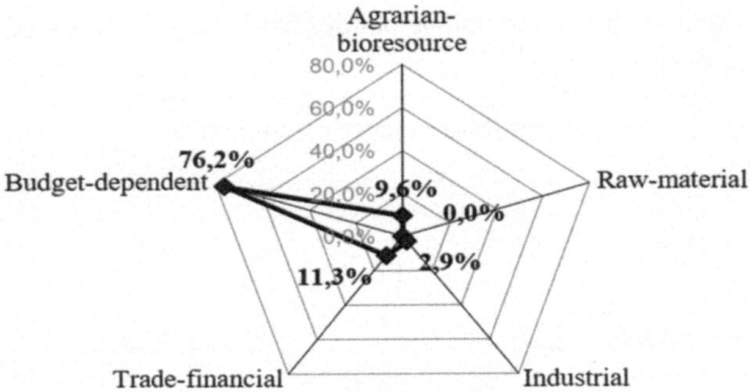

Municipal districts: 1) Bykovsky, 2) Dubovsky, 3) Kikvidzensky, 4) Leninsky, 5) Nekhaevsky, 6) Olkhovsky, 7) Kumylzhensky, 8) Rudnyansky, 9) Serafimovichsky, 10) Staropoltavsky, 11) Surovikinsky, 12) Chernyshkovsky.

Figure 5: Average structure of the GMP and the nominal list of the BD-group with indication of consecutive numbers of the municipalities.

Table 1: Descriptive statistics of the GMP indicator per capita (in thousand roubles). (compiled on the basis of calculations)

GMP per capita	1. Ind&TF-group	2. AB-group	3. BD-group
Mean value	258	146	117
Standard deviation (in % from mean value)	67 (26%)	32 (22%)	19 (16%)
Minimum	184	64	92
Maximum	425	188	160

The industrial and trade-financial municipalities (*Ind&TF-group*) are the most developed ones; the agrarian-bioresource municipalities (*AB-group*) demonstrate the medium level of development; and the budget-dependent municipalities prove to be the most underdeveloped (*BD-group*). The average value of the GMP indicator per capita in the *Ind&TF-group* is 1,77 times higher than the corresponding value in the *AB-group* and 2,2 times higher than the corresponding value in the *BD-group*. The maximum value of the GMP indicator per capita in the *Ind&TF-group* is 2,26 times higher than the *AB-group* and 2,65 times higher than in the

BD-group. The minimum level of economic development for the first group (184,000 roubles per capita) is almost the same as the maximum level of the corresponding value for the second group (188,000 roubles per capita) and exceeds the maximum for the third group (160,000 roubles per capita).

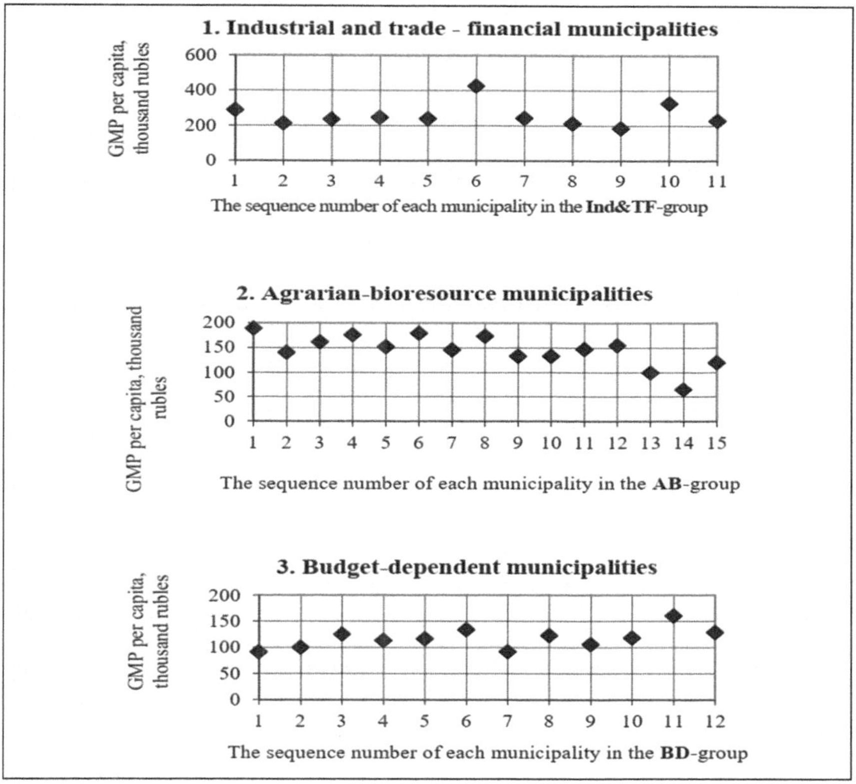

Figure 6: The scatter diagram of the economic development indicator (the GMP per capita, 2015). The consecutive numbers coincide with those in Figs 6-8. (compiled on the basis of calculations)

The intragroup differentiation of municipalities by the levels of economic development is characterized in the second line of table 1 (*Standard deviation*) and is illustrated by scatter diagrams of the GMP indicator per capita.[20]

[20] See Figure 6

3.2 Integrated ranking estimates of municipalities' energy efficiency in the Volgograd region for 2012, 2015 and 2016 and their comparative analysis with account of municipalities' production specialization

The built integrated ranking estimates of EE are shown in figure 7.

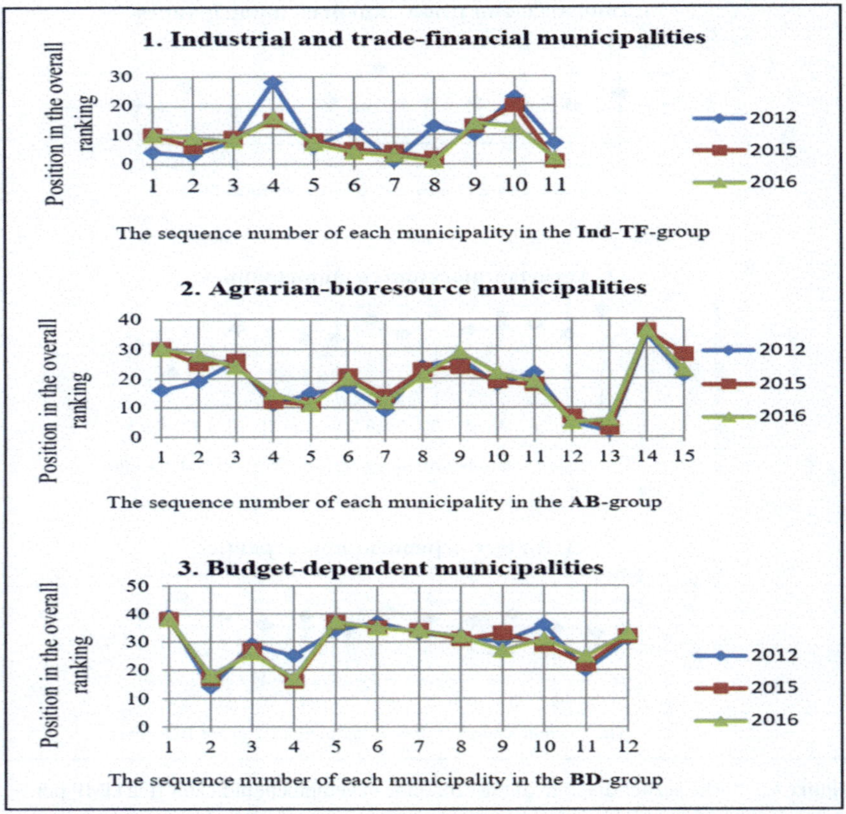

Figure 7: The diagrams of integrated ranking EE estimates of municipalities grouped according to their production specialization. The consecutive numbers coincide with those in figures 3-5. (compiled on the basis of calculations)

3.2.1 Intergroup differentiation of integrated ranking estimates of municipalities' EE

Table 2 presents the indicators which characterize the intergroup differentiation of integrated ranking estimates of municipalities' energy efficiency. For each municipal group we have shown the best (minimum), the worst (maximum) and median ranking estimate among the municipalities which constitute the group.

The median estimate shows that half of municipalities constituting the group have higher ranking estimates than the midpoint, and another half – lower estimates.

As can be seen from table 2, industrial and trade-financial municipalities (*Ind&TF-group*) make up the best group according to all 3 indicators of descriptive statistics; agrarian-bioresource municipalities (*AB-group*) – the median group; and budget-dependent municipalities (*BD-group*) – the worst group.

Table 2: Descriptive statistics of integrated ranking estimates of municipalities' energy efficiency. (compiled on the basis of calculations)

Year / Indicator	2012	2015	2016
1. Industrial and trade-financial municipalities (Ind&TF-group, 11 units)			
Midpoint	8	8	8
The best estimate (min)	1	1	1
The worst estimate (max)	28	20	16
2. Agrarian-bioresource municipalities (AB-group, 15 units)			
Midpoint	18	21	21
The best estimate (min)	2	3	5
The worst estimate (max)	35	36	36
3. Budget-dependent municipalities (BD-group, 12 units)			
Midpoint	32	32	32
The best estimate (min)	14	16	17
The worst estimate (max)	38	38	38

The median estimate for municipalities of the *Ind&TF-group* was equal to 8 over all the periods under consideration, while its value for the *AB-group* made 18 at the beginning of the period (2012) and decreased to 21 by the end of the period (2015, 2016). As for the *BD-group*, the median estimate was stably low and equaled to 32 over all the periods under consideration. The municipalities of the *Ind & TF-group* stably rank the first in the general integrated ranking. The best results of the municipalities from the *AB-group* are the 2nd place among all the municipalities in 2012, the 3rd place in 2015 and the 5th place in 2016. The municipalities of the *BD-group* did not rise above the 14th place in the overall ranking over all the years under consideration.

The worst ranking estimate for the *Ind&TF-group* in 2012 was equal to 28. Then this result was adjusted: in 2015 and 2016, the worst rankings for the *Ind&TF-*

group were 20 and 16, respectively. The worst ranking estimates were significantly lower in the *AB-group*: 35 (in 2012) and 36 (in 2015 and 2016). The *BD-group* was consistently characterized by the lowest 38th place in the overall integrated ranking.

3.2.2 Intragroup differentiation of integrated ranking estimates of municipalities' energy efficiency

Within each group, the interterritorial differences of EE integrated estimates for 2012, 2015 and 2016 are illustrated in figure 7. Among the municipalities of the *Ind&TF-group*, two municipal districts demonstrated consistently high results: the Gorodishchensky (the 1st, the 4th and the 3rd places in the overall ranking for 2012, 2015 and 2016, respectively) and the Kotovsky (the 7th, the 1st and the 2nd places in the overall ranking for 2012, 2015 and 2016, respectively). During the period under study, the largest cities of the region – Volgograd and Volzhsky – lost their ranks: Volgograd dropped from the 4th place in 2012 to the 10th place in 2015, 2016; and Volzhsky dropped from the 3rd place in 2012 to the 6th and 9th places in 2015 and 2016. The most successful trend was demonstrated by the Zhirnovsky municipal district, which moved up from the 13th place in 2012 to the 2nd place in 2015 and to the 1st place in 2016.

In the *AB-group* the following municipal districts showed relatively good results: Ilovlinsky, Kalachevsky, Nikolaevsky, Svetloyarsky, Sredneakhtubinsky. Their integrated ranking estimates of energy efficiency over the whole period were higher than the median estimate. The Svetloyarsky municipal district (the 5th, the 7th and the 5th places in the common ranking for 2012, 2015 and 2016, respectively) and the Sredneakhtubinsky municipal district (the 2nd, the 3rd and the 6th places in the common ranking for 2012, 2015 and 2016, respectively) were the most successful in this group. The worst result in the *AB-group* was shown by the Uryupinsky municipal district (35th place in 2012 and 36th place in 2015, 2016).

Among the municipalities of the third, weakest *BD-group*, the Dubovsky municipal district (14th, 17th and 18th places in the overall ranking for 2012, 2015 and 2016, respectively) and the Leninsky municipal district (25th, 16th and 17th places in the overall ranking for 2012, 2015 and 2016) showed the best results. The worst result, both in the *BD-group*, and among all the other municipalities, was shown by the Bykovsky municipal district taking the last 38th place in 2012, 2015 and 2016.

4 Discussion

The analytical tools presented in the present article allow to estimate the relative levels of municipalities' energy efficiency and to make grounded conclusions about the performance of EE policies implemented at the subregional level. At the same time, it is necessary to point out the limitedness of the proposed methods associated with the following circumstances.

Firstly, today the calculation of the gross municipal product's energy intensity is not possible due to the lack of necessary statistical data both on the volumes of the GMP and on the total energy consumption of the municipalities. Therefore, we may only base our research on integrated ranking estimates of the territories' EE, which do not reflect the real costs of energy resources for the production of a gross product unit.

Secondly, the obtained integrated ranking estimates are based on a number of specific indicators of energy consumption with regard to only two sectors of the economy: housing and utilities sector and the budget sphere. The choice of these industries and their indicators is conditioned by the criterion of data availability. As the available statistical base expands, the results of the EE analysis can be specified.

Thirdly, the Global Urban Observatory (GUO) methodology, which has been used to obtain the authors' estimates of the GMP of the municipalities grouped by production specialization and the levels of economic development, is characterized by significant errors. If necessary, the method of GMP estimation can be improved by combining various currently existing methodological approaches. Besides, the GMP volumes have been calculated only for 2015, since the most recent official data on payroll funds in the SME sector in the municipal context are available only for this year.

Despite the abovementioned limitations, the analytical tools developed and tested in this work allow to obtain grounded quantitative estimates of municipalities' energy efficiency based on the available and accessible data of official statistics. The development of digital economy, digitalization of the energy sector and the housing and utilities sector are supposed to bring big progress in the spheres of energy efficiency improvement and analytical support for monitoring this process.

5 Conclusion

It is argued that intermunicipal comparisons of energy efficiency indicators should be carried out among the territories homogeneous in production specialization and the level of economic development, since this would ensure the correctness of comparative analysis of municipalities' energy efficiency. A grouping of 38 municipal entities of the Volgograd region has been carried out according to the structure of the GMP, which characterizes the production specialization, and according to the GMP index per capita, which reflects the level of economic development. We have put forward the provision on the expediency of expanding the current list of specific indicators of municipalities' energy consumption by supplementing it with indicators 6-13[21], generated and provided by the territorial body of State statistics.

It has been substantiated that the analysis of EE policy performance at the subregional level requires the application of methods of integrated ranking estimates of municipalities. Such methods has been developed and tested in the present research using the example of the Volgograd region. Application of integrated ranking estimation for a number of years has allowed to trace the dynamics of relative energy efficiency of municipalities and hence to evaluate the comparative performance of EE policy. The proposed methods can be easily generalized in case of database expansion. In this case, their application will lead to higher accuracy of estimating municipalities' energy efficiency.

We have obtained the integrated ranking estimates of the energy efficiency of the Volgograd region's municipalities for 2012, 2015 and 2016, taking into account their production specialization. As a result, it has been revealed that the industrial and trade-financial municipalities are the most energy efficient and economically developed. The agrarian-bioresource municipalities demonstrate average performance, while the budget-dependent municipalities are the least energy efficient and economically developed. It is shown that a more detailed analysis of energy efficiency measures at the subregional level can be carried out within the groups of municipalities that are homogeneous in structure of the GMP using the methods of descriptive statistics and graphical visualization. The research results can contribute to enhancing the practice of energy saving management and energy efficiency improvement in the region.

Literature

Baatz, B. (2015). *Why everyone benefits from energy efficiency programs, American Council for an Energy-Efficient Economy.* Retrieved 20.1.2019, from http://aceee.org/blog/2015/06/why-everyone-benefits-energy

Bashmakov, I. (2013). *Development of complex long-term energy saving and energy efficiency programs: methodology and practice. PhD thesis. Institute of national economy forecasting of the Russian Academy of Sciences. (in Russian).*

Bashmakov, I., Myshak, A. (2012). *Russian accounting system to improve energy efficiency and energy savings. (in Russian).* Retrieved 20.1.2019, from CENEF.: http://www.cenef.ru/file/Indexes.pdf

[21] See Table 1

Bashmakov, I., Myshak, A. (2016). Dynamics of energy consumption and energy intensity of GRP in the regions of Russia. Driving with a raised hood. (in Russian). *The Electronic Journal ENERGOSOVET, No. 2.*, pp. 12-20.

Bogachkova, L. (2018). Problems of development of the Russian system of statistical accounting and analysis of energy efficiency indicators of municipalities. (in Russian) *Statistics - the language of digital civilization: collection of reports of the International scientific-practical conference "II Open Russian Statistical Congress": in 2 vols. Vol. 2*, pp. 360-366.

Bogachkova, L., Khurshudyan, S. (2017). *Development of tools for analyzing the effectiveness of energy efficiency policies in the regions of Russia, problems and solutions. Vol 3. No.12.* Retrieved 20.2.2019, from Internet-science. (in Russian): http://internetnauka.com/index.p hp/journal/article/view/233

Bogachkova, L., Zaytseva, Y., Usacheva, N. (2018a). *Tools for Monitoring Energy Efficiency of Municipalities. Housing and Utilities Sector and Budget Sector (the Case of the Volgograd Region.* Retrieved 20.1.2019, from Proceedings of the Int. conf. Competitive, Sustainable and Secure Development of the Regional Economy: "Response to Global Challenges". Advances in Economics, Business and Management Research. DOI: 10.2991/cssdre-18.2018.88

Bogachkova, L., Zaytseva, Y., Usacheva, N. (2018b). *The estimation of structural changes influence on the energy intensity of subregional economy, Regional economy. The South of Russia. (in Russian).* DOI: https://doi.org/10.15688/re.volsu. 2018.3.12

Bogachkova, L., Zaytseva, Y., Usacheva, N. (2019). *The structural changes impact estimation while monitoring the performance of energy efficiency policy at subregional level: Solovev D. (eds) Smart Technologies and Innovations in Design for Control of Technological Processes and Objects: Economy and Production. FarEastCon 2018. Smart Innovation, Systems and Technologies, vol 139, pp.143-150. Springer, Cham. https://doi.org/10.1007/978-3-030- 18553-4_19*

Braungardt, S., Eichhammer, W., Elsland, R., Fleiter, T., Klobasa, M., Krail, M., Sensfuss, F. (2014). *Study evaluating the current energy efficiency policy framework in the EU and providing orientation on policy options for realising the cost-effective energy efficiency/saving potential until 2020 and beyond.* Retrieved 18.1.2019, from Report on behalf of DG ENER.: https://ec.europa.eu/energy/sites/ener/files/documents/2014_report_2020-2030_eu_policy_framework.pdf

Brauweiler, H.-Ch. (2002). *Innovationen im peripheren Raum.* Wiesbaden: Gabler.

Cambridge Econometrics. (2015). *Assessing the Employment and Social Impact of Energy Efficiency, Final report.* Retrieved 25.2.2019, from Volume 1: Main report, Cambridge Econometrics, Covent Garden, Cambridge, UK.: https://ec.europa.eu/energy/sites/ener/files/documents/CE_EE_Jobs_main%2018Nov2015.pdf

EC Directorate-General for Energy. (2016). *The Macroeconomic and Other Benefits of Energy Efficiency. Final report. European Union.* Retrieved 20.1.2019, from https://ec.europa.eu/energy/sites/ener/files/documents/final_report_v4_final.pdf

EPA (Environmental Protection Agency). (2017a). *National Action Plan for Energy Efficiency. United States Environmental Protection Agency.* Retrieved 20.1.2019, from https://www.epa.gov/energy/national-action-plan-energy-efficiency

EPA (Environmental Protection Agency). (2017b). *National Action Plan Vision for 2025: A Framework for Change. United States Environmental Protection Agency.* Retrieved 20.1.2019, from https://www.epa.gov/energy/national-action-plan-vision-2025-framework-change

Gasho, E., Puzakova, V., Stepanova, M. (2013). *Improving energy efficiency in the region. Energy: economics, technology, ecology. (in Russian).* (No. 11).

Government of the Russian Federation. (2009). *Energy Strategy of Russia for the period till 2030, (approved by Decree No. 1715-r of the Government of the Russian Federation of 13 November 2009). (in Russian).* Retrieved 25.2.2019, from https://minenergo.gov.ru/node/1026

Government of the Russian Federation. (2017). *The program 'Digital Economy of the Russian Federation' (approved by the Order of the Government of the Russian Federation No. 1632-p of July 28, 2017). (in Russian).* Retrieved 25.2.2019, from http://www.consultant.ru/document/cons_doc_LAW_221756/

Government of the Russian Federation. (2018). *Comprehensive action plan to improve the energy efficiency of the Russian Comprehensive action plan to improve the energy efficiency of the Russian. (in Russian).* Retrieved 25.2.2019, from https://minenergo.gov.ru/node/1026

IEA (International Energy Agency). (2017). *Energy Efficiency 2017.* Retrieved 20.1.2019, from https://www.iea.org/publications/freepublications/publication/Energy_Efficiency_2017.pdf

Inshakov, O., Bogachkova, L., Popkova, E. (2019). *Energy Efficiency as a Driver of Global Competitiveness, the Priority of the State Economic Policy and the International Collaboration of the Russian Federation. Energy Sector: A Systemic Analysis of Economy, Foreign Trade and Legal Regulations.* (Vol. 44). (O. Inshakov, A. Inshakova, E. Popkova, Eds.) Retrieved from Energy Sector: A Systemic Analysis of Economy, Foreign Trade and Legal Regulations. Lecture Notes in Networks and Systems.

Ivanov, A., Matveev, I. (2017). *The world energy market under geopolitical realities on the eve of 2017.* Retrieved 20.1.2019, from Russian Foreign Economic Journal. (in Russian): http://www.rfej.ru/rvv/id/b0024d9d4/$file/17-31.pdf

Khurshudyan, S. (2018). *Tools for analyzing the energy efficiency of Russian regions: development and application: monograph. (in Russian).* RUSAINS.

Kramer, M., Brauweiler, H.-Ch., Urbaniec, M. (1999). *Einfluß der Umweltgesetze auf Marktentwicklung und Finanzbedarf des polnischen Umweltmarktes. Internationales Umweltrecht - Ein Vergleich zwischen Deutschland, Polen und Tschechien.* (M. Kramer, H.-Ch. Brauweiler, Eds.) Wiesbaden: Gabler.

Makarov, A., Grigoryev, L., Mitrova, T. (2016). *Forecast of the development of the world's and Russia's energy – 2016.* Retrieved 20.1.2019, from Institute of Energy Research, RAS & Analytical Centre at the Government of the Russian Federation, Moscow. (in Russian): http://ac.gov.ru/files/publication/a/10585.pdf

Ministry of Economic Development of the Russian Federation. (2018). *State Report on Energy Saving and Energy Efficiency in the Russian Federation in 2017. (in Russian).* Retrieved 1.2.2019, from http://economy.gov.ru/minec/about/structure/depGostarif/201812103

Ministry of Energy of the Russian Federation. (2015). *State report on energy saving and energy efficiency in the Russian Federation in 2014. (in Russian).* Retrieved 1.2.2019, from https://minenergo.gov.ru/node/5197

Ministry of Energy of the Russian Federation. (2016). *State report on energy saving and energy efficiency in the Russian Federation in 2015. (in Russian).* Retrieved 1.2.2019, from https://minenergo.gov.ru/node/5197

Ministry of Energy of the Russian Federation. (2017). *State report on energy saving and energy efficiency in the Russian Federation in 2016. (in Russian).* Retrieved 1.2.2019, from https://minenergo.gov.ru/node/5197

Naess-Schmidt, S., Hansen, M., von Below, D. (2015). *Literature review on macroeconomic effects of energy efficiency improvement actions.* Retrieved 20.1.2019, from D6.1 report. COMBI. Copenhagen.: https://combi-project.eu/wp-content/uploads/2015/09/D6.1.pdf

Naisbitt, J. (1988). *Megatrends: Ten New Directions Transforming Our Lives.* Published August 16th 1988 by Grand Central Publishing (first published in 1982).

Popov, A., Gainalov, I. (2015). *Assessment of energy and economic development of the region. Fundamental Research. (in Russian)* (No. 7).

Popov, V., Dobrodey, V., Veselova, L., Konyaeva, M. (2012). *Formation of energy efficiency rating of municipalities of the Sverdlovsk region in 2011 and the comparative analysis with the framework period. (in Russian).* Sverdlovsk.

Saldanha, G., Gouvea da Costa, S., de Lima, E. (2016). *Energy efficiency frameworks: a literature overview.* Retrieved 20.1.2019, from 27th Annual Conference Proceedings: Production and Operations. Management Society (POMS).: https://www.pomsmeetings.org/ ConfProceedings/065/Full%20Papers/Final%20Full%20Papers/065-0440.pdf

Strebel, H., Eifler, P., Brauweiler, H.-Ch., et al. (2003). *Umweltorientierung in Betrieblichen Querschnittsbereichen.* Gabler-Springer.

UN. (2004). *Urban Indicators Guidelines: Monitoring the Habitat Agenda and the Millennium Development Goals: UN Human Settlements Programme.* Retrieved 1.2.2019, from http://ww2.unhabitat.org/

Part C: Miscellaneous

Data-driven marketing as a part of a business strategy of Kazakhstani franchise companies

Aida T. Yerimpasheva, Zarema B. Balgabayeva

1 Introduction

The paper documents the basic concepts relating to importance of big data in contemporary data-driven marketing. In an attempt to better understand and provide more detailed insights to the phenomenon of big data in data-driven marketing. The authors consider experience of the global brands entering regional markets. Global brands play important role in the development of entrepreneurship in the Kazakhstani market. Attractiveness of Kazakhstan for global brands can be judged by the wide spectrum of business forms and the country's place in the world franchise rating. Due to franchising companies, the local businesses are being pulled up, the ethical code is identified, new technologies are used and more rapid adaptation to changing market conditions take place. As a result, competition for national specifics is increasing, which in turn makes local brands stronger and gives an opportunity to see the prospects for entering the international market.

Modern reality is transformed under the influence of global megatrends. They are urbanization, the development of digital technologies, new customer behaviors. These trends have an impact on all spheres of life: the state, industry, business, people, and marketing. Experts call today's reality as the "client era". Digital technology has significantly expanded the capabilities of customers. Now the buyer, who has the necessary information, decides what, when, where, and how to buy. Therefore, those companies that make innovation will be able to prevail in the competition.

Today, marketing is strongly linked with digital technology. Primarily, experts draw attention to the importance of understanding what today's client is. Big data as intellectual and predictive analytics play an important role in modern marketing. A comprehensive study of customer behavior and their requests allow creating popular products and services.

We can say that to some extent a modern customer (client) is very "inconvenient" for marketers. He does not rely on direct messages from sellers, but has the opportunity to thoroughly study the characteristics and reviews of the product, to learn the recommendations of other consumers. The client expects a personalized approach, and if he is not satisfied, he/she can even destroy the brand. At the same time, the availability of information and the ability to communicate with

H.-C. Brauweiler et al. (Hrsg.), *Digitalization and Industry 4.0: Economic and Societal Development*, https://doi.org/10.1007/978-3-658-27110-7_23

brands through social networks carry positive points for business: customers are ready to cooperate with organizations to jointly create and improve products. Consumers want to be part of the process and get not only a product or service, but also an interesting experience.

The criteria for a successful brand is easy and comfortable perception, the fascination of the process of interaction with the brand, memorability. For this purpose, new tools are attracted: video, high-quality content, live broadcasts, virtual and augmented reality. This is evidenced by the redistribution of marketing budgets in the world. According to SalesForce, for the last two years video advertising in the B2B segment has grown by 204%, SMS mailings have grown by 197%, native advertising - by 147%, and advertising in social networks - by 130%.[1]

All this poses new challenges to Chief Marketing Officers. In a new competitive environment, they need to increase brand value through customer involvement, which require marketing transformation that is reorganization of departments and marketing functions, as well as mastering a new model. According to the study conducted by authors, the leading channels will be social media, the World Wide Web, mobile apps and a mobile network. Mobile devices and networks, personalization technologies and the Internet of things will become technological trends that will have the greatest impact on marketing in the nearest future.

Big data (BD) is needed for progressive development of the digital ecosystem to achieve sustainable economic growth and increase the competitiveness of the economy.

Big data analytics have to be perceived as a "disruptive technology"[2] that will reshape Business Intelligence (BI), which is a domain that relies on data analytics to gain business insights for better decision-making.[3] Big Data has the potential to 'disrupt' the senior management of organizations, prompting directors to make decisions more rapidly and to shape their capabilities to address environmental changes.[4]

The following objectives of the paper are set:

- To reveal the significance of the big data technology for marketing and management decision making process;
- To explore the prospects of marketing and highlight specific characteristics of business strategy;

1 See Aslanova, 2019
2 (Christensen, 1997)
3 See Fan, Lau, Zhao, 2015
4 See Merendino, et al., 2018

- To study directions of marketing research activities against the background of using the big data technology;
- To identify the main challenges that Kazakhstani companies would face in case not using big data technology and data-driven marketing;
- To conduct qualitative research among specialists on marketing.

2 Literature review

It has been suggested that the big data can change competition in markets by „process transformation, altering corporate ecosystems and innovation".[5] It is often claimed that Big data is „the next frontier for innovation" and „bringing a revolution in science and technology".[6] Erevelles, Fukawa & Swayne claim the same: "Consumer analytics is at the epicenter of a big data revolution. Technology helps capture rich and plentiful data on consumer phenomena in real time".[7]

According to Verhoef, Kooge & Walk "big data in itself is not a revolution but an evolution of the increasing availability of data that has been observed in recent times".[8]

Big data captured by companies change the pace of competition, innovation and productivity in the world. Based on current trends of data doubling every two years, there will be 44 times more data available in 2020 than there was in 2009.[9] The results of the research conducted by Amado et al. "revealed that Big Data in Marketing has seen an increasing interest over the years, with each year doubling the previous one in publication output numbers".[10] At the same time, they found out that most of the research on big data in marketing originates from Europe, North America and Asia.[11] In regard of mixing marketing and big data Xu, Frankwick & Ramirez write that systematization "aims to help firms build strategy to combine knowledge from both marketing and big data domains".[12]

Putting the Big data to work effectively leads to the increasing volume and detail of information used in strategic decision-making process based on Business Intelligence. BI projects have to be implemented and analyzed by BI experts according to their experience. According to MGI research to capture the full potential of Big data companies will be facing a skill shortage gap of people with BI skills[13]

5 (Sen, Ozturk, Vayvay, 2016)
6 (Wamba, Akter, Edwards, Chopin, Gnanzou, 2015)
7 (Erevelles, Fukawa, Swayne, 2016)
8 (Verhoef, Kooge, Walk, 2016)
9 See Johnson, Gray, Sarker, 2019
10 (Amado, Cortez, Rita, Moro, 2018)
11 See Amado, Cortez, Rita, Moro, 2018, p. 6
12 (Xu, Frankwick, Ramirez, 2016, p. 1562)
13 See Benson, Kandasamy, 2019

because "big data... includes collection, storage, preprocessing, visualization and, essentially, statistical analysis of enormous batches of data".[14] Oussous, Benjelloun, Ait Lahcen & Belfkih consider that the traditional static Business Intelligence tools can no longer be efficient in the case of Big Data applications. Big data support decision making through recommendations and automatic detection of anomalies, abnormal behavior or new trends.[15] All the evidence suggests that "such a vast amount of data is useless without plans and strategies" and now it is time 'to cope with its size and complexity...to leverage the information to create value".[16] Sheng, Amankwah-Amoah & Wang consider that „firms need to formulate and implement a data-driven strategy in consequence" of "growing awareness of big data's business values and managerial changes".[17]

Big data influence not only marketing management, but marketing research as well. There are those who argue, "Data collected in a passive, unobtrusive, and non-reactive manner may overcome social desirability bias and other distortions" when researchers directly interact with research subjects. Then Johnson et al. state that detailed data generated as a non-reactive byproduct of digital actions can also complement data collected by researchers through traditional methods of surveys and interviews. Indeed, fine-grained observations of individual and organizational actions are easier and cheaper to collect and analyze than ever before. It is true to say that marketing researchers usually collect secondary and primary data and then marketing decision are made. Big data researchers rarely collect primary data. Typically, they start with computer-based extraction of secondary data, which they then convert into tertiary data to meet their own needs.[18] Yet some researchers as Erevelles, Fukawa & Swayne do not differentiate secondary and primary data. They state: "unprecedented volume, velocity, and variety of primary data, Big Data, are available from individual consumers".[19] It is not so important. For more important is that big data technology helps "capture rich and plentiful data on consumer phenomena in real time".[20]

Some authors as Kun, W., Tong, L., Xiaodan, X. believe that big data "provide services such as decision support, product innovation, quality control, process optimization, service support and risk management and control, thereby enhancing the core competitiveness of enterprises".[21] All the evidences suggest that the use of big data is one of the key factors for finding value proposition, raising

---

14 (Torrecilla, Romo, 2018, p. 15)
15 See Oussous, Benjelloun, Ait Lahcen, Belfkih, 2018
16 (Verhoef, Kooge, Walk, 2016, p. 17)
17 (Sheng, Amankwah-Amoah, Wang, 2017, p. 97)
18 See Johnson, Gray, Sarker, 2019
19 (Erevelles, Fukawa, Swayne, 2016, p. 897)
20 (Erevelles, Fukawa, Swayne, 2016, p. 897)
21 (Kun, Tong, Xiaodan, 2019)

awareness, increasing profitability, and transforming a business model. Organizations focused on working with big data get advantages in all areas of activity. Data-driven marketing as an innovative approach has to be considered as a basic part of a business strategy. Big data technology helps capture rich and plentiful data on consumers. The impact of big data on various marketing activities enables firms to better exploit its benefits.

3 Materials and methods

In-depth interview is a popular research method in marketing. The purpose of in-depth interviews was to uncover some issues that could not be obtained via traditional and online surveys. The first reason why this method was used: to interview a small and hard-to-reach group, representatives of the Kazakhstani business elite. The second reason was interviewing professional people (e.g., industrial marketing research) in the field of big data technology. The interviews took place in the form of free conversation. Respondents had the opportunity to speak freely, since the interviews were unstructured. The interview was held on the results of the Kazakhstan Marketing Conference 2018, which took place on April 27, 2018 in Almaty, where representatives of the Kazakhstani professional marketing community together with businesspersons discussed the future of data-driven marketing and a new generation of consumers. The purpose of the interviews was to obtain a lot of information about Kazakhstani companies using big data technologies. Despite the small number of non-representative cases and non-statistical analysis, the authors were able to develop a richer understanding on the research questions.

During the study, also the case study of the Dostyk Plaza Almaty (Shopping and Entertainment Center (SEC)) was used on how Big Data, artificial intelligence and deep analytics can change the rules of the game and the paradigm of competition among SECs in Kazakhstan.

4 Results and discussion

There can be no doubt that the modern digital systems exist in conditions of tough competition. The only way to make sure that the marketing team works effectively is to analyze the big data, that is, to implement data-driven marketing. More and more marketers use customer data to draw a full portrait of their target audience. This allows them to run more focused campaigns that produce better results. However, the benefits of data-based marketing go beyond the content. Through the data collection and analysis marketers can consider the specific properties of end users. The purpose of the data-driven method is to increase the work's productivity via attracting new customers and retaining old ones.

Data driven marketing does a process by which marketers gain understanding and direction of trends based on comprehensive analysis provided by numbers. Data-driven marketing refers to strategies built on insights pulled from the big data's analysis and collected through consumer interactions and engagements, forms predictions about future behavior. This involves existing data, data that can be acquired, and issues how to organize, analyze, and apply data to make the better marketing efforts. Generally, the intended goal is to enhance and personalize the customer's experience. The data driven marketing research allows for a comprehensive study of preferences.[22] There are those who argue as Anshari et al. that big data can be expected to improve customer relationship as it allows interactivity, multi-way communications, personalization, and customization.[23] The conducted research proved that analytic tools allow to target and personalize marketing to the customer. Approaching an audience with a targeted campaign increases the chances of their conversion. Now marketers can understand the customers' behavior and make informed decisions based on the big data, thus allowing for a relevant targeting that was predicted by academic authors like Malhotra, Peterson, Kleiser.[24] If we consider data-driven marketing's obvious advantages and disadvantages, we can draw following conclusions shown in table 1.

However, despite the complexity and cost of the data-driven approach, it is strongly recommended for implementation, since the markets are changing, users become more demanding, technologies penetrate into the ordinary life. However, it should be understood that data collection is the first stage. The next important stage is data's interpretation, and then making decisions and adjusting business strategies. It is important that solutions based on data have to be consumer-centred, not data-centred.

The cooperation of Dostyk Plaza and the telecommunication company "Kcell" in the field of big data technology made it possible to see the big picture and understand the market based on the "Commercial Report on Geo-location". Dostyk Plaza has begun to use seasonality, which had not been identified before, as it paid more attention to other long-term trends. Now Dostyk Plaza can see and analyze the dynamics of attendance, compare these data with those events that had been held, evaluate the effectiveness of marketing campaigns, etc. In other words, Dostyk Plaza successfully analyzes the behavior of customers and behavioral patterns. Moreover, based on a report from Kcell, Dostyk Plaza analyzes long-term trends, associates them with the macroeconomic situation, and reveals behavioral characteristics. Now the Dostyk Plaza can find clear relationships with

---

22 See Smallbusiness, 2008

23 See Anshari, Almunawar, Lim, Al-Mudimigh, 2018

24 See Malhotra, Peterson, Kleiser, 1999

demographic cycles, which models are typical for different market segments. Otherwise, according to the Director of Marketing and Advertising at Dostyk Plaza Olesya Moskalevich, SEC Dostyk Plaza "would overlook problems, and this is the way to nowhere. Moreover, we could start spending money on those projects that would not bring effect, and we are talking about millions of tenge".[25]

Table 1: Advantages and disadvantages of data-driven marketing

*compiled by authors

Advantages of digital marketing	**Disadvantages of digital marketing**
Data-driven marketing allows offering personalized services due to a deeper understanding of the clients' profile.	Setting data-driven system demands skilled human resources. It is difficult to search for the employees with the necessary qualifications, and it would be expensive.
Data management is becoming increasingly relevant. When using a data-based approach, it becomes much easier to use data in the decision-making process, even online. This can be one of the key competitive advantages.	The data collection infrastructure require the integration process among business units, as well centralized support in training and forming standards.
The coordinated operation of all communication channels allow to message to each client in the right place and time.	If the amount of data exceeds the decision maker's ability to process data, their value is automatically reduced to zero. This is a case when a company is not fully committed to a data-based marketing strategy, is not fully prepared for it, but implements it.
Effective feedback from customers allows providing high quality service, ensuring constant monitoring, and keeping abreast.	Maintenance costs due to a constantly evolving environment.
Product development becomes more sophisticated; it allows developing suitable products for specific markets.	Higher transparency of pricing leads to increased price competition.

Another example of successful using of big data: analysis of the dynamics of attendance at Dostyk Plaza showed the most optimal dates for the marketing campaign. As a result, the growth of trade in the long term to billions of tenge takes place. Big data technologies allow to build a competent marketing strategy, this is confirmation that the Dostyk Plaza is conducting the "right" events and it

25 (Galiyev, 2019)

corresponds to the target audience using communication channels correctly. Due to the "Commercial Report on Geolocation", the Dostyk Plaza can accurately assess the efficiency in digital. Yet, the situation in the developed markets of the world cannot be directly transmitted to Kazakhstan: diverse consumption patterns, cultural differences take place. For example, the share of online purchases is about 10%. In addition, this figure does not change: from year to year all the same 10%. There is no amplitude of a sharp increase in online trading. Perhaps a shift will occur, but in the long run, when the "digitized" generation reaches the age of 25-30 years. Additionally, there should be a mature business providing customers with seamless online purchases with good logistics. To solve these problems Dostyk Plaza used the big data technology.

In the local markets of developing countries, in particular in Kazakhstan, the data-driven approach is only in its outset and represented mostly in large businesses or foreign companies. Therefore, the global brands demonstrate the vector of development of the market but small and medium businesses do not have particular competencies.

The importance of involving small businesses in the process of data-driven marketing is very high, because the goal of the data-driven approach is to increase the productivity in attracting new customers and retaining old ones. In the scale of the national economy of Kazakhstan, entrepreneurship is increasing, but the pace of activity is quite not significant: the level of entrepreneurial activity is two times lower than the world average. To be more precise, small business in Kazakhstan generates 25.6% of GDP, while the share of people employed in small and medium businesses (SME) is 36% of the national labor market.[26]

Global brands play important role in the development of entrepreneurship in the local market. Attractiveness of Kazakhstan for global brands can be judged by the wide spectrum of business forms and the country's place in the world franchise rating.

Due to franchising companies, the local businesses are being pulled up, ethical code is identified, new technologies are used, more rapid adaptation to changing market conditions take place. As a result, competition for national specifics is increasing, which makes local brands stronger and gives an opportunity to see the prospects for entering the international market. Networks of enterprises under a strong brand and data driven marketing strategy easily overcome recessions and crises.[27]

26 See GOV, 2019
27 See Karimova, 2013

Referring to the practice of franchising in Kazakhstan, the following features can be noted:

- In general, there is a sustainable demand for franchises. Franchising is still a peculiar way of doing business in Kazakhstan and this niche is not occupied. Therefore, the market is experiencing an influx of franchises from neighboring countries.
- Franchising often serves as a partner of emerging Kazakh brands.
- In a period of crisis and economic stagnation, it is unprofitable for enterprises to hold branches. They require spending, and the shortage of money leads to the creation of franchise relations with yesterday's branches. This is beneficial to both parties, which stimulates to franchise.
- Kazakhstan has often been discussed in the international market due to the large-scale projects like EXPO 2017; as a result, foreign brands are interested in being in a new market. In addition, Kazakhstan is located in a strategically important region.

Specialized and non-specialized institutions facilitate the development of franchising in Kazakhstan:

- National Institute of Intellectual Property (Kazpatent): regulation of the trademark turnover sector and register franchise agreements.
- Eurasian Franchise Association (EAFRAN): free consultation of entrepreneurs on franchising and licensing issues.
- Damu - Small Business Development Fund: lending of entrepreneurs to purchase a franchise.

Franchising is regulated by a special Law of the Republic of Kazakhstan "On Comprehensive Entrepreneurial License / Franchising" of 2002, Chapter 45 of the Civil Code of RK dated 1999, which regulate franchising, also remains in force.

Kazakhstan today is a leader of the franchise sector in Central Asia. In 2017, according to the data presented by the Union of Franchising Kazakhstan, the share of enterprises launched under the franchise in the structure of SMEs in Kazakhstan was 15% per year. According to Syrlybayeva, Zhadigerova, Zhumanova this indicator can grow up to 30% with active support from the state.[28] Then they claim that the largest number of franchise are in the retail sector (47%), the catering sector (23%) and the service sector (12%). Now, according to experts, more than 450 foreign brands are developing in the country using franchising.[29]

---

28 See Syrlybayeva, Zhadigerova, Zhumanova, 2019

29 See Syrlybayeva, Zhadigerova, Zhumanova, 2019

Regional centers of franchising in Kazakhstan are the cities of Almaty, Astana, Atyrau, Karaganda, Shymkent. They focus small and medium-sized businesses, in the midst of which franchising technologies are developing. More than 70% of franchise projects originate from Almaty: the foreign franchises undergo initial adaptation before being developed in other cities of the country. For example, major international franchise brands such as BaskinRobbins, hotel chains Inter Continental, Hayat, Ritz-Carlton Hotel, etc. are concentrated in Almaty. In Kazakhstan, 75% of franchises exist in the market for no more than 5 years. The share of franchise relations in the volume of SME in the Republic of Kazakhstan is 3.5%. An important factor affecting the franchise market is the reduction of barriers for Russian and Belarusian companies to enter the Kazakhstani market in connection with the creation of the Eurasian Economic Union. Most likely, the number of Russian franchises will increase and may reach 30-40%.[30]

Kisikov states that the great attention to the Kazakhstani market is shown by Russian franchises, which already occupy the lion's share. By the way, in 2015, EAFRAN signed a memorandum of cooperation with the Russian Franchise Association, so now Kazakhstan companies will get a chance to enter the neighboring market. A similar document was signed with Ukraine. It should be noted that Ukrainian brands are especially interested in the Kazakhstan market, because the franchise market is the strongest in the Commonwealth of Independent States (CIS), is currently experiencing understandable difficulties.[31] The big data analytics process is seen as a tool to improve operational efficiency though it has "strategic potential, drive new revenue streams and gain competitive advantages over business rivals".[32]

Syrlybayeva et al. found out that 65 Russian franchisors implemented their business ideas in Kazakhstan. Among them are successful projects as "Orange Elephant", "33 Penguins", "Begemotik", "Econika", "Red Cube", "Chocolate Girl", etc. In the near future 30 more Russian brands are planning to enter the market of Kazakhstan. The United States is developing 36 networks in Kazakhstan, which include 250 franchise outlets. American franchises lost in quantity, but significantly outperformed in terms of turnover. This is not surprising, because mega brands like Coca-Cola, Hilton, Sheraton, Ritz-Carlton Hotel Company are presented. Baskin Robbins also makes a significant contribution to the turnover of American franchising, although a Russian company promotes it. Following Russia and the United States European countries as Great Britain, Germany, France, and Italy represent 82 franchises presenting 276 places. These are mainly fashion boutiques, beauty salons, perfume shops. In addition, investors from Turkey,

30 See Franchayzing v Kazakhstane, 2019
31 See Kisikov, 2019
32 (Sivarajah, Kamal, Irani, Weerakkody, 2017, p. 263)

Israel, Japan, Australia and others promote their business ideas in Kazakhstan Franchising, despite all the difficulties, continues to increase its presence in the economy of Kazakhstan. The annual turnover of enterprises operating on its terms is approaching $ 3 billion per year. Nevertheless, since 2012 cases of bankruptcy among franchise networks have become frequent. Partners do not discuss all the nuances of cooperation. Although the rate of bankruptcies is not great – 5%, but taking into account the level of penetration of franchising in SMEs this indicator is a signal for reflection.[33]

In this regard, it is very important to understand the role of data-driven marketing at each stage of working with a franchise. This is particularly relevant in the markets of developing countries, where the main marketing risk is the discrepancy between the concept of a franchise network and the preferences of the target audience (this risk is greatest when acquiring a foreign franchise, originally developed for another market).

Emerging markets are still far from the saturation and active representation of international franchising, and are an excellent transition platform for the correct entry into backward markets. Therefore, the potential of such markets as Kazakhstan should be used as efficiently as possible and to exclude cases of bankruptcy of franchises.

Despite the potential, emerging markets represent challenges for franchisors who have previously tried their hand in developed countries with stable economies. Franchisors need to reconsider their approach when entering developing markets via effectively integrating data-driven marketing into the international franchise system.

The franchise disclosure document (FDD) should reflect the following mandatory recommendations for working with it:

- Optimization and digitalization of internal business, as well customer service processes. These systems allow watching processes in numbers and identifying narrow and problematic places.
- Training of employees on data driven approach.
- Simplification of big data technologies.[34]

In a result of the introduction of mandatory measures for the collection and analysis of big data, we could obtain the following basic indicators that help to make marketing and managerial decisions:

- Brand awareness: How big the target audience is.
- Test drive: Opportunity to try the product before buying.

33 See Syrlybayeva, Zhadigerova, Zhumanova, 2019
34 See FranchiseLens, 2019

- Customer churn rate: How many customers leave?
- Customer Satisfaction Level.
- The share of attracted consumers: the number of visits online.
- Profit.
- Net present value, Internal Rate of Return, Payback Period, Return on investment in advertising
- Customer Lifetime Value.
- Transaction Conversion.
- Share of failures.
- Word of mouth, personal recommendations.

It is proposed to include these basic data-driven marketing indicators into the analysis to provide the franchisee by recommendations, as well on the use of specific tools, programs, and applications.

The process of using data-driven approach has a very important role at the global level, because it is a preparatory for the implementation of franchise integration, not only in developing, but also in backward markets. Developing markets are a great opportunity for global brands to find the best ways to reach backward ones. This scheme can be described as follows. First, global brands are a powerful driving force for local markets. This is a reference point for global trends, the development of the technological process, an increase in the level of qualification, and the development of local franchising. Local franchising companies are considered as a result and indicator of the success of global brands, whose role in this regard expands further than their own progress and leads to a strengthening of the economies of developing countries.

As the first stage is implemented, it is possible to assess the global brands' settling of developing markets and to work out bottlenecks for further work in backward markets. Specific markets in the developing world should be analyzed, grouped and anchored as a benchmark model to settle backward markets. Here, a data analysis system can be the key to the implementation of this scheme. Mastering backward markets should be expanded to include both global adapted brands and brands from developing countries. Thus, the above scheme can be considered as stepwise and strategically important for the world community as a whole.

Concerning the Kazakhstani market, it is not included into the rating of the most attractive regions due to the low population density, a large distance between cities. Today, Kazakhstan is a leader of the franchise sector in Central Asia, and it should be considered as strategic and potential for further development. Kazakhstan has already reached the largest brands, there is a rudimentary formation of local franchising, and this is the stage when it is necessary to introduce a data-driven marketing approach to optimize the activity of the entire franchise system and prepare a basic model for backward markets with similar specifics.

5 Conclusion

Based on the characteristics of scientific research data of franchise companies, this paper puts forward a direction for building a big data platform for Kazakhstani companies. It can push Kazakhstani companies to pay more attention to data-driven marketing, promote their value proposition to customers personally, and make marketing and managerial decisions. Data-driven marketing on the base of big data technologies will help to realize the collection, collation, processing and analysis of external and internal data resources, transform data into knowledge, provide services, product innovation, quality control, process optimization, service support and risk management and control, set the decision support system, and enhance the core competitiveness of staff.

The modern digital systems exist in a highly competitive environment. The only way to ensure that the marketing team is working effectively is to analyze big data, that is, implement data-driven marketing. Data based method increase productivity by attracting new customers and retaining old ones. Using customer-targeted campaigns allows drawing a full portrait of audience and producing better results.

Data-driven marketing refers to knowledge-based strategies, developed from analyzing big data to predict future behavior. Big data can improve customer relationships because they provide interactivity, multi-channel communication, personalization, and customization. Basic indicators help to make marketing and managerial decisions and data driven marketers can not only understand and predict customer behavior but also make informed strategic decisions.

Literature

Amado, A., Cortez, P., Rita, P., Moro, S. (2018). Research trends on Big Data in Marketing: A text mining and topic modeling based literature analysis. *European Research on Management and Business Economics, 24(1), doi: 10.1016/j.iedeen.2017.06.002*, pp. 1-7.

Anshari, M., et al. (2018). Customer relationship management and big data enabled: Personalization & customization of services. *Applied Computing and Informatics,* Retrieved from Applied Computing and Informatics, doi: 10.1016/j.aci.2018.05.004.

Aslanova, N. (2019). *Kazakhstan Marketing Conference 2018: Sovremennyj marketing neotdelim ot innovacij.* Retrieved 2.4.2019, from https://profit.kz/news/45293/KMC-2018-Sovremennij-marketing-neotdelim-ot-innovacij/

Benson, V., Kandasamy, B. (2019). *Making the Most of Big Data Manager's Guide to Business Intelligence Success.* Retrieved 2.4.2019, from https://bookboon.com/en/making-the-most-of-big-data-ebook

Christensen, C. (1997). *The innovator's dilemma. When new technologies cause great firms to fail.* Boston, USA: Harvard Business Review

Erevelles, S., Fukawa, N., Swayne, L. (2016). Big Data consumer analytics and the transformation of marketing. *Journal of Business Research, 69(2), doi: 10.1016/j.jbusres.2015.07.001*, pp. 897-904.

Fan, S., Lau, R., Zhao, J. (2015). Demystifying Big Data Analytics for Business Intelligence through the Lens of Marketing Mix. *Big Data Research, 2(1), doi: 10.1016/j.bdr.2015.02.006*, pp. 28-32.

Franchayzing v Kazakhstane. (2019). *BRIF Research Group BLOG - blog o marketingovykh issledovaniyakh. (in Russian)*. Retrieved 2.4.2019, from http://www.brif.kz/blog/?p=2370

FranchiseLens. (2019). *All about the Franchise Disclosure Document (FDD).* Retrieved 2.4.2019, from https://www.franchiselens.com/all-about-the-fdd

Galiyev, A. (2019). *Olesya Moskalevich. Dostyk Plaza: poka u vas net dannykh. vy budete prinimat nepravilnyye resheniya. (in Russian).* Retrieved 4.2.2019, from https://tinyurl.com/Galiyev-A

GOV. (2019). *Novosti.* Retrieved 2.4.2019, from https://business.gov.kz/ru/news/?FILTER_ID=15&SHOWALL_2=1

Johnson, S., Gray, P., Sarker, S. (2019). Revisiting IS research practice in the era of big data. *Information and Organization, 29(1), doi: 10.1016/j.infoandorg.2019.01.001*, pp. 41-56.

Karimova, M. (2013). Osobennosti razvitiya franchayzinga v malom biznese Kazakhstana. KazNU Bulletin. *Economics series. 4 (98), (in Russian)*, pp. 154-159.

Kisikov, B. (2019). *Nesmotrya na krizis, ry`nok ranchajzinga v RK v 2016 budet razvivat`sya. (in Russian).* Retrieved 2.4.2019, from https://forbes.kz/finances/markets/bolshoy_mak_i_podzemka_1/

Kun, W., Tong, L., Xiaodan, X. (2019). Application of Big Data Technology in Scientific Research Data Management of Military Enterprises. *Procedia Computer Science, 147, doi: 10.1016/j.procs.2019.01.221*, pp. 556-561.

Malhotra, N., Peterson, M., Kleiser, S. (1999). Marketing Research: A State-of-the-Art Review and Directions for the Twenty-First Century. *Journal of the Academy of Marketing Science, 27(2)*, pp. 160-183.

Merendino, A., Dibb, S., Meadows, M., Quinn, L., Wilson, D., Simkin, L., Canhoto, A. (2018). Big data, big decisions: The impact of big data on board level decision-making. *Journal of Business Research, 93, doi: 10.1016/j.jbusres.2018.08.029*, pp. 67-78.

Oussous, A., Benjelloun, F., Ait Lahcen, A., Belfkih, S. (2018). Big Data technologies: A survey. *Journal of King Saud University - Computer and Information Sciences, 30(4), doi: 10.1016/j.jksuci.2017.06.001*, pp. 431-448.

Sen D., Ozturk, M., Vayvay, O. (2016). An Overview of Big Data for Growth in SMEs. *Procedia - Social and Behavioral Sciences, 235, doi: 10.1016/j.sbspro.2016.11.011*, pp. 159-167.

Sheng, J., Amankwah-Amoah, J., Wang, X. (2017). A multidisciplinary perspective of big data in management research. *International Journal of Production Economics, 191, doi: 10.1016/j.ijpe.2017.06.006*, pp. 97-112.

Sivarajah, U., Kamal, M., Irani, Z., Weerakkody, V. (2017). Critical analysis of Big Data challenges and analytical methods. *Journal of Business Research, 70, doi: 10.1016/j.jbusres.2016.08.001*, pp. 263-286.

Smallbusiness. (2008). *Definition of Data Driven Market Research.* Retrieved 19.2.2019, from https://tinyurl.com/SME-DDMR

Syrlybayeva, N., Zhadigerova, O., Zhumanova, B. (2019). *Franchayzing kak novoye napravleniye razvitiya malogo predprinimatelstva v RK.* Retrieved 2.4.2019, from https://articlekz.com/article/20233

Torrecilla, J., Romo, J. (2018). Data learning from big data. *Statistics & Probability Letters, 136, doi: 10.1016/j.spl.2018.02.038*, pp. 15-19.

Verhoef, P., Kooge, E., Walk, N. (2016). *Creating Value with Big Data Analytics.* London: Taylor and Francis.

Wamba, S., Akter, S., Edwards, A., Chopin, G., Gnanzou, D. (2015). How 'big data' can make big impact: Findings from a systematic review and a longitudinal case study. *International Journal of Production Economics, 165, doi: 10.1016/j.ijpe.2014.12.031*, pp. 234-246.

Xu, Z., Frankwick, G., Ramirez, E. (2016). Effects of big data analytics and traditional marketing analytics on new product success: A knowledge fusion perspective. *Journal of Business Research, 69(5), doi: 10.1016/j.jbusres.2015.10.017*, pp. 1562-1566.

Modeling of the Value added Tax as a Budget-Forming Source

Ulanbek Moldokmatov

1 Introduction

Modelling of the tax to the added cost during the period 2008-2018, also it revealed factors influencing receipt of the tax to the added cost in the budget of the Kyrgyz Republic. Modeling tax revenues in the budget of the value added tax, which can be carried out by different methods, including using regression models, which allow to take into account the influence of one or several signs-factors. The methods of correlation-regression analysis allow, to a certain extent, to assess the influence of one or another accounted indicator-factor on the resultant feature and include it in the model (or exclude it).[1] As an initial hypothesis, it can be assumed that *the basis of coordinated tax relations* between the State Tax Service of the Kyrgyz Republic and taxpayers of all types at the macro and micro levels of the economy can be symmetrical, systematic and mutually beneficial activities based on the use of short-term forecasting and operational monitoring tax revenues in the republican budget.

2 Methodology

When building a model for the receipt of value-added tax (model No. 1), the following factors were selected as the factors forming the tax volumes (Y1 (i)), based on preliminary results of the logical-structural analysis of the taxation process, at the first stage of the simulation:

X1 (i) is the number of enterprises and organizations. Since enterprises, producing products, performing work and rendering services, produce value added, that is, the object of taxation of value added tax. It is assumed that the growth of their number in the region will not increase revenues of this tax to the regional budget.[2]

X2 (i) - accounts payable of enterprises. Its growth reduces the amount of value added tax amounts payable from the budget, thereby increasing the amount of payments to the republican budget.

---

1 See Dougherty, 2010
2 See Shmoylova, Minashkin, 2009, p. 29

H.-C. Brauweiler et al. (Hrsg.), *Digitalization and Industry 4.0: Economic and Societal Development*, https://doi.org/10.1007/978-3-658-27110-7_24

X3 (i) - accounts receivable of enterprises. Its increase is capable (when taking into account proceeds upon payment), on the contrary, to reduce the amount of value added tax paid to the republican budget.

X4 (i) is the average annual number of people employed in the country's economy; determines the composition of the labor resources involved in the production of goods and services subject to value added tax. The factor X4 (i) also characterizes the country's consumer inquiries since the burden of indirect taxa-tion is most often transferred to the shoulders of the employed population.

X5 (i) - Import; goods imported into the territory of the Kyrgyz Republic, with the exception of exempt supplies, are subject to value added tax in accordance with the instructions of the Tax Code of the Kyrgyz Republic, which significantly affects the increase in budget revenues.

X6 (i) - Turnover of inventories by type of economic activity; from the rapid turnover of inventories created a lot of deliveries, therefore, increase the income tax value added.

X7 (i) - rates of value added tax; rate change also affects the flow of payments to the budget.

X8 (i) is the registration threshold for value added tax; from this indicator depends on the number of tax payers who pay value added tax.

3 Results and Analysis

As an effective feature factor (Y1 (i)), we define the volume of value added tax that was transferred to the budget of the Kyrgyz Republic in the period 2008-2018. The initial data for the analysis were taken from the publications "Kyrgyzstan in figures"[3] and "Foreign trade of the Kyrgyz Republic".[4] The coef-ficients of the pair correlation of the statistical relationship, the selected signs-factors with the volume of the value-added tax are presented in table 1. It is advisable to include in the model only those factors for which either the correlation coefficient with the resultant attribute has the highest value, or whose connection is meaningfully flawless, but not assessed as highly as possible by the criterion of closeness.[5]

3 (Committee, National Statistical, 2018)
4 (Committee, National Statistical, 2018)
5 See Shmoylova, Minashkin, 2009

Table 1 shows the sign factor based on the pair correlation coefficient with the volume of value added tax, received by the budget of the Kyrgyz Re-public in the period 2008 – 2018.[6]

Considering that - 1 ≤ r ≤, when r <0, the relationship is inverse, when r> 0 - the relationship is direct. During the analysis, if the correlation coefficient | r (xi y) | ≥ 0.60, then the con-nection between the i-th factor and the resulting attribute is close, then this fac-tor influences the resultant mark and remains in the model.

Table 1: Sign factor based on the pair correlation

Indicators	Factors
X1(i)	0,938335
X2(i)	0,961859
X3(i)	0,950717
X4(i)	0,907442
X5(i)	0,986179
X6(i)	0,851473
X7(i)	-0,68259
X8(i)	0,833929

Table 2: Sign factor based on the pair correlation

	X2	X4	X5	X6	Y
X2	1				
X4	0,9227656	1			
X5	0,9521935	0,87533447	1		
X6	0,7859534	0,8555957	0,7777234	1	
y	0,9618589	0,90744236	0,98617887	0,851473	1

Determine the collinearity between the factors X2 and X4

1) | r (x2 x4) | ≤ | r (x2 y) | | 0.922 | <| 0.961 |

| r (x2 x4) | ≤ | r (x4 y) | | 0.922 | <| 0.907 |

In this case, the conditions are not met, we exclude X 2 - accounts payable factor

6 See Committee, National Statistical, 2018

2) | r (x2 x5) | ≤ | r (x2 y) | | 0.952 | <| 0.961 |

| r (x2 x5) | ≤ | r (x5 y) | | 0.952 | <| 0.986 |

conditions are met, both factors remain in the model.

3) | r (x2 x6) | ≤ | r (x2 y) | | 0.785 | <| 0.961 |

| r (x2 x6) | ≤ | r (x6 y) | | 0.785 | <| 0.851 |

conditions are met, both factors remain in the model.

For the following analysis, the model contains factors x4 - the average annual number of people employed in the country's economy, x5 - imports, x6 - inventory turnover by economic activity. The relationship between the volume of value added tax received by the budget of the Kyrgyz Republic - Y and X4 - the average annual number of people employed in the economy of the country, x5 - import, x6 - turnover of inventories by types of economic activity is closer.[7]

Table 3: Correlation Matrix

	X4	**X5**	**X6**	**y**
X4	1			
X5	0,8753345	1		
X6	0,8455957	0,7777234	1	
y	0,9074424	0,98617887	0,8514727	1

Determine the collinearity between factors X4 and X5

1) | r (x4 x5) | ≤ | r (x4 y) | | 0.875 | <| 0.907 |

| r (x4 x5) | ≤ | r (x5 y) | | 0.875 | <| 0.986 |

conditions are met, both factors remain in the model.

2) | r (x4 x6) | ≤ | r (x4 y) | | 0.845 | <| 0.907 |

| r (x4 x6) | ≤ | r (x6 y) | | 0.845 | <| 0.951 |

conditions are met, both factors remain in the model.

At the next stages of multifactor modeling, such signs-factors were used, which "explained" the taken into account (controlled) fluctuations of value-added tax income in sizes exceeding 50% of the total variation. Therefore, the choice of such a set of explanatory (independent) variables as the signs-factors of the regression model was more appropriate here: the average annual number of people

7 See n.n., 2008-2018

employed in the economy is X4 (i); import - X5 (i). and finally, inventory turnover by economic activity - X6 (i).

The economic-mathematical model applies the following form:

$$Y = A0 + B1X1 + B2X2 + B3X3$$

$$= 9864 + 1.336 * X4 + 0.072 * X5 + 2717.69 * X6$$

The relationship between the value added tax - Y and X4 - the average annual number of people employed in the economics, X5 - import and X6 - the turnover of inventories by economic activity is closer.

Table 4: Regression analysis results

	Coefficients	**Standard error**	**t- statistics**	**P- Value**
Value Added Tax	9864	3965,1	2,4876	0,0376
Average annual employment in the economics	1,3368233	2,61230351	0,51174118	0,622655
Import	0,0718172	0,0063244	11,35558	3,2606
Turnover of inventories by type of economic activity	2717,6945	915,460179	2,96866487	0,017908
Statistical parameters				
Multiple R	0,865447			
Coefficient R^2	0,748153			
Normalized R-squared	0,741509			
Observations	12			
Statistics of Durbin - Watson	1,96			

By t - Student's criterion, the regression coefficients a0, a1, a2 are significant, by Fisher's F criterion, the overall quality of the regression equation is signifi-cant, therefore, this model can be used to make practical decisions for forecasting.

According to figure 1 74.8% of the y-variation is explained by factors X4 - the average annual number of people employed in the economy, X5 - imports and X6 - the turnover of inventories by economic activity, 24.2% are explained by factors that are not included in the model.

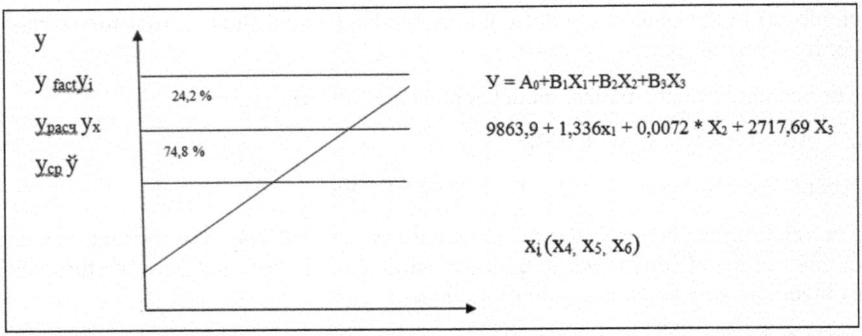

Figure 1: Estimation of the significance of the correlation coefficient and regression (Source: Committee, National Statistical, 2018)

Table 4 shows the results of the regression analysis, when evaluating the model for the receipt of value added tax with the inclusion of all factors. In this regression, as shown in table 4, the R2 coefficient is 0.72.

The most common method for determining autocorrelation is the Durbin – Watson test. Determined by the formula:

dW = ∑ (ei-ei-1) 2 / ∑ ei 2

dW = 6045300,22 / 3082619.96 = 1.96

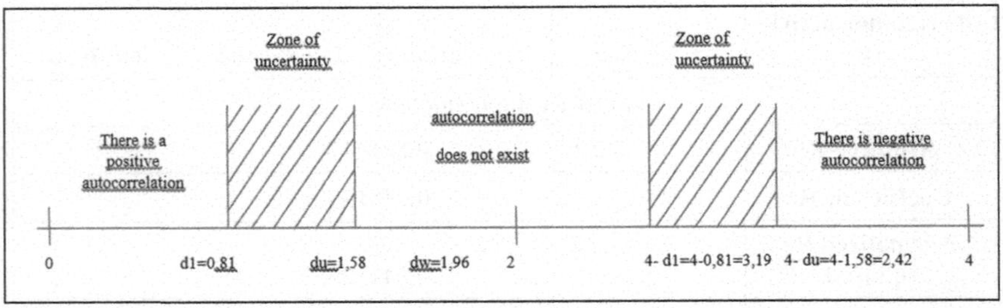

Figure 2: The Darbin-Watson test (Source: Shmoylova, Minashkin, 2009)

As shown in figure 2, the Durbin – Watson statistic is 1.96, that is, its value is between du and 4-du, from which it can be concluded that there is no autocorrelation in the model.

Indeed, it can be assumed that the average annual number of people employed in the country's economy determines the amount of labor resources involved in the production of goods and services subject to value added tax. On the other hand, it also characterizes the country's consumer inquiries, since the severity of the value added tax is most often transferred to the shoulders of the employed population;

accordingly, the greater the number of enterprises a country has, the higher the number of employed people in these enterprises.

Literature

Committee, National Statistical. (2018). *Kyrgyzstan in numbers.*

Dougherty, K. (2010). *Introduction to Econometrics.* Moscow: INFRA.

n.n. (2008-2018). *Finance of Enterprices of the Kyrgyz Republic.*

Shmoylova, V., Minashkin, R. (2009). Workshop on Theory of Statistics. *Finance and Statistics.*

Features of the development of organizational structures of large Russian state-owned companies (based on the example of SC «Roskosmos», SC «Rostekhnologii», SC «Rosatom»)

V. V. Kurchenkov, O. S. Makarenko, M. V. Kurchenkova, H.-Ch. Brauweiler

1 Introduction

State companies have a significant impact on the development of the Russian economy. Their activities are concentrated in strategically important and high-tech industries, where private business does not see the prospects for profit or is simply unable to function and develop a particular production because of the need for large financial investments or the laboriousness of the production process. The state-owned companies (SC) contribute to the development of high-tech industries (SC «Rostekhnologii»), provide national security (SC «Rosatom»), contribute to the growth of innovative potential, attract investment and commercialization of scientific development.

The special legal status of state companies is expressed in statements determined by current legislation. These are: significantly less control by public authorities, low requirements for disclosure of information about their activities, non-distribution of their insolvency (bankruptcy) law on their activities.

The creation of state companies is one of the elements of the policy of managing the state property of any country.[1] Any economic system has branches of economy controlled by the state. The institute of public companies is widely distributed in the US, Canada, Germany, Great Britain, Italy, India, Korea, and Japan as an instrument of modernization and industrialization of state economy. They were created in these states at different periods of time and in different conditions and sectors.[2]

In the Russian economy, at the moment, state companies have passed the stages of creation and formation and are in the process of their development. The purpose of creating of such companies is to support and develop those sectors of strategic importance where private business in the short and medium term does

1 See Kurchenkov, Brauweiler, Ponomareva, 2018; See Kurchenkov, Fetisova, Orlova, Gladkaya, 2017

2 See Brauweiler, 2002, p. 52 ff; See Brauweiler, 2017

H.-C. Brauweiler et al. (Hrsg.), *Digitalization and Industry 4.0: Economic and Societal Development*, https://doi.org/10.1007/978-3-658-27110-7_25

not see attractive opportunities for investing its funds and where the country's positions are steadily falling.

2 Analysis of the organizational structures of Russian state-owned companies «Roskosmos», «Rostekhnologii», «Rosatom»

The concept of «organizational management structure» in the scientific literature is marked by a great variety. Organizational structure is understood as an ordered set of bodies that manage production activities, and a set of relations arising between management in the management process. Also, organizational structure is «the logical interrelationships of the levels of management and functional areas constructed in such a form that allows achieving organization's goals».[3]

Organizational structure of management consists of the composition, correlation, location and interconnection of the individual subsystems of the organization. The formation of such a structure is focused on the distribution among individual units of the organization of rights and responsibilities.

Within organizational structure of management the management process takes place, between the participants of which the functions and management tasks are distributed. From this point, organizational structure of management is a form of division and cooperation of management activities, within the framework of which a managerial process is carried out, which is aimed at achieving certain objectives of the enterprise. Organizational structure of management includes all the objectives that are distributed among various elements, the coordination of their implementation is ensured by the links between them.[4]

Depending on the nature of the links, there are several main types of organizational management structures:

- linear;
- functional;
- linear-functional;
- divisional;
- matrix;
- free.

It should be noted that effectiveness of an organization´s work as a whole depends on correct choice of organizational structure, the correct location of functional elements such as departments, services etc. Thus, according to Henry

---

3 See Skobkin, 2009, p. 44
4 See Vesnin, 2013, p. 215

Mintzberg, "the elements of the structure should be selected in such a way that internal coherence or harmony is achieved and fundamental correspondence of the organizational situation - the size of the organization, its age, the type of environment in which it operates, the technical system usedetc. All these situational factors are often the matter of no less strict "choice" than the elements of the structure themselves".[5]

The larger the organization, the more complex its structure (that is, the work tasks are more specialized, the organizational units are more differentiated, the administrative component is more developed). In addition, the larger the organization, the larger is the average size of its organizational units. Obviously, by hiring more and more workers, the organization is forced to form new divisions and put new managers over them, and over them - other leaders. In other words, it complicates administrative hierarchy. State companies are just such organizations, that create the need for constant analysis of the existing organizational structure, identifying ineffective elements in it and subsequent optimization.

In the process of research of the activity of the institute of state-owned companies in the Russian Federation, we conducted analysis of the organizational structures of SCs «Roskosmos», «Rostekhnologii», «Rosatom», which have a complex management structure typical for large companies with a large volume of production and a high number of employees.

2.1 Analysis of the organizational structures of SC «Rosatom»

The analysis of the organizational structure of the state company «Rosatom», made it possible to conclude that this type of structure refers to the functional-project type of organizational structure. This conclusion was made on the basis of two main factors.

First, the element of the functional structure is clearly traced in the allocation of individual units, departments engaged in specialized activities. So, HR Department deals with issues of hiring, dissmissal of personnel and other functions related to the management of human resources.[6] Accounting, Information Technology Department, Documentation Support Department - contribute to the implementation of other individual functions and tasks of the company.[7] Functional management is carried out by a certain set of units specialized in the performance of specific types of work required to make decisions in the system of linear control. In the organizational structure of SC «Rosatom» there are various departments (Economy Management Division, Control Department, Development

5 Mintzberg, 1993
6 See Makarenko, 2016
7 See Mintzberg, 1993

Department, etc.), that once again confirms the existence of distribution of functions between the components of the general management structure of the company.

The main advantages of the functional management structure include:

- high competence of specialists responsible for the implementation of specific functions;
- release of line managers from solving of some special issues;
- standardization, formalization and programming of phenomena and processes;
- elimination of duplication and overlapping in the performance of management functions;
- reduction of the need for specialists of a wide profile.

However, there are drawbacks of this type of structure, including:

- excessive interest in the implementation of the goals and objectives of "their" units;
- difficulties in maintaining of permanent relationships between various functional services;
- the emergence of tendencies of excessive centralization;
- lengthy decision-making procedure;
- relatively rigid organizational form, responding to changes with difficulty.

Secondly, in the organizational structure of the organization under consideration, 7 project offices (for example, the project office "Development Projects", the project office of the "Radiation Technologies" program, etc.) are allocated, which allows us to speak about the presence of the element of the project organizational structure. These project departments have their structures, and project management includes: definition of its objectives, formation of the structure, planning and organization of work, coordination of the actions of performers. After having completed the project, its structure of the project disintegrates its components, employees go to a new project or are dismissed (if they worked on a contract basis).

In this regard, the advantages and disadvantages of the project management structure should be highlighted.

Advantages of the project management structure are:

- high flexibility;
- reduction in the number of management personnel in comparison with hierarchical structures.

Disadvantages of the project management structure are:

- very high qualification requirements, personal and business qualities of the project manager, who should not only manage all stages of the life cycle of the project, but also take into account the project site in the company's network;
- fragmentation of resources between projects;
- the complexity of interactions of a large number of projects in the company;
- complicating of the process of development of the organization as a whole.

2.2 Analysis of the organizational structures of SC «Rostekhnologii»

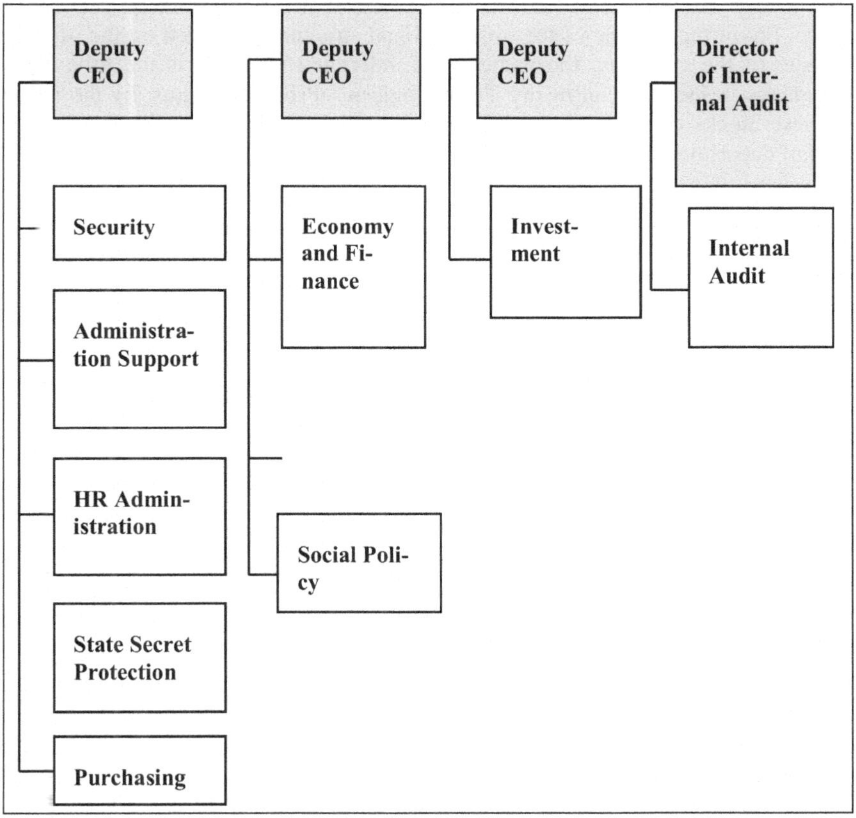

Figure 1: Fragment of the organizational structure of SC «Rostekhnologii»

Currently, SC «Rostekhnologii» includes 14 holding companies (integrated structures), formed according to the industry line (including aircraft, ammunition and special chemical industry, the conventional weapons industry, radio electronic industry) in the defense and civil industries, and also organizations of direct management. The total number of organizations of the company exceeds 700.[8]

Analysis of this structure allows us to conclude that there is a functional management structure with vertical and horizontal hierarchy of subordination. There are no elements of design, matrix or divisional organizational structures in this management structure. In contrast to the structure of SC «Rosatom», this structure has less units, which implies less management personnel, and, accordingly, less financial management costs. However, in the organizational structure of SC «Rostekhnologii» the names of individual structural elements are presented in such a way that it is not clear whether this element is a department, section or office. So, in the scheme of the organizational structure presented on the official website of the company, the name of its individual elements is the following: «Strategy», «Security», «Priority Technologies», «Protocol». Thus, by the name of these blocks of the organizational structure it is difficult to understand what kind of department or section it is and what its function is.

In general, organizational structure of the central office of the company under review is optimal in terms of its composition and elements, it does not reveal repeating or duplicating functions of individual units. However, there is a difference in the number of structural subdivisions subordinate to the Deputy CEO. Thus, in the submission of one Deputy there are five divisions and the other has only one.[9]

The management bodies of SC «Rostekhnologii» are: the Supervisory Council, the Board and CEO, who is appointed by the president of the Russian Federation.

The managerial staff of SC «Rostekhnologii» is represented in the following list:

1. CEO.
2. First Deputy CEO.
3. Deputies CEO (4 people).
4. Executive Director.
5. Chief of the CEO Staff.
6. Director of Internal Audit.
7. Director of Legal Support.
8. Managing Directors.
9. Industrial Directors.
10. Chief Accountant.
11. Executive Secretary.

---

8 See Rostec, 2015
9 See Figure 1

The staff presented in its list and number of managers fully correspond to the scale of the activities of the state-owned company.

According to CEO of SC «Rostekhnologii», Sergei Chemezov: "The new organizational structure will improve the management of the company, motivate staff, use the best market practices. The process of making managerial decisions will become even more transparent and understandable, which will increase the competitiveness of the company".[10]

2.3 Analysis of the organizational structures of SC «Roskosmos»

The structure of SC «Roskosmos», which is the latest state-owned company in Russia, also has its own peculiarities.[11]

In general, organizational structure of the SC under consideration has a functional form, where a clear division of authority over highly specialized functions is clearly visible, taking into account the maximum number of management personnel not more than 500 people.

By December 31, 2015, 35 structural subdivisions (departments, sections), the Scientific and Technical Council, management and control bodies were part of the central office of the SC «Roskosmos».

All structural divisions are formed into blocks managed by the CEO, First Deputy CEO, Managing Secretary - Deputy CEO, 8 Deputies CEO and 3 Executive Directors.

35 structural divisions contain:

- 8 structural subdivisions. subordinated directly to CEO of the company;
- 2 structural subdivisions that are subordinated directly to the First Deputy CEO of the company (the First Deputy CEO of the company also controls the activities of two Deputies CEO and one Executive Director);
- 2 structural subdivisions are subordinated directly to the Executive Secretary – the Deputy CEO of the company;
- 18 structural subdivisions, subordinated to the Deputy CEO of the company;
- 5 structural divisions, subordinated to the Executive Directors of the company.

The number of structural divisions and the structure of positions are formed in accordance with the standards of manageability adopted by the company. The total number of the company's personnel in 2015 was 139 thousand of people.

10 (Rostec, 2015)

11 See Roscosmos, n.d.

The management bodies of SC «Roskosmos» are the Company's Supervisory Council, the Company's CEO and the Board of the Company.[12]

It is important to note that there is a specialized department or unit responsible for strategic management issues in the organizational structures of the company. So in SC «Rosatom» this is Department of Strategic Management, in the structure of SC «Rostekhnologii» this is a separate Block of Strategy that has been singled out, which is represented by the Managing Director for Strategy and Department of Strategic Management and Innovative Development. The main function of these organizational structures is to work out development strategies that each operating company has. Development of long-term strategies covering a period of three to five years, the objectives of which should be defined in sufficient detail, is of great importance. Finally, another specific feature of the strategic management of state-owned company is the reflection of state interests in the process of forming corporate strategies, which is expressed in the development of priority industries and technologies.[13]

Thus, having considered the organizational structures of the three state companies, it can be concluded that they all have an element of the functional structure with the presence of clearly designated units for the performance of certain powers. The most complex and volumetric in terms of composition and number of units is the structure of SC «Rosatom». The SC «Roskosmos» has a less complex structure, but it also contains a large number of structural divisions and departments. As for the most optimal of all the structures examined, this is the structure of SC «Rostekhnologii», whose management carried out measures of optimizing organizational structure of corporate governance.

Organizational structure of any enterprise, whether it is a large company or a small business, plays an important role in the current activities of the organization, and affects the effectiveness of its work. Organizational structure of management is understood as a set of specialized functional units that are interrelated in the process of justification, development, adoption and implementation of managerial decisions. Graphically, it is most often depicted as a hierarchical diagram showing the composition, subordination and connections of the organizational units of the company.[14]

The ability of the organization to adapt to the changing conditions of the external environment depends on the choice of this or that type of organizational structure. The congestion of the structure or the presence of other kinds of shortcomings in it, such as the repeated functional powers of a number of departments or divisions

---

12 See Roscosmos, n.d.

13 See Makarenko, 2016, p. 130

14 See Businessstudio, n.d.

of the company, do not influence the successful operation of the company in the best way. Thus, the success and the final result of the work of the entire organization depends on the correct choice of the organizational structure with the optimal number of management units, functional units and other elements.

3 Proposals on optimization of the organizational structures of Russian state-owned companies «Roskosmos», «Rostechnologii», «Rosatom»

Analyzing organizational structures of the three state-owned companies «Rosatom», «Rostechnologii» and «Roskosmos», we will propose measures to optimize them. Thus, the functional and project management structure of SC «Rosatom» combines the advantages and disadvantages of the design and functional organizational structures. This combination provides a number of advantages, so the lack of flexibility and static functionality is balanced by a high ability to adapt and change its design elements. However, the analysis of the structure of the company revealed some shortcomings and peculiarities. Namely, in different blocks of the structure, there is a repetition of subdivisions of a general functional orientation. In particular, the structure has a HR Department in the block for the Nuclear Weapons Complex (NWC), as well as 3 divisions (HR Department, Personnel Department, Rewards and Staff Work Department) subordinated to the HR Director, who, too is engaged in personnel work. The specifics of these structural elements is very similar in content, and despite the large number of employees of the company (the average number of employees is 256.6 thousand people as of 2017[15]), it seems advisable to combine these divisions into two large ones.

3.1 Proposals on optimizing the structure of SC «Rosatom»

So, it is proposed to connect the HR Department from the NWC and the Personnel Department to a single service - Personnel Management, while reducing the number of employees or transferring them to other departments or project teams. This will also reduce the number of management personnel in these departments. The combination of HR Department with the Rewards and Staff Work Department in the Department of Personnel Policy and Work will also lead to similar results.

In addition, in the organizational structure of SC «Rosatom» there are two divisions with the same name - Department of Economics and Controlling. One of which is subordinated to the Director of Economics and Finance, and the other is subordinated to the Directorate for the Nucleard Weapons Complex. In our opin-

---

15 See Rosatom, 2015

ion, it is necessary to combine these two elements of the organizational structure into one subdivision.[16]

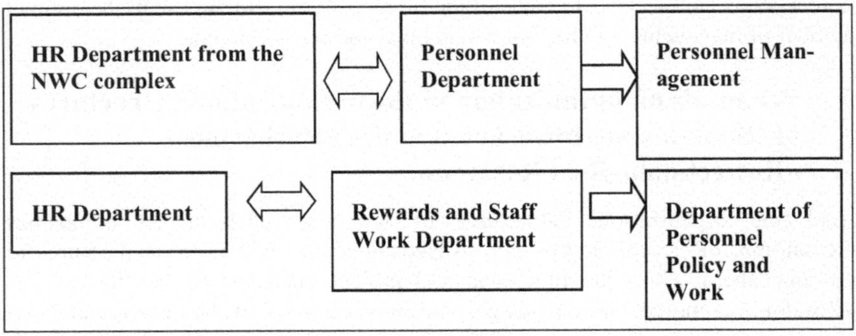

Figure 3: Proposals on optimizing the structure of SC «Rosatom»

3.2 Proposals on optimizing the structure of SC «Rostekhnologii»

The overall task of optimizing the organizational structure of SC «Rostekhnologii» is to reconstruct the internal structure of the company. Key changes in the optimization results should be:

1. Strengthening of shareholders' control in holding companies.
2. Decrease in the number of the central apparatus.
3. Transparency of the management system.

The approved organizational structure includes two levels of management: direct subordinates of the CEO and their functions. Organizational structure has become more modern: hierarchy levels have been reduced, as a result of which any document will be more quickly coordinated and reach the final destination faster. The competences that are strategically important for the company have been transferred to the central office and many similar functions are united within the framework of one management unit. Thus, the tasks of training, development, evaluation, recruitment and motivation of personnel, which used to be in different departments, now are carried out in the single organizational unit. Some processes, in particular, administrative and economic support, organization of exhibitions and IT, were completely transferred to specialized affiliated organizations. Some competencies of the central apparatus are expanded, in particular, control over the execution of programs for capital investments. Reducing the size of the central office should lead to the change in the management culture of the company: reducing bureaucracy and duplicating functions. The result of optimization of the

16 See Figure 3

organizational structure will be a compact company center. The proper distribution of powers will provide effective management decisions and respond to a rapidly changing situation.[17]

In accordance with the new organizational structure, an institute of Industrial Directors was created in 2015 - HR innovation, which requires the involvement of additional qualified personnel.[18]

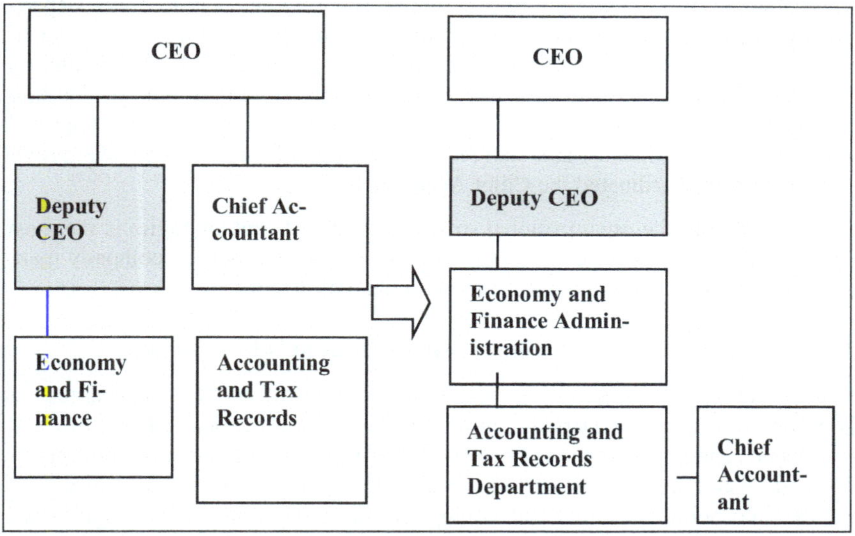

Figure 2: Proposals on optimizing the structure of the SC «Rostekhnologii»

These are the key tasks set for Industrial Directors:

- formation and development of competencies in industrial complexes;
- increase of capitalization and cost of assets, ensuring the growth of dividend flow;
- strategic marketing, development of markets and new directions for the holding companies of the company;
- control of the implementation of the Federal Target Programs.

Creation of the institute of Industrial Directors should also help coordination the product strategies of holdings, identify opportunities for synergy, in order to eliminate possible duplication of production.

[17] See Rostec, 2015
[18] See Kurchenkov, Brauweiler, Ponomareva, 2018

In 2015, the company experienced a planned optimization of personnel. Optimization program aimed at reducing such expense items as transportation services, maintenance of office space, consulting and services. In each holding, the reduction in the administrative and managerial apparatus will be carried out depending on the current structure of the population, since the share of management personnel optimal for the industry is 5-10%.

In addition, it is proposed to introduce the Accounting and Tax Records Department in the Economy and Finance Division, which will speed up the transfer of necessary information and increase the efficiency of their work. Subordination to one leader, represented by the Deputy CEO of the submitted units performing financial and accounting functions, will allow shortening the time for approval and signing of documents, and also reduce the burden from the CEO, who previously directly subordinated the Chief Accountant.[19]

Thus, in general, the organizational structure of SC «Rostekhnologii» is the most optimal of all the structures examined, thanks to the fact that the company management has already carried out the work on its optimization.

3.3 Proposals on optimizing the structure of SC «Roskosmos»

In the organizational structure of the central apparatus of the SC «Roskosmos», it is proposed to unite the Department of Accounting and Corporate Reporting and the Department of Pricing and Financial Control of Investments into one Department of Accounting and Financial Control. This department will also deal with issues of corporate reporting and pricing, but these functions are not highlighted in the name of the department itself, as it was before. In addition, it is also proposed to unite the Department of Economy and Budget Planning with the Treasury Department and create one Department of Economy and Treasury, which will also deal with budget planning issues.[20]

Thus, the proposed combination of the above structural elements will reduce the number of duplicated functions, reduce bureaucracy and accelerate the communication process between the units.

19 See Figure 2
20 See Figure 3

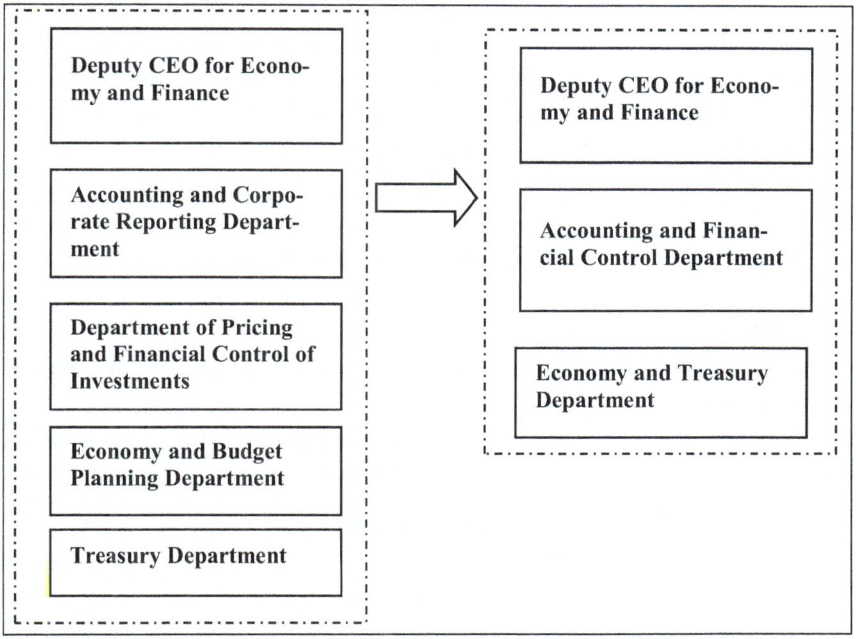

Figure 3: Proposals on optimizing the structure of SC «Roskosmos»

4 Conclusion

So, we summarize the proposals on optimization of organizational structures for the considered companies.

1. As part of the restructuring of the SC «Rosatom» it is proposed to combine four blocks dealing with issues of personnel management in two structural elements. Namely, the department of personnel management from the NWC and Personnel Department were united into a single service - Personnel Management. And Rewards and Personnel Work Department is to be combined with HR department into a single service - Department of Personnel Policy and Work. In addition, it is proposed to combine two offices with the same name into a single integrated management of personnel and controlling. These changes will help to eliminate duplicate functions of the merged departments, which will free up some of the financial and administrative resources. In addition, the time for coordination, interaction, transfer of information between previously existing elements of the structure will be reduced.

2. Optimization of the management structure of SC «Rostekhnologii» included the introduction of the Accounting and Tax Reporting Department in the Administration of Economy and Finance, as well as the specification of the name of all elements of the organizational structure with regard to the status of the division (department, division).
3. The proposals to improve the organizational structure of SC "Rosksmos" are connected with the merger of four departments under the Deputy CEO for Economy and Finance into two Departments: the Accounting and Financial Control Department and Economy and Treasury Department.

Literature

Brauweiler, H.-Ch. (2002). *Innovationen im peripheren Raum.* Wiesbaden: Gabler.

Brauweiler, H.-Ch. (2017) Internal Audit in a Multinational Perspective; Wroclaw University of Economics, Conference Proceedings, 2nd International Research Symposium: "Global Challenges of Management Control and Reporting", in: Research Papers of WUE, Wroclaw, S. 25 -32

Businessstudio. (n.d.). *Organizational management structure. "Business Modeling System".* Retrieved 1.3.2019, from http://www.businessstudio. ru/procedures/glossary/orgstructure

Eberbach, W., Brauweiler, H.-Ch. (1993). *Arbeitsrecht, Systematische Informationssysteme.* Oldenbourg/München.

Hoffmann, F., Brauweiler, H.-Ch., Wagner, R. (1995). *Computergestützte Informationssysteme.* Oldenbourg/München.

Kurchenkov, V., Brauweiler, H.-Ch., Ponomareva, L. (2018). *Formation of the estimation system of the innovative activity in the regions of South Russia. Proceedings of the International Scientific Conference "Competitive, Sustainable and Secure Development of the Regional Economy: Response to Global Challenges"* (Vol. 39). Amsterdam/Paris: Atlantic Press.

Kurchenkov, V., Fetisova, O., Orlova, A., Gladkaya, E. (2017). *The importance of the regions economic activity evaluation in Russia 2012-2016. Revista Galega de Economia.* (Vol. 26-3).

Makarenko, O. (2016). *Features of strategic management of state companies. Materials of the International Scientific and Practical Conference.* Sterlitamak: RIC AMI.

Mintzberg, H. (1993). *Structure in fives: Designing effective organizations.* Prentice-Hall, Inc.

Rosatum. (2015). *Annual report of SC "Rosatom" for 2015.* Retrieved 1.3.2019, from http://www.rosatom.ru/about/publichnaya-otchetnost/

Roscosmos. (n.d.). *Official site of the SC "Roskosmos".* Retrieved 1.3.2019, from http://www.roscosmos.ru/

Rostec. (2015). *Annual report of SC "Rostekhnologii" for 2015.* Retrieved 1.3.2019, from http://rostec.ru/content/files/documents/GODOVOY_OTCHET_2015.pdf

Skobkin, S. (2009). *Management in Tourism: textbook.* Master.

Strebel, H., Eifler, P., Brauweiler, H.-Ch., et al. (2003). *Umweltorientierung in betrieblichen Querschnittsbereichen, in: Internationales Umwelt-management.* Gabler.

Vesnin, V. (2013). *Fundamentals of management: textbook.* Prospekt.

Analysis of Current Kyrgyz Higher Education Based on Lean Principles

H.-Ch. Brauweiler, Zhyldyzbek Zhakshylykov

1 Challenges that Kyrgyz higher education faces

The Kyrgyz higher education system failed to compete with the entire world, except a few undeveloped countries. According to Webometrics ranking system, the world rank of the best university of the country is 4799. Yet, there is no single university in the Times Higher Education World University Rankings database. On the other hand, the country is facing several challenges that can be utilized as new opportunities to keep up with the world's accelerating higher education journey. Is this conception just a goodwill? Is it realistic to get rid of the traps that were put forward by Collier, Acemoglu[1], Robinson[2] et al.? Is it possible to make a real educational miracle? The answer is yes. If Japanese can, why can't we?[3]

Only last two years, the number of private kindergarten has increased from 27 to 297. This statistics shows that the law considering tax exemption, initiated in 2016 and issued in 2017, has triggered private sector to set new schools and kindergarten. The same regulation is being prepared by some parlament members for universities. According to Ministry of the Kyrgyz Republic, there are 32 public and 33 private higher education institutions. In the context of the country, it is expected that private universities enable to accelerate competitive climate for the higher education system. On the other hand, significant number of international donors, such as Erasmus projects, US state department, DAAD etc., are still active and investing in education through variety of mechanisms. Sure, contribution and positive effect of these initiations is indisputable. Furthermore, the current legal arrangements and government efforts against corruption can play an important role to reduce the rate of corruption in universities. In fact, corruption exists in all fields of daily life in Kyrgyzstan. The most occured corruption type in Kyrgyz universities is bribery.[4] In addition, the higher education is suffering from inefficient management and unorganized educational processes. In this study, the Kyrgyz higher education system is analyzed mainly based on the latter challenge mentioned above from the aspect of lean principles.

---

1 Author of the book 'Why nations fail'.
2 Author of the book 'The bottom billion'.
3 Americans widely viewed the NBC documentary: 'If Japanese Can, Why Can't We', June 24 1980.
4 See Nurmanbetova, 2012

H.-C. Brauweiler et al. (Hrsg.), *Digitalization and Industry 4.0: Economic and Societal Development*, https://doi.org/10.1007/978-3-658-27110-7_26

The lean principles were derived from so called Toyota Production System. They are two: continuous improvement and respect for people. These principles consider to focus on process instead of people; to harm nobody while making improvements.

1.1 Inefficient process management in higher education

1.1.1 Improving course quality

After the Soviet Union collapse, the Kyrgyz higher education could not improve courses‘ quality in align with the market demand. Even state standards set for courses were far from the market's reality. In honest, there were very limited successful cases funded by international projects such as Tempus, Erasmus plus etc. Meanwhile, progressive applications for imroving courses were taking place outside. For instance, in the United States, course improvement by applying lean principles and practices was performed at the Rensselaer Polytechnic Institute.

The application of lean principles to the design and delivery of a business course on leadership was implemented. The objectives were to improve consistency between what was taught in the course and how the course was taught, eliminate waste, improve the quality and relevance of course materials, and deliver greater value as perceived by students.[5] Results indicated higher level of student satisfaction, less ambiguity regarding lectures, better management of students‘ time etc. Moreover, Kaizen process was used for ten master degree program courses. In findings of that study, Kaizen was an effective process for improving the value proposition for students. Kaizen could enable Kyrgyz universities compete more effectively against both traditional not-profit and newer for-profit sources of higher education.

The core value providing process in university is teaching. Lean teaching is the application of lean principles and practices to teaching.[6] Lean practices are the tools and methods commonly associated with the Toyota production system[7], while lean principles are continuous process improvement and respect for people. Two surveys conducted by Emiliani show that teaching process contain many types of mistakes. According to these surveys, there is a gap between students‘ perceptions of quality and value and the traditional teaching process delivers. The question is: who is responsible for efforts to improve teaching? The author indicates the importance of faculty engagement as a shared responsibility, while emphasizing that bottom-up approach has less chance than top-down approach urging leadership.

---

5 See Emiliani, 2004

6 See Emiliani, 2013

7 See Monden, 1983; See Ohno, 1988; See Womack, Jones, Roos, 1990

Emiliani's papers[8] show that there is much can be done to improve teaching processes through application of lean principles and practices. It is urgent because of the competition. In addition to competition from existing universities, top managers face new venture capital based startups who believe they can teach better than universities teach. As it is taken seriously by forward-thinking universities, their potential is said to be real and strong. Under these circumstances, Kyrgyz universities may have competitive advantage via successful application of these principles and becoming lean universities.

1.1.2 Improving the education system

A system consists of interacted and interrelated processes having the same goal as the system has. According to this definition, the main processes of the Kyrgyz education system are teaching process, education process, advisory process etc. In this context, it is expected that the process should be improved in never ending cycle. As it is stated previously, inefficient process management is a clear problem of Kyrgyz higher education system. We do not see proper mechanisms, procedures, and instructions that ensure continuous process improvement in the system.[9] However, there are a lot of western studies on lean transformation model for the education system that can be implemented as a good example to establish sustainable process improvement.[10]

According to Steve Yorkstone, who conducted a case study on lean implementation at the university of St Andrews, many universities are pursuing lean thinking. The first evidence of lean initiatives begins in universities in the United States in the early 2000s.[11] The author gives Waterloo University in Canada as an example of transformative power for individuals, businesses, and economies. That, in turn, plays an important role generating 18 billion Canadian dollars in technology sector revenue having great impact on their regions. Alternative early models focused on a limited facilitators who train staff in lean techniques and support them through improvement projects. This approach was seen notably at Cardiff University in United Kingdom. The university of St Andrews founded its lean team in 2006. This was one of the successful lean intervention in higher education. Still today, the unversity continues to practice lean and is supporting other universities in the United Kingdom and worldwide.[12]

---

8 See Emiliani, 2004; See Emiliani, 2005; See Emiliani, 2007; See Emiliani, 2013
9 See Zhakshylykov, 2016
10 See Alp, 2001; See Yorkston, 2016
11 See Yorkston, 2016
12 See Yorkston, 2016

1.1.3 Lean universities

Lean universities implement lean principles: continuous process improvement and respect for people.[13] In many lean applications in universities, we see the non-zero-sum (win win) aspects of lean activity being applied to increase value propositions for students and research outcomes. There are 65 higher education institutions in the Kyrgyz Republic. They are so far from being lean universities. They are currently struggling with inconsistent educational content, lack of vision and mission, lack of leadership, over controlling by the Ministry, corruption, significant number of brain drain, financial shortage etc.[14] The authors of this paper think that all these problems would not have been or at least would have been minimized if only universities would be lean. In other words, if universities pursue to improve their processes continously, those problems would have been detected and prevented on time.

Besides, for many years, the respect for people principle has been understood more narrowly as cooperation, between administration and labor. However, today's managers are aware of that the continuous improvement principle is not applicable without the respect for people principle. On the other hand, still, it is obvious from managers‘ attitudes, common business performance metrics, organizations policies, decision makers behaviours, and even corporate strategy, that they do not understand yet. This principle's context can be better represented by the Toyota definition to express it: respect for stakeholders in a narrow context[15] and humanity in a larger context.[16] It is also great challenge that can be utilized as an opportunity for Kyrgyz universities, as this phenomenon is still common for all.

1.2 Private sector initiatives and competition between universities

Only two of the top five universities in the Kyrgyz Republic are public.[17] It is a strong evidence that private universities have better chance to compete internationally. The other three universities were established by United States, Russia, and Turkey through bilateral agreements. There are also financially strong, well equipped private universities that show better positions.

Recently[18], the newly assigned minister was about to initiate to minimize the number of universities that the authors disagree with. A larger number of univer-

---

13 See Ohno, 1988; See Womack, Jones, Roos, 1990
14 See Zhakshylykov, 2016
15 See Toyota, 2001
16 Blog posting by Jon Miller, Exploring the respect for people of the Toyota way, 2008
17 See Top Universities., 2019
18 Minister's official interview to Maral FM, September 2019.

sities gives only positive impulse to higher education system rather than causing education quality decline as is mentioned in the interview. The Kyrgyz Republic should not make this historical mistake. In fact, we see a lot of successful stories[19] where private sector is encouraged to set universities and to trigger competitive environment.

The primary and secondary education system has already some successes right after the tax exemption decree issued in 2017. In two years, a lot of successful, innovative schools have been established: such as Refal, Abiturient, Bilim Kenchi, Prioritet, Sezimtal, set of schools Bilimkana, Aktilek, Akyltai etc. The same impulse could be given to higher education area in order to launch new universities instead of lessening them.

1.3 International projects integrate the higher education

The international projects have vital role in Kyrgyz higher education. Many transformations[20] were realized under these projects' recommendations: implementation of Bologna process requirements; development of innovative curriculum; establishment of quality assurance bodies; forming a climate for innovations and startups etc. On the other hand, the education system cannot benefit from reported outputs and outcomes of the projects as desired. The final reports of these projects do not meet the expectations and requirements set prior to their launch all the time. A few reasons exist.

First, disorganized management of projects is taking place. No single database of projects where anyone can reach and obtain an information. Second, the Ministry has no long term vision to integrate, sustain, and benefit from these projects.Third, unfortunately, a narrow exclusive group of people control most of these international project channels. Inclusive administration[21] of Ministry of Education and Science of the Kyrgyz Republic could be one of the solutions.

1.4 Government's will and anti-corruption measures

A very strong political will is needed in combating corruption in making the educational policies to be effective. Today, we tend to believe that the top management of the country has this political will and power, as the former president, many prime ministers, members of government are behind bars or in custody for their corruptive actions. It has never happened before in the history of this country. This fact tells and giving hope to us that the following circumstances may take place: strict stable legislative base will be provided; this base will ensure that

[19] USA, India, Turkey, Japan, China, France etc.

[20] Tempus, Erasmus Plus, Asian Development Bank projects.

[21] See Acemoglu, Robinson, 2012

students are not afraid of reporting about bribery; public will be much aware of newly adopted policies; laws will be properly implemented; strict punishments will be imposed or will be taken preventive actions; professors' salaries will be increased and it will decrease the level of bribery; both students and professors will understand and practice academic honesty.[22]

2 Advised lean transformation model for Kyrgyz universities

Purpose of lean transformation in universities is to evolve the application of lean principles and practices to the process of teaching, in time, to other processes, consequently to ensure students satisfaction. Kyrgyz universities are strongly recommended to realize it in order to become competitive. In this section, we will advise a sample transformation model to apply lean principles and practices at universities.

Currently, Kyrgyz higher education is under increasing financial pressure due to rapid declines in enrollment, inefficient operating costs, and cuts both in international organizations and goverment funds. Usually, university management increase tuition fees and layoff faculty to struggle with this pressure. However, we do not see increase in value propositions for students or payers, parallel to these measures. In western universities, some leaders are seeking an intellectual response to this problem by adopting lean principles, though this has been limited mainly to administrative processes. Core academic processes remain untouched.[23] Kyrgyz universities should be careful of being in this trap while initiating to lean transformation. They need to start from teaching process first, and then proceed to other supporting processes step by step: research, new program development, academic advising, academic assessment, new course development, review board, academic integrity, promotion and tenure etc.

On the other hand, lack of leadership is unfortunate in Kyrgyz universities. It will lead to unwillingness to engage faculty in academic processes so that interested people are left to demonstrate their own efforts to achieve what is wanted. In order to engage faculty better, rewards may exist such as new opportunities, higher pay etc.[24] But, it is important to have also intrinsic (usually monetary and right after the improvement) rewards to motivate the pursuit of process improvement effectively.

In the discipline of process improvement, a process is not considered to be improved if the number of steps in a process is reduced but costs remain the same

---

22 See Nurmanbetova, 2012

23 See Balzer, 2010; See Doman, 2011; See Waterbury, 2011; See Svensson, Antony, Ba-Essa, Bakhsh, Albliwi, 2015; See Sunder, 2016

24 See Emiliani, 2016

(or if cost go down but quality is worse). This is called *kairyo* in Japanese, which means improvement on a single dimension.[25] But, according to the *kaizen,* a process should be improved across multiple aspects, while harming nobody during its improvement.[26] Kyrgyz university leaders must understand that adoption of lean principles requires all faculty members involvement. As Edwards Deming said in his list of 14 steps, the transformation is everybody's job.

Literature

Acemoglu, D., Robinson, J. (2012). *Why nations fail: The origins of power, prosperity, and poverty.* Crown Books.

Alp, N. (2001). *The lean transformation model for the education system.* Chattanooga: The university of Tennessee.

Balzer, W. (2010). *Lean Higher Education: Increasing the values and performance of university processes.* Boca Raton: CRC Press.

Brauweiler, H.-Ch. (2017). Erwartungen an moderne Bildung und Universitäten: Notwendigkeit des lebenslangen Lernens und der akademischen Fortbildung. *Vestnik / Science Journal of Volgograd State University, Vol 19 No. 4*, pp. 40-44.

Doman, M. (2011). A New Lean Paradigm in Higher Education: A Case Study. *Quality Assurance in Education, Vol. 19, Is. 3*, pp. 248-262.

Emiliani, B. (2004). Improving business school courses by applying lean principles and practices. *Quality Assurance in Education, Vol. 12 No. 4*, pp. 175-187.

Emiliani, B. (2005). Using Kaizen to improve graduate business school degree programs. *Quality Assurance in Education, Vol. 13, No. 1*, pp. 37-52.

Emiliani, B. (2007). Real Lean: Understanding the lean management system. *The CLBM. Vol. 1.*

Emiliani, B. (2013). *The lean professor: Become a better teacher using lean principles and practices.* Wethersfield: The CLBM.

Emiliani, M. (2016). *Evolution in Lean Teaching.* Retrieved 4.4.2019, from https://tinyurl.com/Emiliani2016

Kato, I., Smalley, A. (2011). *Toyota Kaizen Methods: Six Steps to Improvement.* Boca Raton: CRC Press.

[25] See Emiliani, 2016

[26] See Kato, Smalley, 2011; See Wood, Herscher, Emiliani, 2015

Klenner, M., Grimm, F., Brauweiler, H.-Ch. (2017). Flipped Classroom Educational Methods in International Distant Learning Projects. *International Conference on Education, Dep. of Education, Shyama Prasad Mukherji College, Delhi University.*

Monden, Y. (1983). *Toyota Production System. An Integrated Approach to Just-In-Time.* Springer.

Nurmanbetova, K. (2012). Policies to Combat Corruption in Kyrgyzstan: The Case of Higher Education. Budapest: Central European University. Departement of Public Policy.

Ohno, T. (1988). *Toyota Production System. Productivity press.* Portland

Sunder, M. (2016). Lean Six Sigma in Higher Education Institutions. *International Journal of Quality and Service Science, Vol. 8, Issue 2.*

Svensson, C., et al. (2015). A Lean Six Sigma Program in Higher Education. *International Journal of Quality & Reliability Management, Vol. 32, Issue 9*, pp. 951-969.

Top Universities. (2019). *5 universities.* Retrieved 4.4.2019, from https://tinyurl.com/topunis20

Toyota. (2001). *The Toyota Way. Internal document. Toyota Motor Corporation.* Toyota.

Waterbury, T. (2011). *Educational Lean for Higher Education: Theory and Practice.*

Womack, J., Jones, D., Roos, D. (1990). *The Machine that Changed the World.* New York: Rawson Associates.

Wood, R., Herscher, M., Emiliani, B. (2015). *Shingijutsu-Kaizen: The Art of Discovery and Learning.* Wethersfield: The CLBM.

Yorkston, J. (2016). *Three Craws.*

Zhakshylykov, Z. (2016). Science education: New competences, development prospects and teaching methods. *Research Journal of Pharmaceutical, Biological and Chemical Sciences*, pp. 617-620.

Mapping and Assessment of the Results on Radioecological Monitoring of the Territories in the Absheron Peninsula of Azerbaijan

Gudrat G. Mamedov, Mahamadali A. Ramazanov, Afet A. Mehdiyeva, Jalal A. Naghiyev

1 Introduction

The replacement of all paper-based data to multifunctional electron database is the demand of current time. The special software with a wide arsenal of possibilities are used for realization of this purpose, so huge flow of information coming from various sources, requires the development and implementation of innovative technologies for their operational processing.

The modern science is provided with ultrahigh technologies with a nanoaccuracy, automatic and remote methods of obtaining information, robotization of processes for replacement of the human in remote and dangerous zones, satellite telecommunication, space images of various scale, etc. These achievements simplify a research process, replace mechanical methods of receiving and processing of information, considerably increase quality and accuracy of the received results.

However such intensive rates of technology development and neglect of the environmental standards often lead to adverse and sometimes pernicious consequences for the environment. Each inhabitant of the planet has to use Earth resources sparingly, because it is the main condition of life existence.

Environmental problems of the present time according their scales conditionally are divided to global, regional and local. For the solution each of them the corresponding human and technical potential is involved.

One of the primary ecological problems of modernity is control of a radioecological situation on the Earth and estimation of a real ecological situation, which are possible on the basis of the integrated solutions at the junction of sciences with involving of scientists from different countries. The complexity of the radioecological problem on localization radiation within single country is connected with distribution of dangerous radioactive particles to neighbouring countries by means of wind or water sources.

The real sources of the invisible and the life-threatening radiation distribution possible to detect only by comprehensive studying of a radiation situation of environment. Combination of ground and remote methods allow to promptly

H.-C. Brauweiler et al. (Hrsg.), *Digitalization and Industry 4.0: Economic and Societal Development*, https://doi.org/10.1007/978-3-658-27110-7_27

obtain the reliable information about the Earth's surface objects and processes occurring in the atmosphere, on the land and in the ocean.

2 The purpose and objects of research

The purpose of our investigations was a study of the radiation environment in the Absheron Peninsula of Azerbaijan, where the most oil and gas deposits and enterprises on their production and processing are concentrated. The country's oil industry history has very deep roots.[1] According to ancient historians the oil was exported from Azerbaijan to other countries as early as the 3rd – 4th centuries.

Azerbaijan is known in the world as a country of rich hydrocarbon reserves with a history of the oil industry of 150 years. However only after obtaining of the independence in 1991 the Azerbaijan people have got an possibility to dispose by own natural resources independently.

Specialists of Azerbaijan have added pages of innovative experience to history of world oil and gas production. First in the world, oil was produced by industrial method at the Bibiheybat field (1846), and also in the first time oil was extracted in the high sea (offshore) at the Neft Dashlari field (1949). Azerbaijan to had the highest in the world on oil extracting and processing and gave half of the world oil production in 1899.[2]

Today, the oil industry of Azerbaijan has a wide infrastructure, and the country is becoming a major producer and exporter of hydrocarbon resources.[3]

However the countries which are rich in natural resources are faced with the negative side of this wealth.[4] Intensive oil and gas extraction in Azerbaijan and merciless their using for providing of energy needs of the united Soviet country has brought to the forefront the problem of preventing in technogenic consequences of developed industry.

Despite the improvement in technologies for extraction and processing of natural resources, there are a lot of facts of oil-polluted lakes and swamps, the abandoned obsolete equipment and pipes on the territory, etc. Sometimes these radiation sources are located very close to residential areas. Therefore, Absheron as an important industrial region of Azerbaijan has serious ecological problems which were accumulated during the centuries. Most of them are the results of the environmental pollution by various industrial wastes needing urgent purification.

---

1 See Mir-Babayev, 2007; See n.n., 2009
2 See Zeynalova, 2014
3 See n.n., 2019
4 See Strebel, Eifler, Brauweiler, et al., 2003

Growing interest of world oil companies and foreign investors to the republic natural resources leads to the increasing of volume in the oil and gas extraction and also in their processing. In this connection, the government of the Azerbaijan supports the fundamental programs and research projects on assessment of radio-ecological situation of the Absheron and cleaning the contaminated areas. Many of these projects are implemented under scientific and financial cooperation with international organizations and funds.[5]

The Project named "Radio-ecological investigations of soils around Baku of Absheron Peninsula" has been executed (01.02.2009-02.02.2012) by Baku State University (*BSU*) within these programs by support of the *Science and Technology Center in Ukraine* (*STCU*) and financed by the *Canadian Government (Department of Foreign Affairs and International Trade (DFAIT), G8 Global Partnership Program)*. The main mission of the Project was a radioecological investigation of the soils, surface waters and marshy areas in the vicinity of Baku to identify the sources of radiation, determining their radionuclide composition and parameters, as well as the assessment of radioecological impact of this type of pollution.

The regions located around of Baku on 10 directions from BSU were selected as objects of study: Binagadi, Pirallakhi, Lokbatan, Balakhani, Azizbayev (new name Khazar), Surakhani, Gourd Gapisi, Mashtaga, and also two routes in the direction of the administrative districts of the Republic - to Shamakhi (the west direction from the capital) and Guba (the north direction from the capital).

3 Scientific and experimental basis of the research

As a result of all processes associated with oil and gas (exploration, production, refining, transportation, etc.) the environment is polluted by radioactive waste, composition of which contains the sources of α, β and γ radioactive emissions being harmful for living organisms.

The groundwater pumped with the oil on the Earth surface contains naturally occurring radionuclides ^{238}U and ^{232}Th, and also radium isotopes ^{226}Ra, ^{228}Ra, ^{224}Ra. In addition, groundwater dissolves calcium (*Ca*), strontium (*Sr*), barium (*Ba*) and radium (*Ra*), which are present in the oil layer. As a result of sedimentation and accumulation these isotopes and their decay products are found in huge quantity as sediment in the water, in the bottom sediments, in the soils of oil-producing areas, on the outmoded equipment, in the bottom of channels. Such sources of harmful radiation increase the gamma background of territory. Distributed by wind the radon ^{222}Rn and thorium ^{220}Rn (decay product of radium) gases

5 See World Bank, 2008

penetrate by airway into the organism of employees and local population, becoming a source of internal radiation.

Therefore, scientists in Azerbaijan with ancient history of the oil industry always paid a special attention to study of radionuclide contamination of soil, water and air.[6]

4 Methodology of research

According to long-term studies of the Absheron Peninsula soils for the radiological isotopes presence into them[7] it is possible to analyse the dynamics of arrival and accumulation of radionuclides and their decay products in the different depths of soils, and also to identify regularity of their detecting, to provide statistics on the sources of these contaminations.[8]

Methodology of our researches was based on dosimetric and spectrometric studies and it included the following steps:

- The field dosimetric investigations (dosimeters-radiometers *MKC-AT1125*, *MKC-AT1125A* with scintillation detector *NaI(*Tl)*; radiometer *PPA-01M-01*) on selected routes and a sampling of soil and swampy areas (with higher and normal background radiation) with the registration of their geographical coordinates (Geographical Positioning Systems (*GPS*) of series *eTrex Legend Cx, Garmin AB*) for further analysis;
- The spectrometric investigations (gamma spectrometers "*Progress-2000*" (calibration using standard sources of ^{137}Cs and ^{40}K) and with detector *HPGe* (calibration using isotopes ^{241}Am, ^{137}Cs and ^{60}Co) of samples in the laboratory to identify the sources of ionizing radiation and also to determine their radionuclide composition and radio-ecological parameters (effective activity, the nature of gamma radiation);
- Creation of a dynamic electron digital database of spatial information for radio-ecological parameters of investigated areas, reflecting the level and distribution of radiation.

5 Experimental research

The created database on the Absheron region was added after each field measurements. Using the *Map Source* (*Garmin*) software the routes and the coordinates of measuring points, fixed by *GPS* during field investigations, were transferred to a computer. The electron map of the measurements was generated on

---

6 See Kahramanova, 2012; See World Bank, 2008; See Zeynalova, 2014

7 See Akhmedov, 1986; See Kahramanova, 2012; See Mamedov, et al., 2010

8 See n.n., 2003

their basis, the points and routes were reflected by conventional signs, and the lengths of these routes were calculated. The *BSU* (Baku) was conditionally accepted as a starting point of the measurements routes.

Test samples of soils and marshy areas were taken at the different time of day, in the different weather conditions, from the surface and different depths (80-250 mm) of soils, from points with higher and normal values of background radiation. Field notes of researchers about the peculiarities in the territories of measuring have been used as additional descriptive information in the analysis of experimental data.

The results of dosimetric measurements were analyzed, systematized and mapped.[9] Minimal and maximal values of *Exposure Dose Rate* (*EDR*) for research areas were summarized in table 1.

Experimental researches have shown that the dosimeter readings in some areas were much higher (sometimes 2-3 orders of magnitude) than the background values permissible for the region (5-7 *μR/h*). The geographic coordinates of these areas were fixed by *GPS*.

Table 1: The dose characteristics of the studied areas

№	Route	EDR, μR/h		№	Route	EDR, μR/h	
		min	max			min	max
1.	Baku - Lokbatan	1.7	187.0	6.	Baku - Balakhani	2.5	8.8
2.	Baku - Gourd Gapisi	2.2	7.8	7.	Baku - Mashtaga	2.9	8.5
3.	Baku - Shamakhi	2.5	14.5	8.	Baku - Azizbayev	2.4	37.5
4.	Baku - Guba	2.7	5.8	9.	Baku - Surakhani	31.0	825.0
5.	Baku - Binagadi	2.5	15.0	10.	Baku - Pirallakhi	2.0	4.7

Territories located along the routes indicated in the table 2 are the most polluted by γ radioactive sources.

[9]See Vandergraaf, et al., n.d.

Table 2: Territories with higher EDR values

Baku - Surakhani (abandoned iodine plants)				**Baku - Lokbatan**	
Ramani settlement		Surakhani settlement		Bibiheybat settlement	
1450 $\mu R/h$	459 $\mu R/h$	825 $\mu R/h$	700 $\mu R/h$	187 $\mu R/h$	140 $\mu R/h$

The territories of the soviet period iodine plants at the Ramani and Surakhani settlements have been investigated more thoroughly[10] because the serious ecological problems of these activity still are a threat for the local population even after the cease of the functioning in the plants many years ago. Huge quantity of the waste activated charcoal used for industrial production of iodine is discharged to the territories of these abandoned plants.

a) b)

Figure 1: The measurings on the territory of Ramani plant (a) and object with coordinates N40°26'43,0"; E49°57'51,7", where EDR = 1450 μR/h (b)

For research of radioactive elements migration in territories of these plants the values of *EDR* have been measured in various points of the territory[11] and samples from a surface and from different depths of a coal dump have been taken. One area in the Ramani settlement was investigated with a special attention and is labelled as *M41*.[12] This area is a place of the separator where groundwater accumulated during functioning of a former iodine plant. On the surface of this area the value of *EDR* was detected up to 1450 $\mu R/h$. The results of spectrometric analysis of the samples taken from bottom of separator detected the presence of radioactive sources as ^{235}U, ^{238}U, ^{232}Th, ^{226}Ra, ^{40}K as well as their daughter products - ^{222}Rn и ^{220}Rn gases.

10 See Mamedov, et al., 2010; See n.n., n.d.; See Vandergraaf, et al., 2013; See Vandergraaf, et al., n.d.

11 See Figure 1a

12 See Figure 2b

Findings on Ramani plant also were generated by using the software *Surfer-7* (*Golden Software, Inc. Golden, CO, USA*). To do this, the tabulated values of latitude and longitude on the settlement were converted from the degree format to decimal format. In the figure 2 clearly are distinguished points with higher values of the *EDR*, especially a point *M41* = 1450 *μR/h*.

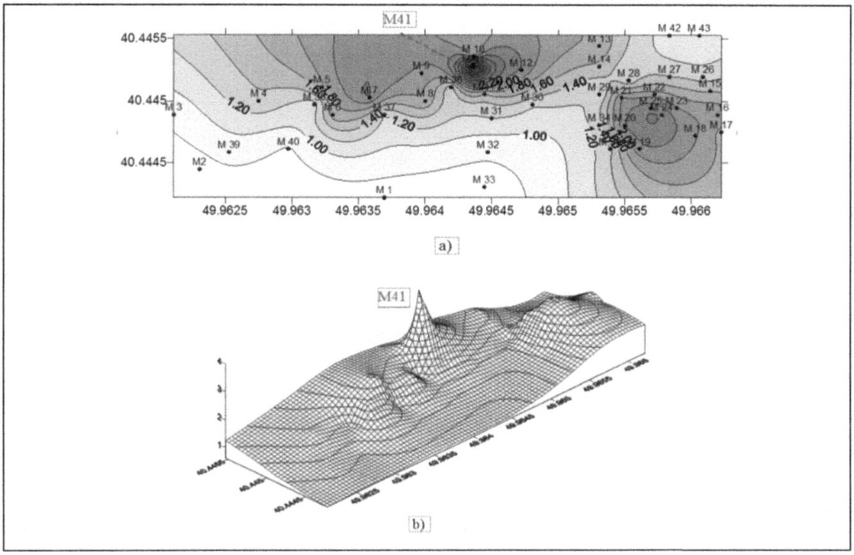

Figure 2: Distribution Plots for Ramani plant including all data, plotting the logarithm of the survey readings: Contour (a); Wire-frame (three-dimensional) (b)

On the basis of laboratory investigations (error was not more than 10%) of soil samples for all 10 routes were analysed[13], prepared by a special technology from the taken samples[14], the radionuclide composition was determined, the activity (A_{eff}) and emission energy of the detected γ-sources were calculated.[15]

In recent years the series ecological legislations and long-term programs on rehabilitation of ecological situation on the Absheron Peninsula have been adopted in the Republic. On the basis of this the nature-conservative measures have been developed and the clearance of radioactive waste in Surakhani and Ramani settlements has been started. Most of these areas were cleared from dangerous pollutants already.[16]

---

13 See Figure 3
14 See Mamedov, et al., 2010
15 See Table 2; See n.n., n.d.; See Vandergraaf, et al., n.d.; See Vandergraaf, et al., 2013
16 See International Atomic Energy Agency (IAEA), 2012

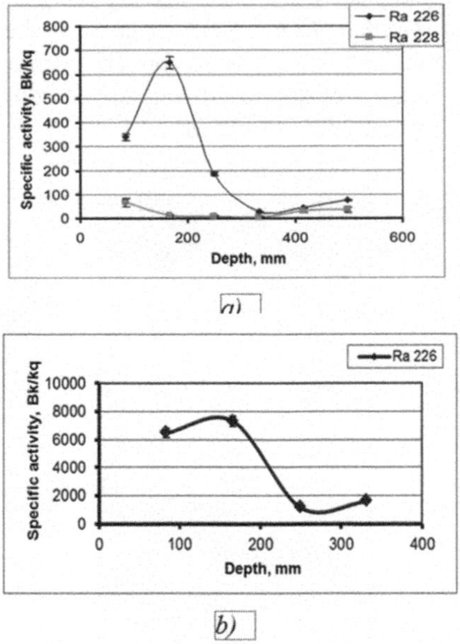

Figure 3: The relationship between the activity of radionuclides in the soil, taken in a certain depth from the points with coordinates: N40°25'13.2"; E50°01'05.9", EDR = 490 μR/h (a); N40°24'47.8"; E50°00'54.2", EDR = 700 μR/h (b)

The government gives a great attention to improving ecological situation in the Republic, so the actions on cleaning and rehabilitation of polluted industrial areas are continued in the Azerbaijan. Within the past five years the cleaning environmental works have been carried out in other regions of the Republic.

During carrying out the scientific radioecological studies along the Baku - Shamakhi route, the areas with high gamma radiation were found in the territories of the Khizi and Shamakhi administrative regions. Chemical and mineralogical composition of soil samples taken from these territories was determined, and a gamma-anomalous map of the study area was drawn. On the basis of this the distribution of natural radioactive elements (*U, Th, Ra, K*) in this territory was studied, and also the *EDR* of gamma radiation was investigated.

According to the results of nuclear-geophysical, geochemical and radio-spectrometric studies, the composition of uranium in the soils of this territory varies in the range of 0.006-0.1%. In soils enriched with uranium, the amount of detected uranium exceeded clark by 1000 times.

In the investigated area 25000 point experiments were carried out, and on the basis of received information the gamma-anomalous maps and also background radiation maps were developed.

Table 3: Activity of radionuclides in various samples

Legend: *Sur1* - waste in pipe with deposits, *Sur2* - soil, *Sur3* - soil, *Sur4* - salt from the bottom of a dry lake, *Sur5* – sediment, *B-Lb* - sign of route Baku – Lokbatan

Code and Coordinates	EDR	^{137}Cs	^{235}U	^{238}U	^{226}Ra	^{228}Ra	^{40}K	A_{eff}
	µR/h	Bq/kg						
Baku-Lokbatan (B-Lb), samples from soil surface								
B-Lb009 N40°19'43.2" E49°48'47.1"	2.5	2.2 ±0.4	1.2	26.04	12,7 ±2,8	18.5 ±1.5	546 ±70	83.3 ±10.7
B-Lb680 N40°19'22.3" E49°49'57.9"	187	MDA = 2.5	206	4470. 2	6476 ±57	937± 47	468 ±61	7743 ±123
B-Lb685 N40°19'05.2" E49°49'35.6"	140	MDA =2.4	153	3320.1	7310,1 ±68,2	197,8 ±37,5	535 ±66	7614 ±122
B-Lb692 N40°19'45.1" E49°49'34.3"	42	3.5 ±0.5	79.8	1731. 7	[illegible] 0 ±18.6	1642 ±19.3	456 ±84	3641 ±51
Surakhani (Sur), samples from different sites								
Sur1 N40°37'37.5"E50 °01'00.3"	210	-	-	-	6526 ± 686	1018 ± 128	1416 ±406	7975 ± 707
Sur2 N40°24'52.9"E50 °00'48.9"	230	-	-	-	6254 ± 459	112 ± 18	1502 ±267	6533 ± 460
Sur3 N40°25'31.8"E50 °01'23.7"	5	-	-	-	24,9 ± 4,5	17,1 ± 3,9	226 ±47	67 ± 8
Sur4 N40°24'58.4"E50 °00'47.6"	50	-	-	-	63 ± 12	17,3 ± 7,2	MDA = 103	85 ± 16
Sur5 N40°24'54.1"E50 °00'47.2"	10	-	-	-	27,3 ± 4,6	10,2 ± 3,3	112 ±33	51 ± 7

For the first time in this area, there was found the extent of a silicon-sulfide layer of limestone (productive layer) containing uranium mineralization with high radiation. In the study area, 763 physical points were noted for 35 profiles, while the distance between the profiles was set at 50 m, and the distance between the points was 20 m. The *EDR* at these points was determined within 6 - 108 $\mu R/h$.

Among these points with high rates 264 samples of ground soil were selected, alpha and gamma spectrometric methods were used to analyze natural nuclear materials, and mapping was performed on indicators of the concentration of uranium in the soil in the study area. Obtained initial encouraging results showed the relevance of continuing research in this area, as well as carrying out geophysical and geochemical work to calculate the territory's nuclear raw material resources after the completion of mapping.

6 Mapping of the radioecological monitoring

Cartographical presentation of results of carried out investigations demonstrates the detected facts clearly. As a rule the procedure for the creation of the electron map consists the certain stages for converting the space image or other graphic material (topographic map) to a specific projection (coordinate system), the objects decoding on the image and the export of vector data to other software to obtain the desired type of information. The possibilities of the constantly improving software allow to perform all necessary complex procedures in a short time and in the same desktop computer.

For cartographic presentation of results on dosimetric and spectrometric studies we used two software specialized for spatial data processing:

- *ERDAS Imagine (Intergraph/Hexagon Geospatial, USA)* - for processing of raster data (images and maps);
- *ArcView GIS (ESRI, USA)* - for operations with vector data (i.e. interpretation, classification and creation of various thematic layers).

According to the international coordinate system of *Universal Transverse Mercator (UTM)*, Azerbaijan covers two zones - *38N* and *39N*.

Using module *"Geometric Correction"* of *ERDAS Imagine* a geo-referencing of all used graphics (the state border of Azerbaijan, its administrative regions and main cities, borders of administrative divisions of Baku (including *BSU*), topographic maps of scale 1:100000 of studying areas, etc.) to a single projection *WGS 84* (*World Geodetic System 1984*).

The dynamically complementing digital map (using the *UTM* system) was created within the *ArcView* software. It displayed the thematic layers as a result of carried out dosimetric works (*EDR* value in accordance with their registered coordinates by *GPS*). Data for all 10 studied routes numbered according to table 1 were displayed on the map.[17]

The criterion for checking of the accuracy in geo-referencing procedure of the created thematic layers (topographic, dosimetric, administrative, etc.) is a maximum coincidence of the same object of research (the building of the former iodine plant) on the different layers of the map. The discrepancy between the coordinates of objects in the various thematic layers is indicator of the random errors in the database (measuring point on the land may be located on the map in the sea).

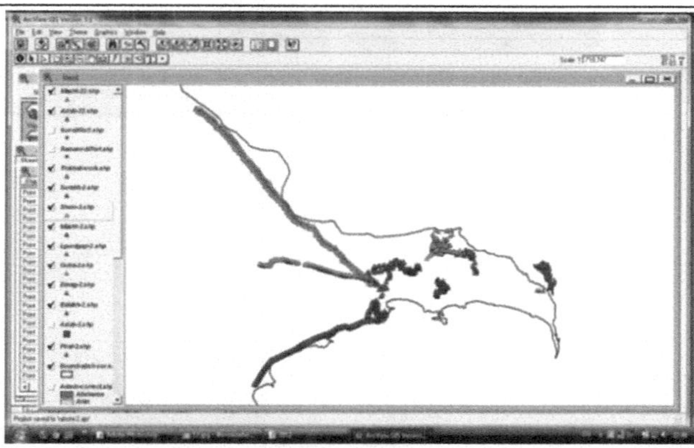

Figure 4: Routes of investigations in digital map

Possibilities of ArcView allows to submit the results of studies on the map as a symbolic labels, colour gradations or sizes labels according the value doses of radiation, and others.[18] Thus, the degree of pollution in the studied areas was clearly reflected on the maps by the scorecard method of estimation.

As consequence of ecological monitoring of dangerous areas in the Republic resently radioecological investigations were carried out on the territory of Adzhichai (Agdara) in the Khizi region. The area of 55 km^2 has been studied, and gamma-dosimetric and gamma-spectrometric search-planning works were carried out there on an area of 1:10000 scale.[19]

As a result, in the soils common in this territory (organic residual clays and shale) the high radioactivity (27-80 $\mu R/h$) was established in Maikop level of Upper Oligocene - Lower Miosennyh age of the Maikop level (27-80 $\mu R/h$), and in some

17 See Figure 4
18 See Figure 5
19 See Figure 6

cases, point radioactivity (relative to the total radiation background 27-80 $\mu R/h$), as well as throughout the clay slate, jarosite plates were sometimes found.

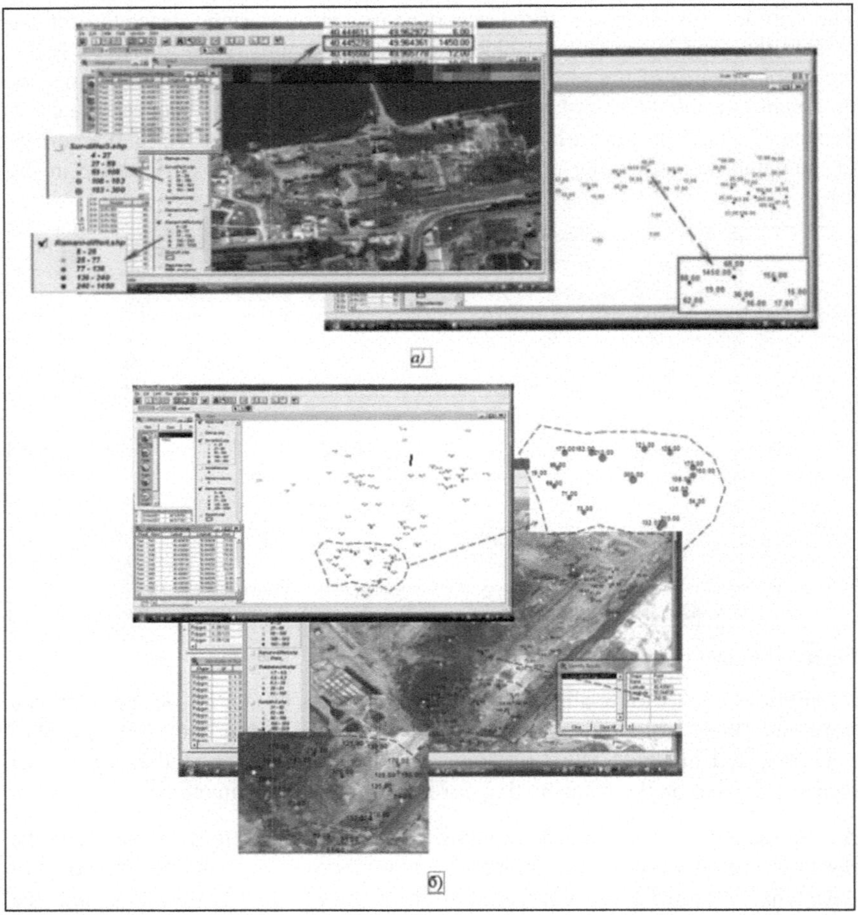

Figure 5: Digital database for the territories of former iodine plants:Ramani district (a); Surakhani district (b)

Radioecological and gamma-anomalous maps of the studied territories were prepared using the Geographix software.[20] The amount of uranium in the soil was established in the range of 0.006-0.07%, and the average amount - 0.05%.

[20] See Figure 7

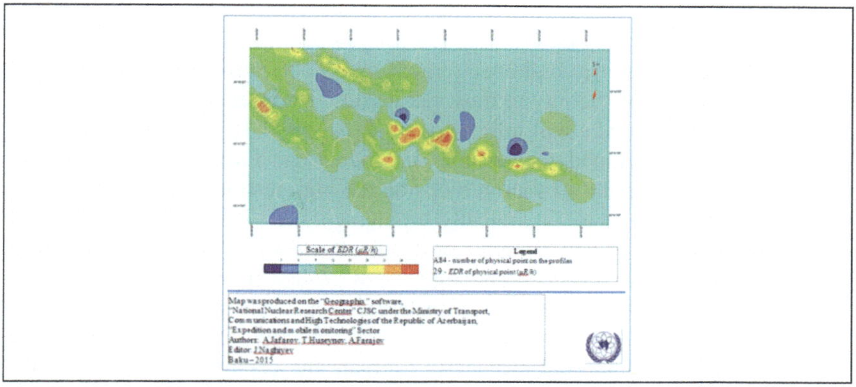

Figure 6: Anomal map of EDR on territory Adzhichai (Agdara) in the Khizi region. Scale 1:25000

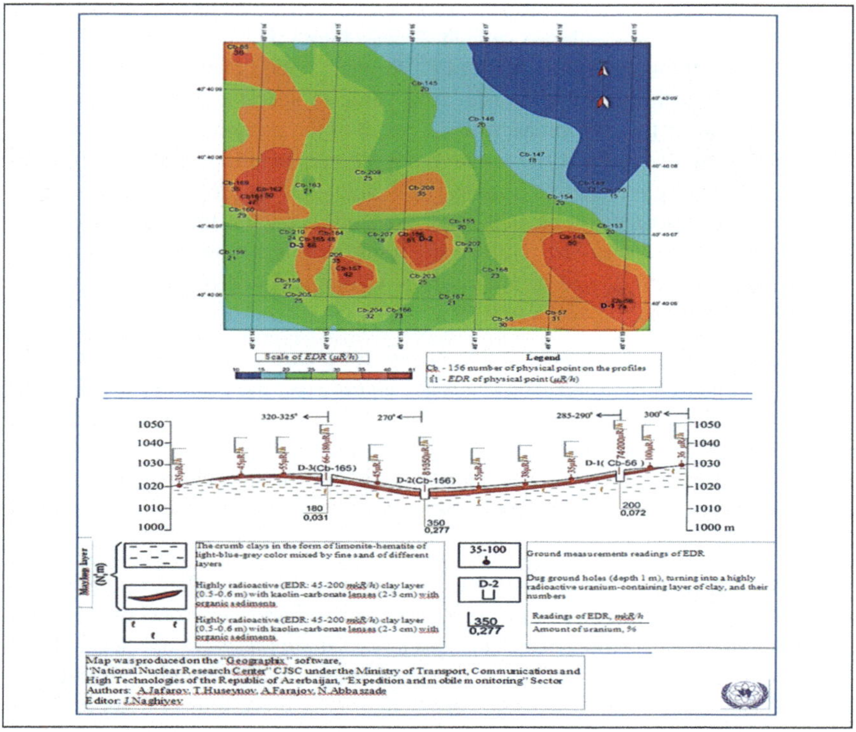

Figure 7: Anomal map of EDR of limestone deposits (Maikop level) with clays of high radioactivity on the territory surrounding Jabani village in the Shamaxi region. Scale 1:500

7 Conclusion

On the basis of dosimetric and spectrometric parameters the areas of Absheron Peninsula around Baku being the most dangerous from radio-ecological point of view were identified and a real informational database of 10 investigated districts was created. It is planned to continue radio-ecological researches of the oil-contaminated areas on the Absheron by using the high resolution satellite images. Used software allows us to dynamically supplement the electron database by new researches in formats of new versions of this level software. Thus, our findings of investigation were based on detailed analysis of ground-based dosimetric (field), spectrometric (laboratory) and remote (satellite) data. It is shown that the effectiveness of radioecological researches can be significantly improved using remote data allowing the prompt and efficiently estimate the ecological situation in the investigating territory. The set of procedures required for joint application radio-ecological and remote methods of investigation is developed.

The features of activity distribution of radionuclides detected in soil samples from the surface and some depth are studied. It was found that in the upper layers of soil the concentrations of radionuclides (^{226}Ra and ^{228}Ra) have higher values. It is a result of the pollution by oil waste. And value of specific activity of radionuclides in the lower layers decreases. It is a result of the mineral composition of the deposits. Based on results of the research the recommendations for cleaning areas heavily polluted by radioactive sources (*EDR* above 40-50 $\mu R/h$) were developed: to remove these sources by physical and mechanical means and securely bury in special pits; refined areas fill with fertile soils; regularly measure a dosimetric parameters; carry out the restoration, bio-physiological and gardening works on the cleaned up areas.

Within the legislations adopted in Azerbaijan for clearing and remediation of the areas contaminated by waste of oil and gas enterprises, the cleaning works at the territories of the former iodine plants in the Ramani and Surakhani districts have been finished[21], and also at the territories former iodine-bromine plant of the administrative district Neftchala. Thus, the degree of pollution in the studied areas was clearly reflected on the digital maps by the scorecard method of estimation.

Since 2014, recreation parks for the population have been installed in the cleared areas at the territories of settlements Ramani, Surakhani and Neftchala with the participation of specialists from *International Atomy Energy Agency (IAEA)*. Environmental monitoring of the polluted territories of the Republic is continuing, and necessary control measures are being taken in various regions of Azer-

21 See International Atomic Energy Agency (IAEA), 2012; See World Bank, 2008

baijan. The environmental policy of Azerbaijan aimed at reducing the production of pollutants to the environment, and rehabilitation the environmental balance in nature. Modern technical achievements allow to diagnose problems at early stages that simplifies their prevention and elimination.

Literature

Akhmedov, V. (1986). *Restoration of soil in the Absheron Peninsula. Chemistry in the agriculture. (in Russian)* (No. 8).

International Atomic Energy Agency (IAEA). (2012). *Appendix to End-of-Mission Report Project No.AZB9005/01/01 "Cleaning up former iodine plants at the Absheron Peninsula, Azerbaijan".*

Kahramanova, S. (2012). *Anthropogenic pollution of soils in Absheron peninsula. (in Russian)* (No. 1). Ekaterinburg: Academician Bulletin Ural.Sc. Res. Project. Russian Acad. Sc.

Mamedov, G., et al. (2008). Radioecological researches of the territories of Binagadi region of Absheron peninsula". (in Azerbaijanian). *Bulletin of Nation.Acad.Sc. of Azerbaijan, Ser. "Physics-Technics and Mathematical Sciences".*, pp. 191-194.

Mamedov, G., et al. (2010). Investigation into Natural and Anthropogenic Radionuclide Contamination on the Absheron Peninsula. *10208, WM 2010 Conference.*, p. 10.

Mir-Babayev, M. (2007). *Shot history of Azerbaijan oil. (in Russian).* Baku/ Azerneshr.

n.n. (2003). *Technologies of restoration of soils, polluted by oil and petrochemicals. Reference Book. (in Russian).* Moscow: REFIA. "Priroda" National Information Agency.

n.n. (2009). *The Baku oil and local communities: a history. Edited by L.Alieva. The center for national and international studies.* Baku/Qanun.

n.n. (2019). *Official web-site of President of Azerbaijan Republic. Oil and gas projects.* Retrieved 2.4.2019, from https://en.president.az/azerbaijan/contract

n.n. (n.d.). Quarterly Progress Report (Q-08 for 8th quarter) of the Project No. 3998. "Radio ecological survey of the soil of the territory of Baku city of Absheron Peninsula". *submitted to the STCU (Ukraine) and DFTAI (Canada).*

Strebel, H., Eifler, P., Brauweiler, H.-Ch., et al. (2003). *Umweltorientierung in Betrieblichen Querschnittsbereichen.* Gabler-Springer.

Vandergraaf, T., et al. (2013). *Distribution of radioactive materials in the Absheron Peninsula.* Azerbaijan: 13567, WM2013 Int. Conf., Phoenix.

Vandergraaf, T., et al. (n.d.). *Determination of the radionuclide contamination on the Absheron Peninsula. ICEM2011.* Reims

World Bank. (2008). *Program on rehabilitation of Absheron of the World Bank. Environmental impact assessment report on "Cleaning of areas polluted with radioactive wastes and oil in territory of Sabunchu and Surakhani districts of Baku"*. Retrieved 2.4.2019, from http://siteresources.worldbank.org/INTAZERBAIJAN/Resources/AARP_MES_EIA-final_Eng.pdf

Zeynalova, M. (2014). *Oil production in ancient and medieval Azerbaijan. (in Russian)*, pp. 32-37. Retrieved 2.4.2019, from J. Black gold, № 1 (67): https://tinyurl.com/irs-az

Trihalogenmethanes in Drinking Water And Non-Carcinogenic Health Risks

F. Božek, A. Pawelczyk, L. Jesonkova-Pavlica†, J. Konečný and S. Vargová

1 Introduction

The disinfection by strong oxidants, carried out with the aim to inactivate pathogens and provide microbial safety of water, produces toxic substances, which may negatively affect consumers′ health.[1] It is caused by the reaction of oxidation agent with organic precursors, which are naturally present in the form of micro-contamination also in ground waters.[2] At the same time, during the distribution of drinking water there is a deposition of particles of various origins with an organic part being a significant component in the areas of the distribution network with favourable hydraulic conditions. The analysis of organic deposits proved that the relevant parts of organic water contamination are humin acids and other alkyl-derivatives with high content of methyl- and ethyl groups. The quantitative data on the composition of organic substances in the distribution water system are stated by Sly et al.[3] Algae, their metabolites and the metabolites of microflora present in water and distribution network may also produce disinfection byproducts. More than 500 different types of halogenderivatives, generally marked as disinfection byproducts (DBPs), were detected by studying the chlorination of untreated surface water containing humin acids. The most significant DBPs identified in water are halogenacetic acids, halogenacetonitriles, chloral hydrate, (2,2,2-trichloro-1,1-ethanediol), chlorophenols, chlorine cyan, bromates and THMs.[4] The most significant DBPs, which occur in the highest concentrations and may seriousunreaten the health of population, are THMs represented primarily by chloroform ($CHCl_3$) and then by bromdichloromethane ($CHBrCl_2$), dibromchloromethane ($CHBr_2Cl$) and tribromomethane ($CHBr_3$).[5]

The requirements for water quality are tackled both on national and international levels. The WHO states in its former Guidelines for Drinking-Water Quality that the national limits for THMs range from 25-250 µg dm^{-3}.[6] The limit of THMs sum in drinking water is 100 µg dm^{-3} in the Czech Republic and complies with

1 See Rook, 1974
2 See Singer, 1994
3 See Sly, et al., 1990
4 See Boorman, et al., 1999; See WHO (World Health Organisation), 2000
5 See Singer, 1994
6 See WHO (World Health Organisation), 2006

H.-C. Brauweiler et al. (Hrsg.), *Digitalization and Industry 4.0: Economic and Societal Development*, https://doi.org/10.1007/978-3-658-27110-7_28

the EU Directive.[7] The THMs limit of 80 μg dm^{-3} is set to be safe to our health by the U.S. EPA.[8]

Besides the total amount of THMs the standards determine also the limit concentrations for individual compounds belonging to the group of THMs. Although the acceptable concentration of THMs sum is higher in the Czech Republic than the limit set by the U.S. EPA, the limits for trichloromethane are lower in the Czech Republic. The WHO does not set particular limits for individual THMs and deals solely with the sum of their concentrations.[9]

Water is currently disinfected through chlorination by chlorine, chlorine oxide, ozonization, or UV radiation. The combination of chlorination and ozonization is also widely applied worldwide. Recently there has been a tendency to disinfect water by UV radiation and ozone for their indisputable advantages. Both methods are, in contrast to chlorination, highly efficient even against resistant pathogens, such as oocysts of *Cryptosporidium,* and incline less to the production of DBPs. However, all disinfection agents are oxidants and produce DBPs.[10]

The composition and concentration of chlorination byproducts depend on the procedure and conditions of disinfection, as well as on physical and chemical parameters of water. The researches carried out by Chinese scientists proved that certain values of pH increase the produced amount of THMs. Temperature is another factor influencing the amount of DBPs. The quantity of DBPs significantly decreases when so called key temperature is exceeded.[11] The amount of produced DBPs is also the function of compositions and concentration ratios of ions in treated water. It has been proved that the cations of Mo^{2+}, Na^{+} and K^{+} increase the summary production of THMs. On the other hand, occurrences of the cations of Fe^{2+}, Mn^{2+} and Ca^{2+} have an opposite effect.[12] The speed of reaction and the range of produced DBPs also depend on the type and dose of applied disinfection agent, the concentration and chemical composition of organic precursors present in water and a distribution system, the time for which water is disinfected, etc.[13]According to some authors the THMs-DBPs ratio ranges from 37% to 58%[14], according to other authors the above mentioned ratio is up to 90% with trichloromethane being a dominant product.[15]

---

7 See CEU (The Council of the European Union), 1998
8 See U.S. EPA (U.S. Environmental Protection Agency), 1989-2004
9 See WHO (World Health Organisation), 2011
10 See Nieuwenhuijsen, et al., 2000
11 See Sun, et al., 2009
12 See Liu, et al., 2012
13 See Whitaker, et al., 2003; See Hamidin, et al., 2008
14 See Colman, et al., 2011
15 See Singer, 1994

There is inhalation, oral and dermal pathways of THMs into human body. They have neurotoxic, immunotoxic, cytotoxic, hepatotoxic and nephrotoxic effects. The carcinogenic, mutagenic, teratogenic and embryotoxic effects are not excluded either.[16] Bromdichloromethane in higher concentration is also suspected to cause spontaneous abortion, the infants′ lower birth weight and increased risk of developmental defects, although these facts have not been sufficiently proved.[17]

2 Applied Methods And Devices

The sampling of drinking water has been carried out from a water supply system in compliance with appropriate standards.[18] The handling of samples followed the standard procedures as well.[19] The concentration of THMs in drinking water was determined by purge-and-trap (P&T) method with the help of Tekmar LSC 2000 concentrator and gas chromatography on a GC Hewlett Packard 5890 device with a flame ionization detector (FID) and a Vocol 105 column.[20] The detection limit for individual THMs was 0.1 $\mu g\ dm^{-3}$ with a combined uncertainty ±20%. Uncertainties related to the accuracy of determination have been calculated as a product of standard uncertainty of measurement in the form of estimating the relative standard deviation and the coefficient of expansion, which equals 2 for the level of significance 95%. The uncertainties do not include the components formed by sampling and concern only the levels over the detection limit.

The health risk assessment was carried out in compliance with national standards[21], which are in compliance with the U.S. EPA methodology.[22] The exposure scenarios were set for three exposure pathways, i.e. ingestion, inhalation and dermal contact during washing, four THMs ($CHCl_3$, $CHBrCl_2$, $CHBr_2Cl$ and $CHBr_3$), and three age groups, i.e. the adults, the children from 6 to 18 and the children up to the age of 6.

Non-carcinogenic risks have been calculated according to the relation (1), where *HQ* represents a hazard quotient, CDI is a chronic daily intake [$\mu g\ kg^{-1}\ day^{-1}$] and RfD is a reference dose ($\mu g\ kg^{-1}\ day^{-1}$) for a particular exposure pathway.

$$HQ = CDI \times RfD^{-1} \qquad (1)$$

---

16 See Larson, Wolf, Butterworth, 1993

17 See Nieuwenhuijsen, et al., 2000; See Colman, et al., 2011

18 See Czech Office for Standards, Metrology and Testing (COSMT), 2007, 2008

19 See Czech Office for Standards, Metrology and Testing (COSMT), 2004a

20 See Czech Office for Standards, Metrology and Testing (COSMT), 2004b

21 See MoE CR (Ministry of Environment of the Czech Republic), 2011

22 See U.S. EPA (U.S. Environmental Protection Agency), 1989-2004

The reference doses *RfD* were adopted from the U.S. EPA documents[23] and are presented in the table 1.

If the reference dose for a given contaminant S was not available, the sum of hazard quotients for inhalation $RfD_{INH,\,S}$ and dermal contact $HQ_{DC,\,S}$ was substituted by the value for ingestion as it is clear from the relation (2):

$$HQ_{ING,S} = HQ_{INH,S} + HQ_{DC,S} \qquad (2)$$

It is clear from the equation (1) that the knowledge of chronic daily intake is the second prerequisite for calculating the hazard quotient. Its value has been calculated individually for each exposure pathway, contaminant and age group according to the following equations, i.e. the equation (3) for ingestion ING, the equation (4) for inhalation INH and equation (5) for dermal contact DC.

$$CDI_{ING} = c_w \times b \times IR_{ING} \times EF \times ED \times BW^{-1} \times AT^{-1} \qquad (3)$$

$$CDI_{INH} = c_a \times IR_{INH} \times ET \times EF \times ED \times BW^{-1} \times AT^{-1} \qquad (4)$$

$$CDI_{DC} = c_w \times SA \times K_p \times ET \times EF \times ED \times C_F \times BW^{-1} \times AT^{-1} \qquad (5)$$

Where c_w [µg dm^{-3}] represents the average concentration of contaminant in water acquired through measurement, IR_{ING} [dm^3 day^{-1}] is the daily rate of consumed water, *b* the rate of consumed water from private sources, *EF* [day year^{-1}] the annual exposure frequency, *ED* [year] the exposure duration, *BW* [kg] the average body weight of population, *AT* [day] the time during which the concentration c_w of contaminant may be considered constant, c_a [µg m^{-3}] the concentration of contaminant in air, IR_{INH} [m^3 hour^{-1}] the rate of air inhaled per hour, *ET* [hour day^{-1}] the daily exposure time, *SA* [cm^2] the skin area which is in contact with contaminated water, K_p [cm hour^{-1}] the coefficient of skin permeability, and finally $CF = 10^{-3}$ dm^3 cm^{-3} is the cm^3 to dm^3 conversion factor.

The concentration c_a can be expressed with the help of concentration c_w according to relationship (6), where *f* represents the fraction of releasable contaminant, *Q* [dm^3 hour^{-1}] the water flow per hour, *t* [hour] the showering time, and finally *V* [m^3] is the volume of bathroom.

$$c_a = c_w \times f \times Q \times t \times V^{-1} \times 2^{-1} \qquad (6)$$

It is possible to express the sum hazard quotient $HQ_{SUM,k}$ for each k-age group according to the relation (7) while assuming the additive effect of non-carcinogenic risk of each i-exposure pathway and j-contaminant:

---

23 See U.S. EPA (U.S. Environmental Protection Agency), 2001, 2010

$$HQ_{SUM,k} = \sum_{i=1}^{n}\sum_{j=1}^{m} HQ_{i,j} \tag{7}$$

where $n = 3$ is the number of monitored exposure pathways and $m = 4$ is the number of assessed contaminants with similar effects. It is clear that the symbols $i, j, k, n, m \in N^{+}$, where N^{+} is the set of all natural numbers.

The life-long non-carcinogenic risk has been determined either as a sum of $HQ_{SUM,k}$ through each k-age category according to the equation (8), or through a weighted average according to the relation (9) considering the duration of exposure in every age category.

$$HQ_{T\,SUM} = \sum_{k=1}^{q} HQ_{SUM,k} \tag{8}$$

$$HQ_{T\,WEIGHT} = \sum_{k=1}^{q} t_k \times HQ_{SUM,k} \times t_{\alpha}^{-1} \tag{9}$$

where $HQ_{T\,SUM}$ is a life-long non-carcinogenic risk as a sum of non-carcinogenic risks of individual k-age categories, $HQ_{T\,WEIGHT}$ is a weighted life-long non-carcinogenic risk according to the duration of exposure in the assessed subpopulations and $q = 3$ is the number of age categories, while symbols $j, q \in N^{+}$. Finally, t_k is the number of years during which the given age category is assessed and $t_{\alpha} = 70$ years is the sum of exposure duration of all three age subpopulations.

When $HQ_{T\,SUM} \vee HQ_{T\,WEIGHT} \leq 1$, the risk is acceptable, when $HQ_{T\,SUM} \vee HQ_{T\,WEIGHT} \in (1; 4\rangle$, the risk is tolerable, and when $HQ_{T\,SUM} \vee HQ_{T\,WEIGHT} > 4$, the risk is unacceptable and it is necessary either to implement corrective measures immediately, or to interrupt the supply of drinking water.

3 Outcomes and Discussion

Drinking water is supplied into the group water system of the assessed region in the Czech Republic with the number of inhabitants approximately 3.84×10^{5} from two aquifers. There are two siphon mains, which consist of drilled wells 12-21 m deep and water is then supplied into the 5×10^{3} m^3 group water tank. The water tank serves for the fixing of hydraulic situation in the siphons and also as an operationally essential accumulation for controlling the water intake from both water withdrawal areas. Permission for water intake from both intake structures is 1.08 m^3 s^{-1}. The ground water is mixed with 5-10% of surface water treated through the technology of preionization, coagulation, flocculation, sedimentation and filtration. The origin of water guarantees its constant quality complying with the requirements of the Directive [10]. Before being supplied into the distribution network the water is the subject to homogenization, aggregation, sedimentation, filtration, and finally disinfection with ClO_2 produced directly in water according to equation (10). Thus it is necessary to monitor the remains of unhealthy chlorite.

$$ClO_2^- + Cl_2 = ClO_2 + 2Cl^- \quad (10)$$

The concentrations of THMs at individual sampling sites are recorded in the table 30. It is clear from the outcomes that the limits for THMs in drinking water set in the EU[24] have not been exceeded at any site. However, it need not mean that the THMs exposure health risks are acceptable.

The calculation of risk for each sampling site separately has been chosen for the needs of risk assessment. The risk is characterized through the value of hazard quotient calculated according to the equation (1), while applying the reference doses presented in table 1 and dependent on the pathway. The relations (3)-(5) were used for calculating the chronic daily intakes for the monitored pathways, contaminants and age groups. The values of exposure factors, shown in tables 3-5 according to exposure pathways and age categories, were acquired from the national methodology[25], the U.S. EPA documents[26] and by expert judgment. The weight of children up to 6 years and the young from 6-18 was acquired as an average weight of girls and boys in individual years of the assessed time period (Our info). The equation (6) was used for calculating the concentration of contaminants in the air of bathroom and the exposure factors required for the calculation are shown in table 6. The concentrations of individual contaminants in drinking water at the assessed sampling sites, acquired by measurement and necessary for calculating the corresponding chronic daily intakes, are presented in table 2.

The calculated values of hazard quotients at the monitored sampling sites are shown in tables 7-12 for each exposure pathway, pollutant and age category, including the summary hazard quotients for the exposure pathways and the monitored pollutants. In order to assess the non-carcinogenic health risks in relation to the sampling site it is decisive to know primarily the value of summary hazard quotients $HQ_{SUM,k}$ for each k-age category calculated according to the relation (7). $HQ_{SUM,k} < 1$ for every sampling site and also every age category. Therefore, the non-carcinogenic risk is acceptable.

It arises from the acquired outcomes that trichloromethane contributes to the risk the most and the children up to the age of six are the most sensitive age category,

---

24 See CEU (The Council of the European Union), 1998
25 See MoE CR (Ministry of Environment of the Czech Republic), 2011
26 See U.S. EPA (U.S. Environmental Protection Agency), 1989-2004

which is in compliance with theoretical assumptions. It may also be concluded that the population near the area of chlorination is the most threatened.

The life-long noncarcinogenic health risk in the form of $HQ_{T\ SUM}$ was calculated according to the equation (8) under the assumption of additive effect of risk across the age categories, or in the form of $HQ_{T\ WEIGHT}$ according to the equation (9) as a weighted average considering the duration of exposure in the assessed age categories. The outcomes for individual sampling sites are shown in table 13 and confirm the previous conclusions. It is obvious from the data in table 13 that the life-long noncarcinogenic health risks significantly differ depending on the way of quantification and the value $HQ_{T\ SUM} \approx 4.2 \times HQ_{T\ WEIGHT}$. We assume that the value of weighted risk reflects the reality more, especially with regard to the existing uncertainties, exposure scenarios and factors. As the value of $HQ_{T\ WEIGHT}$ < 1 at all assessed sampling sites, it may be stated that the life-long noncarcinogenic risk is socially acceptable.

Considering the applied exposure scenarios, the values of hazard quotients characterizing the non-carcinogenic risk resulting from the presence of THMs in drinking water of the assessed region are rather overestimated. The presented outcomes include the following uncertainties:

1. The level of uncertainty of the measured concentrations of THMs is ± 20%.
2. The validity of RfD taken from the U.S. EPA databases, is assessed by the institution itself as "medium".
3. The calculations of CDI are based on the assumption of full absorption of contaminants in the human organism, which is not very likely to happen in practice. This fact increases the values of HQ.
4. There were not found RfD for the intake of CHBrCl2, CHBr2Cl and CHBr3 through inhalation and dermal contact in the available literature. That is why the intake through joint inhalation and dermal pathways was assessed as equivalent to the intake through ingestion, which was in compliance with the recommendation of the U.S. EPA.
5. The calculation of inhalation exposure is burdened by uncertainty when estimating the value of THMs concentration in the indoor air, because the THMs are released during any handling of free water level which is in contact with this air. As a partial compensation of this fact the air exchange was not considered when people stayed in the bathroom.
6. The assumption of the additive effect of THMs when assessing the hazard quotients. The mutual interaction of THMs may show not only synergic, but also antagonistic effects. Such effects have not been analysed in the available literature yet.
7. The interaction of THMs with other compounds present in the analyzed samples of drinking water was not considered either.

4 Conclusion

The non-carcinogenic risk was quantified from the long term consumption of drinking water supplied by a regional group water system to the inhabitants of the Czech Republic. The assessed indicator of risk was the group of four THMs, i.e. chloroform, dibromchloromethane, bromdichloromethane, and bromoform.

The measurements and data analyses lead to the conclusion that toxic THMs, originating during the disinfection of drinking water with the help of chloride dioxide, do not pose any significant system toxic risk to consumers. It has been proved that the most threatened group is the subpopulation of children up to the age of six, living near the area of disinfection, which corresponds to a higher volatility of THMs. However, even in such cases the life-long non-carcinogenic health risk is socially acceptable. Such a conclusion corresponds with the comparison of the values of THMs concentrations with the currently valid limits for their individual and summary concentrations.

Despite the positive facts it is necessary to monitor the concentrations of THMs in drinking water permanently and implement adequate countermeasures in case the increased concentrations are detected. It is also important to inform population of the above mentioned source of hazard and the suitable ways of handling drinking water, which reduce the risks.

It is necessary to emphasize that the risk resulting from the insufficient inactivation of pathogens in drinking water is of higher order priority in comparison with the health risk resulting from the presence of DBPs.

Literature

Boorman, G., et al. (1999). *Drinking Water Disinfection Byproducs: Review and Approach to Toxicity Evaluation. Environmental Health Perspectives 107.*

CEU (The Council of the European Union). (1998). *Council Directive 98/83/EC on the Quality of Water Intended for Human Consumption.* Brusels: CEU.

Colman, J., et al. (2011). *Identification of developmentally toxic drinking water disinfection byproducts and evaluation of data relevant to mode of action. Toxicology and Applied Pharmacology 254.*

Czech Office for Standards, Metrology and Testing (COSMT). (2004a). *Water Quality - Sampling - Part 3: Guidance on the Preservation and Handling of Water Samples.* Prague: COSMT.

Czech Office for Standards, Metrology and Testing (COSMT). (2004b). *Water Quality - Gas-Chromatographic Determination of a Number of Mono-*

cyclic Aromatic Hydrocarbons, Naphthalene and Several Chlorinated Compounds Using Purge and Trap and Thermal Desorption. Prague: COSMT.

Czech Office for Standards, Metrology and Testing (COSMT). (2007). *Water Quality - Sampling - Part 1: Guidance on the Design of Sampling Programmes and Sampling Techniques.* Prague: COSMT.

Czech Office for Standards, Metrology and Testing (COSMT). (2008). *Water Quality - Sampling - Part 5: Guidance on Sampling of Drinking Water from Treatment Works and Piped Distribution.* Prague: COSMT.

Hamidin, N., et al. (2008). *Human Health Risk Assessment of Chlorinated Disinfection By Products in Drinking Water Using a Probabilistic Approach. Water Research 42.*

Larson, J., Wolf, D., Butterworth, B. (1993). *Acute Hepatotoxic and Nephrotoxic Effects of Chloroform in Male F-344 Rats and Female B6C3F1 Mice.* Toxicol. Sci 20, (3).

Liu, X., et al. (2012). Effects of Metal Ions on THMs and HAAs Formation During Tannic Acid Chlorination. *Chemical Engineering Journal 211-212.*, pp. 179-185.

MoE CR (Ministry of Environment of the Czech Republic). (2011). Methodical Instructions for the Risk Analysis of Contaminated Area. *MoE CR Bulletin, XXI, (3)*, pp. 1-52.

Nieuwenhuijsen, et al. (2000). Chlorination Disinfection Byproducts in Water and Their Association with Adverse Reproductive Outcomes: A Review. *Occupational and Environmental Medicine 57, (2)*, pp. 73-85.

Our info. (n.d.). *Children Average Body Weight According to Age.* Retrieved 3.3.2019, from http://www.naseinfo.cz/clanky/tehotenstvi-a-deti/obezita-u-deti/prumerna-hmotnost-deti-podle-veku

Rook, J. (1974). Formation of Haloforms During Chlorination of Natural Waters. *Water Treatment and Examination 23 (2)*, pp. 234-243.

Singer, P. (1994). Control of Disinfection By-Products in Drinking Water. *Journal of Environmental Engineering 120, (4)*, pp. 727-744.

Sly, L., et al. (1990). Deposition of Manganese in a Drinking Water Distribution System. *Applied and Environmental Microbiology 56, (3)*, pp. 628-639.

Sun, Y., et al. (2009). Effects of Operating Conditions on THMs and HAAs Formation During Wastewater Chlorination. *Journal of Hazardous Materials 168, (2-3)*, pp. 1290-1295.

U.S. EPA (U.S. Environmental Protection Agency). (1989-2004). *Risk Assessment Guidance for Superfund (RAGS), Vol. I: Human Health Evaluation Manual.* Retrieved 3.3.2019, from http://www.epa.gov/oswer/riskassessment/ragsa-f/index.htm

U.S. EPA (U.S. Environmental Protection Agency). (2001). *EPA Superfund, Record of Decision. Record: EPA/ROD/R04 01/534.* Retrieved 3.3.2019, from http://www.epa.gov/superfund/sites/rods/fulltext/r0401534.pdf

U.S. EPA (U.S. Environmental Protection Agency). (2010). *Integrated Risk Information System (IRIS). Database of Toxicological Parameters for Human Health.* Retrieved 3.3.2019, from http://www.epa.gov/iris/subst

Whitaker, H., et al. (2003). Description of Trihalomethane Levels in Three United Kingdom Water Suppliers. *Journal of Exposure Analysis and Environmental Epidemiology 13, (1)*, pp. 17-23.

WHO (World Health Organisation). (2000). *Disinfectants and Disinfectant By-Products.* Geneva: WHO (Environmental Health Criteria 216).

WHO (World Health Organisation). (2006). *Guidelines for Drinking-Water Quality. Recommendations. 1st Addendum to 3rd.* (Vol. 1). Geneva: WHO.

WHO (World Health Organisation). (2011). *Guidelines for Drinking-water Quality.* (Vol. 4). Trihalomethanes/Switzerland: WHO.

Attachment

Table 1: Values of Reference Doses for particular pathways and THMs

Reference dose	Unit	$CHCl_3$	$CHBrCl_2$	$CHBr_2Cl$	$CHBr_3$
Ingestion RfD_{ING}	$\mu g\ kg^{-1}\ day^{-1}$	10.0	20.0	20.0	20.0
Inhalation RfD_{INH}	$\mu g\ kg^{-1}\ day^{-1}$	8.6E-02	-	-	-
Dermal contact RfD_{DC}	$\mu g\ kg^{-1}\ day^{-1}$	2.0	-	-	-

Table 2: Concentrations of THMs on individual sites and in various seasons

Sampling Site	$CHCl_3$ [μg dm^{-3}]	$CHBrCl_2$ [μg dm^{-3}]	$CHBr_2Cl$ [μg dm^{-3}]	$CHBr_3$ [μg dm^{-3}]
A	1.80	2.30	2.20	0.60
	1.40	2.30	2.90	0.70
	1.10	1.60	1.90	0.30
B	3.10	2.20	1.90	0.40
	2.10	1.70	1.40	<1.00
	2.40	2.80	2.80	<1.00
	1.30	1.30	1.50	<1.00
	1.20	1.20	1.30	<1.00
C	<0.10	<0.10	<0.10	<0.10
	0.20	0.10	<0.10	Not detected
	0.30	0.20	<0.10	Not detected
	<0.50	<0.50	<0.50	<1.00
	0.60	<0.50	<0.50	<1.00
	0.50	<0.50	<0.50	<1.00
	<0.50	<0.50	<0.50	<0.50
D	<0.10	<0.10	<0.10	<0.10
	0.50	0.20	<0.10	Not detected
	0.70	0.40	0.10	Not detected
	<0.50	<0.50	<0.50	<1.00
	1.00	<0.50	<0.50	<1.00
	<0.50	<0.50	<0.50	<1.00
	<0.50	<0.50	<0.50	<0.50
E	0.13	<0.10	<0.10	<0.10
	0.30	0.15	Not detected	Not detected
	<0.10	Not detected	Not detected	Not detected
	<0.50	<0.50	<0.50	<1.00
	<0.50	<0.50	<0.50	<1.00
	<0.50	<0.50	<0.50	<1.00
	2.15	0.50	<0.50	<1.00
F	0.19	<0.10	<0.10	<0.10
	0.50	0.30	<0.10	Not detected
	1.10	1.10	<0.50	<1.00
	<0.50	<0.50	<0.50	<1.00
	<0.50	<0.50	<0.50	<1.00
	<0.50	<0.50	<0.50	<0.50
	1.10	1.10	<0.50	<1.00

Table 3: Exposure factors for calculating the chronic daily intake through ingestion

Age category	IR [dm^3 day^{-1}]	b	EF [day $year^{-1}$]	ED [year]	BW [kg]	AT [day]
adults	2.0	0.75	350	52	70.00	18 980
children 6-18 years	1.4	0.75	350	12	47.00	4 380
children up to 6 years	1.0	0.65	350	6	15.58	2 190

Table 4: Exposure factors for calculating the chronic daily intake through inhalation

Age category	IR [m^3 $hour^{-1}$]	ET [hour day^{-1}]	EF [day $year^{-1}$]	ED [year]	BW [kg]	AT [den]
adults	0.60	0.20	350	52	70.00	18 980
children 6-18 years	0.55	0.25	350	12	47.00	4 380
children up to 6 years	0.18	0.30	350	6	15.58	2 190

Table 5: Exposure factors for calculating the chronic daily intake through dermal contact

Age category	SA [cm^2]	K_P [cm $hour^{-1}$]	ET hour day^{-1}]	EF [day $year^{-1}$]	ED [year]	C_F	BW [kg]	AT [day]
adults	18 500	0.010	0.20	350	52	0.001	70.00	18 980
children 6-18 years	13 120	0.015	0.25	350	12	0.001	47.00	4 380
children up to 6 years	6 560	0.025	0.30	350	6	0.001	15.58	2 190

Table 6: Exposure factors for calculating the concentration of contaminants in the air of bathroom

Age category	Q [dm^3 $hour^{-1}$]	t = ET [hour]	f	V [m^3]
adults	600	0.20		
children 6-18 years	550	0.25		
children up to 6 years	500	0.30	0.75	9.00

Table 7: The values of hazard quotients, including the summary hazard quotients for the exposure pathways, monitored pollutants and HQSUM, k at the sampling site A

			Adults		
	$CHCl_3$	**$CHBrCl_2$**	**$CHBr_2Cl$**	**$CHBr_3$**	**Sum of *HQ* through exposure pathways**
HQ_{ING}	2.945E-03	2.123E-03	2.397E-03	5.479E-04	8.013E-03
HQ_{INH}	1.370E-01				
HQ_{DC}	3.632E-04	2.123E-03	2.397E-03	5.479E-04	1.424E-01
Sum of HQ through THMs	1.403E-01	4.246E-03	4.794E-03	1.095E-03	***$HQ_{SUM,\,k}$* = 1.504E-01**
			Children 6-18 years		
HQ_{ING}	3.071E-03	2.214E-03	2.499E-03	5.713E-04	8.355E-03
HQ_{INH}	2.679E-01				
HQ_{DC}	7.194E-04	2.214E-03	2.499E-03	5.713E-04	2.739E-01
Sum of HQ through THMs	2.717E-01	4.428E-03	4.998E-03	1.143E-03	***$HQ_{SUM,\,k}$* = 2.823E-01**
			Children up to 6 years		
HQ_{ING}	5.734E-03	4.134E-03	4.667E-03	1.067E-03	1.560E-02
HQ_{INH}	3.462E-01				
HQ_{DC}	2.170E-03	4.134E-03	4.667E-03	1.067E-03	3.582E-01
Sum of HQ through THMs	3.541E-01	8.268E-03	9.334E-03	2.134E-03	***$HQ_{SUM,\,k}$* = 3.738E-01**

Table 8: The values of hazard quotients, including the summary hazard quotients for the exposure pathways, monitored pollutants and HQSUM, k at the sampling site B

Adults					
	$CHCl_3$	**$CHBrCl_2$**	**$CHBr_2Cl$**	**$CHBr_3$**	**Sum of *HQ* through exposure pathways**
HQ_{ING}	4.151E-03	1.890E-03	1.829E-03	9.041E-04	8.774E-03
HQ_{INH}	1.931E-01				
HQ_{DC}	5.119E-04	1.890E-03	1.829E-03	9.041E-04	1.982E-01
Sum of HQ through THM	1.978E-01	3.780E-03	3.658E-03	1.808E-03	***$HQ_{SUM,k}$* = 2.070E-01**
Children 6-18 years					
HQ_{ING}	4.327E-03	1.971E-03	1.907E-03	9.426E-04	9.148E-03
HQ_{INH}	3.775E-01				
HQ_{DC}	1.014E-03	1.971E-03	1.907E-03	9.426E-04	3.833E-01
Sum of HQ through THM	3.828E-01	3.942E-03	3.814E-03	1.884E-03	***$HQ_{SUM,k}$* = 3.925E-01**
Children up to 6 years					
HQ_{ING}	8.081E-03	3.681E-03	3.561E-03	1.760E-03	1.708E-02
HQ_{INH}	4.879E-01				
HQ_{DC}	3.058E-03	3.681E-03	3.561E-03	1.760E-03	5.001E-01
Sum of HQ through THM	4.991E-01	7,362E-03	7.122E-03	3.520E-03	***$HQ_{SUM,k}$* = 5,171E-01**

Table 9: The values of hazard quotients, including the summary hazard quotients for the exposure pathways, monitored pollutants and HQSUM, k at the sampling site C

			Adults		
	$CHCl_3$	**$CHBrCl_2$**	**$CHBr_2Cl$**	**$CHBr_3$**	**Sum of *HQ* through exposure pathways**
HQ_{ING}	7.926E-04	3.523E-04	3.376E-04	5.284E-04	2.011E-03
HQ_{INH}	3.686E-02				
HQ_{DC}	9.775E-05	3.523E-04	3.376E-04	5.284E-04	3.818E-02
Sum of HQ through THMs	3.775E-02	7.046E-04	6.752E-04	1.057E-03	$HQ_{SUM,k}$ = **4.019E-02**
			Children 6-18 years		
HQ_{ING}	8.263E-04	3.672E-04	3.519E-04	5.509E-04	2.096E-03
HQ_{INH}	7.208E-02				
HQ_{DC}	1.936E-04	3.672E-04	3.519E-04	5.509E-04	7.354E-02
Sum of HQ through THMs	7.310E-02	7.344E-04	7.038E-04	1.101E-03	$HQ_{SUM,k}$ = **7.564E-02**
			Children up to 6 years		
HQ_{ING}	1.543E-03	6.858E-04	6.572E-04	1.029E-03	3.915E-03
HQ_{INH}	9.316E-02				
HQ_{DC}	5.839E-04	6.858E-04	6.572E-04	1.029E-03	9.612E-02
Sum of HQ through THMs	9.529E-02	1.372E-03	1.314E-03	2.058E-03	$HQ_{SUM,k}$ = **1.000E-01**

Table 10: The values of hazard quotients, including the summary hazard quotients for the exposure pathways, monitored pollutants and HQSUM, k at the sampling site D

			Adults		
	$CHCl_3$	**$CHBrCl_2$**	**$CHBr_2Cl$**	**$CHBr_3$**	**Sum of HQ through exposure pathways**
HQ_{ING}	1.115E-03	3.963E-04	3.376E-04	5.284E-04	2.377E-03
HQ_{INH}	5.188E-02				
HQ_{DC}	1.376E-04	3.963E-04	3.376E-04	5.284E-04	5.328E-02
Sum of HQ through THMs	5.313E-02	7.926E-04	6.752E-04	1.057E-03	*$HQ_{SUM,k}$* = **5.566E-02**
			Children 6-18 years		
HQ_{ING}	1.163E-03	4.131E-04	3.519E-04	5.509E-04	2.479E-03
HQ_{INH}	1.015E-01				
HQ_{DC}	2.725E-04	4.131E-04	3.519E-04	5.509E-04	1.031E-01
Sum of HQ through THMs	1.029E-01	8.262E-04	7.038E-04	1.102E-03	*$HQ_{SUM,k}$* = **1.056E-01**
			Children up to 6 years		
HQ_{ING}	2.172E-03	7.715E-04	6.572E-04	1.029E-03	4.630E-03
HQ_{INH}	1.311E-01				
HQ_{DC}	8.219E-04	7.715E-04	6.572E-04	1.029E-03	1.344E-01
Sum of HQ through THMs	1.341E-01	1.543E-03	1.314E-03	2.058E-03	*$HQ_{SUM,k}$* = **1.390E-01**

Table 11: The values of hazard quotients, including the summary hazard quotients for the exposure pathways, monitored pollutants and $HQ_{SUM,\,k}$ at the sampling site E

Adults					
	$CHCl_3$	**$CHBrCl_2$**	**$CHBr_2Cl$**	**$CHBr_3$**	**Sum of HQ through exposure pathways**
HQ_{ING}	1.227E-03	3.302E-04	3.082E-04	6.018E-04	2.467E-03
HQ_{INH}	5.708E-02				
HQ_{DC}	1.513E-04	3.302E-04	3.082E-04	6.018E-04	5.847E-02
Sum of HQ through THMs	5.846E-02	6.604E-04	6.164E-04	1.204E-03	$HQ_{SUM,\,k}$ = **6.094E-02**
Children 6-18 years					
HQ_{ING}	1.279E-03	3.443E-04	3.213E-04	6.274E-04	2.572E-03
HQ_{INH}	1.116E-01				
HQ_{DC}	2.996E-04	3.443E-04	3.213E-04	6.274E-04	1.132E-01
Sum of HQ through THMs	1.132E-01	6.886E-04	6.426E-04	1.255E-03	$HQ_{SUM,\,k}$ = **1.158E-01**
Children up to 6 years					
HQ_{ING}	2.389E-03	6.429E-04	6.001E-04	1.172E-03	4.804E-03
HQ_{INH}	1.442E-01				
HQ_{DC}	9.041E-04	6.429E-04	6.001E-04	1.172E-03	1.475E-01
Sum of HQ through THMs	1.475E-01	1.286E-03	1.200E-03	2.344E-03	$HQ_{SUM,\,k}$ = **1.523E-01**

Table 12: The values of hazard quotients, including the summary hazard quotients for the exposure pathways, monitored pollutants and HQSUM, k at the sampling site F

	$CHCl_3$	$CHBrCl_2$	$CHBr_2Cl$	$CHBr_3$	Sum of HQ through exposure pathways
Adults					
HQ_{ING}	1.289E-03	6.018E-04	3.963E-04	6.751E-04	2.962E-03
HQ_{INH}	5.996E-02				
HQ_{DC}	1.590E-04	6.018E-04	3.963E-04	6.751E-04	6.179E-02
Sum of HQ for assessed THMs	6.141E-02	1.204E-03	7.926E-04	1.350E-03	$HQ_{SUM,k}$ = **6.476E-02**
Children 6-18 years					
HQ_{ING}	1.344E-03	6.274E-04	4.132E-04	7.038E-04	3.088E-03
HQ_{INH}	1.172E-01				
HQ_{DC}	3.148E-04	6.274E-04	4.132E-04	7.038E-04	1.193E-01
Sum of HQ through THMs	1.189E-01	1.255E-03	8.264E-04	1.408E-03	$HQ_{SUM,k}$= **1.224E-01**
Children up to 6 years					
HQ_{ING}	2.510E-03	1.172E-03	7.715E-04	1.314E-03	5.768E-03
HQ_{INH}	1.515E-01				
HQ_{DC}	9.499E-04	1.172E-03	7.715E-04	1.314E-03	1.557E-01
Sum of HQ through THMs	1.550E-01	2.344E-03	1.543E-03	2.628E-03	$HQ_{SUM,k}$= **1.615E-01**

Table 13: The values of HQs characterizing the life-long noncarcinogenic risk

	Number					
	1		2		3	
	Sampling site		Sampling site		Sampling site	
Hazard quotient	A	B	C	D	E	F
$HQ_{T\ SUM}$	8.065E-01	1.117E+00	2.158E-01	3.003E-01	3.290E-01	3.487E-01
$HQ_{T\ WEIGHT}$	1.922E-01	2.654E-01	5.139E-02	7.136E-02	7.818E-02	8.293E-02
$HQ_{T\ SUM}$	8.065E-01	1.117E+00	2.158E-01	3.003E-01	3.290E-01	3.487E-01
$HQ_{T\ WEIGHT}$	1.922E-01	2.654E-01	5.139E-02	7.136E-02	7.818E-02	8.293E-02

Applied possibilities of psychometry

Tatiana Vnukovskaya

1 Purpose

The purpose of this research: to promote the development of science in the study of the possibility of a quantitative assessment of quantities, which, in the opinion of many, at first glance, cannot be assessed. In particular, such concepts as reproductive labor, risks and the quality of reproductive labor. However, measurement in the social sciences has a long history. So, Stanley Smith Stevens (1946) proposed a measurement - the assignment of numbers to objects or events according to some rule. Most of the early studies in the field of psychometrics are based on the desire to measure intelligence.[1] Francis Galton, known as the "father of psychometry" has incorporated mental measurements into anthropometric data.[2] Psychometrics - studies the theory and methodology of psychological measurements, including the measurement of knowledge, abilities, attitudes, and personality traits.[3]

Let us apply the laws of psychometry in relation to the new economic category - "risks of reproductive labor".[4]

1.1 The risks of reproductive labor as an economic phenomenon

The risks of reproductive labor as an economic phenomenon significantly reflect the probability of negative (positive) events in the socio-economic life of society in terms of the reproductive process, the reproduction of labor resources and the value of human resources in general.

This is a specific economic category that reflects the objective reality of social and labor relations. The study revealed a contradiction that occurs at the intersection of continuums social and economic risks, consisting in the absence of identification of risks in reproductive activity-their absence in the "pure" economic risks (technical, technological, investment, financial), formed in the production sector in various sectors of the economy, and "purely" social (in particular genetic risk). However, most of the risks are at the intersection of economic and social risks arising within the framework of social and labor relations and associated

---

1 See Stanley Smith, 1946
2 See Bulmer, 2003
3 See Stigler, 2010
4 Vnukovskaya, 2014

H.-C. Brauweiler et al. (Hrsg.), *Digitalization and Industry 4.0: Economic and Societal Development*, https://doi.org/10.1007/978-3-658-27110-7_29

with the interaction in the life of both human resources and means of production. RL risks integrate economic, social, medical, political, technical aspects representing a certain compromise between opportunities and safety of RT, forming at the intersection of economic and social risks. The total part of the risks lying in the field of intersection of economic and social risks is occupied by the risks of RT, which in theoretical and methodological terms do not have their justification. Moreover, the risks of RL are the core of all the risks associated with human activities.

1.2 The introduction of a new economic category "risks of reproductive labor"

The introduction of a new economic category "risks of reproductive work" will allow to improve the process of reproduction of human resources, which is of paramount importance for improving the quality of life of the population, the development of the national economy, competitiveness of the state and the welfare of society as a whole. Man is the Creator of the conditions of his existence. Its risk protection affects the efficiency of its functioning, both in the production and reproductive spheres.5 This category fixes the static state of these relations at each stage of formation and development of human resources, and also, according to the laws of the RT, involves the study of this object of study in dynamics. It is not easy for US to fix the level of risk of RL in a certain period of time, but also to compare the changes of this indicator in the stages of development of the value of human resources, taking into account the influence of each participant of the reproductive process. Tracking these changes will effectively regulate the risks and quality of RL at each stage of development as a single individual, and for any object of interest at the micro-, meso - and macro - levels. Also, the assessment of the risk of RL in dynamics will allow to assess the effectiveness of the activities carried out to regulate the risks and quality of reproductive labor at the previous stage of human resources development and to draw conclusions about the feasibility of using these tools at the next stage, or to indicate the need to replace them.

1.3 The subjects of risks of reproductive labor (RRL), the means of labor, the subject of reproductive labor risks

All involved in the process of emergence of risks of the RL will be called the participants of risks of reproductive labor, and the subjects of reproductive labor in the narrow sense of the word – parents (mother, father) will be defined as the subjects of risks of reproductive labor (SRL).

---

[5] See Vnukovskaya, 2012

It is reasonable to consider the set of labor, material and financial resources (as well as temporary and information) involved in the process of occurrence of risks of the RL as a tool of labor, the main part of which are the means of risks of reproductive labor, namely: the housing conditions of the family, the level of family income, the level of education of parents, the material and technical base of educational institutions, health, culture and sports, as well as the level of qualification of pedagogical, medical and other personnel of the above-mentioned institutions, the business community, the funds allocated by the state for the implementation of the reoriented policy, the society in whole. The subject of reproductive labor risks will be socio-economic relations between the participants of the RL in the process of formation, cultivation and development of human resources. All the consequences of reproductive labor risks entail changes in quantity and quality of human resources and their value.

2 Dynamics of risks and quality of reproductive labor

The paper identifies the factors, conditions of implementation of RL and proved the relationship of conditions and risks of RL. By increasing the value of human resources in each family, we, due to the synergetic effect, provide the country's economy with a vital resource for it, which leads to an increase in the efficiency of the production sector of the economy and the growth of the welfare of the country.

2.1 The contradiction between productive and reproductive labor

The contradiction between productive and reproductive labor arises before entering the labor market. Lack of consideration of RL risks can lead to an increase in overall risk. However, on the other hand, the desire to reduce risks in reproductive activity can lead to an increase in the overall risk in society. That is why it is necessary to maintain the level of risk of RL taking into account the balance of interests of all participants of the reproductive process.

Dynamics of interrelation of risks and quality of RL and the main contradictions are presented in figure 1. The higher the quality of RL in the reproductive sphere, the lower in the productive sphere. The maximum loss in real terms in the reproductive sphere-a consequence of the minimum cost of preventive measures to mitigate the impact of risk of RL; the higher the quality of RL, the lower the risks of reproductive labor.

2.2 The interconnection between Quality of Reproductive Labor (QRL) in reproductive and productive spheres

The process is cyclical, continuous and endless. The movement takes place according to the laws of infinity ("eight") in the sphere of "quality of life" Qi, where i = 1, n, and Qi - quality of life of object of reproductive labor (ORL), its parents and a sort in General (SRL) , its environment in the person of the health care organization, education and culture and sports (DRL), business community (BS), state (G), society at large (S). Economic opportunities to reduce the risks of reproductive labor are not unlimited. The money spent on reducing the risks of reproductive labor can cause damage in terms of the imbalance of the labor-dependent balance, the increase in the burden on the social sphere, the emergence of parasitism and infantilism, which, in turn, can lead to an increase in social and professional risks of participants in the reproductive process.[6]

$$^{QRL}\text{in reproductive sphere} \quad \frac{V - V\,min}{V\,max - V\,min} \tag{1}$$

$$^{QRL}\text{ in productive sphere} = \quad \frac{U\,max - U}{U\,max - Umin} \tag{2}$$

Natural losses (in man-hours)

Figure 1: Dynamics of risks and quality of reproductive work

6 See Figure 1

On the basis of the classical understanding of the outcome of any labor, is advanced and substantiated the thesis that the product RL (productive activities for nurturing human resources (care, education, training, professionalization, socialization)) (it is good) is its value and (or) the usefulness With an increase in the cost of measures to reduce economic risk, social risk increases. However, the understanding that the risks of RL-the core of all risks of human life, awareness of the self-value of human life, changing society's attitude to the problem of risk protection of the human person, actualize the problem of finding solutions to regulate the risks and quality of RL at the national, regional, departmental levels. In order to take into account the development and impact of man-made and anthropogenic components the necessity of considering the RL through the risk category (through the creation of labor protection systems) and the formation of a managed and self-organizing system of risk management and quality of the RL, allowing to have an effective controlled impact on the balance of productive and reproductive labors of developing abilities as a future, a functioning labor force. The result of the RL is not the person himself, but a measure of his value and (or) usefulness for himself, family, organization, city, region, country, that is, the quality of the object of the RL. In order for the quality of the RL facility tosatisfy all stakeholders, it is necessary to find a balance in risk management and quality of the management and quality of the RL.

3 The product of RL, the result of RL, the quality of RL, the quality of the subject of RL

The usefulness of RL is understood as a set of characteristics of the cultivated object of RL related to the ability to meet the established or expected requirements of various stakeholders. The value of RL is a set of physical, intellectual and spiritual characteristics of the object of reproductive work.

The quality of reproductive labor is a measure of the value (usefulness) of the RL, produced in the process of human resources cultivation (their formation and development), taking into account the risks of the RL.

The quality of RL in the reproductive sphere is characterized by the level of increment of the value of the object of RL (formula 1), and the quality of L in the productive sphere is characterized by the level of increment of the usefulness of the object of RL (formula 2) for a certain period of time.

Risks of reproductive labor in the author's interpretation is a qualitative and quantitative measure of danger/consequences in the process of reproduction of human resources, understood as a combination of two elements: 1) the frequency or probability of a risk event associated with subjects, objects and RL in the course of their life in both the production and non-production sectors of the economy and 2) the severity of its consequences (negative / positive) for all participants in the reproductive process.

The concept of quality of the subject of RL is introduced - the level of compliance of individual characteristics of the subject of RL and its reproductive labor activity to requests of the forming personality and perspective needs of society on formation of object of RL of the set level of quality.

Introduction classes of RL, risk RL, quality of constituent entities of the RL has allowed us to Refine and expand understanding of the category "reproductive labor» as a productive activity aimed at the formation of (cultivation) and development of human resources (harmoniously developed individuals) in order to create conditions for the growth of their (her) value (usefulness), taking into account the interests of the object of reproductive labor, subjects of reproductive labor (parents, family, genus, delegated parent labor (reproductive centers, maternity hospitals, other educational institutions, health, schools of development, cultural and sports institutions), the business community, the state and society as a whole.[7]

4 Seven main participants of reproductive process

Along with internal factors influence on the quality of the object RL (ORL), risk assessment and qualitative factors influence on it, which form the key groups of participants of reproductive labor: parents (SRL) (mother (SRLm), father (SRLf), the quality of their health (Hl), intellectual capital (I), spiritual development (D) quality of life (Q), the subjects delegated parental labor (DRL) (next of kin, the genus as a whole (DRLr)), and vocational educational institutions (DRLi), health (DRLhl), schools development, culture and sports (DRLd)), the business community (BS), government (G) and society (S).

The author proves the existence of natural links between the risks of RL (RRL) and risks of 7 main groups of participants of reproductive process. The risk of each depends on 4 factors: physical health (Hl); intellectual potential (I), spiritual development (D) and "quality of life" (Q) the relevant participant of the RL (income level of the employee, material and technical base of the organization, infrastructure of municipality, region, country) (formula 3).

$$
\begin{aligned}
RRL = f(&RRL(ORL\,(Hl,I,D,Q)), RRL(SRLm\,(Hl,I,D,Q)),\\
&RRL(SRLf\,(Hl,I,D,Q)), RRL(SRLm\,(Hl,I,D,Q)), RRL(DRLr\,(Hl,I,D,Q)),\\
&RRL(DRLi\,(Hl,I,D,Q)), RRL(DRLhl\,(Hl,I,D,Q)), RRL(DRLd\,(Hl,I,D,Q)),\\
&RRL(BS\,(Hl,I,D,Q)), RRL(G(Hl,I,D,Q)), RRL(S\,(Hl,I,D,Q)))
\end{aligned} \tag{3}
$$

7 See Vnukovskaya, 2011

Each of the participants in the reproductive process contributes to the formation, development and formation of human resources of the country through various socially responsible actions. At the same time, their actions to regulate the risks of RL are aimed at the sources of reproductive risk associated, one way or another, to some extent, with physical health (Hl), intellectual potential (I), spiritual development (D) and quality of life (Q) all RL participants.

The object of reproductive labor (ORL) influences this process through self-actualization, development and involvement in the process of its formation as a parent (support of physical health, intellectual potential, spiritual development and quality of life). The higher the level of participation, the higher the stage of human resource development. Subjects of reproductive labor (SRL) - parents (mother (SRLM), father (SRLF)) act through socially responsible parenthood. Delegated entities reproductive labor (DRL) influences everyone's priority in their field of activity: health (DRLHL), education (DRLI), culture and sport (DRLD) through delegated socially responsible parenthood. It is advisable to take into account the coverage of objects of the RL, the material and technical database of institutions, staffing, the number of human resources, the level of qualification of staff. The business community (BS) influences the risks and quality of the RL through the level of socially responsible business (development of social policy at the enterprise, professional development of employees, formation of corporate culture.) The state (G), pursuing a reoriented state policy, investing in the infrastructure of the region, affects the level of risks and quality of the RL and contributes to the growth of competitiveness of countries by strengthening the quantitative and qualitative component of human resources. Society (S) represented by public organizations, acting on behalf of the emerging civil society, and the mass media, being socially oriented, forms public opinion that strengthens the image of a strong family, revives its value in society, raises it to the rank of a national idea, strengthens spirituality and faith through spiritual, cultural, educational and cognitive actions.[8]

5 The method of Express-diagnostics of risks of reproductive labor

It allows to analyze the occurrence of risks of RL from micro-level to meso-and macro-level and to diagnose risks of RL at the level of organization of any sphere of economy, institutions of infrastructure of culture, sports) as at the level of the organization, and in the territorial context (in the district, city, region, country as a whole), to forecast changes and dynamics of risks of RL for subsequent generations for certain categories of persons and age groups, taking into account the

8 See Vnukovskaya, Lavrent'ev, 2014

likelihood of health risks, intellectual and spiritual development of each participant of the reproductive process, the risk of the object of RL will look like a code of four digits, where each varies from 1 to 4 (1 – low risk (0-25%); 2 – below average (25 to 50% inclusive); 3-above average (50% to 75%); 4-high risk (the probability of occurrence of a risk event is over 75%). The first figure in the code describes the risk associated with the health of the participant of the reproductive process (Hl); the second – the risk associated with the state and development of intellectual capital (I); the third – – – the risk associated with the level of spiritual development (D); the fourth-the risk associated with the quality of life (Q).

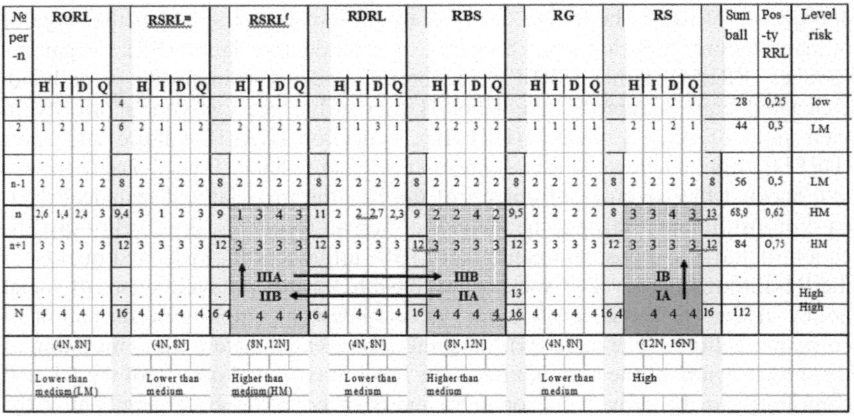

Figure 2: Methods of rapid diagnosis of risks and the quality of reproductive labor of the organization

The degree of involvement of the participant of the delegated RT can be either equal probability or differentiated depending on the importance of the expert opinion for the analysis (it is necessary that the condition that the sum of the probability of all outcomes was equal to 1). Having such a matrix for the period [t; t+1] or [t; t+n], it is possible to obtain a fairly accurate picture of changes in the risk and quality of RL. In addition, such comparisons can be made before and after the implementation of any risk reduction measure, drawing appropriate conclusions about their impact on risk management and quality of RL. If there is a need to obtain a more detailed layout for a specific object of reproductive work in all 14 stages of formation and development, it is possible to supplement the matrix with a road map formed on the object of interest of the RL from the sample. The proposed matrix is recommended to be built at any level in order to obtain information on the risks of RL in the organization (representative of the business community), on all employees of the organization, on the health care institution (for all children who have ever visited this institution (maternity hospital, polyclinic, hospital), on the educational institution (kindergarten, school,

College, Institute), on the district administration for all institutions of delegated parental work in the field of health, education, culture and sports, city, region, country. A methodological example of the use of the matrix of rapid diagnosis of risks and quality of RL for the organization for all participants of the reproductive process is shown in figure 2.

6 Conclusion

Due to the activation of socially-oriented actions of the RL subjects, the humanization of labor increases through the growth of market efficiency, increase of reproductive efficiency of the RL subjects; social efficiency of the delegated RL to improve the economic efficiency of the business community through the interaction of risks of productive and productive work.

The author's understanding of the humanization of labor is to highlight two important characteristics: consideration of the humanization of labor as a complex socio-economic process of reproduction of human resources, experiencing negative, dysfunctional and traumatic consequences and increasing the risks of RL in both productive and reproductive sectors of the economy – on the one hand, and as an economic phenomenon, widespread since the transition to market conditions of management, on the other hand. Exclusion (non-inclusion) of reproductive labor in the national economy, increases the risks of RL, distorts the principles of implementation of humanization of labor, dehumanizes labor, reduces the quality of life and the realization of labor potential of workers, which, in turn, affect the quality of productive labor, determining the efficiency of labor in the productive sector of the economy.

Literature

Bulmer, M. (2003). *Francis Galton: pioneer of heredity and biometry*. Baltimore: JHU Press.

Stanley Smith, S. (1946). *On the Theory of Scales of Measurement". Science.* Retrieved 2.4.2019, from doi:10.1126/science.103.2684. 677

Stigler, S. (2010). Darwin, Galton and the statistical enlightenment. *Journal of the Royal Statistical Society: Series A (Statistics in Society)*, pp. 469-482.

Vnukovskaya, T. (2011). *Managing quality reproductive labour at all stages of formation and development of human capital: theoretical and methodological issues: monograph.* Yekaterinburg: publishing house of the Ural Institute economics, management and law.

Vnukovskaya, T. (2012). Resource-process-effective models for assessing the quality of the object of reproductive work, taking into account reproductive risks. *National interests: priorities and security. Finances and credit. №3 (144)*, pp. 44-54. Retrieved from National interests.

Vnukovskaya, T. (2014). *Theory and methodology of reproductive work risks: monograph.* (Financial publishing house "Delovoy Express") Retrieved 2.4.2019, from http://izd-n.com/PDF/001MNG14.pdf

Vnukovskaya, T., Lavrent'ev, I. (2014). The mechanism of regulation of risks of reproduce-tive labor: theoretical aspect. *Problems of risk analysis.*, pp. 42-50.

Qualitätsverbesserungen unter Einfluss von Ultraschall auf die Produkte der Glasindustrie und ihre Reflexion in den finanziellen Angelegenheiten der Produktion

Hajymuhammet Geldiyev, Patshakuli Atayev, Nuraly Hudaykuliyev, Durjahan Atayeva

Es ist bekannt, dass externe Effekte auf möglicherweise instabilen Systemen immer solche Effekte verursachen, die das System in einen stabileren Zustand führen. Zu diesen äußeren Einflüssen zählen die Auswirkungen von Wärmefluss, Strahlungsenergie, elektrische und magnetische Felder sowie die Auswirkungen von Ultraschall. Ihre Auswirkungen können je nach Situation einzeln oder gemeinsam organisiert werden.

Die aktive Wirkung des Ultraschalls auf eine Substanz, die zu irreversiblen Veränderungen führt, oder die Auswirkung des Ultraschalls auf physikalische Prozesse, die den Verlauf beeinflussen, ist in den meisten Fällen auf nichtlineare Effekte im Schallfeld zurückzuführen. Eine solche Auswirkung wird häufig zur Lösung von Problemen der industriellen Technologie eingesetzt. Hier unterscheidet sich der Mechanismus der Ultraschallbelastung für verschiedene Umgebungen.

Technologische Prozesse der Verarbeitung von Festkörpern unter Verwendung von Ultraschall basieren auf den folgenden Effekten: Verringerung der Reibung zwischen sich voneinander weg bewegenden Oberflächen während Ultraschallschwingungen einer von ihnen; Verringerung der Streckgrenze; die Plastizität des Materials erhöhen; Härten oder Zerstörung eines Ultraschallinstruments. Der einstellbare Ultraschalleffekt beeinflusst die Reibungskraft und den Prozess der plastischen Verformung sowohl bei paralleler als auch normaler Ausrichtung der Schwingungsverschiebung relativ zur Grenzfläche.

In dieser Arbeit haben wir das Verhalten des Oberflächenreliefs von technischem Glas unter der Wirkung einer Ultraschallwelle mit einem Sondenmikroskop untersucht. Um solche experimentellen Arbeiten durchzuführen, haben wir ein spezielles Setup zusammengestellt, mit dem wir die Probentemperatur gleichzeitig kontrollieren und mit einem Piezo-Transducer beschallen können. Die Probentemperatur wurde mit einem Thermoelement direkt auf der Probenoberfläche gemessen. Damit sich der piezoelektrische Wandler nicht zu sehr auf eine kritische Temperatur erwärmt, wurde er mit einem speziellen Wärmeisolator isoliert. Die Ultraschallbehandlung wurde bei einer Resonanzfrequenz durchgeführt, um die umgewandelte Energie effizient für die Verarbeitung zu nutzen.

H.-C. Brauweiler et al. (Hrsg.), *Digitalization and Industry 4.0: Economic and Societal Development*, https://doi.org/10.1007/978-3-658-27110-7_30

Derzeit nehmen Glas und andere Glasmaterialien einen sehr wichtigen Platz beim Bau von Gebäuden ein. In vielen Ländern der Welt wird Glas beim Bau von mehrstöckigen Gebäuden hauptsächlich für die Außenbeschichtung der gesamten Oberfläche verwendet. Aufgrund natürlicher Phänomene, wie beispielsweise Niederschlag, Wind, Temperaturunterschiede der Umgebung, treten an der Außenfläche von Glasbeschichtungen schlamm- und schlammpigmentartige Anhäufungen auf, die in den meisten Fällen auf Staubansammlungen in mikroskaligen Unregelmäßigkeiten zurückzuführen sind. Das Verfahren zur Reinigung von Glasbeschichtungen von mehrstöckigen Gebäuden ist für die Versorgungsunternehmen sehr zeitaufwändig und teuer. Die Ansammlung von Staub auf der Oberfläche des Glases - ist das Ergebnis natürlicher Sedimentation oder Anhaftung der Staubteilchen an den mikroskopischen Unregelmäßigkeiten, Erhebungen und Rauheiten des Oberflächenreliefs des Glases.

Wenn es möglich wäre, die Glasoberfläche so zu glätten, dass der Staub sowie die Staubkörner, aus denen sich Staub zusammensetzt, nicht ausfallen oder an seiner Oberfläche haften bleiben können, würde die Mühsamkeit des Reinigungsprozesses der Glasoberfläche auf ein Minimum reduziert, und möglicherweise ist eine Reinigung überhaupt nicht erforderlich.

Glas ist bekanntlich ein amorphes Material. Daher ist ihr Zustand instabil. Wenn Sie sich die Glasflächen der Gebäude ansehen, die vor einem halben Jahrhundert und früher gebaut wurden, werden Sie feststellen, dass die Dicke des oberen Teils des Glases viel geringer ist als im unteren Teil. Dies ist ein Beleg für die Fließfähigkeit von festem amorphem Material im Fall unseres Untersuchungsglases.

Die Oberfläche des Glases auf einer horizontalen Oberfläche wird im Laufe der Jahre viel glatter als im Moment. Dieser Prozess kann durch den Einsatz von Ultraschall beschleunigt werden. Es ist bekannt, dass die Atome und Moleküle, die die mikroskopischen Unregelmäßigkeiten und die Rauheit ausmachen, in einem instabilen Zustand sind. Der Einfluss von Ultraschall trägt zu einem gewissen Grad dazu bei, dass der stabilisierte Zustand der molekularen Lokalisierung maximal beschleunigt wird.

Wenn wir eine molekulare Glättung der erforderlichen Oberfläche erreichen können, haben wir darüber hinaus die Möglichkeit, die Reibung auf das maximale Niveau zu reduzieren, das auftritt, wenn solche Substanzen mit einer festen, flüssigen und gasförmigen Struktur der Struktur der Oberfläche ausgesetzt sind, und auch die Widerstandsfähigkeit gegen mechanische Strömungen, die daraus entstehen, beseitigt werden Betrieb von technologischen Maschinen, Gas- und Dampfturbinen, Lüftungs- und Verdichtereinheiten sowie Rohrleitungen für verschiedene Zwecke. Dies ist ein äußerst wichtiges Thema, insbesondere bei der Herstellung, Installation und dem Betrieb von Öl- und Gaspipelines sowie Öl-

Abbildung 1: Gesamtansicht eines forschungsnanotechnologischen Komplexes eines Rastersondenmikroskop

und Gasspeichern. Die molekulare Glättung der Oberfläche trägt auch dazu bei, die Möglichkeit eines frühen oder schnellen Verschleißes sowie der Bildung von Defekten auf den Oberflächen von technologischen Teilen zu beseitigen.

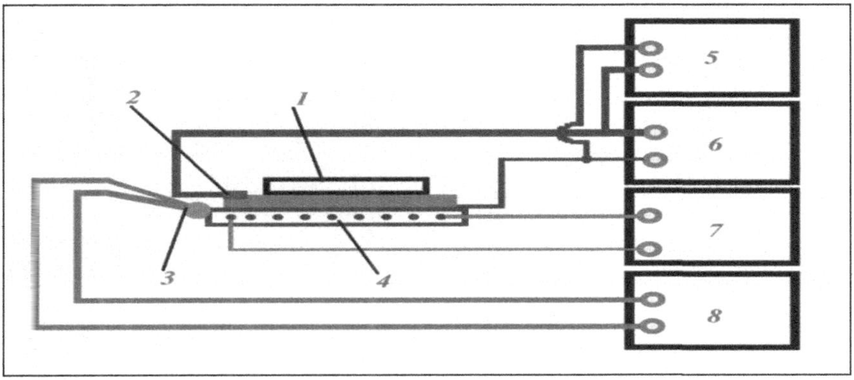

Abbildung 2: Schema des Hardware-Komplexes, der für die Implementierung der Ultraschall-Exposition zusammengestellt wurde. Dabei bezeichnen die Zahlen: 1 – die zu untersuchende Probe und die zu bearbeitende Probe, 2 – ein Piezoelement, 3 – ein Thermoelement, 4 – einen elektrischen Heizofen, 5 – ein Oszilloskop, 6 – einen Ultraschalloszillator, 7 – eine elektrische Stromquelle, 8 – ein Voltmeter

Das Ziel der wissenschaftlichen Forschung auf diesem Gebiet ist: die Untersuchung der Wirkung von Ultraschall mit einer durchschnittlichen Leistung auf das Mikrorelief der Oberflächenschicht und auf andere Parameter amorpher Materialien unter Verwendung eines Rastersondenmikroskops; die Entwicklung einer mikroskopischen Glättungstechnologie unter Verwendung eines Sondenmikroskops; Entwicklung einer Technologie zum Glätten der Oberfläche fester amorpher Materialien auf atomarer Ebene unter Verwendung kontrollierter Ultraschallwellen.

Die Neuheit der Forschungsarbeit besteht darin, dass die Eigenschaften und physikalischen Parameter des Mikroreliefs der Oberflächenschicht aus Glas durch Anwendung der neuesten Entwicklungen auf dem Gebiet der Nanotechnologie in 3D untersucht wurden. Unter Verwendung eines Rastersondenmikroskops wurden verschiedene Variationen des intrinsischen Verhaltens der Oberflächenschicht aus amorphem Material bei verschiedenen äußeren Einwirkungen untersucht. Die optimalen Ultraschallbehandlungsmodi, deren Dauer sowie Temperaturen, die die Verringerung der molekularen Erhöhung effektiv beeinflussen und zu einer gründlichen Glättung der Oberflächenunregelmäßigkeiten der untersuchten Probe beitragen, wurden ausgewählt.

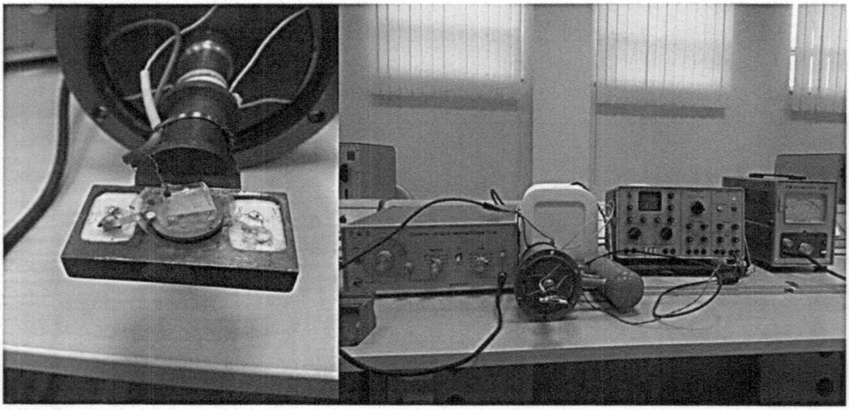

Abbildung 3: Allgemeine Ansicht des Hardware-Komplexes, um Unregelmäßigkeiten und Rauheiten auf der Oberfläche der untersuchten Probe mit Ultraschall auszugleichen

Wie bekannt, ist jede physikalische Welle, einschließlich Ultraschall, eine der Möglichkeiten, Energie über eine Distanz zu übertragen. Bei dieser Untersuchung haben wir mit einem Generator ein elektrisches Signal bei einer Ultraschallfrequenz erhalten. Dann mit einem piezoelektrischen Element in Ultraschall umwandeln. Aufgrund der elektrischen Wirkung des piezoelektrischen Elements erzeugt es eine mechanische Beanspruchung und erfasst Bewegungen bei der Ultraschallfrequenz, wodurch Ultraschall erhalten wird. Dieses physikalische Phänomen ist auch charakteristisch für einige Kristalle, wie zum Beispiel Quarzkristalle sowie für einige keramische Materialien. Um es auf dem Material zu identifizieren, müssen positive und negative Ionen sein. Die elektrische Wirkung dieser Ionen zeigt die mechanische Belastung in ungleichen Zuständen. In unseren Studien haben wir ein keramisches Piezoelement in Form einer Platte verwendet.

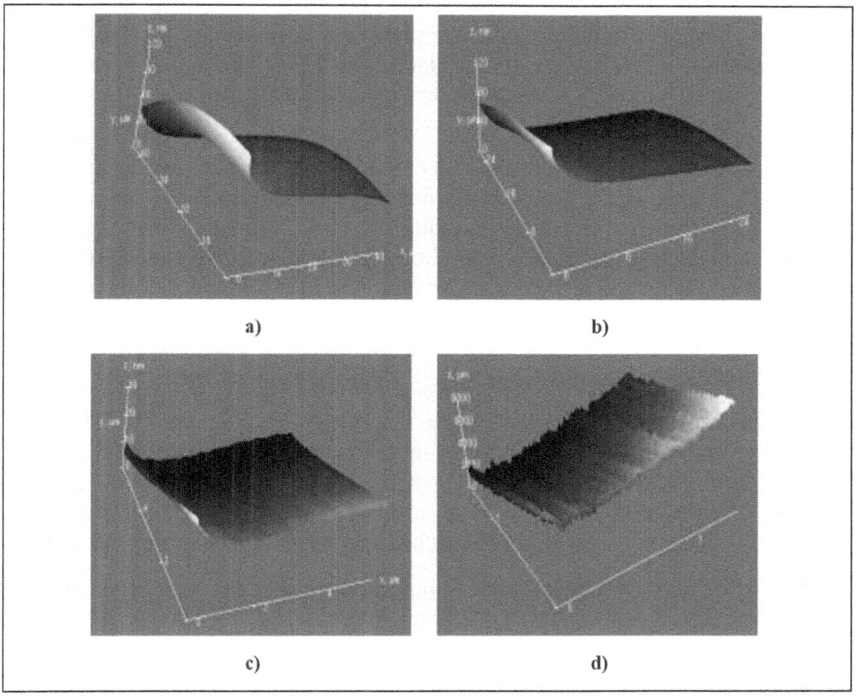

Abbildung 4: Bilder von Unregelmäßigkeiten mit unterschiedlicher grafischer Auflösung auf der Oberfläche des untersuchten Glases: a) 40x40 Mikrometer; b) 24x24 Mikrometer; c) 4x4 Mikrometer; d) 1x1 Mikrometer

Bei Experimenten mit Ultraschallwirkungen auf amorphen Materialien wurde die Wirkung auf das Mikrorelief der Oberflächenschicht der Proben sowie auf andere Eigenschaften unter Verwendung eines Sondenmikroskops untersucht und forschtet. Abbildung 4 zeigt die erhaltenen Bilder des Oberflächenreliefs einer Glasprobe im Verlauf der Experimente, a) mit einer Scanauflösung von 40x40 Mikrometer scheint die Probenoberfläche gleichmäßig zu sein; b) Wenn die Scanauflösung 24 x 24 Mikrometer beträgt, erscheinen kleine Unregelmäßigkeiten und Rauheiten auf der Oberfläche. c) Beim Scannen eines 4x4 Mikrometer Scans sind Unregelmäßigkeiten und Rauheit auf der Oberfläche deutlich sichtbar; d) Bei einer Scanauflösung von 1x1 Mikrometer werden Unregelmäßigkeiten und Rauigkeiten deutlicher sichtbar.

Die Herstellung von Mustern wurde wie folgt durchgeführt. Ein Glasmaterial wurde ausgewählt, das als außenliegende dekorative Glasbeschichtung von mehrstöckigen Gebäuden verwendet wurde, und dann in drei Proben mit Abmessungen von 10x2 mm geschnitten. Die Proben wurden mit warmem destilliertem Wasser gereinigt, getrocknet und dann erneut mit einem in technischem Alkohol getränkten weichen Papier gereinigt. Sie waren mit Klebepapier nummeriert. Das örtliche Zentrum der Proben mit einer Fläche von 10 Quadratmikrometern wurde zum Rasterkraftmikroskop verwendet, um topographische Bilder in 3D zu erhalten.

Das Scannen von lokalisierten zentralen Stellen der Proben wurde mehrmals durchgeführt. Dies wurde gemacht, um den Zustand der Scans des ausgewählten Bereichs zu ermitteln. Es ist sehr wichtig, es beim Scannen sauber zu halten. Jegliche mechanische Partikel können die Qualität des resultierenden Bildes beeinträchtigen. Daher wurden die Experimente in einem speziellen Nanotechnologielabor mit dem fortschrittlichsten Luftreinigungssystem durchgeführt. Falls die kleinsten Partikel auf die untersuchte Probenoberfläche fallen, können sie wie zusätzliche Höhen mit häufig wechselnden Koordinaten aussehen.

Wie in den ersten Bildern zu sehen, sehen Unregelmäßigkeiten und Rauheiten aus wie stufenförmig gewellte Formationen mit abrupten Änderungen der Koordinaten der Oberseite und der Tiefe der eigenen Struktur. Bei der Verwendung von Glas mit solchen Mikroreliefs können sich Staubpartikel oder andere mechanische Formationen wie natürliche chemische Emulsionen leicht darauf absetzen.

Die Probe Nr. 1 wurde in einen speziell hergestellten Kryostaten gegeben und auf eine Temperatur von 400°C erhitzt und auch Ultraschall mit einer Frequenz t = 0,5 MHz und einem Pegel von 0,2 dB für 5 Stunden ausgesetzt.

Probe Nr. 2 wurde ebenfalls auf eine Temperatur von 350°C erhitzt und 3 Stunden lang Ultraschall ausgesetzt.

Probe Nr. 3 wurde ebenfalls auf eine Temperatur von 450°C erhitzt und 2 Stunden lang Ultraschall ausgesetzt.

Probe	Temperatur, °C	Frequenz	Db-Ebene	Dauer
№1	400		0,3	5 Stunden
№2	350	0,5 MHz	0,2	3 Stunden
№3	450		0,1	2 Stunden

Nach der Einwirkung von Ultraschall wurden erneut Bilder des Oberflächenreliefs der äußeren Schicht der Proben erhalten. Sie wurden mit einem Atomkraftmikroskop abgetastet, wonach die erhaltenen topographischen Bilder durch Vergleich und geometrische Analyse untersucht wurden.

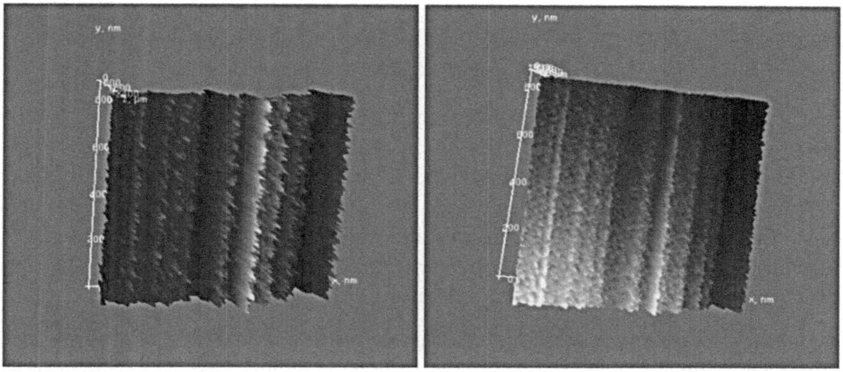

Abbildung 5: Bilder des Oberflächenreliefs von normalem technischen Glas vor (links) und nach (rechts) Ultraschallbelichtung

7 Zusammenfassung

Basierend auf dem Einsatz moderner Nanotechnologie-Forschungsgerätekomplexe wurden die Eigenschaften der Oberflächenschicht von Glasproben, bei denen es sich um amorphe Materialien handelt, untersucht, indem dreidimensionale Bilder des Reliefs der mikroskaligen Oberflächenbereiche erhalten wurden. Die Eigenschaften der Oberflächenschicht von Glasproben wurden in verschiedenen Betriebsmodi untersucht. Es wurden optimale Bedingungen für Ultraschall, seine Dauer sowie für zusätzliche Temperatureffekte ausgewählt, die unter bestimmten Bedingungen die Verringerung von Unregelmäßigkeiten und Rauigkeiten auf der Glasoberfläche wirksam beeinflussen. Die Wirkung von Ultraschallwellen auf das Relief ist besonders stark spürbar, wenn die Temperatur der thermischen Belastung zunimmt, wodurch sich das Relief auf der Glasoberfläche derart ändert, dass die mikroskaligen Erhebungen abnehmen und die Ebenheit zunimmt.

Bei höheren Temperaturen (T>450°C) treten unter dem Einfluss von Ultraschall neue Erhebungen, Unregelmäßigkeiten und Rauheiten auf den untersuchten Probenoberflächen auf. Dies ist ein Indikator für die Fähigkeit des Ultraschalls, neue Unregelmäßigkeiten zu erzeugen, die auf Faktoren wie strukturelle Instabilität von amorphem Material zurückzuführen sind, das bei thermischer Wirkung weich wird und infolge der Bildung mechanisch aktiver Wellen im gesamten Materialvolumen, das durch eine Quelle stabilen Ultraschalls erzeugt wird, Unregelmäßigkeiten auftreten. Daher ist es sehr wichtig, den optimalen Temperaturindikator zu wählen, der für die kombinierte Anwendung zusammen mit Ultraschall bestimmt ist.

Es wurde festgestellt, dass der Glättungsgrad der entsprechenden Oberfläche umso höher ist, je länger der Ultraschall auf die Oberfläche der amorphen Oberfläche bei der optimalen Temperatur (T=400°C) anhält.

Es wurde festgestellt, dass bei Abwesenheit der restlichen Parameter des Experiments auch bei der Dauer der Ultraschalleinwirkung t = 5 Stunden keine Veränderungen an der untersuchten Oberfläche festgestellt wurden. Dies ist ein klares Beispiel dafür, dass nach einer gewissen Zeit, wenn Ultraschall auf die Oberfläche aufgebracht wird, ein stabiler Zustand erreicht wird und alle molekularen Aktivitäten der Komponenten der äußeren Schicht der Oberfläche aufhören. Das heißt, es gibt auch einen optimalen Indikator für die Ultraschallbelastung.

Es wurde experimentell festgestellt, dass mit zunehmender Frequenz und Amplitude der Einwirkung von Ultraschall auf höhere Indices das untersuchte amorphe Material durch "extreme" deformierende Vibrationen auf molekularer Ebene im gesamten Material versagen kann. Dies ist besonders bei niedrigen Temperaturen sehr bemerkbar, wenn die Ultraschallbehandlung die Anzahl der fehlerhaften Zonen und Versetzungen auf der untersuchten Oberfläche erhöhen kann.

Unter Verwendung des Rastertunnelmikroskops eines Atomkraftmikroskops wurde das Oberflächenrelief und die Morphologie des nativen Oxids (Ga_2O_3) der n-GaAs (100) -Halbleiterstruktur untersucht.

Wenn die Ergebnisse dieser Forschungsarbeiten verwendet werden, können die mit der Reinigung und Wartung von Glasbeschichtungen von mehrstöckigen Gebäuden zu verschiedenen Zwecken verbundenen finanziellen und materiellen sowie zeitlichen Kosten gesenkt werden. Bei der Einführung der vorgeschlagenen Technologie zum Glätten der Glasoberfläche für die industrielle Produktion wird es zudem möglich sein, die Anforderungen an das Glasrecycling zu senken und die damit verbundenen finanziellen Kosten um ein Vielfaches zu senken.

Literaturverzeichnis

Atayev, P., Alymbayev, A. (2014). Einfluss des Ultraschalls auf das Oberflächenrelief amorpher Materialien. Die wissenschaftliche und technische Kreativität junger Menschen ist der Weg zu einer auf Wissen basierenden Gesellschaft. *Sammlung von Berichten der IV. Internationalen Konferenz über Wissenschaft und Praxis*.

Geldiyev, H., Atayev, P. (2016a). Technologie zur Schaffung einer transparenten und gut leitenden Schicht für das sichtbare Spektrum der Sonnenstrahlung. (Ylym, Hrsg.) *Technologiezentrum. Wissenschaftliche Konferenz "Innovative Technologien in der Transformation des Landes"*.

Geldiyev, H., Atayev, P. (2016b). Deep Cadmium Telluride Multi-Level-Zentren. *Volumen der internationalen wissenschaftlich-praktische Konferenz von Studenten, Diplomanden und Doktoranden. "Markt- und Produktivitäts-effizienz-13"*.

Melebayew, D. (2010). *Ultraviolett-Fotodetektoren basierend auf Au-Oxid-n-GaP-Nanostrukturen. Verfahren der Internationalen Wissenschafts- und Technikkonferenz. "Nanotechnologie funktionaler Materialien (NFM-10)"*. Petersburg.

The manufacturer's authorised representative in the EU is Springer Nature Customer Service Centre GmbH, Europaplatz 3, 69115 Heidelberg, Germany. If you have any concerns regarding our products, please contact ProductSafety@springernature.com

Printed and bound by CPI Group (UK) Ltd, Croydon, CR0 4YY
22/09/2026
02220979-0001